ER   ELL   ALS
NTEMPORARY   1Y

THE POWER OF

INTELLECTUALS

IN CONTEMPORARY

GERMANY

Edited by **Michael Geyer**

THE UNIVERSITY OF CHICAGO PRESS
CHICAGO AND LONDON

MICHAEL GEYER is professor of contemporary European history at the University of Chicago. He is coeditor of *Resistance against the Third Reich, 1933–1990* (1994, with J. Boyer), also published by the University of Chicago Press.

The University of Chicago Press, Chicago 60637
The University of Chicago Press, Ltd., London
© 2001 by The University of Chicago
All rights reserved. Published 2001
Printed in the United States of America
10 09 08 07 06 05 04 03 02 01   1 2 3 4 5

ISBN: 0-226-28986-9 (cloth)
ISBN: 0-226-28987-7 (paper)

Library of Congress Cataloging-in-Publication Data

The power of intellectuals in contemporary Germany / edited by Michael Geyer.
   p. cm.
   Includes bibliographical references and index.
   ISBN 0-226-28986-9 (alk. paper)—ISBN 0-226-28987-7 (pbk. : alk. paper)
   1. Geyer, Michael.

  DD290.26 .P69 2001
  943—dc21   2001027899

♾ The paper used in this publication meets the minimum requirements of the American National Standard for Information Sciences—Permanence of Paper for Printed Library Materials, ANSI Z39.48-1992.

Acknowledgments   ix

MICHAEL GEYER
Introduction: The Power of Intellectuals in
Contemporary Germany   1

PART 1
Intellectuals and the Politics of Culture in the
German Democratic Republic

DIETRICH HOHMANN
An Attempt at an Exemplary Report on H.   27

FRANK TROMMLER
German Intellectuals: Public Roles and the
Rise of the Therapeutic   35

DOROTHEA DORNHOF
The Inconsequence of Doubt: Intellectuals
and the Discourse on Socialist Unity   59

SIMONE BARCK, MARTINA LANGERMANN,
AND SIEGFRIED LOKATIS
The German Democratic Republic as a "Reading Nation":
Utopia, Planning, Reality, and Ideology   88

KATIE TRUMPENER
La guerre est finie: New Waves, Historical
Contingency, and the GDR "Rabbit Films"   113

DAVID BATHRICK
Language and Power   138

PATRICIA ANNE SIMPSON
Syntax of Surveillance: Languages of
Silence and Solidarity   160

LOREN KRUGER
Wir treten aus unseren Rollen heraus:
Theater Intellectuals and Public Spheres   183

ALEXANDER KLUGE
It is a Mistake to Think That the Dead
Are Dead: Obituary for Heiner Müller   212

PART 2
Intellectuals in Transit: Toward a Unified Germany

DIETRICH HOHMANN
The Consequences of Unification According to H.   221

PATRICIA ANNE SIMPSON
Soundtracks: GDR Music from "Revolution"
to "Reunification"   227

ANDREAS GRAF
Media Publics in the GDR: Unification and
the Transformation of the Media, 1989–1991   249

KONRAD JARAUSCH
The Double Disappointment: Revolution,
Unification, and German Intellectuals   276

MITCHELL G. ASH
Becoming Normal, Modern, and German
(Again?)   295

ANDREAS HUYSSEN
Nation, Race, and Immigration: German
Identities After Unification   314

JOHN BORNEMAN
Education After the Cold War:
Remembrance, Repetition, and Right-
Wing Violence   335

MICHAEL GEYER
The Long Good-bye: German Culture Wars
in the Nineties   355

ALEXANDER KLUGE
The Moment of Tragic Recognition with
a Happy Ending   381

List of Contributors   395
Bibliography   401
Index   445

It is a pleasure to acknowledge that this volume had its origins in a conference sponsored by the Goethe-Institut Chicago, the Department of German Literatures and Languages, and the Interdisciplinary Program for the Study of Europe at the University of Chicago. The conference explored the relations between the State Security Service (the Stasi) and writers, artists, cultural workers, academics, and ministers (what we called, in short, "intellectuals" or the intellectual classes) in the late German Democratic Republic (GDR). The responsibility of intellectuals in the face of state power and the fallibility of moral and aesthetic authority were its main concerns. It was co-organized by Robert von Hallberg, Michael Geyer, and Hans-Georg Knopp (of the Goethe Institut). Subsequently Neal Enssle, Gale Erie, Michael Latham, Devin Pendas, and Annette Timm provided translations and research assistance that accompanied the emergence of this volume. They deserve high praise and heartfelt thanks.

MICHAEL GEYER

Introduction: The Power of Intellectuals in Contemporary Germany

This book of essays focuses on the intellectual class of the defunct German Democratic Republic (GDR). Taking the troubled transition to a unified Germany as a starting point, the essays explore the public debates surrounding the role of intellectuals in the process of unification and reflect on the challenges of this momentous event. The responsibility of intellectuals in the face of state power and the fallibility of their moral and aesthetic authority are the contributors' major themes. The controversies that surrounded relations between the State Security Service of the GDR (the Stasi) and writers, artists, cultural workers, and academics shaped the public culture of the newly unified country to a remarkable degree. The essays in this volume read these controversies as markers of a struggle over the makeup of culture in the new Germany and the "spirit of our age."[1]

The relations between East German intellectuals and the Stasi have a history that is now being explored in ever finer detail.[2] After an initial media frenzy, revealing all manner of Stasi ties, this emergent history establishes meticulously and, one hopes, truthfully the degree of their collusion and collaboration with the East German regime and its ruling Socialist Unity Party, the SED. Above and beyond the record, however, the entwinement of intellectuals and the repressive regime is of signal importance in the ongoing debates on German culture. At stake is the relation of culture to power, which, for all intents and purposes, is the key concern of modern intellectual life—and surely of German intellectual life in the twentieth century.

The complex genealogy of this issue need not concern us.[3] What matters is the hope invested in a separation of the spheres of power and spirit. The presumption of and insistence on the autonomy of culture was justified

1

as a check against state power on one hand and as a counterweight to commerce and industry on the other.[4] In the German system of checks and balances, culture ascertained moral justice. The control of intellectuals over the sphere of culture guaranteed not just the reign of good taste but social betterment and *Bildung*.[5] Even if it had not been for this elevated role of intellectuals, their collusion with a repressive regime and their subsequent abandonment by the reading public would still have mattered. However, because of the special role of intellectuals as both guardians against the state and as tutors of the nation, the actual betrayal of their role (misbegotten as this role may appear in hindsight) destroyed not only the credibility of individual informers and of the whole class of collaborating intellectuals but also the legitimacy of an idea.

This collection explores the power of the idea of the tutelary intellectual and the social and cultural configuration from which it sprang.[6] For the GDR intellectuals and especially the writers were highly regarded, irrespective of their individual merits, because they came to articulate this idea of culture as a realm of justice most compellingly. The contributions in this volume explicate two kinds of entanglement. One has to do with what has become past, the GDR and its culture—a past that has a weighty presence. The other has to do with the evolution of a post-"revolutionary," post-unification German nation and the place of culture and, more so, the public and political role of intellectuals in the new state and its emergent media and information society. The two lines of inquiry are intimately linked in that the past is revisited as the present is made to change. The controversies about the Stasi ties of East German intellectuals were but the starting shot for a procession of spectacular debates on the nature of culture and the power of intellectuals in the newly unified country.[7] These debates ranged over an extraordinarily wide terrain and they amounted, at times, to a free-for-all. In a genteel spirit, one might treat them as miscellaneous discontents about Germany and modernity or even as a kind of *Weltschmerz*—or all of the above wrapped up into one, as Peter Handke's writings of the mid-nineties suggest.[8] Or one might treat them as a quest for truth amid a world of lies, with a national media public as a sort of truth commission that eclipsed the state-sponsored effort at national accounting in the form of the Enquete Commission.[9] I suggest that we think of these debates and their entwinement of past, present, and the future as rites of passage from one world to another.

The essays collected in this volume were written and rewritten at various stages during the 1990s. They make apparent the emotional nature and the insecurities of the transition to a new Germany. Writing them was an exercise in the production of thought in the process of moving and settling into a new world, to borrow loosely from a signal essay by Heinrich von Kleist nearly two centuries ago.[10] Thus, the essays offer a running commentary on the turmoil unleashed by unification. They trace the unraveling of one intellectual culture and its institutions and the simultaneous emergence of another and yet incomplete one. Because the disappearing intellectual culture held a special status in the remaking of the individual and society and gained its public role from ascertaining the right of intellectuals to give meaning and purpose to the self-realization of individuals in society, the stakes were extraordinarily high. The authors approached their respective themes with concern and, not infrequently, with a wistful look at what was left behind. At the same time, the essays also reflect the labors and the excitement of bringing a past to closure and opening up a space for a new beginning. If there is a bias in this volume, it is that the contributors were altogether more fascinated and less perturbed by the possibilities that arose from unification than many of the subjects they were thinking and writing about.

The Native as Stranger

That a great deal of soul-searching and uncertainty resulted from unification is now undisputed.[11] The daunting nature of the transition came as a shock, however, because the East Germans had hoped for nothing so much as the continuation of the Federal Republic's good life as their own. All the while, the East Germans had been affirming West Germans' very high assessment of their own achievements. This horizon of expectation was firmly lodged in an imaginary that pictured the present as a natural extension of the West German past, which was the de facto common ground for an otherwise quite mythical German *Volk*.[12] Hence, the main thrust of the unification process had been to preserve the old by means of co-optation, integration, and assimilation. This was the case in politics as well as culture and in economic as well as social relations. The extraordinary initial success of Chancellor Kohl's unification program rested on the simple but effective premise that there would be more of the same (West German) abundance and that it would now be for all Germans.[13] Its inverse, of course, was the disappearance or, as it subsequently was put, the wanton destruction of the GDR as a way of life, which was not what the majority of East Germans had anticipated when they bought into the West German dream. But things did not happen quite that way.[14] It is not just that the East Germans discovered that they had something to lose. At the moment of unification, in 1989–90, West Germany itself was caught in an accelerated process of transformation. The state and the economy the East Germans wanted to join was disappearing.

It was a case of double jeopardy. The GDR was abandoned, its institutions dissolved. Meanwhile the transformation of West Germany, notwithstanding the assurances of its chancellor and increasingly desperate efforts to ward off change, gained velocity and, after a moment of hesitation and disorientation, moved ever faster. It took nearly a decade for the recognition of this acceleration to set in. But once the two political stalwarts of the old Federal Republic, the Social Democrat Oskar Lafontaine and the Christian Democrat Helmut Kohl, were removed from politics, the shift suddenly seemed self-evident. By the beginning of the new century, the debate on intellectuals had begun to disappear as a marker for the transition from one state to another. In a world of new signs defined by economics, one might take Daimler buying Chrysler and going global and a recently founded British communications company by the name of Vodafone buying a brand name like Mannesmann and going European as the signature events of this development—a process capped by the attempted but ultimately rejected merger of the London and Frankfurt exchanges. Only at this point, and with this kind of action, was the unified Germany becoming the "truly normal" country that unification was supposed to bring about. The irony is that "normalcy," contrary to what it was made up to be by the inventors of the concept, turned out to be an entirely unpredictable, market-driven, and consumption-oriented state of affairs.

The new Germany was neither the way East Germans expected it to be nor the way West Germans knew their Federal Republic. Hannah Arendt described such moments of reckoning as a "loss of world" and thus captured the essence of a manifest and unhappy collective experience.[15] Mostly debated as an issue of the cultural difference between East and West (which is real enough), the cognitive dissonance between what easterners and westerners were used to and what they actually confronted stands out most clearly as the dominant experience of the nineties.[16] It was the disappearance, dissolution and, indeed, collapse of a common space, of meaningful structures within which to act, that marked first the East Germans' and then the West Germans' rite of passage. It should be noted that this loss of world was not, for the most part, accompanied by material hardship and surely not by an implosion of institutional structures—a collapse of the state—as was the case in eastern Europe and, especially, in the former Soviet Union. But for all the material advantages accrued through unification and for all the maintenance of reconstructed institutions, the harsh reality of losing one's world and the resulting disorientation cannot be underestimated.[17]

An everyday sense of estrangement was first articulated by the East Germans who joined the old Federal Republic and discovered that nothing in this world was quite the way they had imagined it. Massive unemployment, the erosion of GDR social and gender arrangements, the remaking of norms of conduct were overwhelming—and it was quite naturally presumed that the burden of change was to be carried by the East in exchange for lavish monetary transfers. This clash of worlds generated both an involution, a nostalgic turn to the familiar ways of the GDR (which were increasingly seen as the more traditionally German), and a great deal of rage in eastern Germany. It was acted out against anyone and anything that appeared strange, notably "foreigners," but also against West Germans and, perhaps most prominently, against locals who did not fit. It quickly engendered an entire literature on East-West sensibilities.[18]

None of this bothered the West Germans, at least initially. Still, they too had to discover that their world was changing. Jürgen Habermas, the West German philosopher whose role as the consummate public intellectual of Germany has yet to be fully appreciated in the English-speaking world, had, in 1985, coined the phrase *neue Unübersichtlichkeit* (a novel lack of clarity or vision) for this condition.[19] He wrote of the decline of utopian energies that he made responsible for the challenges to the welfare state—a nexus that gives one pause in hindsight. In the nineties, the notion of *Orientierungslosigkeit* (lack of orientation) was sprouting. The angst about the fraying of community was not just a figment of the imagination. The imaginary community of the West Germans ran up against a dual challenge from both the easterners and the world. The sheer truculence of comments that nothing happening in the East could possibly affect Munich, Frankfurt, Düsseldorf, or Bonn indicates that the exact opposite was the case.[20] The rampant deutschmark nationalism might as well be read as a defensive gesture against the "contamination" of West German success in an age of perceived "globalization" and a very real Europeanization of national economies.[21] But things were changing irretrievably, and the decision to move the seat of government to Berlin marked the turning point of public perception. By the middle of the nineties the German public was engulfed in a debate about the construction of Berlin as the new center of Germany.[22] By the end of the decade the new Berlin had begun to take shape as the crowning achievement of unification. Of course, at the beginning of the new century, Frankfurt stepped out of the shadow of a national bank in order to become a global marketplace, which tells us one thing or another about nations and their centers.

The old Republic was slipping and with it went a way of life and, more slowly, a way of thinking of and perceiving the world. Resistance to change was tremendous and, at times, seemed overwhelming. If East Germans raged against strangers, West Germans railed against globalization, gene technology, and the media society, but above all against anything and anyone that did not quite fit the "lite" fusion of humanism and efficiency of the late Federal Republic. The refusal to change seemed to paralyze the entire nation, and quite a few commentators spoke of a *nation bloquée* similar to the late French Third Republic.[23] A decade after unification, East and West were thoroughly disunited, while going through a corresponding experience. As East German institutions and an eastern German way of life were wound down in the process of unification, the Germany that was being united was itself in transit.

In a universe full of complaints, intellectuals were among the first to feel put upon.[24] They also expressed their alienation more vociferously than almost anybody else. They felt they had been rendered superfluous.[25] Collectively, they saw themselves as a casualty of unification: the first ones to go were the East German intellectuals, but their West German counterparts were carried away by a similar, if somewhat delayed, downward spiral. If the East German intelligentsia was caught in never-ending revelations about secret ties to the Stasi, West German public intellectuals felt entrapped in the onrush of an entertainment and information society that was described quite melodramatically as "panic in the face of a meaningless world; fear that media-capitalism will usher in a yet more banal culture."[26]

All the while they fought like cats and dogs. It was not just that easterners and westerners discovered that they had little in common and that, even when they agreed, they were miles apart, as an exchange between Christa Wolf and Jürgen Habermas indicated.[27] More frequently, long-standing quarrels among eastern and western intellectuals broke wide open with unification. The personal and the political were inextricably linked in this public airing of what occasionally turned out to be very dirty laundry. When the poet and songwriter Wolf Biermann, whose expulsion in 1976 from the GDR helped galvanize a new wave of dissent, called Sascha Anderson, the Prenzlauer Berg poet-entrepreneur, an "asshole" because of Anderson's Stasi connection, he attacked Anderson as informer and as poet. He set in motion an investigation into Anderson's past *and* cast doubt on avant-garde aestheticism.[28] When Frank Schirrmacher of the *Frankfurter Allgemeine Zeitung* (FAZ) wondered aloud about Christa Wolf's accommodation to the SED regime, he wanted to challenge the good conscience of a literature of moral uprightness that he considered suspect, but in fact he rode on a frenzy of allegations about Wolf's career in the GDR.[29] And when the West German author Martin Walser expressed his unease about a culture of German contrition, he not only expressed publicly a popular German sentiment that had previously been heard only in private, but also ended up in a nasty spat with his friend

Ignatz Bubis, the head of the German-Jewish community.[30] The latter now found support among many of the Frankfurt radicals who, in the seventies, had accused him of being a (typically Jewish) real estate speculator.[31] The procession of debates and controversies just never seemed to end.

Undoubtedly, the happenings were driven by the media's interest in scandal. Brawls among intellectuals make good copy, which itself is a rather intriguing phenomenon that the Germans at last had come to share with the French. Easterners and westerners confronted the demons of their respective pasts just at the moment when the familiar maps of animosity began to collapse. What all the debates had in common is that they should have been resolved twenty or thirty years ago, when they were fresh and new. Now, they became the baggage of a disappearing age. Rather than having West German culture affirmed, "traditions" that had accrued in East and West during the long postwar era were challenged. It came as quite a surprise in the process that both easterners and westerners were deeply committed to their respective traditions, which they had so often considered ephemeral, ready to be discarded. Eastern nostalgia gained a certain notoriety as *Ostalgie*.[32] The far more serious bout of West German nostalgia (starting with the retro cult of the eighties) is yet to be fully explored.[33] But nostalgia was really only one side of the coin. Equally important was the recognition that distinct postwar East and West German cultures had come about in the first place, which set in motion a process of sorting out and remaking them as distinct legacies—some to be displayed in museums as artifacts of a different time and others to be carried over and carried on.[34] If the intellectual brawls themselves are more or less exciting, the fact that there is so much "culture" to be fought about, before it is lost or discarded, is truly striking.

The sheer act of sorting and remaking a legacy is noteworthy and may well have been one of the most promising things to happen in Germany after unification.[35] Although the contestation was fierce (and in many ways remains undecided) it stayed public and civil. The significance of this hard-won civility becomes evident if we recall the century-long history of culture wars that began with Bismarck's *Kulturkampf* (and, if one so wishes, with the antirevolutionary legislation in the context of the post-Napoleonic restoration), reached its zenith as an all-out war of purification in the Third Reich, and ended with the persecution of deviant intellectuals in the GDR and the *Berufsverbot* (the prohibition of employment for members of left-wing radical groups) in the Federal Republic. This is not to say that they all are the same thing but that there was a persistent pattern of violent confrontations over ways of thinking and ways of living. Hence, we may take the postunification controversies as an indication that culture wars can, indeed, be fought metaphorically.

One might then further speculate whether this is the German version of the ending of an era of revolutions that François Furet had proclaimed some time ago for France.[36] More to the point and more specifically geared to the latest stage in the long German history of purification campaigns are two observations concerning the making of a legacy that are at the center of this volume. The first one concerns the literary scene of the defunct GDR; the second deals with the legacy of the West German culture of memory and the challenge of developing a German national identity. Both together raise questions about the status of postwar German culture and its future in the new Germany.

One of the most positive aspects of unification was the chance and the challenge—for both easterners (who had been too isolated to canvass the range of activities) and westerners (who never really cared)—to discover, as it were, the East German cultural scene in its complexity and richness. It was only after the collapse of the SED regime that the range and creativity of East German intellectuals could be taken in. This scene turned out to be far more diverse and far more differentiated than had generally been assumed. Prevailing assessments and established pecking orders tumbled and began to give way, slowly, to a broad reassessment of East German culture.[37] In the course of this decade-long exploration of what proved to be surprisingly unfamiliar and unknown worlds, it furthermore became obvious that these intellectual cultures were so deeply imbricated in modern German culture that getting rid of one entailed amputating the other. It proved to be quite difficult to abandon the GDR intellectuals without abandoning a good part of modern German identity.[38]

This insight, in turn, raised the stakes in the fierce—and all too often verified—accusations of collaboration with a repressive regime and its punitive politics. While accusations and counteraccusations were flying, the question emerged: What was it about German culture or, for that matter, about intellectuals, about their particular brand of emancipatory cultural politics, that made them such blind and willing instruments of repression? What made eastern German intellectuals accommodate to the SED regime, and what made western German intellectuals so oblivious to this accommodation? Here we enter a realm of debate that transcends scandal-mongering. Was the emancipatory utopia of German intellectuals a jaundiced illusion whose time has come and gone, as some observers already noticed in 1989?[39]

Simultaneously, the West German politics of memory came under renewed scrutiny. The scene was perplexing. For *Vergangenheitsbewältigung* only now reached a state of popular saturation. In the long run-up to the fifty-year anniversary of the end of World War II—starting with D-Day and ending with May 8–9—it seemed as if the (West) German nation was over-whelmed by memory.[40] A culture of memory that had been a left-liberal intellectual domain in the old Federal Republic entered the broad stream of popular debate, which, for all the attending controversy (exemplified most clearly in the mass contestations over a traveling exhibition that challenged the image of the Wehrmacht),[41] had become a national and mass-mediated event. It is easy enough to point to the many infelicities and blind spots of this memory culture, but the main point is that it came into being in the first place. It is altogether more important that, as a ritual of transition, it marked a generational shift. For those born between the 1920s and 1940s it was a cathartic experience, whereas it was "history " and, more likely, a movie for the younger generation born into (West) Germany. It is a measure of the distance traversed in the nineties that so heartfelt and intimate an experience also began to transcend national confines to be discussed as a global phenomenon. It was now treated as "your memory culture and ours" in a comparative perspective.[42] Memory became at one and the same time subject and object of public debate. It became memory culture, to be watched and commented on, compared with what happened elsewhere in the world. The culture of memory thus gained a level of "metanarrativity" that was the surest sign of experience being transposed into the realm of objects. Typically, East Germans now came to admire their own past in everyday life museums, while West Germans put theirs into monuments and, apart from fostering their own museum culture, dis-played it on television. Television, with its reruns of old movies—Eastern, Western, Third Reich, and Weimar—and the endless documentaries about the "way we lived only ten years ago," side by side with soaps and world cinema, is perhaps the most perfect rendition of contemporary German memory culture.[43]

As ever more books, articles, and exposés were published on the culture of memory, however, and as scholars cast about for comparisons, it turned out that, as troubling as the past was, the present was in disarray. There were bouts of nationalist exuberance in the wake of an otherwise unremarkable world championship in soccer in 1992; a mounting xenophobia and racism both in East and West with effects on the political debate on asylum and citizenship; a worsening of unemployment, primarily in the East but also the West, and the resulting controversies about German competitiveness; and revulsion against the American bombing in the Gulf War followed by the debate about the out-of-area use of the Bundeswehr on one hand and a growing consensus about humanitarian intervention in the former

Yugoslavia on the other. The list could be continued. The basic trouble was that no amount of *Vergangenheitsbewältigung* had prepared the Germans for the present. In part this was debated as a matter of how to learn the "right" lessons from the past and, particularly, from a past that includes Auschwitz.[44] But there was more at stake. The difficult discovery to be made was that, after unification, the Germans faced the world and themselves on their own without the borrowed securities of the cold war.

The procession of literary, political, and cultural debates flows into a much broader stream of sentiments and resentments that come as result of a happy ending. Together, they articulate the joys, pains, and anger that accompany the remaking of subjectivities and identities. Although Germany is unified and the cold war has come to an end, the Germans and, for that matter, Europe have yet to find their peace and, in view of the accumulating acrimony, one might as well say, their civility. What is tested and challenged in the avalanche of controversies and debates are the bonds that hold society together and the forces that pull them asunder. One might well call this challenge *Gegenwartsbewältigung*, because coping with the present is the unresolved and, in the German context, novel experience.

Traditionally, the use of language to constitute bonds of belonging (and to tear them apart) and to give meaning to social action has been the privilege of intellectuals, a privilege they derived from the juxtaposition of power and culture. Whether intellectual can and should retain this privilege is the subject of the current debates on culture. They articulate in many competing and conflicting ways what ties people together and who does it. The "production of the nation" has become the academic shorthand for this phenomenon, which fits the German scene in more than one sense.[45] Inasmuch as the German debates of the nineties are any indication, the issue of the nation is formed by a far broader array of material and symbolic strategies of societalization (*Vergesellschaftung* is the venerable German word from another turn of the century) designed to cope with the unsettlement that resulted from the remaking of two German states into one nation.

Once again, this issue was raised on a grand scale by François Furet in his challenge to the "idea of communism."[46] Although Furet's book had little impact on the American scene (it was not published in English until 1999), it became the center of an extraordinarily heated debate in Germany and France. Much of that controversy had to do with Furet's treatment of communism and fascism as twin evils and his peculiar revival of the notion of totalitarianism, an argument that reminded many German observers of the apologetic writing of Ernst Nolte.[47] In debating the passing of an illusion,

German and French intellectuals did not quite know whether to declare communism a mirage or a "specter." They reaffirmed their opposition to fascism, which the Germans, in particular, came to separate more carefully from national identity. But most of all they discovered that they disliked the alternative, American- or British-style free-for-all market liberalism. Over time the debate on the illusions of the past transmogrified into a controversy about European versus American culture as the challenge for the present and the future.[48] Only if we consider this transition can we begin to fathom the kind of transformation intellectual cultures underwent during the nineties. What started out as a debate about the East and its intellectuals and the Germans and their past ended up as an exploration of Europe after the end of the cold war.

Intellectual Cultures Between Worlds
Initially, the unification debates were entirely focused on the East and on the eastern intellectuals, at that. As these literature debates have become subjects of an instant historiography, one phenomenon stands out, because it is so contrary to the intention of these debates. They have put what for all intents and purposes was the not very well known regional literature of the GDR (if compared, for example, to the Austrian one) into the mainstream of German literary traditions. In a way, these debates have created a GDR literature as part of the German canon. The first part of this volume discusses key dimensions of this reconsideration.

The departure from the GDR, the writer Dietrich Hohmann explains in the lead-off essay, was as hard as the arrival in the new state. The old one was bankrupt and the new one strange and in its strangeness hurtful and unwelcoming. Hohmann's short story about the writer's exit from the GDR and his loss of voice was written in 1992–93. The story captures contradictory emotions that were difficult to accept at the time but have since been amply confirmed as the quintessential experience of the citizens of the former GDR. Hohmann was willy-nilly tied to a state that he otherwise considered as a contrivance, if not a nuisance, that one had to work with. What he could not live with and what made it difficult for him to live with himself was the disappointment of hopes and expectations invested in creating a better and more humane society in the GDR. This had been the horizon of the new state and the new society to be built on German territory. Like many intellectuals of his generation, he felt betrayed and, worse, he fears that he may have betrayed himself. The questions Hohmann raises for himself and about himself were questions intellectuals were bound to confront. The response was key to the paramount issue of "what remains"—What would be the legacy of all those hopeful attempts to build a German society from the ruins of war and genocide?[49]

Frank Trommler makes an important distinction that sets the stage for the subsequent essays by challenging an understanding of the role of intellectuals in relation to (repressive) state power that had gained prominence after 1989. As at the peak of the cold war, it has become common again to invoke Julien Benda's "treason of the intellectuals"—their abandonment of reason and truth in favor of partisanship on behalf of a class, nation, or party.[50] Furet reintroduced a strong version of this charge into the debate.[51] But Trommler contends that the notion of treason, though useful for describing one dimension of the communist experience, elides the quandary of GDR literary culture. A manichean dualism and a compulsive projection of right and wrong, typical of intellectual betrayal according to Benda, did characterize the generation of exiles, Stalinists as much as anti-Stalinists. Their politics of treason, moreover, perceived the people as a constant source of threat and considered treason, not as some exceptional act but as the order of the day. However, this was just one element in a more complex lay-out of the GDR. The main thrust of GDR culture in the sixties and seventies was to be found in a different and, as far as Stalinist righteousness was concerned, regime-critical remaking of the social agenda in a project in which literature acquired the mission of "social work." The public role of intellectuals consisted in articulating the social space in which a wounded society could heal and individuals could recover and regenerate a postfascist identity.[52] Their purpose consisted in creating a tight public sphere that would prevent escape from the past and induce cathartic renewal. Heinrich Böll in the West and Christa Wolf in the East were the main protagonists of this type of intellectual culture. One might well conclude that this aesthetics of interiority and therapy, which both created and justified the public role of intellectuals, was "the spirit" of late twentieth-century Germany. Was it an illusion? And what, if anything, was its betrayal?

The older and starker conflict of reason versus treason is captured in the contribution by Dorothea Dornhof. She treats this conflict as a "historical" problem, quite remote from her own efforts to find a way out of GDR literary criticism and into a unified Germany which, at the time of writing, appeared to her as yet another "system" to master. She reminds us of the vindictiveness of the Stalinist regime of the early GDR and its relentless pursuit of partisan truths. Dornhof analyzes the fears and hopes that accompanied what one might best describe as rectification campaigns. The trouble is that the norms and standards of this moral righteousness were derived from Schiller and Goethe as much as from Lenin and Stalin. The classic German heritage served the reeducation of the East Germans. In turn, the transformation of GDR cultural politics along the lines Trommler suggests is succinctly captured in the transition from imagining the GDR as a "literary society"—a de facto reeducation dictatorship—to the GDR as a "reading nation" and eventually to the presumption of a "readers' paradise." Simone Barck, Martina Langermann, and Siegfried Lokatis point to the discrepancies of image and reality at each stage of this design. The new communal nation did not emerge, at least not the way it was represented. In the end, its most memorable failure was that those who actually wanted to read never got the books they wanted, not even those that fit the canon. Quite as telling, though, are the unmistakable traces of sadness that the laudable notion of a nation of readers just did not come to fruition and was gone for good even before unification.

The first set of essays raises a difficult issue for all those who see the GDR literati "dead and gone." The GDR of the fifties—that is, the high Stalinist GDR—not only attracted some of the finest writers and thinkers but also adopted an immaculately humanist canon. Its cultural policy was moved by a deep concern for reeducating the German nation. The regime's concern for the moral betterment of the working men and women was, for all intents and purposes, quite well received, although the clash of literary and plebeian cultures and the discrepancy between material goods and spiritual uplift remained notorious issues. One might well argue that Stalin and Goethe did not go together well, but lest there be any doubt, they were brought together, and the commitment to a classical humanism was genuine. The regime aspired to be a "tyranny of books" in the felicitous phrase of Barck et al., even when it abandoned its initial course and moved toward a therapeutic discourse of self-improvement. What we need to know, then, is captured neither by the notion of treason nor by the idea of communism as a delusional form of antifascism. We rather have to rethink the issue of how the accommodation of bolshevism and humanism worked.[53]

One way to approach this problem is to ask how opposition could be organized and legitimated under these conditions. Katie Trumpener and David Bathrick make perfectly clear that in the GDR the most spirited opposition against the communist regime came from Marxist and socialist heretics until well into the eighties, but by then the regime was crumbling and, with it, the opposition. Critics of the regime, such as Wolf Biermann, remained tied to a commitment to remake society and, if anything, their opposition was motivated by the desire to go one better than their calcified Stalinist elders. East Germany thus differs quite profoundly from other eastern European countries in that its main dissenters were Marxist apostates.

Incidentally, this may help explain why expulsion to West Germany was perceived as punishment in the first place.

Trumpener discusses the most prominent and, by all accounts, most promising of these oppositions. In two successive waves, some of the most accomplished filmmakers of the GDR attempted to create a new film culture whose main mark was an appeal to a socialism from below that matched the therapeutic discourse analyzed by Trommler. Of course, this movement annoyed the party stalwarts who appeared as the bad guys in films in which the young and the beautiful were always already the better socialists. But typically, what set the party on edge was the modernist aesthetic experimentation. The party, it turns out, was genuinely worried about Kafka, above and beyond being upset about the characterizations of its functionaries as old, fat, and nepotistic. But why should anyone, let alone the SED, worry about aesthetic modernism? At issue was, as Trumpener shows, a way of seeing and listening, a changed and changing perception of the world. Trumpener points to the potential of this move-ment, which saw in art the starting point of a new way of experiencing the world rather than consolidating and restoring an old one. Had the works of these filmmakers not been denied distribution, they might have broken the SED's restorative grip on everyday life. The possibilities become evident when Trumpener puts the GDR in the context of the eastern Eu-ropean experience. Alas, all that remains are high-quality archival copies of films, never shown in their time, that made it into a quite different world in 1990. Still, the fact that experimental art was understood as a challenge to the regime is worth our attention. If the functionaries were wrong, one wonders why; and if they were right, one might question what it is about art—and aesthetic experimentation, at that—that challenges state power.

Bathrick focuses on the moment when writers such as Christa Wolf or Christoph Hein, who had maintained a critical stance toward the regime but had willingly tempered their aestheticism, came under attack from a mostly younger generation of writers. This opposition consisted of several groups that themselves were at loggerheads.[54] But it is this opposition that quickly turned into dissidence and fed into the grassroots mobilization of 1989.[55] Bathrick focuses on the challenge from one of these groups, which became associated with the Prenzlauer Berg milieu and, at least initially, was subsumed under a much broader if highly segmented resistance against the regime by peace, environmental, and feminist groups with whom it shared a space.[56] As oppositional congeries, these literary groups—and in this they agreed with the new social movements—held that the regime's language of progress and therapy was intimately tied to its repressive structure of power. Artists who bought into this language inevitably succumbed to the state's power structures. Attempts to break out of this nexus of culture and power led these groups to the margins of the regime and to an exploration of "alternative" institutions. What emerged was an underground culture that refused to enter and be co-opted by official institutions. In deliberately putting themselves at the margins of society in order to escape the regime, however, they quickly encountered the one institution that occupied this space habitually: the secret police. As it turns out, there was no exit from the regime. The margins were riddled with informers.

It is this situation of living and writing at society's edge that Patricia Anne Simpson illuminates in her close reading of some of the haunted texts that emerged from this scene. They show a frighteningly fragile world of clandestiny in which trust was everything—and was regularly betrayed. In some of the most difficult texts, those by Gert Neumann and Gabriele Stötzer-Kachold in particular, we discover the linguistic imprint of the very real violence in a world on the margins. It seems reasonable to follow the thrust of Simpson's argument that it is in this kind of linguistic labor against violence—violence that issues from the regime as much as from fellow dissidents—that a new aesthetic of resistance was articulated. It remains to be seen how this aesthetic squares with the politics of alternative movements that occupied the same marginal space.

Only if we enter the world of dissidence from the margins and liminal spaces of East Germany can we fathom how already out of touch the official world of writers and artists was when, late in 1989, they stepped up their own opposition to the regime. Loren Kruger's essay highlights the pushes and pulls of oppositional discourse among theater people and shows, in the pivotal moment of the protest rally on November 4, 1989, the disparate tendencies of opposition and conformity in the GDR. Theater was the space in which the GDR was performed as socialist nation. This in any case was what the theater intellectuals wanted to believe, picking up a venerable German enlightenment tradition. Because they were attuned to the power of performance, they realized keenly and quickly—not unlike the Stasi—that the mass protests of 1989 were the revolution that the GDR never had and that they, as theater intellectuals, so desperately had tried to generate or, as the case may be, simulate over the past forty years. They also recognized their impotence, for the street had become the stage, with Leipzig, as usual, being "holier than thou," Berlin playing the impudent, and beer and schnapps, difficult it is to imagine, being even more important than in Rainald Götz's plays.[57] The theater intellectuals realized that in this lay theater of street protesters the presumed union of theater and social action was broken—an indication of the crisis of intellectuals to come.

The defeat of the intellectuals—and it was a defeat—spelled the end of neither literature nor of the theater, but it did bring to an end a twentieth-century project of remaking the world by cultural means that had taken on a particular urgency in postwar Germany. At times this cultural project was an illusion, but at times it was not. At times it was communist, at other times it was not. Any theory about the illusion of this culture and, for that matter, of communism as it applies to Germany will have to engage with the quintessential theater intellectual Heiner Müller and try to make sense of his oeuvre. Alexander Kluge, who conducted a series of interviews with Müller for his television program, thinks of him as the first intellectual of the twenty-first century.[58] What is sure, though, is his proletarian gestus (inspired, no doubt, by Bertolt Brecht) and his "it-takes-two-to-tango" attitude toward the SED regime and the West German media, which made him an instant hero in the postunification transition, because the young loved him and the older ones had always found this kind of German genius irrepressible. The very old one, of course, thought of Brecht himself. Müller's gestus was calculated, Kluge argues, to confront a reticent public with the legacy of this century—the experience of war and warriors that he had begun to think, write, and perform anew toward the end of his life. Kluge is right: The power that German culture did battle with is the armored existence of the state and the subjectivities this existence generated.

What we discover is that this battle was a dirty one that left loyalties betrayed, principles toppled, and the best intentions marooned—in the Third Reich and in exile, in the GDR as well as the Federal Republic. But inasmuch as the sobering reality of the imbrication of power and culture leaves a dent in the implacably good conscience of its main defenders, the historical labor on GDR culture is well spent. For it is this kind of labor that is vital for the transition to another Germany. Rather than being the abject part of German intellectual life, the GDR intellectuals are the symptomatic expression of the spiritual situation of our time. East German intellectual culture and, for that matter, eastern Europe cannot be given over to oblivion without a serious loss for everyone, including "our" selves.

As with all historical labors, the danger of digging into the past is that we get stuck in it. There is a good argument to be made that this is what happened to German intellectuals in the nineties. Hence, Part II deals with this temptation of antiquarianism and simultaneously suggests exit strategies. For the purposes of this book one might have wished that German intellectuals had taken on such exit strategies a bit more vigorously than they actually did. This would likely have left an altogether more definite oeuvre, where in fact transient writing and thinking predominated. Still, the debates of the nineties are well worth more detailed scrutiny, if we look at them as controversies over a culture under construction. Inasmuch as the authors of the second part of the volume have a common voice, they tend to agree that overcoming the legacy of unification—which has amounted to very real impediments and obstacles—is the greatest challenge on the horizon. The task of Part II is to take measure of the balance of metaphors to be carried over into a new century, an effort that must begin by thinking out the navigational charts of those who moved themselves into a new century after November 9, 1989.

Part II opens with the continuation of the story by Dietrich Hohmann. Hohmann's account of his "free fall"—coincidentally, the title of a book by one of the leading German intellectual historians about the fate of East German intellectuals[59]—shocked and upset readers of the manuscript by the sheer violence of the emotion. They now may cherish the clairvoyance with which the writer diagnosed the vertigo generated by unification among East Germans.[60] It is the disaster-prone effect of encountering oneself as another, alienation, that is both so prescient an insight into the contemporary German situation and so archetypical a figure of German thought. Hohmann's short story suggests the distance to be traversed before the country can be united. Alexander Kluge's concluding contribution, in turn, redefines the stakes of the transition—the inadvertent difficulties that come with happy endings such as unification.

In order to size up the role of intellectuals in the collapse of the GDR and the transition to a new Germany, a walk on the wild side, into the underbrush of unification, seems appropriate. It keeps the story about intellectuals down to the ground and the metaphors honest at a moment when intellectuals easily flew off the handle and metaphors went into overdrive. If Heiner Müller fantasized after unification about an interment ending in complete chaos (he had Felix Guattari's funeral in mind), the punks just a short walk away from his *Schauspielhaus* acted out the chaos days and put them on record. Patricia Anne Simpson takes them on in her second contribution to this volume. The punks performed the end of the GDR as the last days of Pompeii. Although their noise could undoubtedly be heard among the dissenting intellectuals of the Prenzlauer Berg, the twain did not ever meet—although, again, they lived pretty much in the same space. The punks knew, or so it appears in Simpson's history of unification as seen or heard through the noise of the local scene, what the dissenters only discovered the hard way and after the fact. Unification soon dried out the margins of the GDR. It destroyed the family scene at the edge of society in an eruption of privatization and propelled "the people" straight to the supermarket. The revolution of 1989 was unfathomable for oppositional intellectuals and dissenters alike because it was, "totally," a revolution of private wants and desires. Not unlike their British models nearly twenty years earlier, the East Berlin punks discovered the truth about the disappearance of a culture of resistance (in the British case it was a working-class culture) before anyone else did. The screams of *Keynkampf* (no more battles, no more *Mein Kampf*) make up the funeral march for the German century. It is now left to the French to debate whether this culture was a good thing or not.[61]

The onslaught of privatization was unwelcome news as well for Andreas Graf, the dissident historian of anarchism. He was in the right place to stem the tide, participating in the (futile) efforts of the East German democracy movement to remake the state-run media sector of the GDR. He fervently hoped that a public sphere could be forged after the destruction of a repressive state. But he shows why and how this did not happen. Graf's essay portrays the destruction of the media monopoly by the state and the subsequent inability to rebuild it. The outcome was a massive move toward the privatization of the media with the collusion of the East German technical intelligentsia and in the absence of any effective role of public intellectuals. Contrary to what one might expect, however, rapid privatization produced not efficiencies but so cumbersome a corporate mechanism (Jens Reich spoke on another occasion of the "cloning of a dinosaur") that it actually set back the mediatization of society. By consolidating and rolling over the old-fashioned West German media sector into that of eastern Germany, unification made the transition to a future media society that much harder. It is this kind of logic that haunts unification.

Konrad Jarausch gives intellectuals, both the oppositional literati and the dissidents, a great deal of credit in creating the language and the networks necessary for the popular mobilization in 1989. Dissidents, he insists, took the public lead and, lest it be forgotten, conquered and brought to light the Stasi—an act whose signal importance can only be gauged in comparison and contrast with developments in eastern Europe and especially in Russia, where the same did not happen. For with the destruction of state authority the power of the secret parastate grew everywhere—except in the transitional GDR. This said, however, it is also clear that the dissenters and the intellectuals lost their mass following almost overnight in the process of unification. The people wanted a unified nation and free and uninhibited consumption, while the intellectuals shunned both. The fallout was far-reaching. Unification with its twin features of a popular national self-assertion and a consumer identity undercut the language of political and moral concern that had created and justified the public role of intellectuals in the first place.

The following essays by Mitchell Ash on the politics of higher education, by Andreas Huyssen on the politics of national identity, by John Borneman on the politics of memory after the cold war, and by myself on the culture wars of the nineties, pick up on Jarausch's concluding comment that intellectuals should move on, because there is plenty of work to be done. If only the intellectuals would stop whining, they might recognize the power they actually have. The four essays have a common approach and a common sense of urgency. A nation, a culture, a community of people need rebuilding—this is the main conclusion since initial hopes and dreams about a revolution that would make everyone happy (except the men and women of the old regime) have dissipated. Rather than with the intellectuals, the challenge started with Germans at large, who did not grow together but set themselves apart and found considerable pleasure in disparaging each other. It seems that the impatience of the four authors caught on in Germany during the second half of the nineties, spawning a recognition of both the prevailing paralysis of postunification Germany—a widespread sense of being stuck and going nowhere fast—and an incipient sense of the possibilities that emerge from entering a post–cold war world.

The four essays make clear that such a step cannot be taken without a thorough reorientation of postwar eastern, western, and common German identities. Hence, they reach back into postwar history in order to show what has been, but no longer is. Ash highlights the West German paradigm of mobilization, which creates havoc when applied to East Germany and confusion and arbitrariness when used to reform higher education. Huyssen discusses the peculiarly West German antinationalism as a condition and a result of the cold war (but not of Auschwitz, as was asserted by postwar intellectuals). Borneman revisits East German education after Auschwitz, which he considers more successful than is commonly assumed, but insufficient to cope with the present. All three are unanimous in stressing the high cost of unloading the West German experience onto the East. I discuss the fallout of debates between conservatives and liberals about the course of West German cultural politics that gained new valence with Stasi revelations. All of the debates of the nineties discussed in these four essays, which range from the literary to the political, shared an initial refusal to recognize the enormity of the social experiment that unifying Germany amounted to. The essays, in turn, insist that nations do not happen but have to be constituted and articulated. For better or for worse, this remains the task of intellectuals, whose number, as 1989 suggests, is called quickly when they are too far off the mark.[62] What they discover is that they did not create their public role as "critical" intellectuals, but it was given to them by a public that proved to be far more critical and far more conscious of its needs and desires than the intellectuals would ever have suspected. Still, the essays also suggest that it matters what intellectuals do with their role. If anything, the history of East and West Germany suggests that they made a difference—and there is no reason to presume that there is no need for them now.

The nature of the challenge has changed, though. For one thing, the media are remarkably different from what they were in East and West Germany and will continue to change as Germany enters the electronic age. For another, Germany needs a national public sphere, geared not only to coping with the past but suitable for and responsive to an age in which the world is connected in a flash but in which connections fail to be made. In a world ruled by regimes of privacy public intellectuals become the floating authority that translate subjective emotions into public action. This is the gist of Alexander Kluge's speech on the occasion of his acceptance of the Lessing Prize of the city of Hamburg in 1992. Intellectuals—not as purveyors of utopia, but as mediators and net-workers—are needed as urgently as ever.

A Propos the Power of Intellectuals

If I am less pessimistic about the impending transition than are some of the German pundits, this has not least to do with the fact that so wonderfully convincing a theorist of the public sphere as Alexander Kluge does brisk business with his television spot *Prime Time Spät Ausgabe* (sic), which is aired at eleven o'clock on Sunday night and has a viewership of anywhere between 500,000 and 900,000 people on private television.[63] This is not a mass public, but it is no mean feat, either. Time and again, I am also impressed by the give-and-take of public debate in a thick and rich colloquy in all media. The pervasiveness and openness of public debate is striking—and the very persistence of debating intellectuals had more than one American visitor gasping. It seems that wherever one turns there is a talking head explaining the world or any part thereof—and behind every talking head is a writing hand. I am well aware that this is not the way a Pierre Bourdieu would like his intellectuals to be.[64] Hauke Brunkhorst has raised similar concerns.[65] But if the theorists of the public sphere are right to think that coffeehouses were good for public discourse in the eighteenth century and served an emergent class of intellectuals well, one cannot but wonder if the contemporary mediascape might not do the same for the twenty-first.

Notes

1. Karl Jaspers, *Die geistige Situation der Zeit* [1931] (Berlin, 1979) (Man in the modern age, trans. Eden and Cedar Paul [New York, 1978]).

2. Joachim Walther, *Sicherungsbereich Literatur: Schriftsteller und Staatssicherheit in der Deutschen Demokratischen Republik* (Berlin, 1996).

3. Wolfgang Bialas, "Ostdeutsche Diskurse und die Weimarer Republik: Variationen zum Verhältnis von Geist und Macht," in *Die Weimarer Republik zwischen Metropole und Provinz: Intellektuellendiskurse zur politischen Kultur,* ed. Wolfgang Bialas and Burkhard Stenzel (Weimar, 1996); Wolfgang Bialas and Eckhardt Fuchs, eds., *Macht und Geist: Intellektuelle in der Zwischenkriegszeit* (Leipzig, 1995); Pierre Bourdieu, *Die Intellektuellen und die Macht,* ed. Irene Dölling, trans. Jürgen Bolder (Hamburg, 1991); Peter de Mendelssohn, *Der Geist in der Despotie: Versuche über die moralischen Möglichkeiten der Intellektuellen in der totalitären Gesellschaft* (Frankfurt am Main, 1987).

4. J. P. Nettl, "Ideas, Intellectuals, and Structures of Dissent," in *On Intellectuals: Theoretical Case Studies,* ed. Philip Rieff (Garden City, N.Y., 1969), 53–122; Christophe Charle, *Les intellectuels en Europe au XIXe siècle: Essai d'histoire comparée* (Paris, 1996).

5. Aleida Assmann, *Arbeit am nationalen Gedächtnis: Eine kurze Geschichte der deutschen Bildungsidee* (Frankfurt am Main, 1993); Wolf Lepenies, *Between Literature and Science: The Rise of Sociology* (New York, 1988).

6. Zygmunt Bauman, *Legislators and Interpreters: On Modernity, Post-Modernity, and Intellectuals* (Ithaca, 1987).

7. The newest literature on the subject includes Stephen Brockmann, *Literature and German Unification* (Cambridge, U.K., 1999), and Jan-Werner Müller, *Another Country: German Intellectuals, Unification, and National Identity* (New Haven, 2000).

8. The stretch of the imagination is captured by Peter Handke. See his *Mein Jahr in der Niemandsbucht: Ein Märchen aus den neuen Zeiten* (Frankfurt am Main, 1994), *Eine winterliche Reise zu den Flüssen Donau, Save, Morawa und Drina, oder, Gerechtigkeit für Serbien* (Frankfurt am Main, 1996), *Sommerlicher Nachtrag zu einer winterlichen Reise* (Frankfurt am Main, 1996), and *Zurüstungen für die Unsterblichkeit: Ein Königsdrama* (Frankfurt am Main, 1997).

9. John Borneman, *Settling Accounts: Violence, Justice, and Accountability in Postsocialist Europe* (Princeton, 1997); Anne Sa'adah, *Germany's Second Chance: Trust, Justice, and Democratization* (Cambridge, Mass., 1998); Enquete Kommission, ed., *Materialien der Enquete Kommission "Aufarbeitung von Geschichte und Folgen der SED-Diktatur in Deutschland,"* 9 vols. Aufarbeitung von Geschichte und Folgen der SED-Diktatur in Deutschland im Deutschen Bundestag (Frankfurt am Main, 1995).

10. Heinrich von Kleist, "Über die allmähliche Verfertigung der Gedanken beim Reden," in *Sämtliche Werke und Briefe,* ed. Heinrich von Kleist (Munich, 1983), 2:315–18.

11. Günter Gaus, *Kein einig Vaterland: Texte von 1991 bis 1998* (Berlin, 1998); Peter Glotz, *Die Jahre der Verdrossenheit: Politisches Tagebuch 1993/94* (Stuttgart, 1996); Alison Lewis, "Unity Begins Together: Analyzing the Trauma of German Unification," *New German Critique* 64 (1995): 135–59.

12. Konrad Jarausch, *The Rush to German Unity* (New York, 1994).

13. Andrea Böhm and Stefan Willeke, "Nichts als die Wahrheit?" *Die Zeit* 27, 10 February 2000.

14. Daniela Dahn and Barbara Erdmann, *Wir bleiben hier, oder, Wem gehört der Osten: Vom Kampf um Häuser und Wohnungen in den neuen Bundesländern* (Reinbek, 1994); Daniela Dahn, *Westwärts und nicht vergessen: Vom Unbehagen in der Einheit* (Berlin, 1996).

15. Hannah Arendt, *The Human Condition* (Chicago, 1958).

16. Lothar Probst, ed., *Differenz in der Einheit: Über die kulturellen Unterschiede der Deutschen in Ost und West* (Berlin, 1999).

17. Annette Simon, "Fremd im eigenen Land" *Die Zeit* 25, 17 June 1999, 7.

18. Wolfgang Hardtwig and Heinrich August Winkler, eds., *Deutsche Entfremdung: Zum Befinden in Ost und West* (Munich, 1994).

19. Jürgen Habermas, *Die neue Unübersichtlichkeit* (Frankfurt am Main, 1985).

20. Wolf Lepenies, *Folgen einer unerhörten Begebenheit: Die Deutschen nach der Vereinigung* (Berlin, 1992).

21. Jürgen Habermas, "Yet Again: German Identity—A Unified Nation of Angry DM-Burghers," *New German Critique* 52 (1991): 84–101.

22. Brian Ladd, *The Ghosts of Berlin: Confronting German History in the Urban Landscape* (Chicago, 1997).

23. Rudolf Herzinger, "Staubwolken im Nichts," *Die Zeit* 28, 5 July 1996, 36.

24. Wolfgang Jäger and Ingeborg Villinger, eds., *Die Intellektuellen und die deutsche Einheit* (Freiburg, 1997).

25. Martin Meyer, ed., *Intellektuellendämmerung: Beiträge zur neuesten Zeit des Geistes* (Munich, 1992).

26. Thomas Assheuser, "Was ist deutsch?" *Die Zeit* 40, 30 September 1999.

27. Christa Wolf, *Auf dem Weg nach Tabou: Texte 1990–1994* (Cologne, 1994).

28. Wolf Biermann, *Der Sturz des Dädalus oder: Eizes für die Eingeborenen der Fidschi-Inseln über den IM Judas Ischariot und den Kuddelmuddel in Deutschland seit dem Golfkrieg* (Cologne, 1992). See also Peter Böthig and Klaus Michael, eds., *Macht-Spiele: Literatur und Staatssicherheit im Fokus Prenzlauer Berg* (Leipzig, 1993).

29. Hermann Vinke, ed., *Akteneinsicht Christa Wolf : Zerrspiegel und Dialog* (Hamburg, 1993).

30. Frank Schirrmacher, ed., *Die Walser-Bubis-Debatte: Eine Dokumentation* (Frankfurt, 1999).

31. Andrei S. Markovits, Seyla Benhabib, and Moishe Postone, "Symposium on Rainer Werner Fassbinder's 'Garbage, the City, and Death,'" *New German Critique* 38 (1986): 3–27; Janusz Bodek, "Ein 'Geflecht aus Schuld und Rache'? Die Kontroversen um Fassbinders Der Müll, die Stadt und der Tod," in *Deutsche Nachkriegsliteratur und der Holocaust*, ed. Stephan Braese et al. (Frankfurt am Main, 1998), 351–84.

32. In lieu of a long literature: Uwe Steimle, *Uns fragt ja keener: Ostalgie: Texte für Ilse Bähnert und Günter Zieschong* (Berlin, 1997).

33. Axel Schildt, *Ankunft im Westen: Ein Essay zur Erfolgsgeschichte der Bundesrepublik* (Frankfurt am Main, 1999), is a good starting point.

34. Michael Geyer, "Geschichte als Wissenschaft für ein Zeitalter der Unübersichtlichkeit," in *Nach dem Erdbeben: (Re)Konstruktionen ost-deutscher Geschichte und Geschichtswissenschaft*, ed. Konrad Jarausch and Matthias Middell (Leipzig, 1994), 38–65.

35. Frank Trommler, "What Should Remain? Exploring the Literary Contributions to Postwar German History," in *Beyond 1989: Re-reading German Literary History since 1945*, ed. Keith Bullivant (Providence, 1997), 153–76.

36. François Furet and Pierre Rosanvallon, eds., *La République du centre: La fin de l'exception française* (Paris, 1988).

37. Rainer Land and Ralf Possekel, '*Namenlose Stimmen waren uns voraus*': *Politische Diskurse von Intellektuellen aus der DDR* (Bochum, 1994); Wolfgang Emmerich, *Kleine Literaturgeschichte der DDR: Erweiterte Neuausgabe* (Leipzig, 1996).

38. Heinz Ludwig Arnold, ed., *Literatur in der DDR: Rückblicke* (Munich, 1991).

39. Horst Domdey, "DDR-Literatur als Literatur der Epochenillusion," in *Die DDR im vierzigsten Jahr* (=22. Tagung zum Stand der DDR-Forschung in der Bundesrepublik) (Cologne, 1989), 137–48; Cora Stephan, ed., *Wir Kollaborateure: Der Westen und die deutschen Vergangenheiten* (Reinbek, 1992).

40. Klaus Naumann, *Der Krieg als Text: Das Jahr 1945 im kulturellen Gedächtnis der Presse* (Hamburg, 1998).

41. Kulturreferat, Landeshauptstadt München, ed., *Bilanz einer Ausstellung: Dokumentation der Kontroverse um die Ausstellung "Vernichtungskrieg: Verbrechen der Wehrmacht 1941 bis 1944"* (Munich, 1998); Hamburger Institut für Sozialforschung, ed., *Besucher einer Ausstellung: Die Ausstellung "Vernichtungskrieg. Verbrechen der Wehrmacht 1941 bis 1944" in Interview und Gespräch* (Hamburg, 1998).

42. Helmut König, Michael Kohlstruck, and Andreas Wöll, eds., *Vergangenheitsbewältigung am Ende des zwanzigsten Jahrhunderts*, Leviathan 18 (special issue) (1998).

43. Andreas Ludwig, "Objektkultur und DDR-Gesellschaft: Aspekte einer Wahrnehmung des Alltags," *Aus Politik und Zeitgeschichte* B28 (1999): 3–11; Rainer Gries, "Nostalgie—Legende—Zukunft? Geschichtskultur und Produktkultur in Ostdeutschland," *Universitas: Zeitschrift für interdisziplinäre Wissenschaft* 51 (1996): 102–15.

44. Mary Fulbrook, *German National Identity After the Holocaust* (Cambridge, 1999).

45. Ronald G. Suny and Michael D. Kennedy, eds., *Intellectuals and the Articulation of the Nation* (Ann Arbor, 1999); Herfried Münkler, Hans Grünberger, and Kathrin Mayer, eds., *Nationenbildung: Die Nationalisierung Europas im Diskurs humanistischer Intellektueller; Italien und Deutschland* (Berlin, 1998).

46. François Furet, *The Passing of an Illusion: The Idea of Communism in the Twentieth Century* (Chicago, 1999), originally *Le passé d'une illusion: Essai sur l'idée communiste au XXe siècle* (Paris, 1995). The German translation was published in 1996.

47. François Furet and Ernst Nolte, *"Feindliche Nähe": Kommunismus und Faschismus im 20. Jahrhundert* (Munich, 1998).

48. Pierre Bourdieu, *Acts of Resistance: Against the Tyranny of the Market* (New York, 1998).

49. Christa Wolf, *What Remains & Other Stories*, trans. Heike Schwarzbauer and Rick Takvorian (Chicago, 1995).

50. Julien Benda, *The Treason of the Intellectuals* (New York, 1969); Margaret Boveri, *Der Verrat im XX. Jahrhundert*, 4 vols. (Reinbek, 1956); Urs Jaeggi, *Versuch über den Verrat* (Neuwied, 1984); Werner von Bergen and Walter H. Pehle, eds., *Denken im Zwiespalt: Über den Verrat von Intellektuellen im 20. Jahrhundert* (Frankfurt am Main, 1996).

51. Furet, *Passing of an Illusion*.

52. This is brilliantly analyzed by Julia Hell, *Post-fascist Fantasies: Psychoanalysis, History, and the Literature of East Germany* (Durham, N.C., 1997).

53. Maurice Merleau-Ponty, *Humanism and Terror: An Essay on the Communist Problem* (Boston, 1969).

54. Gerda Haufe and Karl Bruckmeier, eds., *Die Bürgerbewegungen in der DDR und in den ostdeutschen Bundesländern* (Opladen, 1993); John C. Torpey, *Intellectuals, Socialism, and Dissent: The East German Opposition and Its Legacy* (Minneapolis, 1995); Ehrhart Neubert, *Geschichte der Opposition der DDR 1949–1989* (Berlin, 1997).

55. Helmut Müller-Enbergs, Marianne Schulz, and Jan Wielgohs, eds., *Von der Illegalität ins Parlament: Werdegang und Konzepte der neuen Bürgerbewegungen* (Berlin, 1992); Christian Joppke, *East German Dissidents and the Revolution of 1989: Social Movement in a Leninist Regime* (New York, 1995).

56. Barbara Felsmann and Annett Gröschner, eds., *Durchgangszimmer Prenzlauer Berg: Eine Berliner Künstlersozialgeschichte in Selbstauskünften* (Berlin, 1999); Philip Brady and Ian Wallace, eds., *Prenzlauer Berg: Bohemia in East Berlin?* (Amsterdam, 1995).

57. Heiner Müller, "Das Leben stört natürlich ständig: Ein Gespräch mit Heiner Müller," *Freibeuter* 47 (1990): 91–98.

58. Alexander Kluge and Heiner Müller, *"Ich schulde der Welt einen Toten": Gespräche* (Hamburg, 1995); Alexander Kluge, *"Ich bin ein Landvermesser": Gespräche mit Heiner Müller* (Hamburg, 1996).

59. Wolfgang Bialas, *Vom Unfreien Schweben zum freien Fall: Ostdeutsche Intellektuelle im gesellschaftlichen Umbruch* (Frankfurt am Main, 1996).

60. See most recently Wolfgang Hilbig, *Das Provisorium* (Frankfurt am Main, 2000).

61. Tony Judt, *Past Imperfect: French Intellectuals, 1944–1956* (Berkeley, 1992).

62. Ronald G. Suny and Michael D. Kennedy, eds., *Intellectuals and the Articulation of the Nation* (Ann Arbor, 1999).

63. Peter C. Lutze, *Alexander Kluge: The Last Modernist* (Detroit, 1998).

64. Pierre Bourdieu, "L'emprise du journalisme," *Actes de la recherche en science sociales* 101–2 (1994): 3–9; Pierre Bourdieu, *On Television* (New York, 1998).

65. Hauke Brunkhorst, *Der entzauberte Intellektuelle: Über die neue Beliebigkeit des Denkens* (Hamburg, 1990).

PART 1

Intellectuals and the Politics of Culture

in the German Democratic Republic

DIETRICH HOHMANN

Translated by Devin Pendas

An Attempt at an Exemplary Report on H.

H. is a writer from Brandenburg. He has published two novels, a collection of short stories, and a book of travel essays. His texts have appeared in many anthologies, he has dabbled in screenwriting, and he has translated verse and prose from Scots into German. He has done all this in a country whose very right to exist has been heatedly debated within and without its own borders since its birth and—consequently?—no longer exists.

H. explicitly insisted on the question mark after "consequently." He informs us that he cannot agree with the idea that there were from the outset democratic majorities in the country who would have supported the abolition of this unique creation on German soil. Rather, he believes that following the war, for which the Germans were so fundamentally to blame, these citizens had hoped that they might be able to risk making a new start. They hoped to atone for the most heinous crimes against humanity in history, as well as the crimes against their fellow country-men, Christians as well as communists, Social Democrats as well as free thinkers. This desire for atonement bound H. to an active humanism that entailed antifascism and a desire for greater social justice than the postwar bourgeois order was ready to practice. He was young then, on his way to adulthood. The multitude of possibilities inherent in a society of equals and the seductive appeals to one's youthful aspirations could easily sway an adolescent. He felt particularly vulnerable when he remembered that great catastrophe, which, although in the distant past, was still present in ruins and graveyards everywhere. The sight of the Buchenwald concen-tration camp, which was near his home and, later, of the remnants of the Warsaw Ghetto had made a deep impression on him. These sights led to an oppressive confrontation with utterly abhorrent contempt for human life and the sheer helplessness of the individual. These experiences had determined the course of his life for decades. He believed in the possibility of a social order that could realize the lofty goals for which people of different centuries, different races, and different religions and worldviews had suffered and died.

Today, he is almost apologetic about his formative experiences, which nevertheless still seem to move him deeply. It is as if he wants to say it is no longer appropriate to refer to such experiences. Every media commentator with any influence between Hamburg and Munich refers to people like him as "hobbyhorse anti-fascists." H. has long been cognizant of the ways in which people reproach authors of his background: The authors were privileged, supportive of the government, cowardly, and, above all, irrelevant to German literature.

It is hard to get H. to face up to "such vicious slander," as he puts it. He is the product of an age dominated by clichés about and prejudices against people like him. Like the representatives of the church, intellectuals were proclaimed the least "loyal citizens" whenever the "leading comrades" of the Unity Party held internal discussions. The leading comrades, always assuming the longevity of their regime, denounced the opponents of their all holy *Kulturpolitik* (cultural and educational policy). And so insult is added to injury; this at least has not changed. Any retaliation against these sorts of pat judgments, which are loudly propagated and well suited to the current political climate, is a futile gesture at best.

If, in the GDR, it was a privilege to live modestly from one's books and literary activities, then, says H., he was privileged. If one were a coward for not calling, either in speech or print, for the overthrow of a system that had squandered its historical chance—and this was precisely his critique of the system—then H. was a coward. Furthermore, if one characterizes H.'s vision of a humane society as "ideological prostitution," a state in which freedom, justice, and solidarity are not degraded into mere phrases (and precisely this is the accusation), then he is guilty and stands convicted of such prostitution.

No, there is no "but . . . ," no further reply to the accusations. The reader might try, H. suggests quietly, to put himself momentarily in H.'s shoes and then assess the sum of his own courage or take measure of his own caution.

H. asserts that it was possible to write what one wanted to write in the GDR between 1945 and 1989. Anyone who did not seek an audience—particularly through publication—did not face any constraints; one could write merely for oneself, as some writers have occasionally claimed.

Doing so would create literature that did not intend to have an impact, and in this respect the assertion is for the most part correct. Writing would serve only self-understanding and self-clarification, without any expectation of finding a correspondence with the "external world." This would mean permanent intellectual masturbation, according to H., and quite simply the end of literature.

Since the statement "writing for oneself" is only rarely applicable, indeed is usually just a mechanism to protect the work, these same defenses are effective not only for those who allegedly write for themselves but also for those who delivered their texts to the public as homages, meticulous descriptions, reform proposals, didactic examples, sources of friction, accusations, barrages of curses, or tirades of hatred. H. says it is the purpose of writing to be published. Publication is a necessary piece of luggage whenever anyone takes the great journey toward a readership. Not all writers can be their own publishers. During the thirty-year history of the GDR, at least, that goal was out of reach. Only institutions (such as libraries) were allowed to have a photocopier. Moreover, in these institutions every copy was registered and documented. H. did not even dare consider other modes of duplication. Self-publication would only have been possible through illegal means. Thus, it would have presupposed a conspiratorial society and, naturally, the conscious desire to be punished for one's literary impact.

And the publishing houses? How did one deal with them?

According to H., publishers as well as editors were required to select their titles according to certain criteria and to assign them a purpose, a theme. In the GDR there were party apparatchiks everywhere, including the publishing houses, which discovered these themes or deduced such guidelines from party documents. This meant that the all-powerful SED, which in the words of a popular marching song was "always right," also determined what art and literature ought to achieve. Documents to this end were everywhere; tons of paper were used to print them. But this much was always true: the publisher was free to decide how broadly or how narrowly to interpret these guidelines. It was one of the advantages of these guidelines that they were quite abstract; and, as everyone knows, the more abstract guidelines are the more ambiguous they become. A precept such as "literature should serve the working people of our country" could just as well accommodate a work that did nothing but castigate the inconsistency of the system. This presupposes that the publisher was an accommodating sort. His leniency was, among other things, a function of the stability of his position and his courage, since he risked the wrath of both known and unknown censors at the Ministry of Culture. Assuming that he was not part of the power apparatus, that he was not dependent on their decisions, that he adhered only so far to their unwritten rules, he could effectively steer criticisms of the status quo through the censor, if they were mixed with praise for powers that be or at least provided a way out for the party.

This is fundamentally nothing more than the German demand for something positive in literature, comments H. This demand is not an invention of "actually existing socialism." It was amplified to the point of excess by the state, though.

In this sense, once there was a consensus between authors and publishers, once the "playing field" was defined, it became possible for one's work to develop. The author only cut what he or she deemed "unspeakable at the time," "not speakable at all," or absolutely "hostile" with mental scissors. It would have required much courage to save words, sentences, and titles from this self-censorship! It is indisputable that all, "under the burden of responsibility for the whole," became their own strictest censors. This was accomplished, H. explains, through experience, through education, and through "propaganda work"—the cynical circumlocution for indoctrination. As an author one knew, every time one wrote anything, what one was getting involved in and what one would have to put up with. Writers had to live with a divided soul—driven on one hand by the growing number of unbearable burdens and hopes for reform while, on the other, being pulled by the demands for patience, for slow breathing, for hope for the future. And the future—how far ahead dared one venture? What battles in an often too timid heart!

In the GDR, there was nothing cheaper and more abundant than hope for the future. The incomplete socialist society—whose ideologues spoke apologetically of the "actually existing socialism" as if this were not yet true socialism—was open to the future. It could only gain in maturity, in beauty, and in all the grand humanist goals that had been envisioned for generations and had only acquired power and direction through strenuous debate. In this regard, what were three, four, five decades! He had heard this often from like-minded people, even friends, and had said as much himself. People considered themselves very far away from reality, and perhaps it was once again utopia, the "principle of hope" that had taken hold of him and made the days bearable.[1]

In the end, there were only years and then days. The supply of hope was expended much more quickly than anyone could have expected. It seemed that the intellectuals' concept no longer fit reality when the GDR simply disappeared from the map, from history. Without further ado, the people, the "working masses," the readers once so lauded and beloved by writers, decided otherwise. According to H., when individual interest mercilessly supersedes ideology, religion, or just the notion of community, anyone who promises "happiness on earth" within a single life span—anyone who daily projects prosperity, generosity, and success on a screen but cannot actually provide them at the table, on the street, or in the marketplace—is done for. That is the rhythm of modernity according to German standards. This is the battlefield: The individual is trained in Darwinist survival techniques and only the healthy, determined, and ruthless have any chance for success, influence, or power. Being clever is always "in." Money is everything. Consumption is an idol—the "golden calf"—which, according to H., is slaughtered on foreign shores. One learns things like this in the Five New States, and learns them quickly.

As an author, H. became acquainted with new publishers and with new criteria that his writing would have to meet if he wanted it to "go to market." Perhaps he had rid his soul of its heresies, recapitulated his own prodigal path, named the injuries. But he also sought the "achievements" of socialism that, despite all the warnings from an inquisitorial press, he still could not do without. And now it was time to take the three or four hundred pages to the people. (He no longer thought only of "his people" but, rather, hoped that the millions of old, established *Bundesbürger* [citizens of the Federal Republic] who were openly striving for understanding might also be interested in the kinds of mundane things that were striking to an educated East German, if only as a memorial of where indifference toward power might lead.) And so his novel went to various publishers, new West German ones and recently privatized East German ones. Each of them had their criteria, of which salability and marketability were the most important—if sheer novelty and sensationalism could not be promised—and failure to meet these criteria meant the end. Of course, if the author decided to write more sensationally, to compose a sort of thriller, with more action and clichés, to write exposés à la "sex and crime and royalty in the former GDR," then he might approach, with success, the sort of publisher who understood trivial, and thus desirable, entertainment but understood it to perfection.

H. admits that in his relations with publishers in the new Germany, he was preoccupied with profit and loss. Is this how it was supposed to turn out? Is this how, he asks, it becomes impossible to live as a writer?

Yes, quite probably. And justly so, intoned the tabloids. There were too many of these people in the GDR anyway and who knows if they understand what life in a true democracy means, in terms of hardship, sweat, and humiliation.

Too many people have discovered this in the meantime, H. asserts. Among them are authors who have still not learned to be ashamed of their past, no matter how hard they try. But the learning process is not over, says H., irritated and annoyed at his own emotional outburst.

His privilege in the fallen state was truly thus: After many years of hard work, he had become financially independent, had always written what was important to him, and only then gone to the publisher, who said yes or no and who sometimes withheld a book from publication for years. Only now, many of these East German presses no longer exist; the old cultural landscape is desolated. Now H., who before the *Wende* had never sought out any West German publishers, is, like hundreds of other authors in the new states, once again, in his mid-fifties, a literary neophyte. In submitting a manuscript, he can no longer be satisfied with the often irritating but ultimately successful dialogue with a state-owned editor. Rather, he must be content with the terse rejection of an editor who "craves sensation and curiosity." And not just occasionally but, so far, incessantly. No longer willing to "go door to door" or "to rely on a lobby, on protection," as he says, he has found a job in which he feels useful, even indispensable. It is precisely this: As an author in the country of three initials—which was sometimes only so-called and sometimes only in quotation marks—he was certain that he was needed. He was able, through his texts, to communicate to interested people that which, in the absence of a free press, they could only learn "from outside." He could count on a readership that could read between the lines. The East Germans were masters of this skill. Many books, he claims, consisted of one important sentence, one important scene for him as a reader. As an author, he had, for example, conveyed the particularities of his own country's homemade social situation, its truly antagonistic contradictions, which had sharpened themselves to the breaking point, while the ideologically powerful continued to attribute such conditions exclusively to bourgeois societies. He was able to outwit the censors by disguising himself in the fairy tale, the allegorical, and the historical. The alert readership and listening audience, trained in every kind of allusion, felt as if they were in the know and at one with him—what could be better for an author?

H. doesn't wait for an answer; his question is meant rhetorically. He recalls the intellectual satisfaction of his writing, and only then does he become conscious of the distortions, the fears, the difficulties, and the injuries which he inflicted on himself, which he accepted as part of the bargain and which he had long repressed. He disguises as question what he already knows about his conduct: Why are people more inclined to accommodation than to opposition? Because there is no better motive for accommodation than self-conscious agreement with ideas and visions that appear entirely plausible and in no way criminal. At the time one could hide behind such ideas and retreat to them when daily life no longer corresponded to them. And wasn't an individual more susceptible to error than society at large? This also means that an individual might not overestimate himself and, consequently, cannot underestimate society if he wants to be taken seriously. Is any of this tenable in the face of the increasingly obvious tendency to conceive of society as merely the sum of extremely self-absorbed individuals?

Certainly, his struggle with the past remains visible. How does one come to grips with the fact that the country in which he lived "will become nothing more than a footnote to the history of the world"? He read that assessment of an old, spiteful author who had fought to the bitter end for a better GDR.[2] Does this "nothing more than a footnote to the history of the world" also apply to those who lived in this country? If not, what can they bring along with them into the new order, which has descended upon them overnight with innumerable ordinances, with new faces, concepts, and maxims, with different rules, with an unfamiliar scale of values, with unknown ways of relation and mutual dependencies, with the colossal dimensions of this globe, whose most distant point is now within reach so long as one fulfills the necessary prerequisites? Oh, yes, all these newly surfacing prerequisites for survival, for a better life in the united republic, which, H. asserts, cannot altogether remain the old after this joining but does not yet recognize that grave changes will be necessary—from the North Sea to the Alps—if it is serious about equal living conditions and equal opportunities for all Germans. The great apportionment remains to be accomplished.

H. is asked whether he wanted the unification. It all happened too fast, he answers. He sees the danger that, in this flight forward, Germans can neither win the now necessary insight nor manage that quiet self-contemplation, that necessary grieving process, which psychology describes as vital. Many of his compatriots currently find themselves suddenly delivered without having arrived. This proves itself to be a giant Pandora's box, from which, along with all the wishes, hopes, and expectations, has crept an all-too-real loss of self-esteem as a result of unemployment and a renewed powerlessness in the face of scarcely less oppressive power structures. H. is certain of one thing: ideology's right to govern has followed money's right to power, and anyone who refuses to pay homage . . .

Well, anyone with an imagination can picture the consequences for himself, H. explains impatiently.

Editor's Notes

1. Ernst Bloch, *Das Prinzip Hoffnung* [1954–1959] (Gesamtausgabe vol. 5), 3 vols. (Frankfurt am Main, 1977) (The principle of hope, trans. Neville Plaice, Steven Plaice, and Paul Knight [Cambridge, Mass., 1986]).

2. See Stephan Heym, "Ash Wednesday in the GDR," *New German Critique* 52 (winter 1991): 31–36, esp. 31.

German Intellectuals:
Public Roles and the Rise of the Therapeutic

The Language of Treason

The revelation of their widespread collaboration with the State Security apparatus (the Stasi) in East Germany before 1989 has given new momentum to the debate whether twentieth-century intellectuals have been more often perpetrators of universal treason rather than carriers of universal reason. Julien Benda's juxtaposition of reason and treason in *La trahison des clercs* has gone through a spirited revival.[1] Benda makes a distinction between upholding ideas of truth, justice, and enlightenment on one hand and selling out to political partisanship on behalf of nation, class, or party on the other. Benda's distinction has been used in order to articulate a moral response vis-à-vis the entanglement of the intelligentsia with the state security and has given expression to entire population's disgust over the loss of trust and civility. Commentators equated Benda's concept of treason with the moral corruption of the SED regime and of its intellectuals.

Yet, with every new revelation, exposure, accusation, and admission of complicity it has become more apparent that the concept of treason, which had been the public perception of intellectual politics in Germany since World War I, is no longer an adequate framework for the issue at stake. There can be no doubt that the accusation of treason has been one of the crucial political weapons in the battles between National Socialism, Communism, and Western democracies. However, although the cold war prolonged and temporarily even enhanced the weight of this accusation,[2] treason has become less central to the West's definition of the intellectual. The recent encounters with the phenomenon of betrayal, even when focused on intellectuals, does not produce the ideological sound waves that accompanied the public accusations and confessions in an earlier period. The disclosure of the Stasi files unraveled a fabric of lies and deception on which many public careers were built in the German Democratic Republic. But with these lies, the giant screen on which individual conduct could be enlarged and redeemed for socialism or history has vanished as well. What remains is the betrayal of personal or intellectual loyalties. Despite its broad and emotion-laden publicity, this kind of betrayal has no redeeming qualities.

The much-debated cases of prominent East German writers such as Christa Wolf and Heiner Müller who were contacted by the Stasi and of writers who became active informants confirm the frailty of Benda's universalist distinction of reason and treason. Although the public roles of authors who chose to stay in the German Democratic Republic always invited a comparison with the roles that writers of an earlier generation (most prominently Bertolt Brecht, Anna Seghers, and Johannes R. Becher) had played in the establishment of the state, the change in the language of political commitment cannot be overlooked. Though still a moral discourse that builds on the onerous heritage of twentieth-century German history, this language constructs identities whose components bear little resemblance to the compulsive projection of right and wrong in the language of the generation of exiles. More than two decades ago, Gerhard Zwerenz, summarizing his generation's attitude toward the language of the older colleagues, bade farewell to their ritualistic self-positioning in the minefield of ideological right and wrong:

> The old authors continued battles that had long been anachronistic and did not really concern us anymore. Brecht treated Thomas Mann who lived in Switzerland with irony; Arnold Zweig ignored the present situation with admirable contempt; Lukács and Kurella continued to write their accusations against Brecht, Bloch, Eisler; while they, in turn, confronted Lukács and Kurella, although the adversaries did not always call themselves by name.[3]

During the 1970s, confrontations between writers and SED officials suggested the increasing shallowness of the languages of treason that the party continued to employ. Most revealing were the SED accusations against the writers who protested the expulsion of Wolf Biermann from the GDR in 1976. Even more disturbing was the unrelenting use of this language against nine prominent authors who were expelled from the writers union in a show trial in 1979.[4] The arguments with which in the following years well-known authors justified their allegiance to the GDR while others (among them Günter Kunert, Sarah Kirsch, Thomas Brasch, Hans-Joachim Schädlich, Jurek Becker, and Reiner Kunze) left East Germany, were clearly distant from the language of treason. At the end of the 1980s, this language had exhausted itself. In spite of the many revelations of betrayal, the language of treason failed to provide a measure for the understanding of emergent political identities.

The exhaustion of this language is even more obvious if one turns to the younger generation of writers. This generation found its own voice in refusing both the language of the Politburo and the moral claims of a Wolf, a Müller, or a Christoph Hein. Sascha Anderson's seemingly postmodernist line of defense for his collaboration with the Stasi—"I have no clear point of view"[5]—presents the antidote to Ignazio Silone's famous line: "The final struggle will be between the communists and the ex-communists." The only message that could still be derived from Silone's prediction is the expectation that the final word on the entanglement with party, state, and Stasi will arise from the debates between the writers who left the GDR before 1989 and those who stayed.

Nonetheless, the shock of individual tragedies revealed by an exploitive media and the sense of remoteness from the unfolding events in the East contributed to the revival of Benda's concept of intellectual treason in the West. West German critics, aware of the half-hearted attempts after 1945 of getting to the bottom of the corruption of intellectuals under National Socialism, were quick to refer to the intellectuals' responsibility to uphold the values of truth and reason under all circumstances, including the constraints of a dictatorial regime. Positive models were mostly taken from earlier periods when Emile Zola's *J'accuse* in the Dreyfus Affair and Heinrich Mann's antiwilhelmine and prodemocratic stance in and after World War I inspired a minority of German writers to engage in the fight against the reactionary Right and National Socialism. The less West German critics had concerned themselves with the realities of life in the GDR and the challenges that East German writers faced in their literary work, the more they tended to frame their analysis of the latter group within the concept of failure of intellectual politics vis-à-vis Nazism and Stalinism. This concept reflects the difficulties of playing public roles under adverse circumstances yet confirms the language of treason's penchant for demarcating absolutes in a sea of relativity.

Although distance from the events undoubtedly has its heuristic advantages, it also enhances the desire for dramatizing the seemingly innocuous, causing every personal, political, and aesthetic encounter to appear to be the result of conspiratorial strategies and counterstrategies. What emerges is a different screen, one of familiar proportions on which intellectuals and their conflicts figure in a continuous replay of events that were too quick to be registered by the unsuspecting eye. It is hardly surprising that the most gripping dramatizations of treason as a betrayal of personal and political loyalties originated in countries that never knew occupation and the concomitant entanglements of collaboration: England and the United States. From George Orwell's visionary dismantling of totalitarianism to Britain's successful exportation of spy novels and films about the 1940s and 1950s, from John le Carré's master thrillers to the Hollywood fabrications of cold war Berlin, there is an astounding continuity in the imaginary topography of treason still lingering behind many useful journalistic documentations of life under communist regimes.[6] The fascination with tracing "the other" in daily life leads to one or another version of what George Steiner described in the essay "The Cleric of Treason" in 1980:

> I would like to think for a moment about a man who in the morning teaches his students that a false attribution of a Watteau drawing or an inaccurate transcription of a fourteenth-century epigraph is a sin against the spirit and in the afternoon or evening transmits to the agents of Soviet intelligence classified, perhaps vital information given to him in sworn trust by his countrymen and intimate colleagues. What are the sources of such a scission?[7]

Setting a morning of intellectual routine against an evening of treason provides more than just a plot for spy thrillers. Steiner's fascination has been shared by many Western writers who were in search of exciting material as well as clues to their less-than-exciting identities in the confrontations of the cold war. They generally overlooked the fact that much of their dramatization corresponded with the language of treason that the communist parties had tried to maintain. Since the breakdown of these parties in 1989, the writers' need to serve a broader market will guarantee further exploration and exploitation of the concept of treason.

The changes registered in the moral self-positioning of participants in literary discourse reflect a transformation of the social predicament of intellectuals that took place long before the opening of the Berlin Wall and are not exclusive to East German writers. It is one thing to illustrate the power of the paradigm of treason with the increasing distance from the events; it is another to follow up on the moral ambiguities of German public life, be it during or after a dictatorship, and assess critically its reflection in the ensuing dialogue of writers and intellectuals with a thoroughly disenchanted audience. The fact that such figures as Heinrich Böll and Christa Wolf were praised as creators of an effective language of moral concern helps situate this phenomenon historically. The language of treason, with its sparks of intellectual heroism, tends to obscure the predicaments of creating and justifying a public role for the literary intellectual.

Since World War II, a new communicative attitude has arisen among writers, on the basis of which they have established a moral authority that eschews heroic distinctions and creates a discourse both of scrutinizing and healing the effects of history. This is what I would like to call the rise of a therapeutic mode of discourse as part of the transformation by means of which modern societies have redefined political conflicts as social concerns. As the social welfare state has expanded both in capitalist and socialist countries, and socialist welfare policies have corresponded closely to the growth of the welfare thinking in the West, the rise of a therapeutic mode in the public and aesthetic discourse followed. It was not limited to one or the other side. The concept of literature as social work underwent similar transformations in East and West Germany. Thus, the therapeutic attitude can be traced both in Böll's and Wolf's narrative.

Of course, the differences cannot be overlooked. In retrospect, even an understanding of the "social" cannot be defined without reference to the rather peculiar kind of social work in which the Stasi engaged. It is note-worthy that this institution, which originally was charged with surveillance of the population in order to prevent and reveal treason, became itself an agent of "social" work, eventually monitoring and exploiting a therapeutic mode as a crucial vehicle of political integration.

The West German Debate

Although the phenomenon of the university 'mandarins'—the academics who reluctantly shared published opinion with nonuniversity intellectuals after World War I—has received considerable attention in recent studies of German intellectuals, there is still not enough information about the mandarinate's effort to recoup its influence after 1945.[8] Neither the postwar encounters between writers and academic mandarins nor their separateness as distinct publics have been analyzed by the intellectual histories of that period. Thus, the conflict between writers and sociologists that surfaced in the earlier part of the century, taking a dramatic turn in the student revolt of the late 1960s and then in the subsequent debates about the influence of intellectuals of the 1970s, has been largely overlooked. This conflict is generally a clash of idiosyncrasies and an expression of contempt rather than an open dialogue. But at its core lie the competing interests of sociologists and writers in how to assess the general well-being of society. The conflict figures centrally in the shifts of the intellectual discourse from an exchange over ideas and ideological positions to an exchange over social and psychological concerns.

Once a matter of different forms of prestige, this conflict always entailed an uneasy acknowledgment of the other discipline's insight, as was the case in Max Weber's and Thomas Mann's renditions of the Protestant ethic and the spirit of capitalism, respectively.[9] Later, the conflict evolved into a hostile clash when a peculiarly German brand of anti-Enlightenment so-ciology called for German culture to be cleansed of the "sociological" view of Weimar's left-wing intellectuals. The rivalry over society and its well-being remained one of the important areas in which the Left and the Right intersected. There is a close correspondence between the missionary disposition of Weimar writers, who revitalized literature's potential for social intervention, and sociologists such as Hans Freyer, who propagated the new sociology as "value-oriented political therapy."[10] The continuities of these debates after Nazism are most prominently displayed in the two famous treatises on the state of German society, *Zur geistigen Situation der Zeit* (Man in the modern age, 1931) and *Die Schuldfrage* (The question of German guilt, 1946).[11] In these treatises Karl Jaspers linked diagnosis and therapy in an aesthetically charged language of moral concern. In his assessment of German guilt in 1946, Jaspers set the stage for a public debate about carrying the burden of German history as an act of individual responsibility. To that end, he chose a language of empathy rather than one of distance. Like the writers of the journal *Der Ruf*, Jaspers maintained an allegiance to a certain national sense of duty that results from "participation in German spiritual and emotional life."[12]

In short, throughout the twentieth century there was a stratum of converging and diverging approaches of writers and sociologists to society's fabric, a competition between academic mandarins and writers in representing the historical moment. Thus it cannot surprise that the sociologist Helmut Schelsky singled out Heinrich Böll as the embodiment of the moral claims with which West German writers had promoted themselves to positions of power. In his broadside against Böll, he articulated the frustrations of the mandarin who felt that the writer had the unfair advantage of personalizing the therapeutic approach to Germany's ills. Although Schelsky's book *Die Arbeit tun die anderen: Klassenkampf und Priesterherrschaft der Intellektuellen* (1975)[13] has been recognized as the quintessential declaration of West German conservatism, its furious digression on Böll can be read as an informative treatise on the rise of the therapeutic discourse among cultural critics as well as on the post-Freudian mandarins.[14] In Schelsky's digression, Böll is seen as a high priest of a social messianism (*soziale Heilsreligion*). Böll is represented as both the cardinal and the martyr: on one hand, Böll undermines the political system of the Federal Republic; on the other, he claims to suffer pain and persecution inflicted by it. In particular, Schelsky is irritated by Böll's assertion that he seeks not to acquire political power but rather to proclaim and establish whatever he considers morally "positive":

> The fact that this moral and social religion of salvation is very vague and subjective, not only accounts for his persuasive writing power with his "idealistic" reading audience, but also for the invaluable possibility to apply it, at any time, to reality according to his own casuistry. Nobody but he himself determines the occasion and the inner duty when and where he should morally intervene in the social and political reality and when he can remain

silent, yet his claim of condemning "society" rests on this "innermost self-understanding as a warning voice and conscience in opposition to the ruling establishment."[15]

Schelsky's indictment is the exact antithesis of the statement with which the Swedish Academy bestowed the Nobel Prize for literature on Böll as the representative of a new generation of German writers who were "ready so soon to shoulder their country's and their own essential task in the spiritual life of our time."[16] What Schelsky called illegitimate posturing as cardinal *and* martyr, the academy praised as Böll's ability to connect a sensitive representation of individual endurance with a far-reaching engagement in the moral recovery of German society. The recognition of Böll as the proponent of German self-criticism also in communist countries—an important element of the Swedish Academy's citation—added to Schelsky's displeasure.

The mandarin's insistence that the glass was half empty, not half full, reflected his obsession with the political power of intellectuals. By exposing Böll's techniques as those of a high priest of social therapy, Schelsky curiously affirmed the writer's extraordinary influence in the public domain. His affirmation came at a time when the student rebellion of 1968, mostly using a sociological rhetoric, had declared literature dead and the whole fuss about the influence of the Group 47 passé. It was an ironic move that he repeated in his defense of sociology. While highlighting the centrality of the discipline, he destroyed the authority of sociologists who, in his view, represented a vulgar scientific sociologism. Schelsky wrote this attack as the foremost sociologist in postwar Germany.

In his intellectually stimulating though empirically flawed vendetta against the left-wing intelligentsia, Schelsky interprets the increase in psychosocial doctrines of salvation as a maneuver of the Left to exert effective thought control over the private sphere—and thus prevent the rise of the social (as the proper domain of sociologists). Although he is mostly concerned with demonstrating the de-motivating influence of these doctrines of interiority (*Innerlichkeit*) on the work habits of the "productive part of the population," he also considers the use of depth psychology as a doctrine of social action to be part of this maneuver. Apart from Böll, Alexander Mitscherlich is a particular target of this polemic: having rejected the warning that "the psychoanalytic physician cannot assume the authority of the physician of the entire society," Mitscherlich, "as a critical writer, as a political partisan, . . . has attempted with the means of psychoanalysis 'to impose the therapy on the masses,' i.e. to control them."[17]

Even a short discussion of the rise of the therapeutic cannot skip these accusations from the conservative mandarinate, which used to blame the tyranny of the consumer ideology over the life of the individual for society's decline. What Schelsky excluded from his assessment is a reflection on the predicaments of a society in which the therapeutic approach could assume such importance for the inner well-being of the country: the experience of war and the nonexperience of the Holocaust, both of which haunted Germans for decades afterward. Both Böll and Mitscherlich are key examples of intellectuals who developed their professional self-understanding and public roles in response to this predicament. They linked, albeit in different ways, the realm of the individual emotions to the collective experience, and they used this link to forge a public sphere designed to form a barrier against the prevailing tendency to escape the past without cathartic renewal.

Böll's early narratives about survivors of the war are filled with an array of emotional triggers of sights, sounds, smells, joy, melancholy, and *Angst* from past and present experiences. These emotional triggers are repeated in *Wo warst du, Adam?* (Where were you, Adam?), *Und sagte kein einziges Wort* (And never said a word), and *Haus ohne Hüter* (The unguarded house).[18] The redundancy of emotional signals was meant to set a therapeutic awakening in motion. In subsequent works, this momentum builds to a forceful resentment (perhaps even hatred) toward those who forge ahead in their lives without moral reflection or regret. One can find the influence of Riesman's observation that inwardness yields to "the social" in Böll's development as a writer.[19] In *Ansichten eines Clowns* (The clown, 1963)[20] the author abandons his preference for mythologizing everyday situations in favor of analyzing these situations with a sociological, even journalistic eye. In this highly successful novel, the narrator scrutinizes the involvement in the Nazi regime of a well-to-do family in the Rhineland. Böll builds his cathartic message, relying on a certain ironic redundancy of the emotional triggers. While carefully pacing the emotional recovery of the past within the everyday present, he nonetheless conveys the impression that he is running out of patience with the present. If the buildup of resentment and aggression was initially, in the forties and fifties, part of a therapeutic recovery, he increasingly came to articulate them directly, especially during the seventies, as part of his political intervention.

Although Mitscherlich's essayistic contributions to contemporary life were lively, consequential, and often brilliant, he was measured against the reestablished corps of academic psychologists, therapists, and analysts. These mandarins rejected his agenda of reintegrating Freud's cultural theory into the therapeutic practice of everyday life. Their arguments were similar to Schelsky's: that Alexander and Margarete Mitscherlich's step from individual psychology to a social-psychological analysis in *Die*

Unfähigkeit zu trauern (The inability to mourn, 1967) was unscientific, mere politics.[21] In turn, the Mitscherlichs insisted that individual psychology had to be transcended in order to gain the appropriate historical reference for the crisis of the individual. A mere generalizing of individual psychology without a sociohistorical perspective could not enable one to come to terms with the traumatic aftereffects of the collective disaster of National Socialism.

The Mitscherlichs were eager to emphasize that *The Inability to Mourn* was meant as a scholarly contribution to the current debates. In 1967, the German public's attention was not only focused on the students' movement and their awakening as political activists but also on right-wing and neo-Nazi organizations whose activities revealed the shortcomings of the politics of silence about the Nazi past. Some of their critics conceded that the Mitscherlichs, owing to their intellectual engagement in the public discourse, had done more to integrate psychoanalysis in the postwar dispute over Germany's responsibility for the past than their mandarin colleagues in their various university institutes. Yet, the polemic tended either to trivialize or to demonize their work. The discipline's aversion to linking their professional outlook to the engagement with the recent past echoed Schelsky's aversion to including an examination of German sociology during the Nazi period in the redefinition of the discipline. Administering the fortresses of *Wissenschaft*, whether those of sociology, psychology, or history, with their traditional claim for Truth as a coat-of-arms, seemed to suffice. That a particular historical event, even one of the magnitude of National Socialist rule, should be able to derail a science contradicted the mandarin sense of scholarly legitimacy.

In contrast to the attempts of academics to rebuild their disciplines along the lines of acceptable continuities, and with the help of the occasional import from the West, postwar West German writers of the war generation had convened under the banner of a new beginning. This emphasis on "Hour Zero" could be interpreted as an illusionary shedding of responsibilities. But owing to Hans Werner Richter's stern command over Group 47, an agenda had emerged that clearly responded to the failure of German writers and intellectuals to resist National Socialism. The main impulses for this group came from France and Italy, in particular from Sartre's definition of resistance as an existential act that went far beyond the predicament of the totalitarian control of everyday life. It helped reinstate the conviction that after World War II writers could regain legitimacy through their commitment to resisting any recurrence of Nazism. A key part of this kind of resistance, *nachgeholter Widerstand*,[22] was the constant effort of integrating the experience of war and complicity into the narrative of the present. There were other influences that contributed to the emergence of the attitude of resistance in the works of such authors as Alfred Andersch, Wolfgang Koeppen, and Hans Magnus Enzensberger—less visible at the time, but noteworthy nonetheless. The aesthetic attitude (*Haltung*) of both Gottfried Benn and Ernst Jünger, despite their implication in the rise of National Socialism, caught on among writers. From very early on, this attitude contributed to an almost existential opposition to the diluting of aesthetic and intellectual challenges within the new middle-class society of West Germany.

Although Böll never engaged in this kind of a masculine aestheticism in the manner of a Jünger or a Benn, he shared with these writers the conviction that the author's function had to be redefined in the wake of the moral and aesthetic fall of German writers. He rethought issues of memory in their individual and social dimensions and found in the need to remember the new legitimacy for his public intervention as a writer. Avoiding labels such as "therapy" and "social work," Böll wrote about how literature could recover from a disastrous past through its service to the moral recuperation of a whole society. The strategy he suggested was slow and unassuming, yet it contributed to the success with which writers of the war generation were able to engage a considerable segment of the reading public in their first reckoning with the Nazi past in West Germany.

The Twilight of Literature and Sociology

During the early sixties, the works and public appearances of Günter Grass, Heinrich Böll, Hans Magnus Enzensberger, Peter Weiss, Martin Walser, and Uwe Johnson created a sense that the dominance of conservative politicians, the cold war, and the continuities to the Nazi period could be successfully challenged. The prerequisite for this efflorescence of therapeutic literature was the growth of an institutional and professional network from the cooperation of private publishing houses and public broadcasting stations. The political elites were upset by the fact that part of this network was supported by taxpayer's money, but this was clearly in keeping with the German tradition of public funding for intellectual work.

That the postwar efflorescence of literature was so short-lived is not hard to understand if one compares it with the reign of Expressionism in the post–World War I period. Expressionism appealed to writers' and artists' desire to create a new art, even a new society. It did at least help to launch a new culture of modernity. In 1961, by contrast, the writers helped engage in a discourse about the ways in which the past was still closing in on the Germans. The erection of the Berlin Wall attested not only to the lack of a vision for the future under communism, but also to the longevity of Hitler's legacy. One might even draw an analogy between the writers' concern about this legacy and the federal government's commitment to vindicating itself through a social welfare policy for the victims of the war. Although separated by contrasting languages and public attitudes, both endeavors drew their legitimacy from the impulse to reconnect the present with the past. The energies the Expressionists were able to muster for an aesthetic foray into the future, cutting their links with the past, were beyond the grasp of writers of the war generation in the Federal Republic.

Such a foray into the future, engendered by the student movement, followed hard on the heels of the literary revival. Although it was directed against literature, among other things, it was not unlike the more radical utopianism of Expressionist writers. The rhetorical self-liberation that once had been shaped by aesthetic eccentricity was now inspired by the rediscovery of the Enlightenment as a phenomenon that reached far beyond the commitment to catching up with history. When Enzensberger, in a famous article in *Kursbuch* (1968), wrote about the death of literature, he confirmed the victory of the socio-revolutionary paradigm in the public discourse on contemporary society. He also commented on the interplay of the languages and warned against entangling literature in the sociological rhetoric of revolution.[23]   The uses of a language of *Wissenschaft* as the conduit to a rationally reconstructed society had its own poetry, as the ritualized use of Marcuse's and Adorno's sentences showed in innumerable variations. In the mantra-like reference to these classics, literary and scientific pursuits merged. Thus, a new German *Wissenschaftssprache* emerged with the belief that the new self-empowerment through the language of rational discourse would finally establish a truly social avant-garde.

Neither sociology nor literature recovered from this denouement of the seventies and eighties. West Germany's enormous economic expansion allowed the disillusionment of a younger generation to become a worthwhile oppositional experience, even a movement. This new movement centered around competing practices of rediscovering the individual subject. Resonating, though often inadvertently, with another expansion of the social welfare state, the intellectual discourse tended to yield to an agenda of therapeutic debates that catered to individual needs for self-realization and collective needs for security and a safe environment. But academics did not come to the rescue in his situation. By vilifying rationalism and left-wing enlightenment as the cause of all the evils of modernization, Schelsky reinvented, rather, a traditional cultural pessimism and thus failed to halt the rise of the therapeutic that he so vividly documented.

A decade later, Ralf Dahrendorf, the leading liberal sociologist, wondered whether the sociology of the eighties had completely succumbed to the individualization, losing entirely its ability to generalize empirical facts and deliver knowledge concerning the institutions and structures of social action. According to Dahrendorf, contemporary sociologists had shifted the focus of their discipline away from the institutions—as "materialized forms of norms, authorities of decisions and sanctions"—and toward everything "that crawls and creeps underneath the institutions," for which they even found a name: "life world" (Lebenswelt).[24] The innovations of the 1980s, Dahrendorf added, had occurred in politics, economics, ecology without any evident input from the social sciences. Other critics voiced less dissatisfaction with the consequences of these innovations but also pointed to the withering of the social sciences from intellectual life.[25]

Literature underwent similar transformations. Individualization diminished the capacity to generalize stories, plots, and personal experiences. In one of the most insightful assessments of this retreat from the center of the intellectual debate, the Swiss writer Adolf Muschg immersed himself in the study of therapy, which he considered to be the only viable way to reach the younger generation. His lectures, Literatur als Therapie? (Literature as therapy?), were intended to raise consciousness and expectations of literature, in order to defend literature against the accusation of being a mere compensatory strategy for the ills of modernity. "I was interested in liberating the engagement with literature from the blemish of flight and treason, if possible even to embed it with the sense of withstanding."[26] Few other writers went as far as Muschg did in rationalizing the new closeness of literature and therapy. Most authors internalized the shift from social to individual concerns more as an attitude than an intellectual project. In order to successfully establish public legitimacy, the sense of a moral withstanding had to be hardwired to a sense of therapeutic understanding. The literary works of established authors such as Peter Härtling, Martin Walser, Walter Jens, Siegfried Lenz, and many younger writers began to center on problems that allowed this attitude to become a freestanding concern of its own.

Taken as a key to the less-than-exciting literary production of the eighties, this attitude might help explain why writers deferred their own internal disputes in favor of an encompassing and all-embracing solidarity movement for peace in the early 1980s, when the cold war seemed to return with the NATO decision to install new medium-range missiles in central Europe. West German critics even put off disputes with East German writers such as Hermann Kant, whom they had counted as part of the political inventory of that state, hardly worth a thorough literary critique. Although Günter Grass, who was a driving force behind the demonstration against the renewed arms race of the big powers, insisted that the East-

West consensus of writers not overpower the protest against the brutal crackdown on intellectuals in Poland, he could not prevent the dissension of well-known authors, especially of those who had left the German Democratic Republic as the victims of its restrictive cultural politics. Even Julien Benda's accusation, *La trahison des clercs*, was quoted as pertaining to these endeavors—and rejected.[27] The accusation of treason led nowhere in a situation in which Erich Honecker, as the representative of the GDR, was officially received both by Chancellor Helmut Schmidt in 1981 and Chancellor Helmut Kohl in 1987.

Against the Western Therapists of an Eastern Past

The speeches by Christa Wolf, Christoph Hein, Stefan Heym, and others during the mass meeting at Berlin's Alexanderplatz on November 4, 1989, have been considered (along with the proclamation *Für unser Land* [For our country]) the moment of truth for East German intellectuals in their precarious wanderings between the realities of the Stasi state and the hopes for a better version of a socialist society. Whether these addresses were the logical result of the troublesome commitment of GDR loyalists to this state or an attempt to articulate the warnings of intellectuals against the unification of the two Germanies (which Grass and other West German authors echoed with different arguments shortly thereafter), the event supplied critics with a rich source of polemic for and against the accommodationist attitude of East Germany's intellectuals. One is tempted to argue that, if it had not been for these controversies, the West German debate about the fall of the GDR, at least in the initial stages, would have drowned in economic grandstanding and neighborly sympathizing with a population deprived of the amenities of Western life. After the *Runde Tische* (Round tables) with their refreshing medley of people and interest groups had ceased to function as a conduit for the variety of East German views, and once the technical intelligentsia, which was instrumental in dismantling the ideological claims of the regime, worked on its new acculturation, the intellectuals' reflection on the end of a state-supported cultural establishment in the GDR served as a focus for the more painful questions regarding the social achievements, the moral legitimacy, and the intellectual heritage of this state. Even the popular press felt obliged to comment on the fact that Christa Wolf published her autobiographical text, *Was bleibt* (What remains), in 1989, not in 1979, when the events it recounts—the frustrating experience of being a target of Stasi surveillance—actually happened.[28] For a while, it seemed that the cultural heritage of this state would have to be sifted from among the thousands of files that the Stasi had collected on the writers.

The language of treason helped, at this point, to stimulate a dramatic view of the disastrous consequences of the death of the GDR for its intellectual and academic elites, but it did little to realign the assessment of the plight of the intellectuals with that of the population at large. The latter had become the domain of economic and psychological deliberations. The fact that the revolt of 1989 had returned a progressive meaning to the term *Volk*, as a living, thinking, and fighting organism *(Wir sind das Volk, Wir sind ein Volk)* reinforced the tendency to choose diagnostic tools that already reflected the holistic—or, rather, psychological—language of the envisioned recuperation. Though credited with regaining its identity by shedding the dictatorial regime, this *Volk*, so it was thought, would complete its "turnaround" *(Wende)* with an economic recovery and, equally important for many Western critics, with a psychological recovery. Both expectations were of course intimately tied to Western help.

"Patient DDR" was the appropriate title of a therapeutic assessment that Reimar Hinrichs published in the journal *Kursbuch*.[29] The piece reads like a satire on the therapeutic reductionism applied to the deceased GDR, but it means to present a serious and convincing list of significant events of the past as markers of the peculiar neurosis that the East Germans had gone through and that now required a sensitive balance of love and mourning. In the same year the East German psychotherapist Hans-Joachim Maaz published the widely successful account of this neurosis, *Der Gefühlsstau*.[30] Although Western psychoanalysts criticized Maaz for going overboard—or, alternatively, for being naive—in modeling the whole population into one big patient, his studies became the focus of a broad-based discussion in East and West. Maaz, despite his idiosyncratic call for a "psychic revolution," set a measure for the successful integration of macro and micro factors without which the history of the GDR, including the accommodationist pattern in the situation of distress in the 1980s, cannot be understood. With its broad applicability, the therapeutic paradigm became the favorite shorthand in the West for what already in the 1980s had been cultivated in the search for a sensitive approach toward the East. Obviously, the very success of this paradigm after the fall of the Wall also had to make up for its earlier preponderance over more critical—and political—perceptions of the communist system.

The concept of treating a whole society as a patient has its traditions, especially in the United States, where conventional ways of dealing with foreign countries had lost credibility owing to the inability to contain Nazi Germany and Japan.[31] The fact that Schelsky and other critics viewed the American attempts at reeducation after 1945 as part of this therapeutic mindset, and took pleasure in associating it with the cold war fear of brainwashing, might explain the older generation's deep-seated suspicion toward the new interest in the therapeutic in the seventies and eighties. For them, the totalitarian features of rewriting collective as well as individual pasts that Orwell had unmasked so vividly overshadowed the possible psychological benefit from exposing oneself to the recollection of the past. The resolution to oppose these exploratory techniques draws heavily on fears of an omnipotent state or political system that had been invigorated by the cold war. Considering the increasingly critical reaction of the East German population to the Western suggestion that it had better go beyond psychological analysis and actually engage in a process of collective therapy, these associations should not be overlooked. Though directed toward the past, the Western suggestions tend to overlook the actual experience of this past as a reality that included the presence of the Stasi and other intrusive political organizations. After all, the ubiquity of the Stasi as an organization that devoted itself to the thoughts and not just to the actions of the individual still has an Orwellian ring. Who were those Westerners who claimed the legitimacy to administer the therapy for coming to terms with a dubious past?

In contrast to the writer Monika Maron's complaint against the "therapeutic attitude" of the West Germans,[32] the theologian and politician Richard Schröder differentiated between two forms of therapeutic commitment. He distinguished between the immense need for therapeutic treatment, be it with professional therapists, social workers, or church representatives, on one side, and programs for *Vergangenheitsbewältigung*, of coming to terms with the past, on the other. Schröder considered the latter an extension of the West German project of coping with the Nazi past, which, in his words, was undertaken mainly by the children who wanted to make up for the failure of the parents: "Now, in the GDR, another dictatorship has collapsed. It seemed to be an appropriate opportunity for some contemporaries in the West to offer their experiences: We come to terms with your past, for we already did the same for our parents." Schröder's rejection of this offer is unambiguous. He views the expectation that *Vergangenheitsbewältigung* would produce a therapy of society as dangerous: "For therapy means cure, and cure is a restoration of health. The assumption is that someone knows what constitutes a healthy society and how a sick society can be cured. This sounds familiar to me: the rotting capitalism and the healthy development of the socialist system. The demand for a therapy of society veils a massive claim for domination."[33] Schröder's distinction of the program of *Vergangenheitsbewältigung* from the therapeutic engagement as social work treaded explosive terrain in Germany, where the remembrance of the Holocaust and of persecution holds a clue to the moral legitimation of a national politics. Yet, this distinction seems appropriate, not least because it has been an important tool of critics who refer to the German population as the object and interject themselves as the subject of the moral discourse. The breaching of the walls of silence concerning the Nazi past, for which the Mitscherlichs generated the therapeutic reference in the 1960s, has become the confabulation of moral mastery whose power to ordain intellectual identities reaches far beyond Germany.

Schröder's distinction helps us understand why, in his response to Habermas's essay *Die andere Zerstörung der Vernunft* (The other destruction of reason),[34] he concentrates so much on the author's complaint that the addition of the former GDR to the Federal Republic spoiled the established ways of making and reflecting democratic politics.[35] West German intellectuals had to readjust their identities and their mission: this was, for Schröder, the reason for their complaint about the East. However, assessing the arrogance with which Western intellectuals had imposed the therapeutic paradigm on the East, Schröder concluded that this adjustment had not progressed very far. Or had it? In a satirical comment, Lothar Baier asserted that West German intellectuals had indeed embarked on a transformation, albeit only in their self-perception.[36] Realizing the extent to which the East German intellectual had been coopted by the homey and muggy universe of social work, West Germans felt the need to demonstrate their distance from a life of the social worker. Their new ideal was a life of constant confrontation, the life of a fighter, exposed to the cold winds of Modernism. While the East German intellectual had held a secure position by giving the state a hand in providing mental comfort to the population, the West German had pursued the course of reason and democracy on a high wire, without a net. Baier's conclusion: Since this self-perception drew on the encounter with the GDR as social workers' paradise, it would have been preferable if that state had been maintained in order to assure the permanence of perception.

The Last Chapter Is Still Being Written

In her first major prose work, *Der geteilte Himmel* (The divided heaven), Christa Wolf recounted the attitude, pro and con, of a young woman toward the GDR before the Berlin Wall had made a freely chosen departure impossible.[37] Rita travels to West Berlin to see her fiancé, Manfred, who had left the GDR but now asks her to live in the West with him. She says no—as it turns out, only a few days before the erection of the Wall on August 13, 1961. After her return, Rita attempts to commit suicide. The book begins when she wakes up in the hospital and recapitulates the attempt to justify her decision to remain in East Germany without her fiancé. The book ends with the completion of Rita's recovery as a fully adjusted citizen who has gotten over her emotional breakdown through "precise thinking," as she calls it.

In the following works, beginning with *Nachdenken über Christa T.* (The quest for Christa T.), Wolf grounded her narrative of individuation within East German society in a more sophisticated use of the therapeutic paradigm.[38] Whereas the recovery in *Der geteilte Himmel,* in which Rita settles her mourning with a political rationalization of her case, is still close to earlier exemplary transformations of human beings into socialist heroes, the case of Christa T. reflects both a clear departure from and an explicit critique of these transformations for which Wolf's political disillusions in the mid-1960s provided the momentum. Wolf made the case for the self-realization of the individual in this society with the help of an informed reflection on Freudian categories. She highlighted the encounter with the past (including the Nazi past) within a therapeutic framework.[39] In this respect, her work is similar to that of Franz Fühmann, Günter de Bruyn, and other, usually younger authors.

Western critics welcomed this development as an important step toward some measure of literary autonomy in the GDR. They noted that Wolf was not merely catching up with the stylistic experiments and psychological introspection in the West but engaging in a genuine rethinking of the potential for individualization in East Germany. Günter de Bruyn acknowledged that Heinrich Böll was the author who had always provided important impulses for this endeavor: "Böll's admonishing memories were also necessary here, as was his defense of individual self-determination against the political apparatuses and his strict rejection of enemy projections, war and the military. He was read, loved and understood, and his sincerity and courageous nonconformity have served as a model."[40] Yet, while Böll helped justify the moral integrity of the therapeutic attitude in narrating stories of survival and recovery, the political predicament was so constricting that the concept of self-realization, even in its Freudian turn, took a very different form. Both its achievements—providing access to the individual experience—and its limitations—correlating, though often *ex negativo*, the individual experience with a surmised socialist self-realization on the part of this society—deserve closer scrutiny.

A historical approach might take up this task at the earlier observation that a different language replaced the compulsive projection of right and wrong in the literature of returned exiles. Distancing his generation's work from the anachronistic battles of the older writers, Zwerenz indicated the end of an era in which treason meant life or death for the individual in fact. Using the case of Alfred Kurella, one of the most powerful men of that era, Zwerenz diagnosed what separated the older communist intellectuals who went to prison or had fled Germany during the Nazi regime from the younger ones who became adults in the communist state. The concept of treason was crucial for this separation between old and young, because it signaled the decision that the older generation had to make: to leave the bourgeois class in order to join the proletariat. Or, according to Georg Lukács in *Geschichte und Klassenbewußtsein* (History and class consciousness): Whoever intends, as a bourgeois, to become a communist, must first become a traitor to his class.[41] Kurella, in Zwerenz's diagnosis, is the quintessential communist intellectual who had to make up for this treason: "The bourgeois intellectual, as Kurella himself once was, out of disgust with this origin and class affiliation, jumped into the marxist fountain of youth and reemerged from it as an executioner."[42] Not surprisingly, the language of the ideological executioner masks a persistent feeling of insufficient service to the movement. "The revolutionary as an unhappy martyr who again and again offered to sacrifice himself for history—yet was rejected. However, when he was not allowed the great unique act of existential extermination, he did away with himself in portions, put his ego, as it were, under the guillotine in small pieces, slice by slice."[43] This is obviously not a language of recovering the self from the "residue of history" (*Bodensatz der Geschichte*), as Christa Wolf formulated it in *Der geteilte Himmel*, but rather of sacrificing the self in ever-renewable acts of loyalty, always invoking the specter of treason.

It is ironic—but may have been meant as an act of consolation—that Wolf chose a word from that most notorious, gifted, and unhappy communist intellectual of bourgeois origin who guided the East German cultural policy through the Stalinist years, Johannes R. Becher, when she introduced *Nachdenken über Christa T.*, her fictional manifesto for a therapeutic recovery of the self. Becher's word, used as a motto for the work, was also highlighted in a previous *Selbstinterview* (Interview with myself) in 1966 when she said: "For this deep unrest of the human soul is nothing but the faculty to sense and to divine that man has not yet come to himself. This coming-to-oneself—what is it?" Wolf answered by replacing Marx with Freud as guide, yet she retained the socialist frame for the psychological construction of the self: "This is a great thought—that man does not rest until he has found himself. I see a deep-seated accord between genuine literature and socialist society, which is rooted in this very feature: both aim to help man arrive at self-realization."[44] In pursuit of this agenda the function of the writer consists in mediating between two very different forms of self-realization. The trials of the self have to be authenticated in the socialist claim of a self-realization of society. An older generation of communists felt compelled to utilize literature for constructing and simultaneously in-ternalizing the socialist camp, which may account for the preponderance of topics featuring sabotage, wrecking, treason, and sacrifice—given the fact that the process of interiorization was bound to be fickle and prone to subjective error. Wolf's generation, on the other hand, had seen the Wall go up around this camp and felt compelled to expand and deepen the inner space of the socialist self. By drawing on the romantic, utopian, and realistic traditions of German culture, this generation helped readers rediscover literature as a mediating experience for the trials of the self. Re-flecting a long tradition of German inwardness (*Innerlichkeit*), these writers overcame the barrier that separated postwar audiences and the message of the returned exiles, among them Anna Seghers, Bertolt Brecht, Arnold Zweig, and Friedrich Wolf.

When the Wall was erected in 1961, it was proclaimed an antifascist protective wall. The fact that literature or, more specifically, reading was held in high esteem in the walled-in East German state was usually under-stood by literary critics as a direct consequence of this event. Protective it seemed to be, though less against the vague phenomenon of fascism than against what was labeled the Coca-Colonization of German society. Literature received a last reprieve in East Germany before the onslaught of Western mass culture. The developments since the fall of the Wall in 1989 have confirmed this perception. The *Leseland GDR* is no more. Poems and statements of the young writers of the Prenzlauer Berg scene already implied that much in the 1980s. By removing the moral trappings of poetic language, these authors disentangled themselves from the therapeutic use of literature and from the opposite incriminations of both "serving" and "disturbing" the interests of socialism, actions that had helped literature gain the limelight. They could not care less for *Innerlichkeit*.

When Wolf, Hein, Heym, and other authors at the demonstration on November 4, 1989, five days before the Wall fell, proposed that a better edition of the GDR be created, their attachment to the precarious fortunes of the *Leseland* might have played an important role. The interest in reform shown by these writers was, in any case, different from that of the engineers and other members of the technical intelligentsia who had to cope with the *Reformvermeidungspolitik*[45] (policy of avoiding reforms) of the SED. Their frustration with the outdated equipment and anti-innovative command structure in industrial production, together with a loss in social status, had reached alarming proportions. The writers' interest was also different from that of the intelligentsia in the natural sciences whose leading spokesper-son, Jens Reich, soon began to express grave doubts about the reform potential of the system. In his assessment of the role of the intelligentsia in the demise of the GDR, *Abschied von den Lebenslügen*, Reich showed little patience for the concerns of writers.[46] In a public discussion with Heiner Müller, Reich reiterated his thesis that the most valuable contribution of the technical and scientific intelligentsia had been the liquidation of the exhausted system without bloodshed.[47] The intelligentsia had rebelled against its own privileged status at the side of the party nomenclatura.

Although Reich's thesis has been contested, it helps explain why the secondary position of literary intellectuals in the events of 1989 received more attention than the "turn-around" of the technical and scientific intelligentsia. The latter may well have decided the November revolution of 1989 as far as the course of events was decided in the GDR. But the dramatization of the writers' quest remains intimately tied to a central aspect of the liquidation of that state: the dissolution and, more important, the much slower phase-out from within of the Stasi as thought police. Although such close parallels between the fate of the writers and the fate of the Stasi were never desired or even thought of by the writers, it was the flip-side of their public engagement in the intellectual life of the people, of their close relationship with the readers as individual beings. Once a younger generation of writers had established their legitimacy as intimate observers with a public mission, they were no longer alone in their musings about mastering life in a socialist society. On one hand, they shared much of the stage with the church; indeed, the church provided the only stage when they tried to address the public directly—uncensored—in readings, discussions, and performances. On the other hand, they also shared with the Stasi, if unwittingly, a concern for a therapy of and for the people. While the church has been engaged in softening the shocks of the social transformation after 1989, the writers have had a hard time to situate themselves vis-à-vis the dismantling of the Stasi. A statement such as *Dieses Mißtrauen gegen mich selbst* (This suspicion against myself),[48] which was used by the highly regarded author Günter de Bruyn in order to deal with his failure to recollect the extent of the contacts with the Stasi, contains more information about their practices of intimidation and deception than lengthy investigations. De Bruyn compared his personal recollection with the entries in the Stasi files. Neither account is reliable, but he has to live— and write—with them, as he states, for the rest of his life.

The prerogative of the literary intellectual to articulate a public perception within the GDR was secured by the antisociological self-understanding of the SED. Christa Wolf's question as to the coming-to-oneself was directed toward the individual as part of a socialist community. Her individual is that of the German *Bildungsroman*, not the focus and instigator of social conflicts. Under these auspices, the party resigned itself to privileging writers and not social scientists to create the discourse on the inner life of this society, but simultaneously empowered the Stasi to act as social investigator and social worker. Without the institutional infrastructure that made the writers into beneficiaries of this peculiar system of welfare and surveillance, the literary intellectuals would not have been able to take over some of the sociologists' traditional tasks.

This arrangement was the second choice of the SED after a comprehensive attempt to integrate literature into the transformation of the industrial system, the so-called *Bitterfelder Weg,* had failed. Ulbricht's investment in the various activities of the *Bitterfelder Weg* were motivated by the idea that a broad involvement of workers in writing campaigns would help enhance industrial productivity. Although the therapeutic turn of literature in the capitalist West—at least until the late 1980s—accompanied high productivity, in the East, after a period in the 1960s when writers were punished for not joining the productivist effort, this turn was increasingly recognized as a compensation for the low productivity of the system. As a consequence, literature has been quite limited in its documentary scope, neglecting the developments in the sector of industrial productivity. This is why writers, little involved in the industrial realities of the GDR, still maintained utopias of a reformed socialism at a time when most members of the technical intelligentsia had given up these hopes.

In the summer and fall of 1989, when thousands of young families succeeded in forcing their exit from the GDR via Hungary and Czechoslovakia, writers were particularly shocked by the *Sprachlosigkeit* (speechlessness) with which the young people turned their backs to this state.[49] They were not victims of the Stasi, nor were they respondents to the activities of the civil rights groups, let alone to the reasoning of the writers. Their actions were a testimony to the failure of language, official as well as literary. Was there any language left? When Honecker heard of the end of the German Democratic Republic, he is reported to have reacted with the one word that shaped the language of his generation of communists, whether intellectuals or not: "Treason."

Notes

1. Johano Strasser, "Intellektuellendämmerung? Anmerkungen zu einem Machtkampf im deutschen Feuilleton," *Neue Deutsche Literatur* 40, no. 10 (1992): 110–27, here 122; Klaus Hartung, "Im Spiegelkabinett der Vereinigung: Die neue deutsche Täter-Opfer-Ordnung und die alten Fluchten aus der Realität," in *Wir Kollaborateure: Der Westen und die deutschen Vergangenheiten,* ed. Cora Stephan (Reinbek, 1992), 154; Stefan Hornbostel, "Kein Land in Sicht—Von den neuen Schwierigkeiten,

ein Intellektueller zu sein," *Leviathan* 24 (1996): 493–520; Werner von Bergen and Walter H. Pehle, eds., *Denken im Zwiespalt: Über den Verrat von Intellektuellen im 20. Jahrhundert* (Frankfurt am Main, 1996).

2. Raymond Aron, *The Opium of the Intellectuals* (Garden City, N.Y., 1957); Margret Bovery, *Treason in the Twentieth Century* (New York, 1963).

3. Gerhard Zwerenz, *Der Widerspruch: Autobiographischer Bericht* (Frankfurt am Main, 1974), 133–34.

4. See Joachim Walther et al., eds., *Protokoll eines Tribunals: Die Ausschlüsse aus dem DDR-Schriftstellerverband 1979* (Reinbek, 1991).

5. Holger Kulick, "Grautöne: Der Amoklauf Sascha Andersons. Aus drei Gesprächen," in *MachtSpiele: Literatur und Staatssicherheit im Fokus Prenzlauer Berg*, ed. Peter Böthig and Klaus Michael (Leipzig, 1993), 197.

6. George Orwell, *Nineteen Eighty-Four* (New York, 1949); John le Carré, *The Spy Who Came in from the Cold* (New York, 1963). On Hollywood fabrications of cold war Berlin see Stephen J. Whitfield, *The Culture of the Cold War* (Baltimore, 1991).

7. Quoted in Bruce Robbins, "Espionage as Vocation: Raymond Williams's Loyalties," in *Intellectuals: Aesthetics, Politics, Academics*, ed. Bruce Robbins (Minneapolis, 1990), 274.

8. Fritz Ringer, *The Decline of the German Mandarins: The German Academic Community, 1890–1933* (Cambridge, Mass., 1969); Hauke Brunkhorst, *Der Intellektuelle im Land der Mandarine* (Frankfurt, 1987). See also Brunkhorst, "The Intellectual in Mandarin Country: The West German Case," in *Intellectuals in Liberal Democracies: Political Influence and Social Involvement*, ed. Alain G. Gagnon (New York, 1987), 121–42; a survey for the period after 1945 is Walter H. Pehle and Peter Sillem, eds., *Wissenschaft im geteilten Deutschland: Restauration oder Neubeginn nach 1945* (Frankfurt am Main, 1992).

9. Wolf Lepenies, *Die drei Kulturen: Soziologie zwischen Literatur und Wissenschaft* (Reinbek, 1988), esp. "Motive Max Webers im Werk von Thomas Mann," 357–75.

10. Wolf Lepenies, "Epilog: Soziologie und Anti-Soziologie im Nationalsozialismus und danach," in ibid, 403–22.

11. Karl Jaspers, *Die geistige Situation der Zeit* (Berlin, 1931), *Man in the Modern Age* (New York, 1978), and *The Question of German Guilt* (New York, 1961).

12. Karl Jaspers, *Die Schuldfrage* (The question of German guilt) (Heidelberg, 1946), 71 f.

13. Helmut Schelsky, *Die Arbeit tun die anderen: Klassenkampf und Priesterherrschaft der Intellektuellen* (Munich, 1977).

14. The most comprehensive definition of the adjective *therapeutic* used as a noun is to be found in Philip Rieff, *The Triumph of the Therapeutic: Uses of Faith After Freud* (Chicago, 1966). Though stimulated by the broad historical contextualization of "the therapeutic" as a concept, I do not share Rieff's views on society and culture.

15. Schelsky, *Die Arbeit tun die anderen*, 464.

16. Bernhard Weinraub, "Heinrich Böll Wins Nobel for Literature," *New York Times*, 20 October, 1972, p. 6, col. 3.

17. Schelsky, *Die Arbeit tun die anderen*, 383.

18. Heinrich Böll, *Wo warst du, Adam?* (Opladen, 1951) (Where were you, Adam? trans. Leila Vennewitz [London, 1970]); *Und sagte kein einziges Wort* trans. Leila Vennewitz (Cologne, 1953) (And never said a word, trans. Leila Vennewitz [London,

1978]); *Haus ohne Hüter* (Cologne, 1954) (The unguarded house, trans. Mervyn Savill [London, 1957]).

19. David Riesman, *The Lonely Crowd: A Study of the Changing American Character* (New Haven, 1950).

20. Heinrich Böll, *Ansichten eines Clowns* (Cologne and Berlin, 1963) (The clown, trans. Leila Vennewitz [London, 1965]).

21. Alexander and Margarete Mitscherlich, *Die Unfähigkeit zu trauern* (Munich, 1967).

22. I have given a more extensive analysis of this phenomenon in "Die nachgeholte Résistance: Politik und Gruppenethos im historischen Zusammenhang," in *Die Gruppe 47 in der Geschichte der Bundesrepublik*, ed. Justus Fetscher et al. (Würzburg, 1991), 9–22. See also my "Between Normality and Resistance: Catastrophic Gradualism in Nazi Germany," in *Resistance Against the Third Reich, 1933–1990*, ed. Michael Geyer and John Boyer (Chicago, 1994), 119–38.

23. Hans Magnus Enzensberger, "Gemeinplätze, die Neueste Literatur betreffend," *Kursbuch* 15 (1968): 187–97.

24. Ralf Dahrendorf, "Einführung in die Soziologie," *Soziale Welt* 40 (1989): 1–10, here 4–5. The term *Lebenswelt*, of course, is taken from Husserl.

25. Hauke Brunkhorst, "Das Verschwinden der Sozialwissenschaften aus dem 'geistigen Leben,'" *Literaturmagazin* 15 (1985): 69–81.

26. Adolf Muschg, *Literatur als Therapie? Ein Exkurs über das Heilsame und das Unheilbare: Frankfurter Vorlesungen* (Frankfurt am Main, 1981), 19.

27. Fritz J. Raddatz, "Es geht. Geht es? Eindrücke vom zweiten Berliner Ost-West-Treffen der Schriftsteller," *Die Zeit* (U.S. ed.), 6 May 1983, 14.

28. Christa Wolf, *Was bleibt* (Frankfurt am Main, 1990) (What remains and other stories [New York, 1993]).

29. Reimar Hinrichs, "Patient DDR," *Kursbuch* 101 (1990): 57–65.

30. Hans-Joachim Maaz, *Der Gefühlsstau: Ein Psychogramm der DDR* (Berlin, 1992).

31. See Lawrence K. Frank, *Society as the Patient: Essays on Culture and Personality* (New Brunswick, 1948), esp. 298–307 ("The Historian as Therapist"). A prominent example is Richard M. Brickner, *Is Germany Incurable?* (Philadelphia, 1943).

32. See Stephan Speicher, "Die gekränkte Würde der Ostdeutschen: Monika Marons Angriff auf ihre Landsleute. Eine Diskussion in Potsdam," *Frankfurter Allgemeine Zeitung*, 15 September 1992.

33. Richard Schröder, "Die Gesellschaft läßt sich nicht therapieren: Was heißt Vergangenheitsbewältigung im Osten?" *Frankfurter Allgemeine Zeitung*, 2 February 1993.

34. Jürgen Habermas, "Die andere Zerstörung der Vernunft: Über die Defizite der deutschen Vereinigung und über die Rolle der intellektuellen Kritik," *Die Zeit* 20, 17 May 1991, 19.

35. Richard Schöder, "Es ist doch nicht alles schlecht. Einspruch gegen Jürgen Habermas: Auch im Faktischen steckt manchmal ein bißchen Vernunft," *Die Zeit* 23, 7 June 1991, 17.

36. Lothar Baier, "Fighter und Sozialarbeiter oder die neue Kunst des rechten Einteilens," *Freibeuter* 53 (1992): 44–52.

37. Christa Wolf, *Der geteilte Himmel* (Halle, 1963) (Divided heaven [New York, 1976]).

38. Christa Wolf, *Nachdenken über Christa T.* (Halle, 1968) (The quest for Christa T. [New York, 1970]).

39. See Bernhard Greiner, " 'Sentimentaler Stoff und fantastische Form': Zur Erneuerung frühromantischer Tradition im Roman der DDR," in *DDR-Roman und Literaturgesellschaft*, ed. Jos Hoogeveen and Gerd Labroisse (Amsterdam, 1981), 249–328; Uwe Wittstock, *Über die Fähigkeit zu trauern: Das Bild der Wandlung im Prosawerk von Christa Wolf und Franz Fühmann* (Frankfurt am Main, 1987).

40. Günter de Bruyn, "Als der Krieg ausbrach," *Liber: Europäische Kulturzeitschrift* 1 (October 1989): 4.

41. Georg Lukács, *Geschichte und Klassenbewußtsein* (Berlin, 1923) (History and class consciousness [Cambridge, Mass., 1971]).

42. Zwerenz, *Der Widerspruch*, 135.

43. Ibid., 139.

44. Christa Wolf, "Interview with Myself," in *The Author's Dimension: Selected Essays*, ed. Alexander Stephan (New York, 1993), 16–19, here 17.

45. The term comes from Sigrid Meuschel, "Überlegungen zu einer Herrschafts- und Gesellschaftsgeschichte der DDR," *Geschichte und Gesellschaft* 19 (1993): 5–14, here 12.

46. Jens Reich, *Abschied von den Lebenslügen: Die Intelligenz und die Macht* (Berlin, 1992). See also the critical overviews in Wolfgang Bialas, *Vom unfreien Schweben zum freien Fall: Ostdeutsche Intellektuelle im gesellschaftlichen Umbruch* (Frankfurt am Main, 1996).

47. Jan Ross, "Abschied von den Lebenslügen: Jens Reich und Heiner Müller diskutieren in Berlin über die Rolle der Intellektuellen," *Frankfurter Allgemeine Zeitung*, 2 April 1992; Reich, *Abschied von den Lebenslügen*, 164.

48. Günter de Bruyn, "Dieses Mißtrauen gegen mich selbst: Schwierigkeiten beim Schreiben der Wahrheit. Ein Beitrag zum Umgang mit den Stasi-Akten," *Frankfurter Allgemeine Zeitung*, 18 February 1993.

49. Albert O. Hirschman, "Abwanderung, Widerspruch und das Schicksal der Deutschen Demokratischen Republik: Ein Essay zur konzeptuellen Geschichte," *Leviathan* 20 (1992): 330–58, here 351–52.

DOROTHEA DORNHOF

Translated by Michael Latham

The Inconsequence of Doubt:
Intellectuals and the Discourse on Socialist Unity

Doubt is the Beginning of Wisdom.
—René Descartes

Doubt is Sin and Eternal Death.
—Martin Luther

Inconsequence: lack of proper sequence
in thought, speech or action
—*Webster's Collegiate Dictionary*

Who Speaks?

With the arrival of a new state, we were confronted with a new set of institutional constraints after more than forty years of predictability, central planning, and paternalistic welfare. Whereas institutional pressures to adjust and to acculturate came overnight, my everyday affairs are changing much more slowly. There are psychological ruptures. I encounter the diffusion of new lifestyles and a new intellectual habitus. These changes are uneven and unbalanced. They create new hierarchies of wants and demands. In lieu of the centrally planned and altogether predictable life in the collective of old, I am now asked to be efficient and to perform. I am counted as an individual. All the same, I am the subject of interrogation as an East German intellectual.

For East German intellectuals, the current remaking of their existence means that their present and their future are radically changing. The course of events, however, depends on the evaluation of their past. What they did or did not do will decide what they may or may not do henceforth. Negative stereotypes about "the guilt of intellectuals," of the "symbiotic links between intellectuals and power" in the GDR or of a "moral monopoly" of intellectuals in the twentieth century have been circulating in the media— all nourished by the media's assessment of the role of intellectuals in the GDR. This media circus happened with obvious relish on one side and with dire consequences on the other. In 1989 East German intellectuals had appeared, at long last, on the stage of the revolution. They have since fallen silent under the pressures of relentless summons to self-criticism and the brazenness of their condemnation.

Having a past as a young academic in the late GDR, how should I perform? My first reaction is predictable: it is to question the interrogators. Where did these critics come from? In whose name do they speak? Have not a few Western intellectuals acquired a new monopoly of interpretation in this spectacle of the disappearance of all others? Is there no longer a space for East German intellectuals who were neither victims nor culprits, accommodating themselves within the confines of the regime much as the majority of the population did and sharing their illusions and compromises, dissatisfaction and opportunism? To be sure, the salient qualities of intel-lectuals as we know them from a bourgeois age—the public nature of their criticism, their autonomy, and their political engagement—applied only conditionally to the intellectuals of the former GDR. But their continuing difficulty in speaking—after these conditions had become reality—is cause for concern. It is an indication of a general crisis of their self-understanding as intellectuals in the tradition of the Enlightenment. "Those who remain silent draw the suspicion of a distance to the world upon themselves, al-though they may still be utopians who reject the idiom which is demanded, refusing to be satisfied with a politics dominated by an ever increasing degree of coercion."[1] Does this apply to the old world or the new?

The difference between cultures becomes particularly evident if one examines the prevailing debates in the East and in the West. A postmod-ern West had come to dismiss intellectual enlightenment that is tied to political activism. The reverse was true for the intellectuals in socialist states. They returned to politics after years of muted debate. With their demands for democracy and liberalization, Eastern intellectuals set them-selves against cynicism and lies. They have put their societies and them-selves on trial and have reclaimed moral authority.

> In Central and Eastern Europe, intellectuals have attained their positions of power and even highest public offices not by virtue of their economic competence or on account of their political expertise. They have achieved such status on the basis of their moral authenticity and their courageous commitment to human rights—the great legacy of eighteenth century Euro-pean Enlightenment. These intellectuals are moralists who have presented

the rest of Europe with a new culture of political engagement and public debate. As enlightened intellectuals they are participants in a culture of complaint; they are the seasoned melancholics who have unmasked the official optimism of the socialist regime as an imposition.[2]

Wolf Lepenies finds the future of European politics in a clash between the political cultures of experts and moralists, respectively. Behind this vision we see the general problem of the role of intellectuals and their debates in different social and political environments, as these are shaped by distinct historical circumstances and theories of society. These settings will have to be scrutinized in some detail if we want to understand the current ambivalence of intellectuals who have emerged from a socialist state and attempt to escape its intellectual universe.

There are difficult questions to master on the way. What are the sources of the peculiar inconsequence of enlightened doubt[3] among intellectuals in the GDR? Why did the critical potential within Marxist theory not lead to a radical challenge of the regime? It is true that the SED possessed a monopoly of power in the state and over society. But the SED was never able to control society completely. The regime was certainly unable to control its intellectuals. The alert vigilance of the regime in relation to its intellectuals suggests continuous misgivings as to the loyalty of this heterogeneous group. Moreover, intellectuals confronted decisions for or against the regime during every decade of its existence—in 1953, 1956, 1968, 1971, 1976, 1985, and 1989. They articulated doubt time and again, and this habitus of doubt cannot and should not be taken lightly. And yet radical doubt frequently was softened into an apparent reconciliation with the regime. Why is it that the critical potential of doubt did not transgress the boundaries of the regime?

There is a tradition—a certain Protestant habitus—that may help explain this hesitance. A deeply entrenched moral code encouraged hope beyond reason that a system, even though incapable of learning, could reform after all. This hope muted opposition even in the face of inhuman practices. Time and again, it led to a reconciliation with the regime. It was self-deception. Sad to say, the issue is not laid to rest by pointing to a discrepancy between thought and action. The very notion of intellectual doubt had much to do with the toleration of the regime. The labors of doubt themselves had a tendency to create a false candor that absorbed the dissatisfactions and excused the inhuman practices. The utopia of solidarity, of a better society to come, was written into humanist and aesthetic discourses and assuaged discontents that the very real expectation of the utopia had helped articulate. If reality was bad, it could always be improved. What emerged was not doubt suppressed or marginalized, but a false openness among doubters, a deception that created its own reality and helped to stabilize the regime, and that ultimately underwrote its inhumanity. The problem is the nature of doubt and of the doubters. Casting a critical eye on the regime, intellectuals could always perceive themselves as being marginalized and thus overlook their stabilizing function in society. They could doubt as much as they wanted, as long as they expected change to come from the regime.

In his book *Abschied von den Lebenslügen*, Jens Reich drew a connection between the intelligentsia as a *structure-forming* and the nomenclatura as a *power-forming* force. Writers, social scientists, engineers, bureaucrats, and functionaries formed a strong and politically influential group in the GDR. They were the champions and executors of "the chimera of a rational project of society." But "we acted under the illusion that we, as a class, were repressed and oppressed in a society run by the nomenclatura, party functionaries and aided by party minions like the state bureaucracies, the State Security and Armed Forces. Caught in this illusion, we presumed that we defended the people against the powers of the state. In reality, intellectuals were not so much oppressed as they were duped."[4]

Literary scholarship, much like other spheres of intellectual life, was dominated by the state.[5] Official political pronouncements set the tone for the study of literature—as we shall see, a very privileged arena in the discourse on culture. This much is evident and quite unsurprising. Hence, yet another outline of the rhetoric of the regime, or a look behind the scenes in order to find out "how it really was," is not very helpful, even though it might reveal one secret or another. It seems of much greater interest to study both the effects of the official discourse on intellectuals and the role intellectuals played in informing discourse—in this case, that on literary scholarship as part of the humanities, or, as the GDR would have it, as part of the *Gesellschaftswissenschaften*, the social sciences. The powers of the state cannot be explained solely by reference to either the steering and control mechanisms of the state, including the State Security, or official statements of the party concerning intellectuals and academics. Rather, there was a space in between control and acquiescence that facilitated interaction, a communicative exchange between "above" and "below"— so much so that the humanities eventually moved in the direction of a self-governance of professional elites in the seventies and eighties without ever shedding their subordination to the regime. In fact, what needs to be explained is the process of the ever more elaborate self-control of an altogether professional community of scholars that made literary scholarship so readily a part of the regime, even when and where it appropriated the posture of objective scholarship and expressed doubt about the regime.

In this context, Foucault's notion of power proves useful. He sees power not as a rigid tool or object of those in power but as dependent on how it is enacted in social relations. These power relations extend beyond the boundaries of the state and thus are potentially beyond the control of the state: "The state, notwithstanding its manifest apparatus of power, is unable to control the field of actual power relations. In fact, state power can only operate within the context of pre-existing power relations."[6] Hence, the single-minded concentration on the study of the surveillance mechanisms of the State Security and the party that has become popular since the *Wende* could well be understood as yet another deception. It only prevents us from seriously considering the actual *web of power relations* which sustained the regime and entrapped critical thought.

Foucault's notion of power can help us reformulate our initial concern. How is it possible that intellectuals who pride themselves on an emancipatory self-understanding would not only enter into these power relations of their own free will but sustain them despite increasing doubts about their ability to realize any of their emancipatory goals? I suggest that the historical roots of this development must be sought in the nascent self-consciousness of intellectuals within the GDR during the fifties and sixties.

"We Are Not Pacifists, We Are the SED"

The founding myth of the GDR was shaped by returning émigrés with their therapeutic discourse on the *Kulturnation*.[7] They were instrumental in renewing a fatally apolitical and idealistic tradition of German political culture in intellectual circles and particularly in academia. "Both aspects, transcendent norms of a cultured and educated German bourgeoisie and the opposition against the idea and reality of the citizen, are woven into the political and cultural self-consciousness of the German *Kulturnation*."[8] The elision of these destructive elements of a German humanist and antifascist tradition had repercussions for subsequent perceptions of reality, political attitudes, and, above all, the eager loyalty of the social-scientific and artistic intelligentsia toward the regime.

This was an act of deliberate forgetting, because there were voices that had warned against the dangers intrinsic to this tradition, and they had been outspoken about the violence inherent in the notion of the *Kulturnation*.

> Some émigré philosophers and social-psychologists like Walter Benjamin, Max Horkheimer, Herbert Marcuse, and Erich Fromm recognized the ambiguity of the [inherited] bourgeois notion of culture. They interpreted this ambiguity as the outcome of the persistence of "two Germanies." They pointed to the contradictions of a culture based on social inequality and to its con-

sequences of endlessly dichotomizing in an effort to capture inequality, as the basic fact, in words. They warned against the potential of violence, the authoritarian structures and symbolic hierarchies which this notion of culture engendered. But the majority of returning authors and writers supported an idealistic concept of the *Kulturnation*. Their idealism carried along, together with its emancipatory message, the repressive elements inherent in the notion of *Kultur*.[9]

The structural ambiguity of the German notion of culture was exacerbated by the very real historical conditions under which the returning émigré intellectuals labored. From the beginning they faced a political leadership of Communist antifascists who had returned from their exile in Moscow. Both sides eagerly anticipated the chance to realize socialism after two world wars, after Auschwitz, Hiroshima, and Nagasaki. Writers such as Anna Seghers, Bertolt Brecht, or Johannes R. Becher were dedicated Communists notwithstanding the experience of Stalinism. The epochal illusion of returning émigrés consisted in their longing for a radical alternative to the catastrophic realities of the twentieth century. Their expectation of creating a better world proved to be resistant against all experience, including their own, with the deformation of socialism. It kept them from acknowledging the dictatorial tendencies implicit in their own educational project, which they conceived as an attempt to salvage the German nation by balancing power with culture.

In 1945, these two groups stood poised to create a new elite. In this they differed quite profoundly from their West German counterparts. The identity of the elites was to change radically in the GDR, whereas the Federal Republic built on a continuity of elites, retaining its intellectuals from the past with only limited purges. Antifascist rhetoric served the elites of the GDR as a remedy for "overcoming" National Socialism, although they knew well that the majority of the population whom they met as returnees had been fellow travelers of the National Socialist regime.[10] Thus, the first social contact between political and intellectual elites on one hand and the populace on the other was constituted by a simple exchange. The majority traded its responsibility for the Nazi regime—as well as its guilt—for the opportunity for a minority of political cadres to rule and for intellectuals to educate. This exchange was predicated on the assumption that Germans, if properly ruled and educated, could not help but change. The antifascist hope rested on the notion of transformation from above. For this to happen, the unity of politics and culture was required—and this is where the émigré intellectuals got caught.

Johannes R. Becher reflected this sentiment most clearly when he praised Marxism as "a scientifically based universal system" that facilitates "objective research into truth [objektive Wahrheitsforschung]." In his book *Education for Freedom* (1946) Becher asserted: "We have emphasized Marxism, because Marxism represents the perfection and completion of all objective thought. It is this concrete foundation of truth, and a world view based on these foundations, which lends intellectual support and cohesion, which provides a cognitive structure that preserves human thought from sinking into nihilism and anarchy, into purposelessness and meaninglessness, and which will show a debilitated humanity the means of elevating themselves toward worthwhile human thought, toward truthfulness, and toward the affirmation of life."[11] The evident religious hyperbole and resultant moral demonism in these lines reflect a discursive fusion of antifascism and humanism that formed the intellectual basis of official antifascism.[12]

Antifascism and its constituent idea of the unity of all social, cultural, and political forces made for a powerful foundational program that implicated intellectuals in a web of power relations. Insofar as intellectual elites emerged as critics of the regime, they always returned to the initial social contract and its intellectual foundation in Marxism as an education for freedom. Doubt became an issue of debating the form of pedagogy and the pedagogical role of intellectuals was never questioned. Subsequent generations of intellectuals were to elaborate the founding exchange in metanarratives of Marxism as narratives of progress and emancipation. Marxism-Leninism could thus appear as a discourse that established unity and coherence. This discourse of unity was linked to older Marxist traditions, hypostatizing concepts from the twenties and thirties; traditions proved "scientifically" that bourgeois imperialism was a decaying social formation and would inevitably lead to the victory of socialism as a law of history—underwriting a rhetoric of the superiority of the GDR.

Ironically, the intellectuals who helped sanctify this discourse also proved to be the first to be affected by it. Their very own images of capitalism and its disintegrating decadent culture, as well as of modernity as chaos and the archnemesis of civilization, made them susceptible to the political uses of this argument by the SED leadership. Had not many of the intellectuals themselves come from bourgeois backgrounds and, hence, could they be entirely free of decadence? The SED leadership thought not. Political leaders quickly projected onto intellectuals every sort of stereotype from the "dictionary of barbarians." They were called "intellectual agnostics" or "degenerate critics."[13] Later on they became more simply "grumblers and nags," who had to be cast out or surveilled as foreign and inimical elements in the interest of preserving the imaginary progress toward socialism as an ever more advanced unity of politics and culture.[14]

The idealist unity of the nation hardened into a power monopoly of the party, stages in this development being the transition of power from the Soviet Military Administration to a German administration in 1947–48, the elimination of the social-democratic elements in the SED, and the creation of a centralist party along Stalinist lines. In fact, a monopoly of power rather than spiritual renewal integrated the country, although there was always room for partial institutional autonomy and the individual initiatives of intellectuals.

At the very moment in which initial doubts could have arisen in view of the beginning purges of intellectuals, intellectuals as a group got ever more deeply entrapped by the regime. Already in 1947, the initial antifascist alliance between political and intellectual elites had acquired the quality of an entrenched political myth. It was the intellectual justification of this myth that undercut the very foundations on which open debate among intellectuals rested. Campaigns against idealism, existentialism, formalism, decadence, and revisionism and the classification of all modern philosophy since the arrival of "scientific Marxism" as "proto-fascist"[15] opened the door for the defamation of potentially all academics and intellectuals.[16] They could be labeled as proponents of Fascism. Thus, the initial campaign against bourgeois academics was camouflaged as a "de-nazification" campaign.

The intellectual tools for this campaign were provided in a master narrative that can be traced back to the work of Georg Lukács during his Moscow exile. These studies set up a stark juxtaposition of rationalism and irrationalism in German thought.[17] The ensuing historical-philosophical narrative of the course of German history allowed Lukács to portray romanticism as a movement counter to German classicism and as a persistent challenge to progress and enlightenment. As an irrational countermovement, romanticism was responsible for the eclipse of German thought and fed into antimodern, antienlightened tendencies in German society. According to this narrative, the nadir, reached with Nietzsche, lead from Nietzsche straight into National Socialism. Hence, anyone accused of Nietzschean or romantic leanings was not just an aberrant thinker but a political danger.

In this fashion, a powerful discourse arose in the Soviet Occupied Zone that conjoined elements of Marxism, classicism, and contemporary politics and insisted on the "unity of politics, economics and culture."

> The unrealistic and utopian elements of moral and political thought in Marxism were hypostatized—ideas which Marx had used, borrowing from preceding historical epochs and transferring them onto the economic evolution of capitalism. Now, the superannuated elements in Marx's works be-

came the decisive ones—Lenin's interpretation of Marx fits this pattern
very well—and the scientific element of Marx's thought was eviscerated.
Lenin's theory of imperialism, the theory of revolution and of the political
dictatorship [of the proletariat]—all of this was the outgrowth of utopian
elements of Marxism which resulted, already in Marx's own days, from the
crisis of the workers' movement.[18]

The social theory based on these ideas ignored any and all complexities
in thought and political action. Because truth is not debated but objectively known, this social theory eliminated difference and refused to engage
in debate. In 1947, this discourse was used to postulate a state socialism that
rested on the dominance of a political bureaucracy over everything else.
The result was a process of social and intellectual de-differentiation and
homogenization in the name of unity and rationality that reached its high
point in the fifties. Incidentally, this process of de-differentiation can even
be observed in the above quotation before its author very clearly rejects
the Lukacsian master narrative, but in his rejection still adheres to the
juxtaposition of rationalism and irrationalism, claiming that what had been
labeled as "rational" had in fact been irrational. There was and is no easy
escape from this kind of thinking.

The Reality of Antifascism
The dominance of a bureaucratic political regime intended to ensure unity
meant that the diverse elements of society had to be accommodated within
the state. Typically, this effort led to the revival of a pre-modern language of
community-building. Like the *paterfamilias* of the pre-bourgeois family, the
party, with its centralized structure and its general secretary serving as the
"father of the people," assumed the right to speak for and to represent the
people. Ideas of social equality and justice found highly stylized expression
within the context of these paternalistic principles. As much as this paternalistic state socialism championed claims of equality and emancipation,
it picked up on the traditional antifeminism of the workers' movement and
the equally traditional animosity toward intellectuals, subordinating both
under the imperatives of staying the rational course of unity on national
and social issues. The state took on the role of a tutelary power.

Representation always entails an element of silencing the manifold interests of those who are represented. But in this case, it meant the very
real repression of autonomous political publics and their ability to articulate their own interests, and so the destruction of an essential component
of a "civil society." The absence of such political publics had instanta-
neous consequences for the relation of the intellectuals to the state. The
ideological constructions of a harmonious, conflict-free society and of its

"new (wo)man" as "will and imagination," as Bourdieu called it, fed into a populist mobilization against intellectuals, reducing their autonomy.[19] While Anton Ackermann, then a member of the Central Committee of the SED, proclaimed the freedom of the arts and sciences,[20] former members of the Social Democratic Party were excluded and persecuted, and the first preparations for a major purge of party members were under way as part of the fight against social democratism. Simultaneously, the *Kulturbund zur demokratischen Erneuerung Deutschlands* (Cultural Alliance for the Democratic Renewal of Germany), founded in 1945 as a nonpartisan organization of the intelligentsia, was increasingly instrumentalized by the SED. By the end of the forties, a "front of the German intellectual workers [*Geistesarbeiter*]" was propagated, combining efforts for intellectual renewal and education with a politics of schisms and partisan divisions.

In all this, the notion of the *Kulturnation* figured centrally both as a justification and as a way of hiding very real forms of violence. The advanced state of collaboration between political and intellectual elites can be gauged from what at first sight appears to be a remarkable gesture. After the uprising of June 17, 1953, the executive council of the *Kulturbund* passed a twelve-point program in which the authority of the SED in cultural and scientific matters was explicitly *rejected*. The program called for the complete autonomy of the *Kulturbund* as "a comprehensive nonpartisan organization of democratic self-determination [*Selbsttätigkeit*] of the intelligentsia."[21] General Secretary Walter Ulbricht commented on this debate among intellectuals at a subsequent meeting of the central committee of the SED: "The members of the intelligentsia cooperated loyally in the days of the fascist provocation [June 17, 1953]. The majority embraced the new course of the party and the government. The implementation of this political course means that the key points of the *Kulturbund* program can now be realized."[22] This entailed, in accordance with the demands of the intellectuals, dissolving the notorious *Staatliche Kunstkommission* (State Art Commission). The role of the commission was taken up, however, by the censorship office within the Ministry of Culture, which was established in 1954. Because the intellectuals cooperated with the party against the people, they regained some autonomy vis-à-vis the party—which they were to lose again shortly thereafter.

After the Twentieth Party Congress of the Soviet Communist Party in 1956, the SED's monopolist claim to power stood, once again, at the center of attention among reform-minded socialist intellectuals. The Aufbau Verlag was one of the centers of the reform efforts promoted by its director, Walter Janka, and the editors of the *Kulturbund* journal *Sonntag*, Gustav Just and Heinz Zöger. But these initiatives came to an abrupt end with the suppression of the Hungarian uprising and the subsequent trials of Wolfgang Harich in March 1957 and Walter Janka in July 1957. The executive council of the *Kulturbund* distanced itself from the "anti-republican goals"[23] of the group surrounding Harich and later from Janka as well.[24] The behavior of the president of the *Kulturbund*, Johannes R. Becher, may in part be explained by his character. Like many party intellectuals, he had a tendency toward self-denial and showed a remarkable lack of solidarity, against his own better knowledge. But unwittingly he also acted according to a script that can be found in the disciplining rituals that undergirded the Stalinist trials. Becher's self-critique was published in the party newspaper *Neues Deutschland* in October 1957. After Becher had distanced himself from the "criminal agent organization Harich-Janka" and censured Alfred Kantorowicz's "hostile attitude" and his "flight from the republic" (*Republikflucht*), he addressed himself to the deficient political vigilance of the *Kulturbund*,

> which watched Bloch's activities and stood by while Bloch insulted the president and the other members of the presidential council [*Präsidialrat*], and which fears to speak a word about this whenever Bloch is present. . . . This is not an application of the power that the proletariat has placed in our hands. It contradicts the counsel of the party to engage this power. When we yield, we soften. This is a crucial lesson. In my opinion we need to understand better than has been the case that certain manifestations need to be taken seriously. I didn't take Harich and his ideas seriously. Hitler's *Mein Kampf* was also not to be taken seriously. But precisely because from a certain standpoint he was not to be taken seriously, it was possible for him to implicate the people and incite unspeakable crimes. The great lesson for us is this: it is necessary to exercise power, in order to maintain power; if one lets go of power, one is driven into a position of powerlessness, in which one loses control over the laws of action.[25]

In order to educate and to emancipate the masses, the intellectuals needed power. But in order to have power against an untrustworthy population, they had to close ranks and join the party—a party that might very well take away power from the intellectuals in the name of progress and unity.

If subsequent waves of doubt concerning the course of the party resulted in disillusionment about the system's ability to reform, the rituals of affirming power by closing of ranks on one hand and by exclusion on the other were repeated time after time. Ernst Bloch, Hans Mayer, Robert Havemann, Rudolf Bahro, and Wolf Biermann, much as the reform-minded members of the Writers' Union in 1979, followed one after another in a long procession of expulsions. All of them had doubted the wisdom of the regime, but their doubt was always accompanied by hope. They left not because they resisted the regime but because they were forced out as political and intellectual elites closed ranks, hoping yet again to preserve the basic antifascist compromise that had brought them to power in the first place. If you want to educate, you need power; if you want to stay in power, you need to educate—and both cannot be done without the discipline of the party.

The Social Tasks of Marxist Literary Science

Literary scholarship was treated as a social science in the GDR. The protagonists of this scholarship set out to distinguish themselves from the predominantly aesthetic scholarship in the other Germany and its emphasis on the autonomy of art and culture. Literary scholars championed a new, scientific paradigm, a radically altered thematic focus, and alternative forms of expression for the humanities. The price to pay for such innovations was a wholesale break with scholarly and institutional traditions. The search for new foundations led to the transfusion of prefabricated notions of history and society into the new humanities disciplines. On the basis of presumed laws of history and scientific truth, a set of binary models and antinomies—such as capitalism/socialism, progress/reaction, rationalism/irrationalism, realism/modernism—were now writ large. These oppositions were carried over from Marxist literary scholarship of the twenties and thirties. In practice, this meant that the historically contingent interests of the SED dictatorship were read as general laws of history— much as a hypostatized universal consciousness, represented by Marxism-Leninism, was now claimed to be the truthful representation of actual life. "In the philosophy of real existing Socialism, the scientific element of Marxism was displaced by a dogmatic metaphysics. Its main principle consisted in insuring that whatever was to be represented [in scholarship] unfolded from a general Law that was presumed to be present as a silent code behind all manifestations [of actual life]."[26]

The privileging of the Marxist tradition was accompanied by a veritable cult of the German classical heritage. The classics were set against late-bourgeois cultural and artistic developments of all kinds. Such divisions established unequivocal identities. They united diverse research strategies in one overarching interest—the presentation, in scholarship, of the socialist character of the nation and of its antecedents. Inasmuch as other cultures, including the "other culture" of a bourgeois past, were studied, these efforts served the elaboration of the socialist and national character of the nascent GDR.

Humanist and antifascist discourses proved to be particularly effective in this context. They facilitated elaborately encoded images of the (socialist) self and the (capitalist) other. In passing, we might note that this juxtaposition conveniently elides the destructive experience of modernity on one hand and of the National Socialist past on the other. This was not quite by chance. The humanities in the GDR quite faithfully reflected the same threefold anachronism that Eberhard Lämmert had elaborated for literary scholarship in National Socialism. During the famous 1996 German Language Association meeting, "National Socialism in Germanic Literary Studies and Poetics," Lämmert had characterized the key features of Germanic literary studies under the Nazi regime and their unreflected continuity in the Federal Republic. He pointed, first, to the humanities' claim to universality as normative and identity-forming disciplines (and the resulting emphasis on the unanimity of the discipline); second, to the servility and dependence of literary studies on political programs and agendas; and, third, to the predominance of pedagogical claims for improving the nation and ridding it of the ills of decadence.[27]

Both in the GDR and in the Third Reich, the "others" for these "humanities" were capitalism and imperialism, against which all resources of *Kultur* were mobilized. It is difficult to understand the almost religious veneration of culture and art and the dreamlike belief in scientific rationality, if one does not recognize how common this juxtaposition of culture and market was. For GDR intellectuals, especially at the height of the Cold War, things were made very simple. Either one chose unfettered capitalism or the humanities and the arts—*Kultur*. And if one chose the latter, one was hard put not to choose the actually existing socialism, even if one did not like all of it. Thus the institutional reorientation of the humanities in the GDR led to a permanent fixation on its supposed opposite, the "bourgeois" humanities and their decadent literary scholarship, which betrayed the *Kulturnation*.[28] This trope was to become the standard reference for all subsequent debates.

For a Social-Scientific Literary Scholarship
The hegemony of social-scientific discourse in history, in the humanities, and in literary scholarship in particular, can be traced in the documents of the Office of Sciences and Culture (*Abteilung Wissenschaft und Kultur*) at the Central Committee of the SED. Research in these documents amounts to a veritable archeology of power, because the evidence reveals not only the steering and control apparatus—planning and financing of scholarship and research at the universities and at the German Academy of Science (*Deutsche Akademie der Wissenschaften der DDR*)—but also concurrently the cooperation and collaboration between members of the academy, university professors, party secretaries, and officials of the research and education bureaucracies.

The key decisions about the future of scholarship in the GDR were made between 1947 and 1957. Shortly after 1945, scientific research had been divided between an Office of Propaganda and Agitation (*Propaganda und Schulung*) and an Office for Culture and Education (*Kultur und Erziehung*). Immediately after the university reform of 1951, an Office for Science and Higher Education was established, which was run by Kurt Hager. After being elected secretary of the Central Committee in 1955, Hager served as the top party administrator for science and culture until the end of the GDR. The Office of Sciences (*Abteilung Wissenschaften*) of the Central Committee was established under this name only in 1957. Following a resolution of the Central Committee's Secretariat, its immediate forerunner, the Office of Science and Propaganda was dissolved. Its functions were moved into a new and separate Office for Agitation and Propaganda. As the mere enumeration of the various offices suggests, the basic institutional patterns and discourses were set after a period of intense confrontations over the future role of scholarship between 1945 and 1957. They were to remain basically unchanged until the end of the GDR. The labels further suggest that the major divisions concerned the nature and function of scholarship. Within a period of roughly ten years, "science" was released from its linkage to politicization—but subjected to the tight control of the party all the same. By the end of the fifties, scholarship administration had become both more purely "science"-oriented and more dependent on the supervision of the Central Committee of the SED.

The founding of the Institute of Marxism-Leninism in 1949, following the Soviet model, was of equal importance. This initiative created a system of academies separate from universities and colleges. The establishment of the Institute for Social Sciences (*Institut für Gesellschaftswissenschaften*) at the Central Committee of the SED in 1951, the foundation of Centers for National Research and Commemoration of Classical German Literature (*Nationale Forschungs- und Gedenkstätten der klassischen deutschen Literatur*) in Weimar in 1953, and the publication of the journal *Weimarer Beiträge* and of the series *Contributions on the German Classics* completed the cycle of academic-political institution-building. All these innovations were to serve political claims to leadership in the sciences and the humanities and established the dominance of Marxism-Leninism (M-L) in scholarship. They came in close conjunction with the emphasis on classicism as the national German heritage and the exemplary articulation of cultural and scientific ideals. Typically, Johannes R. Becher proclaimed at the Fourth Writer's Congress in 1956 "a new period of German Art and Culture . . . in the service of workers and peasants" and as "signal for the [new] internationalism of socialist realism."[29]

Universities quickly became subject to ideological control. Order 333 of December 1946, issued by the Soviet Military Administration, had mandated the foundation of social science divisions at the universities in Leipzig, Jena, and Rostock.[30] The introduction of mandatory general education courses in Marxism-Leninism made M-L, as it was called, an integral part of university curricula from the late forties onward. Simultaneously, Soviet publications provided the intellectual and ideological underpinnings for social science scholarship.[31] They served the antimodernist campaign against "decadent" Western culture and legitimized the political battle against the relative autonomy of art and culture, the aesthetic sphere in bourgeois society. In addition, this literature provided the underpinnings for a Marxist-Leninist social science in colleges and universities. Michail Lifshitz's edited volume *Marx und Engels über Kunst und Literatur*, which saw its Russian publication in 1934, was issued in German in 1948.[32] This volume quickly became a fount of quotations for all cultural and literary scholarship at the universities. It was only replaced when the Party University Karl Marx at the Central Committee of the SED published its own material for its "Language and Literature" chair to serve in the training of SED functionaries. *Marxism-Leninism on the Role, the Essence, and the Meaning of Literature and Art* presented excerpts that canonized certain texts as Marxist-Leninist aesthetics and, hence, scientific knowledge about the laws of aesthetics and of artistic thinking.[33]

The sum total of these initiatives points to the persistent effort to mold scholarship according to official dogma. In view of the overwhelming power of, first, the Soviet Administration and, subsequently, the SED regime to enforce compliance, the transformation of humanist scholarship seems to be an open-and-shut case. But throughout the late forties and fifties, institutional development and reality did not correspond well, as the many conflicts over the orientation of literary scholarship attest. Where one might expect the one-sided avowal of an ideological creed, one finds in fact a combination of collaboration and resistance. Doubt and hope characterized the thought and action of leading scholars—and the universities of the GDR attracted some of the most prominent minds who had returned from exile.

The case of Hans Mayer, who survived National Socialism in exile, gives us an indication of what happened. Mayer accepted a professorship at the University of Leipzig in 1948, following the advice of his colleague Werner Krauss. He served as chair both in the social sciences and in the philosophical faculty. From the autumn of 1948 until February 1951, Mayer was professor of cultural sociology at the Franz Mehring Institute. The institute belonged to the university's newly constituted social science faculty, which was founded under Soviet authority in 1947. The Leipzig social science faculty was commissioned to teach a new generation of "progressive" (that is, Marxist-Leninist) students in order to advance them into leadership positions in the economy as well as in culture and politics.[34] It was, in short, a key institute for M-L agitation and an elite-factory, at that. This is to suggest that Hans Mayer entered Leipzig University via the highly politicized "social science" route. In September 1951, he moved on to a chair for the history of national literature at the Karl Marx University in Leipzig—the key position from which to articulate the classic German heritage, or so it was set up to be. At the time, Mayer was already in-volved in a running controversy with the party apparatus over his lec-ture "Masterpieces of Nineteenth Century World Literature." However, if he did not get his own institute—an Institute for World Literature and Comparative Literary Scholarship—this was not owing to the SED but to the power of two of his colleagues, Theodor Frings and Hermann Au-gust Korff. Only after the retirement of Korff in 1956 could he become director of the Institute of Modern German Literature (*Institut für neuere Deutsche Literatur*) and of the Institute for the History of National Liter-atures (*Institut für die Geschichte der Nationalliteraturen*). This was not the institute of world literature that he had hoped for, but clearly it was one of the most powerful and influential positions in literary scholarship in the GDR.

Mayer was a major player at a key university and he got, by and large, what he wanted. He began his career not simply as an antifascist intellec-tual returning from exile but as a Marxist academic who was to crack open the bourgeois university structure. Moreover, he entered the university and managed to establish himself as a literary scholar via the social sciences, which were the main battering ram of a Marxist-Leninist scholarship. He had the picture-perfect career of an aspiring Communist intellectual—but it turned out quite differently. His tenure as a professor at Leipzig was rocked by conflict, ending with Mayer's departure for West Germany. He was, from the start, involved in a running dispute over the extent of coop-eration (as far as the SED was concerned) and the dangers of exclusion (as far as literary scholarship was concerned). This confrontation between the antifascist and Marxist scholar and the Marxist-Leninist party bureaucracy articulated in exemplary fashion the mixture of attraction and rejection that brought intellectuals and politics together and set them apart. It left a legacy of bitterness. In hindsight, Hans Mayer recounts both the extraor-dinary expectations and the deep despair: "The obvious transgressions of this state and of the rulers who went down with it cannot undo the hopes, achievements, and the expressions of a democratic common will."[35] Mayer had hoped and fought for a radical reformation of scholarship, but what he got was party rule.

During the early fifties, Mayer became one of the most popular university professors in the GDR. His lectures on modern German literature also attracted the keen attention and controlling instincts of the party. A confidential report to the Central Committee of the SED reveals the peculiar combination of attraction and distance from the vantage point of the party—and not least the pedestrian problems of surveilling a high-caliber professor. "In the context of the Institute for Germanics . . . in Leipzig, Professor Hans Mayer's lecture is currently the only one which deserves the label Marxist. However, this cycle of lectures [German Literature in the Second Empire] could be checked only on the basis of often very deficient notes. . . ."[36] As an independent antifascist and Marxist scholar, Mayer was considered a troublemaker. He remained under surveillance throughout his tenure, long before he was to become the ideological enemy at the university, to be fought by all means. Troubles began to intensify in 1956, generally a threshold year in the development of the relation between the SED and literary scholars.

The first victim of the ideological offensive that began in 1956, however, was not Hans Mayer. The director of the Institute for Philosophy at the University of Leipzig, Ernst Bloch, was accused of being the spiritual leader of the "counterrevolution" at the university. The conflict with Hans Mayer escalated when Mayer protested against the suspension and early retirement of Bloch. Mayer had problems of his own, though. He had come to polemicize against the canon of socialist realism and strongly supported a positive evaluation of "decadent" literature. A scheduled radio lecture titled "On the Current Condition of Our Literature" was to give him a chance to extol his views before a national audience. This radio talk must be seen in the context of the hopes for reform that the Twentieth Party Congress in Moscow had engendered in 1956.[37] Picking up on Soviet debates about sectarianism and the decay of literature, Mayer pointed to administrative restrictions on literature and scholarship and castigated the stagnation and sterility of GDR literature. His talk was to be broadcast on November 28 in the *Deutschlandsender* but was canceled shortly before the broadcast. However, on December 4 the complete text was printed in the weekly culture magazine *Sonntag*. As a result the two editors of the magazine, Gustav Just and Heinz Zörger, were apprehended and, a few months later, were sentenced to lengthy jail terms. The newly hired editorial staff of *Sonntag* instantly organized polemical articles countering Mayer's critical assessment,[38] Alfred Kurella being the main leader of the charge.[39]

The consequences of the canon of M-L literature were far-reaching. Increasingly, Mayer's books and essays could only be printed in the West. His ability to work and to speak were curtailed. He was persistently harassed. Yet, Mayer stayed in Leipzig until 1963. Despite his enemies in high places, and surveillance and encroachments on his activities, he felt a sense of obligation and experienced an excitement that he did not encounter in Tübingen, where he resided after his departure from the GDR. He felt that students and colleagues needed him and counted on him. Only after the local FDJ (Free German Youth) magazine challenged him with an article titled "One Scholarly Opinion Too Many" and confronted him, his staff, and his students with the choice to put up or shut up, did he feel that his influence as a teacher was in jeopardy.[40] When his students and assistants came under fire, he felt responsible for them and their misfortunes. Their fate outweighed the hopes for outlasting the regime. Mayer capitulated and left.

Mayer's career in the GDR was at one and the same time immensely successful and evidently heretical. It is full of contradictions, exhibiting a quest for power and influence, as well as gestures of impotence. Mayer's call for a social scientific foundation to literary scholarship, his Marxist dialectics, and his historical thinking had little to do with the official discourse of the Marxist-Leninist social sciences. And yet, he was part of it. The utopian moment inherent in Marxist theory nourished his doubt and held it in abeyance—until he was forced to face the irrevocable choice of being silenced or having to leave. Until this point, he had doubted—and stayed.

The career of Werner Krauss, who survived National Socialism on death row, shows a rather similar pattern. Krauss accepted a chair at the University of Leipzig in 1947. From the very beginning, he made his name among literary scholars by insisting on the urgency of a methodological reconsideration of literary scholarship and by calling for the application of historical and dialectical materialism to the study of literature. He demanded a wholesale reorientation of his department, Romance Languages and Literatures, in the expectation that "the historical task of literary history could only be fulfilled if the highest levels of achievement of the victorious class were reached."[41] He was vociferous in pleading for the abolition of "idealist" approaches to literature in favor of integrating literary studies into the social sciences. He may well have been sensing the implicit dangers of this demand when he added that the "new scientific orientation of literary studies should not divert from genuine literary scholarship by using cheap, surrogate knowledge."[42] Of course, this was a less than subtle reminder of his opposition to the M-L citation mania. A social-scientific orientation eschewed dogmatic references, Krauss insisted. He was no pluralist, to be sure. However, in his view only the emphasis on scholarship guaranteed the success of a social scientific approach. Hence, "the transformation of our literary science must start with the scholarship in the individual disciplines. They need to be transformed from within in order to achieve a new level of scientific quality."[43]

Together with like-minded scholars such as Hans Mayer, Ernst Bloch, and Walter Markov, Krauss laid the foundations for a remarkable upswing of scholarship in East Germany. He never questioned the partisan character of Marxism, which would lead to superior scholarship if paired with the enlightened quest for truth and objectivity. The link between the two is explained in his famous essay "Literary History as Historical Mission" (1950), which is a brilliant argument against both positivist and idealist traditions in German literary scholarship and the disastrous consequences of their accommodating and, indeed, facilitating the Nazi past. In contrast, Krauss called for a literary scholarship cognizant of its own historicity and of the historicity of literature, without which neither literature nor politics could flourish. "[I]t is the historical testimony of literature that matters. If human beings are indeed social beings, this suggests that literary scholarship is called upon to create from the literary record a comprehensive picture of the contradictions of humanity, as they were once experienced. Literature above all possesses the power of memory which brings to light all those moments that constitute society."[44] It was literature that mattered—literature understood as the aesthetic trace of human endeavors in constituting society.

During the fifties Krauss increasingly withdrew into scholarship, abandoning the more explicit political stance of his early days in Leipzig. In his eyes the whole debate on canonical positioning as a prerequisite for research seemed rather to diminish the newly gained scope of scholarship, instrumentalizing the universities for narrow political and ideological goals. In 1955, Krauss created for himself what he called a "workspace" (*Arbeitsstelle*) for German and French Enlightenment, in fact an institute replete with its own series of publications, at the German Academy of Sciences in Berlin. His research focused on the Enlightenment in France, Spain, and Germany. His withdrawal into "pure" scholarship was a reflection of his growing doubts about an increasingly sclerotic political system. He managed to create the profile of a literary scholarship that was shaped by four elements: a more encompassing notion of literature including all manner of nonliterary texts; the study of readers and audiences as actors and mediators in literary history; research into the contextual conditions of scholarship such as publishing and censorship; and the recognition that any research on past literary production happens in the present and is therefore shaped by the present. Long before a "historical" approach was (re)invented by Western scholarship, it had become the very foundation of Marxist and, indeed, Communist literary scholarship in the GDR. Krauss managed to pursue his scholarly program. The price he had to pay for this was increasing isolation.

The difficulty consisted in defending this "social-scientific" (in fact, historicist) approach against its Eastern and Western detractors. In the West, the preeminent scholar in Krauss's field, Ernst Robert Curtius, had withdrawn from the present into the literary past—and lived it. Literary scholarship that would acknowledge the present was unheard of. A scholarship that would deal with noncanonical texts was shunned as demeaning the treasured heritage of the Occident. In the East, the present was really not for scholars to define, as the much more cantankerous Hans Mayer had to experience at first hand. Krauss could well insist that "Enlightenment scholarship is a chapter in current history," as he did to Kurt Hager,[45] but it was Hager and the Politburo who defined what current history was to be. Theirs was not so much an orthodox but a literal Marxism that allowed for neither creative scholarship nor political reflection on the present. Krauss was never banished for his critique of the provincialism and banality of the prevailing scholarly discourse. Nor did he achieve what he set out to do: "Marxist method must start with the current state of scholarship. It cannot start from the subject position of Marx's own time."[46] Creative Marxist scholarship was never appreciated in the GDR.

Classicism as Hegemonic Knowledge

Literary scholarship was not constituted along the lines that Hans Mayer or Werner Krauss had suggested. They had insisted on radical reform, even revolution from within scholarship and from within the disciplines of literary studies. It was literature that was to shine—to be the supreme testimony of human endeavor and class struggle. But the reverse was the case. What emerged was a Marxist-Leninist social science with a dogmatic ideological posture concerning periodization, a canon of its major texts, and a way of judging literature. Social-scientific dogma subordinated literature and literary studies to a set of beliefs concerning the nature of history and progress.

The dominant system of education and scholarship was transfixed by the legacy of bourgeois culture that was heralded by the Weimar Centers for National Research and Commemoration of Classical German Literature (*Nationale Forschungs- und Gedenkstätten der klassischen deutschen Literatur*). It focused on the so-called progressive traditions of bourgeois culture, that is, on all the traditions that could be associated with classicism. In Weimar,

Lukács's classicist aesthetics was turned into a veritable cult. It was used to legitimate a German literary scholarship whose claim to fame consisted in being a socialist national philology. In this capacity, it formed the hegemonic science in literary scholarship. Notwithstanding the criticism of its reductivist Marxism by the Leipzig School of Krauss, Markov, Mayer, and Bloch, literary scholarship, prior to Werner Mittenzwei's call for revision in the first genuine debate on classicism in the seventies, constituted a canonical orthodoxy that relied on Goethe's and Schiller's works.[47] Ultimately, it was the combination of classicism and the national philology of the Weimar school, rather than the Marxism of the Leipzig school, that accommodated the M-L of the SED.

According to the tenets of official Marxist-Leninist self-perception, socialist society was not only the inheritor of bourgeois achievements, transferring them in a new scientific-technological revolution. Marxist social science history was also an absolute and complete scientific view of the world and of history, the one and only correct perspective of the working class. Literary scholarship and particularly German literary scholarship had a prominent place in this architecture of knowledge. It was allotted a leading role as the national science of literature. German literary scholarship shaped the cultural self-understanding of the early GDR with its synthesis of Marxist and classical bourgeois knowledge systems. This synthesis entailed an authoritative universalism that is characterized by the slogan "Encouragement of the Positive and the Disparagement of Decadence," coined by the Soviet philosopher Michail Lifshitz.[48] This universalist architecture of knowledge defined modernity strictly as decadence. It ignored the diversity of modern interests and value orientations, denigrated alternative worldviews and religion, and rejected the differentiated cultures and lifestyles in the post–World War II era. It actively destroyed the intellectual force field of the era that had brought forth, within the GDR, such diverse representatives as Hermann August Korff, Hans Mayer, Werner Krauss, Gerhard Scholz, Ernst Bloch, Alfred Kurella, Wolfgang Harich, Alfred Kantorowicz, and Leo Kofler.[49]

The concentration on the national literary heritage and on the construction of a socialist national literature, celebrating socialist realism as the high point and end point of German classicism, entailed well into the seventies both a cultural-political and a literary-theoretical opposition to modernism and the avant-garde. The roots of this aversion lie, on one hand, in a Soviet model of the construction of Socialism and, on the other, in the tendency inherent in the German labor movement to disparage the autonomy of art and literature in favor of their strict political instrumentalization. The programmatic unity of science and politics was called for—

and with this constitution of an "official scholarship," the misidentification of Marxism-Leninism with Marxist scholarship was set in place.[50] Literary scholarship became the study of *German National Literature*—a course of scholarship, moreover, that synchronized political and literary history and politicized aesthetics.

> The rational methodology of the social sciences was destroyed by its dependence on a canonical text. It created a homey intellectual atmosphere, which put an anti-scholarly norm of an idealized allegiance to the canon in the place of an analytic methodology and a critically rational structuring of the subject matter at hand. In lieu of the criteria of logical argumentation and the search for agreement in scholarly dispute, we find an experiential community of the always already convinced This mechanism created the mental disposition of intellectuals to accept the fact that non-scientific institutions regulated scholarship.[51]

In fact, we find a huge bureaucratic scientific apparatus whose sole purpose was the reproduction of canonical knowledge, creating a tremendous amount of activism in terms of scholarly and administrative committees and councils but ultimately leading to nothing. Nothing exemplifies the actual structure of scholarship better than the 1951 draft of the Office of Sciences on the "Statute for the Promotion and Intensification of Research at Universities and Colleges in the GDR," which mandated the following regulatory mechanism:

> As far as the Social Sciences are concerned, the State Secretariat for the Universities, in conjunction with the German Academy of Sciences, the State Planning Commission and the National Ministry for Education, elaborates directives for research in the context of long-range planning and passes them on to the Institutes at the University . . . with reference to the available means. The institutes develop concrete research proposals on the basis of these directives, taking into account personnel and material costs. Upon consultation with the faculties they are combined in university and college-wide plans for the humanities and social sciences, and upon further consultation with the faculty senate, they are passed on to the State Secretariat for the Universities. The State Secretariat for Universities rearranges these proposals according to the needs of an all-encompassing coordination of projects and the correct mission of individual institutes and balances them against the research plans of the Academy of Sciences, the State Planning Commission and the National Ministry for Education.[52]

The demand for a fusion of scholarship and politics boiled down to a horrendously complex process of elaborating national plans for literary research. Such plans could only flourish in the pursuit of gigantic projects. Thus, literary scholars from all universities and from the Academy of Sciences were brought together under the umbrella of the SED in a grand collective research project, which was to develop a history of German national literature. This project was intended to counter the much-deplored retrogression of German literary scholarship during the overall advance of socialism. An encompassing prospectus for German literary scholarship was the first product of this venture. As might be expected, it set the task of developing the study of national literature on the basis of Marxist social theory. The 1958 prospectus expressed this goal in the following way: "Correct approaches cannot deflect from the fact that dialectical and historical materialism, as the foundation for a theoretical perspective and as a general principle for scholarly and educational work, have not yet succeeded in shaping literary scholarship as a whole." As yet-to-be-developed scholarship on German literature and language, "[these studies] are to make a prominent contribution to the education of our people toward a socialist consciousness, toward the development of new ethical norms in the co-existence among people, and toward the heightening of their culture within socialist society."[53]

The central task of research was seen as "the development of a scientific image of the history of German national literature on the basis of Marxist-Leninism, to unveil the laws of historical development in German literature, to make effective the grand humanist and revolutionary traditions of German literature—especially of the literature of socialist realism—for socialist education, to generalize literary phenomena on the basis of Marxist-Leninist literary theory into a unified literary theory and, with this tool available, to effect the broader development of socialist literature."[54] The institutionalization of Marxist literary scholarship was predicated on "the leading role of the Party in all research and educational facilities concerned with German literary history,"[55] as well as on the permanent confrontation with revisionist tendencies among its own ranks and with bourgeois literary scholarship.

The key elements of a Marxist-Leninist literary scholarship can be seen against the foil of all the tendencies that were denigrated as revisionist after 1956. The revisionism of a Hans Mayer or an Ernst Bloch was castigated for the denial of the leading role of the party, the depreciation of the role of the masses, the defamation of the accomplishments of socialist literature, and the rejection of a theory of reflection (of material reality in literary production). In order to assure compliance, a conference, arranged by the Office of Sciences, was held at Humboldt University for the purpose of counteracting inimical and revisionist positions of literary scholarship. The cream of Marxist-Leninist scholarship assembled and made Georg Lukács and Hans Mayer their scapegoats. The intellectual godfathers of social-scientific and classicist scholarship, respectively, were debunked. Once this hatchet job was done, the scholarship machine was cranked up. Research was now dedicated, full-time, to the study of German national literature and contemporary socialist literature. The result was a twelve-volume anthology titled *The History of German National Literature* (1965–1983), which came under critical scrutiny only in the eighties.[56] Its tenor was predictable. It favored the classical German heritage and a socialist-realist national literature as the culmination of classicism. It denounced any and all modernist affects, leading to the wholesale exclusion of all modernist literature from literary scholarship. What was left was a totalized classicism, fitted into the laws of historical progress, that found its apogee in the GDR.

The Marxism-Leninism in German literary studies did not succeed in creating the "new scientific methodology" that Werner Krauss had so adamantly supported. The analysis of literary production and historical reality did not begin where they might have added to knowledge, with doubt about the singularity of the unified architecture of socialist knowledge and with the exploration of the literary articulation of contemporary life. Rather, literary scholarship was cast into a rigid frame, wherein society was predetermined by class structures and lived social experience was reduced to a series of neatly calibrated essential and peripheral "contradictions." Literary history was reduced to an ideological history that elaborated the imaginary totality of a socialist nation and of a socialist conscience.

If we believe the West German critics of intellectual life in the GDR, this might be a good enough conclusion. But powerful and enduring as this kind of simplistic scholarship was, it did not last. Underneath the M-L discourse on unity and progress, there was room for lateral movement. The standard scholarship, as it was expressed in the twelve-volume *History of German Literature: From the Beginnings to the Present*,[57] came under sustained attack.[58] New forms of cooperation, favoring interdisciplinary and comparative approaches, were explored. The strictures of canonical scholarship were circumvented, for example, in the study of the literature and art in the Weimar Republic, which necessarily had to deal with a good bit of "decadent" art. New channels of communication with the international scientific community did develop. In short, a process of differentiation set in, which undercut the M-L narrative. But as daring as many of these initiatives appeared at the time, doubt about the canonical knowledge of scholarship remained without consequence. Those who challenged the unitary discourse outright, such as Robert Havemann, Rudolf Bahro, and Wolf Biermann, were cast out. The majority of intellectuals did not dare to doubt, with the radical consequence that Descartes suggested. It would have meant to question the very foundation of knowledge, the utopian spirit of progress that had engendered so much hope for a more enlightened future, and an imaginary community that found its legitimacy in overcoming and combating fascism. Such doubt would have destroyed the very identity that few of us were willing to forsake. The lack of a critical public among whom doubt could be raised against the reigning discourse and the lack of a debate over the "good life" led to the interiorization of the tensions that found only faint expression in scholarship. The more deadlocked literary scholarship was in its attempt to transpose its messages from the past into the present or to support a new literature, which would work out the contradictions of society in its writing, the greater the contradiction between the claim for a community of enlightened individuals and the reality of dependence and self-induced tutelage. "The consequence of incompatibility remained concealed in the life-world. One can accomplish a lot without reconciliation, with the exception of living. If we had not experienced this reconciliation of the irreconcilable, we would have, in actual fact, become schizophrenic."[59]

Notes

1. Jörg Magenau, "Strukturelle Befangenheiten: Die Intellektuellen-Debatte," in *Verrat an der Kunst? Rückblicke auf die DDR-Literatur*, ed. Karl Deiritz and Hannes Krauss (Berlin, 1993), 48–53, here 51.

2. Wolf Lepenies, "Das Ende der Utopie und die Rückkehr der Melancholie: Blick auf die Intellektuellen eines alten Kontinents," in *Intellektuellendämmerung*, ed. Martin Meyer (Munich, 1992), 15–26, here 22–23.

3. Compare the historical survey of this theme in Michael Walzer, *The Company of Critics. Social Criticism and Political Commitment in the Twentieth Century* (New York, 1988).

4. Jens Reich, *Abschied von den Lebenslügen: Die Intelligenz und die Macht* (Berlin, 1992), 23.

5. See Dorothea Dornhof, "Von der 'Gelehrtenrepublik' zur marxistischen Forschungsgemeinschaft an der Akademie der Wissenschaften: Das Institut für deutsche Sprache und Literatur," in *Deutsche Literaturwissenschaft 1945–1965: Fallstudien zu Institutionen, Diskursen, Personen*, ed. Petra Boden and Rainer Rosenberg (Berlin, 1997), 173–203.

6. Michel Foucault, *Sexualität und Wahrheit.* (Frankfurt am Main, 1986), 1:113 (History of sexuality: An introduction, trans. Robert Hurley [New York, 1978]).

7. The heading is from Walter Ulbricht, "Beratung mit Genossen Gesellschafts-wissenschaftlern." 18 April 1954. Zentrales Parteiarchiv (ZPA), in *Stiftung Archiv der Parteien und Massenorganisationen der DDR beim Bundesarchiv* (SAPMO-BA), Bestand Abteilung Wissenschaft beim ZK der SED, IV/2/904/33.

8. Sigrid Meuschel, *Legitimation und Parteiherrschaft in der DDR: Zum Paradox von Stabilität und Revolution in der DDR, 1945–1989* (Frankfurt am Main, 1992), 16.

9. Lutz Winkler, "Der Geist an der Macht? *Kulturnation* und intellektueller Hege-monieanspruch," in *Les intellectuels et l'état sous la république de Weimar*, ed. Manfred Gangl and Hélène Roussel (Rennes, 1993), 219–31, here 225.

10. Jeffrey Herf, "German Communism, the Discourse of 'Antifascist Resistance,' and the Jewish Catastrophe," in *Resistance Against the Third Reich, 1933–1990*, ed. Michael Geyer and John Boyer (Chicago, 1994), 257–94.

11. Johannes R. Becher, *Erziehung zur Freiheit: Gedanken und Betrachtungen*. (Berlin, 1946), 128.

12. Manfred Riedel, "Die Sage vom guten Anfang: Über ein Kapitel deutscher Literatur-Geschichte," *Sinn und Form* 44, no. 4 (1992): 520–34.

13. These terms appeared in a series of articles in the Heidelberg journal *Die Wandlung* by Dolf Sternberger, Gerhard Storz, and Wilhelm Emanuel Süskind (1946–1948), which along with Victor Klemperer's *LTI: Notizbuch eines Philologen* (Leipzig, 1946) is among the first ideological-critical analyses of the language of National Socialism. In 1957, the first revised publication of the article from "Die Wandlung" appeared in Hamburg in book form. Dolf Sternberger, Gerhard Storz, and Wilhelm Emanuel Süskind, *Aus dem Wörterbuch des Unmenschen* (Hamburg, 1957); and the expanded version, *Aus dem Wörterbuch des Unmenschen*, with a report of the debate on the critique of language (Munich, 1970).

14. Klaus Städtke, "Beispiele der Deformation wissenschaftlichen Denkens in den Geisteswissenschaften der frühen DDR," *Zeitschrift für Sozialwissenschaft* 19, no. 1 (1991): 32–43, here 37.

15. Gerhard Harig, "Die Erkenntnistheorie des Marxismus (1945)," in *Ausgewählte philosophische Schriften 1934–1959* (Leipzig, 1973), 61–75, here 65.

16. Wolfgang Schubardt, "Zur Entwicklung der marxistisch-leninistischen Philo-sophie," *Deutsche Zeitschrift für Philosophie* 5, no. 6 (1959): 701–20, here 705.

17. Georg Lukács, *Die Zerstörung der Vernunft* (Berlin, 1953) (The destruction of reason, trans. Peter Palmer [Atlantic Highlands, N.J., 1980]).

18. Gerd Irrlitz, "Ankunft der Utopie," *Sinn und Form* 42, no. 5 (1990): 930–35, here 943.

19. Pierre Bourdieu, *Sozialer Raum und Klassen* (Frankfurt am Main, 1985), 37.

20. Anton Ackermann, "Rede vor Angehörigen der Intelligenz," 15.10.1946; SAPMO-BA, ZPA NL/109/14: 40.

21. "Präsidialratssitzung am 3. Juni 1953," in *SED und Intellektuelle in der DDR der 50er Jahre: Kulturbund-Protokolle*, ed. Magdalena Heider and Kerstin Thöns (Cologne, 1990), 16.

22. Walter Ulbricht, in *Das 15. Plenum des Zentralkomitees der SED vom 24. Juli bis 26. Juli 1953. Nur für den persönlichen Gebrauch bestimmt*, ed. ZK der SED Berlin (Berlin, 1953), 82.

23. Stenographisches Protokoll der 30. Tagung des ZK der SED, IfGA; ZPA IV/2/1/252: 109.

24. Wolfgang Harich, *Keine Schwierigkeiten mit der Wahrheit: Zur nationalkommuni-stischen Opposition 1956 in der DDR* (Berlin, 1993).

25. Johannes R. Becher, "Vom sinnvollen Einsatz der Macht," *Neues Deutschland*, 26 October 1957: 4.

26. Gerd Irrlitz, "Ein Beginn vor dem Anfang: Philosophie in Ostdeutschland 1945–1950," in *Wissenschaft im geteilten Deutschland*, ed. Walter H. Pehle and Peter Sillem (Frankfurt am Main, 1992), 113–24, here 114.

27. Eberhard Lämmert, "Germanistik: Eine deutsche Wissenschaft," in *Nationalismus im Germanistik und Dichtung: Dokumentation des Germanistentages im München vom 17.–22. Oktober 1966*, ed. Benno von Wiese and R. Henß (Berlin, 1967), 15–36.

28. On the discourse of *Kulturnation* as the founding myth of the state, see Winkler, "Der Geist an der Macht?"

29. Johannes R. Becher, "Von der Größe unserer Literatur der Arbeiterklasse," in *Gesammelte Werke*, ed. J. R. Becher Archiv der Akademie der Künste (Berlin, 1981), 18:499–534, here 533.

30. "Befehl Nr. 333 der SMAD über die Gründung von Gesellschaftswissenschaftlichen Fakultäten vom 2. Dezember 1946," in *Dokumente der Sowjetischen Militäradministration in Deutschland zum Hoch- und Fachschulwesen 1945–1949*, Studien zur Hochschulentwicklung, vol. 57, ed. Gottfried Handel and Roland Köhler (Berlin, 1975), 56–61.

31. Rainer Rosenberg, "Der ritualisierte Diskurs: Das Modell der offiziellen sowjetischen Literaturtheorie der 50er Jahre," *Zeitschrift für Germanistik*, n.s. 3, no. 1 (1993): 99–109.

32. Michail Lifshitz, *Marx und Engels über Kunst und Literatur: Eine Sammlung aus ihren Schriften* (Berlin, 1948).

33. *Der Marxismus-Leninismus über die Rolle, das Wesen und die Bedeutung für Literatur und Kunst*, ed. Parteihochschule Karl Marx beim ZK der SED (Kleinmachnow, 1953).

34. Hans Uwe Feige, "Hans Mayers Vertreibung von der Karl-Marx-Universität Leipzig," *Deutschlandarchiv* 24, no. 7 (1991): 730–32. See also *"Hoffnung kann enttäuscht werden": Ernst Bloch in Leipzig*, ed. Volker Caysa, Petra Caysa, Klaus-Dieter Eichler, and Elke Uhl (Frankfurt am Main, 1992). On the "case" of Hans Mayer, there is presently only the extensive academic historical study by Petra Boden, "Universitätsgermanistik in der SBZ/DDR: Personalpolitik und struktureller Wandel 1945–1965," in *Geschichte der Deutschen Literaturwissenschaft 1945–1965: Fallstudien zu Institutionen, Diskursen, Personen*, ed. Rainer Rosenberg and Petra Boden (Berlin, 1996), 119–56.

35. Hans Mayer, *Der Turmbau von Babel: Erinnerungen an die Deutsche Demokratische Republik* (Frankfurt am Main, 1993), 16.

36. SAPMO-BA, Bestand Abteilung Wissenschaft beim ZK der SED, IV 2/904/225: 32–33.

37. Hans Mayer, "Zur Gegenwartslage unserer Literatur" (1956), in Hans Mayer, *Zur deutschen Literatur der Zeit. Zusammenhänge. Schriftsteller. Bücher.* (Hamburg, 1967), 365–73.

38. With his defense of Western modernism, Mayer directed himself in the essay "Zur Gegenwartslage unserer Literatur" (On the present condition of our literature) —as he had previously at the Konferenz zu Fragen der Literatur und Literaturwissenschaft (May–July 1956)—against the Stalinist position of Ulbricht, which conceived of the writer as an "engineer of the human soul." Above all, he opposed Becher's notion that the literature of the GDR had developed out of the literature of the working class, as well as his idealistic conception of a "socialist literary society" (see Becher's address at the Fourth Writers' Congress in *Von der Größe unserer Literatur* [Berlin, 1956], 8). Mayer lamented the diminished standards of contemporary German literature in the East and the West and recalled the literary opulence of the twenties. He saw the raising of artistic standards of GDR literature as a decisive

turn toward bourgeois and nonbourgeois modernism, and thus placed the nascent GDR literature in the context of world literature. "If one wishes to change our literary climate, a comprehensive confrontation and engagement with modern art and literature will finally have to begin." (Mayer, "Zur Gegenwartslage," 371). Compare Günter Erbe, *Die verfemte Moderne: Die Auseinandersetzung mit dem "Modernismus" in Kulturpolitik, Literaturwissenschaft, und Literatur der DDR* (Opladen, 1993).

39. Alfred Kurella (1895–1972) served as director of the Institute for Literature in Leipzig (1954–1957) and as vice president of the German Academy of the Arts in Berlin (1965–1974). In the aftermath of the arrest of Wolfgang Harich, Walter Janka, and the editorial staff of the *Kulturbund* journal *Sonntag*, Kurella became a key figure in the continuing campaign against "decadence" and "revisionism," in which context he argued against Hans Mayer, among others. In *Sonntag*, Kurella took a strong position against Mayer's ideas and sharply rejected the "recuperation of the experiments of the twenties." Alfred Kurella, "Einflüsse der Dekadenz," *Sonntag* 29 (1957); also in *Dokumente zur Kunst -, Literatur- und Kulturpolitik der SED*, ed. Elmar Schubbe (Stuttgart, 1972), 471. See also Alfred Kurella, "Ästhetische Restauration?" *Sonntag* 6 (1947): 12. Compare Erbe, *Die verfemte Moderne*, and Norbert Kapferer, *Das Feindbild der marxistisch-leninistischen Philosophie in der DDR 1945–1988* (Darmstadt, 1990).

40. Cited in Hans Mayer, *Ein Deutscher auf Widerruf: Erinnerungen* (Frankfurt am Main, 1984), 2:255. After the construction of the Wall, the reprisals against Mayer were resurrected and intensified. Under increasingly difficult circumstances, he was able to arrange speaking engagements and discussions at his institute even for *Unpersonen* (nonpersons) such as Günter Grass and Peter Hacks, who at that time stood in the spotlight of party criticism for his play *Die Sorgen und die Macht*. In the autumn of 1963 Mayer's work *Ansichten zur Literatur der Zeit* (Reinbeck, 1963) was published by the Rowohlt Verlag. Shortly thereafter Werner Bahner, who had succeeded Werner Krauss as director of the Romance Language Institute, received instructions to investigate Mayer's "party-hostile views." Mayer had now become a "case" and his expulsion a closed matter. As an "enemy" of socialist cultural politics who attached little value to socialist literature and in his teachings emphasized the work of "modernist" authors, he was no longer welcome at the socialist Karl Marx University (see Hans Uwe Feige, "Hans Mayers Vertreibung von der Karl-Marx-Universität Leipzig," *Deutschlandarchiv* 24, no. 7 [1991]: 730–32). A press campaign was begun against Mayer that persisted in the university newspaper of the Karl Marx University from January to July 1963. The opening salvo, "Versäumnisse und Aufgaben unserer Germanisten" (Sins of omission and tasks of our Germanists, January 1963), came from Mayer's student Klaus Schuhmann. There followed articles by Werner Bahner and Kurt Schnelle (4 April), Siefried Streller (25 April), Walter Dietze and Wolfgang Neubert (16 May), Erhard John (6 June), and Harri Jünger (11 July). All expressed the opinion that at the Institute for German Literary History, there had been one opinion too many: the opinion of Hans Mayer.

41. Werner Krauss, "Literaturgeschichte als geschichtlicher Auftrag," in *Werner Krauss: Das wissenschaftliche Werk*, vol. 1, *Literaturtheorie, Philosophie, Politik*, ed. Manfred Naumann (Berlin, 1984), 7–61, here 61.

42. Werner Krauss, "Der Stand der romanistischen Literaturgeschichte an der Leipziger Universität," in *Werner Krauss: Das wissenschaftliche Werk*, vol. 1, *Literaturtheorie, Philosophie, Politik*, ed. Manfred Naumann (Berlin, 1984), 62–66, here 63.

43. Krauss, "Der Stand der romanistischen Literaturgeschichte," 64.

44. Werner Krauss, "Literaturgeschichte als geschichtlicher Auftrag," 57.

45. Typescript of letter, Werner Krauss to Kurt Hager, 28 December 1958, *Archiv der Berlin-Brandenburgischen Akademie der Wissenschaften*, Werner Krauss papers.

46. Typescript of letter, Werner Krauss to Dr. Schrickel, 17 July 1956, *Archiv der Berlin-Brandenburgischen Akademie der Wissenschaften*, Bestand Akademieleitung 115.

47. Werner Mittenzwei, "Brecht und die Probleme der deutschen Klassik," *Sinn und Form* 25, no. 1 (1973): 135–68.

48. Michail Lifshitz, *Karl Marx und die Ästhetik* (Dresden, 1960), 15.

49. A new "inter-philological" orientation was exhibited by the *Neue Beiträge zur Literaturwissenschaft*, established in 1955 by Werner Krauss and Hans Mayer (and continued after Mayer's expulsion by Krauss and the Germanist and *Vormärz* specialist Walter Dietze). This series produced about forty volumes. A similar orientation informed the *Arbeitsstelle für Geschichte der deutschen und französischen Aufklärung*, which Krauss had organized in Berlin in 1955. Representative volumes of the former include vol. 1: Werner Krauss, *Grundposition der französischen Aufklärung* (Berlin, 1955); vol. 2: Hans Mayer, *Studien zur deutschen Literatur* (Berlin, 1955); vol. 3: Ernst Schumacher, *Die dramatischen Versuche Bertolt Brechts 1918–1933* (Berlin, 1956); vol. 4: Marian Szyrocki, *Martin Opitz* (Berlin, 1956); vol. 5: Werner Bahner, *Beitrag zum Sprachbewußtsein in der spanischen Literatur des 16. und 17. Jahrhunderts* (Berlin, 1956). A Festschrift published in honor of Werner Krauss's sixtieth birthday, *Literaturgeschichte als geschichtlicher Auftrag* (Berlin, 1961), contained contributions by his colleagues and students. The research of the Weimarer Gedenkstätte zur Erforschung der deutschen Literatur concentrated on German classicism, neglected the Enlightenment, and was caught up in the notion of a "philological nationalism" in the construction of an alternative, socialist national philology (cf. Leo Spritzer, "Das Eigene und das Fremde: Über Philologie und Nationalismus," *Die Wandlung* 1, no. 7 [1946]: 576–94). Compare also the series of interviews with GDR Germanists in the *Zeitschrift für Germanistik* 2, no. 1 (1982) to 5, no. 3 (1985).

50. Hans Peter Krüger, "Rückblick auf die DDR-Philosophie der 70er und 80er Jahre," in *Demission der Helden: Kritiker von innen, 1983–1992*, ed. Hans Peter Krüger (Berlin, 1992), 79–103.

51. Irrlitz, "Ankunft der Utopie," 936.

52. "Verordnung über die Förderung und Intensivierung der an den Universitäten und Hochschulen der DDR betriebenen Forschungen," SAPMO-BA, ZPA, Bestand Abteilung Wissenschaft beim ZK der SED IV2/904/373: 36–37.

53. Ibid., SAPMO-BA, ZPA IV2/904/225: 353.

54. Ibid., SAPMO-BA, ZPA IV2/904/225: 327.

55. Ibid., SAPMO-BA, ZPA IV2/904/225: 324.

56. Wolfgang Thierse and Dieter Kliche, "DDR-Literaturwissenschaft in den 70er Jahren: Bemerkungen zur Entwicklung ihrer Positionen und Methoden," *Weimarer Beiträge* 31, no. 2 (1985): 267–308.

57. *Geschichte der deutschen Literatur: Von den Anfängen bis zur Gegenwart*, ed. Hans-Günter Thalheim, Günter Albrecht, Kurt Böttcher, Hans Jürgen Geerdts, Horst Haase, Hans Kaufmann, Paul Günter Krohn, and Dieter Schiller. 12 vols. (Berlin, 1965–83).

58. Thierse and Kliche, "DDR-Literaturwissenschaft in den 70er Jahren."

59. Hans Peter Krüger, "Ohne Versöhnung handeln, nur nicht leben: Zur Diskussion um DDR-Intellektuelle," *Sinn und Form* 44, no. 1 (1992): 40–50, here 49.

SIMONE BARCK, MARTINA LANGERMANN,
AND SIEGFRIED LOKATIS
Translated by Michael Latham and Devin Pendas

The German Democratic Republic as a "Reading Nation": Utopia, Planning, Reality, and Ideology

The GDR as a "Reading Nation"?

In early 1991 we came across a text montage in the literary journal *Neue Deutsche Literatur*. Formerly the official magazine of the East German Writers' Union, the *NDL* had reprinted the flip side of an East Berlin brochure titled "The Politics of Housing & Squatting." The reproduction showed a passage from Brecht's exile poem "Resolution of the Communards," spraypainted on the wall of a squat.

> In Erwägung, daß da Häuser stehen
> Während ihr uns ohne Bleibe laßt
> Haben wir beschlossen, jetzt dort einzuziehen
> Weil es uns in unseren Löchern nicht mehr paßt.

> [Considering that houses stand there
> while you leave us without shelter
> we have resolved at this time to move into them
> since we are no longer at home in our hovels.]

The editors of the *NDL* ironically titled this reproduction of graffiti "Reading-Nation [*Lese-Land*]."[1] Some readers may have smirked, while others frowned, catching the scent of nostalgia. In any case, this sort of text montage called forth vivid memories and associated personal experiences. Conceptions of a reading nation" or of a literary society (*Literaturgesellschaft*) represented a point of intellectual contention within the GDR, in which identities were articulated in opposition to or defense of the concept. This was because the notion of a reading nation was at once an imaginary design for a new and communal nation and the reference point for the description of reality in the GDR.

Immediately after 1989–90 some spectacular disputes arose concerning the way in which the reading nation was to be interpreted. Some declared it to be an outright myth, pointing to the changes in book-buying and reading behavior after 1989. But it seems rather sardonic and a little arrogant to reproach East Germans for only wanting to buy "travel literature, self-help books and non-fiction works."[2] The demise of the entire sociocultural and political environment that had supported a culture that treasured art and literature is hardly mentioned. It remains unsaid that many former East Germans are suffering from severe economic and psychological hardships—conditions that make it difficult for them to have an active cultural life. Changes in infrastructure have limited their access to literature, particularly in rural areas. As a result, cuts in the well-established GDR library system and the very high level of unemployment in some regions have disrupted the customary ways of getting books through bookstores and libraries. Access to books by the so-called average reader has changed dramatically.[3]

The NDL intervened in this running debate on the GDR as a reading culture in a most provocative manner, raising intriguing questions. With its ironic montage the journal highlights young squatters who have appropriated Brecht in an everyday and matter-of-fact way and wonders whether this is a trace of the former reading culture. Is this not an indication of a specific understanding of literature, now a matter of the past—a literature that insisted the world could be changed? The editors use these questions in order to pose a more interesting question: Which of the attitudes, literary ambitions, and practices that originated in the GDR would continue to work in contemporary Germany?

The Reading Nation

In its time, the ability of East German culture to develop independently of the market had been a source of fascination for many intellectuals, including Western intellectuals. The country seemed to provide an environment in which the old dichotomy of culture and market could be overcome and in which "a culture encompassing all of society" could arise. Certain groups in West Germany, such as the *Kulturbund zur demokratischen Erneuerung* (The Cultural Alliance for Democratic Renewal of Germany), had demanded similar programs into the early sixties.[4] In the GDR, the concept of the *Lese-Land* (reading nation) was rather more typical for the seventies and even the eighties. Previously, the notion of the GDR as a literary society had been more common. This term illustrates much more clearly the utopian horizon that the cultural politics of the GDR envisaged. It was coined by Johannes R. Becher at the Fourth German Writer's Congress in January 1956.[5] Becher used it to sketch out his vision of a harmonious pan-German communion of art and people, to be developed on new social foundations and based on the German classics, which he valued above all. He developed the notion of the ensemble character of literature, extending this to the notion of community. "To the extent that literature has a social character . . . , it is particularly suited to further the process of the development of social beings [*Gesellschaftlichwerden*] and of association-building [*Sich-Assoziieren*] in a transitional socialist society."⁶ Literature was for Becher "the most highly developed organ of a people in the service of forming their self-understanding and developing consciousness. In literary works people have at their disposal the subtlest organ of feeling and touch; through literature empathy can penetrate to the deepest levels of their being, revealing the least irregularities in heartbeat, able to feel its way toward the possibilities that might serve for good or ill."⁷ In order for a "collective organism of literature" (*Kollektivwesen Literatur*) to develop, Becher believed, all social groups, including those previously excluded, needed to partake in the cultural process and develop a new democratic understanding of their role in this process. The ultimate goal was an "educated nation," an association of educated readers.

This agenda appealed to many intellectuals in the fifties and sixties, not least because it retained the dream a of democratic renewal for all of Germany. The attraction of Becher's ideas lay in their systematic nature, wherein the idea—despite its focus on literature—could acquire a high degree of allegorical validity. The socially encompassing pursuit of art thus became an agent of democratization. Becher held that thinking and writing about the social forms that democratization would take in an era of mass culture was a worthy undertaking. How are opinions formed, and how can they develop democratically? What is the role of the arts in these processes? How do societies organize knowledge about themselves? What about self-reflexivity? These questions have lost none of their validity.

Nonetheless, the idea of a literary society is problematic, because it was never merely a utopian project. It was, rather, employed by leading cultural politicians in the GDR as a description of a supposedly already existing reality. The whole idea congealed into a cultural-political cliché, becoming a "concept for ideological struggle."⁸ Thus, the moral imperatives inscribed into the program mutated with a sleight of hand into an instrumental description of existing circumstances that entailed a great deal of wishful thinking. The necessary precondition for a literary society, as outlined by Becher, got lost in the process; that is, that this society of educated readers could only exist democratically and that it developed from the convictions of citizens as readers rather than from following the orders of a literary apparatus. Becher saw in this the Achilles heel of the literary society.

In the later canonization of the concept, this important aspect retreated into the background. Hans Koch elaborated the concept in 1965, for example, in his treatise on literary society.[9] Other more differentiated treatments of the concept of literary society, like the one by Dieter Schiller, emphasized the metaphoric meaning of the idea. Schiller underscored the "model quality" of Becher's idea and rightly pointed to the mass communications angle of Becher's work.[10] In the 1973 book *Gesellschaft-Literatur-Lesen*, which founded a functional-communicative approach to literary history in the GDR, literary society appears as the "desired working relation" (*angestrebte Funktionsweise*) between literature and society.[11]

In contrast, the idea of a reading nation, while resembling the notion of a literary society, reflects a less normative and more pragmatic-political understanding. Erich Honecker was the first to endorse the idea at the Tenth Party Congress of the SED in 1981, replacing the earlier slogan of the "Book-Nation GDR." In its subsequent career as a convenient political cliché, the concept was more often misappropriated for propaganda than used as an analytic tool. But the notion carried a certain understanding of the GDR that was to become quite common.

> We can, with complete justification, describe the GDR as a "Reading Nation." Publishers, book stores and libraries have done a great deal to increase the reading pleasure of our citizens. In 1970, our readers received nearly 5000 titles with a total production of 122 million copies and in 1980, there were 6100 titles and a production run of 148 million copies (9 volumes per person). In the last five years, the more than 700 people's bookstores increased their turnover by 32%. Every citizen has spent roughly 40 marks on books. . . . In the past year, the number of volumes in our libraries reached 80 million. More than 100 million volumes were borrowed. Two thirds of the children and young people in our country are regular borrowers at the library.[12]

Apart from such statistical exercises painting the GDR as a reading nation, there were other formulations, like the one by "Book Minister" Klaus Höpcke (1981), which superinscribed the notion of an "educated nation" upon the statistical literature on readership in the GDR. "Our state is appropriately characterized as a 'Reading Nation' because it concerns itself—from pre-school, kindergarten, elementary and high school, through the professional and working years, into retirement—with augmenting the level of culture of its citizens by encouraging an ever more regular contact with books and an ever broader circulation of reading materials."[13] The problem is that Höpcke did not simply cherish a nation of bookworms but had some rather specific ideas about what the ideal reader might be.

The "New Reader"

The "new reader" was the point of mediation between program and reality, as far as Becher was concerned. This new reader exhibited a "fundamentally altered relationship to literature." In order to prove his case, Becher referred to the large number of letters to newspapers and to the high sales figures for books. He took the existence of the new reader as an indication that a new social and cultural reality was in the making. He argued:

> Literature is not simply a house with an infinite number of separate apartments. . . . All the people who are truly interested in literature partake in the social linkages, as they are created in literature. . . . Neither publishers, editors, nor booksellers should be excluded from this process, nor especially the reader. Readers are not simply consumers, but the silent partners of the writers. They do not stand opposite the writer, but are immanent to them as a never ceasing voice, an invisible corrective—the writers' better half, their conscience. This literary society reaches far beyond actual literature.[14]

Although the "new" reader did not yet correspond to the programmatic ideal of an educated reader, in practice the reader was granted the authority of this ideal construct. Thus actual readers were encouraged to place requests with and to formulate commissions for artists. The new reader assumed the role of a "democratic censor" and thus was meant to take over the role of the administration of literature from the state apparatus. This could be done with the help of letters to the editor or as the result of active participation in literary circles or, indirectly, through the appeal to conscience, which demanded self-censorship from the author. In this fashion—if one trusts cultural policy makers and literary scholars—a high level of the "socialization of the artistic process" would be achieved. Readers accompanied authors through the process of producing texts, particularly in the period of the *Bitterfelder Weg* (1958–65), when they were given access to authors as much as they introduced authors to work sites. Previews in daily papers and popular magazines served not merely as information about upcoming work, as they did later. Rather, the prepublication texts were considered provisional. It was generally understood that the author required "public opinion" feedback in order to complete his work.[15]

Literary circles and letters to the editor were strongly encouraged during the early sixties. All of the resulting discussions were intensely politicized and principled. Politicians would repeatedly find themselves in the position to acknowledge the opinion of the "masses" or, alternatively, would.be challenged by some provocative literary statement. The SED had an interest in activating society and in bringing all social groups into the process. This was impossible unless a public sphere was created and legitimated in which individual voices would and could be heard. The Brigade movement of

1959–60 was one of these sites for a public literary debate.[16] The petition law of 1961, according to which letters to the editor were to be handled like petitions, was another aspect of the same movement.[17]

The political leadership quickly appropriated these discussions for its own ends, interpreting them as the expression of a new habitus (*neues Lebensgefühl*). Whatever they thought this new habitus might be, many readers held onto the very real experience that these literary circles and debates had generated a political public that had something to do with their own lives. This kind of literary publicity provoked vigorous debates in which the critique of art not uncommonly stood in for the critique of reality, and in which the official criteria used to evaluate art were repeatedly questioned—although it remains quite unclear why certain literary works actually gained public attention while others did not.[18] Loud reactions to particular books were not necessarily due to authors' addressing public taboos. It might be said instead that readers, inasmuch as they participated in these debates, either put forth their own fiercely held ideological convictions or made occasionally denigrating comparisons between art and life, usually at the expense of the artist.[19] Literature had a way of not getting things right, as letters and discussions pointed out. Literary works were either not realistic enough or not ideological enough. Still, the engagement and participation of diverse segments of the population in the literary process made a great deal of sense in the early sixties. It was the very power of popular opinion, and the rather ambivalent consequences that it had for authors as well as for politicians, that led to the curtailment of the literary debate. Readers spoke their minds, and that was difficult for both groups to take.

There was an ongoing battle over who was empowered to speak. The shifts in defining and, hence, authorizing a "new reader" suggest changes in the cultural-political program and more or less subtle ways of handling the situation. Implicitly, they also indicated changing notions of how to order society. During the "classic" phase of the *Bitterfelder Weg* the proletariat stood at the center of attention. This meant that the educated worker, the "advanced worker-reader,"[20] was at the pinnacle of all efforts to form a literary society. But already in the mid-sixties this focus became increasingly attenuated; indeed, it was tacitly adjusted. The new reader increasingly lost the authority that derived from a particular social location. The very fact of being a worker no longer quite authorized intervention into the literary process, although the writers were not necessarily the beneficiaries of this process. The political elite did their best to undermine the authority of the proletariat that they themselves had empowered only a few years earlier, in order to authorize themselves as the ideal readers of the republic.

Starting with the seventies, the entire debate and the very notion of a literary society were no longer supported by the SED. Literary circles lost their authority, as did readers. Where would it end, Walter Ulbricht had asked at the famous Eleventh Plenum in December 1965, if writers instead of the party determined politics?[21] Also, other media, such as television, began to compete with the book market and with literary circles as sites for negotiating interests and articulating public concerns. In spite of considerable excitement surrounding some literary debates during the seventies and eighties—the debate over *Die neuen Leiden des Jungen W.* (The new sufferings of young W.) is a good example—these discussions can hardly be viewed as a continuation of the debates of the sixties.[22]

By the early seventies, ever new definitions of the new reader were created. Terms such as the "appropriate," "intervening," "engaged," or "empathetic" reader were in circulation. The notion of a "duly qualified [*zuständig*] and mature reader" (D. Schlenstedt) using some of Becher's earlier conceptions, took hold. These were reader models that were less concerned with what was happening in society and at the workplace than with the creation of a new type of literature. "This literature—at least if one takes its most outstanding works—links a literary public originating from society at large to a demanding literature which sets out to engender a process of social self-understanding."[23] Taking up Becher's vision of a literary society, as well as the concept of "cultural socialism" coming out of the social democratic tradition, gave this understanding of literature (as opposed to the reader) a distinctly critical and, indeed, normative and correcting role within society. Above all it reflected a desire not so much to strengthen the association of individual citizens but to further the vision of an educated and relatively homogeneous society, achieved through literature as an agent of emancipation.

Literary Politics Between Censorship and Planning

If the desire to inculcate a love of books in the masses was the general interest in the GDR, there was always a large gap between the demand for and the supply of books. While politicians spoke of generous support for literature, their critics used the shortage of books to speak of a preclusion of literature. There was a great difference between the perceptions of what the idea of "reading nation" meant, what it never embodied, and what it revealed or covered up. In any case, Becher and his followers were far more interested in the new reader than they were concerned with the actual production and distribution of books. But ultimately production and distribution mattered in a situation that was characterized by persistent scarcities. There were never enough books—books that readers actually bought—even though statistics show that lots of books with remarkably high production runs were published. This discrepancy leads us to a reconsideration of censorship and, above and beyond, to the ever-present issue of planning book production

The files of the GDR's Ministry of Culture stretch more than a mile. These records document more than forty years' work by the central censor's office, the Main Administration for Publishing and Booksellers (*Hauptverwaltung Verlage und Buchhandel*) within the Ministry of Culture, which was geared to the systematic planning of the literature of an entire state.[24] These files form an incomparable set of data, offering a tremendous opportunity for research into the conditions, instruments, difficulties, successes, and limits of a literary-political experiment of unique proportions. It was an experiment to create a "national literature" in the GDR that would be completely separate from that of West Germany.[25]

The state's efforts to manipulate texts on this scale raises new and urgent questions—and not simply about the notorious issue of suppressing certain texts. Which texts can be assigned to their authors in the traditional sense of the word and which texts, due to their complex production process, including the contributions of editors and literary officials, have to be deemed collective products? The archives contain more or less extensive dossiers that detail the production of literary works. The individual dossiers indicate the numerous deletions, revisions, correspondences, evaluations, and reports in which a multiplicity of institutions and individuals participated.[26] What emerges is a book-writing "combine" of writers, editors, officials, and censors of unprecedented dimensions.

From very early on, the efforts of the censors far exceeded their original task of preventing the production of Nazi or militaristic literature. They contributed to the elimination of critics of the regime and the preservation of more or less clearly defined social and political taboos. Thus, rapes committed by Soviet soldiers could not be mentioned in any publication.[27] The regime could not be criticized publicly and directly. In order to understand the full consequences for the credibility of literature of such officially enforced erasures, we do well to study not only criteria for censorship in their historical context but also the way in which this apparatus worked. For it is one thing to establish clear-cut prohibition, but it is an entirely different matter to subordinate an entire national literature to censorship.

In reality, the latter resulted in quite extraordinary difficulties. There were not enough cadres who were both ideologically reliable and professionally qualified to do the job. The administration of literature needed specialists in the various areas of scientific and technical literature, political books, children's books, art, and music, as well as literary texts. Since the number of manuscripts submitted to the various offices could hardly be mandated, some censors would be swamped with work while others had scarcely enough to do. Depending on circumstances, censorial intervention could be heavy-handed or perfunctory. The jurisdictions of various censors were constantly modified. It also proved to be necessary to evaluate classics differently from contemporary novels, or political books differently from music literature. In general, one can see a learning curve in which the work of the censors "improved." They became more effective, more expeditious, and less conspicuous as they went along. The censors read a lot and learned a great deal in the process. They also became less capricious and more predictable.[28]

The whole system was predicated on a complex set of checks and balances because, ultimately, the individual censors and the Main Administration as a whole were in a precarious position. A single slip, that is, one book that seemed to the SED leadership to be insufficiently censored, could cost the censor his job. In turn, his hard-won experience would be lost to the Main Administration, which had no interest whatsoever in disrupting bureaucratic routines. Under these circumstances, it became common practice for various individual censors to distribute responsibility in critical cases in order to guard against the Central Committee and the Politburo. For this reason, and in order to limit their workload, the Censor's Office tried to unload as much preliminary work onto the publishers as they possibly could. The publishers were supposed to submit the manuscripts in exemplary condition and to provide abridged versions and recommendations. As a result, censorship was not a one-shot deal. Rather, editors and officials often supervised the whole development of a manuscript quite intensively. They suggested themes, knew and counseled the prevailing language rules and, in many cases, had entire chapters rewritten.[29] One should not forget that working-class authors were particularly encouraged to write. Such authors were often especially dependent on help from their editors. In certain cases it is not easy to determine whether ideological or stylistic considerations lay behind interventions. Editing and censoring were, in any case, ongoing processes.

The publishers themselves handled their responsibilities in an uneven manner, if one trusts the Main Administration. Some were stricter censors than the officials of the censorship office—or so it appeared. This is because in terms of the publishers' relations with writers, it was quite convenient for publishers to justify rejecting unwanted manuscripts or asking for repeated revisions citing censorship as the reason, even when this was unwarranted in the eyes of the Main Administration. Publishers, in short, tended to use censorship as an excuse.[30] By the same token, publishers that were deemed politically reliable often had a greater flexibility than those that were known to be politically unreliable, such as denominational publishers, which were under close scrutiny by the authorities. The latter tended to overcompensate.[31] A great deal also depended on informal, personal relationships between individual censors and publishers.

Publishers could also be subordinated to the State Security Service—a growing tendency in the late years of the GDR.[32] This looks like a general stepping up of surveillance and a tightening of state control. But, in fact, Stasi control was a result of the increasing decentralization and relaxation of censorship procedures, at least as far as they were exercised by the Main Administration. The delegation of censorial responsibility to the publishers, what officials called the "democratization of assessment," led to the increased use of informers of all kinds. If censors controlled literary production, the Stasi attempted to keep the writers under control. If the literary scene was permeated by con men, this was not least a result of the overall fraying of the apparatus of censorship and literary administration in the context of the redefinition of the role of literature during the seventies and eighties.[33] Altogether, censorship functioned in a very diffuse and erratic manner. It is difficult to find unequivocal criteria. All the more important, therefore, were the "scissors in the mind" of the authors, the anticipation of censorship. The study of bureaucratic procedures and the interplay of responsible apparatuses and their presumed and real, anticipated and actual interaction with the authors concerned seem to be more important for an understanding of censorship in the GDR.[34] "The role of self-censorship was judged differently from one author to author. Some considered it much more a West German phenomenon."[35]

The Control of Publishing
Actual censorship was supplemented by a system of literary control that included the recruiting and education of writers, the determination of how many books were to be printed, support through reviews and advance copies, and the channeling of sales. This work was also done by the Main Administration, which supervised the book and magazine production of the nearly eighty publishers (the number remaining roughly constant after the mid-fifties) in the GDR, their supply of paper and their printing capacity, the central book wholesaler LKG, the network of people's bookstores, public libraries, and the import and export of literature. Within this huge literary apparatus, political censorship mixed with all kinds of other considerations. Economic constraints and bureaucratic bargaining shaped the reading nation no less than did the cultural-political considerations of the SED or even the antagonism between writers and censors. A book is

only a book once it is published in sufficient numbers, once its publication is advertised, and if and when it is actually available in the bookstores. None of this was guaranteed, even after a book had undergone censorship. The reading nation suffered, above all, from a bad case of production and circulation problems.

In principle, though clearly not always in practice, the planned economy for publishing worked as follows: every publisher was assigned a certain field of work and a corresponding production profile. The nearly eighty publishers drew up a so-called Thematic Plan *(Themenplan)* at the beginning of each planning year that listed working titles and proposed the number of copies to be printed. The Main Administration decided whether or not to authorize the publication of each individual book and established the number of copies to be printed within the limits of the overall paper supply for each publisher. Its main guiding principle was the usefulness of the literature.

Individual thematic plans of publishers were collated by the Main Administration into an overall thematic plan that sought to "profile" the various publishers as clearly as possible, although it never quite managed to achieve its goal. Profiling established each publisher as a working part of a functionally consolidated system, an overall plan. It aimed at coordinating and differentiating the various publishing plans in order to avoid overlap and duplication. This principle applied to the various specialized publishers, which produced technical, economic, medical or, like the *Akademie-Verlag*, scientific texts. It also applied to the military, farmer's, women's, and church publishers; and naturally, it was also supposed to apply to the publishers of literary texts.

As far as the latter were concerned, terminology borrowed from the Soviet Union was employed in order to classify literature, distinguishing between what was considered to be the "classical heritage" on one hand and critical and socialist contemporary literature on the other. As a result of profiling, many literary and fine arts publishers in the GDR gained a reputation that was the envy of any bourgeois publisher. Profiles were evident in the very names of publishing companies. Thus, Kultur und Fortschritt (Culture and Progress) published Soviet literature; Volk und Welt (People and World) published contemporary critical literature from abroad; the Aufbau-Verlag (Reconstruction Publishers) guarded the singular legacy of the emigration as well as classic and bourgeois literature. The Weimarer Volksverlag (The Weimar People's Publishing House) put out editions of Goethe, Eulenspiegel was in charge of satire, Neues Berlin produced detective literature and science fiction, and the FDJ publishers Neues Leben (New Life) published adventure novels for young people. The list goes on.

Contemporary socialist literature came mostly from Dietz, the trade union publishers Tribüne, and the Mitteldeutscher Verlag.

As a result of this system of thematic planning, it appears easy enough to gain an overview of the working parts, as it were, of the reading nation. However, things were less settled than meets the eye. There were always idiosyncrasies that undercut the planning process, but most of all the individual publishers had their own interests to expand and differentiate, if only to increase their paper contingent or to mute censorship. The bigger a publisher, the more powerful it was, the better it was able to adhere to the planning process, the happier the bureaucrats in the Literature Administration, the better the fix on the thematic plan for the following year. Publishers had every reason to expand, even though profitability was not an issue.

As a result, publishing in the GDR was continuously in flux. Take the example of the Mitteldeutscher Verlag. After 1959, the Mitteldeutscher Verlag, which had been a minor publisher of administrative pamphlets and amateur writing in 1950, became the leading publisher for the *Bitterfelder Weg* with authors such as Volker Braun, Günther de Bruyn, Erik Neutsch, and Christa Wolf. Such steep ascent would have been unthinkable, were it not for the dwindling reputation of the Aufbau Verlag.[36] In the early 1950s, the Aufbau-Verlag had been the showpiece for the GDR, since it had all of the prominent authors from the emigration period. It suffered a serious setback with the apprehension and trial of Walter Janka in late 1956.[37] A few years after the demise of the *Bitterfelder Weg* yet another shift became evident. In the late sixties, the Hinstorff Verlag, which had previously specialized in regional literature from Mecklenburg, began to dispute the Mitteldeutscher Verlag's leading role.[38]

Because of profiling, the politics of literature was always also the politics of publishing. The shifting political preferences of the Main Administration were either challenging or infringing upon the interests of individual publishers. In turn, publishers used policy shifts in order to advance or upgrade their own profile. What appeared to be highly political turnabouts boiled down, in practice, to tough negotiations over the allocation of paper. The latter was the single most important practical means of literary-political control. There was an intense competition between publishers for the best quality paper that was as inventive as it was unpleasant, leading to intrigue, flattery, hypocrisy, and denunciation.[39] The Main Administration, which assumed the function of regulatory arbiter in this struggle, had no choice but to take into account the publishing system's actual hierarchy when making decisions. The way in which this system worked becomes evident if we look at the situation in the late fifties. At the time, the seventeen literary publishers received roughly five thousand tons of paper per year.[40] After the allocation of paper for contemporary socialist literature was tripled in 1958 (in conjunction with the *Bitterfelder Weg*), there naturally had to be a corresponding decrease in the share given to critical foreign literature and classics. By the early sixties, there was hardly any paper left for Goethe, Heine, or Schiller.[41]

East German publishers were by no means helpless victims in the struggle over paper allocation. The most powerful of them were certainly in a position to influence the policies of the ministry in their favor. In any case, there were considerable differences between publishers, and not just in terms of their profiles or the status of the books they produced. The actual hierarchy of publishers was, in fact, quite different from the way it appeared, especially if we take the notion of a reading nation as a yardstick.

Publishers normally had to rely on their export revenue to acquire the hard currency that was necessary in the competition for paper. However, the so-called organizational, that is, mass-organization–owned (*organisationseigene*) publishers assumed a more or less prominent position as a consequence of the fact that they were exempt from this provision.[42] In addition to the publishers mentioned above, almost all of the political parties and mass organizations had their own publishers, as did state and scholarly institutions and the churches, which, taken together, constituted a public sphere of social and cultural powers quite distinct from the reading nation. Moreover, organizations such as the FDJ (Free German Youth), the FDGB (Trade Union), and the NVA (Armed Forces) were in a position to guarantee their publishers every possible privilege, because they had direct ties to the Politburo.

As the official organ of the SED, the Dietz Verlag was undoubtedly the most prominent and most privileged publishing house in the GDR. Dietz was directly subordinate to the Central Committee of the SED and therefore higher in rank than even the Ministry for Culture and its Main Administration. Consequently, Dietz was not even subject to censorship by the Ministry. It also received as much as five thousand tons of paper every year, approximately as much as all of the literary publishers combined.[43] This means that the paper shortage that served as the justification for the entire system of economic planning had distinctly political origins—but none that had to do with censorship per se. The persistent overproduction by Dietz and other mass-organization publishers automatically led to shortages of all other kinds of books.[44] In fact, one might well argue that the paper shortage was a result of the structural exigencies of this system of book production in the GDR.

The distribution system faced similar problems. Books were in high demand in the GDR. Reading was encouraged. A network of people's bookstores was created. Every effort was made to provide for the rural population, which was organized through machine and tractor stations into agricultural cooperatives. Booksellers cooperated with mass organizations and factories to facilitate the distribution of books. Books were also advertised in the press and on radio. Even the state railway made announcements in the trains about the publication lists of various publishers. Reading groups and book bazaars became quite popular, and a political rally without a book table was the exception. Books were given as productivity bonuses, as tokens of appreciation for the regular attendance of meetings, as prizes at the lottery, and at festivals such as the Youth Fairs.[45]

But there was a permanent shortage of books, and not simply because of the preeminence of Dietz. Among publishers and booksellers, there was widespread consensus that the responsibility for the persistent book deficit lay with the mismanagement of the LKG, which acted as the wholesaler for the GDR. The LKG was a large party-owned bookstore in Leipzig that had come to monopolize book distribution. This monopoly quickly destroyed well-established distribution routines that had previously facilitated the flexibility of the book market. Many publishers complained that the LKG had severed their ties with bookstores and readers. Bookstores also had a major complaint. For many years the LKG would not allow a functioning system of used bookstores or provisions for the remittance of unsold books, factors that would have minimized the economic risks for booksellers. (This is where the Dietz overproduction came into play, because Dietz books were hard to sell.) Bookstores therefore refused to order hard-to-sell books outright. Not wanting the books they could order, they had no assurance that they would get what they did order.

In part, this was because there were not enough desired books being produced. But the distribution system of the LKG further exacerbated the structural shortcomings of the publishing system. A significant portion of the yearly book supply went to army bookstores, another portion to libraries, and, finally, many of the more desirable works were reserved for export.[46] This meant that barely half of the copies of a given work were earmarked for regular bookstores. Hence, even if a particular book had a large production run, there were often only one or two copies for each bookstore, whether they had ordered more or not. To further complicate matters, the distribution system tried to cover the whole country in an egalitarian fashion. The bookstores in Berlin, although they served as windows to the West, did not get the number of copies they actually wanted or needed. Yet there might be numerous copies of a book languishing in some remote bookstore in Mecklenburg or in the enormous LKG warehouse system. Typically, tens of thousands of books were discovered in 1989, stashed away in improvised storage facilities and left to the elements.

What matters is that in addition to the political crisis of publishing there was a structural crisis of distribution. If the first crisis led to a situation in which masses of books were produced that the people did not care to read, the second crisis exacerbated the problem in that the people could not even get the books that might have entered the LKG distribution system. In a country that prided itself on being a reading nation this was a major problem. The SED generated an image the nation could not hope to actualize.

A brief look at the party-owned Dietz Verlag may help illuminate this system of double jeopardy. The significant reform effort of the 1950s was likely set in motion by the fortunes of Dietz, which found itself in the midst of a sales slump. Although book sales had increased sixfold after the recession of 1950–56, for the Dietz Verlag sales shrank in 1956 to 30 percent of their 1952 level. Unsold inventory made up nearly 90 percent of that year's production.[47] The most powerful publishing house in the GDR found itself shut out of the general boom in book publishing.

This turn of events led to disturbing conclusions about the outlook of the people that could hardly leave the SED indifferent. In 1957, the ideological hardliners in the SED began a cultural-political offensive in reaction to the Hungarian uprising and, in this context, dedicated themselves to remedying the Dietz sales crisis. The Politburo and the Central Committee formed a Cultural Commission and ordered a systematic "investigation of all institutions involved in the distribution of literature."[48] During subsequent meetings, bookstores were admonished to sell more Dietz literature. People's bookstores were expected to reach a fixed quota in their sales of Dietz publications.

Until that time, the bookstores' ability to fulfill their sales quotas had been measured solely in quantitative terms, with rewards being given for success. The main emphasis was on a rapid turnover in inventory, since the LKG's warehousing capacity was limited. However, in 1958 a more elaborate subvention system was developed, with "qualitative reference numbers" to indicate the literary and ideological quality of the works. These numbers were used to give bookselling and publishing plans a distinctly political slant. Also, a new pricing policy was implemented in order to make ideologically desirable literature more affordable. Reviews in newspapers and journals were also improved. Dietz literature was not alone in profiting from these measures. Soviet books and, more notably, the hard-to-sell contemporary socialist literature (but also poetry!) profited. These and similar infrastructural measures, designed to control demand, shed a peculiar light on the *Bitterfelder Weg* as a large-scale experiment in creating a reading nation focused on "contemporary socialist literature." It was motivated by a variety of concerns, above all that of creating a literary society. But it was also a means to get readers to buy the works that the political leadership (and, not least, its publisher, Dietz) deemed useful and therefore published in great numbers.

None of this helped Dietz, and it did not really advance the party's control over popular taste and popular opinion, either. The general animosity toward the Dietz Verlag could not be rectified. Hence, the Mitteldeutscher Verlag was pushed into the foreground. In April 1959, the Mitteldeutscher Verlag organized the programmatic *Bitterfeld* Conference. The criteria for publishing and distributing books, created between 1958 and 1965 for cultural-political steering and for the control of demand, remained largely in place even after the *Bitterfeld* experiment had started. The structures for selling and distributing books outlived the literary-political program they were designed to support. This system never really changed until 1989, making desired books extremely scarce and highly prized commodities while generating a huge output of unwanted books.

The "Real" Reader

It was one thing to set "qualitative reference numbers" for bookstores. It was an entirely different matter when these criteria clashed with the desires of book buyers. Not that party officials and bureaucrats really considered giving in to those wants, but in order to influence readers' tastes, one first had to get to know them. Only then could tastes be changed and the success of these pedagogical efforts evaluated. This is when the era of reader discussions and of reader research began, which in turn facilitated the notion of the GDR as a reading nation.

The research results of East German literary sociologists and library scientists provide a quite different picture of the GDR as a reading nation from the one envisioned either by Johannes Becher or by the party bureaucrats responsible for book production and distribution. Empirical studies of the reading culture in the GDR, of the book supply, of the reading climate, of the development of readers' wants and reading interests, and of reading sophistication and reading behavior are available for periods from the seventies onward.[49] In order to deduce reading habits from these statistics we should, however, remember that reading and publishing imperatives cannot be easily separated.

The core of the literary canon was "contemporary socialist literature." The fact that this canon was not as widely accepted as had been desired in the early sixties[50] remained largely unnoticed both by the literary sociologists and in cultural-political comments during the seventies and eighties. This omission became the main bone of contention of a West German literary scholar, Richard Albrecht, who set out to critique the study *Funktion und Wirkung* (1978), which had set the standards of reader research in the GDR. Although the reception of contemporary socialist literature was made the test case for the GDR analysis and interpreted as a measure of the basic level of literary competence, the relatively low reputation of the genre was passed over by reading researchers in the GDR, Albrecht argued. They had accepted the list of important works and authors of this genre cited by survey subjects as proof of the high level of prestige accorded to it, without further reflection. That is, the readers obviously knew well which literature was "politically correct," but this did not mean, according to Albrecht, that they had come to like it. The surveys did not inquire to what extent the readers' responses entailed an appreciation of the genre as a whole or of specific works within it. The fact that some books were well received was taken as proof that the genre of socialist contemporary literature was an overall success.[51]

If such dubious methods suggest—as Albrecht notes—that contemporary socialist literature as a genre was not in very high demand, one might easily conclude that conditions were hardly favorable to the kind of literary debate the regime wanted to generate with its appeal to the reading nation. However, irrespective of their weaknesses the surveys demonstrate that there was a general readiness for literary debate. Dislike for the genre did not necessarily mean that the readers actually dismissed literature or, for that matter, the socialist canon. For one thing, the school system had established a relatively stable literary canon, which is why readers knew how to respond to the polls in the first place. But the commonality of references to the canon also points beyond political correctness to a situation to which the *Neue Deutsche Literatur* had alluded. The widely shared knowledge of a literary canon led to a situation in which the expression of one's aspirations and opinions through literary references could become a general practice. People not only identified with their literary heroes and antiheroes but used literary references in everyday life. A vernacular literary debate was thus made possible. The vernacular, however, was politically charged. If the public's interest was focused on relatively few works, this was due largely to the publishing practices we have described. It was almost always possible—when an interesting new book appeared—to get a public debate going. However, such discussions were not generally spontaneous developments. Whether this or that book would be the subject of debate was contingent on predeterminations of varying sorts—the number of copies printed, the decision to issue advance copies, public signals regarding the acceptability of the author or the book's theme, interviews with literary critics and scholars—and all this could launch a book and a debate. There were only very few cases when this kind of predetermination was absent. In any case, there was more of a reading nation than the disinterest in the genre of contemporary socialist literature would suggest.

There was also less of a genre than meets the eye. Readers named the "correct" socialist or bourgeois-humanist literature in the surveys, but a more subtle evaluation of their preferences reveals that, in ranking, they seemed strongly oriented toward perennial literary tastes such as travel, action, romance, regional (*Heimat*) literature, and detective stories.[52] The surveys show the decisive impact of the scholastic canon as well as the public appreciation, even adulation of specific authors. These tended to fit socialist categories in a general way. But when it came down to actual books and real authors, a much more conventional picture emerges. It is not just that traditional forms prevailed within the socialist genre; the novels that every student read in school generally employed exceedingly effective and long-established techniques of moving the reader. Their relatively widespread effect can be traced, primarily, to the combination of compelling moral questions and traditional aesthetic forms. Within the genre of contemporary socialist literature, then, readers had distinct preferences, although not entirely of their own making—and these preferences had more to with long-standing conventional tastes than with the dictates of cultural policy.

If the readers' interests proved to be more traditional than the genre of *sozialistische Gegenwartsliteratur* would suggest, this insight is only one aspect of the necessary deflation of the vaunted reading nation. It still presumes that the people in the GDR were, in fact, avid readers—and, more important, read as a nation. This presumption, however, proved to be wrong. In the GDR's final year, the previously scattered publications of literary sociologists were collected in the volume *Buch, Lektüre, Lesen*, with the intention of providing an "overview of nearly two decades of literary sociological research in the GDR."[53] This volume shows that the development of reading habits had proceeded differently than had been envisioned in the sixties and seventies. The detailed surveys suggest a process of differentiation between groups and indicate the multifaceted structure of reading tastes.[54] In June 1989, Dietrich Löffler, researcher for the literary sociology project, went so far as to argue that it was necessary to abandon a major thesis that he and his colleagues had held that "the social and cultural development of the Republic will generally support reading. We assumed that reading would necessarily increase as a result of the steady growth in general education accompanying the implementation of the ten-year polytechnic schools, the further integration of rural and urban life-styles, the creation of a cultural infrastructure and of the publishing system."[55] They had expected that the people of the GDR would grow together into a reading nation, but found instead an ever more differentiated readership. The central assumption of the GDR's cultural-political program proved to be untenable. It had been one of the axiomatic beliefs of the regime that scientific and technical progress would alter the character of work and create more leisure time in a relatively short period, which would profit reading and, by implication, create a nation. This was the basic justification for the enormous educational and political efforts to raise the general level of education. Reading was supposed to serve as the measure of cultural attainment and to provide a new impulse for encompassing social development. Despite unquestionable progress, however, the "new reader" as part of a reading nation remained a fiction.

As with the conceptualization of the reader and the theories about the nature of literary publics, East German literary scholarship betrayed uncertainty when it came to claiming that the GDR "represented a single reading people." By the end of the 1970s, literary sociologists conceded that various social groups had very different communicative habits. Despite all educational and political efforts, there was nothing resembling a common cultural basis uniting classes and groups. Some 1982 data substantiate the fact: In 1971, 25 percent of adults were nonreaders; in 1979 the number had shrunk to 19 percent. But by far the most active readers were schoolchildren, students, and members of the intelligentsia. Among workers, 30 percent were nonreaders; among farmers, 50 percent. To further illustrate differences between groups, only 10 percent of workers and 4 percent of farmers belonged to the group of active readers. There were, on average, 143 books per family in the GDR (not counting schoolbooks), but this average neglects tremendous differences in the size of family libraries. Moreover, the writers whose books were most often borrowed from libraries (in 1979) were not exactly the authors one might expect (or whom Johannes Becher or the *Bitterfelder Weg* had come to expect). They included Jules Verne, Harry Thürk, Jack London, and Stanislaw Lem.[56] Despite all educational and political efforts, there was nothing resembling the homogeneous national-cultural foundation that would have unified different social classes in the reading nation, and what there was did not necessarily reflect the cultural attainment that Becher had once envisaged with his literary society.

The literary sociologists responded to this stunning discovery with a most peculiar argument. Artistic communication, they now said, should not be viewed as a special instance of social communication but rather categorized as a "normal" part, among others, of general social communication. Literary debate would no longer be an exclusively postreceptive process mediated by a specific work or genre of literature. "In socialism, public communication about art is, as the phrase implies, publicly oriented and will fundamentally address *everyone*."[57] This was to say: "Briefly, neither a commonalty in literary experience, nor . . . a specific literary interest are prerequisites to participation in literary discussions. The distinctive desire or, as may be, need of each individual to examine reality is far more important. . . . The requisite minimum of literary experience for this can generally be found even among the so-called nonreaders."[58] With this kind of absurd-sounding formulation, literary sociologists attempted to salvage the reading nation in the face of a limited integration of citizens into the GDR as a republic of letters. The literary sociologists simply declared nonreaders to be part of the reading nation, because they could be assumed to adhere to the cultural standards if, indeed, they would only read. It was hoped that the very incantation of the concept of a reading nation would by itself provide an integrating and identity-forming element. Whatever people actually did, the GDR as a nation read.

It was strenuously argued that it was untenable "to infer a wide-spread split between the 'masses' on the one hand and a small, literary elite on the other" from the different cultural behaviors of the social classes and groups. "The 'uniformity of books' available under socialism precluded the necessary conditions for such a division."[59] Behind the formulation of the "uniformity of books" in socialism there hid the inconspicuous admission of a mass reception of entertainment literature.

The notion of a reading nation thus could become an image for advertising the GDR. The very insistence that the GDR was a nation of readers and the resulting emphasis on cultural values as a particular heritage of the GDR became a means to demarcate the country from other nations, particularly Western ones. Just at the moment when it became apparent that the GDR was not going to be a homogeneous reading nation, it began to distinguish itself from the West with this image. In the end, the effort to distinguish the GDR from "philistine imperialism" was the one element of the reading nation that remained intact.

Thus, it was the proudly cited statistics, which in fact concealed an overproduction of unwanted books, that provided the main indicator for what the GDR was not—a reading nation as envisioned in the fifties. But it was a nation in which more people read more books than most anywhere else. Under certain circumstances, specific books could generate a public literary debate that reflected social tensions and aspirations. The problem was that the books that people read or liked to read were not usually those that were produced—and therein lies the main problem of censorship. Therein also lies the main frustration of all those who had so avidly supported the concept and continued to adhere to it, long after surveys suggested that the future of the worker's and peasant's state rested on nonreaders. They firmly believed and hoped that the concept could be realized after all, whereas the people had come to associate the regime with a tyranny of books: books they coveted but could not have and books they could have had but did not want—and books they had standing on their shelves while watching Western television.

The distinct aftereffects of the ambitious reading nation program can be found in an opinion survey conducted after 1990 by the Mainz *Stiftung Lesen*. According to this survey, the East Germans were considerably ahead of the West Germans with regard to book buying, library visits, and the number of books they read. In our opinion, this doesn't seem at all a bad contribution to the "uniform" German *Kulturnation*.[60]

1996–1998

Notes

1. "Lese-Land," *Neue Deutsche Literatur* 39, no. 1 (1991): 172.

2. Wolfgang Emmerich, "Die Literatur der DDR," in *Deutsche Literaturgeschichte von den Anfängen bis zur Gegenwart* , ed. Wolfgang Beulin et al. (Stuttgart, 1992), 462.

3. Petra Böhme, "Öffentliche Bibliotheken in den neuen Bundesländern," *Mitteilungen aus der kulturwissenschaftlichen Forschung* 32 (1993): 452–59, special issue, *Kultur in Deutschlands Osten*.

4. Jost Hermand, *Kultur im Wiederaufbau: Die Bundesrepublik Deutschland: 1945 bis 1965* (Frankfurt am Main, 1989), 263–72.

5. Johannes R. Becher, "Von der Größe unserer Literatur," 4. *Deutscher Schriftstellerkongreß* (January 1956), ed. Deutscher Schriftstellerverband (Protokols 1 and 2, 1956): 11–39.

6. Quoted in Wolfgang Emmerich, *Kleine Literaturgeschichte der DDR*. 5th ed. (Neuwied, 1989), 21–22.

7. Johannes R. Becher, "Macht der Literatur," in *Von der Größe unserer Literatur: Reden und Aufsätze* (Leipzig, 1971), 224–33, here 224.

8. Pierre Bourdieu, "Die historische Genese einer reinen Ästhetik," *Merkur* 46, no. 11 (1992): 967–79, here 973.

9. Hans Koch, *Unsere Literaturgesellschaft* (Berlin, 1965).

10. Dieter Schiller, "Zu Begriff und Problem der Literaturgesellschaft," in *Studien zur Literaturgeschichte und Literaturtheorie*, ed. Hans Günther Thalheim and Ursula Wertheim (Berlin, 1970), 291–332.

11. Manfred Naumann, ed., *Gesellschaft-Literatur-Lesen: Literaturrezeption in theoretischer Sicht* (Berlin, 1973), 291–98, here 298. See also the summary by Jürgen Scharfschwerdt, *Literatur und Literaturwissenschaft in der DDR* (Stuttgart, 1982).

12. Erich Honecker, *Bericht des ZK der SED an den X. Parteitag der SED* (Berlin, 1981), 104.

13. Klaus Höpcke, *Probe für das Leben* (Halle, 1971), 210.

14. Becher, "Von der Größe unserer Literatur," 276.

15. Gudrun Klatt, "Schriftsteller-Literatur-Leser: Zur Literaturdiskussion am Beginn der sechziger Jahre in der Zeitschrift 'Junge Kunst,'" *Weimarer Beiträge* 23, no. 10 (1977): 23–44; Therese Hörnigk, "Die erste Bitterfelder Konferenz: Programm und Praxis der sozialistischen Kulturrevolution am Ende der Übergangsperiode," in *Literarisches Leben in der DDR 1945 bis 1960,* ed. Inge Münz-Koenen (Berlin, 1980), 196–243.

16. Jörg Roesler, "Gab es sozialistische Formen der Mitbestimmung und Selbstverwirklichung in Betrieben der DDR? Zur Rolle der Brigaden in der betrieblichen Hierarchie und im Leben der Arbeiter,"*Utopie Kreativ* 31–32 (1993): 122–39.

17. Ellen Bos, *Leserbriefe in Tageszeitungen der DDR* (Opladen, 1992), 227.

18. Inge Münz-Koenen, ed.,*Werke und Wirkungen: DDR-Literatur in der Diskussion* (Leipzig, 1987).

19. Martin Reso, *Der geteilte Himmel und seine Kritiker* (Halle, 1965).

20. Horst Oswald, *Literatur, Kritik und Leser* (Berlin, 1969), 99.

21. Günter Agde, ed., *Kahlschlag: Das 11. Plenum des ZK der SED 1965. Studien und Dokumente* (Berlin, 1991), 331–34.

22. Gudrun Klatt, " 'Modebuch' und Diskussionen 'über das Leben selbst': Ulrich Plenzdorfs Die neuen Leiden des Jungen W.," in *Werke und Wirkungen,* ed. Inge Münz-Koenen (Leipzig, 1987), 361–98.

23. Dieter Schlenstedt, *Wirkungsästhetische Analysen* (Berlin, 1979), 92.

24. In 1990, Robert Darnton visited this office and interviewed several of its staff members. See Robert Darnton, *Berlin Journal, 1989–1990* (New York, 1991); see esp. "The Viewpoint of the Censor," 202–17. See also Robert Darnton, "Censorship, a Comparative View: France, 1789–East Germany, 1989," *Representations* 49 (winter 1995): 40–49. For the early history of censorship in the Soviet Occupied Zone see Jean Mortier, "Ein Buchmarkt mit neuen Strukturen: Zur Verlagspolitik und Buchplannung in der SBZ, 1945–1949," in *Frühe DDR-Literatur,* ed. Klaus Scherpe and Lutz Winckler (Hamburg, Berlin, 1988), 62–80.

25. Ernest Wichner, " 'Und unverständlich wird mein ganzer Text': Anmerkungen zu einer zensurgesteuerten 'Nationalliteratur,' " in *"Literaturentwicklungsprozesse": Die Zensur der Literatur in der DDR,* ed. Ernest Wichner und Herbert Wiesner (Frankfurt, 1993), 199–216.

26. Siegfried Lokatis, "Verlagspolitik zwischen Plan und Zensur: Das 'Amt für Literatur und Verlagswesen' oder die schwere Geburt des Literaturapparates in der DDR," in *Historische DDR Forschung,* ed. Jürgen Kocka (Berlin, 1994), 303–25.

27. For example, there were prohibitions against Boris Djacenko's *Herz und Asche,* Bd. 2 (1958) and Werner Heiduczek's *Tod am Meer* (1978). The prohibition against the latter followed a protest by the Soviet embassy. See *Zensur in der DDR,* ed. Ernest Wichner and Herbert Wiesner (exhibition catalogue of the Literaturhaus Berlin) (Berlin, 1991), 57–59.

28. Lokatis, "Verlagspolitik zwischen Plan und Zensur," 315–24.

29. A prominent example of the latter practice is the nineteenth chapter of Christa Wolf's *Nachdenken über Christa T.* Konrad Franke, "'Deine Darstellung ist uns wesensfremd': Romane der 6oer Jahre in den Mühlen der DDR-Zensur," in *"Literaturentwicklungsprozesse": Die Zensur der Literatur in der DDR*, ed. Ernest Wichner and Herbert Wiesner (Frankfurt am Main, 1993), 101–27, here 115.

30. "Hausmitteilung des Amtes für Literatur und Verlagswesen vom 20.10.1955," *Bundesarchiv* DR [Druckgenehmigungsvorgänge] 1/1906.

31. Richard Zipser, ed., *Fragebogen: Zensur* (Leipzig, 1995), 110 (Volker Ebersbach): "It seems important to me that censorship was exercised directly by the Politburo . . . and the Ministry for Culture only to a certain extent—albeit the weightiest. It was always broadly compartmentalized and extensively differentiated. Publishing directors, directing editors, even simple readers practiced it, often as a kind of anticipatory duty, and even the block parties LDPD, CDU, and NDPD had their own appointed censors in the publishing houses connected to them, who served to maintain good conduct with the SED. But there were also many readers who struggled on the authors' behalf to get around the censors."

32. On the question of the Stasi and literature, see Siegfried Bräuer and Clemens Vollnhals, eds., *"In der DDR gibt es keine Zensur": Die Evangelische Verlagsanstalt und die Praxis der Druckgenehmigung 1954–1989* (Leipzig, 1995), 11. See also Ulrich Plenzdorf, Klaus Schlesinger, and Martin Stade, eds., *Berliner Geschichte: "Operativer Schwerpunkt Selbstverlag." Eine Autoren-Anthologie: Wie sie entstand und von der Stasi verhindert wurde* (Frankfurt am Main, 1995); and Karl Corino, ed., *"Die Akte Kant," "Martin," die Stasi und die Literatur in Ost und West* (Hamburg, 1995).

33. Peter Böthig and Klaus Michael, eds., *MachtSpiele. Literatur und Staatssicherheit im Fokus Prenzlauer Berg* (Leipzig, 1993).

34. Erich Loest, *Der vierte Zensor* (Cologne, 1984); see also his *Der Zorn des Schafes* (Künzelsau and Leipzig, 1990).

35. See Zipser, *Fragebogen: Zensur*, 68 (Matthias Biskupek): "It would be infantile to edit yourself as a free author while still in the process of writing, if you know there are so many with this responsibility above you."

36. Carsten Wurm, *Jeden Tag ein Buch: 50 Jahre Aufbau-Verlag* (Berlin, 1995).

37. Walter Janka, " . . . *bis zur Verhaftung": Erinnerungen eines deutschen Verlegers* (Berlin, 1993).

38. This had much to do with the productive activities of the directing editor, Dr. Kurt Batt, after whose sudden death in 1975 the publisher again lost its importance for contemporary literature. See Fritz Rudolf Fries and Kurt Batt, *Bemerkungen anhand eines Fundes oder das Mädchen aus der Flasche: Texte zur Literatur* (Berlin and Weimar, 1985), 10–12.

39. See, e.g., the "Protokolle der Literaturarbeitsgemeinschaft der belletristischen Verlage von 1958," *Bundesarchiv*, DR-1/1224.

40. This number includes children's books as well as books on art and music. For 1959, this number broke down as follows: literary texts, 3,000 tons; children's and young readers' books, 1,400 tons; art and music, 1,400 tons. *Bundesarchiv*, DR-1/1223. Abteilung Schöne Literatur, Kunst und Musik, 21.1.1958.

41. As of 1958, the tonnage for "socialist German contemporary literature" increased from 778 to 1,508 tons and that for "socialist literature from abroad" from 567 to 1,021 tons. At the same time, tonnage for the "cultural heritage" decreased from

958 to 630 tons. *Bundesarchiv*, DR 1/1275, Nachtrag zur Statistik über die Entwicklung der belletristischen Buchproduktion, 13.10.1960.

42. Siegfried Lokatis, "Zur Rolle der Massenorganisationen in der Diktatur: Praktische Probleme der Kunstverbreitung in der DDR," in *Auf der Suche nach dem verlorenen Staat: Die Kunst der Parteien und Massenorganisationen*, ed. Monika Flacke (Berlin, 1994), 78–89.

43. The Dietz allotment ranged from 2,000 to 5,000 tons (e.g., 1952: 2,400 tons; 1953: 4,800 tons). See Lokatis, "Verlagspolitik zwischen Planung und Zensur," 313.

44. See Siegfried Lokatis, "Dietz: Probleme der Ideologiewirtschaft im zentralen Parteiverlag der SED," in *Von der Aufgabe der Freiheit: Festschrift für Hans Mommsen*, ed. Christian Jansen, Lutz Niethammer, and Bernd Weisbrod (Berlin, 1995), 533–48, here 547.

45. On the book lottery, see Walter Victor's address to the Ministry of Culture, 10 July 1959 (*Bundesarchiv*, DR-1/1278); on advertising in trains, see the *Hauptreferat Buchhandel, 22.5.1954:* "Werbung für Bücher durch den Zugfunk" (*Bundesarchiv*, DR1/1896). The Leipzig "Börsenblatt für den deutschen Buchhandel" provides many further examples of ingenuity in bookselling.

46. Erwin Strittmatter, *Die Lage in den Lüften, Aus Tagebüchern* (Berlin, 1990), 217. About his novel, *Der Wundertäter*, Strittmatter writes: "The so-called distributor ratio was completed. We were ready to begin delivery. Then representatives of the army arrived and demanded that the army be supplied first. (A trick to have part of the edition vanish). . . . I wanted to know how many copies the army had purchased. The publisher's director said he didn't know. But he told Eva five thousand. In the meantime, a friend who should know enlightened me on the telephone: Be careful, the army buys up entire printings!" According to the contract, Christa Wolf's *Nachdenken über Christa T.* was to have an edition of twenty thousand copies. Of these, five thousand were exported. Of the remainder that were printed, only four thousand copies were initially bound. *Landesarchiv Merseburg*, Bezirksleitung der SED Halle, IV/B-2/9.02/699: 164–167.

47. See Lokatis, "Dietz," 544.

48. The "Untersuchung über die literaturverbreitenden Institutionen" followed a resolution of the Thirty-second Plenum of the Central Committee of the SED (10.–12.7.1957). See *Börsenblatt für den deutschen Buchhandel, 16.11.1957*, 738–39: "Wie steht es mit der Verbreitung sozialistischer Literatur?"

49. Dietrich Sommer, ed., *Funktion und Wirkung: Soziologische Untersuchungen zur Literatur und Kunst* (Berlin, 1978); Dietrich Sommer, *Leseerfahrung-Lebenserfahrung: Literatursoziologische Untersuchungen* (Berlin, 1983).

50. An opinion poll taken in 1968 showed among "40.1% of book readers" a 7 percent share for "novels about problems and conflicts in the process of constructing socialism." See Heinz Niemann, *Meinungsforschung in der DDR: Die geheimen Berichte des Instituts für Meinungsforschung an das Politbüro der SED* (Cologne, 1993), 31.

51. Richard Albrecht, *Das Bedürfnis nach echten Geschichten: Zur zeitgenössischen Unterhaltungsliteratur in der DDR* (Frankfurt am Main, 1987): 27–41.

52. Ibid., 35–36.

53. Helmut Göhler, ed., *Buch-Lektüre-Leser: Erkundungen zum Lesen* (Berlin, 1989).

54. Zentralinstitut für Bibliothekswesen, ed., *Internationale Beratung der Spezial-*

isten sozialistischer Länder für die Forschung auf dem Gebiet des Lesens und der Biblio-theksbenutzung, November 17–22, 1980 in Berlin (Berlin, 1982); *Leserförderung im Sozialismus: Ergebnisse einer internationalen wissenschaftlichen Konferenz anläßlich der iba [Internationale Buchkunst-Ausstellung], May 19–20, 1982 in Leipzig* (Leipzig, 1983).

55. Dietrich Löffler, "Perspektive des Lesers im Zeitalter der Medien," in *Leser und Lesen in Gegenwart und Zukunft: Beiträge einer internationalen wissenschaftlichen Konferenz des Institutes für Verlagswesen und Buchhandel der Karl-Marx-Universität anläßlich der iba 1989,* ed. Jutta Duclaud (Leipzig, 1990), 90–105, here 98.

56. See Helmut Göhler, *Stand und Tendenzen des Lesens in der DDR* (Berlin, 1983), 1–72, here 38.

57. Sommer, *Funktion und Wirkung,* 466.

58. Sommer, *Leseerfahrung-Lebenserfahrung,* 289, emphasis added.

59. Sommer, *Funktion und Wirkung,* 466.

60. See *Leseverhalten in Deutschland 1992/93: Repräsentativstudie zum Lese- und Meinungsverhalten der erwachsenen Bevölkerung im vereinigten Deutschland.* Survey conducted by the Stiftung Lesen (Mainz, 1993), 9–16.

La guerre est finie: New Waves, Historical Contingency, and the GDR "Rabbit Films"

Walter Ulbricht: . . . And now I return to the question of democracy here and of democracy at DEFA [Deutsche Film Aktiengesellschaft, the GDR state film studio]. Since we knew that there were some people (for the moment I won't name any names) who have declared—in the spirit of this "opposition party" [the parliamentary opposition proposed by regime critic Robert Havemann] that they would use every means to ensure a [cinematic] run for the *Rabbit* [Kurt Maetzig's DEFA film *Das Kaninchen bin ich (I am the Rabbit)*, condemned at the Eleventh Plenum], because they wanted it to set political goals—

(Erich Honecker: They planned to present the Party with a fait accompli.)

(Kurt Hager: They even said directly that they wanted to force us into it.)

we said: of course the Politburo could simply have withdrawn the film, from the point of view of the Party statutes, we would have the right to do so. But it was clear to us that the stake was not simply this "Rabbit" but a few dozen other rabbits. We therefore decided to present all the material to the Central Committee. The Central Committee is to decide.

(Member of the audience: Since our name is not Rabbit.)[This interjection puns on a proverbial protestation of innocence: *Mein Name ist Hase, ich weiß von nichts*—My name is rabbit, I don't know anything.]

Yes, the Central Committee is to decide. How it will go, who will force whom, and who will determine whom in the German Democratic Republic, this is what we want to test.

—Walter Ulbricht, "Closing Speech," 11. Plenum of the SED Central Committee, 1965

This essay takes its title and its guiding questions from a famous 1966 Alain Resnais film that epitomizes, both politically and formally, the many cinematic New Waves of the 1950s and 1960s. Scripted by Jorge Semprun, the film's story centers on the relationship between the Old and the New Left, both in their political tactics and in the structure of their political commitments. Forced into exile in France at the end of the Spanish Civil War, a group of Spanish communists are still working from their

Parisian suburbs, thirty years later, to undermine Franco's dictatorship and to keep the cause—and the hope—of Communism alive in Spain. But while their political activities (undertaken at considerable personal sacrifice and risk) continue to be crucial to the Spanish resistance, their increasing, inevitable distance from Spain's present, day-to-day situation causes their political thinking to become calcified, their analysis to become formulaic (guided by Moscow and classic lines of Marxist political prediction rather than by the latest reports from Madrid on local conditions), their planning to become unrealistic and therefore dangerous to the actual "undercover" workers who are to put them into action. The film's central character is one such rank-and-file revolutionary, a middle-aged courier who for decades has moved back and forth between Spain and France, between the realms of actuality and analysis. Increasingly critical, yet still deeply loyal both to the Republican cause and to the comrades who have spent or given their lives in its name, he reacts defensively when the party's work is attacked by a younger generation of ultraleftists, who reject the cautiousness of its resistances in favor of violent frontal attack. Resnais's film situates itself somewhere between the two positions: although the film's voice-over narration culminates in a lyrical and moving evocation of political self-sacrifice, in a eulogy that continues to deploy a Communist rhetoric of martyrdom and triumph, the experimental formal structure of the film—particularly the recurrence of narrative loops that stage an array of possible, alternative outcomes—decisively breaks with the teleological thrust of orthodox Marxism. At the same time, for the film as a whole, these formal experiments with narrative temporality and contingency catalyze a set of wide-ranging meditations on the historical epistemology of Communism, on the historicity, future, and temporality of socialist commitment, particularly on the dangers of its constant, teleological sublimation of the present to the distant hope of a different futurity.[1]

Old Left against New Left, content against form, the redeployment of the formal techniques of high modernism as a means for new kinds of epistemological and political speculation about the contemporary world: Resnais's film crystallizes some of the crucial concerns that bind together the many otherwise disparate and internally heterogeneous New Waves and New Cinemas that arose in France, Italy, and West Germany, in Poland, Czechoslovakia, Hungary, and the Soviet Union, in Britain and the United States, in Québec, Latin America, and Japan. As has often been argued, what shaped many of these New Waves was the renewed influence of avant-garde and documentary aesthetics on narrative film, as well as a belief in filmmaking as a committed, socially critical activity. Acutely concerned with their own national histories, and with a specific national shaping of political, institutional, and historical questions, the cinematic New Waves represented, at the same time, a truly international phenomenon that crossed many geopolitical divides. Around the world, the New Waves reflected one another and the global developments of the sixties: they were influenced alike by the residue of existentialism and the advent of the psychedelic, by new forms of youth culture and by the phenomenon of consumerism, by anxieties about a newly identified Third World, by official utopian rhetoric of scientific progress and universal prosperity, and by the oppositional utopianism and millenarianism of emerging countercultures, protest movements, and the New Left. Seen as an ensemble, the New Waves derived their perspective, their pace, their rhythms from the driving energies of a specific shared period. Within individual national cinemas, indeed, the arrival of New Wave aesthetics signaled the advent both of a self-conscious embrace of contemporaneity and of a self-conscious inter-nationalism. In their announcement of the end of cold war isolationism, however, the New Waves proved short-sighted as well as prophetic.

For despite their determined internationalism, the cinematic New Waves of Eastern Europe remained vulnerable to local reprisals and acutely dependent on the mood of local governments. Due both to their perceived cosmopolitanism and to the local force of their critiques, these cinemas repeatedly ran afoul of national authorities. At different moments between 1956 and 1970, all the Eastern European New Waves came under sustained government scrutiny and attack, usually during periods of large-scale social or political unrest: films were censored and banned, directors harassed, the development of an experimental aesthetic temporarily or permanently impeded. Hungary, Czechoslovakia, and Poland each experienced at least one such clampdown, with drastic consequences, at least in the short term, for the role of the cinema in national life, both as a site of vanguard political analysis and as a space of aesthetic alterity, refuge, and resistance. Yet over the long run, despite the ruptures represented by 1956, 1968 or 1970, the new cinemas in these countries were able to maintain much of their original momentum and broke decisively with the socialist realist aesthetics of the early fifties.

Between 1956 and 1965, the cinema of the German Democratic Repub-lic saw two successive waves of cinematic innovation, similar both in tim-ing and in political impetus to the New Waves in neighboring countries. But both waves proved short-lived, crushed by the sustained attacks of the SED (the ruling Socialist Unity Party) on the state-controlled film studio, DEFA *(Deutsche Filmaktiengesellschaft)*. Convoking a so-called *Kampfkon-ferenz* (battle conference) on film in 1958, the SED condemned a number of current films (including youth-oriented films by Kurt Maetzig, Heiner

Carow, Gerhard Klein, and Konrad Wolf) insisting that film production be realigned with the 1952 standards that the party had established for the cinema. And in 1965, the Eleventh Plenum of the SED Central Committee accused a second wave of contemporary youth problem films of pessimism, pornography, and decadence, of promoting *Rowdytum* (hooliganism) among GDR youth.

The Central Committee's sustained attack on DEFA had devastating consequences, both in the short and the long term.[2] To begin with, the studio pulled from circulation an entire year's worth of feature film production (eleven finished or almost finished films by directors including Kurt Maetzig, Gerhard Klein, Jürgen Böttcher, and Frank Beyer, all representing important aesthetic departures from their previous work). Virtually all became *Regalfilme*, banned or kept from release for more than two decades. Known collectively as *die Kaninchenfilme* ("the rabbit films"), after the Kurt Maetzig film singled out for particular denunciation by the SED, their only influence in the GDR was as underground legends. Maetzig's *Das Kaninchen bin ich* (I am the rabbit) had explored the inequitable love affair between an opportunistic Stalinist judge and a young working-class woman, who finally realizes that she has been trapped like a rabbit beneath a hunter's gun. The lingering nickname *Kaninchenfilme* translates Maetzig's anti-Stalinist analysis into a critique of the Eleventh Plenum itself, hinting at a parallel between the abusive relationship of the film's ill-matched couple and the relationship of a repressive state with the critical filmmakers who seek its reform and find themselves, in return, sacrificed like laboratory rabbits (*Versuchskaninchen*), in the name of the general good.

As once before, in 1958, the government intervention of 1965–66 had serious consequences not only for future film planning and for the working atmosphere of the film studio but also for the careers and creative development of individual filmmakers. Böttcher never made another fiction film, Beyer was blacklisted for several years, and other directors were relegated to work in "safe" genres such as antifascist films, as in the wake of the 1958 crackdown. The cumulative effect of 1958 and 1965 was to crush New Wave tendencies within GDR filmmaking even before, at either moment, they had fully emerged. The break with socialist realism, initiated by the GDR in the late fifties as in other Warsaw Pact cinemas, was thus never finalized.

Had a GDR New Wave survived the crackdown of 1965, in particular, it might well have developed in advance of or in interesting counterpoint to the New German Cinema just getting under way in the Federal Republic at the time of the Eleventh Plenum. In the immediate postwar period, DEFA had produced films that were aesthetically and politically much stronger than the comparable films being made in West Germany; even as late as 1965 it represented the stronger of the two postwar German cinemas. Without the Eleventh Plenum, the GDR New Wave might have continued to be preeminent. Forced, instead, back into realist narrative and visual codes, and forced into a lasting political cautiousness, GDR cinema got further and further out of step with other European national cinemas. Far from achieving *Weltoffenheit*, the openness to international currents and participation in world cinema to which the 1965 filmmakers had aspired, GDR cinema after 1965 occupied an increasingly marginal place even within the European film world.[3]

Why was the emergence of a New Wave in the GDR so belated and so truncated, particularly if compared to other Eastern European cinemas? The explanations offered in this essay will be primarily historical, institutional, and sociological. Yet as Resnais's film itself constantly reminds us, our ability to grasp political causalities or patterns of historical development remains deeply dependent on historically contingent repertoires of aesthetic forms and epistemological conventions. Despite the effort of Resnais's own looping narrative to imagine simultaneously alternative possible presents and futures, and despite New Wave attempts to represent the complexly layered temporality of the present, the subsequent historiography of the sixties tends to flatten out and reteleogize the epoch it chronicles. Even the metaphor of the New Wave, which in its own moment connoted both forcefulness and fluidity, cannot be deployed, in retrospect, without reinforcing an anachronistic sense of directionality. For with hindsight, of course, the apparently self-propelled New Waves prove to have been dependent on invisible currents and a complex system of tides, advancing only to retreat again.

If what was at stake in the individual films and in the collapse of the GDR New Wave was the survival and the shape of a political modernism, that stake is raised again in the narratives that surround the recent excavation and reanimation of these films, now that their moment, their culture, the film tradition they came out of and the socialism they wanted, all seem to have died. Within a few months of the fall of the Honecker government in 1989, filmmakers and film scholars began working together to reconstruct and restore the *Kaninchenfilme*. In the political climate of 1990 and 1991, the films' reappearance functioned at once as belated rehabilitation for the filmmakers, as the retrieval of a repressed history, meant to launch a collective political working through of the GDR, and as an act of mourning for "the alternative" GDR that which had never come to be. Broadcast on German television, showcased (with international press coverage) at the Berlin Film Festival, and sent around the world by the Goethe Institute as a series titled "Forbidden Films," the films of 1964–65 have gained a strong retroactive coherence. At the same time, as a group of artistic texts almost completely deprived of audience or influence during the period of their creation, they continue to pose a central problem for the retrospective historiography of GDR aesthetics.

The poignance of these films for present-day Eastern and Western viewers alike lies in the way they suggest alternative historical, political, and aesthetic paths not taken by the GDR—and that might have led somewhere else than to what we now know to have been the final outcome of the GDR: its spectacularly sudden collapse as a state, the long-term economic impoverishment and psychic disorientation of its citizens, and the reemergence of a German Question apparently more unsolved and more dangerous than ever. The post-1989 reception of the *Kaninchenfilme* has emphasized their status as uncompromising, uncompromised records of the GDR's history of political crisis. Yet these films demand a synchronous as well as a retroactive reading. Seen within the context provided by contemporary international filmmaking as by the existing tradition of DEFA cinema, these films look very different than they would in isolation, and we may be able to assess more accurately what is genuinely daring about them and what is thoroughly typical, their radicalness and their ultimate loyalty to what they criticize so searchingly. The recent release of the GDR *Kaninchenfilme* from the mid-1960s has, on one level, strengthened the retroactive criticism of socialism as it really existed. But these films might fulfill an opposite function as well, reminding us of the noninevitability of the present moment and giving critical contours, once again, to a socialist tradition in which commitment and critique battle each other constantly and stand side by side.

For the state-controlled cinemas of Eastern Europe, the official de-Stalinization initiated by Khrushchev in 1956 also signaled the beginning of a short period of political liberalization, economic restructuring, social reform, and aesthetic experiment that lasted into the early 1960s. And in virtually every country in Eastern Europe, as in the Soviet Union itself, this brief interval of cultural "thaw," which saw the emergence of new aesthetic movements and cinematic New Waves, was followed (the precise dates and triggering causes varying from country to country) by countermovements of political reaction and government repression, with serious consequences for the cinema as for every other national institution of aesthetic and intellectual life. In Poland, for instance, a new "Polish School" of socially critical filmmaking flourished between 1956 and 1962, winning international acclaim. This cinema was catalyzed, in large part, by the dramatic political developments in Poland: Wladyslaw Gomulka's rehabilitation and return to power; the dissolution of the collective farms; the Communist accord with the Catholic Church; the rehabilitation of the Home Army (the nationalist, non-Communist Resistance, which had fought the Nazi occupation). The ensuing atmosphere of reassessment and debate began to create a new kind of public sphere in Poland, as well as a new kind of film culture. A slackening of censorship enabled Polish audiences to see a larger and more diverse body of foreign films, while Poland's burgeoning film societies fostered political as well as aesthetic discussion of contemporary film. And the Polish film industry itself underwent a major economic restructuring and administrative decentralization; after 1955, the studios were divided into semiautonomous production units, each with its own directors and production crews. This restructuring was an unqualified success from a financial as well as from an artistic standpoint. The new autonomy enjoyed by the production units encouraged the growth of new filmmaking styles and genres. And with the critical success of Andrzej Wajda's *Kanal* (Canal) at the 1957 Cannes film festival, Polish films began to receive international attention and distribution. The huge increase in productivity under the new studio system led in turn to an equally huge expansion in the scale and scope of its productions.

By the early 1960s, however, the official encouragement of reform had given way to a climate of retrenchment, and for the rest of the decade, the cinema was repeatedly criticized for its pessimism and "revisionism." And despite a significant degree of preemptory self-censorship, the cinema still came under official attack during the period of government clampdown after the widespread social unrest of 1968. Accused of "commercialism" and of a failure to reflect socialist values, the cinema was forcibly reorganized once again, and the formerly autonomous production units were reassembled to ensure tighter government surveillance and control. Yet already in 1970, the studio underwent renewed decentralization, and by the middle of the decade, the new cinema was back in full swing.[4] The Polish case is worth detailing both because it represents an early and paradigmatic case of the development of a New Wave cinema in Eastern Europe and because it makes clear, in comparison, the GDR cinema's relative lack of aesthetic autonomy and political resilience.

Both in the political and in the aesthetic realm, the GDR had a different, slower, and more encumbered path to de-Stalinization than any of its neighbors. Unlike other countries in the Warsaw Pact, the GDR was self-evidently not an integral nation-state. Whereas communists saw the GDR as the logical successor to the defeated Third Reich, the political concretization of "*das andere Deutschland*" (the alternative Germany, the Germany of antifascist resistance), the Western European states questioned the legitimacy of the GDR, seeing it more as an accidental by-product of regrettable historical circumstances. Continually on the defensive, and continually worried about GDR's political autonomy and integrity, the SED government was strongly predisposed against the large-scale historical reassessments, reform debates, and structural changes that took place in surrounding Warsaw Pact countries in the late 1950s. Their anxieties assumed a different form during the 1960s, as the GDR's Warsaw Pact allies began to condone various forms of cultural and economic Westernization and showed an open interest in developing economic and diplomatic ties to the newly rich Federal Republic as well as to other countries in Western Europe. The SED government, in contrast, continued to preach communist isolationism and to polemicize against the dangers of Western influence, even from the midst of its own Western-style modernization program. On several fronts and over several decades, then, the perilously alluring proximity and prosperity of West Germany reinforced the SED's belief in the necessity of continuing a hard-line course for the GDR.

Within a few months of Stalin's death in 1953, furthermore, the attempt to initiate a new economic course for the GDR had catalyzed a large-scale workers' uprising, which was crushed only by military force and government repressions. Although in the short term the "17th of June" actually initiated a brief period of economic reassessment (and with it, aesthetic reorientation), it also remained a lasting trauma for the SED government. Later in the decade, the SED followed Nikita Khruschev's example in renouncing the Stalinist cult of personality. Yet it refused to engage in Soviet-style self-criticism about its own actions or policies during the Stalinist era. Khruschev's 1956 denunciation of Stalin catalyzed a bloc-wide thaw, with reform discussions and initiatives, historical revelations, and rehabilitations continuing in some countries for as long as six or seven years.[5] In the GDR, the thaw lasted less than a year and ended, in the aftermath of the Hungarian Uprising, with the show trial of Wolfgang Harich (as with the public denunciation of "dissident" academics such as Ernst Bloch and Robert Havemann). From within the SED itself—and in open consultation with Walter Ulbricht—Harich had attempted to outline a program of political reform in which the Central Committee's monopoly on power would have been replaced by a new, broad-based party organization. In the wake of Harich's trial (and in view of his ten-year prison sentence) any impetus for political reform, as for the reevaluation of the political legacies of Stalinism, was effectively forced underground.[6] This was the political context in which the SED called their 1958 *Kampfkonferenz*, denounced a first wave of social problem films, and demanded a renewed commitment to political loyalty from the state film studios.

As a result, the GDR cinema changed direction for the third time in less than a decade. Between 1950 and 1953, DEFA had embraced socialist realism and participated fully in the political campaigns of the cold war.[7] The more open "new course" followed after 1953 gave individual directors greater choice and responsibility in their selection of subjects; it also encouraged international co-productions, a large-scale increase in the number of films produced, and a greater effort to make films that would meet the actual tastes of GDR audiences. The 1958 film conference then turned against such "new course" films, criticizing their general political indecisiveness. In the case of the films of Gerhard Klein and others of his generation, party officials complained particularly of a "misapplication" of techniques from Italian neorealism: developed in order to show the fundamental contradictions within capitalist society, neorealism was emphatically unsuitable to suggest the existence of parallel contradictions and alienations within socialism. From 1958 onwards, DEFA therefore reaffirmed its explicit commitment both to socialist realism and to "socialist filmmaking."[8]

With the 1959 proclamation of the *Bitterfelder Weg*, the SED attempted a kind of cultural revolution, which realigned artistic life to production and to working-class culture and realigned socialist realism with the production aesthetics of the late twenties.[9] The 1963–64 inauguration of the economic modernization program known as the "New Economic System" *(Neues Ökonomisches System)* implied a similar realignment of ideological priorities and political alliances. The 1961 erection of the Wall (and the ensuing SED campaign against "ideological border-crossing") had worked explicitly to shut the West out, to lock the GDR into itself, and to increase SED control over the country's political, economic, and social development. Paradoxically, however, the establishment of firm territorial boundaries also made it possible for the GDR to reconsider its long-standing resistance to intellectual influences from the West and to the economic strategies of capitalism.

Placing a new emphasis on profit as well as productivity, and on domestic consumption as well as export manufacture, the New Economic System introduced a modified version of Western market and managerial strategies into the GDR, decentralizing, reorganizing, and rotating much of its economic coordination. With a parallel rhetoric of modernization, the SED called on GDR universities to take up (often long-forbidden) Western research fields and research methods, from cybernetics to systems theory, and to adapt their research programs to the current needs of industry. In the realms both of production and of research, then, a new liberalization was accompanied by an increasing emphasis on functionalization. A similar paradox became visible as well in the public sphere and the political realm of GDR life. For as the state began to support the development of consumer culture, it was forced also to condone the emergence of new "lifestyle" subcultures, particularly among young people, and to permit new arenas of consumer, social, and aesthetic choice.

The shift in official attitude was perhaps most visible in the SED's new youth policy, formulated in 1963 and 1964, which argued that the goal of socialist education was to produce constructively critical citizens rather than conformists. Rather than being seen as *Erziehungsobjekte*, more or less intractable objects of education, GDR youth should be addressed as already moral, often deeply idealistic individuals. They needed to be permitted a private sphere in which to work out their own beliefs, to make their own choices and their own mistakes. Their critical challenges to authority needed to be encouraged rather than punished, as the best defense against official complacency and hypocrisy. Noting the obvious parallels to the anti-authoritarian movements then gaining momentum in the Federal Republic, some recent commentators have read this youth policy as the GDR's most important opening to a new democratization. Others, more cynically, have read it as a sign, in a uniquely market-driven epoch, of increasing government indifference to real social consensus.[10]

Unsurprisingly, substantial groups with the SED opposed the New Economic System and the changes it catalyzed in GDR social and cultural life during the early 1960s, on grounds both idealistic (for the new policies threatened to dilute socialist economic principles and the country's hard-won political autonomy) and pragmatic (for officeholders deemed unable to meet the demands of the new system were either removed from their positions or forced to undergo extensive retraining). In December 1965, only two months after Khruschev's fall from power in the Soviet Union, the SED Central Committee met to decelerate the modernization program and to condemn some of the undesirable social effects it had helped produce. Among the principal targets of their plenum, of course, were what members of the Central Committee dubbed the *Kaninchenfilme*, the 1965 wave of youth-oriented films made very much in the spirit of the SED's own 1963 youth directives. Caught out by a change in governmental direction, the *Kaninchenfilme* inadvertently confronted the SED with its own next-to-last rhetoric.

In the wake of the SED's previous 1958 crackdown on GDR cinema, the political reinstrumentalization of film had led to an evident loss in its quality. Then, in the early sixties, after the erection of the Wall and a series of critical public discussions about the future of DEFA, GDR cinema made room for so-called *neue Tendenzen* (new tendencies), while prominent directors argued that the GDR public be allowed to see a much broader selection of contemporary world filmmaking.[11] Already in the late fifties, a new generation of directors had begun to move the cinema into new styles and subjects. The early films of Wolf, for instance, manifest the influence both of visual Expressionism and of existentialist philosophy. And the early films of Klein, which in many ways belong to the new international "youth problem" genre then developing simultaneously in many different cinematic contexts,[12] also work to reintroduce into GDR filmmaking a documentary neorealism—including the use of lay actors and an acute attention to the texture of locales and milieus—which had been programmatically absent from GDR filmmaking since 1946 (and which was denounced anew in 1958 together with Klein himself).[13] By the mid-1960s, DEFA films quite consistently show the direct impact not only of new trends in Soviet, Polish, Hungarian, and Czech filmmaking but also of the contemporary Western European art film and of Western mass culture. They suggest an attempt, at least on the part of some directors, to align GDR filmmaking with the new "progressive" film movements emerging in the West, or to adapt various Western critiques of capitalism, whether contained in pop art or in pop culture itself, to the critique of industrial society in the GDR.[14]

Beginning in 1961, the institutional structures of DEFA itself (like many other sectors of industrial and agricultural production) had undergone an important modification, with production reorganized and decentralized in several phases. Initially proposed by Maetzig, the changes were modeled on the highly successful restructuring of the Polish film studios five years earlier. Under the new dispensation, seven *Arbeitsgruppen* (teams of directors, scriptwriters, technicians, and cultural functionaries) were each empowered to design and produce films with virtual autonomy. Arguably, the impact of this reorganization was equivalent to the concurrent restructuring of the film subsidy system in West Germany. There, pressure from the signatories of the 1962 Oberhausen manifesto and the subsequent reorganization of government funding proverbially created the conditions for the New German Cinema, a cinema preoccupied, throughout the 1960s, with the critique of West German institutional structures.[15] In the GDR, similarly, the reorganization of DEFA appears to have redirected and concentrated the critical energies of the cinema, and by the mid-sixties, to have turned them (fatally, as it proved) on the political legacies of Stalinism, on major contradictions in really existing socialism, and on the ossified power structure of GDR schools, workplaces, and government.

Already at the beginning of the sixties, a number of films suggest the emergence of new political sensibilities. Klein's 1960 *Der Fall Gleiwitz* (The

Gleiwitz affair) presents history, political power, and the Nazi prise-du-
pouvoir in analytic terms clearly influenced by structuralist Marxism and
utterly devoid of the redemptive optimism that had traditionally accompanied DEFA's antifascist films. In a very different register, Beyer's 1960
Spanish Civil War drama, *Fünf Patronenhülsen* (Five empty cartridges),
recast Henri-Georges Clouzot's 1953 *Salaire de la Peur* (The wages of fear)
to rederive socialist solidarity out of existentialism. Despite the obvious
influence of new French filmmaking and new French thought on these
films, they continue to retain the narrative and political transparency of
1950s realist filmmaking.

The advent of the New Economic System, however, somewhat increased GDR access to contemporary Western European and even American
filmmaking. By 1965, GDR films had become often dizzyingly eclectic in
their range of intertextual references and suggest, in contrast to films made
even a few years earlier, a much more thorough and profound reconception
of received socialist plot forms and visual styles, under the pressure of international influences. Opening with an homage to Fellini's *La Dolce Vita*,
and with a plot derived in equal part from the Czech New Wave (Vojtech
Jasny's 1963 *The Cassandra Cat*), Jerry Lewis movies, and Hollywood musicals, Egon Günther's *Wenn du groß bist, lieber Adam* (When you're grown
up, dear Adam, produced 1965, immediately banned, and released in 1990)
suggests the coexistence of many alternative worldviews, each with their
own epistemologies and their own ethical rules: what the film itself tries to
develop is a fairytale logic, at once whimsical and stringent, through which
to view and judge the moral and political landscape of the GDR.

Under the very different but equally strong influence of the British and
French New Waves, Böttcher's *Jahrgang 45* (Born in '45, produced and
banned 1966, released 1990) presents a remarkable verité-style portrait of
GDR youth culture, itself strongly influenced by the icons and the philosophical stance of contemporary American popular culture. The film's ado-
lescents express themselves in the way they slouch in their Levis, in the way
they ride their motorcycles around a deserted courtyard to a rock-and-roll
song played on a portable record player, in the way they flirt in an ice cream
parlor, pick each other up at big frenzied public dances, or sing together
around a guitar in a deserted construction site. Popular music, from folk
ballads to bossa nova, serves as the crucial background and motivation for
everyone's mood; even the dog is named Elvis, as if to mark the complete
incursion of American music, and a music-based youth culture, into the
production-oriented world of the mid-sixties GDR. The movie does make
nominal concessions to socialist thematics: its plot moves its hero toward
an understanding of socialist responsibility and a final symbolic embrace,

in the maternity ward, of a responsible and better future. Yet the real energy and emphasis of the film are elsewhere, as it documents and participates in the dreamy, narcissistic presentism of sixties youth, seeking adventure, sensation, and authenticity, amid a high-tech socialist landscape of prosperity, consumption, and high-rises. As the film suggests in its closing homage to *Saturday Night and Sunday Morning* (Karol Riesz, Britain, 1960), there are strong congruities between sixties youth culture in the GDR and in the UK, between working-class life under socialism and working-class life under capitalism.

The mid-sixties also saw a parallel critique, in East and West, of bureaucratic calcification. Probably without direct influence in either direction, Kurt Maetzig's *Das Kaninchen bin ich* (I am the rabbit, produced 1965, released 1966) shares both key visual motifs and central political concerns with an exactly contemporaneous West German film, Alexander Kluge's *Abschied von Gestern* (Yesterday girl, produced 1965, premiered 1966), the first international breakthrough film of the New German Cinema. Although each film literally takes a different Germany as its primary object of analysis, both understand the division of Germany as a determining circumstance for life on either side of the Wall. Kluge's film follows a young refugee from East Germany as she tries, and fails, to find a place for herself in the West. Maetzig's film centers on a young East Berliner denied entrance to the university because on the eve of the building of the Wall, her brother made critical remarks about the GDR and was sent to prison for defaming the state; from the calmer political atmosphere of the post-Wall period, the harshness of his sentence becomes ever clearer in retrospect. Both films call attention to the chilly architecture of state, in which individuals find themselves reduced to bureaucratic traces. Disillusioned by their treatment at the hands of ostensibly benevolent state institutions, both heroines eventually try to break away toward a different future. Walking in circles and pulling her earthly possessions behind her, Kluge's Anita G. moves aimlessly across West Germany, until at the end of the film she is finally caught and "institutionalized" once more. Battered by her brother, Maria Morzeck leaves home at the end of Maetzig's film to begin her studies at last. Yet her own sense of purposefulness and renewed optimism in the final shot of the film, as she pulls her personal possessions down the streets of Berlin toward a new life, is undercut both visibly (as her passage through the scene is obstructed by a long succession of leering and jeering men) and audibly (as we hear, in voiceover, a male bureaucrat "processing" her for admission to the university). In her new life as in her old, she will be subject at once to "personalized" sexual harassment and to bureaucratic depersonalization.

Surveying West Germany as an institutional landscape, Kluge's film repeatedly satirized the conformist goals of West German education and cultural life, most famously in a sequence in which a bureaucrat observes dog-obedience classes after a request for government support of dog training as a cultural activity, enjoyed by trainers and animals alike. Maria Morzeck's account of her schooling, in Maetzig's *Kaninchen*, suggests a similar critique of GDR education: "Went to secondary school and learned everything one needs: Why Pavlov's dogs drooled when the bell rang; why the Second International sank into the swamp of revisionism . . ." The students themselves are conceived of as Pavlovian dogs, trained to recite memorized political formulas on command.[16] Even the school's attempts to expose students to aesthetic experience seem compromised by its underlying interest in fostering conformity. If Maria continues, for a variety of private reasons, to remember the concerts she attended with her Berlin school class (and the music of Bach's Brandenburg Concertos in particular) as the beginning of her initiation into adult emotional life, we are reminded by the soundtrack's subsequent deployment of the concertos that they were composed not only for aesthetic enjoyment but also, quite literally, as a music of state for a previous absolutist government of Brandenburg.

In its very emphasis on the sufferings of an individual character, Maetzig's *Kaninchen* underlines the authoritarian rigidity of the GDR state and of the institutional structures in which all its citizens are caught. Although Maetzig's film was singled out for special critique at the Eleventh Plenum, what unites the so-called *Kaninchenfilme* of 1965–66 is their attempt at a belated de-Stalinization and institutional reform, their wish for a society in which individual voices—and conscience—might really matter. From Gerhard Klein's *Berlin um die Ecke* (Berlin around the corner), which was banned before completion in 1966 and released in 1990, and Hermann Zschoche's *Karla* to Frank Vogel's *Denk bloß nicht ich heule* (Just don't think I'll cry), banned 1965 and released in 1990, and Beyer's *Spur der Steine* (Traces of stones), released and banned 1966 and re-released 1989, these films consistently criticize the calcification of GDR political life from the standpoint of their central characters, impatient young idealists who refuse to make their peace with the status quo. Despite its often commodified forms, these films argue, the new international youth culture of the sixties is underpinned by genuinely utopian desires. The prophetic vision and the energies of youthful reformers need to be harnessed, not crushed by the state—and the constant failure of the system to find a place for them is a self-indictment, a sign of structural inflexibility, of the system's acute inability to reproduce and to improve itself.

What these films ultimately argue for, of course, is the radical reform, not the replacement, of a state socialism. In many ways, these films work with, as well as against, the tropes of a socialist realism itself usually concerned with figuring—in order to solve—contradiction and crisis within the socialist movement. Where socialist realism often worked to suspend crisis and contradiction within an inclusive and directive narrative logic, these films experiment with looser, less authoritative narrative and visual forms. Even so, they represent not only a break with or challenge to the established GDR aesthetic tradition but also a logical extension (even perhaps a telos or terminus) of its underlying critical tendencies. At the same time, they also represent an updating—and Westernizing—of socialist realism. They rewrite its standard plot of disagreement, reform, and reconciliation so that it reflects that quintessential phenomenon of the 1960s, the "generation gap." And they rethink the problem of reform itself in new terms and on a new scale, using the structural models that then pervaded all aspects of Western institutional thinking. The systems theory and structural-functionalism of the 1950s and 1960s emphasized that a system's cardinal goal was self-maintenance and self-preservation. Under the influence of this thinking, the socialist realist plot of ostracization, belated recognition, and reintegration (in which all suffering was eventually rewarded by the progress of socialist ideals) is rethought as a plot of martyrdom, as the system succeeds (for the moment, at least) in restabilizing itself through the expulsion or destruction of its critics.

As if to prove the accuracy of the analysis, the SED reacted to these films with an unprecedented crackdown on cinema and other cultural forms. Although convoked primarily to discuss a partial retraction of the New Economic System, the Eleventh Plenum of the SED Central Committee actually opened with screenings of the two most "objectionable" recent DEFA films (*Das Kaninchen bin ich* and *Denk bloß nicht ich heule*) and devoted much of its public energies to a denunciation of the tendency of recent—and as yet unreleased—GDR films, which it linked both to the decadences of Western "beat" culture and to specific incidents of youthful "Rowdytum" and political protest within the GDR itself.[17]

The GDR's new filmmaking was sociologically very different from virtually all of the other New Waves (including those in other parts of Eastern Europe), and this magnified the repressive effects of the plenum. Elsewhere, a rising generation of filmmakers catalyzed a new cinema by introducing into filmmaking a new ethos and a new aesthetic. Here, a new cinematic movement was inaugurated primarily by well-established older directors.[18] Many of them had started making films during the "new course" of the mid-fifties, and a few had helped build up DEFA from its very beginnings.[19]

As both detractors and defenders of DEFA noted during the polemics of the 1965 plenum, most of the directors under attack had previously been awarded every possible recognition for their work on behalf of the state; many were *Nationalpreisträger* (recipients of the National Prize, the GDR's highest civil honor). Against this background, the New Wave of the mid-sixties has to be seen as an effort to achieve aesthetic and political renewal *from within* the system, and one that accompanied a parallel liberalization within film journalism.[20] The failure of this reform movement, the withdrawal of the critical films and the subsequent muffling of many of DEFA's most prominent directors, was therefore a particularly serious and permanent blow to GDR film life.

As most post-1989 assessments of DEFA's history agree, the feature film studio never fully recovered, aesthetically or politically, from the 1965 clampdown. Most of the 1965 directors were eventually allowed to work again, and they stood behind several subsequent bursts of cinematic innovation, in particular a revival of the social problem film in the late 1970s and early 1980s. Compared to the films of 1965, however, these later films are deliberately, defensively, small in scale, presenting their social critique only on a micro-level, as individual (if perhaps exemplary or emblematic) case histories, the chronicles of individual failures and despairs.[21] In West Germany, the voluntary turn of the early 1970s from the overtly political toward a more subjective analysis of social life (after the failure of the student movement and after government clampdowns on radical activities) is usually taken to mark the ultimate victory of reaction. Here, the tendency is much the same, under pressures far more direct and far more prolonged.

If the artistic and political horizons of feature filmmaking thus contracted visibly in the wake of the Eleventh Plenum, the aesthetic experimentation and political questioning of the 1960s found some continuation at DEFA's documentary studios: over the next twenty-five years, the documentary and short-film units not only sponsored the work of a number of innovative documentarists but even harbored a few "material" filmmakers as well who were engaged in experimental manipulations with the surface and medium of film itself.[22] Under different political and institutional circumstances, this reabsorption of socially critical, documentary, and avant-garde impulses back into the genres from which they had originally arisen might be read simply as the natural life cycle of a New Wave.

Similar tendencies, in fact, were observable in many of the Western New Cinemas as well: if by the mid-sixties experimental narrative forms, a documentary approach to character, avant-garde visuals, and cinema-verité camera style began to appear quite regularly in mainstream and commercial feature films as well as in independent films, by the end of the seventies most feature filmmaking had reverted to a pre-sixties "realism" in its narrative and visual techniques. However critical one might be of the integration, appropriation, or cooptation of experimental and "independent" techniques by mainstream feature film industries in the West, the unquestionable effect of the brief period, in the mid and late 1960s, of rapprochement between "art" cinema, nonnarrative, and mainstream feature filmmaking was to expose tens of millions of "ordinary" filmgoers to unfamiliar and "difficult" kinds of films. The 1970s, however, saw an almost complete return, in studio-based feature filmmaking, to the old visual and narrative "realism." The renewed ghettoization of art film and experimental film spelled not only the end of their mass impact but also the aesthetic and intellectual impoverishment of the average movie-goer, now left without easy or regular access to the new modes of visual and conceptual stimulus that even the most mainstream films had provided so routinely during the preceding decade. What was true of the movies was equally true of consumer and political life as well, as the expansive climate of the 1960s gave way to the economic retraction and the renewed authoritarianism of the 1970s.

In its futurism, its techno-euphoria, its utopian striving, its optimism and openness to new social forms, the decade of the 1960s was deeply reminiscent of the 1920s: indeed it saw not only the critical reclamation of the art and aesthetic theory of the 1920s but also sustained attempts to mimic its artistic, intellectual, and political revolutions. Dada, futurism, and constructivism were thus reincarnated in Fluxus, in pop art, in lettrism, in new kinds of collage and montage; Wilhelm Reich's Sex-Pol movement was rehabilitated as a model for the new antipsychiatry and for the new movement for sexual liberation, while Frankfurt School analyses of fascism, mass culture, and the alienations of modernity fed a new critical sociology, and student and social movements all over Europe situated themselves in explicit relation to the revolutionary movements and heroes of the early twentieth century, from the Russian anarchists to Rosa Luxemburg.

Within the GDR, and within DEFA filmmaking, the influence of the twenties on the sixties was more subtle but nonetheless ubiquitous. At the famous 1963 Kafka conference at Liblice, most of the GDR delegates had watched the socialist rehabilitation of an alienated modernism with stiff disapproval or silence.[23] Yet the early sixties had actually seen the emergence of a new socialist modernist literature in the GDR (as represented by Johannes Bobrowski, Christa Wolf, and Volker Braun) whose formal innovations and relativization of realist forms reflect an understanding of socialism itself as historically contingent. At the same time, even the more mainstream tradition of committed realism began to show clear signs of the rediscovery and reassessment of the Communist political struggles and Communist political culture of the Weimar Republic. In Beyer's *Fünf Patronenhülse*, set in the Spain of the 1930s, it is thus the spirit of an old Spartacist revolutionary that presides over the rebirth of political ideals.

And in Hermann Zschoche's 1965 *Karla*, the high point of joyful solidarity between Karla, the idealistic young teacher (soon to be driven out of the school system for her resistance to institutional hypocrisy), and her rebellious but equally idealistic students is marked by a moment of festive dancing that explicitly recalls and rethinks the committed filmmaking of Weimar. In the famous closing shot of Piel Jutzi's 1929 *Mutter Krausens Fahrt ins Glück* (Mother Krausen's journey to happiness), the paradigmatic socialist realist film of the Weimar Republic, the contradictions and tragedies of daily working-class life find symbolic resolution as the film's heroine falls in with a Communist protest march, fumbles for a few paces, begins to catch the rhythm of the other marchers, and (as the camera shows in closeup the lines of marching feet) begins to march in step with them.[24] Zschoche's *Karla* restages this scene in a way that at once respects and overturns almost all of its terms. For as the students show their teacher how to perform the latest rock-and-roll dance steps, and as she attempts, fumblingly, to fall in with their dance, the dance lesson undermines the hierarchical distance that separates her life from theirs, showing a young authority figure how to move to the rhythm of an even younger generation.

Here, at the other end of a socialist revolution, the collectivity that the film's heroine joins is composed not of party members, committed despite all political persecution, but rather of idealistic youthful opponents of the socialist status quo, committed despite all party persecutions to honesty and conscience. In *Mutter Krausen*, the socialist collectivity formed itself in the act of marching and in shared dreams of a better future. No longer marching forward but moving instead to form a circle, the collective in *Karla* organizes itself nonteleologically and nonhierarchically, finding its utopia (at least temporarily) contained within itself, in the here and now, and in the fluid rhythms of the dance step rather than the regimented pace of the march.[25]

A socialist collective that encouraged individual expressiveness: like the other *Kaninchenfilme*, *Karla* both represents and expresses a moment of critical utopianism that the Eleventh Plenum, in the name of a more regulated and predictable progress, then did its best to suppress. Now, after the fall of the SED government and the re-release of the *Kaninchenfilme*, amid new efforts to reconstruct the historical context of the Eleventh Plenum, the 1965 moment of critical utopianism seems at once much more tangible than before and irrevocably lost. Indeed, as the post-1989 revelations of profound corruption within the GDR literary and political leadership of the 1970s and 1980s lead to generalizing Western denunciations of an "aesthetics of commitment" and of utopian rhetoric as the alibi of collaborators, it might seem that the lessons of 1965, and its mode of historical thinking, had all been forgotten completely. Yet what the explosive political developments in Germany over the past decade have called into question are not only the fatuously confident 1989 pronouncements of Germany's teleological arrival "at the end of history" but also the status of postmodern thought among West German intellectuals, as an explanatory model that, particularly in its Baudrillardian emphasis on the discursive construction both of "history" and of the "real world," enabled a stance of increasing intellectual distance. At a moment in which continuing, xenophobic political violence in a tenuously united Germany is perceived in the rest of world as an eerie replay of the 1930s, there is a pressing need to recover the optimistic energies of the Enlightenment and indeed of modernism itself, both in its 1920s and in its 1960s incarnations.

In twentieth-century Germany, cultural renaissances seem to be built not only on changes in material conditions, but even more important, on the ability of intellectuals to develop an expanded sense of possibilities, to recover a sense of contingency as well as of teleology, and thus to stretch the temporal limitations of their moment. Bleak and crisis-ridden for those actually living them, the years of the Weimar Republic nonetheless appeared in retrospect to the intelligentsia of the 1960s as an era of enormous vitality and of tragically unfulfilled promise. Both the aesthetic life and the political reform movements of the 1960s derived much of their strength from their sense of a looping return to and reconnection with the interrupted modernist past. Perhaps, as we work now to understand the *Kaninchenfilme*, we may in turn derive from them both the spirit of their utopian energies and their vivid sense of historical possibility.

Notes

The research for this essay was conducted primarily at the Filmarchiv-Bundesarchiv (Berlin), the principal film and document collection from DEFA; many thanks to the archive staff for their generous hospitality and assistance. My thanks also to the DAAD (German Academic Exchange Service) for a short-term travel grant and to the Hochschule für Film und Fernsehen (Berlin) for access to their library.

1. Semprun's 1963 autobiographical novel, Le Grand Voyage, makes clear that his own impulse to depict the coexistence of numerous temporal layers stems from two aspects of his wartime experiences: the mental discipline he and other Resistance fighters tried to cultivate to help them resist the brutalities of interrogation and

captivity (the deliberate attempt to block out the present situation by calling up memories in series or in loops, or by mentally reconstructing *Swann's Way* in correlation to autobiography, all as a way of trying to move through and out of time) and the lasting, involuntary, post-traumatic flashbacks he and other former concentration camp prisoners continued to suffer after the war, in which almost any event in the present could trigger an involuntary memory loop. Jorge Semprun, *The Long Voyage*, trans. Richard Seaver (New York, 1990), esp. 72, 126–27. Extrapolating from Semprun's own relationship to time, it could be argued that the sixties' sense of temporal fluidity derives, ironically, from the collision between a technology-induced "future shock" and a trauma-induced inability to work through or leave behind the wartime past. For related attempts to stage the historical unevennesses and political clashes of the twentieth century through experiments with temporality and mise-en-scene, see the films of Nagisa Oshima (especially his 1960 *Night and Fog in Japan* and his 1970 *The Ceremony*), Miklos Jancsó (especially his 1968 *The Red and the White* and his 1969 *The Confrontation*), and Theo Angelopoulous (*The Travelling Players*, 1975).

2. Christiane Mückenberger, ed., *Prädikat: Besonders schädlich. Das Kaninchen bin ich. Denk bloß nicht, ich heule. Filmtexte* (Berlin, 1990), 355–56, lists some of the legal repressions suffered by filmmakers, studio executives, and film scholars (including Mückenberger herself) in the wake of the Eleventh Plenum. For the overall effects of the plenum on DEFA filmmaking, see Erika Richter, "Zwischen Mauerbau und Kahlschlag, 1961 bis 1969," in *Das zweite Leben der Filmstadt Babelsberg: DEFA Spielfilme 1946–1992*, ed. Rolf Schenk (Berlin, 1994); Joshua Feinstein, "The Triumph of the Ordinary: Depictions of Daily Life in the East German Cinema, 1956–1966" (Ph.D. diss., Stanford University, 1995); Hans Kaufmann, *DEFA-Frühling findet vorläufig nicht statt* (Köln, 1966); Südwest 3 Filmreihe, *Verbotene Filme der DDR* (Baden-Baden, 1991); Regine Sylvester, ed., *The Forbidden Films* (Goethe Institute, 1992). For fictionalized accounts of the Stasi-orchestrated cinema riots preceding the 1966 banning of Frank Beyer's *Spur der Steine*, see Thomas Brasch, "'Und über uns schließt sich ein Himmel aus Stahl,'" *Vor den Vätern sterben die Söhne*, ed. Thomas Brasch (Berlin, 1977), 27–60, and Jurek Becker's *Sleepless Days*.

For contemporaneous West German journalistic reactions to the effects of the Eleventh Plenum, see, e.g., the defense of *Spur der Steine* in Siehard Schiewe, "Zurück zum Dogma," *Spandauer Volksblatt Berlin*, 20 July 1966, and especially Heinz Kersten's three-part article "Schatten über Babelsberg," *Filmkritik* 10, no. 3 (March 1966): 164–66, 10, no. 4 (April 1966): 232–34, and 10, no. 5 (May 1966): 250–53. For the long-term political consequences of the plenum for Christa Wolf, as one of the few Central Committee members who defended the works under attack, see Angela Drescher, ed., *Dokumentationen zu Christa Wolf, "Nachdenken über Christa T."* (Hamburg, 1991), esp. 9.

3. As Elke Scherstjanoi points out in "'Von der Sowjetunion lernen . . .'" (which traces the parallel history of aesthetic thaws and freezes in the Soviet Union itself), the years 1956–65 came to be seen in the Soviet Union, too, as "the last period, in which world cinema still counted on us." Günther Agde, ed., *Kahlschlag: Das 11. Plenum des ZK der SED 1965. Studien und Dokumente* (Berlin, 1991), 39–51, here 40.

4. See Bolesław Michałek and Frank Turaj, *The Modern Cinema of Poland* (Bloomington, 1988), esp. 19–35. For parallels in the Czech cinema, see Peter Hames, *The Czechoslovak New Wave* (Berkeley, 1985). On DEFA's relation to these new waves, see my "Moving DEFA into Eastern Europe" (forthcoming). The standard survey of

Eastern European cinema in the postwar period remains Mira and Antonin Liehm, *The Most Important Art* (Berkeley, 1977); for a more differentiated account see David Paul, ed., *Politics, Art, and Commitment in the Eastern European Cinema* (New York, 1983). For the subsequent course of Eastern European filmmaking, see Daniel J. Gould, ed., *Post New Wave Cinema in the Soviet Union* (Bloomington, 1989), particularly Sigrun D. Leonhard's sympathetic reading of the GDR films of the seventies and eighties, "Testing the Borders: East German Film Between Individualism and Social Commitment," 55–101.

5. For a particularly lucid introduction to the shape of GDR history, see Dietrich Staritz, *Geschichte der DDR 1949–1985* (Frankfurt am Main, 1985). For a helpful comparison between post-1956 political discussions in the GDR and in the other Warsaw Pact countries, see especially pp. 113–16, as well as the articles in the first section of Agde, *Kahlschlag*, "Wirtschaft und Kultur nach dem Mauerbau," 15–68.

6. For a vivid evocation of the political atmosphere in the GDR in the wake of the Hungarian Uprising and at the time of Harich's arrest, see Walter Janka's memoir of 1956, *Schwierigkeiten mit der Wahrheit* (Reinbek, 1990). "Old Communist," antifascist, exile publisher, and then, in the postwar period, director of the Aufbau Verlag (the Reconstruction Publishing House, the most important GDR press during the 1940s and 1950s) and sometime director of DEFA itself, Janka was arrested soon after Harich and sentenced on related conspiracy charges, spending three years in solitary confinement. Officially rehabilitated shortly before the fall of the Wall, Janka became a *cause celèbre* once more with the 1989 publication of his memoirs, which indicted several prominent GDR writers, friends who although convinced of Janka's innocence had failed to come forward in his defense.

7. In 1952, for instance, the SED convoked a conference of filmmakers to call for more films about present-day problems (particularly "disturbance factors" from the West) as well as about the problems of the working-class movements.

8. For the history of DEFA from its beginnings to the sixties, see Thomas Heimann, *DEFA, Künstler und SED-Kulturpolitik: Zum Verhältniß von Kulturpolitik und Filmproduktion in der SBZ/DDR 1945 bis 1959* (Berlin, 1994); Christiane Mückenberger and Günther Jordan, *"Sie sehen selbst, Sie hören selbst . . .": Die DEFA von ihren Anfängen bis 1949* (Marburg, 1994); Schenk, *Das zweite Leben der Filmstadt Babelsberg;* Albert Wilkering, *DEFA; Betriebsgeschichte des VEB DEFA Studio für Spielfilme* (Potsdam, 1981), 3 vols., esp. vol. 1, *Geschichte der DEFA von 1945–1950: Auf Neuen Wegen. 5 Jahre Fortschrittlicher Deutscher Film* (Berlin, [1951?]); *Der Deutsche Film. Fragen-Forderungen-Aussichten: Bericht vom ersten Deutschen Film-Autoren-Kongreß 6–9 Juni 1947* (Berlin, n.d.); *Auf Neuen Wegen: 5 Jahre Fortschrittlicher Deutscher Film* (Berlin, [1951?]); Christiane Mückenberger, ed., *Zur Geschichte des DEFA-Spielfilms 1946–9: Eine Dokumentation,* 2 vols. (Potsdam, 1976 and 1981); *Für den Aufschwung der fortschrittlichen deutschen Filmkunst* (Berlin, 1952); Heinz Baumert and Hermann Herlinghaus, *20 Jahre DEFA-Spielfilm* (Berlin, 1968); Rolf Richter, *DEFA und ihre Kritiker: Spielfilmregisseure,* 2 vols. (Berlin, 1981). For a complete filmography of DEFA feature film production through 1964, see Günther Schulz, ed., *Film-Archiv 4: DEFA-Spielfilme I: 1946–1964. Filmographie* (Berlin, 1989). For good overviews of the development of the GDR cinema, see Peter W. Jansen and Wolfram Schütte, eds., *Film in der DDR* (Munich, 1977), esp. Heinz Kersten, "Entwicklungslinien," 7–56; Wolfgang Gersch, *Film und Fernsehkunst der DDR: Traditionen-Beispiele-Tendenzen* (Berlin/DDR, 1979); Wolfgang Gersch, "Film in der DDR: Die verlorene Alterna-

tive," in *Geschichte des deutschen Films*, ed. Wolfgang Jacobsen, Anton Kaes, and Hans Helmut Prizler (Stuttgart, 1993), 323–64; and Harry Blunk, Dirk Jungnickel, and Berend von Nottbeck, eds., *Filmland DDR: Ein Reader zur Geschichte, Funktion und Wirkung der DEFA* (Köln, 1990). For a sense of the cold war context in which DEFA arose, see Heinz Kersten, *Das Filmwesen in der sowjetischen Besatzungszone* (Bonn, 1954), which includes as an appendix a charting of individual films according to whether they fit particular categories of content ("antifascist; anticapitalist; anti-Western; building up of new life; role of the working class; socially critical") and particular categories of function ("primarily entertainment; didactic entertainment; agitational"), as well as *Die Spielfilm-Produktion in der SBZ* (Bonn, 1964).

9. On the *Bitterfelder Weg* as a general aesthetic direction, see Wolfgang Emmerich, *Kleine Literaturgeschichte der DDR, 1945–1988*, rev. ed. (Frankfurt am Main, 1989), esp. chap. 4, "Literatur in Auseinandersetzung mit der 'neuen Produktion' (1949–61)," 91–159, as well as chap. 5, "Unterwegs zum Widersprung gegen die ökonomisch-technische Rationalität (1961/63–71)," 160–232.

10. On new government attitudes toward young people and their effect on cultural life, see Agde, *Kahlschlag*, esp. Michael Rauhut, "DDR-Beatmusik zwischen Engagement und Repression," 52–63, and Leonore Krenzlin, "Vom Jugendkommuniqué zur Dichterschelte," 148–58, as well as the 1965 "Beratung der Arbeitsgruppe zur Vorbereitung eines Beschlusses über die ideologische Arbeit unter der Jugend in der jetzigen Zeit," 284–88.

11. During the 1961 public discussions about the loss of quality in DEFA films, writer-director Wolfgang Kohlhaase criticized DEFA's "primitive sociological procedure in the depiction of people," while Kurt Stern diagnosed a "fear of psychology" in the cinema (Kersten, "Entwicklungslinien," in *Film in der DDR*). For even more vociferous mid-60s complaints and criticisms, see Mückenberger, *Prädikat*, 10–14. During the early years of the decade, practitioners of the other arts also voiced important complaints about the party's formulaic approach to aesthetic questions. Hanns Eisler complained in 1962 that the SED's functionalization of art amounted to a "retraction of secularization . . . we need potatoes, therefore a potato cantata," while Fritz Kremer called in 1964 for an end to the SED's use of derogatory formulas such as "formalism" and "decadence" to condemn whole directions in the visual arts. (Agde, *Kahlschlag*, 233, 278).

12. See Ingmar Bergman's *Port of Call* (1948), *The Devil's Wanton* (1949), and *Summer with Monika* (1952); Nagisa Oshima's *Cruel Story of Youth* (1960); Poland's "Black Series"; Hollywood's juvenile delinquent films, from Nicholas Ray's *Rebel Without a Cause* (1955) and Richard Brooks's *Blackboard Jungle* (1955) to John Frankenheimer's *The Young Stranger* (1957); and in West Germany, the films of Georg Tressler, Helmut Käutner's *Himmel ohne Sterne* (Sky without stars, 1955), Bernhard Wicki's *Die Brücke* (The bridge, 1959), and Herbert Vesely's *Brot der frühen Jahre* (Bread of the early years, 1962).

13. But see also Feinstein, "Triumph of the Ordinary," esp. chap. 2, "Whose reality? Berlin-Ecke Schönhauser Straße and a Novel Look at Socialism," 63–118.

14. A mid-60s account of DEFA production, Kaufmann's *DEFA-Frühling findet vorläufig nicht statt*, makes clear DEFA's self-conscious connection to new developments in world cinema. An article in the second issue of *film-wissenschaftliche mitteilungen* (an issue eventually banned by the authorities) reported on the findings of a questionnaire answered by twenty-two DEFA directors, writers, camera-

men, and functionaries. Asked to list the most important current foreign films in the socialist world, they cited films from the Soviet New Wave (Mikhail Romm's *9 Days in One Year*; Andrei Tarkovsky's *Ivan's Childhood*; Grigori Chukrai's *Ballad of a Soldier*; Mikhail Kalantazov's *The Cranes are Flying*), as well as films from the Polish (Wajda's *Ashes and Diamonds*) and Czech New Waves (Elmer Klos and Jan Kadar's *The Accused*). Asked about which international films they have found most important, they cite films such as Luchino Visconti's *Rocco and His Brothers*; Stanley Kramer's *Judgement at Nuremberg*; Alain Resnais' *Hiroshima Mon Amour*; Robert Wise and Jerome Robbins's *West Side Story*; Luis Bunuel's *Viridiana*; Michelangelo Antonioni's *L'Aventura*; Tony Richardson's *Tom Jones*; Federico Fellini's *La Dolce Vita*; Jean Cocteau's *Orpheus*; François Truffaut's *The 400 Blows*; Stanley Kubrick's *Dr. Strangelove*; Billy Wilder's *The Apartment*; and several recent West German films, including Wolfgang Staudte's antifascist *Rosen für den Staatsanwalt* (Roses for the district attorney) and Wicki's anti-war *Die Brücke*. Asked who has had the greatest influence on his filmmaking, DEFA director Roland Gräf lists a veritable roll-call of New Wave cineastes—Richardson, Antonioni, Fellini, Visconti, Karol Reisz, Jean-Luc Godard—while other directors mention Sergei Eisenstein and Bertolt Brecht, Charlie Chaplin and Vittorio De Sica, Michael Romm and Billy Wilder. (On the government ban on the issue in which these results appeared, see Heinz Baumert, "Das verbotene Heft: Film-wissenschaftliche mitteilungen, 2/1965," in Agde, *Kahlschlag*, 189–200.)

During the mid-60s, as Kaufmann reports, the Filmkunst-Theater Camera, East Berlin's most serious art cinema, ran retrospectives of Antonioni, De Sica, Roberto Rossellini, and Fellini, as well as the works of several Swedish directors (including Victor Sjöström and Alf Sjöberg), and even *Smiles of a Summer Night*, the first GDR screening of a film of Ingmar Bergman, long held to be the embodiment of Western decadence. In the mid-60s this was the only cinema of its kind in the GDR. Yet its programming (taken together with DEFA directors' own lists of favorites) suggests that at least the GDR film elite (directors, writers, film functionaries, film scholars) had considerable exposure to many of the new cinematic developments in the West as well as in other parts of Eastern Europe. Before the building of the Wall in 1961, DEFA directors, scriptwriters, and dramaturges crossed to West Berlin in order to watch films there. At least one major art cinema gave special discounts to GDR film students and film workers. Babelsberg's Deutsche Hochschule für Filmkunst (formed 1954) regularly screened foreign films for its students that never received general release in the GDR. And the annual Leipzig film festival, one of the major world venues for documentaries and experimental shorts, gave both GDR filmmakers and sections of the GDR public sustained exposure to foreign and experimental films. See Christiane Mückenberger, "Die Leipziger Dokumentar- und Kurzfilmwoche," in Günther Jordan and Ralf Schenk, eds., *Schwarzweiß und Farbe: DEFA Dokumentarfilme, 1946–1992* (Potsdam, 1996), 364–82.

15. For a more sustained account of the Rabbit films as reflections on these changed conditions of production, see my *The Divided Screen: The Cinemas of Postwar Germany* (forthcoming). For the West German situation, see also Thomas Elsaesser, *New German Cinema: A History* (New Brunswick, 1989); Eric Rentschler, *West German Cinema in the Course of Time* (Bedford Hills, 1984); Eric Rentschler, ed., *West German Filmmakers on Film: Visions and Voices* (New York, 1988), as well as Alexander Kluge, ed., *Bestandsaufnahme: Utopie Film* (Frankfurt, 1983).

16. "Ging zur Oberschule und lernte alles, was man dazu braucht: Warum

Pawlow's Hunden die Spucke läuft, wenn's klingelt; warum die Zweite Internationale im Sumpf des Revisionismus versank. . . ." My translation from "Das Kaninchen bin ich," in Mückenberger, *Prädikat*, 23–177, here 27. On the parallel metaphoric significence, in Kluge's *Abschied von Gestern*, of dog training, cultural training, and the architecture of state, see Miriam Hansen, "Space of History, Language of Time: Kluge's *Yesterday Girl* (1966)," in *German Film and Literature: Adaptions Transformations*, ed. Eric Rentschler (New York, 1985), 193–216, as well as Katie Trumpener, "Reconstructing the New German Cinema: Social Subjects and Critical Documentaries," *German Politics and Society* 18 (fall 1989): 37–53.

17. See Agde, *Kahlschlag*, for excerpts from the plenum debates themselves as well as for retrospective assessments of the plenums' political background and their long- and short-term impact on GDR cultural life. (For the relationship between economic and cultural agendas at the plenum, see particularly Detlef Eckert, "Die Volkswirtschaft der DDR im Spannungsfeld der Reformen," 20–32, and Nikola Knoth, "Das 11. Plenum-Wirtschafts- oder Kulturplenum?" 64–68.) Excerpts from the Eleventh Plenum debates are also available on an audiocassette released by the Studio für elektro-akustische Musik at the Berlin Akademie der Künste: *Kahlschlag: Auswertung eines Plenums, oder Paul Verner liest "Die Kipper" von Volker Braun. Aus dem Tonbandprotokoll des 11. Plenums des ZK der SED vom 15. bis 18. Dezember 1965* (Berlin, 1990).

18. Kurt Maetzig (born 1911) had directed his first film in 1947. Gerhard Klein (born 1920) directed his first film in 1953; Jürgen Böttcher (born 1931) and Frank Beyer (born 1932) had been directing since 1957. Of the filmmakers whose films were banned in the wake of the Eleventh Plenum, only a few—most notably Egon Günther (born 1927, first feature 1964) and Hermann Zschoche (born 1934, first feature 1965)—could really be considered novice directors. On the "generation" question, see also Mückenberger, *Prädikat*, 15.

19. Kurt Maetzig, whose "Kaninchen" film was singled out for particular attack at the Eleventh Plenum, had been one of the signatories of DEFA's initial charter. Maetzig began his filmmaking career with newsreels and documentary film, including the 1946 *Einheit SPD-KPD;* see Mückenberger and Jordan, *"Sie sehen selbst."* In the 1940s and 1950s, he was arguably DEFA's most successful director of antifascist films: his 1947 melodrama *Ehe im Schatten* (Marriage in the shadows), about the Nazi persecution of assimilated German Jews, was by far the most popular film of the immediate postwar period, viewed by more than ten million people in all four occupation zones. During the same period, he also directed a number of highly acclaimed epics of working-class family life—*Die Buntkarierten* (The girls in gingham), *Familie Benthin* (The Benthin family), and *Schlösser und Katen* (Castles and cottages), all of which simultaneously offered SED-Marxist analyses of historical events in German history from the rise of fascism to the division of Germany and the 1953 workers' uprising— as well as the epic 1954 *Ernst Thälmann, Sohn seiner Klasse* (Ernst Thälmann, son of his class), the "biggest" biopic of the 1950s. Between 1954 and 1964, in addition, Maetzig served as rector of the GDR's film school. A member of the Communist Party since 1944, Maetzig enjoyed the particular trust of the studio and of the SED from the initial rebuilding onward, as someone of sterling political reliability. See Kurt Maetzig, *Filmarbeit, Gespräche, Reden, Schriften*, ed. Günther Agde (Berlin, 1987). Gerhard Klein and Frank Beyer had also received strong government acclaim during the 1950s and early 1960s; their films—particularly Beyer's 1964 *Karbid und Sauer-*

ampfer (Carbide and sorrel), a comedy about the postwar occupation, and Klein's 1963 *Sonntagsfahrer* (Sunday drivers), an uneasy comedy about the building of the Wall—concur explicitly with the SED in blaming both the cold war and the political division of Germany on the Allied Occupation Forces.

20. See, e.g., Baumert, "Das verbotene Heft."

21. This is true even for antifascist films, the traditional strength of the studio. The enormous loss of political daring from DEFA's beginnings to its end is suggested by a comparison of one of the final films made in the GDR, Siegfried Kühn's 1988 *Die Schauspielerin* (The actress), a brittle, subjectivist account of German identification with Jewish suffering during the Nazi period, with its famous prototype from the very beginning of DEFA production, Maetzig's *Ehe im Schatten* (Marriage in the shadows), with its implicating identification structures. A parallel comparison of Günther Ruckert and Günther Reisch's 1980 *Die Verlobte* (The fiancée) with Ryszard Bugajski's 1982 *Interrogation*, one of the most important banned Polish films of the Solidarity period on a similar topic, suggests the relative political, aesthetic, and philosophical timidity of DEFA films made during the past two decades. Centered on the personal suffering of a jailed Communist resistance fighter in the high-security prisons of the Third Reich, the German film is innovative, within the DEFA context, for its emphasis on subjective experience—except that the viewpoint is that of a saintlike Communist martyr, whose only moment of true despair comes at the news of the Hitler-Stalin pact. The Polish film, in contrast, uses the travails of *its* jailed heroine, a nightclub singer inadvertantly caught up in the Stalinist show trials of the early 1950s, to mount a stinging indictment of the Polish gulag archipelago and to reflect on the way the postwar Stalin cult depended, for its belief structure, on the prior collapse of traditional notions of destiny in light of the randomness and intensity of wartime suffering.

22. Throughout the 1970s, DEFA remained an important training ground for young writers such as Ulrich Plenzdorf, Jurek Becker, Helga Schütz, and Klaus Schlesinger and as such continued to play an important secondary role in developing new literary talent. See my essay "Old Movies: Cinema as Palimpsest in GDR Fiction" (forthcoming).

23. See Werner Mittenzwei, "Zur Kafka-Konferenz 1963," in Agde, *Kahlschlag*, 84–92, as well as Emmerich, *Kleine Literaturgeschichte*.

24. On the central position of *Mutter Krausen* within Weimar committed film-making, see Rudolf Freund and Michael Hanisch, eds., *Mutter Krausens Fahrt ins Glück: Filmprotokoll und Materialien* (Berlin/DDR, 1976); Gertraude Kühn, Karl Tümmler, and Walter Wimmer, eds., *Film und revolutionäre Arbeiterbewegung in Deutschland 1918–1932* (Berlin/DDR, 1975), 2 vols., esp. 1:93–127; Bruce Murray, *Film and the German Left in the Weimar Republic* (Austin, 1990).

25. Ulrich Plenzdorf's script for *Karla* appears in his *Filme* (Frankfurt am Main, 1990).

Language and Power

The removal of an unjust system, the liberation from the supervision of a secret police which penetrates everything and which with petty-cold perfection outdoes anything that Foucault's image of a panoptic society had ever sought to grasp about our reality—that is what is normatively decisive about this "revolution."

—Jürgen Habermas, *Vergangenheit als Zukunft*

The three major post-Wall debates about the political and moral legacy of East German literary culture were all framed by controversies involving the writer and the secret police. The first occurred in June 1990, when the belated publication of Christa Wolf's fictional "story" *Was bleibt*,[1] written in 1979 and depicting the writer's harassment by the Stasi, resulted in strong public rebuke of the author for her depiction of self as victim and her failure to speak out against state repression during the decade prior to the fall of the regime.[2] The following year the issue of the Stasi and the poets was brought again to the fore when it was revealed that two leaders of the younger poetic underground, Sascha Anderson and Rainer Schedlinski, had been working as unofficial informants (IMs) for the Stasi.[3] Not surprisingly, to have the leading spokesperson and chief literary entrepreneur of the dissident Prenzlauer Berg artists, Sascha Anderson, unmasked as a Stasi agent was taken by some as further proof of an all-pervasive, ever-corrupting control of GDR intellectuals from above.[4]

But the Anderson scandal would not be the end of it. The revelations in January 1993 that Christa Wolf and Heiner Müller had also spoken with the Stasi, the former over a three-year period, seemed to confirm once and for all the moral and political bankruptcy of the literary avant-garde in the GDR. It was one thing for Müller and Wolf to have naively worked within a dictatorial system in hopes of reforming it, quite another to have crossed the line into a realm of unadulterated evil. For in the social imaginary of post–cold war and post-Wall German politics, the Stasi had become precisely that: a metaphorical monster whose tentacles enveloped and indeed poisoned every aspect of East German public and private life. Again Habermas:

> Today this sovereign authority, organized to perfection by German profes-
> sionalism, is symbolized in the image of the *Krake* [Octopus]. This image also
> expresses the feeling on the part of those who are caught up in it that freeing
> oneself is not simply a matter of a single act of liberation, but rather a process
> of gradual decontamination [*Entgiftung*] in which no one knows how long it
> will last. One slays a dragon, an octopus simply perishes [*verendet*]—and not
> everything caught in its clutches is let go of. Therefore some things survive
> which are not particularly worth keeping. The new beginning is burdened
> with false continuities."[5]

The image of the Stasi as *Krake* did not originate with Jürgen Habermas. In March 1990, three months prior to the interview in which both of the above quotations appear, *Der Spiegel* ran a cover story titled "The Long Arm of the Stasi" with a giant picture of a sinister-looking octopus looming out of the dark with a tiny East German flag clutched in its massive tentacle.[6] In the phantasm of the culture industry and the frenzy of post-Wall allegations, the GDR had already become metamorphosed into the Stasi as a monster sea serpent.

What is significant because uncharacteristic of Habermas here, however, is the somewhat frivolous slippage of metaphor as he struggles to articulate the uniquely horrifying, yet equally pedestrian nature of power configu-ration in the GDR. On one hand, we find the familiar tropes from an Orwellian world of mind control and a one-dimensionally deformed bu-reaucracy: the Foucauldian panoptic eye, detached from the violent body, which with "petty-cold perfection" and "German professionalism" pene-trates to the very core of its would-be knowing victim. Here is the logic of modernization run amok; the Weberian iron cage, coded now teutonically and in the service of dictatorship, as a monument of absolute philistine efficiency. If there is evil here it is characterized, in Hannah Arendt's sense of the term, by its banality.

Yet coexistent with its aura of technological perfection is an image of the Stasi as gargantuan and mythological, as evil incarnate. Indeed, the figure that will reembody this apparatus emerges out of a very different tropic system. The sinister *Krake* is a metaphysical beast from the oceanic depths whose formidable powers to invade and infect an organism would seem to defy any hope for the kind of purgative quick fix suggested in the notions of "revolution" or "liberation." There is something not so much pre-modern as antediluvian in the depiction of a body politic released by the dying serpent and subject to the slow and painful process of decontamination. Such an image shifts the emphasis from a clinical focus on spatial control (the panopticon) to the problem of a temporal rehabilitation that which must allow for the organism to restore and purify itself, morally and psychologically, over time.

The point, of course, is not to delimit the "meaning" of the Stasi interpretively to one signifying system or form of discursive analysis. Nor should we concern ourselves as to whether either of these metaphorical families has anything to do with the "reality" of a surveillance system that had become mired in inefficiency and overproduction and whose increasing capacity to gather trivia had rendered it almost incapable of "knowing what it knew." Rather, the tension in Habermas's mixing of metaphors will be helpful in reminding us of the contradictory meanings, discourses, and phantasms that have circulated around the process of Stasi revelation. The story of the Stasi and the poets is not just about individual literary figures or the empirical workings of an intelligence service. It is also about reconstructing and reclaiming one's history; the nature of complicity, control, and dissent in the processes of everyday GDR life; the search for new and different norms of morality and value; and confronting the twin legacies of Fascism and Stalinism. Understanding the story of the Stasi and the poets takes us to the very heart of questions concerning the relationship of intellectuals to the Stalinist state.

What Happened?

In comparing the Stasi connections and activities of Christa Wolf, Heiner Müller, Sascha Anderson, and Rainer Schedlinski, notable differences emerge that are important for evaluating them individually and as representatives of different generational experiences. In the cases of Anderson and Schedlinski, it is clear that they both took an active and damaging role in reporting on the activities and views of friends and colleagues, some of whom were on the front lines of political resistance in the GDR. Anderson worked as an IM for approximately twenty years, beginning as a seventeen—year-old in 1970 and continuing even after his exile to the Federal Republic in 1986.[7] A prolific poet and social extrovert, he was the center of an enormously active scene of writers and artists, facilitating the development of the entire Prenzlauer Berg movement through contacts and publication arrangements both inside the GDR and with Western publishing houses. Simply by talking casually about his own day-to-day experiences, which is all that Anderson claimed (or wanted to believe) he was doing, he was in a position to provide a virtual panorama of information and interpretive impression about a whole generation of young intellectuals in the GDR. But Anderson, who operated under the code names "David Menzer," "Fritz Müller," and "Peters," did more than just talk. In contrast to his highly allusive and esoteric fictional writing, Anderson's numerous written IM reports were a model of thoroughness, clarity, and precision, providing a wealth of potentially incriminating detail. Since his discovery in November of 1991, Anderson has either denied having worked "officially" for the Stasi (despite overwhelming evidence to the contrary) or sought to belittle the allegations being made against him.

Rainer Schedlinski was considerably less well known than Anderson, if in some quarters more respected as a sophisticated theorist of postmodern culture. Under the code name "Gerhard" he worked for the Stasi from 1974 until 1989. His reports differ markedly from Anderson's in their general dearth of empirical information, as well as in their emphasis on subjective interpretive impression. Schedlinski has used this difference to claim that he purposely avoided providing any "information" that might incriminate anyone. One look at a Stasi report based on "Gerhard's" recounting of a New Year's eve party at the house of dissident Lutz Rathenow reveals how thin the line can be between fact and interpretive fancy:

> Rathenow then set off some giant fireworks with his son and after that everybody played "monopoly." A few days later Rathenow sent to the IM [i.e., Schedlinski] by way of Detlev Opitz the following items:
>   1. Copy of "Dialog" with articles massively antagonistic toward the GDR Schädlich, Duwe, Fuchs.
>   2. Copies of "Ost-West-Diskussionsforum" Nos. 3 and 4 as well as other written materials of western origin which he had gotten hold of illegally.[8]

The possession of any one of these materials would have been grounds for arrest, if the security system were so disposed. But had the Stasi intervened at this point, it would probably have destroyed its own elaborate system of surveillance and control. Convincing Schedlinski and Anderson that as informers they themselves were actually using the Stasi for their own purposes was one of the means this organization employed to keep the upper hand. Since the revelations, neither Anderson nor Schedlinski has seemed able or willing to acknowledge the enormity of their actions. Anderson often lied about his activities or said it didn't matter anyway.[9] Schedlinski has "confessed" publicly on several occasions, excusing himself at every turn.[10]

Regarding the Stasi's contacts with Heiner Müller and Christa Wolf, there is no evidence to date that either of them ever informed on friends or colleagues or divulged information that was not already available from other published sources or the public media.[11] The archival material in the case of Müller consists of a few index cards and some handwritten notes which indicate that during the 1980s he was registered first as "IM Cement," in what was called a *Vorlauf* (preparatory status), and later as "IM Heiner." To date no IM files for Müller have been found, nor has he appeared in anyone else's file as an IM.

In an interview with *Spiegel TV*, Müller admitted to speaking with the Stasi and gave as his reasons a desire to lobby for the publication of his work in the GDR as well as an attempt to criticize and influence what he considered to be the disastrous domestic politics of the Honecker regime during the Gorbachev era. He also confessed to seeking "material" about the working methods of an organization that had remained a mystery to the population at large.

The motivations and circumstances in the case of Christa Wolf are markedly different.[12] Unlike Müller, there is an IM file record of her contacts with the Stasi containing, for the most part, reports of conversations. These meetings occurred over a period of thirty years prior to the time of the revelations, from 1959 to 1962, when as a committed member of the party she was rapidly becoming a leading figure within the literary socialist public sphere. Although the "voice" to emerge from the file clearly adheres to the sectarian rhetoric of SED cultural policy of the 1950s, the information given to the Stasi (for example, about the politically misguided and "labile" attitudes of other writers) did not differ, in tone or content, from the views she was expressing publicly as a literary critic writing in the mainstream press. Furthermore, although Wolf knowingly took the code name of "Margarete," she appears to have written only one report and to have eventually insisted that her meetings take place at her home in the presence of her husband, rather than in a "conspiratorial apartment," as was the usual practice. Although the latter fact does not excuse Wolf of anything, the "normalizing" of the situation (an admitted Stasi strategy) does help explain why Wolf was able to repress any memory of having worked officially as an IM or of the fact that she had a code name. It is also clear from written comments by her interrogators about her excessive "caution" and "discretion" that she was not giving them much of what they needed, which may explain why they decided to close her file.

Three years after this episode Wolf was to emerge as an outspoken critic of the regime's domestic policies, and by 1968 the Stasi had opened a "victim" file on her and her husband Gerhard under the code name "Doppelzüngler" (forked tongue), which by 1980 had expanded to forty-two volumes. Wolf discovered the existence of "Margarete" while reading her victim file in the spring of 1992. The reason she gave for waiting nine months before announcing it publicly had to do with her fear of the witch hunt atmosphere, which "would block rather than promote a debate about the complex reality of the GDR as well as self critical working through of our experiences in this country."[13]

Generational Differences and the Language of Power

Although neither Wolf nor Müller was found guilty of the sorts of behavior attributed to Anderson or Schedlinski, aspects of *all* the cases and their aftermath reopened important issues about the highly complicated and ambivalent status of literary dissidence in the GDR. Indeed, the seemingly oxymoronic notion of *Stasidichter* threw into question the very identity of GDR dissidents as the bearers of a genuine, antifascist alternative to the Stalinist version propagated by the regime. Was it possible to work "inside" an authoritarian system in any critically viable way? Was there even a credible distinction to be made between "inside" and "outside"? What had been the role of language and rhetoric, and, metonymically, the poet in defining difference and power?

It is significant that the framing of the discussion around inside and outside, language and power had already emerged in the GDR with the radical disavowal of any working within the system by the Prenzlauer Berg poets in the late 1970s. The political role of this group is important, less for any programmatic positions than for the questions these poets asked. As a rhetorical strategy, my concern will be to stage a debate between the "older" and the "younger" oppositional generations, loosely defined, as a way of exploring the historical presence of alternative voices within what since 1989 has increasingly come to be characterized as a monolithic, closed society, one devoid of any alterity or disruptive fervor and more totalitarian in some ways than the Third Reich. As the exposition to such a discursive drama, let me briefly outline a history of literary opposition in the GDR as it emerged prior to the 1980s.

The initial period of GDR literature was centered within the official party institutions and the discourse of Marxism-Leninism. From 1949 to roughly the mid-1960s, most major and minor writers viewed themselves as integral members of and even as spokespeople for the official socialist public sphere. They published in major journals and publishing houses, participated in the state writers' organizations, and produced their stage and television plays as part of an orchestrated public life. The writer, it was held, spoke as a mediator of social values and served to enlighten and communicate, in aesthetic media, policies forged within the higher reaches of the party hierarchy.

To be sure, even in the 1950s there were "uncomfortable" writers, such as Peter Huchel, Erich Arendt, Peter Hacks, Heiner Müller, and Günter Kunert, whose aesthetic proclivities or ideological nonconformity challenged or wished to broaden the norms of official aesthetic doctrine. But if these few experimentalists were in any way oppositional, then it was only by virtue of stylistic transgression. They did not consciously question the epistemological premise that linked one's knowledge of reality to the collective reproduction of the system in its entirety. Nor did their view of history contest the notion that the development of industrial production, technology, and science inevitably led to the emancipation of the society as a whole. What they did suggest—and this was the *limit* of their nonconformity—was the necessity for a greater plurality of "progressive" cultural voices within the body politic: not the end of one-party hegemony, or even the legal guarantee of freedom of speech, but a kinder, gentler articulation of monolithic rule.

The period from the mid-1960s through the Biermann expulsion in 1976 marked a significant turning point in the nature of dissent and opposition among the literati in East Germany. Whereas most writers in the earlier period had sought merely to broaden the framework of debate within a structure of shared ideological values concerning the primacy of production, the inevitability of socialist history, and the validity of proletarian truth, a number of leading writers now began to question those discursive paradigms. At the center of their critique was a repudiation of the instrumental reason guiding official socialist policy. What these writers had begun to understand is the extent to which the *language* of a supposedly progressive, scientifically rationalized, dialectical materialism was irrevocably linked to repressive structures of power in the GDR, and that any genuine struggle for social change would also mean a recasting of the entire value system around which it would cohere.

Perhaps it should not be surprising that intellectuals such as Kunert, Braun, Müller, Wolf, and Morgner, though critical of official ideology, would nevertheless choose to ground their critiques in the language of a deviant Marxism. The first GDR publication of the early writings of Marx in 1968,[14] coupled with growing reference to such unorthodox thinkers as Jean-Paul Sartre, Walter Benjamin, Ernst Bloch, Antonio Gramsci, the Frankfurt School, and even the young Georg Lukács, provided a medium with which to launch an assault from *within* the framework of Marxism in order to transform the entire tradition itself. Thus the GDR dissidents of the 1970s were caught in the classic aporia of the "renegade."[15] Committed to speaking within the ever-shifting boundaries of permissible public expression, they drew on a discourse that they hoped would at once be acceptable to and yet subversive of the language of power itself.

It is precisely this symbiotic discursive status that proved so repugnant and unacceptable to the youngest and, as it turns out, last generation of opposition to emerge in the GDR. Born for the most part in the 1950s, which is to say subsequent to the founding of the GDR, the Prenzlauer Berg writers and artists defined themselves in opposition to the older, now established literary generation precisely in terms of what they saw as the latter's naive attempt to fight from within to reform the system.

A strong articulation of this position may be found in an essay by the poet Uwe Kolbe titled *The Homeland of Dissidents: Afterthoughts Concerning the Phantom of GDR Opposition*, written after 1989, in which the author bluntly states that there never was an opposition in the GDR.[16] Kolbe compares East German intellectuals to their colleagues in the rest of the Eastern bloc and finds the former wanting in the extreme. Whereas Soviet and East European oppositional writers risked their lives in unequivocating struggle against the system as a whole, often ending up in jails and insane asylums, the East German "dissident" elite articulated the dream of reform socialism—a utopian third way between Stalinism and capitalism, beyond the existing two-bloc system. In contrast to the genuine "anti-socialist" opposition of a Vaclav Havel, who, precisely because he had refused compromise with the foreign Soviet dictatorship, was morally and politically able to unify a postcommunist Czechoslovakia, leading GDR writers unmasked themselves as hopelessly out of touch with the needs of the general populace. Exemplary for Kolbe of such naiveté was Christa Wolf's plea to a downtrodden GDR populace on the very eve of total collapse: "Help us build a truly democratic society," she intoned, "one which will retain the vision of a democratic socialism" (34).

For Kolbe and the other Prenzlauer Berg dissidents, even the most radical forms of intellectual resistance throughout the postwar GDR cannot be called genuine opposition. This is true of Wolf Biermann, who was prohibited from making public appearances for twelve years and then exiled, or the physicist Robert Havemann, who lived his latter days under house arrest and permanent harassment, or even Jürgen Fuchs and Rudolf Bahro, both of whom were jailed and then exiled into the BRD, Bahro for his book *Die Alternative*, critiquing socialism as it really existed[17] and Fuchs for his protest of the Biermann affair. To Kolbe and others, none of these people represent an opposition. The reason for this is very simple: Havemann, Biermann, Fuchs, Bahro, the writers Brecht, Müller, Wolf, Heym, or Franz Fühmann—regardless of their physical or mental suffering and despite their desire for fundamental political change—were *dissidents* acting out of a desire to build an alternative form of socialism. Dissidents, then, in this category were those who had been excommunicated from the church but remained true to the faith. More important for our present analysis, dissidents for Kolbe were the renegades whose very effort to speak in the language of the faith at the moment of its greatest corruption leant a powerful legitimacy to the status quo.

In response to Uwe Kolbe, let me first argue historically. The tendency of East German intellectuals to speak within an alternative Marxist discourse was clearly connected to their situation vis-à-vis German fascism and the history of the Third Reich. Whereas other Eastern bloc intellectuals drew on nationalist and religious discourses to articulate an anticommunist or antisoviet form of resistance, the coupling of nationalism with the ideology and criminality of Nazism during the Third Reich had effectively foreclosed any move to such a tradition within German postwar political culture. Seen from this perspective, the appeal of Marxism for dissident intellectuals in East *and* West Germany may be viewed historically as a logical means by which they strove to open up an oppositional discursive space within the frozen contours of central European cold war culture: in the West, between a conservative, potentially nationalist anticommunism on the Right and a helpless, ultimately apologetic anti-anticommunism on the Left; in the GDR, between existing forms of Stalinism and a restoration of what were perceived to be the socioeconomic conditions that had led to Nazism in the first place.

In the GDR the turn toward a critical Marxism permitted an incipient intellectual opposition the means by which to challenge the prevailing Marxist-Leninist dogmas concerning gender, ecology, freedom of speech, the role of science, and technological and industrial progress, and to do so as potentially constituent of civil society and within the framework of an existing socialist public sphere. To that extent, Kolbe is absolutely right when he borrows the language of ecclesiastical history to label the East German dissidents *Abtrünnige*, defectors from the faith. Like Luther, their original intent was very much a move toward reformation or revision and not a total abandonment of doctrinal adherence, or even a break with the institutional church. And again like Luther, the political consequences of such heresy led them far afield of their imagined political goals. Certainly it was the existence of such a heretical discourse that provided the language and means for public dialogue that in turn was initially to help galvanize a broadly based civil rights movement around issues of peace, freedom of speech, freedom to worship, juridical due process, ecology, feminism, gay rights, and freedom to assemble. Simply to dismiss the East German cultural opposition on the basis of their philosophical roots within a political culture of Marxism or their efforts to work from within is to ignore their function within the evolution of a much broader, democratizing process.

Yet having made that point, I would nevertheless maintain that there is more to be learned from pursuing our staged confrontation between the two generations. For what is important about the younger generation of poets is precisely the radicality with which this group of intellectuals has stressed the issues of language and discourse, discourse and power for an understanding of the complicated process of political articulation within a system devoid of officially constituted structures of civil society. Their reading of Foucault and of Deleuze and Guattari onto the symbiotic discursive network of real existing, that is to say, real discursive socialism opens up a dimension of the opposition question that forces us to explore more thoroughly issues of complicity and resistance beginning at the level of the speech act itself.

Contours of Accountability: Müller and Wolf Take Stock

Focusing on the question of complicity and speech within the framework of our debate and in the light of Stasi allegations, let us return for a moment to the two authors who because of their fame as writers and as public political personae have most come to represent the paradigm of GDR literary dissidence in its now classical phase: Heiner Müller and Christa Wolf. Although the poetic and political voices of Müller and Wolf are different in many significant respects, their shared generational experiences and institutional relations to the state are not. Born in 1929, Müller and Wolf were socialized under two dictatorships in ways that shaped much of their intellectual and political lives: regardless of any perceived shortcomings, the highly authoritarian forms of GDR antifascism remained for both authors the necessary antidote to what was feared to be a probable return to fascism under conditions of capitalism. Moreover, both saw their work develop into increasingly critical and even dangerously confrontational exchanges with the status quo.

Following 1989, Müller and Wolf both published "autobiographical" works that sought to explore that inchoate subliminal region of social life where an individual self and the power of the state become proximate, where the political as a language of being is imbibed and reinvented in the struggle to constitute a separate identity or even to justify one's location within a set of conflicting and not easily observable political coordinates. In both these texts, one "fictional" (Wolf) and the other in the form of staged interviews (Müller), the issue of the poet and the Stasi reemerges at a deeper register as the question concerning the extent to which one is able to trace in memory and through *language* the contours of accountability in relation to a state and a party with which one is at once profoundly at odds and deeply entangled—and whose absent presence after unification continued to provide the defining framework for political self-understanding.

In Müller's *War Without Battle: Life Under Two Dictatorships*, the "voice" of the author appears at times almost compulsively driven to explain its relationship to the ruling elite and the reasons for having preferred to stay in the GDR. "Partisan commitment to the GDR was connected to Brecht," he says emphatically. "Brecht was the legitimation for why one could be for the GDR . . . a proof for the superiority of the system was its better literature. I never thought about leaving."[18] As articulated here, Müller's choice to stay in the GDR does not emanate from a set of political beliefs or social values. Whereas writers such as Franz Fühmann, Christa Wolf, Stefan Hermlin, and Günter Kunert often stressed the moral authority of an antifascist leadership that had actually engaged in the struggle against Nazism as providing the basis for their initial commitment to the GDR, for Müller, the dramatist, the GDR supplied *Erfahrungsdruck* (the pressure of experience) for his production of literature:

> Living in the GDR was above all living in a material. It's like architecture, architecture also has more to do with the state than painting does, and drama also has more to do with the state than other literary genres. Here there's a particular relationship to power, a fascination with power, a rubbing up against power and taking part in power, even perhaps submitting oneself to power in order to take part. . . . For a dramatist a dictatorship is more colorful than life in a democracy. (113)

Several points emerge in the above citation that are significant for understanding Müller's own highly dramatized, intensely performative relationship to the GDR. First, the playwright's elaborate representation of the pre-modern, semifeudal, indeed Elizabethan conditions of real existing socialist dictatorship, familiar enough from the highly allegorical staging of his own version of *Macbeth* in 1982, unfolds an almost physically erotic relationship to "power," revealing much about its seductive pull on intellectuals, particularly male intellectuals, in the GDR. Müller also suggests a contrast to the less "colorful" life of a writer under capitalist liberal democracy, whose market-mediated relationship to the status quo operates within a highly insulated buffer zone in relation to the state. In the GDR, writers were more vulnerable precisely because of their proximity to power. This is not, of course, due to any disposition over the means of state security or their participation in political decision making. Rather, it stemmed from the importance of the role writers played in generating a language of legitimation. Given the accelerating devaluation of official ideology as a means for constituting political consensus in the 1970s, the writer in the GDR became increasingly vital as a medium for the creation of "authentic" speech in a world of nonspeech. Indeed, it was precisely within this growing discursive power vacuum that literary discourse was able to provide what for Müller becomes an erogenous zone within the interstices of power, a place, in his own highly metaphorical formulation, where poet and power "rub up" against one another, where one "submits oneself in order to take part."

If the sensual gratification of cavorting with state power provided titillation at times, the direct and altogether personal violence of state oppression also delivered the terror, and thereby the "material" for his work as a professional dramatist. Müller's emphasis on the priority of material" over political attitude or moral stance as the starting point for his "production" as a thinker and writer appears repeatedly throughout his autobiography and is a familiar theme in much of his work. For instance, asked about his fascination with the neoconservative Carl Schmitt, Müller replies: "Carl Schmitt is theater. His texts are performances. I am not interested in whether he is right or not" (272). Similarly, in response to a question concerning Ernst Jünger receiving the Goethe prize in 1980, we are told that "for me Jünger was never a hero . . . I am interested in his literature. I can't read things morally, just as I can't write morally" (281).

Müller's theory of an "aesthetics of material" is basic to his self-understanding as a political artist. Like Brecht, who preferred the "bourgeois" works of Franz Kafka and the expressionist Georg Kaiser to the political correctness of nineteenth-century naturalism or even socialist realism, Müller too claims to be drawn by properties inherent to the solution of formal aesthetic problems; he was drawn by their performative dimension, rather than by any overriding interest in the political or philosophical views of the authors.

Particularly revealing in this regard are the comments he makes about his major clash with the party concerning the production of his play The Peasants in 1961. Müller's dramatic depiction of the brutal and anarchic conditions of the early collectivization campaign in the province of Mecklenburg (which premiered in most untimely fashion four weeks subsequent to the building of the Wall) so infuriated the party that the production was canceled after one performance and Müller himself expelled from the official Writer's League and denied publication rights in the GDR. What becomes significant in Müller's autobiographical recounting of the events is not the severity of the punishment or even the cowardice of his literary colleagues, many of whom denounced him publicly and almost all of whom, with the exception of Peter Hacks and Hans Bunge, voted for his expulsion.

Far more striking is Müller's description of how he subsequently stood before his colleagues to practice self-criticism: "I looked at the whole thing as dramatic material, I myself was also material, my self criticism is material for me. It was a mistake to believe that I was a political writer" (183); "It definitely had an aspect of the theater about it, how people simply walked right by me without saying hello. I was not hurt by that, I observed the whole thing with detached interest" (181).

At one level, the voice of the text can be rightfully accused of massive denial, topped off with a touch of apologetics. Faced initially with the full terror of the state, Müller's subsequent narration of the events resorts to self-aggrandizing, ironic distance, at once stylizing himself performatively as above the fear and shame of the moment but also playing down the fact that other writers had ended up in jail for far lesser "crimes."

Yet what we also see in the above is the extent to which Müller's "erotic" relationship to the state indeed derived from his being permitted to perform and take part, from being provided the truly dramatic material of what was a moment of extreme humiliation for himself and the entire literary community. Moreover, as is obvious from the text of his self-criticism, which he still refuses to disavow, this was born precisely out of his strong bond to the system: "I wanted to write a play that would be useful for socialism. . . . My wish was a hard discussion. A discussion which would help me to keep working on a higher plane, more than before, better than before, productively."[19] In his subsequent twenty-eight years in the GDR, Heiner Müller's position was never really to change. He remained to the very end, as he acknowledged when confronted with the Stasi allegations, dedicated to dialogue. Paradoxically, however, it was always his unsuccessful efforts to achieve a genuine dialogue with power, and the "material" such failures and humiliation provided him as a performer of his own abjection, that kept him "working on a higher plane." What better source for his hapless representation of intellectuals in such figures as the young Friedrich the Great or Hamlet in *Hamletmaschine?* And what better testimony to his own *discursive* seduction by power than Müller's anecdotal insight into the fate of socialist renegade intellectuals from Bukharin down to the author himself:

> If a criminal is blamed for something unfairly he will not refute it, he simply says nothing. An intellectual, on the other hand, can't hold back if he is blamed for something unfairly. He can't stop himself from disagreeing. And at that moment he joins the game/play (Spiel), the dialogue begins, and you've got him. An intellectual always wants to play a part, all you have to do is offer him a part. That is the point about Bucharin, the point about the Moscow trials. That's how you get an intellectual. A criminal knows better. (184)

That, unfortunately, is not the only point about the Moscow trials, where the raw savagery of Soviet state power and Stalinist paranoia simply ground up any form of "participation," regardless of individual attitudes concerning dialogue or criminality. But it is, interestingly, a most revealing confessional point about Müller himself, as well as others of his generation. For in point of fact, the double bind of many GDR intellectuals lay very much in their inability to accept themselves as having been criminalized. The most profound forms of public mistreatment or humiliation were viewed by many right to the very end as part of a dialogic process in which the powers that be might be brought to see the error of *their* ways.

Christa Wolf's first post-Wall publication reveals a similar narrative compulsion. In *What Remains*, written about a time of crisis between the exile of Wolf Biermann in 1976 and the expulsion of other authors from the Writers' Union in 1979, Wolf portrays a day in the life of a female author being observed by the Stasi: three uniformed men sit in a car in front of her house, ostentatiously watching and waiting. In the highly volatile post-Wall atmosphere in which it appeared, this work was either criticized for its self-serving glorification of Wolf herself as victim or was praised as posing "a radical critique of real existing socialism."[20] As Herbert Lehnert has rightly argued, certainly any blanket identification of Christa Wolf with the central figure ignores the obvious "fictionality" of the text and leads to a distorted reading of the story.[21]

Of interest to me is less the question of the text's "critical" attitude toward the state, although clearly that is a theme of the book, than what it reveals about the narrator-writer's tortured struggle to situate herself—cognitively, emotionally, psychically—in relation to a system within which she is both willing participant and an object of ostracism. Indeed, in my view this text is not concerned at all with establishing complicity or resistance, with whether the writer is a fellow traveler or a victim of persecution. What it seeks instead is to confront the *already* internalized discursive "system" as a functioning and invasive presence in the mental processes of *this* intellectual's everyday life.

Wolf presents the phenomenology of surveillance as a process of shared communication. If Foucault's panoptic eye registers the power of the look as one-sided, an epistemological upper hand, in *Was bleibt* the viewer (the Stasi) is also the viewed: "And so I stood, as I did every morning, behind the curtain that had been put there so that I could hide behind it, stood and looked, hopefully unseen, across to the parking place on the other side of Friedrichstraße. . . . By the way, they weren't there" (10). Here we have a game of cat and mouse, played out within a regime of domesticated terror, told by a narrator who must perforce deny the full implications of the violence unfolding before and within her. One night the "victim" flashes a light in the window in an attempt to signal her pursuers, "whereupon they blinked their car lights three times in return. They had a sense of humor. We went to bed that night a little more relaxed, a little less intimidated" (20). On other occasions, the narrator catches herself wanting to bring them hot tea (19), or not wishing to demonize the "three gentlemen" by thinking of them in "leather coats" (18), or simply boasting of the fact that from her window above them she is able to notice a balding spot on one of the officers, "even before his own wife might have, who has never gotten a chance to view him from this angle" (16).

This narrative compulsion to domesticate and de-demonize is significant, because it shifts the focus from a simple depiction of victim and victimizer to the more complicated question concerning the victim's own *investment* as speaker and actor in the social text. For what this work is exploring are the fragile emotional and discursive fault lines binding and separating the self in relation to an apparatus with which the central figure had once considered herself at one. The story's internal dialogue entails a struggle to press against the truth of an author's persecution and what an acceptance of that truth would mean for her own political and moral identity. Her desire to understand and even nurture her oppressors, to converse with them about the weather and their family life, her "shameful need to get along with any kind of people" (20) give startling voice to the gendered mechanisms of internalization and rationalization that have *self-admittedly* hindered the acquisition of a new "language, which is there in my ear, but not yet on my tongue" (7).

Rather than a record of repression, this is the search for another voice as a means for finding another self. If her story begins with anxieties concerning the Stasi sitting in front of the house, the centerpiece of this work is the struggle to come to terms with the Stasi within. In a 1974 interview, Wolf spoke of "the mechanism of self-censorship" as being more dangerous than the official censor, "for it internalizes constraints which can hinder the birth of literature" and "entangles an author in mutually exclusive demands."[22] *What Remains* radicalizes and works through this insight performatively in a fictional internal dialogue among competing voices of the self, one of which is her "Self-censor" (52) (now serving as her *better* self rather than as a "mechanism" of outer control!), whom she intermittently calls "Judge," "Partner," and "Companion." "Incensed I demanded to know who had placed him (the Companion) there and he answered calmly: you yourself sister" (56–57). The succeeding passage brings us to the nexus of inner and outer forms of censorship and control: "I myself. It took me a long time to get beyond those two words. I myself. Which of the multiple beings, of which "I myself" constructed me? The one that wanted to know itself? The one that protected itself? Or that third one, that was always tempted to dance to the same tune as the young gentlemen out there in front of my door?" (57). By splitting the "I," the narrator deconstructs a single self, and with it the authority of "that third one . . . always tempted to dance to the same tune," and does so as a prerequisite for moving forward. The acknowledgment of a fragmented, multiple self, once the marker of an alienated being, now provides the regenerative terrain for discursive renewal.

In their "autobiographical" works, Heiner Müller and Christa Wolf have sought to confront the rhetorical and dialogic grounds of the writer's relationship to the state. Müller's self-stylization as cynical performer in the drama of his own abjection would seem a distant cry from Wolf's depiction of a highly personal, tentatively groping struggle to extract oneself from or extract from oneself "that third one" (jenen Dritten). What links the two, however, is an effort to explore the extent to which separation or opposition of self had to begin in dialogue with and even subjection to the (internalized) powers that be. It also confirms even as it challenges the radical critique by the Prenzlauer Berg poets of the older dissidents.

Prenzlauer Berg and Beyond

What then would be a "genuine" opposition in the eyes of the newest generation? In her preface to the poetry anthology of young writers from the Prenzlauer Berg subculture titled *Berührung ist nur eine Randerscheinung* (Touching is only a marginal thing), Elke Erb articulates what amounts to a manifesto concerning the younger generation vis-à-vis their elders, one that proves helpful for understanding the self-declared differences between the two: "The new literature reflects a social consciousness which no longer wants or is even able to be the object of an inherited civilization. . . . They (the authors) refuse to be infantilized by its utopian contents and they resist its compromises. Nor are they seduced into feckless criticism and confrontation. Their social maturity is the result of a total withdrawal [Austritt] from the authoritarian system, an absolute release from the tutelage of subordinated meanings."[23]

The "maturity" of the Prenzlauer Berg poets, in Erb's definition, reverses the Freud-inspired paradigm whereby emotional and political sovereignty would occur through internalization, in all of its dialectical complexity, of the ideological superego. Whereas the elders, such as Wolf, Müller, Heym, and Biermann, remain "infantilized" by their compromisings with the socialist Vater-Staat as well as through their adherence to the telos of a utopian philosophy of history (Geschichtsphilosophie), the young ones dare to stage their Vatermord not as an act of aggression, but rather as an evacuation from any kind of historical continuity or paternal heritage: no confrontation, no shared linguistic space, no Hegelian *Aufhebung.* "I attempted not to live in this system," says Sascha Anderson in his notorious interview in *Die Zeit.* "Perhaps it was wrong, but it was a kind of *Abwehr* [defense mechanism]." Schedlinski describes this relationship narcissistically in terms suggesting a kind of Habermasian uncoupling of system world and life world: "What the others do, does not interest me, what my friends think is important."[24]

Central to this construction of an autonomous second culture, one that was oblivious and disdainful of all state institutions, was the priority attributed to a critique of language as a *prerequisite* for a critique of social and ideological structures. In contradistinction to the older dissident writers who labored in what has been described as "the web of public lies" (*das Gespinst der öffentlichen Lüge*),[25] the Prenzlauer Berg poets saw themselves driven to the margins of society, *outside* the "dictatorship of linguistic simulations" and immune to the conventions of a language that binds the speaker "to a hermetic discourse, robbing him/her of the freedom of one's senses."[26] Only a language free from the clichés of ideological polarities, a language, finally, in close and intimate proximity to the material "thingness" of things, may break the vicious circularity of discursive oppression. Gert Neumann's notion of "clandestine" speech, a poetics of silence speaking between the signs, signals the absolute bankruptcy of the language of power while claiming to restore and reconnect a relationship between language and truth, public and private speech.[27]

Having established the premises of the linguistic critique emerging from the younger generation, let us return now to our staged debate and to the question concerning literary opposition as it emerged in the GDR of the 1970s and 1980s. First, it is clear, at one level, that what the Prenzlauer Berg poets were able to see and thematize in both their theory and their poetry— in a way that Müller, Wolf, Hein, and others were not—was the extent to which the decay of ideology (*Ideologieverfall*) had severely discredited *any* form of Marxism as a positioned discourse of opposition. This is not to underestimate the important role of the socialist literary opposition historically, nor does it ignore the significance of their own "poetic speech" as a locus of authentic alterity. Rather, it recognizes the extent to which the ultimately *symbiotic* relationship of this inner opposition to the central powers substantially inhibited writers such as Wolf, Heym, Braun, and even Hein from *actively* calling for modes of reform that lay outside or at ideological variance with the normative discourse of socialist institutional life: for the abolition of censorship, for a multiparty system, for a genuinely representative parliament, for total freedom of speech, for the institution of civil society.

As a second point, it is also the case that the linguistic turn within the "Prenzlauer Berg connection" (Endler) made them far more sensitive to the bipolar deep structures of a classically articulated, dialectical discourse and its potential for communicating beyond or even in contradiction to what it thinks it is communicating. Schedlinski's essay "The Dilemma of the Enlightenment" presents us with an elaborate critique of what he calls an "enlightenment discourse of protest" (der aufklärerisch protestierende Diskurs), which in his view is always limited to articulating what the ruling discourse has always already been silent about—and for that reason is always contained as a mirror reflection of a higher discursive power.[28] The young poet offers an incisive, indeed brilliant linguistic variation on Marcuse's somewhat shopworn theory of repressive tolerance, turning it now against socialist as well as capitalist forms of discursive control. Significantly, he also reveals in his rhetorical turns a fundamental dislocation lying at the heart of the younger poets' credo.

What intrigues me about the Prenzlauer Berg poets is not that they claimed to be the only real opposition in the GDR, while simultaneously some of their leadership was consorting with the Stasi. It is clear that most of this group was *not* involved in IM activities, nor is there evidence, as some journalists were wont to argue, that the Stasi completely controlled or corrupted the poets' activities.[29] Of far greater importance is the contradiction at the very basis of their notion of what it means to launch an opposition in the first place. On one hand, they ridicule the older generation for believing in confrontational dialogue and, employing a discourse theory rooted in French poststructuralism, present a "radical" critique of the "encrastic" (Barthes) language and metanarratives (Lyotard) of the socialist status quo and its power to subvert any potential resistance. In accordance with this position and in agreement with Foucault, there is no such thing as a linguistic archimedean point outside or marginal to a dominant discourse from which to speak the "truth." Any discourse, regardless of its intention or political gesture, is situated necessarily within the interstices of power. It is through language and language alone that one is interpellated into the system. The poet Stefan Döring makes this abundantly clear when he says: "Durch die Sprache wird Person erzogen, hat man die Sprache gefressen, dann auch die Ordnung." (People are formed by language—if one has devoured the language, then one has eaten the order as well.)[30]

Yet as much as these poets go beyond the linguistic innocence of the older generation—which in their eyes still clung to the possibility of an "enlightened discourse of protest"—their own self-stylizations reveal them to be asserting *nolens volens* the viability of a self-conscious, autonomous, subject-centered, indeed, archimedean locus outside of the dominant discourse within which to develop an "authentic" language. When Gerhard Wolf and Elke Erb, both GDR poet-critics from the older generation, wax euphoric about this "second culture," which "as an independent artistic movement" (G. Wolf)[31] had seemingly transcended the confines of a feckless clinch with the SED power structure, they are not just projecting themselves as an older generation that has been worn down by their own failure to resist. They represent as well the illusions of the upstarts, who, in stylizing their poetic struggles into the status of the "Outcast,"[32] have repressed the basic insights of their own highly theorized experience: that there is no such thing as the absolute outside, spatially or linguistically.

For if we examine the actual *function* of the Prenzlauer Berg poets, we see that the forms of revolt are positioned in an obvious contextual relationship to the prevailing discourse, as well as to the institutionalized formations of power in the GDR. For example, as a result of their proliferating modes of distribution and performance, these poets were able to create a counter public sphere, which, though tolerated and even infiltrated by the Stasi, nevertheless marked out a powerful cultural articulation precisely as a response to what they viewed as "the one dimensionality of the prevailing discourse" in the GDR.[33] The publication of such underground journals as *Mikado, UND, SCHADEN*, and *Ariadnefabrik* were integrated into an emerging network of semipublic (unofficial) readings, exhibitions, film showings, concerts, cabarets, and performances, that saw itself as an expression of a new kind of "autarkic urban feeling":[34] an assertion of "autonomy," "authenticity," and "critical life practice" that became "a resistance against and at the same time a contradictory product of a centralized, administered, and increasingly alienated Public Sphere."[35] This contradictory dimension is important. Clearly these poets' *sense* of autonomy provided an important impetus to an organizational formation, which, while thoroughly under the surveillance of the security apparatus, nevertheless was able to self-define a cultural position within the breakdown of cultural legitimacy as a whole. The official decision to tolerate (that is, not repress) such activities was simply the other side of a growing helplessness on the part of the regime to itself negotiate satisfactory modes of productive culture within a deteriorating state apparatus.

But even at the level of poetic utterance, the Prenzlauer Poets were in dialogue, regardless of their disavowal of any participatory role within what they disparagingly called a *Gesprächskultur*. Despite Gert Neumann's articulated refusal to speak, his call to all for a "language of non-power," a "voice of silence" spoke nevertheless from within and against a culture in which "conversations take place, in order to numb thought."[36] Michael Thulin's insightful analysis of a "critique of language" as "counter-culture" catalogues a manifesto of the various "intentions" driving what he would even call the "language critical school of Prenzlauer Berg Berlin/DDR": these poets are against "the false appearance of linguistic continuity," "the everyday language of power," "the authoritarian institution of meaning," and so on.[37] Even a language of silence, it would seem, must define itself against the distorted discursive system that has necessitated it. The failure to accept the essentially contextual and ultimately political relationship between poet and state has led to dangerous naiveté on the part of those who would want to resist the state by claiming to ignore it. Conversely, the aggression of a *Sprachkritik* that understands the extent to which "all social norms are at the same time norms of language" (240) has much to offer a generation of writers still struggling to reach, in Christa Wolf's terms, "a language which is there in my ear, but not on my tongue."

Our image of the Stasi as *Krake* at the outset served metaphorically to conjure up a post-Wall GDR body politic released from the grasp of a dying organism and subject to the slow, painful process of social and political renewal. For the present analysis, what was important about such a reading was less a notion of the Stasi as evil incarnate, as was often enunciated in the Western press, than what such an image communicated about the all-embracing, thoroughly internalized nature of social control under the conditions of a modern society. The Foucauldian panoptic society has been vastly outdone, it would seem, by a social organization in which there can be no pristine, "outside" subject whose body and mind might elude the grasp (or the gaze?) of political involvement. The fact that oft-proclaimed dissident writers, many of whom saw themselves at varying "odds" with the status quo, were nevertheless found implicated *discursively* contains an important lesson about the immanent nature of any relationship in that society.

The activities of individual oppositional writers of any generation in the GDR must be judged in light of the historical context from which they spoke. The powers of their speech were always part of a double-edged evolutionary process: on one hand, they were the enabled voice of a self-legitimating status quo; on the other, they sought to articulate, from within the official language and power relationships, the challenge to a repressive system. Like language itself, this system will release its hold not through a single act of revolutionary rupture or conscious renewal, but by means of a gradual working through over time of its forty-year experience. Certainly GDR writers of all generations will continue to play a role in any such process.

Notes

An earlier version of this essay appeared in The Powers of Speech: The Politics of Culture in the GDR *(Lincoln: University of Nebraska Press, 1995), 219–42. Copyright © 1995 by the University of Nebraska Press; reprinted by permission of the University of Nebraska Press.*

1. Christa Wolf, *Was bleibt* (Frankfurt am Main, 1990). The book is subtitled *Erzählung.* All subsequent quotes from this work will be cited by page number in the text.

2. For anthologies of articles dealing with the debate that erupted around Wolf and the book, see Karl Deiritz and Hannes Krauss, eds., *Der deutsch-deutsche Literaturstreit oder "Freunde, es spricht sich schlecht mit gebundener Zunge"* (Frankfurt am Main, 1991); Thomas Anz, ed., *Es geht nicht um Christa Wolf* (Munich, 1991); Andreas Huyssen, "After the Wall: The Failure of German Intellectuals," *New German Critique* 52 (winter 1991): 109–43.

3. The German term for this is *"Inofizieller Mitarbeiter"* (lit.: unofficial co-worker) and is often signified by the initials "IM," which I shall use in my subsequent discussion.

4. Frank Schirrmacher, "Verdacht und Verrat: Die Stasi-Vergangenheit verändert die literarische Szene," *Frankfurter Allgemeine Zeitung,* 5 November1991.

5. Jürgen Habermas, *Vergangenheit als Zukunft* (Zurich, 1990), 45–46.

6. "Der lange Arm der Stasi," *Der Spiegel* 44, 26 March 1990.

7. For an excellent discussion in English of the Anderson and Schedlinski affairs, see Jane Kramer, "Letter from Europe," *The New Yorker,* 25 May 1992, 40–62.

8. Lutz Rathenow, "Operativer Vorgang Assistent: Stasi," *Stern,* no. 3, 9 January 1992.

9. Jürgen Fuchs and Klaus Hensel, "Heraus aus der Lüge und Ehrlichkeit herstellen: Der Schriftsteller und die Stasi-Spitzel," *Frankfurter Rundschau,* 21 December 1991.

10. Rainer Schedlinski, " 'Dem Druck, immer mehr sagen zu müssen, hielt ich nicht stand': Literatur, Staatssicherheit und der Prenzlauer Berg," *Frankfurter Allgemeine Zeitung,* 14 January 1992.

11. See Manfred Jäger, "Auskünfte: Heiner Müller und Christa Wolf zu Stasi-Kontakten," *Deutschlandarchiv* 26, no. 2 (February 1993): 142–46.

12. For full documentation of Wolf's Stasi files between 1959 and 1962 as well as the discussions subsequent to their revelation in January of 1993 see Hermann Vinke, ed., *Akteneinsicht Christa Wolf: Zerrspiegel und Dialog* (Hamburg, 1993).

13. Christa Wolf, "Eine Auskunft," *Berliner Zeitung,* 21 January 1993.

14. Karl Marx and Friedrich Engels, *Werke, Ergänzungsband Erster Teil* (Berlin, 1968).

15. See Michael Rohrwasser, *Der Stalinismus und die Renegaten: Die Literatur der Exkommunisten* (Stuttgart, 1991).

16. Uwe Kolbe, "Die Heimat der Dissidenten: Nachbemerkungen zum Phantom der DDR-Opposition," in Deiritz and Krauss, *Der deutsch-deutsche Literaturstreit*, 33–39.

17. Rudolf Bahro, *Alternative: Zur Kritik des real existierenden Sozialismus* (Frankfurt am Main, 1977).

18. Heiner Müller, *Krieg ohne Schlacht: Leben in zwei Diktaturen* (Cologne, 1992), 112. Further references appear in the text.

19. Reprinted in Müller, *Krieg ohne Schlacht* under the title "Selbstkritik Heiner Müllers (an die Abteilung Kultur beim Zentralkomitee der SED)," 407–10.

20. Huyssen, "After the Wall: The Failure of German Intellectuals," 124.

21. Herbert Lehnert, "Fiktionalität und autobiographische Motive: Zu Christa Wolfs Erzählung *Was bleibt* ," *Weimarer Beiträge* 3 (March 1991): 423–44.

22. Christa Wolf, "Interview," *Weimarer Beiträge* 6 (1974): 90–112, here 102.

23. Elke Erb, "Vorwort," in *Berührung ist nur eine Randerscheinung: Neue Literatur aus der DDR*, ed. Sascha Anderson and Elke Erb (Cologne, 1985), 14–15.

24. Sascha Anderson, " 'Das ist nicht so einfach': Gespräch von Iris Radisch mit Sascha Anderson," *Die Zeit*, 45, no. 1 November 1991; Rainer Schedlinski, "Dem Druck, immer mehr sagen zu müssen," *Frankfurter Allgemeine Zeitung*, 14 January 1992.

25. Antonia Grunenberg, "In den Räumen der Sprache: Gedankenbilder zur Literatur Gert Neumanns," in Text + Kritik (special issue) (1990): 207.

26. Michael Thulin, "Sprache und Sprachkritik: Die Literatur des Prenzlauer Bergs in Berlin/DDR," in Arnold and Wolf, *Die andere Sprache*, 236–37.

27. Gert Neumann, *Die Klandestinität der Kesselreiniger* (Frankfurt am Main, 1989).

28. Rainer Schedlinski, *Die Arroganz der Ohnmacht* (Berlin, 1991), 18–28.

29. Karl Corino, "Vom Leichengift der Stasi: Die DDR-Literatur hat an Glaubwürdigkeit verloren. Eine Entgegnung," *Süddeutsche Zeitung*, 12 June 1991.

30. "Introview: Egmont Hesse—Stefan Döring," in *Sprache & Antwort: Stimmen und Texte einer anderen Literatur aus der DDR*, ed. Egmont Hesse (Frankfurt am Main, 1988), 100.

31. Gerhard Wolf, "Gegen sprache mit sprache—mit-sprache gegen-sprache: Thesen mit Zitaten und Notizen zu einem literarischen Prozess," in Arnold and Wolf, *Die andere Sprache*, 15.

32. Gerrit-Jan Berendse, "Outcast in Berlin: Opposition durch Entziehung bei der jüngeren Generation," *Zeitschrift für Germanistik*, n.s. 1 (1991): 21–27.

33. Thulin, "Sprache und Sprachkritik," 237.

34. Rainer Schedlinski, "zwischen nostalgie und utopie," *ariadnefabrik* 5 (1989): 29.

35. Peter Böthig, "Differenz und Revolte: Literatur aus der DDR in den 80er Jahren. Untersuchungen an den Rändern eines Diskurses" (Ph.D. diss., Humboldt University in Berlin, 1993), 80.

36. Gert Neumann, "Geheimsprache 'Klandestinität,' " in Hesse, *Sprache und Antwort*, 135.

37. Thulin, "Sprache und Sprachkritik," 237.

PATRICIA ANNE SIMPSON

Syntax of Surveillance:
Languages of Silence and Solidarity

A text is an encounter with the reader, which creates language; truth lives in the respect for this encounter. The encounter is a difficult matter: in it, communication takes place almost silently, because it has to free itself from the meanings of public language . . . ; and, I've often dedicated my work to this theme.

—Gert Neumann, "Anfangstexte einer Lesung"

During the 1980s, the "unofficial"[1] writers of the former GDR sought and set up alternative means of publication, not to "resist" or "defy" the state, but simply to bypass its mechanisms of literary and artistic production.[2] In the process of realizing alternative means of production (the self-publishing of the *Ariadnefabrik* [ariadne factory] is one example), the poets of Prenzlauer Berg and others (of different generations and residences), whose work became a cornerstone of the alternative cultural *Szene* (scene), developed their literary styles with a focus on the relationship between languages of power and the collective unconscious. Under the circumstances of censorship and control, the signification of silence becomes crucial to an examination of this literature.[3]

The first step demands a reading of the abstract language assumed to be coded and subversive. The relationship between language, silence, and potential political resistance is at the center of this discussion of the East German "avant-garde." The associative lyrics of Elke Erb, Rainer Schedlinski, and Gabriele Stötzer (formerly Kachold), as well as the prose of Gert Neumann, highlight the relationship between thought and society with a high degree of specificity to the GDR (see the appendix at the end of this chapter). Their individual attention to the function of language within a power structure places them on common ground. The work is frequently self- or cross-referential: the common denominator of this work is the constant interrogation of the capacity of language to tell the truth under any and all conditions. These writers examine the material conditions of linguistic meaning: material in both a Marxist and a poststructuralist sense. Each poet arrives at the "truth" through a seemingly random process of association that turns out to be highly motivated and, finally, imperative. I first examine briefly excerpts from the poets' works, then turn to the prose of Gert Neumann.

Poetry and Power: Writing the "Political Unconscious"

The poetry produced in and around the Prenzlauer Berg "scene" is frequently characterized as "avant-garde"[4] and associated with a specific political resistance. These and similar assumptions about poets such as Sascha Anderson and Rainer Schedlinski must be more closely examined after the documentation of their respective degrees of Stasi involvement.[5] Still, the rigorous interrogation of meaning, both political and poetic, revolves around the search for a communicative truth. Communication is constituted in this context by silence and must be examined with reference to sociopolitical conditions that prohibit or control communication. This search on the surface of language, this insistence on basic elements of signification, provides a starting point for the analysis of three radically different poets, Elke Erb, Rainer Schedlinski, and Gabriele Stötzer. Erb's associative lyrics locate her aesthetically in the Prenzlauer Berg; Schedlinksi, a member of a younger generation "born into" socialism (Uwe Kolbe), produces poetry of revealing-concealing of meaning that can now be approached in the light of his Stasi affiliation. Gabriele Stötzer, who is not "in" the scene as such, works in Erfurt but thematizes the relationships of a generalized scene in her poetry, which pays explicit attention to questions of sexuality, power, and language. Gert Neumann relates the issue of language, silence, and communication to a specifically German absence of language. All these linguistic processes constitute a kind of private sphere in the absence of public discourse.

Elke Erb has never been known for easily accessible poetry, but in her recent volumes, the poet brings together poetry and prose commentary effectively, not to explain or justify poetic inscription, but to distribute more evenly the burden of meaning.[6] In her work, the poet absents herself as subject and tries to allow the language of things to be heard. Part of her purpose in writing is to probe the linguistic unconscious and bring its preprogrammed social content to light. This act of relating the conscious to the unconscious is manifest in the poem "Das Unternehmen Schreiben" (The writing enterprise), which is situated midway through the volume

Winkelzüge oder nicht vermutete, aufschlußreiche Verhältnisse (Shady moves or not anticipated, conclusive relationships):

Für das Schreiben als z gilt:
x und y, das Unbewußte und das Bewußtsein,
wirken aufeinander in z als zx und zy.

Das heißt, das Schreiben,
obwohl es ein bewußt geführter Prozeß ist,

gleicht jedem anderen Zusammenhang,
in dem x und y aufeinander wirken.[7]

For writing as z applies:
x and y, the unconscious and the conscious,
effect each other in z as zx and zy.

That means, writing,
although it is a consciously directed process,

is equal to every other relation,
in which x and y effect each other.

In this slender excerpt from an expansive and rich text, Erb continues a lyrical deliberation on the logical relationship between letters, literally, and meaning. Elsewhere in *Winkelzüge* [Shady moves], she traces the "illumination" of the unconscious by language in the form of light as it travels from life to writing: *"Nicht über das Papier: / durch das Herz!"* [Not over the paper / through the heart!][8] and generally performs the relationship between language, life, and representation, specifically, poetic language. She posits a dialectical relationship between "Reden und Schweigen" (speaking and being silent), implying that these are interdependent and mutually defining. Erb sets out her own system of signification according to the materiality of certain signifiers, specific letters. In the above excerpt, the poet inverts and reinscribes the language of algebra to yield an equation in which the final letter is writing.

Of importance is Erb's description of writing as a process, and not one with predictable or intended "meaning." In other words, Erb does not trust or glorify the intentionality of the author; rather, she lets language "work" according to its own subjectless stratagems. Erb writes an associative process in which intention and meaning are independent. She deliberates on the occurrence of an "unintended" mistake. In calibrating the relationship between *Sinn* and *Unsinn* (sense and nonsense), Erb points to the mistake of reading mistakes too quickly: " . . . zu leicht / als Fehler gesehen und entwertet wird" (" . . . too easily seen / as a mistake and devalued").[9] Further, in the continuation of the above passage, she writes: "Für einen Text, der einen Assoziationsstrom fixiert, / ist allein

Offenheit verbindlich" ("For a text, which fixes a stream of association, / only openness is binding").[10] Finally, she resolves this play with a con-nection between "verbindliche Offenheit" (binding openness) and "offene Verbindlichkeit" (open obligatoriness).[11] If errors occur in an associative process, they cannot be dismissed or devalued. In a similar way, association must remain paradoxically open and binding, *verbindlich*. The paradox is not resolved but suspended in the alternation between a compulsory open-ness and an open yet binding force. At this point, the paradox opens onto the association between the text and the context, the x, y, and z of writing and the context, she mentions in the final line cited above: "gleicht jedem anderen Zusammenhang, / in dem x und y aufeinander wirken" ("is equal to every other relation, / in which x and y effect each other"). Erb's relation-ship to language is finally self-consciously playful, serious, and associative. Her "lyrisches Ich" ("lyrical I") is conditionally linguistic, a grammatical category of processing life and art.[12] This approach she has in common, to a certain degree, with the associative process at work in Schedlinski's poetry.

Rainer Schedlinski writes what Michael Thulin (Klaus Michael's pseu-donym) has called "die nüchterne sprache der dinge" ("the sober language of things").[13] In a review of the volume of verse *die rationen des ja und des nein* (the ratios/rations of the yes and the no), Thulin, with a strong sense of semiotics and contemporary French poststructuralist theory, describes the effect of Schedlinski's poetry: "die wirklichkeit ist eine gesamtheit vieler sprachen. die dinge sprechen. sie haben ein eigenleben" ("reality is a totality of many languages. objects speak. they have their own life").[14] As Thulin points out, Schedlinski tries to fuse the sign and the signified to allow the things themselves to speak. The context is both provided and problematized by the "I" or "subject" in the poems. This tension leads to the decentering of the lyrical subject, as well as to linguistic innovations with inevitable—if unintended—political import. According to Thulin, "das ist der kernpunkt jeder innovation des poetischen; die verantwortung des sprechenden gegenüber dem sprachlosen" ("that is the central point of each innovation of the poetic; the responsibility of the speaking towards the speechless").[15] The reader can decide what is "speechless." In this way, not unlike Erb, Schedlinski relies on a semiconscious process of association to achieve the desired end.

Thulin's general characterizations of Schedlinski's poetry allow for the inclusion of a potentially "language-critical" element: "es sind texte, deren zeichenhafte und metaphorischen einzelheiten in einen assoziationsstreit geraten und die ihre sprachliche existenz reflektieren" ("there are texts, whose signifying and metaphoric elements get into an associative fight and that reflect their linguistic existence").[16] Erb's "associative stream" becomes in Schedlinski an "associative fight," escalating the degree of aggression in the work itself. Thulin goes on to distinguish Schedlinski from Papenfuß-Gorek, who begins with semes and phonemes as the basic components of poetic language. Schedlinski, Thulin observes, begins with individual words or a linguistic image. Sometimes the associations are obvious, as in the stanza from which the book takes its name. In the poem (etmal) ("x-times"), Schedlinski writes:

> die ration zigaretten zum beispiel
> die rationen des ja und des nein
> an die ich geglaubt
> dann das aber und überhaupt
> so handelt man sich ein thema ein.[17]

> the ration of cigarettes for example
> the rations of the yes and the no
> which i believed in
> then the but and the overall
> thus does one catch a theme.

Schedlinski moves from the material act of rationing in the sense of allotting an object or limiting distribution, to ration as in ratio, the ground or nature of a thing as determined by its relation to other objects. Finally, Schedlinksi brings these two semantic layers together in the act of "rationing" ration. This moment of doubled meaning is clarified by the use of a rhetoric of argumentation, here inscribed in the "but" and the "overall." What is at stake in this poetry is the relationship between logic, grammar, and rhetoric as well as the "grounds" of interpretation based on relations. In other words, this representative poem, when taken with the self-conscious attention to secondary sign systems found in the rest of the work, forces a reading of the relationship between thought and language and objects. Schedlinski seems in fact to decide that words themselves are the grounds of reason and rationing.

This premise is echoed in a poem which seems to cite daily speech, essentially empty retorts uttered when no argument or opinion is required:

> man kann verschiedener meinung sein aber
> man muss wissen wo man steht was
> das wichtigste ist erstens&zweitens
> wem nützt das natürlich

> kann man geteilter meinung sein das
> kann man ganz offen sagen das
> ist das eine die realität ist das
> andere das muss man mal festhalten

er legt eine hand auf den tisch
das ist so.[18]

one can be of different opinions but
one must know where one stands what
the most important thing is first & second
what good it is to whom naturally

one can be of divided opinions that
one can say openly that
is the one thing reality is the
other that one must record occasionally

he puts one hand on the table
that is so.

When strung together, otherwise empty utterances take on a resonance in their meaninglessness. The poem is about logic without thought, language without argument, automatic utterance. Schedlinski indicts a language without associative contexts in which the words would mean something or anything.

In the final section of the collection, Schedlinski explores the "gesetz / der brechung" ("law / of refraction or breaking").[19] If, in the earlier sections, he establishes the unstable ground of logic as part of communicative language, then he also destabilizes the grounds of communication in a context of surveillance. One poem in this final cycle refers to *sender* and *gegensender* (sender and counter-sender),[20] news reports, and "die fenster des ministeriums" ("the windows of the ministry"), which "arbeiten sich schwarz" ("work themselves silly").[21] When in the last three stanzas of the poem "wir lösen die fragen mit hängenden fahnen" (we solve problems with hanging flags), Schedlinksi turns his attention to the larger network of communication, the result is chilling:

das ist bekannt, wir lesen
die zeitungen selbstredend, sie sprechen
in der tat, was ich dir schreibe

bleibt postgeheimnis, das auge
hört mit, das ist das gesetz
der brechung, es liegt

ein schweigen über dem schweigen &
damit es jeder erfährt
haben wir endlich das sprechen gebrochen.[22]

that is known, we read
the newspapers self-speakingly, they speak
in fact, what i write to you

> remains a postal secret, the eye
> eavesdrops, that is the law
> of the breaking, it lies
>
> a silence over the silence &
> so that each learns
> we have finally broken the speaking.

The open silence echoes Erb's "open obligatoriness," but this version of the signified silence is sinister. The eye that hears, an obvious reference, constitutes the "law of the breaking" rather than a "breaking of the law." The result of the open, communicated silence is the ultimate breaking of language, "das sprechen gebrochen" ("the speaking broken"). The poems in this section weave in and out of Western myth (*theseus zur rolle der frau* [theseus on the role of woman]),[23] the role of the Stasi in society (DIE EINZIGEN DIE NICHT BEI DER STASI SIND / SIND DIE DIE DABEI SIND [the only ones who are not with the Stasi / are the ones who are with them]),[24] and especially self-conscious attention to words: "auch das schweigen ist aus worten" ("silence also consists of words")[25] and "als wären es alles nur worte, in scherben / zerfallende evidenzen . . ." ("as if it were all only words, in shards / shattering evidences . . .").[26] The final poem ends with reference to a figure for silence that, I think, is the quintessence of Schedlinski's use of language in this collection: "wie ein engel ohne argumente immer / schweigend" ("like an angel without arguments always / silent").[27] In this volume, Schedlinski brings together the possibilities and limits of communication in a context where surveillance and codified silence prevail, where yes and no, rational thought itself, was rationed. Yet, after the accusations and documentation, this poetry can only be read as an effort to conceal by revealing.

The theme of male-female relations in language and limbs from the end of Schedlinski's book is conceptualized and represented with a vengeance in the long poem "Das Gesetz der Szene" ("The law of the scene") by Gabriele Stötzer. The poet indicts the "scene" and the "associations" in a gender-specific way.[28] The poem makes the most concerted effort to control the associative process and reveal the painful logic behind the words. The law of the scene, according to Stötzer, is again betrayal.

Her associative process in this sprawling, sharp-edged, and enraged poem escalates the indictment of the "scene," whether it refers to the GDR or to society in general. The "law of the scene" echoes, intentionally, the "law of the jungle" and emphasizes the unwritten code that constitutes the trap of the collective. Though the lines in each roughly hewn stanza do not necessarily make sense syntactically, they make sense tactically and semantically. A representative example is the self-demonstrating effect of the first line: "das gesetz der szene / setz dich reiß auf setz dich" ("the law of the scene / sit down tear open sit down"),[29] in which the mention of the law of the scene is followed by a string of imperatives. The morphological units in the words themselves release their own associative logic, as in the line: " . . . die tiere sind so wach wie wachsam heilsam streitsam einsam / die polizisten spitzen fußes . . ." ("the animals are as awake as watchful healing quarrelsome lonely / the police on pointed toes"),[30] in which the sounds emerge from the preceding words, and the insane logic of rhyme dominates the semantic axis of the stanza. The poet, though, seems to be in control of the words, not the reverse, especially in the following:

> . . . also guten tag spaziergängerin hier ist das schlaraffenland des verrats
> hier ist das gaffenland das schaffensland
> wo der betrug sich enttrollt und zum blatt wird am baum
> wir schaffen alle mit am baum der verführung weiß
> vom blatt zur frucht vom ficken zum kinderkriegen der baum spaltet
> sich zur krone einender zweiender dreiender keinender die hirsche
> röhren die affen springen von ast zu ast.[31]

> . . . so good day
> a woman walking here is the shangri-la of betrayal
> here is the gawking land the land of creation
> where deception untrolls and becomes a leaf on a tree
> we all create the tree of seduction know
> from leaf to fruit from fucking to having kids the tree splits
> to the crown oneender twoender threeender noender the stags
> roar the apes leap from branch to branch.

The progression-regression in this section is fraught with bitterness related to knowledge. The "shangri-la of betrayal" is also the "gawking land" and the "land of creation": a motif picked up from the tree of knowledge in the Garden, the tree of seduction that leads the poet in a bizarre logic to the fruits of fucking until, finally, the signifier "apes" contained within all the designations of this tortured topography stand alone just as the apes, the signifiers of the stanza, leap from branch to branch.

This itinerary recurs further along in the poem in which the law of the scene is unfolded:

> das gesetz der szene ist verrat
> das gesetz der szene ist klatsch
> das gesetz der szene ist alle wissen alles
> das gesetz der szene ist gruppe
> das gesetz der szene ist verbündete
> das gesetz der szene ist vielwissen durch allestun und alles
> weitersagen

das gesetz der szene ist sich durch nähe an die wortfolgen
heranbringen.[32]

the law of the scene is betrayal
the law of the scene is gossip
the law of the scene is everyone knows everything
the law of the scene is the group
the law of the scene is allies
the law of the scene is know a lot through doing everything and
passing it all along
the law of the scene is bringing oneself to the sequences of words
through nearness.

If there is a community constituted by shared language and the survival of sanity, that community is brutal and radically exploitative of its members. The law of the scene is spoken and linguistically motivated, for language is knowledge is power in this stanzaic equation. But the nature of the words themselves in Stötzer's composita stands in direct opposition to the investment of truth in language found still in Erb's poetry, for language is a means of unearthing the social unconscious; even in Schedlinski, language is given back to things and objects are resignified. In Stötzer's linguistic topography, words are lies, extended, elaborated, and powerful. In the stanza quoted above, the "nearness" is defined as *ein wortefreßsog* (a word devouring undercurrent).[33] Is the satirized *Szene* thus made up exclusively of *lochbrüder* (cunt brothers) and *schwanzschwestern* (dick sisters)?[34] And is this sexualized linguistic community beyond the reach of the truth?

If there is a search for the truth, it is controlled by the brutality of power relations. The "scene" is divided within and against itself; the truth is constituted by this division:

die szene fällt auseinander in blinde und sehende
die sehenden wollen den anderen die augen ausstechen
es gibt eine blinde und eine wache wahrheit
blind ist innen-sehend ist außenwahrheit
die blinden sind triebhaft schamlos
die sehenden sind bewußt schamvoll . . .[35]

the scene falls apart into the blind and the seeing
the seeing want to gouge out the eyes of the others
there is a blind and a vigilant truth
blind is inner-seeing is outward truth
the blind are compulsively shameless
the seeing are consciously shameful.

In the economy of vision and blindness, truth and violence, the "vigilant truth" is not reincorporated into the linguistic carnage.

The "truth" in a pale and polluted form returns at the end of the poem:

. . . wenn die wahrheit
in der buttertrommel ist und noch
mal durchgedreht wird mit weiß
spüler und rotationsachse quer
überm abgrund.[36]

. . . if the truth
in the butter churn is and still
is churned again with bleach
and rotation axis diagonally
across the abyss.

When the truth is churned like butter with bleach, it ends up suspended diagonally across the abyss. The truth value of language, then, does not return to the objects but remains suspended in a chemically poisoned form, a mix of innocuous dairy product and a "bleached" or processed substance.

It would seem that the postmodern subject inscribes contextual silence into an associative process that unearths sub- or unconscious relationships between power, language, and society in a complex interplay of revealing and concealing the truth; these processes are not, however, confined to lyrical experimentation. The same processes of determining the social significance of a politicized silence, which constitutes a breach between public and private speech so often conflated with communication in the GDR, are at work in the prose of Gert Neumann.

Silent Solidarity

In his literary production, the writer-worker Gert Neumann thematizes the relationship between socialism and language. From the novel *Elf Uhr*, published only in the West, through *Die Klandestinität der Kesselreiniger*,[37] as well as in *Die Schuld der Worte* (The guilt of words), the only of his work published "officially" in the GDR, and the essayistic publications of the early 1990s, Neumann develops the dialectic of speech and silence in a specifically GDR context.[38] His presentation of work and workers, his interpretation of the social syntax of his surroundings, and his persistent attempt to overcome the radical split between public and private speech locate him at the foreground of what was the literary underground or avant-garde in the GDR. The topics of his essays, printed in self-published journals, in *ariadnefabrik*, for example, and, as is in case with the essay and photographs titled "Die Stimme des Schweigens" (The voice of silence) in *Selbstverlag*, are consistent with his concept of language as the weapon with which one wages war against the state and the dominant language of its lies. Language, as an expression of truth, he argues, is set against the

"Versteinerung der Materie Wirklichkeit" ("fossilization of the material of reality").[39] He interrogates relentlessly the criminalization of writing, the effects of censorship and self-censorship, and the relationship of thought to the idealized and ideologized "everyday life" in socialism, while trying to maintain logic in the representation of reality *through* thought. In other words, Neumann articulates the political *with* the aesthetic. But more than belonging to a literary avant-garde[40] or establishing a language of opposition, Neumann radically reconceptualizes, rather, resignifies the "silence" of really existing socialism as its dominant mode of both communication and solidarity. The question remains: Is this relationship between the state's *Sprachmacht* (language power) and Neumann's *Klandestinität* truly one of opposition?

Neumann posits a language of silence that is to be understood as imperative for survival and solidarity in the face of "observation." He is preoccupied with thought, language, and the expression of the relationship between the two. A virtually random sample of titles corroborates this assertion—from *Schuld der Worte* (Guilt of words): "Die Namen" (Names), "Gesang" (Song), "Poesiebeweis" (Poetry proof); from the recent collection "Die Wörter des reinen Denkens" (The words of pure thought): "Die Stimme des Schweigens" (The voice of silence), "Brief ohne Antwort" (Letter without answer), "Das Buch des Lesens" (The book of reading), "Die Schuld der Worte" (The guilt of words), "Die Ethik der Sätze" (The ethics of sentences), among others. His general concern with the *Verfall der Dinge* (decline of things) includes, as he specifies in "Die Wörter des reinen Denkens," the *Verfall der Gegenwartssprache* (decline of contemporary speech).[41] This relationship between thought and its articulation provides the space of silence. His figure for this silence is *Klandestinität*. Silvia Morawitz points first to the borrowing from Deleuze and interprets the gesture as follows: "Clandestinity . . . is the name the author has given to his premonitions and certainties of the secret inherent in all things and of the possibility to allow for something of their essence to appear in a dialogue with them."[42] In the collection of essays written between 1982 and 1991, Neumann insists on a political dimension to the meaning of the word. In a section of the prose pieces titled "Übungen jenseits der Möglichkeit" (Exercises beyond possibility), from which the volume takes its name, Neumann addresses a letter to the imprisoned Adam Michnik that is described as a text for the truth. He characterizes his interpretation of linguistic authority:

> Power cannot force the truth. It is amazing that the human being always keeps coming back to this idea. The language of power is so reduced that it can no longer reach the things. The language of power has to orient itself on

the existence of the enemy; and its completion is the death sentence, which lives on the insane hope that it will have forced the truth definitively into the object by destroying the argument living in people against a *ruling* praxis of truth.[43]

Somewhat idealistically, Neumann declares the incapacity of authority to force the truth, as well as its paranoid compulsion to realize its version of the truth-in-praxis by destroying opposing arguments. The defensive nature of this response precludes, according to Neumann, the coincidence of language and truth, or, of authority and its opponents. Neumann specifies the silence he advocates as a German silence, and distinguishes between the Polish *Solidarność* and his own praxis:

> For my thinking . . . it follows from this analysis, which is necessary, in my opinion, because it inevitably is and will be the case, that real socialism exists: the support of the praxis of *clandestinity*, which is a culture I have encountered in my life as a worker, that has to live without solidarity . . . : and it is either destroyed by this extraordinary test, or begins to anticipate and speak a language within the signs of praxis, which attempts carefully to come closer again to responsibility.[44]

Crucial in this passage are the conditions under which the author encounters *Klandestinität*: as a worker. Neumann himself learns this language that speaks between signs. The responsibility to which he alludes is a general therapy for the working class:

> Clandestinity contemplates a therapy which would be capable of preventing the disaster. It is the growing secret among people, who assure themselves of their *living* worth. Their medium is the concrete, daily encounter, which may put its trust in the syntax of clandestinity, because it is not burdened with the translation questions of the respective ruling languages.
> These have only one possibility: to learn to speak the clandestine language, which requires them to relinquish their claim to dominance for a long time; probably for such a long time that they no longer can understand it in the midst of the clandestine thinking. (I hope you share my sense of humor?).[45]

The subversive potential of this clandestine language is constituted by the exclusion of authority, which, if it were to learn to speak this secret language, would no longer be able to think itself. Apart from the bravely attempted levity, the seriousness of Neumann's position relies on the representation of work, of everyday encounters, of a silence that must be understood. As such it is an ideal language that communicates without linguistic signs but is at the same time dependent on an external system, syntax, of signification that it opposes. This theory is the subject of the text *Die Klandestinität der Kesselreiniger* (The clandestinity of the boiler cleaners). In this text, as in all his work, Neumann posits a close connection between the material context of writing and the truth that the language of the text can tell, even if that truth is to admit that it cannot be told. It is clear from response within the GDR that this silence and its political dimension are subject to severe criticism. In samizdat, Cornelia Jentzsch responds to the theory of communication in Neumann's essay "Die Ethik der Sätze" with a pointed question: "But how should communication occur about apparently urgent, immediate, life-and-death decisions, concerning the (re)organization of a social body, which indeed should at least be unambiguous and also appropriate and, third, meaning all equally?"[46] Jentzsch raises the questions about the possibility of this language: Can a language be founded on a moral integrity that is "outside" that of the state? Would it constitute sufficient opposition? And how would it change social structures?

Neumann's indirect response is his use of clandestine language, the speech that occupies the absence demarcated by the reigning *Sprachmacht* (language power). Clandestine language and dominant language are mutually exclusive, though users of the former are capable of understanding the latter. The former is, in fact, both an inclusive and exclusive response to the latter. Clandestine language *is* solidarity. That is the point Neumann develops as *Klandestinität der Kesselreiniger* unfolds. Difficult to categorize generically, the work is a speculation on the relationship between language and society. It is a political poetics. The "Poetik dieses Schweigens" ("poetics of this silence")[47] is contingent on the working relationship between Gert Neumann and his Bulgarian co-worker Angel. At work, they speak their own language, "weil unsere Sprache ein Rotwelsch war" ("because our language was pidgin"),[48] as well as their own silence. They cover for each other. Neumann assiduously avoids sentimentality, however. This silence is not the pathos of the unspoken:

> I speak, certainly not of that silence of which one can be easily assured if one observes the present landscape for a language: that is a ruined socialism, which, until the eighth decade of this century, wastes itself on the obligation to a wayward text fossil, which sometimes: suddenly, it receives its shape in public and also private sentences: . . . "The teaching of Karl Marx is omnipotent, because it is true!"[49]

The silence of which he writes is not to be found in the present landscape: the resonance of the words "a ruined socialism" indicates the absence of truth in the present state of socialism, as well as the conventional connotation of the words. Such textual residues and the attempt to resignify these "fossils" occupy the center of the work. Neumann elsewhere in the text indicts the pleonasms of such slogans, all of which contain some transformation of the omnipotent and totalizing *all*: " 'Alles für das Volk' "

("Everything for the people").[50] Here, however, he is defining the silence that crosses over both public and private language, constituted by empty signs. He intends something different from mere meaninglessness: "I mean naturally that silence which then begins when it is in the brightness of dangers: 'The dictatorship does not represent the absent!' "[51] That which and those who are absent from public discourse are the subject of this text. Representation, political and aesthetic or linguistic, by definition evacuates that which is being represented. Neumann makes this connection in the assertion: "The dictatorship does not represent the absent!" On one level, Neumann thematizes the language of the dictatorship, inverts it, and reinscribes it into his poetics of silence. However, the language of silence attributes dialectically to official rhetoric the status of falsehood, rendering truth mute and silence a political stance. Neumann's texts inhabit this paradox. The thematization of silences must be inscribed, represented even in clandestine solidarity. The text is therefore highly citational. The author incorporates the language of state institutions into his own writing in an act of appropriation for the purpose of critique, though he expressly denies the possibility of written criticism in a language that is not a dialogue. Still, he includes letters written by the state lawyer who is assigned to represent his son, arrested for insulting a policeman;[52] he cites (ostensible) medical reports on the death of Angel,[53] as well as numerous political clichés and socialist slogans. The citationality of the text alludes heavily to a literary past: Neumann cites Mallarmé, Hamann, the Bulgarian poet Christo Botew, his own diaries. The point of these quotations becomes clear in the reading, the self-consciousness of the writing, and the direct addresses to the reader: all things, including history, enter discourse in the form of language. For Neumann, this entrance into discourse is contingent on, is literally and figuratively based on, work.

As a craftsman, a worker, a writer, the character Gert Neumann and the author coincide in the text. Writing, thinking, speculating, philosophizing are all as much a part of the daily routine as is manual labor. This text, ironically silenced in the GDR, epitomizes the success of the writer-worker, but with a twist:

> For this inescapably our tools had become files, hammers, wire brushes, glasses, hand brooms, and shovels, notebook and ball point pen. The writing tools . . . I hid in the beginning under a fire brick stone if I wasn't writing with them. I thought I had to protect even this text, which was originating through it, from an encounter with the observation, because indeed the goal of this very uncertain text was the defense of our possibilities, which I, in the morning, when I came into the shop from writing . . . , thought to have recognized in a message which lay forgotten on the boiler and which the observation with its contract for boiler cleaning thought to be able to

occupy . . . , in order to be able to suspend the nothing of our possibilities which offered itself freely to its eye. I thought that our possibilities, which had no language at all, would not be protected, if the observation could finally force my *writing* into illegality.[54]

This passage is centered on vigilance: Neumann's own "observance" with regard to observation; his care to place nothing in the gaze of the wide-open eye. More significant, however, is the positing of the actual boiler as the workplace. The enumeration of hammers to pens points to yet another connection between the *Handwerkzeuge* and the *Schreibzeug*. The writer, to play on the double meaning of *Zeuge* as used here as "witness," bears witness to work. Language is used as a metaphor for possibilities. As such, it must be protected, *bewahren* also containing the stem of truth, against its criminalization. Written silence, the silence that leaves a trace, that bears witness to the rhythm, syntax, and clandestine language of work and workers, must leave a trace, a written trace in order to counter "das Geflecht dichter werdender alltäglicher Lügen" ("the network of daily lies becoming ever more dense").[55] One of the ways of opposing the "daily lie" is to posit the possibility of a German language, which, Neumann concludes, is doubtful. His doubt, however, aligns with his convictions of the contextual specificity of the text. He begins the fourth part of this story of concentration[56] with an epigraph from Jacques Lacan's "Für Jakobson": " 'Daß man sage, bleibt vergessen hinter dem, was sich sagt in dem, was sich versteht' " ("that one would say, stays forgotten behind that which is said in that which is understood").[57] This quotation presides over the section about the speculations he made while on a trip to a nonsocialist foreign country,[58] West Germany, which begins with the confiscation of his manuscript by GDR customs, which is later retrieved at the German-German border. The German-German bureaucracy, landscape, and experience are frequently supposed to be suspended in the singular German language and its interpretation. This, Neumann suspects, is not the case. The German silence erases language, history, Germany. Regarding the role of interpretation and its historical specificity, Neumann writes:

In Germany, or however it would be to say, the drama exists without doubt in completely disparaging meanings of one and the same material: which probably only through this elegy, hopefully sharing with the reader or the reading in this writing, will again have to be brought together with thought, in order to take from this land its horrible pain, which threatens it like insanity: that these meanings of things do not exist in any language.[59]

Neumann laments the absence of a language adequate to the German condition and contrasts the situation of West to East, plenty versus lack, and the qualitatively differing powers of perception that result. The task of the reader or the reading is to be able to, to have to reconstruct the German dialogue in the thought process of reading the manuscript. The elegy is written not for a country divided or a lost landscape but for a language that cannot accommodate the interpretation of things: "And, it is not only a pity that this dialogue about the essence of this perception does not take place between the Germans; or, not yet: as it probably wants to exist through the aforementioned observation."[60]

This dissonance is resolved, finally, in an address given in 1991 in Ansbach, where Neumann was a fellow of the Lion's Club. His consideration, his speculation, his philosophizing remains, even after the *Wende*, the relationship between language and truth. Here, however, he adds the historical dimension of a specifically German history to his address. Neumann ultimately asserts that the clandestine language he advocated is transferable, in fact, imperatively transferable to the *new* conditions of a united Germany.

His final positing of what I have called a socialist resignification of silence is based on the forty years of silent history he perceives as German. Just as he describes the relationship between writing and reading as a *Begegnung* (encounter), as in the epigraph to this paper, so he defines the current political conditions between East and West Germany: "I think, the encounter of the Germans in the space of possible German unity waiting for them for forty years offers sufficient opportunity to return to the questions which Germany until then could only banish into the responsibility of history either not taking place or having taken place."[61] German unity, in other words, requires a new language, a linguistic place, corresponding to a geography, where the questions of silence in the form of German history are finally asked. He continues:

> However I want to dare [this assertion], in order not to have to let the search for Germany end already in the concept of unity; where this muzzle hinders the possibilities of speaking, which banishes from the conscious realm of guilt the encounters of the questions of truth that led, no contest, to the point of catastrophe in Germany again and again; where German speaking happily resides, when language is necessary for the name of the encountered.[62]

Germany does not end in German unity: it begins with a question of guilt and consciousness that can only take place in language. The act of writing, under the conditions of observation, can become an act of resistance. The clandestine language of Neumann's texts—the abstract speculations on the everyday, the language designed, written, silenced in order to evacuate itself from the official language of censorship—this is the language that occupies and represents the absence imposed and reassures Neumann that there is a place of language—the language of resistance, the language of silence—that subverts dictatorship, no matter what its guise. "This poetics of resistance which has become familiar to me as given . . . is in my opinion worthy of creating reality in the dialogue of the Germans."[63]

Neumann knows that geographic and constitutional unity is only the beginning for a German-German dialogue. Consistent with his theory of clandestine language, reality is constituted by the language of things, of silence, and of solidarity, rather than one of political divisiveness. His work, read against that of Erb, Schedlinski, and Stötzer, indicates the degree of damage that the muteness of the German-German dialogue has inflicted. The resignification of the GDR language of silence, solidarity, and resistance now must include a consideration of the competing language of betrayal, unstable subjectivity, and secrecy. Somewhere between these two lies a language of dialogue. That language, its syntax and semantics, is desperately needed, and has yet to be translated.[64]

Appendix: Authors' Biographies and Works

Elke Erb   Born in 1938 in the Eifel, Erb moved to the GDR in 1949. She has been living as a writer since 1967 and has produced many volumes of poetry, prose, and translations. The volume she edited with Sascha Anderson, *Berührung ist nur eine Randerscheinung* (1985), marked the first significant collection of "new" lyric from the GDR. She won the Peter-Huchel-Preis for the volume *Kastanienallee* in 1988. *Unschuld, du Licht meiner Augen*, a collection of poetry, appeared in 1994. The following year, Erb also published a volume of essays, *Der wilde Forst, der tiefe Wald* (1995). Since then, Erb has published a volume of poetry and diary entries, *Mensch sein, nicht* (Basel, 1998), and a poetry/prose collection, *Sachverstand* (Basel, 2000). She lives in Berlin. (Adapted from her *Winkelzüge oder nicht vermutete, aufschlussreiche Verhältnisse*, 1991.)

Gert Neumann   Born in Heilsberg in 1942, Neumann has worked as a tractor operator and a metal worker, among other things. He went to the Johannes R. Becher literary institute in Leipzig but was exmatriculated in 1969 and excluded from the SED. He then worked at various trades in Leipzig. Since 1986, he has been an independent writer in Berlin (GDR). He edited *Anschlag* and *Zweite Person* and contributed to other self-published journals. His works include the novel *Elf Uhr* (1981), published only in the West (1981), *Die Klandestinität der Kesselreiniger. Ein Versuch des Sprechens* (The clandestinity of the boiler cleaners: An attempt at speaking) (1989), *Die Schuld der Worte* (The guilt of words), his only work published "officially" in the GDR (1989), and his more recent essayistic publications, *Übungen jenseits der Möglichkeit* (1991), the last published by Koren and Debes, a publishing house he helped found. Throughout the 1990s, Neumann received a number of literary sponsorships, including the first international stipend awarded by the Robert Bosch Foundation and one from the Deutschen Literaturfond. In 1998, he held the inaugural lectures on poetics for the Dresden series "Literature in Central Europe," published in *Verhaftet*, with essays by Martin Walser and the literary scholar Walter Schmitz (Dresden, 1999). He recently published a novel of a post-reunification attempt at East-West communication, *Anschlag* (Cologne, 1999). (Adapted from *Verhaftet*, 91.)

Gabriele Stötzer   Born in 1953 in Emleben, Stötzer now lives in Erfurt. She studied to be a medical technician and did her *Abitur* at night school. From 1973 to 1976 she studied German and art education in Erfurt and was exmatriculated. She spent time in prison. Since 1980, she has been living as a freelance writer and filmmaker, has worked in women's groups, and is involved in the art center in Erfurt. Her first volume of poetry, *zügel los*, appeared in 1990. She has since published *grenzen los fremd gehen* (1992) and *erfurter roulette* (1995).

Rainer Schedlinski   Born in 1956 in Magdeburg, Schedlinski grew up in the region and moved in 1994 to Berlin, where he currently resides. He trained as a *Wirtschafts-kaufmann* until 1974 and held a variety of jobs before he became active in the literary scene in Berlin. His publications include *die rationen des ja und des nein* (1990), *letzte bilder* (essays, 1990), *die arroganz der ohnmacht* (essays, 1990), and *die männer/der frauen* (poems, 1991). From 1986 to 1989 he edited the *ariadnefabrik*. Schedlinski edited the *Abriss der ariadnefabrik* along with Andreas Koziol. He was a co-founder of Galrev, a publishing house for poetry from the East and the West. His leadership was suspended when his involvement with the Stasi came to be known. He later resumed this position. His poetry has been translated and anthologized.

Notes

All translations, unless otherwise indicated, are my own. I thank Frauke E. Lenckos for her assistance with difficult passages. I would also like to thank Roger Blood, whose insights into the category of the aesthetic inform my own.

1. The terms "unofficial," "avant-garde," "alternative culture," "scene," and "literary subculture" have been used to describe the literary production by writers of the GDR in the 1980s. Klaus Michael, in "Feindbild Literatur: Die Biermann-Affäre, Staatssicherheit und die Herausbildung einer literarischen Alternativkultur in der DDR," *Aus Politik und Zeitgeschichte. Beilage zur Wochenzeitung Das Parlament B* 22–23, no. 93 (28 May 1993): 23–31, points out the difficulty of applying *"Subkultur"* and *"Gegenkultur"* to the self-published journals of the 1980s in light of the documented Stasi involvement. He suggests the term *"ausgegrenzte Kultur"* (excluded or marked off culture, 28) instead. It is clear that the individual authors require individual treatment, though certain similarities in their theory of language and its relation to society emerge.

2. For an overview of this type of literary production, see Luise von Flotow, "*Samizdat* in East Berlin," *Cross Currents: A Yearbook of Central European Culture* 9 (1990): 197–218, esp. 212. Von Flotow notes that Neumann was editor of the journal *Anschlag* and a frequent contributor to other publications. She cogently summarizes his language theory as follows: "Neumann's critique of meaninglessness, and his response to the realization that 'die Materie, in der Wahrheit lebt, ist vernichtet' [the material in which truth resides has been destroyed], must, he assumes, constitute him as an opponent since any view or use of language which places communication and

dialogue at its center frees language from official control and interpretation, and in so doing enters the realm of the political" (212–13).

3. For a compelling work on censorship and self-censorship, see Ernest Wichner and Herbert Wiesner, eds., *"Literaturentwicklungsprozesse"*: *Die Zensur der Literatur in der DDR* (Frankfurt am Main, 1993), esp. the contribution by Gert Neumann, "Gespräch und Widerstand: Das nabeloonische Chaos," 144–65. See Thomas Beckermann, " 'Die Diktatur repräsentiert das Abwesende nicht': Essay on Monika Maron, Wolfgang Hilbig and Gert Neumann," in *German Literature at a Time of Change: 1989–1990: German Unity and German Identity in a Literary Perspective*, ed. Arthur Williams, Stuart Parkes, and Roland Smith (Bern, 1991), 97–116, esp. 108–11 for a specific analysis of Neumann's use of silence as a form of communication.

4. See Anneli Hartmann, "Schreiben in der Tradition der Avantgarde: Neue Lyrik in der DDR," *Amsterdamer Beiträge zur neueren Germanistik* 26 (1988): 1–37 (special issue: *DDR-Lyrik im Kontext*, ed. Christine Cosentino, Wolfgang Ertl, and Gerd Labroisse). In this essay, Hartmann points out the contradiction of an "avant-garde" tradition and locates the production of GDR poetry in a historical framework that includes futurism, dadaism, and expressionism; she also marks the moments of difference, particularly in the *Zwangsläufigkeit* (inevitability) of the contemporary, self-conscious experimentation of the GDR poets (esp. 16). The application of the term "avant-garde" is persistently problematic, owing to the difficulty of documenting influence.

5. See Peter Böthig and Klaus Michael, eds., *MachtSpiele: Literatur und Staatssicherheit* (Leipzig, 1993). For a thorough and sustained presentation of the Stasi's involvement in the literary life of the GDR see Joachim Walther, *Sicherungsbereich Literatur: Schriftsteller und Staatssicherheit in der Deutschen Demokratischen Republik* (Berlin, 1996). Of particular interest is the characterization of Anderson's duty to "depoliticize" the Prenzlauer Berg scene (640–41).

6. See my "Die Sprache der Geduld: Produzierendes Denken bei Elke Erb," in *Zwischen Gestern und Morgen: Schriftstellerinnen der DDR aus amerikanischer Sicht*, ed. Ute Brandes (Berlin, 1992), 263–76. Erb and Sascha Anderson co-edited the volume *Berührung ist nur eine Randerscheinung: Neue Literatur aus der DDR* (Cologne, 1985), which made texts by relatively unknown authors available. Some authors were to have been represented in an "Akademie-Anthologie," the repression of which Klaus Michael views as the beginning of criminalization of younger authors. See Klaus Michael, "Eine verschollene Anthologie: Zentralkomitee, Staatssicherheit und die Geschichte eines Buches," *MachtSpiele*, 202–16, esp. 202, 213. On Erb's role as a "model" or "mentor" for the poetics and personalities of the Prenzlauer Berg see Friederike Eigler, "At the Margins of East Berlin's 'Counter-Culture': Elke Erb's *Winkelzüge* and Gabriele Kachold's *zügel los*," *Women in German Yearbook* 9 (1993): 146–61, and Birgit Dahlke, "Avant-gardist, Mediator, and . . . Mentor?" *Women in German Yearbook* 13 (1997): 123–32.

7. Elke Erb, *Winkelzüge oder nicht vermutete aufschlussreiche Verhältnisse*. Illus. Angela Hampel (Berlin, 1992): 171 ff., here 171.

8. Ibid., 142.

9. Ibid., 172.

10. Ibid., 173.

11. Ibid., 174.

12. For a reading of Erb's work since the *Wende*, see Barbara Mabee, "Footprints

Revisited or 'Life in the Changed Space That I Don't Know': Elke Erb's Poetry Since 1989," in *Studies in 20th Century Literature* 21, no. 1 (winter 1997): 161–85 (special issue on contemporary German poetry, ed. James Rolleston). Erb's own poetological essay, in which she interrogates her poetic relationship with sociopolitical changes, appears in the same volume. See "Fundamentally Grounded (Gründlich mit Grund)," trans. James Rolleston et al., 187–218, which first appeared in her prose volume *Der wilde Forst, der tiefe Wald* (Göttingen, 1995), 353–79. She has also published a volume of poetry titled *Unschuld, du Licht meiner Augen* (Göttingen, 1994). More current work includes *Mensch sein, nicht* (Basel, 1998) and *Sachverstand* (Basel, 2000).

13. Michael Thulin, *Abriss der Ariadnefabrik*, ed. Andreas Koziol and Rainer Schedlinski (Berlin, 1990), 83.

14. Ibid. See also Erk Grimm, "Rainer Schedlinksi," *Kritisches Lexikon zur deutschsprachigen Gegenwartsliteratur 42. Nachlieferung* (forthcoming). He notes the relation between speaking and silence and refers to Thulin's reception of Schedlinski's work.

15. Thulin, *Abriss*, 88.

16. Ibid., 85.

17. Rainer Schedlinski, *die rationen des ja und des nein* (Frankfurt am Main, 1990), 41. This volume is a reprint, with one added chapter, of an Aufbau edition from 1988.

18. Ibid. (Aufbau Verlag, 1988), 32.

19. Ibid., 131.

20. Ibid., 134.

21. Ibid.

22. Ibid., 135.

23. Ibid., 137.

24. Ibid., 150.

25. Ibid., 139.

26. Ibid., 153.

27. Ibid., 154.

28. Gabriele Kachold, "Das Gesetz der Szene," *Kontext* 5 (March 1989): n.p., reprinted in *Alles ist im Untergrund Obenauf . . . eine Auswahl aus Kontext 1–7* (Everything in the Underground is at the top . . . a selection from *Kontext* , 1–7), ed. Torsten Metelka (1990), 64–72. A different version of this poem also appeared in Gabriele Stötzer, *grenzen los fremd gehen* (Berlin, 1992), 133–36. I thank Stötzer for her generous response to my inquiries about the specifics of the poem. She indicates that the poem could refer to the Prenzlauer Berg scene as a literary object of interest to her, but she also includes her own Erfurt environment. The meaning of the poem, I think, offers a more generalized interpretation of the topography of sexual and social relations. See also Beth Linklater, "Erotic Provocations: Gabriele Stötzer-Kachold's Reclaiming of the Female Body?" *Women in German Yearbook* 13 (1997): 151–70.

29. Kachold, *Alles ist im Untergrund*, 64.

30. Ibid.

31. Ibid.

32. Ibid., 67.

33. Ibid.

34. Ibid., 68.

35. Ibid., 69.

36. Ibid., 72.

37. See Antonia Grunenberg, "In den Räumen der Sprache: Gedankenbilder zur Literatur Gert Neumanns," *Text + Kritik* (special issue, *Die Andere Sprache: Neue DDR-Literatur der 8oer Jahre*, ed. Heinz Ludwig Arnold) (1990), 206–13, esp. 210–11. Grunenberg connects the activity of clandestine writing to the secret spaces in Neumann's work. See also Walter Schmitz, "Über Gert Neumann," in *Verhaftet* (Dresden, 1999), 97–131, for an extensive treatment of Neumann's intellectual biography in the contexts of the GDR and an undivided Germany. Schmitz also attends to issues of writing, work, and silence. On clandestinity, see 122 f. This work also contains a useful bibliography of Neumann's literary production.

38. Gert Neumann, *Elf Uhr* (Eleven o'clock) (Frankfurt am Main, 1981); *Die Klandestinität der Kesselreiniger: Ein Versuch des Sprechens* (The clandestinity of the boiler cleaners: An attempt at speaking) (Frankfurt am Main, 1989); as well as in *Die Schuld der Worte* (The guilt of words), his only work published "officially" in the GDR (Rostock, 1989), and *Übungen jenseits der Möglichkeit* (Exercises beyond possibility) (Frankfurt am Main, 1991).

39. Neumann, *Elf Uhr*, 5.

40. See Günter Saße, " 'Der Kampf gegen die Versteinerung der Materie Wirklichkeit durch die Sprache': Zur Systematik sprachthematisierender Literatur aus Anlaß von Gert Neumanns *Elf Uhr*," in *Die Schuld der Worte*, ed. Paul Gerhard Klussmann and Heinrich Mohr (Bonn, 1987), 196–219, here 201.

41. Neumann, *Übungen jenseits der Möglichkeit*, 27–56, 13.

42. Silvia Morawitz, "Die Freiheit des Gesprächs . . . ," in *ariadnefabrik* 3.89, reprinted in Thulin, *Abriss*, 255–58, here 258. "Klandestinität . . . ist der Name, den der Autor seinen Ahnungen und Gewißheiten von dem Dingen innewohnenden Geheimnis und der Möglichkeit, in einem Gespräch mit ihnen von ihrem Wesen etwas erscheinen zu lassen, gegeben hat."

43. "Gewalt vermag die Wahrheit nicht zu zwingen. Es ist erstaunlich, daß der Mensch immer wieder darauf verfällt. Die Sprache der Gewalt ist so reduziert, daß sie die Dinge gar nicht mehr zu treffen vermag. Die Sprache der Gewalt muß sich an der Existenz eines Feindes orientieren; und ihre Vollendung ist das Todesurteil, das von der wahnsinnigen Hoffnung lebt, mit der Vernichtung des im Menschen lebenden Arguments gegen eine *herrschende* Wahrheitspraxis die Wahrheit endgültig ins Objekt gezwungen zu haben . . ." (Neumann, *Übungen jenseits der Möglichkeit*, 50).

44. Ibid., 53. "Für mein Denken . . . folgt aus dieser Analyse, die meiner Meinung nach notwendig ist, weil es unausweichlich der Fall ist und sein wird, daß der Realsozialismus existiert- : die Unterstützung der Praxis der *Klandestinität*, die eine Kultur ist, der ich in meinem Leben als Arbeiter begegnet bin, das ohne Solidarität zu leben hat . . . : und an dieser außerordentlichen Prüfung entweder zerbricht, oder eine Sprache innerhalb der Zeichen der Praxis zu ahnen und zu sprechen beginnt, die sich, vorsichtig, bemüht, der Verantwortung wieder näher zu kommen."

45. Ibid., 53–54. "Die Klandestinität denkt über eine Therapie nach, die das Verhängnis abzuwenden vermag. Sie ist das, wachsende, Geheimnis zwischen den Menschen, die sich ihrer *lebendigen* Würde vergewissern. Ihr Medium ist die konkrete, alltägliche, Begegnung, die auf die Syntax der Klandestinität vertrauen darf, weil sie mit keinen Übersetzungsfragen in die jeweils herrschenden Sprachen belastet ist. Diese haben nur eine Möglichkeit,: die klandestine Sprache sprechen zu lernen, was von ihnen verlangt, ihren Herrschaftsanspruch auf sehr lange Zeit aufzugeben;

wahrscheinlich auf solche eine lange Zeit, daß sie ihn gar nicht mehr, inmitten des klandestinen Denkens, verstehen können. (Ich hoffe, Sie teilen meinen Humor?!)."

46. Cornelia Jentzsch, "Eine Anmerkung" (A comment), in Thulin, *Abriss,* 293. "Wie sollte aber die Kommunikation über anscheinend lebenswichtige, unmittelbare Entscheidungen, die die (Re)-organisation eines gesellschaftlichen Körpers betreffen, erfolgen, die ja zumindest eindeutig sein müßte und des weiteren zutreffend und drittens alle gleichsam meinend?"

47. Neumann, *Die Klandestinität der Kesselreiniger,* 11.

48. Ibid., 93.

49. Ibid., 14. "Ich spreche, ganz sicher, nicht von jenem Schweigen, dessen man sich leicht vergewissern kann, wenn man sich die gegenwärtige Landschaft für eine Sprache betrachtet: die ein verwahrloster Sozialismus ist, der einem, bis ins achte Jahrzehnt dieses Jahrhunderts, verirrten Textfossil verpflichtet zu sein vorgibt, das manchmal: plötzlich, seine Gestalt in öffentlichen und auch privaten Sätzen bekommt: . . ."Die Lehre von Karl Marx ist allmächtig, weil sie wahr ist!"

50. Ibid., 103.

51. Ibid., 14. "Ich meine, natürlich, jenes Schweigen, das denn beginnt, wenn, im Glanz der Gefahren, gesagt ist: " 'Die Diktatur repräsentiert das Abwesende nicht!' "

52. Ibid., 16.

53. Ibid., 175 ff.

54. Ibid., 85–86. "Deshalb waren unausweichlich unsere Handwerkzeuge Feilen, Hämmer, Drahtbürsten, Brillen, Handfeger und Kehrschaufel, Notizheft und Kugelschreiber geworden. Das Schreibzeug . . . versteckte ich anfangs unter einem Schamottstein, wenn ich nicht damit schrieb. Ich meinte, auch diesen durch es entstehenden Text vor einer Begegnung mit der Observation bewahren zu müssen, da doch das Ziel dieses sehr unsicheren Textes die Verteidigung unserer Möglichkeiten war, die ich, am Morgen, als ich vom Schreiben in die Werkstatt gekommen war . . . , in einer, auf dem Kessel kaum mehr zu erinnernden, Nachricht zu erkennen meinte und die die Observation mit ihrem Auftrag zum Kesselreinigen meinte besetzen zu dürfen . . . , um so das sich ihrem Auge freilich bietende Nichts unserer Möglichkeiten aufheben zu können. Ich dachte, daß unsere Möglichkeiten, die überhaupt keine Sprache hatten, nicht verteidigt wären, wenn die Observation mein *Schreiben,* schließlich, in die Illegalität zwingen konnte."

55. Ibid., 100.

56. Ibid., 119.

57. Ibid.,

58. Ibid., 120.

59. Ibid., 128. "In Deutschland, oder wie zu sagen wäre, existiert ohne Zweifel das Drama vollkommen auseinandertreibender Deutungen ein und desselben Materials: die wahrscheinlich nur durch diese, dem Leser oder dem Lesen sich hoffentlich in diesem Schreiben mitteilenden, Elegie wieder zum Denken zusammengefügt werden können: oder zusammengefügt werden müssen; um diesem Land seinen schrecklichen Schmerz zu nehmen, der ihm wie Wahnsinn droht: daß diese Deutungen der Dinge in keiner Sprache existieren."

60. Ibid., 129. "Und, es ist nicht nur schade, daß es dieses Gespräch über das Wesen dieses Wahrgenommenen zwischen den Deutschen nicht gibt; oder, noch nicht gibt: da es wohl durch die soeben vorangegangene Bemerkung existieren will."

61. Neumann, *Übungen jenseits der Möglichkeit,* 161. "Ich denke, die Begegnung

der Deutschen im sie vierzig Jahre erwartenden Raum möglicher deutscher Einheit bietet genügend Gelegenheit, zu Fragen zurückzukehren, die Deutschland bis dorthin in die Verantwortung nicht stattfindender oder stattgefundener Geschichte zu verbannen wußte."

62. Ibid. "Ich will sie [diese Behauptung] aber wagen, um die Suche nach Deutschland nicht schon im Begriff Einheit enden lassen zu müssen: wo dieser Knebel die Möglichkeiten des Sprechens hindert, die von Deutschland unbestritten wieder und wieder bis in die Qualität der Katastrophe geführten Berührungen der Fragen der Wahrheit aus dem Bewußtseinsraum der Schuld zu vertreiben-, wo sich das deutsche Sprechen ganz gern aufhält, wenn Sprache für den Namen des Berührten notwendig ist."

63. Ibid., 164. "Diese mir als selbstverständlich bekanntgewordene . . . Poetik des Widerstands ist meiner Meinung nach würdig, im Gespräch der Deutschen Wirklichkeit zu stiften."

64. See Klaus Humann, ed., *Schweigen ist Schuld: Ein Lesebuch der Verlagsinitiative gegen Gewalt und Fremdenhaß* (Frankfurt am Main, 1993).

Wir treten aus unseren Rollen heraus:
Theater Intellectuals and Public Spheres

The Intellectual Spectacle: Conscience or Complicity?

"We cast off our roles." At once exhortation and performative utterance, this call to abandon the roles and rules prescribed by the state was the motto of the Initiative 4 November, the group of theater and film professionals who organized the last and largest demonstration in the German Democratic Republic in Alexanderplatz, East Berlin, on 4 November 1989. Taking its cue from statements issued by the informal independent group, the New Forum, and the official writers' association,[1] the initiative was led by (primarily younger) members of metropolitan cultural institutions such as the Deutsches Theater, Volksbühne, and the Berliner Ensemble. It called for public debate on the authority of the Socialist Unity Party (SED) and its control over political, socioeconomic, and cultural practice, while reiterating their commitment to preserving *a* socialist society against the incursions of capitalism and the perceived social Darwinism of West Germany.[2] Mindful of police attacks on demonstrators protesting the celebration of the GDR's fortieth anniversary on 9 October, many participants at the demonstration invoked the GDR constitution's articles on freedom of speech and assembly. They wished to protest arbitrary restrictions on those freedoms and to challenge the authority of laws criminalizing the dissemination of news from unauthorized sources or the establishment of unauthorized meetings as "dangerous to the state"(*Wir treten aus*).[3]

Against the attempts by the state security apparatus to repress unauthorized speech as illegitimate and therefore seditious, this demonstration appeared at the moment to offer an extraordinary coincidence of life and art, performance and representation, theater and public sphere, a utopian space in which the intellectual, particularly the theater intellectual, might be agent par excellence of social change. Especially for those old enough to have participated in the founding of the GDR and who identified with its claim to be the only antifascist German state (such as Stefan Heym and Christa Wolf), the event constituted a revolutionary encounter between progressive intellectuals and a people belatedly come of age (*Wir treten aus*, 219–21, 223–35). In their eyes, this encounter might exorcise the specters of failed revolution, disengaged intellectuals, and an indifferent populace, which had haunted German history since the French Revolution, from Georg Büchner's indictment of the idealized revolution of the young Germans in the 1840s to Bertolt Brecht's regret that the transformation of East Germany came about without the "cleansing effect of revolution."[4]

Younger participants in the demonstration (those born into the GDR) may not have invoked revolution, but they tended nonetheless to share with those who did a sense that the events of the moment vindicated the role of the intellectual in general, and of the theater intellectual in particular, on the forefront of social change. They saw themselves casting off the role of performers whose reliance on state support helped legitimate the SED as source of that support and taking on the role of a vanguard testing out new roles in advance of their general enactment in society. With the possible exception of Heiner Müller, who read a statement—on behalf of an uninvited group of workers pushing for independent unions— criticizing the privileges that protected artists from the deprivations of daily life in the GDR,[5] the theater intellectuals assumed for the most part the political *transitivity* of the theater as well as the value of their mediation between the state and the people and thus acted in the belief that theater was also and immediately politics. But, if "theater intellectuals" here refers to practitioners of theater and other forms of performance who are critically engaged with the role of social interpreter, it also implicitly poses the question of the *intransitivity* of this activity and of the limited political agency of theater intellectuals. How much of a vanguard for social change was this group of people whose relative freedom of movement, even of criticism, was a function less of radical dissent than of their privileged status as more or less state-sponsored cultural practitioners?

Today, the utopian union of theater and social action may seem little more than the reflection—not the critique—of privilege. Since the unification of Germany in 1990, socialist intellectuals who treated as a betrayal of socialism the general if not unanimous shift in the last months of the GDR toward the promise of economic well-being and conservative politics offered by the West have been castigated (often by former GDR intellectuals) for expressing the arrogance of privilege.[6] More recently, West German critics, including those once identified with the Left, have indicted GDR intellectuals who persist in defending socialist ideals, arguing that their advocacy for the idea of socialism necessarily grants "unlimited credit to a corrupt and repressive 'actually existing socialism.' "[7] Theater writers who have argued that the public occasion of theater enabled the adumbration of a counter public sphere (*Gegenöffentlichkeit*) against the party's attempt to monopolize legitimate speech in the electronic and print media[8] have been attacked on the grounds that the subsidized theater in the GDR offered a mere imitation public sphere (*Ersatzöffentlichkeit*) or, worse, publicity for the SED state.[9]

The problem with this scenario is that it assimilates the actions of GDR intellectuals to the agency of the SED state and attributes totalitarian power to a state that was in fact subject to internal contradictions as well as external pressures. Attacking GDR intellectuals for associating with a Stalinist party, the accusers beat them with the bluntest of Stalinist instruments, the charge of "enemy of the people."[10] This charge fixes in an eternal, diabolically controlled present the histories of a range of cultural institutions and practices whose links to the armature of the state varied across time and place. The SED attached great importance to the contribution of culture to "building socialist society," as is indicated by the maintenance of sixty-eight stationary theaters and more than two hundred cultural venues and by the Ministry of Culture's boast of ten million yearly theater visits by sixteen million inhabitants by the 1980s.[11] It is also arguable that, especially since the detente of the 1970s, the SED state gained prestige and hard currency from the Western publication and performance of work by writers critical of the status quo, such as Heiner Müller and Ulrich Plenzdorf.[12] It does not, however, inevitably follow that those who stayed in the GDR out of a commitment to socialism or at least to a noncapitalist alternative to West Germany reinforced the SED's version of "real socialism" (*Realsozialismus*) by their mere presence, nor that any contact between cultural practitioners and party bureaucrats amounted necessarily to "*unlimited* credit" for the regime.

While misrecognizing the attachment of GDR intellectuals to their country as mere submission to the SED regime, this scenario also misreads the departure of dissidents as nothing more than evidence of the illegitimacy of the GDR. This reading ignores the testimony of dissidents such as Freya Klier and Stephan Krawczyk, expelled in 1988, who defied the legitimation monopoly of the SED by treating taboo subjects such as the indifference of GDR youth to SED pieties, but who refused to abandon the hope of transforming the GDR under the aegis of a reinvigorated socialism. It also leaves out the GDR theater intellectuals who attempted to negotiate the terrain between these extremes, to carve out critical space within existing institutions, especially in regions outside Berlin, or those whose work in institutions less prestigious than the flagship theaters (chil-

dren's theater, community cultural centers, or the churches) challenged
SED cultural policies marginalizing the representation on stage or elsewhere of current social problems. This range of activities, places, and occasions of performance suggests that the public spheres animated and inhab-
ited by GDR theater intellectuals in the 1980s should not be completely
reduced to a dichotomy between a uniformly oppressive state and a tiny,
persecuted underground, but should be understood as a complex of substitute public spheres, occasionally clearly adversarial, more often elements
of a *virtual* public sphere, a site and discourse of subjunctive action within
a thoroughly circumscribed frame of indicative legitimacy.[13] This essay will
sketch key moments in the formation of this dichotomy as well as the
scattered but not insignificant traces of public spheres between them.

**The Commitment Melodrama: Aesthetics,
Conviction, and the Cold War**
The scenario that is bent on translating commitment into capitulation, on
reducing identification with a future socialist society to loyalty to its actual
parody, is not the drama of recognition and historic reversal it pretends to
be but, rather, a rerun of a familiar if half-remembered cold war melodrama.
Although the protagonists, the audience, and the immediate issues at stake
at the formal conclusion of the cold war in Germany were by no means
identical with those at the start, the echoes in the script are noteworthy.
West German critics at the forefront of the attack on the remnants of
GDR culture have argued that their own Western affiliation is immaterial
in the face of East German intellectual complicity with power,[14] but the
ongoing attack on an aesthetics of conviction remains intimately bound
up with the history of West German ambivalence about its Eastern Other.
Ulrich Greiner's dismissal of an aesthetics of moral conviction (*Gesinnungsästhetik*), like Frank Schirrmacher's disdain for the engaged literature
of West Germany,[15] bears a significant resemblance to the attacks of Martin
Esslin, Hannah Arendt, and others on the Stalinist contamination of art by
politics. Before we can differentiate the roles of theater intellectuals within
(and occasionally without) state institutions in the final years of the GDR
from the roles assigned them in the commitment melodrama, we need an
outline of the drama of solidarity and betrayal played out between the two
German states in the first decade or so of the cold war.

   Played with particular intensity by the Congress on Cultural Freedom
(funded by the CIA), the melodrama of commitment portrayed the engagement of artists as at best the corruption of art by politics and at worst
as the sign of madness. As in 1990, the primary charges leveled against East
German intellectuals in the 1950s were self-delusion and willing suppres-

sion of morality due to dogged loyalty to a totalitarian state.[16] The figure of Brecht as exemplary committed artist became, as André Müller, author of *Crusade Against Brecht*, has pointed out, a lightning rod for attacks on the legitimacy of the GDR as a whole at moments of crisis, especially in 1953 (the year of Stalin's death and the workers' rebellion in East Berlin), 1956 (Khrushchev's denunciation of Stalin at the Soviet Communist Party Congress, followed by the Soviet suppression of the Hungarian uprising), and 1961 (after the erection of the Berlin Wall).[17] At their most hysterical, the crusaders demanded that Brecht be banned from West German stages on the ground that any expression from him amounted not only to communist propaganda but also to the production of "means to bring about the destruction of the West by the East," augmenting the "immediate threat of the Red Army."[18] The more familiar strategy, however, especially in the United States, has been the attempt to rescue the "artist" Brecht from the misguided communist functionary. The thesis of Martin Esslin's *Bertolt Brecht: A Choice of Evils* (1959), which attributes Brecht's personal amorality to marxism and his artistic achievements to the triumph of the talented practitioner over the dogmas of socialist theory,[19] remains enormously influential, as an anti-intellectual reflex as much as a specifically anti-marxist argument, as its reappearance in a recent textbook and its regurgitation in the *New York Times* confirm.[20]

For its part, the SED exhorted socialist intellectuals to contribute to the GDR's struggle against capitalist encroachment and used their loyalty, however ambivalent, to bolster the legitimacy of the state on the international stage. The SED's cultural policy, especially in the first decade, routinely dismissed deviations from a narrowly functionalist definition of socialist realism—"the ideological reeducation of the working masses in the interests of socialism"[21]—including Brecht's work from the *Lehrstücke* to the parables, as "formalism," "alien *(volksfremde)* decadence," or "nostalgia for Weimar modernism."[22] The policy went as far as to associate artistic experimentation with the "warmongering of American imperialism."[23] Nonetheless, even in this climate of hysterical antimodernism, party ideologues from General Secretary Walter Ulbricht on down did not hesitate to appropriate the work of Brecht and his successors such as Heiner Müller as evidence for socialist reconstruction in the arts and as a weapon in the cold war.[24] This cold war discourse persists well into the era of thaw and detente: as late as 1988, in a speech commemorating Brecht's ninetieth birthday, the GDR minister of culture was praising Brecht as a "fighter against capitalist exploitation" whose work is testimony to the possibility of "mobilizing reason in the struggle against irrationalism and SDI [Strategic Defense Initiative]."[25]

Brecht's contribution to the discourse of *Kulturpolitik* in the founding decade of the GDR offers ample testimony to the persistent, indeed
constitutive, tension in GDR intellectual engagement between loyalty to
socialist ideals and doubts about their reification as instruments of SED
hegemony. Whereas Ulbricht placed the blame for growing pressures on
East-West coexistence squarely on "American imperialism," Brecht appealed to the possibility of intellectual cooperation across borders. In the
"Open Letter to German Artists" (1949), for instance, he invokes the
possibility of peaceful reunification in a climate of artistic and political
freedom, but, in insisting on the restriction on the freedom of those celebrating "warmongering and racial hatred," raises the question of the arbitrary extension of this restriction to other critics of SED hegemony
(GW, 19: 495–96). Furthermore, while expressing qualified support for
the SED in the wake of the uprising on 17 June 1953, Brecht, along
with contemporaries such as Stefan Heym and Wolfgang Harich, used the
occasion to challenge SED dogma on the "progressive arts" (*fortschrittliche
Kunst*).[26] In "Cultural Policy and the Academy of Arts," Brecht argued
that the cultural functionaries' version of socialist realism amounted to
a kitsch reduction of the Soviet tradition (GW, 19:541). Attacking this
dispensation as the tyranny of anachronistic forms over a realistic reassessment of the current situation (GW, 16:933), Brecht turned the SED's
campaign against formalism against itself, contending that cutting artistic
representation against a prefabricated yardstick was not merely an aesthetic
error but a social and political one because it resolved conflicts in fiction
rather than in reality and thus provided illusory solutions to real problems
(GW, 19:542).

Critical though he was of the functionalism of the party line, Brecht
nonetheless called on intellectuals, especially in the theater, to contribute
to the "self-understanding of the nation" (GW, 16:931). Calling this participation a "privilege" rather than a burden, Brecht invoked the authority
of the "working masses" as the "new, determining theater public" (931).
Even as he saluted the working masses as the vanguard of a new publicity, however, Brecht registered doubts about the resistance of actual
audiences (AJ, 2:596), as well as their ambivalent response to change
from above:

> The cleansing [*reinigende*] process of revolution was not granted to Germany.
> The great transformation that otherwise follows a revolution arrived without
> it. . . . [I]n the context of a new way of life which was changing daily and
> for which substantial sections of the population still lacked appropriately
> new ways of thinking and feeling, art cannot appeal simply to the instinct
> and emotions of its motley audience. It cannot allow itself to be led by

the audience's applause or displeasure; on the other hand, representing the interests of the new vanguard class, art cannot allow itself to be cut off from the audience it must lead. (16:907)[27]

Vacillating between the socialist intellectual's attachment to the ideally determining role of the critical audience and the somewhat paternalistic regret that this audience needs to be led to "new ways of thinking and feeling," this passage betrays a fundamental contradiction. The "new determining public" (bestimmendes Publikum) that is to inaugurate a new socialist and democratic public sphere is figured here as a passive audience whose role is to endorse the "great transformation" led by intellectuals rather than to challenge it. In this dispensation, theater is no longer a site of virtual publicity, a site for the symbolic invocation of utopia, but rather the reification of critical publicity in the form of the already-arrived Arbeiter-und-Bauern-Staat.

"A Family Business": Benevolent Despotism as Cultural Policy

Brecht's contradictory representation of the people as "determining public," as a vanguard that is nonetheless only an audience, has proved remarkably tenacious, as Heym's and Wolf's alternation between celebration and execration of the "mob" confirms. Although, in its utopian formulation, the socialist public sphere ought to replace the degraded publicity of advanced capitalism with forums for ongoing direct democracy from local workplace to Central Committee,[28] the actual practice of "democratic centralism" tended to be authoritarian and unaccountable, disallowing or disarming activity that challenged the axiom of the SED's claim to legitimate authority (Führungsanspruch).[29] For all their ambivalence toward the actual cultural and social policy of the SED, intellectuals of the generation who remembered the chaos of the "rubble years" and the hopes of the "socialist reconstruction" could not quite abandon the notion of an exclusive claim to legitimate authority according to which the SED would be not merely the ruling party but the effective horizon of legitimate publicity.

At their most affirmative, GDR theater intellectuals summoned the authority of the SED as Staatspartei to secure the prestige of central cultural institutions. Manfred Wekwerth, member of the Central Committee of the SED, formal Stasi informant, and former general director (Intendant) of the Berliner Ensemble, was the affirmative intellectual par excellence, one whose multiple institutional roles reflected the subordination of cultural institutions to political domination. Wekwerth's tenure, from 1977 to 1990, was characterized by resistance to the critical treatment of Brecht by directors from Benno Besson and Peter Palitzsch to B. K. Tragelehn, Manfred Karge, and Matthias Langhoff (all of whom left the GDR) and by productions that favored the heroic portrayal of historical figures.[30] In his commemoration of the fortieth anniversary of the ensemble in 1989, Wekwerth claimed that the company, established the same year as the state (1949), would endure as the state had endured. Titling the speech "The World Needs Change," he tried to appropriate the rhetoric of change while resting on the monumental weight of the Brecht institution, which had long lost its claim to be a vanguard theater.[31]

If Manfred Wekwerth represented, as a member of the SED's Central Committee, an embodiment of the identity of state and cultural institutions, he was by the 1980s no longer typical. Far more typical were functionaries attempting to appropriate initiatives for social and cultural transformation and to render inappropriate cultural activity illegitimate by refusing publicly to acknowledge its existence. In an interview in 1988 with the influential West German theater magazine *Theater Heute* titled "The Most Certain Thing Is Change," Hans Joachim Hoffmann, minister of culture from 1971 to 1990, assured the editors that the GDR theater institution was elastic and enlightened enough to accommodate dissent.[32] Acknowledging the much-lamented stagnation of GDR culture in the early 1980s, he praised above all as signs of GDR glasnost dramas on historical themes, from Alexander Lang's irreverent and, if anything, antihistorical productions—such as his pairing of *Theodor, Herzog von Gothland*, Grabbe's rambling play on the chaos of war, and *Iphigenia*, Goethe's paean to the reason of peace (1983), at the flagship Deutsches Theater—to the Berliner Ensemble's 1988 production of Volker Braun's *Lenins Tod* (written and shelved in 1970), directed by Christoph Schroth, and Heiner Müller's 1988 revival of his 1957 indictment of SED labor relations, *Der Lohndrücker* (The wagebuster) at the Deutsches Theater.

Although neither Hoffmann nor his West German interviewers mention theater outside the capital, his account of new GDR theater was supplemented in the same volume with comments on theater outside Berlin, in particular, the work of Wolfgang Engel at the Dresden State Theater (an institution with the same "A" status as the Deutsches Theater).[33] At Dresden since 1980, Engel had staged GDR premieres of taboo authors such as Beckett (*Waiting for Godot*, 1987) as well as darkly contemporary versions of more or less canonical German texts (Friedrich Hebbel's *Nibelungen*, 1984) or those on the outer fringes of the SED canon (Heinrich von Kleist's *Penthesilea*, 1988). In April 1989, he would direct what would become the emblematically critical "spectacle of the state": Christoph Hein's *Knights of the Round Table*. Whereas the West German reviewer mentions in passing that Hans Modrow, SED secretary for Saxony (and later briefly prime minister), was "open-minded and interested in theatre," as though this fact were incidental, in a later interview, Engel notes that his relative artistic freedom and access to privileges denied most GDR citizens—not least, frequent travel abroad—directly depended on the enlightened patronage of Modrow and General Director Gerhardt Wolfram.[34] Engel's acknowledgment of Modrow's support, in his version of the familiar claim that the theater functioned as a virtual public sphere in a state that officially refused to admit any legitimate publicity outside itself, is also an acknowledgment that the Dresden State Theater's critical repertoire reflected the power of SED paternalism (in this case an enlightened version) rather than a radically democratic alternative to the status quo. Although these rare examples of toleration could and did enable some bold new work, and although personal networks and telephone communications helped deflect (but not diminish) some of the effects of state surveillance, the model for this dissident communication network is less the public sphere (virtual, incipient, counter) than, as East German theater chronicler Knut Lennarz has since remarked, "for good or ill, a kind of family business."[35]

As a "family business" dominated by paternalist discretion, rather than a public sphere in the making, the tolerance of the SED was structurally inseparable from its tyranny. Hoffmann's representation of his ministry's benevolent guidance of GDR theater has to be juxtaposed with the aversion to social and theatrical experiment that characterized his administration in the late 1970s, after the expulsion of Wolf Biermann in November 1976 shocked artists and intellectuals and inaugurated another period of repression. Not only did he cancel the production of contemporary political dramas, such as Jürgen Groß's *Parteifreund* (1977), but he also supported legislation designed to "protect" the designation "writer" by granting it only to those earning six thousand marks (GDR) yearly and withholding it from those receiving royalties from abroad or earning a living by other means.[36] His colleague Werner Lamberz, member of the Politburo and minister for agitation and propaganda, was responsible for stripping Biermann of GDR citizenship in his absence, for the calumny against Biermann that appeared immediately afterwards in *Neues Deutschland*, and, directly or indirectly, for withholding work from those who submitted a modest protest to the action against Biermann. His response to the protest is striking for its combination of the presumption of "socialist" family loyalty (marked by the compulsory use of the familiar "du" among party members) and a refusal to countenance a public sphere other than that regulated by familial consultation (by telephone and private chats rather than by publication).[37]

There is an undeniable continuity between the SED policy of legitimation and illegitimation in the 1970s and Hoffmann's dismissal in 1988 of attempts by small, unauthorized performance groups to democratize the-

ater administration as the residue of "1968 experimentalism." In treating
as "sensationalist journalism" even the authorized production of a play
dealing with touchy social problems such as homelessness and the abuse
of women, as in Ulrich Plenzdorf's *Freiheitsberaubung* (Robbed of freedom)
(performed in 1988 after being banned the previous year), Hoffmann himself exposed the limits of official tolerance.[38] Based on a story by Günther
de Bruyn, *Freiheitsberaubung* offers, in monologue form, the experience of a
woman in police custody attempting to explain why she was turned out of
her apartment. Hoffmann's objections are undefined but probably pertain
to the character's comments on unemployed youth, single women, and
other "asocial" types and to the publicity granted this "negative" play by the
status of the author (*the* exemplary chronicler of alienated GDR youth) as
well as the performance venue: the Theater im Palast der Republik, which
generally targeted younger audiences.

A/social Resistance: Intellectuals on the Margins
of Legitimate Publicity

More telling, perhaps, than the culture minister's ambivalent remarks
about dissident performances within official institutions was his silence
about those excluded from legitimate publicity altogether, even in an era
of partial glasnost. The editors of *Theater Heute* amplified this silence by
framing and interrupting the interview with official photographs of high
points in GDR history alongside images of officially unmentionable events.
Among the latter was a photograph of a performance of *Pässe/Parolen*
(Passports, passwords), a series of satirical skits by director Freya Klier
and singer-songwriter Stephan Krawczyk. As a record of their last major
project before their imprisonment after a demonstration commemorating
Rosa Luxemburg's defense of the freedom of those "who think differently"
in January 1988 and their expulsion a month or so later, this image—
and the accompanying photograph of that demonstration—was deployed
by *Theater Heute* editors as an ironic comment on Hoffmann's claims for
glasnost in GDR theater.

    This image pays tribute to the courage of performers who challenged
the official interpretation of the socialist legacy as well as SED taboos on
chronic problems in the contemporary GDR, and who attempted to wrest
at least the idea of a counter public sphere from the pseudo publicity of
the state. But it does not show the progress of these performers from their
relative privilege as graduates of elite institutions through their dissidence
and ostracism from official cultural institutions to their ultimate expulsion.
The directing career of Klier (b. 1950) is particularly interesting because it
charts the consequences of a constitutive contradiction in the production

of GDR intellectuals. Klier, like many of her contemporaries, ran up against the state's actual resistance to the critical engagement with socialism in the theater and GDR society that was nominally promoted in its educational institutions. While still a student at the Theater Institute, Klier was reprimanded for her involvement in unauthorized peace initiatives and for her student production of Fernando Arrabal's antiwar play, Picnic (1982). Despite this reprimand, her production of Plenzdorf's Legende vom Glück ohne Ende in Schwedt the following year was transferred to Leipzig as an entry in the annual GDR Theater Workshop and earned praise from Hans Rainer John, editor-in-chief of Theater der Zeit (the organ of the Association of Theater Practitioners) and long-time SED loyalist, as well as a prize for directing and an appointment to the GDR Theater Jury.[39] At the same time, however, she was subject to increasingly intrusive Stasi surveillance for participation in unofficial peace initiatives as well as an unauthorized survey of GDR women.[40]

Klier's last commissioned production was a revival in 1985, on the occasion of the fortieth anniversary of the Soviet Army's arrival in Berlin, of Optimistic Tragedy (1934), Vsevolod Vishnevsky's patriotic but ambivalent treatment of a clash between a female Bolshevik commissar and anarchist sailors during the Russian Civil War of 1921; it provides a noteworthy case of SED appropriation and containment of critical socialist engagement. Working under the auspices of the Mecklenburg State Theater in Schwerin with none-too-enthusiastic students from the Acting Institute in Berlin, Klier attempted to use the complexity of the engagement between Bolsheviks and anarchists in the first two acts to cast an unsparing light on the patriotic pathos of the final act, in which the commissar's military errors and the slaughter of the battalion are redeemed in the name of the impending Bolshevik victory.[41] According to Klier, the production was criticized by the otherwise liberal Christoph Schroth, then director in Schwerin (who had himself used the clash between Bolsheviks and anarchists in an "agitation evening" in honor of Solidarity in 1980), for playing down the pathos of the commissar's death and for pessimism deemed "inappropriate for the occasion."[42] After a private hearing with Schroth and the director of the theater school, Hans-Peter Minetti, the production was taken out of Klier's hands, and directing projects of hers under consideration in Berlin and Dresden were canceled.

Although not quite an official exclusion from the profession (Berufsverbot), this reprimand effectively deprived Klier of the legitimate institutional base she had taken as her due.[43] In the next two and a half years, Klier and her partner Krawczyk, who had been officially banned for alleged sedition (Staatsverleumdung), including public readings of Rosa Luxemburg on freedom of speech, performed satirical sketches on GDR life in informal venues ranging from the Church of Zion in Prenzlauer Berg to rural barns and private apartments. *Pässe/Parolen*, their most visible production, included material on illegal immigration, the militarization of GDR education, and the difficult lives of GDR women despite official gender equality. It managed to tour for about a year (1986–87), despite Stasi surveillance of the performers and intimidation of the facilitators (through mounting fines) and the audience (through disruption of performances by "skinheads" shouting "pornography" and other insults).[44]

The heroic representation of Klier and Krawczyk in *Theater Heute* after their expulsion contrasts with relative Western indifference earlier on and tends to reinforce their own accounts of a lonely struggle against overwhelming odds. Although it is now generally acknowledged that GDR theater intellectuals offered only limited solidarity for those ostracized by the SED, it is not the case that Klier's and Krawczyk's was the *only* independent theater group, nor that the gap between authorized and unauthorized performances was always absolute and unbridgeable. Commenting on the marginally visible independent (*freie*) theater scene, Peter Waschinsky, noted puppeteer and self-described entertainer, suggests that independent groups tended to be hampered less by lack of subsidy (given the low cost of living) than by the scarcity of venues and the rationing of publicity in a parastatal field divided between the Free German Youth (FDJ) and authorized culture clubs.[45]

In addition to cabaret and other motley entertainments that were granted sporadic access to youth halls and community venues in the 1980s, there was a significant, if fragile, line of descent marked by informal performances under the aegis of unofficial peace initiatives, such as "Swords into Ploughshares." *Pässe/Parolen* could be said to inhabit the same incipient public sphere as an event organized by this group three years earlier at the Wittenberg Church Conference. On this occasion (24 September 1983), a blacksmith slowly beat a sword into a ploughshare, accompanied by the pastor reading a modernized version of Isaiah to an audience informally gathered in front of the Lutheran assembly house.[46] The event was significant not only for its challenge to SED orthodoxy on several fronts—the doctrine of "peace through defense," the concentration on heavy industry at the expense of domestic welfare—but for its *redeployment* of official socialist iconography in the shape of the muscular "model worker" forging the future of the socialist nation, and for its appeal to young people at best indifferent to official socialist pieties. It was the reproduction of this icon on buttons and posters, as well as the performance itself, that provoked the retaliation of the SED, which made possession of these objects a criminal offense.

Klier and Krawczyk have also been compared to Zinnober, a puppet theater turned relatively independent performance group active in Prenzlauer Berg from the early 1980s on. Like Klier and Krawczyk, the members of Zinnober were products of elite institutions but, unlike them, began work in the relatively underprivileged arena of puppet and children's theater and later survived on intermittent labor, ticket sales, and social security rather than regular state support.[47] In the 1980s, Zinnober members worked both outside and within authorized if not quite centralized institutions such as radio (state-owned and -operated in the GDR but subject to less systematic state surveillance than the more central and ideologically powerful institution of television). Iduna Hegen, for instance, took part in Heiner Müller's radio version of Brecht's *Fatzer* material, broadcast on Berliner Rundfunk in February 1988.[48]

The longevity of Zinnober may have been due in part to the relative immunity of the Prenzlauer Berg literary scene, with which Zinnober occasionally shared space, or to the intervention of more prominent partners such as Heiner Müller.[49] But it owed its audience also to the less spectacular but no less significant presence of puppet and other "youth" theater in the GDR cultural field. As "community" rather than "state" theaters, as "public services" or "educational" institutions rather than metropolitan showcases of culture fit for export to the West, these theaters enjoyed less subsidy but also less scrutiny than the major metropolitan institutions. Although many reproduced the FDJ version of youth culture, others, such as Theater unter dem Dach, a community cultural center in Prenzlauer Berg since 1986 and, unlike many others, still going, managed to address issues—such as punk culture, problems with parents, or sexual exploration—of interest to allegedly asocial young people.[50] The linked (but not identical) institutional spaces of groups such as Zinnober or spaces such as Theater unter dem Dach imply a certain limited porousness in the borders between authorized and unauthorized activity, rather than an absolute distinction between approved and forbidden cultural practice. Moreover, they suggest the potential for a critical socialization of underprivileged young people on the margins of official youth organizations.

Dissidence as Privilege? The Pitfalls of Authorized Critique

In this light, it is perhaps not surprising that, in the period between the New Forum's articulation of a visibly dissident publicity and the spectacular legitimation of that dissidence with the November demonstration, youth and puppet theaters reacted more promptly and more bluntly than did more prestigious institutions to state violence and coercion. The statement of the Berlin Puppet Theater (29 September), for instance, provides a sharp contrast with that of the Berliner Ensemble released the same day. The latter offered a convoluted acknowledgment of the "current situation of crisis" only to resort to resolution by cliché, in its invocation of "open dialogue without taboos" (a phrase used by Erich Honecker to inaugurate the "thaw" in 1971) and a "restoration of a relationship of trust between leadership and populace" (*Wir treten aus*, 22). The Berlin Puppet Theater, on the other hand, referred to the crisis as an "unbearable contradiction" between the "values which we are communicating to children and those actually existing in society" and denounced SED policy for "manipulat[ing] citizens from childhood . . . by criminalizing the very critical attitude that it publicly proclaims" (19). Released before the change of leadership and subsequent moratorium on police violence after 9 October, this statement exposed its signers to the threat of retaliation, not least because it launched the attack on the militant paternalism of the SED state from the vantage point of an institution traditionally associated with children.

We should nonetheless be cautious about using this contrast to reinforce a melodramatic opposition between authorized and forbidden culture. Although *Wir treten aus unseren Rollen heraus*, the collection of documents by theater intellectuals at and around the demonstration with which I began this essay, may suggest this scenario in its juxtaposition of critical and affirmative statements, subsequent replay of the event elides the vanguard authority of the underprivileged youth theaters and locates the source of dissent paradoxically in the privileged dissent of certain state theaters. The variants of this document and later views of the event suggest that the structural hierarchy of prestige and privilege and the representative roles of the personnel may have survived the demise of "real socialist" paternalism and has perhaps been shored up in a more or less united Germany.

This realignment of dissent with prominent members of elite institutions emerges already in this apparently catholic compilation of statements. The representative statement—and the title of the book—does not directly indict the state for "criminalizing" critical inquiry and political engagement and for infantilizing the population, but rather appeals to a general crisis:

> We cast off our roles
> The situation in our country compels us to do so
> A country that cannot hold its youth endangers its future
> A party leadership that no longer examines the practicability of its principles
>   is condemned to decline . . .

We are making use of our platform to demand:
We have a right to information
We have a right to dialogue . . .
We are duty bound to demand that our state and party leadership restore
    trust in the populace.

(*Wir treten*, 39)

This statement (Dresden State Theater, 6 October) is striking for three reasons. First, it departs from the direct indictment of the state present not only in the Puppet Theater statement but also in an early version of the Dresden statement, which pointedly challenged the SED "family business"—"Is the claim to legitimate authority (*Führungsanspruch*) of the SED a matter of privilege and birthright?"—and made more concrete demands: "release of all political prisoners / analysis of the faulty policies of forty years / abolition of every form of disenfranchisement . . ." (29). Second, the coexistence of these two versions suggests the privileged position of the Dresden management (watched over by the benevolent Modrow) but also the force of self-censorship and the habits of *Sklavensprache*, the subversive but subaltern language of slaves. Third, the all-embracing "we" that opens the statement implies a unanimous shift from one role to another, from subaltern to vanguard, from nonage to people's tribunes, obscuring the muffled criticism of privilege and the divergent levels of political risk taken by groups that were party to the manifesto.

Although dubbed the "theatrical and political event of the season,"[51] the demonstration marked the end of unanimity among GDR theater intellectuals. Already in early 1990, the initiative's members were casting doubt on the effects of the new political dispensation, media explosion, and economic dislocation on any future social role for theater.[52] By the end of the first season after the opening of the Wall, the wave of interest among East German audiences in formerly forbidden or marginalized plays and themes had largely ebbed in the wake of competition from the electronic media and, after unification, dramatically higher prices. The waning of audience interest left the field to intellectuals of the former GDR who were absorbed in anxiety about the fate of theater in a capitalist *Germoney*, a Germany in which the domination of the cash nexus apparently left no place for critical theater.[53]

Rationalization and Its Discontents: Theater After the Fall

Although the changes in the German theater institution after unification in 1990 corresponded in large part to Western rather than Eastern priorities, they cannot nonetheless be reduced to a mere reflection of laissez-faire capitalism, in the nightmarish vision conjured up by some former

GDR intellectuals. To be sure, theaters have been closed and regional networks cut back, and theater workers (artistic and technical) have lost the lifetime tenures provided by the GDR Cultural Ministry, but the terms of this rationalization are not quite those of simple profit or loss in a "free" market. Instead, the new *Länder* in the east have been brought in line with the Federal Republic's regulation of cultural production, in particular, its emphasis on the generation of cultural capital in the form of national and international prestige and a secondary accent on education. Although the cultural and economic configuration of contemporary Germany is complex and the theater activity diverse, the logic of rationalization—the consolidation of shrinking resources within already large and expensive "stable" institutions rather than its distribution to more numerous, cheaper, and arguably more efficient theater organizations—has dominated practice and commentary in the decade since unification and therefore remains the organizing principle of this final section. The conflict between the generation of cultural capital, which requires expenditure to maintain prestige, and the logic of rationalization is especially visible in Berlin, the new federal capital, where, especially in Mitte, the area at the heart of the former capital of the GDR, the transitional mix of national institutions such as the Staatsoper, the Deutsches Theater, and the Berliner Ensemble, community institutions, such as Theater unter dem Dach, and new groups occupying dilapidated buildings of uncertain ownership, such as Tacheles and the Pfefferberg, gave way over the course of the decade to a high-rent, high-prestige commercial and government hub with few open spaces for experiment. My object is to sketch the institutional restructuring of the postunification theater, but my concluding remarks on the institutions of theater in contemporary not-quite-united Germany by way of Berlin, the capital city in the making, are, like the city, very much under construction.

Initially, the process of rationalization reduced the stagnation endemic in the East German theater system by closing some theaters and bringing others in line with West German structures. By 1991, most theaters in the new *Länder* were offering the educational and entertainment mix characteristic of most West German provincial houses: textbook classics for education and the reproduction of cultural capital, on one hand, and light comedies and musicals for entertainment, on the other.[54] The initial exceptions, as in West Germany, were the metropolitan showcase theaters in Berlin, especially the Deutsches Theater and the Volksbühne, and key state theaters, such as Dresden, but the elite system did not escape rationalization, as the closure of the Schiller Theater, the biggest state-subsidized house in West Berlin, indicates. Further reductions in state subsidy have also compelled major metropolitan institutions in all *Länder* to cut expenditures and raise funds rather than rely on subsidy. The Berlin Senator for Culture in the 1990s, Ulrich Roloff-Momin, argued for "less state and more responsibility": the major Berlin theaters should ultimately raise up to 50 percent (compared to a previous maximum of 18 percent) of their budget from higher ticker prices and television rights.[55] In 1996, public funding for major theater institutions was cut by one million marks and subsidy shifted from buildings and salaries (previously at 80–90 percent) to support for short-term projects. The idea of compelling institutions including the Hochschule der Künste (West) and the Ernst-Busch-Schauspielschule (East) to compete in the same market was greeted by former GDR theater intellectuals such as Käthe Reichel, Brecht's last leading lady (Gretchen in his 1953 Faust) and now instructor at the Busch-Schauspielschule, as the "dictatorship of the market" and, recalling the rhetoric of Hoffmann, as the "excess of democracy."[56] Nonetheless, excesses of subsidy remained: in 2000, his successor Christof Stöltzl had to announce a deficit of more than DM 15 million.[57]

In comparison with the market-driven rationalization in Great Britain, however, in which formerly subsidized flagships such as the National Theater must now compete for the most lucrative tourist audience by producing musicals and similar spectacles that had been the fare of the West End, the rationalization of German theater has not been purely economic but rather modified by the authority of cultural capital.[58] The evolution of the Berliner Ensemble offers a striking case of the superior force of cultural capital over fiscal considerations. While closing the Schiller Theater in 1991, the Berlin Senate judged the Berliner Ensemble's historical association with Brecht more important than its recent and moribund existence under Wekwerth and Barbara Brecht-Schall and thus moved to rescue the theater and promoted its volatile and decidedly inefficient management under five major directors: Peter Palitzsch, Peter Zadek, Fritz Marquardt, Matthias Langhoff (who left almost immediately), and Heiner Müller, who remained until his death. Even before the departure of his chief rival, Zadek, in early 1995, Müller had effective control over the repertoire, sponsoring, in addition to revisions of his own GDR work, Einar Schleef's spectacularly irreverent production of Wessis in Weimar, a play by Rolf Hochuth, West Germany's most notorious exponent of "documentary theater" in the 1960s, on the topical theme of Western appropriation of East German assets.[59] When Hochhuth denounced the production and attempted to buy the Berliner Ensemble out from under the city by negotiating with the heir apparent, a Jewish exile in New York, the city's lawyers dismissed the case. Müller treated the occasion as an opportunity to remark that no one knew any longer what theater was for.[60] Yet the city of Berlin was willing, despite overall reductions in funding, to subsidize the work of directors such as Schleef, whose fame and commodity value depended on a rivalry driven by *succès de scandale*, and the rather inefficient administration of Heiner Müller, whose plays and adaptations and stagings of Brecht dominated the repertoire until his death in 1996. Even with reduced subsidy, the Senate was apparently willing, more recently, to support as new intendant Claus Peymann, formerly intendant of the Burgtheater, Vienna's flagship, although without recourse to Brecht to justify the expenditure. Peymann has all but banished Brecht from his old house in favor of Peymann's favorite playwright, the late Austrian Thomas Bernhardt, alternating with Franz Xaver Kroetz and Shakespeare.[61]

What drives this cultural economy as a whole is less the conflict between legitimate and emergent public spheres than the competition among producers of cultural capital regulated in part by the state and in part by influential cultural brokers such as the reviewers and editors of *Theater Heute*. This competition may sometimes, in the form of the occasional performance that resonates with the perception of social or political crisis, overlap with and even sharpen conflict over legitimate publicity, but it more often derives profit from the regulated display of social and political dissent within the proper institutional frame. Shortly before unification, Wolfgang Engel's *Faust* (1990), for instance, which portrayed a Mephisto inventing paper money (the signature of the set), functioned less as a critique of capitalism than as an early but visible sign of cultural rejuvenation after the fall of the Wall. Nearly a decade after unification, Klaus Emmerich revived Brecht's communist *Lehrstück*, *Die Massnahme* (*Measures Taken*) for Brecht's centenary in 1998. Fifty years after Brecht had banned professional productions of a text written for education and self-critique of activists, on the grounds that productions made a spectacle, or *Schaustück*, out of the *Lehrstück*, this revival, however aesthetically pleasing, nonetheless confirmed Brecht's fears by creating a spectacle, even a museum piece, of Communism, which would ironically bring in the crowds and increase the box-office receipts of a theater now reliant on capital.

In this economy, the iconography of *Ostalgie* (nostalgia for East [Germany]) as a marketable image takes precedence over critical working through of the recent past. At the end of the decade, GDR board games and reissues of satirical and even official songs of the old regime sold better than the thorough, invaluable, but weighty tomes of Christof Links Press series of studies based on Stasi and other recently released GDR archives, and stage images tended to be likewise kitschy and nostalgic. For instance, *Helden wie wir* (Heroes like us), Thomas Brussig's best-selling comic novel about the good-for-nothing son of a Stasi underling whose outsize member allegedly broke the first hole in the Wall, became after the opening of the film version (directed by Sebastian Peterson, who got his start at Theater unterm Dach) and the stage adaptation (by Peter Dehler) on 9 November 1999 (exactly fifty years after the founding of the GDR state and a decade after the fall of the Wall) a prime exhibit of *Ostalgie*.[62] Returning to the Deutsches Theater stage on 3 October 2000 to commemorate the tenth anniversary of unification, the play encouraged a sentimental response to the *Ostalgie* object-commodity, which Brecht would have called culinary. More ambiguously, perhaps, Frank Castorf, who had made a reputation of wrapping post-Brechtian critical theater texts such as Heiner Müller's *Bau* (1986 in Karl-Marx-Stadt) in scenographies consisting of the plastic bric-a-brac of GDR modernity as a late-model version of the Western 1960s pop, continued in the 1990s to use the iconography of GDR (pre)modernity (from local fashion to the old SED songs) to draw former GDR audiences to the Volksbühne's deconstructions of modern classics such as Hauptmann's *Weber* (1999) and *A Streetcar Named Desire* (in this version, *Endstation Amerika*, 2000).

The differentiation between provincial public service institutions providing entertainment and education and elite metropolitan institutions run by star directors represents the *normalization* of East German theater, in other words, its integration into an advanced welfare capitalist state able to support cultural activity relatively independent from the market or from direct political manipulation. Normalization entails not the abandonment of theater to unbridled capitalism, as some GDR theater intellectuals feared, but the rationalization of subsidy according to prevailing norms of cultural capital, which penalize institutions unable or unwilling to generate cultural capital while rewarding the few that do, even if the ongoing subsidy contradicts the logic of rationalization and leads to even greater deficits.[63]. The fact that the reward takes the form not only of regular and stable subsidy but also of critical attention couched in *artistic* rather than explicitly ideological terms (praise for avant-garde testing of the limits of theater art rather than for generating international prestige) strengthens its function in the production of cultural capital since it reinforces the aura of artistic autonomy that is an essential part of cultural prestige.

The casualty of this normalization is above all the institutional legitimacy of groups that lack the capital or the inclination to generate prestige. Theater groups attempting to articulate a counter publicity or a "new concept of sociability"[64] tend, in the new as in the "old" *Länder*, to be those whose institutional ambiguity (the *freie Szene*), specialization (such as the Theater unter dem Dach), or regional particularity (as in Frankfurt-Oder on the Polish border) limits their general impact but may concentrate their efforts to lend publicity to communities marginalized by unification. Some theaters have disappeared under pressure from the economy of selective subsidy and cuts in funding that have affected youth theaters in the new *Länder* as a relatively undeserving part of the cultural sphere. Others have responded to this economy of scarcity by making theater for educational and social as well as aesthetic uses, such as Theaterpatie in the early 1990s (comprised of some members of Zinnober), Theater unter dem Dach (surviving, just), or, more recently, Ramba Zamba (whose mentally challenged actors perform evocative renderings of classics from *Woyzeck* to *Medea*), but these too have struggled to acquire the survival skills needed to maintain a presence in the alternative theater scene since unification—from low-technology performance techniques and a mobile staging apparatus to procedures for dealing with scarcity of funding and skeptical cultural bureaucrats to the collaborative development of new venues like the Kulturbrauerei in an as yet only partly gentrified part of Prenzlauer Berg.

The groups struggling to maintain their foothold in Berlin-Mitte share with other small-scale "free" performance groups that are operating on the margins elsewhere in Western Europe not only material problems of limited and irregular subsidy and the tricky negotiation of the links (if any) between theatrical experimentation and the desire to seek out non-theatergoing audiences such as young people or ethnic minorities, but also the perhaps immaterial problem of normalization, in that they are forced to adopt the language and processes of capital in creating niche markets for their work and in persuading investors that they are worthy instruments. As the now traditionally leftist Berlin biweekly, *Die Zitty*, stated recently, "those who want to survive [the investors driving out arts organizations] need to professionalize themselves."[65] But, whereas "free scenes" in long-standing nation-states such as Britain and the United States can and do reinforce their claims for cultural legitimacy (if not hard cash) by appeals to a long history of the alternative theater that usually takes in the workers' theaters of the 1930s as well as the counterculture of the 1960s, the institutional memory of the Berlin equivalents remains bifurcated. Despite the ongoing efforts of the now-independent Theater der Zeit to highlight the theater of the new *Länder* and of Berlin institutions that survived the *Wende* and thus challenge the still narrowly Western picture of *Theater Heute*, the larger circulation *Zitty*, despite its leftist line and catchy slogan "I am the city," still promulgates a history of the alternative scene in Berlin over the past twenty years that deals *exclusively* with West Berlin from the 1970s squats to unification in 1990, writing critical institutions and unofficial dissidents of East Berlin out of history and thus repeating the cold war picture of monolithic totalitarianism.[66] Restoring this history does not merely balance the record; it also provides pertinent examples of institutions and groups that created theater in the space between the SED dictatorship and the regime of global capital. At issue here is not the restoration or (re)unification of one history or the spectacle of *one* people or *the* people, but rather a more probing navigation of what a theater intellectual under similar institutional constraints in another country has called the "brink of performance efficacy"[67] at the interference of these public spheres.

Notes

All translations are mine, unless otherwise stated.

1. For the New Forum statement, "Aufbruch 1989," and the declaration of the writers' association, see the dossier, *Wir treten aus unseren Rollen heraus: Dokumente zum Aufbruch 1989*, compiled by Angela Kuberski (Berlin, 1990), 11–13 (cited in the text as *Wir treten aus*).

2. I distinguish between the SED state and GDR society to acknowledge the conceptual and historical differentiation made by GDR intellectuals between the official SED line on "actually existing socialism" and the possibilities, however circumscribed, of realizing a socialist alternative to West German capitalism.

3. Art. 27: "Every GDR citizen has the right to express his opinion freely on the foundations of the constitution. Nobody may be penalized for exercising this right. Freedom of the press, radio, and television is guaranteed"; and art. 28: "All citizens have the right, in accordance with the foundations and goals of the constitution, to assembly freely," *Wir treten aus*, 200. These constitutional rights were restricted by criminal law: para. 99 refers to the distribution of unauthorized news as "treasonous" *(landesverräterische Nachrichtenübermittlung)*, para.106 to "attacks on the socialist social organization of the GDR" as "agitation against the state" *(staatsfeindliche Hetze)*, and para. 107 to the establishment of unauthorized organizations as "association endangering the constitution" *(verfassungsfeindlicher Zusammenschluss)*. First invoked by Deutsches Theater actors Ulrich Mühe and Johanna Schall (Brecht's granddaughter), the contradictions between the constitution's nominal defense of civil rights and the SED's suppression, marginalization, and illegitimation of free speech was raised throughout the demonstration.

4. The expression is Brecht's. See "Einige Irrtümer über die Spielweise des Berliner Ensembles," *Gesammelte Werke* (Frankfurt am Main, 1967), 16:907 (hereafter *GW*). Büchner's letters to Young German propagandist Franz Gutzkow express his scorn for the attempt "to change society from the educated classes down" and his engagement as a committed intellectual; Georg Büchner, *Werke und Briefe* (Munich, 1980), 287.

5. See Müller's statement in *Wir treten aus*, 231–32, the hostile reactions to it in the SED organ, *Neues Deutschland* —(Dr.) Oskar Hauser, "Demagogie oder nur Unkenntnis," (Dr.) Hans Lüttke, "Sonnabend-Demo Positives und Negatives entnommen" (7 November 1989)—and Müller's rejoinder, "Plaidoyer für den Widerspruch," *Neues Deutschland*, 14 December 1989.

6. Compare Stefan Heym, "Hurrah für den Pöbel," *Der Spiegel* 45 (6 November 1989): 30–31, with Heym, "Aschermittwoch in der DDR," *Der Spiegel* 49 (4 Decem-

ber 1989): 55–56. See also the statement "Für das Land" (December 1989), signed by Heym, Wolf, and others, which presents a stark opposition between working to make the GDR a "society of solidarity and social justice" and "selling out morally and materially . . . giving in to annexation by the Federal Republic," quoted in "DDR-Literatur: Eine Chronik." Appendix to Heinz Ludwig Arnold and Frauke Meyer-Gosau, eds., *Literatur der DDR: Ein Rückblick* (Munich, 1991), 301. The most emphatic initial attack on intellectual privilege was that by ex-GDR writer Monika Maron, "Die Schriftsteller und das Volk," *Der Spiegel* 7 (12 February 1990): 68–69.

7. Thomas Schmid, "Pinscherseligkeit: Über die deutschen Intellektuellen und ihre Unfähigkeit mit der jüngsten Geschichte zurechtzukommen," *Die Zeit*, 10 April 1992, 13.

8. See, e.g., the comments of GDR playwrights Völker Braun, "Die Kunst als Streit der Interne," *Theater 1988* (Yearbook of *Theater Heute*), 130–31, and Christof Hein, "Warum ich in der DDR geblieben bin," *Theater Heute* (April 1992): 40–41. These sentiments are not peculiar to the first generation to grow up in the GDR; see also Leander Haußmann, thirty-something director of Ibsen's *Nora* in Weimar in 1991, "Man wechselt nicht so leicht die Feinde," *Theater 1990*, 31–32.

9. Peter von Becker, "Theaterspielen im neuen Deutschland," and Rolf Schneider, "Selbstmitleid und Selbstbetrug," *Theater 1990*, 128, 138–40. See also Hartmut Krug, "Auch Theater sind sterblich," *Theater Heute* (January 1992): 3.

10. For a (rare) reminder of the Stalinist pedigree of this charge, see Lothar Baier, "Selbstverstümmelnde Literatenschmäh: Über den neuen deutschen Intellektuellenhaß," *Freitag* 5 (29 January 1993): 9.

11. For general propaganda, see Hans-Joachim Hoffmann (minister of culture), "Culture in the GDR: Unity and Diversity," *World Marxist Review* 30 (1987): 94–100; for specific claims about theater, see his interview with *Theater Heute*, "Das Sicherste ist die Veränderung," *Theater 1988*, 10–20. Note, however, that West German expenditure on theater was always higher (per spectator) than the subsidy in the GDR; see Friedrich Dieckmann, "Von der Volksbühnenbewegung zum Subventionstheater," *Theater der Zeit* (August 1991): 4–6.

12. Compare Hoffmann's assertion of the GDR's support for critical theater ("Das Sicherste ist die Veränderung," 12) with Rolf Schneider's counterclaim that the relationship between artists, however critical, and the state that sponsored them could only be described as "parasitical" ("Selbstmitleid und Selbstbetrug," 139). As demonstrated by Joachim Walther's comprehensive study *Sicherungsbereich Literatur: Schriftsteller und Staatssicherheit in der Deutschen Demokratischen Republik* (Berlin, 1996), there were more than 170,000 "informal collaborators" for the Stasi by 1989, one spy for every 120 citizens (554).

13. For a suggestive, but brief, discussion of the distinction between subjunctive and indicative action, see Raymond Williams, "Brecht and Beyond," in *Politics and Letters* (London: 1981), 219–24; for an adumbration of the implications of this distinction for the concept of virtual public sphere, see Loren Kruger, "Placing the Occasion: Raymond Williams and Performing Culture," in *Views Beyond the Border Country: Essays on Raymond Williams*, ed. Dennis Dworkin and Leslie Roman (New York, 1993), 51–73.

14. Ulrich Greiner, who launched an early and effective salvo in the battle over GDR intellectual conviction and complicity—"Die deutsche Gesinnungsästhetik. Nocheinmal. Christa Wolf und der deutsche Literaturstreit," *Die Zeit* (9 November

1990): 15—later disclaimed any interestedness on the part of West German critics, even as he appealed for an end to the debate he had helped stir up: "Plädoyer für Schluß der Stasi-Debatte," *Die Zeit* (12 February 1993): 15. See also Karl-Heinz Bohrer, "Die Ästhetik im Ausgang ihrer Unmündigkeit," *Merkur* 44 (1990): 851–65.

15. Frank Schirrmacher, "Abschied von der Literatur der Bundesrepublik," *Frankfurter Allgemeine Zeitung*, 2 October 1990.

16. See Herbert Lüthy's lengthy inaugural account of Brecht's progress from anarchic rebel to emasculated court poet in thrall to the fatal illusion of "communist humanism," in "Vom armen BB," published in the organ of the Congress of Cultural Freedom, *Der Monat* 4, no. 44 (May 1952): 115–44, here 144, 134 (reprinted in the British equivalent, *Encounter*). Hannah Arendt's essay on Brecht, first published in *The New Yorker* in 1966, repeats these claims more than a decade later, using as evidence odes to Stalin that have yet to be traced. See Arendt, *Men in Dark Times* (New York, 1968) and commentary by John Willett, "Two Political Excursions," in *Brecht in Context* (London, 1985), 210–21.

17. André Müller, *Kreuzzug gegen Brecht: Die Kampagne in der Bundesrepublik 1961/62* (Darmstadt, 1963).

18. See Friedrich Torberg, "Soll man Brecht im Westen spielen?" *Der Monat* 14, no. 159 (1962): 56–62, and responses in "Soll man Brecht spielen: Antworten an Friedrich Torberg," *Der Monat* 14, no. 161 (1962): 57–64.

19. Martin Esslin, *Bertolt Brecht: A Choice of Evils* (London, 1962). Although it avoids Esslin's psychodrama of the deluded artist, T. W. Adorno's critique of Brecht in "Engagement," in *Noten zur Literatur* (Frankfurt am Main, 1980) rehearses the classic cold war dichotomy between artistic autonomy and political instrumentalization, as the title of the original radio broadcast, "Engagement oder Autonomie von Kunst" (Radio Bremen, March 1962) attests.

20. See John Fuegi's *Bertolt Brecht: Chaos According to Plan* (Cambridge, U.K., 1989), which expatiates on the thesis that Brecht's genius as a director developed in inverse proportion to his theoretical and political pronouncements; see also opera critic John Rockwell's casual dismissal of the "naive leftist idealism" allegedly marring the "artistic vitality of Brecht's Berliner Ensemble" in "Berliner Ensemble in the 90's: Brecht's Old House Is Divided," *New York Times*, 8 February 1993, B1; for critical commentary on Rockwell's own political naiveté, see Warren Leming, "Tui-Memorandum: Brecht and the *New York Times*," *Communications from the International Brecht Society* 22, no. 1 (1993): 5–6.

21. Walter Ulbricht, "Der Kampf gegen den Formalismus in der Kunst und Literatur: Für eine fortschrittliche deutsche Kultur," in *Dokumente zur Kunst-, Literatur- und Kulturpolitik der SED*, ed. Elmar Schubbe (Stuttgart, 1972), 178–86, here 182.

22. Fritz Erpenbeck, editor of *Theater der Zeit* and primary critic of Brecht, led the attack on *Mother Courage*, the Berliner Ensemble's first performance in the GDR (1949), for its "volksfremde Dekadenz" in "Formalismus und Dekadenz," in Schubbe, *Dokumente*, 109–13; Kurt Hager (Secretary for Science and Culture) attributed this tendency to "Weimar nostalgia" in his speech to the plenum of the Central Committee of the SED, July 1957, *Dokumente*, 540.

23. Ulbricht, "Der Kampf gegen den Formalismus," 180.

24. See Ulbricht, "Der Weg zur Sicherung des Friedens" (1959), in Schubbe, *Dokumente*, 543, and "Einige Probleme der Kulturrevolution" (1957), in ibid., 534.

25. Hans Joachim Hoffmann, "Commemorative Address on Brecht's 90th birth-

day, 10 February 1988," *Theater der Zeit* (April 1988): 6–9. The term SDI, referring to former president Reagan's Strategic Defense Initiative, was cited by Hoffmann in the original English abbreviation.

26. Brecht's statement "Kulturpolitik und Akademie der Künste" was published in *Neues Deutschland* (12 August 1953) as a response to the academy's declaration of solidarity in the "fight against fascism," published in *Neues Deutschland* on 30 June 1953. Brecht's statement shared with those by Heym and Harich (published in the *Berliner Zeitung*, 29 and 14 July 1953, respectively) an emphasis on a critical realism encompassing the ongoing exploration of new forms appropriate to the new realities; see Wolfgang Harich, "Es geht um den Realismus," and Stefan Heym, "Das Volk will echten Realismus!" in Schubbe, *Dokumente*, 292–96 and 298–99.

27. Brecht's private comments, in his working journal, *Arbeitsjournal* (Frankfurt am Main, 1981), 2:596 (hereafter *AJ*), combine doubt about the reality of the vanguard class (criticizing not only the "petit bourgeois character" of contemporary audiences but also the "depravity" of the 17 June rebels) with a note of regret and frustration echoed by later GDR intellectuals such as Heym and Wolf.

28. The *locus classicus* is Lenin's "State and Revolution," in *Lenin Anthology*, ed. Richard Tucker (New York, 1985), esp. 368–80. The utopian moment in Lenin's solution to the failings of "bourgeois talking shops" may be difficult to discern at this point in time, but his diagnosis of the problem—that popular participation in advanced capitalist societies is largely illusory—resonates even in the analysis of decidedly *un*-Leninist critics of the degraded publicity of advanced capitalism, such as Jürgen Habermas and Noam Chomsky.

29. Although the GDR constitution allowed for representation of other parties in the *Volkskammer*, it also secured the SED's permanent dominance of the Central Committee and the Politburo; see *DDR-Handbuch*, edited by the Federal Republic of Germany's Ministry for Intra-German Relations (Cologne, 1985).

30. A good example is Wekwerth's production of *Galileo Galilei* in 1971. Arguing that Brecht's final version of *Leben des Galileis* (1956) focused too much on Galileo's weakness and so ignored the heroic dimension of Galileo's fight for the truth, Wekwerth returned to the more positive portrayal of the earlier version (1938–39). See Werner Hecht, ed., *Materialien zum Leben des Galilei* (Frankfurt am Main, 1977). On Wekwerth's long-standing work for the Stasi as "collaborator for special missions" beginning in 1969, see Walther, *Sicherungsbereich Literatur*, 622–75.

31. Manfred Wekwerth, "Die Welt braucht Veränderung," *Theater der Zeit* (December 1989): 8. Under Brecht in the 1950s and, to a certain degree under Helene Weigel's administration in the 1960s, the Berliner Ensemble was a vanguard institution that shaped the course of European and world theater. By the 1980s, however, under "Multifunktionär" Wekwerth, monitored by Brecht heirs Barbara Brecht-Schall and lead actor Ekkehart Schall, the theater was little more than a Brecht museum. The (only) two new Brecht productions of the 1980s, *Der Untergang des Egoisten Fatzer* (1986) and *Baal* (1988) broke little new ground, preferring to harness these thoroughly *asocial* texts to the platitudes of "real socialism."

32. Hoffmann, "Das Sicherste ist die Veränderung," 12.

33. Peter von Becker, "Nach Sachsen, nach Sachsen: Eindrücke in Dresden und Leipzig, über Aufführungen der beiden größten Schauspielhäuser außerhalb der Hauptstadt," *Theater 1988*, 36–41.

34. Engel himself acknowledges this contradiction while arguing for its value

within the confines of the GDR. See "Diesseits der Hoffnung, jenseits der Furcht," interview with Engel conducted by Isabel Bayer, *Theater 1990*, 47–51.

35. Knut Lennarz, "Das Theater und die Wende," in *Vom Aufbruch zur Wende. Theater in der DDR* (Velber, 1992), 61. In "A Postmodernized Brecht?" *Theatre Journal*, 45, no. 1 (1993): 1–19, Marc Silberman argues for the GDR theater as a site "relatively free from direct intervention from the Stasi" (17). Silberman acknowledges the price (conformity, indirect criticism, silence about the persecution of colleagues) of this relative freedom and the power of the paternalist state as the final arbiter of that freedom, but he remains reluctant to conclude that the paternalism and structural arbitrariness of the "family business" made legally secured civil and artistic rights impossible, even if occasionally allowing for independent expression.

36. On the implications of this legislation (stymied by external publicity), see Petra Boden, "Strukturen der Lenkung von Literatur: Das Gesetz zum Schutz der Berufsbeschreibung Schriftsteller," in *MachtSpiele: Literatur und Staatssicherheit*, ed. Peter Böthig and Klaus Michael (Leipzig, 1993), 217–27.

37. Biermann was not expelled, strictly speaking, since he was in West Germany on a concert tour, but rather *ausgebürgert*, or stripped of his citizenship, in a procedure based on a Nazi-era law used against against Jews, Communists, and other undesirables. For the effect of the singer-songwriter's expulsion on GDR theater, see Lennarz, "Der Fall Wolf Biermann," in *Vom Aufbruch zur Wende*, 46–49; for an indictment of Lamberz in his own words, see the transcript of the conversation between Lamberz and several of the protesters, including Heiner Müller and Christa Wolf, who signed a statement protesting Biermann's disenfranchisement in the name of a socialist public sphere that was secretly recorded by one of the signatories, the actor Manfred Krug, in his *Abgehauen: Ein Mitschnitt und ein Tagebuch* (Düsseldorf, 1996), 7–112. In Lamberz' view, the public(ation of) "protest" by GDR citizens through a Western press service (after the GDR service had ignored them) was tantamount to betrayal; in the transcript, he explicitly associates this betrayal with the behavior of children toward strict fathers, apparently without any sense of irony, see ibid., 18–19, 62–64.

38. "Das Sichere ist die Veränderung," 13, 24. For less diplomatic expressions of SED hostility to the "experimentalism" and "democratism" associated with 1968 (the Prague Spring and Western student movements), see Karl Schneider (general director of the Magdeburg Theatre), "Das Ensemble," *Theater der Zeit* (February 1989): 3–4 and H. P. Enderlein (secretary of the Artists Union), "Zusammenarbeit schließt Meinungsstreit ein," *Theater der Zeit* (August 1989): 10.

39. Plenzdorf's sequel to his well-known play and filmscript, *Die Legende von Paul und Paula* (dir. Heiner Carow, 1979) placed the eponymous hero in situations that highlighted the stagnancy of GDR society and was therefore originally rejected by the Deutsches Theatre. John's review, in *Theater der Zeit* (January 1984): 4, praised the production for its light execution but faulted it for its "cabarettish" treatment of serious subjects such as military training.

40. See Freya Klier, *Abreiß-Kalender: Ein deutsch-deutsches Tagebuch* (Munich, 1988), 20–60.

41. Written at a moment in the Soviet Union at which the history of the Bolshevik rise to power was being rewritten by Stalin, Vishnevsky's play cautiously acknowledges flaws in Bolshevik strategy but allows those flaws to be explained away at the end by the prestige of the party and the charisma of the commissar (played in Alexander Tairov's original Moscow production by the glamorous Alissa Koonen).

Klier's critical intervention lay less in being "faithful to the text," as Patricia Anne Simpson claims ("State of the Art: Alternative Theatre in the GDR," *Modern Drama* 33, no. 1 [1990]: 131), than in cutting away the pathos of the original to expose the contradictions embedded in the text between the military exigency of the moment and the axiomatic infallibility of the party that finally wins out. For Klier's comments on the play, see *Abreiß-Kalender*, 80–100.

42. See Klier, *Abreiß-Kalender*, 99, 103. For a rather different (Western) view of Schroth as a young turk and facilitator of critical theater in Schwerin, see Hartmut Krug, "Aufbruch-stimmung, Morgenluft? Aspekte jüngerer DDR-Dramatik," *Theater 1988*, 59 and, for a brief account of Schroth's "Solidarity Evening," see Lennarz, "Abschied vom Realismus," in *Vom Aufbruch zur Wende*, 52–53. The difficulty of corroborating events surrounding this production is itself testimony to its erasure from public view.

43. Klier, *Abreiß-Kalender*, 19, 106–7.

44. For a detailed account of this production, see Simpson, "State of the Art," 129–38. For comments on SED pressure, see the interview with Krawczyk, originally published in the underground *Umweltblätter* shortly before his imprisonment (January 1988): "We'll keep playing," trans. Winton Jackson, *Across Frontiers* 4, 2–3 (1988): 39–40.

45. Peter Waschinsky, "Die Off-Theaterszene vor und nach der Wende," *Theater der Zeit* (August 1990): 8–10, and "Die real existierende (?) freie Theaterszene," 11–16.

46. See Wolfgang Büscher and Peter Wensierski, *Null Bock auf DDR: Aussteigerjugend im anderen Deutschland* (series sponsored by *Spiegel* magazine) (Hamburg, 1984), 133–34. The performance lasted about thirty minutes.

47. See the curricula vitae accompanying "traumhaft," the collectively composed Zinnober text in Harald Mueller, ed., *DDR-Theater des Umbruchs* (Berlin, 1990), 272–73.

48. For commentary on this radio version of *Fatzer*, see Loren Kruger, "Heterophony as Critique: Brecht, Müller and Radio Fatzer," *Brecht Yearbook* 17 (1992): 235–51; for an analytic account of GDR media from 1949 to the mid-1980s, see Gunter Holzweißig, *Massenmedien in der DDR* (Berlin, 1984).

49. See photographs of the *Zinnober-Laden* in Klaus Michael and Thomas Wohlfahrt, eds., *Vogel oder Käfig sein: Kunst und Literatur aus unabhängiger Zeitschriften in der DDR, 1979–1989* (Berlin, 1991), 290. Whether marginalized cultural groups were compromised by relying (often unwittingly) on facilitators with links as "unofficial collaborators" to the Stasi remains an unsolved question. The denunciation of Müller in January 1993 by an erstwhile and unsuccessful acolyte, Dieter Schultze, was met by Müller with a mix of ambiguity (his "conversations" with the Stasi were both "well-known" and ripe for dispatch as a "piece of GDR history") and uncharacteristic self-pity (the ongoing experience of "slander and persecution"), while younger colleagues, B. K. Tragelehn and Lothar Trolle, argued that Müller used contacts to actively protect political dissidents as well as artistic rebels. For Müller's self-defense, see "Gegen die Hysterie der Macht," *Tagesspiegel*, 15 January 1993, 14; for an initial report (in the melodramatic manner), see Robin Detje, "Heiner Müller und die Stasi: Der große Dichter schrumpft," and Detje, Iris Radisch, and Christian Wernicke, "Heiner Müller,"*Die Zeit* (15 January 1993): 49, 2. For a rebuttal, see B. K. Tragelehn and Lothar Trolle, "Rechtfertigungsreden sind überflüssig: B. K. Tragelehn und Lothar

Trolle über die Stasi-Vorwürfe gegenüber Heiner Müller," *Berliner Zeitung*, 20 January 1993. In "Literatur und Staatssicherheit," *Frankfurter Allgemeine Zeitung*, 28 January 1993, Frank Schirrmacher argues that Western critics denouncing Müller's dealings with the Stasi had in the bad old days of the GDR invested these dealings with the "seductiveness of the forbidden." This seductiveness is reflected in the comments of Michael Merschmeier, "Heiner und 'Heiner': Im Dickicht der Stasi. Ein deutsches Leben?" in *Theater Heute* (February 1993): 2–3; Merschmeier regrets that Müller's pained response did not live up to the cynical and equivocal persona fostered by influential cultural brokers such as the *Theater Heute* editorial board.

50. See Martin Morgner's interview with Liane Düsterhöft, "Theater unter dem Dach," *Theater der Zeit* (March 1991): 36–41; for some indication of opportunities and difficulties facing youth and community theaters before 1989, see Gunhild Lattmann, "Jetzt ist die Kraftprobe unerhört," *Theater der Zeit* (October 1989): 19–21.

51. Ingrid Seyfarth, "Die Saison 1989–90," *Theater der Zeit* (September 1990): 4. See also Hans-Ludwig Böhme, "Dresden im Herbst—eine Fotodokumentation," *Theater 1990*, 132–37.

52. See the statements by Initiative 4 November: Henning Schaller, "Neu anfangen, unsere Chance," *Theater der Zeit* (February 1990): 11–12; "Standpunkte," *Theater der Zeit* (March 1990): 28.

53. See Günther Rühle (former director of the Frankfurt State Theater and supporter of GDR dissidents such as Klier), "Die Zeit des Übergangs," *Theater der Zeit* (June 1991): 1–2; contributions to *Deutschland, Deutschland* in *Theater 1990*, including Harald Mueller, "Deutschland, ein Fernsehmärchen," 23–24, Sewan Latchinen, "Germoney: Die BRDigung der DDR," 30–31, Leander Haußmann, "Man wechselt nicht so gerne die Feinde," 31–32, and Cornelia Schmaus, "Wie spiele ich weiter?" 32–33.

54. Traute Schölling, " 'On with the Show?' The Transition to Post-socialist Theatre in Eastern Germany," trans. Marc Silberman, *Theatre Journal* 45, no. 1 (1993): 30–31.

55. See "Weniger Staat, mehr Verantwortung," Ulrich Roloff-Momin's interview with Franz Wille, *Theater Heute* (May 1993): 46–47. Roloff-Momin's prescription is harsh by German standards, but it is notable that he and other would-be financial reformers do not go so far as to tout commercial sponsorship as the primary solution. The prevailing understanding of the relations among theater, capital, and the patron state in Germany stands in sharp contrast to, say, the British Arts Council's assault on the so-called doctrine of subsidy and its promotion of "business partnerships" whose explicit goal is to "improve public perception" of the *sponsoring*, rather than of the sponsored organization; see Baz Kershaw, "British Theatres and Economics, 1979–1999," *Theatre Journal* 51 (1999): 267–83.

56. See Miriam Hoffmeyer, "Krieg der Metaphern: Götz Friedrich in Klausur, Käthe Reichel wettert gegen die Demokratie. Kulturniks sind wegen Entwurf zum Nachtragshaushalt schockiert," *Die tageszeitung* (electronic ed.), 15 March 1996 (at: http:www.taz.de).

57. Christine Richter, "Das Defizit wird immer grösser: Berliner Bühnen rechnen im Jahr 2001 mit einem Minus von 15,7 Millionen Mark," *Berliner Zeitung*, 4 October 2000; at: http://www.BerlinOnline.de/wissen/berliner_zeitung/archiv/2000/1004/feuilleton/0162/index.html?keywords=theater%20unter%20dem%20dach&ok=OK%

21&match=strict&author=&ressort=&von=1.9.2000&bis=30.10.2000&mark= dach%20unter%20theater%20dem&start=20.

58. Although he does not compare the aggressive commodification of theater pro-duction in Britain in the 1990s with theater elsewhere in Europe, Kershaw's recent analysis of the transformation of theater from a subsidized institution dedicated to "improving knowledge, understanding and practice of the arts" into a market-driven "entertainment provider" of cultural commodities for a fickle market defined above all by the tourist sector's consumption of "heritage culture" in Britain is useful in this context because it highlights just how much further the "dictatorship of the market" can go; see Kershaw, "British Theatres and Economics, 1979–1999," 269, 271–75.

59. Hochhuth is best known for *Der Stellvertreter* (The deputy), which was first produced by Ernst Piscator at the Freie Volksbühne in West Berlin and scandalized audiences worldwide with its dramatization of the Catholic Church's collaboration with the Nazis in World War II. By the time *Wessis in Weimar* was produced (1993), however, Hochhuth had faded from most German repertoires, although *Die Hebamme* (The midwife, 1974) was recently revived (2000) at the Berliner Ensemble.

60. For a summary of the debate, see Fritz-Jochen Kopke, "Wem gehört Brechts Theater?" *Wochenpost*, 20 April 1995, and, for English-language commentary, Stephen Kinzer, "Duelling Playwrights: Bertolt Brecht's Berliner Ensemble," *New York Times*, 25 June 1995, sec 2:5, 18.

61. Even before Peymann took over in 1999, reduced subsidies compelled the ensemble to raise ticket prices much higher than those at other subsidized theaters, such as the resolutely cheap Volksbühne, but tourists—at least—seem willing to pay them.

62. Although enlivened by the remarkable comic talents of Götz Schubert as the hapless Klaus Ultzsch and enriched by the witty program, a parodic re-creation of *Trommel*, the newsletter of the Young Pioneers, the GDR children's organization, the one-man stage adaptation at the Deutsches Theater offers a rosily sentimental view of a GDR childhood. The film, *Sonnenallee* (1999, directed by Leander Haußmann, who had previously directed theater exclusively), likewise softened the rough edges of GDR adolescence with the hues of 1970s sex, drugs, and rock and roll, to the horror of older, more politically focused dissidents, but succeeded nonetheless in capturing the contradictory, anarchic aspirations of the younger generation more effectively than *Helden*. For comment on the films, see Christiane Peitz, "Alles so schön grau hier: Leander Haußmanns *Sonnenallee*, Sebastian Petersons *Helden wie wir*: Der Osten ist jetzt Kult—auch im Kino," *Die Zeit*, 28 October 1999 (at: http://www3.Zeit.de).

63. See Richter, "Das Defizit wird immer grösser."

64. Schölling, " 'On with the Show?' " 32.

65. Claudia Waljudi, "Subkultur am Ende?" *Die Zitty*, no. 10 (20 April 2000), at: http://194.42.82.244/2000/10/index.htm; and her follow-up article, "Gegen das Kaputtsparen: Die lange Nacht der Off-Kultur," *Die Zitty*, no.24 (15 November 2000), at: http://www.zitty.de.pubs/aktuell/pageviewer.asp?TextID=1953.

66. Waljudi, "Die History," pt. 4 of "Subkultur am Ende?" http://194.42.82.244/ 2000/10/zitty4.html.

67. Baz Kershaw, *The Politics of Performance: Radical Theatre as Cultural Interven-tion* (London, 1992), 243. The (British) institutional context of Kershaw's interven-tion as theater intellectual (director, writer, academic) is in many ways harsher than that in Germany. Although (New) Labour has come to power since Kershaw wrote

his book, current cultural policy in Britain, with its reliance on business sponsorship more aggressive and more visible than in the United States, is still shaped by the legacy of the (post) Thatcherite Arts Council. Despite these different histories, the strategies developed by alternative theaters in Britain in negotiating the not always compatible currents of theatrical innovation and transformation of the social occasion and impact of performance in a fractured political and cultural environment are certainly applicable in present-day Germany.

ALEXANDER KLUGE

Translated by Michael Latham

It Is a Mistake to Think That the Dead Are Dead: Obituary for Heiner Müller

The funeral and burial of someone dear is a bitter and wrenching experience, but also something extremely real.[1] Yet to speak on the occasion of
Heiner Müller's death strikes me as something quite unreal. He said a great
deal about death.[2] With time comes death.

He spoke of the gravity of the dead. In Müller's specific conception,
the living are only half of reality. The dead are the other half. And the
dead have their established locations. These locations help determine the
place remaining for the living. He also said that it is a mistake to believe
that the dead are dead. Taking this into account, it is very difficult, in fact
impossible, to conduct a eulogy for Heiner Müller.

What you have accomplished here in this theater is something very
much alive.[3] For several days you have been reading his writings aloud.
This cannot be considered a leave-taking. It is, rather, a beautiful means
of making acquaintance. I don't know how you are feeling, but I feel in
this theater as though I can see him bowing around the corner, making his
way toward us with the little sacrament in one hand and his cigar in the
other. Armored by his wit. On the day of his interment, this is certainly
something unreal. All the same, it is a very real desire.

This contradiction of emotions—in loving someone, you do not want
to be parted from him—led Heiner Müller to remark that all successful
interments must go wrong. His poem "Mommsen's Block" is dedicated
to the late philosopher Felix Guattari, whose burial in the Père Lachaise
cemetery in Paris went wrong majestically, ending in complete chaos.[4] And
that pleased Heiner Müller . . .

Character Armor

He was born in 1929. An author of this sort always adopts the mother's perspective. That is to say, he regards the twenty years before his birth through the eyes of his parents. The sixty-seven years thereafter he saw on his own. He sees, as has been said, the cipher of the twentieth century, the purpose of the people of this century. His friend Andrei Bitov, who has also come here today, once remarked that the twentieth century begins in 1914 and ends in 1989.[5] We are already in the twenty-first, and already in the process of transferring our heritage to our heirs.

In 1914 we experience the division of the workers' movement, and its constituents are never again able to reunite. This division occurs because the workers and their organizations can do nothing to prevent the first World War. A short while later we have the slaughterhouse of Verdun, which for Heiner Müller will remain a cipher: Europe's leading industries poised against each other in this kind of battle involving poisoned gas and industrial genocide. And subjectively, the internal armoring this caused, not only for the dead, but for the living who returned from Verdun. The most terrible result of this, Müller said, is that there are only two alternatives when one adopts an internal character armor and outwardly begins to travel the rails. This is not only Heiner Müller's personal opinion, but what he likely read as the cipher of the twentieth century: that people, once set in motion, can no longer escape the rails subjectively. And these rails lead like railway traffic into Auschwitz.

Then there is the other alternative, the milder form of misfortune: the withdrawal from history, from reality, from the public sphere; the premature end of a life experience that is now no longer equipped for any further life. This kind of derailment, this confiscation of history, is also cheerless and bled of experience.

I am only mimicking Heiner Müller's way of addressing these issues. I once asked him whether he was more a prophet or a land surveyor. He replied, "A land surveyor, but even more a seismograph." He is a seismograph, one that measures minutiae, and measures as precisely as a quantum physicist. This is what an author does.

Block and Push

In November 1989 Heiner Müller works as if possessed on the mammoth play *Hamlet/Hamlet-Machine* while outside, history takes its course: a mixing of necessities but also of a great many chance occurrences.[6] Then a kind of blockage overcomes him. He described this in his poem "Mommsen's Block." He described how the great historian Mommsen was unable to complete the fourth volume of his imperial history, then his house burned to the ground, taking the manuscript with it. Actually, he claimed, Mommsen simply did not want to describe this continuation of republican Rome.[7] It has been suggested that Heiner Müller was describing his own block here. It is true that he always experienced these blocks, throughout the course of his life. . . . Then there would always be a push to productivity, and I would insist that he experienced another enormous burst of productivity in the three years before his death.

He stages *Tristan* in Bayreuth.[8] One hears sentences form him one would not have heard before. For example, he quotes Nietzsche: Without music all of life would be a mistake. In his writings he achieves a kind of generalization, in the sense of a progression from the abstract to the concrete. His texts become denser, more compressed. One might call it crystalline. He would like to write as Tacitus wrote, very concisely—abbreviated sentences, expressive fragments. The emotions and experiences that course through the subterranean channels—that is what is essential. Words can only accompany them.

How and when, at what time, did Heiner Müller actually produce this enormous body of work? One always sees him looking quite composed. He sits, drinks, observes, reacts, responds—usually not to the question that has been posed, but to something else. Then you see his famous nod. It could mean a number of things: yes, no, absolutely not, under no circumstances, really good. It had a thousand meanings, each in its own context. His Slavic way of expressing himself. A Roman from Saxony and at once a Prussian. To him this is no insult. He calls himself a Prussian—what he means by that is as uncertain as his nod. In any case, he works as if possessed at unusual hours. As if motorized. He is someone whose body also works when he writes. He stands before his work table. He hammers on his iron typewriter, a very old and loud machine. In this way, as if powered by a motor, his texts come into being. He developed especially in his final years dramatic poems that begin to replace theater, as Pushkin did, but that are also the raw materials of theater. That is, they come forth as text. There are no longer any stage directions. The dialogue is, as it were, entirely suspended at times. Then the plot is suspended, and yet it is still dramatic.

In the intensive care ward, two things saved his life. His wife, who watched over him and got him out, like Leonore in Beethoven's *Fidelio*. And more austere texts. He says that against the threat of death and in the face of irrevocable diagnoses, the only help is harder rhythms and even rhyme. It was not customary for him to rhyme. . . . And besides, he is a patriot, he said so himself. I asked him what he considered patriotic. He stared at me in surprise and said, "What do you mean by that?" I said, "Patriotic, what would you risk your life for?" He answered, after a pause,

"For my daughter." And that has nothing to do with him protecting her in some park, mind you; he meant that his writings were intended to help us pass on a heritage from this century to the next.

Heiner Müller possessed many qualities, and each of you here can surely speak of certain facets of them. I will only select examples. He was the very opposite of an opportunist. Opportunism, the fundamental illness of this century, was the only thing that occasioned his loathing. He is generally a friendly man, but on this point he is unyielding.

Author or Poet

He was now in Verdun. He attached great importance to this, and he wanted to see the play *Gespenster am Toten Mann* performed at the Verdun theater festival.[9] He traveled there, took the trouble, and then he made his opinion known: these charnel houses, this museum, the attempt to honor the dead by monumentalizing them, he said, this is death kitsch. He was asked to leave by the mayor. It was all right with him. . . . You will note that here, too, it is a matter of a certain severity to him. Another conspicuous element is his self-assurance. He describes television saying: "Television, daily repulsion, prepared babble, give us this day our daily murder."[10] He despises the inferiority complex that inhabits a number of institutions, including the major media, driven by the notion of actuality in daily affairs, with little patience for the substance of experience.

There is the designation "author" and there is the designation "poet." One designates those who, like independent contractors, assume responsibility for the words they publish. This is the author. The designation "poet" goes a bit further. It refers also to the process of production: even if I lose everything that is valuable in my work, I have still made it. In a radical manner, he exhausted this second possibility.

There are few authors in Europe who play realities against each other in words and sentences, take hold of them, and create an almost crystalline structure, a form of compression. This process comes out in his work, which is admittedly not an easy body of work. Who would in fact read his entire output painstakingly? And yet one can, and one must; it is a unified body of work. And this radical and truly avant-garde work will prove very helpful in the twenty-first century as a summary and translation of the experience of our own century; so much so that this work, upon the death of its author, releases its echo. This should give us all cause to think. He really did nothing to make his work accessible or to bring it to the public at a discount. Yet it is precisely to those who conduct themselves almost hermetically in this manner, and as a result also professionally, that the people themselves will come.

There is a strong emotional current in our entire country right now, also a unifying current in this case, working toward him in this sad moment where we now stand. But we must not be discouraged even on this unhappy day where we take our leave. He has provided us with a surplus of commissions and instructions . . . In his last conversation he said: "You know what the street that runs through here is actually called? It's called 'At the Circus.' Why don't we include with the actors of language also the artists of the body, like those at the circus?" The first circus proprietor in England was arrested, he said, because he produced a drama in his circus, using stunts and horses. This wasn't allowed; there was to be no competition. This division between the trivial, simple, and visceral on one hand and the spiritual, intellectual, and linguistic on the other—that is, the division between theater and circus—must be abolished. The separation of musical theater and dramatic theater has to be loosened. Theaters, he says, are repair shops for unroadworthy classics, but also for unroadworthy operas. This particular theater here is the site where the *Three Penny Opera* was performed and generally where operettas were performed . . .

Categorical Imperative
He had an abundance of ideas that prepare the theater for the transfer of experience from the twentieth to the twenty-first century. When a century ends, he said, one must balance accounts. A balance not of numbers, as in businesses transactions, but a balance of metaphors. A balance of receptacles, bottles, pots, and pans in which human experience can be transported through the desert. I asked him whether he believed in a return. He had thought about that. The idea had been welcome to him—for just a moment. . . . Then he came back to it again and suddenly criticized very severely Immanuel Kant's proposition: "Always act in such a manner that your action could be the object of a universal law."[11] And he said: We are simply not created or engaged as lawgivers. If everyone is a legislator, what an excess of legislation. He had an aversion to that. He said there is a different perspective, and with it one can tell whether or not one is true (*identisch*) to oneself: Always act in your life in such a way that, if you were to return, you would act in precisely the same way, be able to write the same texts, create the same plays. I would maintain that he had a great degree of identity.

There is a moment in a film that impressed him deeply. Jean-Luc Godard has an entire minute of black leader edited into one of his films.[12] That means that the theater goes dark. The audience listens to its own breath for an entire minute, hears that it is alive. And they honor the images by accepting this moment—and a minute is a very long time in a film—where there is no image at all. I think it would please him if we expressed our thanks to him by rising for a moment and offering a minute of silence.

Editor's Notes

1. This obituary was delivered on 16 January 1996 in the Berliner Ensemble. See Friedrich Dieckmann, "Trauersache Geheimes Deutschland: Wanderer über viele Bühnen im zerrissenen Zentrum: Totenfeier in Berlin," *Frankfurter Allgemeine Zeitung* (18 January 1996), 27; Petra Kohse, "Ein sächsischer Römer: Gestern wurde der Dichter und Theaterleiter Heiner Müller auf dem Dorotheenstädtischen Friedhof in Berlin beerdigt. Ein angemessener ratloser Abschied," *die tageszeitung*, 17 January 1996. A somewhat different translation is in Alexander Kluge, "It Is an Error That the Dead Are Dead," trans. Andy Spencer, *New German Critique* 73 (1998): 5–11.

2. Death is the main subject of the two volumes of conversation between Heiner Müller and Alexander Kluge. See Alexander Kluge and Heiner Müller, "*Ich schulde der Welt einen Toten": Gespraeche* (Hamburg, 1995), and *Ich bin ein Landvermesser: Gespraeche mit Heiner Mueller* (Hamburg, 1996).

3. Between January 3 and January 9 Müller's texts were read at the Berliner Ensemble. See "Die Müller Überschwemmung," *Der Spiegel*, 51, no. 3 (15 January 1996). Heiner Müller, "Texte gelesen von 42 Berliner Schauspielern: Live-Mitschnitt der öffentlichen Lesungen vom 3.–9.1.1996 im Berliner Ensemble," ed. Berliner Ensemble-Henschel Schauspiel Theaterverlag and Radio Brandenburg. 3 CDs. [1996].

4. Heiner Müller, "Mommsens Block," in Heiner Müller, *Drucksachen I des Berliner Ensembles* (Berlin, 1993).

5. Among Andrei Bitov's most recent translated works are *Pushkin House*, trans. Susan Brownsberger (Ann Arbor, 1990); *Ten Short Stories* (Moscow, 1991); *A Captive of the Caucasus*, trans. Susan Brownsberger (New York, 1992); *The Monkey Link: A Pilgrimage Story*, trans. Susan Brownsberger (New York, 1995).

6. Heiner Müller, *Hamletmachine and Other Texts for the Stage*, ed. and trans. Carl Weber (New York, 1989).

7. Theodor Mommsen, *Römische Geschichte*. 2d ed. 3 vols. (1857–85; reprint, Berlin, 1954). A fourth volume, consisting of two previously published articles, was published in Vienna in 1877. A fifth volume is on life in the provinces during the imperial period: *Die Provinzen von Caesar bis Diocletian*. 3d ed. (Berlin, 1866).

8. *Tristan* premiered on 25 July 1993.

9. Heiner Müller, *Germania 3: Gespenster am Toten Mann*, ed. Stephan Suschke (Cologne, 1996).

10. "Give us this day our daily murder," quoted from Müller's 1977 play *Hamletmaschine*, cited above.

11. Immanuel Kant, "Grundlegung zur Metaphysik der Sitten," in Immanuel Kant, *Werke*, ed. Wilhelm Weischedel (Darmstadt, 1961), 6:11–102.

12. *Band à Part (Outsiders)*, dir. Jean-Luc Godard, France, 1964, 95m, b/w. The scene consists of (almost) a minute of total silence on the soundtrack.

PART 2

Intellectuals in Transit:

Toward a Unified Germany

D I E T R I C H   H O H M A N N

Translated by Devin Pendas and Michael Latham

The Consequences of Unification
According to H.

H. puts the text of a short story on the table, hoping that it finds an audience. He is asked if this text really can be published in conjunction with what is altogether a fictive report about himself. He responds that, definitely, he wants people to know about the state of emotions here and now.

Everyday Events

This was the first day when no one stood in front of him and said, "You look like shit."

He doesn't even know where to begin, what to do with himself. What's happened? What in the world could make him not look like shit? He usually looked like shit. He had a right to that. Every day he reexperienced this looking like shit. And today he had been denied this essential fact, which had become so important to him that he needed to hear it every day in order to go on living. He looked like shit. Just like any other human achievement, this fact had to be acknowledged. We have a right to a simple nod of acknowledgment. And what else should he cling to in these lousy times?

He wanted to look like shit so that he wouldn't look like nothing, like the absence of a being, a nonentity. Looking like shit, he said to himself, meant being perceived among the masses, plucked out from among the nameless, and he was afraid of nothing so much as his own worthlessness. But today it happened; no one took notice of him. No one said this, "My God, he looks like shit" or "Heavens, you look like shit" or "The way you look makes me want to barf."

He was disturbed to the core of his being. He contemplated leaving this world altogether. If only he could make up his mind to throw himself into the cold river. Or plunge from the bell tower of the restored church like someone pretending to fly, swooshing through the air and hitting the night-cold pavement with a pious ditty on his lips.

He was so confused that, in these minutes, he was hardly in control of himself. In the midnight hours, all he wanted to do was convince himself that he did possess that quality which had, up to now, never been denied him. He told himself that he looked like shit. He still, thank God, looked like shit, he murmured. He did not have the least doubt that now he had to find some person in this world who would give him satisfaction, acknowledging his customary look. The day would be a disaster if the entire world refused him this essential right. He demanded this justice the way one demands the most important things in life—with vigor, with painful determination.

With nothing but the most important sentence in his head, ringing louder and louder, he walked barefoot across the river bridge straight into a lamppost and the post tilted suddenly and broke, crashing to the earth. The light died with a timid whimper. He clutched at the throat of a stray dog and the animal gave a death rattle, grew to the size of a dinosaur, collapsed with a siren cry, and was suddenly a mossy cobblestone.

He drew near the bell tower of the colossal church, which stood there in the glaring floodlights, an example of excess. For a moment he contemplated being likewise excessive and demanding more from the city and the world than the opinion that he looks like shit, which overrates him in any case. He thought about demanding that he be called a leper. After all, anyone prevented from holding a "regular" job—he intoned this "regular" sharply—deserved nothing more than the judgment "leprosy." Yes, that would suit him just fine, he cried through the emptiness of the tower with its stone spiral staircase and silent bells. He was a leper, grown ill overnight, felled at exactly fifty, smashing into the paving stones after the wild autumn that he had hoped would be the day of German unity. He who is no longer needed is a leper.

He was completely out of breath as he stood on the platform with the new wrought iron railing, as the spotlights fixed him with their honey gold light, the self-accused son on the way to crucifixion. He sensed satisfaction, even ecstatic bliss as he, still barefoot, stomped around along the tower walls and railings. With each wild step, the walls broke apart as he hit them in his desperation until, in the end, he stood unscathed on that gigantic heap of rubble to which the tower, the city, and—it seemed to him—the world had been reduced. He thought he must be crazy since there was still nobody in the vicinity who could have at least whispered to him, "You look like shit" or "You scumbag, people should let you die." At least that meant that they wanted to get rid of him.

No, there was nobody there who would have even wanted to bump him off. He had to take everything on himself. He had to survive the night which followed the day when the disgrace befell him that there was nobody who could assure him: "You look like shit, just like shit."

Thus tossed from his path, he dared not think about the coming morning. He was stunned, motionless, as if dead.

H. confesses that he finds it difficult to discern the things worth preserving in the past, the things that he would like to find again in the great unified republic. The disappointment is too deep, the paralysis too overwhelming in the face of the degenerations, yes, crimes, of which, he insists, he was unaware and which, had he learned of them, he would hardly have believed. He should have recognized them, the Mielke orders to Main Office XX of the Ministry for State Security that were intended, and he quotes, to "ensure implementation of the state and party's *Kulturpolitik* in the central cultural institutions by means and methods of political security." This office kept more than 350 part-time informers (read: snitches) active in the area of culture, literature, people who are still largely unknown and who understood themselves to be "the main weapon against the enemy."[1] Their tools against unsuitable authorship included the "systematic discrediting of public reputations, psychological destabilization, engendering mistrust and mutual suspicion within groups, exploitation of personal weaknesses, subversion, perturbation, deliberate indiscretion, and defamation." H. has read that in Berlin alone, the central archive of this ministry contains eighteen thousand meters of personal dossiers and eleven thousand meters of "operative dossiers," which served for the surveillance of individual people. And each meter of dossiers had more than ten thousand pages, containing information along the lines of the above-mentioned order.

H. was shocked by the realization of just how thoroughly the hired hands had done their work. The mutual mistrust among authors is still considerable, and many suspicions have not yet been laid to rest. Yes, H. would like to know what this perfidious apparatus had gathered concerning him; he sent his request for access to his files a year ago. So far the office has had to put him off; the list of applicants is too long. He may well have to wait another year.

No, he does not feel like a victim, but he feels deceived, betrayed, and misused. And in the new *Association of German Authors* the clarification of these various connections is far from finished. In the fall of 1991, a conference of more than thirty authors whose title was "The Stasi Accusation and How to Proceed?" did in fact bring this or that tardy confession. But not one of those gathered identified him- or herself as someone who had, until recently, been associated with the Stasi. It seems that the principle that one is innocent until proven guilty applies here as well. But who wants to promote him- or herself to investigator or judge, so long as everyone and everything is being put upon "from outside" by virtue of the fact that, for whatever reason, so and so was required to spend forty years of his or her life in this eastern part of Germany?

In this way, mistrust remained in society at large and among authors, and complete bewilderment arose in the face of countless retrogressions. Former members of the SED, including authors of both sexes, have, as members of a new "turncoat" (*gewendete*) party, by no means distanced themselves yet from their earlier view that the effects of their Leninist-Stalinist dogmas could no longer be discerned. For H., this phenomenon is part of the present problem: old know-it-alls are once again on hand to hold forth on the great crisis of capitalism, from which only the extreme Left (or the extreme Right?) can rescue the citizenry, the German people. But does this crisis actually exist?

There is insecurity in the face of rising unemployment and the high cost of living. There is the nonsensical provision in the unification treaty dealing with the dissolution of nationalized property, including state-administered houses and lands, that stipulates "return before recompense" for property claims by former owners. Thus, in the state of Brandenburg alone, there are three thousand claims for compensation, which affect nearly half the population of the state. There is the "new division" among the population into an immediately dominant *Besitzstand* (class of owners) and a *Nährstand* (class of producers), condemned to humility, who have nothing to put on the market but their labor power, if there were a market for it. These provide the best soil for right-wing and left-wing extremist forces and parties. H. fears that, on this fertile ground, evil seed will flourish.

H. is asked if this sort of cultural pessimism is a German peculiarity. Isn't he just another whiner whose petulance comes from an unreconstructed mindset and from attitudes, both combining with an element of uncertainty in the face of new living arrangements as well as new constraints and opportunities that, admittedly, are difficult for him to fathom?

H. admits that he could easily want simply to putter on, to be there for the things that he wants to have around him and the few people to whom he feels bound and whom he needs; that he could imagine himself withdrawing to his study in order to let whatever is inside him flow out, probably without any plan, randomly filling page after page, yet secretly hoping that a sort of *Ulysses* would result. Yes, he suspects that answers might be found in ancient myths, as for example to the question that moves him regarding the villains and victims of all times (and yes, he believes that being a villain does not exclude being a victim and vice versa) or to the question of the continual fascination with the—as he still and always anew hopes—eternally valid, yet to be redeemed human values. Without hope, he adds, he is lost and, when he really thinks about it, unable to accept himself and the world around him, too.

He is asked whether he has participated in the diverse support measures that his state has provided for literature. He acknowledges the efforts of the government in Brandenburg for the preservation of arts and literature, for the survival of artists and literati. He is participating in the effort to improve the climate for his guild but not in the distribution of various hundred-thousand-mark stipends, which have so far been awarded to roughly fifty authors in his state. He would much rather have seen his latest book, published in late autumn 1991 (the first German novel about Robert Burns), given a fraction of the promotional support expended on a new laundry detergent or a soft drink.[2] Of the first printing of three thousand copies, exactly three hundred have so far found their way into bookstores. In the country with three initials, whose name many today coyly preface with the word "former," none of his books had an initial printing of fewer than ten thousand copies, and these were always quickly sold out.

Nevertheless, he is happy that good literature gets published and, in his state, is even honored with prizes. The Brandenburg literature prize and three promotional stipends were awarded for the first time in 1991. The award ceremony for 1992 suggests that the prize has gained a good reputation.

He adds that he hopes the time has passed when tons and tons of books were dumped on waste-disposal sites like the one near Espenhain in Saxony. Among them were cloth-bound books printed on high-grade, acid-free paper, editions of Goethe, Schiller, Hegel, and Shakespeare, much as titles by authors who were well known and respected in the West but happened to come from a country that has disappeared from the map.

Also, he hopes the time has passed when being an author in the GDR meant for the opinion makers in the old German states that he or she was suspect of ideology and had betrayed art for nonliterary ends, as the popular and catchy reproach went.

The time has come, H. hopes, when what belongs together can grow together, as one of the great men of postwar Germany has said.[3] And perhaps the time will also come when being an East German intellectual simply means being part of a new Europe of regions. And, of course, H. hopes that occasionally, this Europe will let him publish and will take note.

Editor's Notes

1. The number of 350 part-time informers refers to the IMs employed by Division 7 of Main Office XX, which covered mass media as well as arts and literature. See David Gill and Ulrich Schröter, *Das Ministerium für Staatssicherheit: Anatomie des Mielke Imperiums* (Berlin, 1991), 51.

2. Dietrich Hohmann, *Ich, Robert Burns* (Berlin, 1991).

3. Brandt's famous statement is reprinted in Willy Brandt, *". . . was zusammengehört": Reden zu Deutschland* (Bonn, 1990).

Soundtracks: GDR Music from "Revolution" to "Reunification"

Die Luft brannte auch irgendwo. Das war eine geile Zeit. Kein Law-and-Order, gar nichts. Da dachten wir so, wir mußten den wirklichen Ostberliner Underground dokumentieren in Form von einem Sampler. Und da haben die im Eimer gesagt, im Klub da, im Eimer, in diesem besetzten Haus, wir machen hier zur Währungsunion drei Tage die völlige Aktion, die letzten Tage der Ostkohle, "die last days of the East Mark," da habe ich gedacht, wir nennen das die letzten Tage von Pompeji. Das ist ganz klar, wir machen das aber richtig opulent, denn man weiß im Grunde, alles geht zu Ende. Das war das Feeling auch, dementsprechend wurde auch gespielt, dementsprechend ist der Sound auf dem Album auch. Der ist ziemlich katastrophal, aber es ist okay, so war das, es war nicht anders, das ist ein absolutes Zeitdokument.

There was also something almost burning in the air. It was a totally wild time. No "law and order," nothing. So we thought, we had to document the real East Berlin underground in the form of a sampler. And the guys from the "Eimer" said, you know, in the club there, in the "trash can," in this squatted house, we're going to have three days of total action for the currency union, the last days of the East dough, "the last days of the East Mark," and I thought, we'll call it the last days of Pompeii. It made total sense, but we'll really do it up, lavish, because everyone knows that basically everything comes to an end, and that was the feeling as well. The bands played in that mood, and the sound on the album also corresponds to it. It was catastrophic, but that's okay, that's how it was, an absolute documentary of the time.

—Rex Joswig, "Herbst in Peking"

With the conversion of the East Mark on 1 July 1990, a segment of GDR life came to an end. With that change, the possibility of a marginal, in-expensive, collective existence for GDR bands vanished—not to be con-verted into or exchanged for hard currency. In anticipation of that final time, a trinity of cult bands played for a trinity of days. The live recording *Die letzten Tage von Pompeji* (The last days of Pompeii) constitutes the vinyl remains of a time suspended in the parenthesis between documentary and history, between the immediacy of the everyday and the prediction of its erasure. As he reported in an interview (7 June 1995), Rex Joswig acted on this impulse and documented the event in all its chaos and technical imperfection for posterity. This album, along with retrospective CDs, books, and songs, documents the "wild time" in a chronicle of apocalyptic, irreverent, and chaotic moments. These notes from the margin attest to the existence of a cultural community shaped by politics, music, and republics.

The album in "celebration" of the currency union features the bands IchFunktion, Die Firma, and Freygang and their fans, whose numbers swelled to such proportions that by the third night, they were standing in the street.[1] These bands and their members occupied (and in some cases, retain) a place of prominence in the East Berlin music pantheon. In this chapter, I argue that the music and texts provide an imperative counterhistory to the fall of the East and the fast-forwarded process of reunification. I refract the texts of songs and statements through an historical lens and tailor a theory of the public sphere and civil society in an effort to demonstrate their capacity to resist the totalizing rhetoric of the West, the compulsion of which is to erase all traces of what was the East.

It would be presumptuous and silly to argue that politics is main muse of this music; the "scene," its stage, is elaborately and incestuously constructed, the players interrelated, and the story written in retrospect, only after the eruption or intrusion of history. The "everyday" was suddenly interrupted, elevated; it crashed, and another routine—making a living under the rigorous conditions of West German (cultural) capitalism—ensued. Nevertheless, music marked the historical moment of the Eastern fall, and others have documented the impact of musical culture on political events.[2] The texts I examine here ask to be read differently—not as sociological evidence of rock's politics, but as they are: sometimes clueless, quirky, and historically specific. They reclaim a highly politicized and problematized identity that refuses to be silent. For, according to Joswig, the bands formed a political entity to the extent that they were against the system; the band IchFunktion acknowledges that the state provided the greatest source of inspiration.[3] Politics, then, is involved, however unintentionally or contingently. In this piece, I sketch the chaotic semiotics of the musical texts of the late GDR as partial expressions of socioeconomic conditions and the political production of signs. The provisional political consciousness of the "wild time" at the end of the GDR is expressed in the aesthetics of catastrophe, the argot of the apocalypse. Under these significative circumstances, chaos, in a highly organized system, constitutes a moment of resistance—under the conditions of both socialism and capitalism—and is thus politicized.

Since the fall of the Wall, the German-German elections, *Währungs-union* (currency union), and "reunification," the remnants of the GDR's shipwreck have begun to surface and wash ashore—into a "public sphere" of sorts.[4] The political shift Westward realigned the top, bottom, center, and margins of musical signification in the former East. An irresistible trend in the West to politicize all music is countered, or at least frustrated, by the random and provocative signifying processes of some GDR musicians, or destabilized by the political activism of some members of the Stasi informant network. In the idiom of prophecy and publicity, however, many bands sang the dialect of apocalypse and anarchy. With irony, self-effacement, and nostalgia, they marked the death of a state and their own place in it; they play on and play on meaning.[5] Much depended on the bands' ability to create and occupy new stages for their music and their audience. While some groups have successfully (this is a polyvalent term, as success must be measured differently in East and West)[6] negotiated the loss of their "home," their stabilizing narrative—the fiction of their "national" identity as German citizens of a socialist state—others have broken up or gone under (such as Die Firma), gone private or commercial (such as Bobo in White Wooden Houses or the better-known Rammstein, formed after the *Wende*), or reconfigured (such as Freygang, now a composite of bands past).[7]

In the process of recasting the GDR past, one can ask about what was lost. Was there a GDR-specific music culture? How did it sound? Is it possible to reconstruct a narrative of GDR musical culture with notes from the margins and the cultural artifacts that have surfaced in a small collector's market?

I attempt to answer these questions with reference to several interrelated texts from the late GDR. The first text is the above-mentioned live recording *Die Letzten Tage von Pompeji* (The last days of Pompeii), the album that documents the final days before the *Währungsunion* as celebrated in a squat (illegally occupied house) in the center of Berlin. The three bands, the "unholy trinity" (so described in the promotional material) Firma, Freygang, and IchFunktion, secure their place in posterity for East German music.[8] The album was recorded in the Eimer, located on Rosenthaler 68, the "royal residence" of the punk rock scene in the center of Berlin. The album, released on Peking Records,[9] an independent label founded by Joswig (of Herbst in Peking, performers of the famous and often-anthologized "Bakschischrepublik"),[10] documents a three-day concert—"without overdubbing," in all its atrocity and honesty: "Diese Platte ist das was sie ist— ein Frontalangriff auf hochgezüchtete HIFI-Ohren" (this album is what it is—a frontal attack on the finely tuned hi-fi ears), according to the ladies and gentlemen of Peking Records. The promotional material, the songs, the autobiography—from different enterprises and personalities—have an attitude, the essence of which is captured in the sign-off on this album's promotional flyer:

> Gesungen wird natürlich deutsch und es sind Songs, die den Schreiberlingen westdeutscher Musikgazetten sicher nur ein konsterniertes, gar ein arrogantes "Ostrock . . ." entlocken werden.
> Aber was soll's—wir wissen es besser.

> It's sung in German naturally, and these are songs that will certainly elicit nothing but an arrogant "Ostrock" from the penpushers of West German music magazines . . .
> But what the hell, we know better.

These words, fighting words that throw down the gauntlet before the Western audience, seem to articulate pride before the fall, articulating both a sign-off and a send-up of the Western music critics and pen-pushers who seem, judging by the resonating silence generated in response to so much sound, to be suffering from a politically transmitted selective deafness. This frontal attack on hi-fi ears and the West German music press struts its arrogance and thereby turns the tables on the *Besserwisser* (know-it-all) cliché. On the turf of "Ostrock"—even if the columns are crumbling—the *Besserwessis* (a derogatory term for West Germans, indicating an assumed arrogance in their self-proclaimed superiority) lose their "home" advantage.

The next object of reference in this study is a book published by an alternative press in East Berlin. In Key Pankonin's *Keynkampf*, the author, who wrote songs for Die Firma and performed in the band, as well as in IchFunktion, founded by Tschaka, reports and fantasizes on the moods and music of his life in the sounds, the surreal everyday, and the marginality of the time in transition, in question.[11] His autobiographical account of the "scene" takes the form of fairy tale (in some ways, it is an unconventional story of his search for the only woman, "FF," who assumes various shapes on earth, such as those of a glow-worm, a witch, a queen of darkness, and various human females, the *Kartoffel* [potato]), science fiction (in some ways, the time travel is completely disorienting and extraterrestrial), and essay (in other ways, it offers wisdom with an attitude about everything from political birth to a philosophy of life known as *Rock gegen Mittelmäßigkeit* [rock against mediocrity]), in which he explicates the imponderable abstractions of love, hatred, time, and freedom.[12] The text is coded with names of other band members, abbreviated places, and some unreadable references. Dreams and history (from the crossing of Czech borders to his first visit to the West) meld with fantasy and fiction.

The narrative constant is provided by the negative philosophy that dominates the text (and, by extension, interprets a life-strategy for the former GDR). Pankonin's title echoes and negates Hitler's Mein Kampf[13] and appropriates the phrase for his own form of late twentieth-century living under whatever system predominates. Pankonin wants to be a hero; he has the imagination for it, but not the means. Perhaps the only act of heroism in his time and place is no act at all. Significantly, the text ends with a dream of inspired battle, of taking a stand, of pushing unwanted visitors down the stairs, after thirty years of silence. He is "Key—der Kampf" (108) only in a dream, in which the Rolling Stones play at the award ceremony and Johnny Rotten, the great inspiration for the author and for Punk East, attends. The negativity of dreams, however, is in some ways the source of songs. The passive resistance of Keynkampf was (and could be?) a disruption to the systems: it is the friction in the machine; it opposes the mediocrity and boredom supplied by daily life. Not to fight is the only way to live Pankonin's narrator's philosophy of punk. If, in an act of flagrant dialectical recuperation, this amounts to politicized passive resistance, so be it. This posture is a leftover from his GDR upbringing, which—politics aside—effectively fragments the totalizing rhetoric of unification. This text is full of philosophy, fantasy, documentary, history, and personal narrative, all of which combine to give the reader a time telescope into the private past of a pivotal player in the music scene. Music provides the reference point for his narrative lifeline.[14]

The cover of Keynkampf features a male figure, fast asleep on the back of the rear end of a gigantic pig (the head, predictably in this topsy-turvy world, is depicted on the back cover). This image advertises the inverted world within: the author, guitarist, songwriter, and now autobiographer of the alternative music scene in Berlin/DDR sends news from "far away worlds," according to the back flap. And while he was sleeping, history happened. His voice is that of the eyewitness, his narrative unreliable. In his waking moments, Pankonin sketches his own precarious subject position, tossed in the tumult of historical events. He does not, however, invest the narrative with anything more courageous than his own lyrics. Despite his dreams, his socialist conditioning, his idealism, his dedication to "Trashfoodpunk," Pankonin is a sublime hero of negativity, a philosopher of friction and of the music that is its expression.[15]

Here, in his post-unification description of himself and the events that marked his nation and generation, we the readers find ourselves immersed in a kind of "court" culture, complete with a king, a queen, a royal residence, courtly intrigue, and courtly love—all are imagined or experienced by the antihero Pankonin. His tales of fictional dragons, princesses, and other figments and figures of the real and the imaginary populate the narrative that straddles his personal and political history. This account frequently blurs the distinction between the worlds—not surprising, since his response to the upheaval of his time is to go to bed with comic books (39). Pankonin's adventure explores with innocence and hindsight (and without apology or ideological window-dressing) the relationship between music and politics in the demise of the East as it succumbs to prevailing politics. Still, once the fairy-tale dust of the "revolution" settles, a correspondence emerges between political categories and popular culture.

The third product is a CD by Die Firma called *Kinder der Maschinenrepublik* (Children of the machinery republic) that is significant on its own, but especially so in this context. Pankonin wrote the lyrics to four of the twenty-one songs on the release. The music is consistently aggressive, occasionally aggravating, and persistently underproduced. The songs, too, aggress, transgress, and tyrannize. The victims: corruption, filthy fascists, boredom, mediocrity, revolutionaries, old-guard heroes. There is an audible intertextuality between *Keynkampf*, the CD, and the album. The "scene" evolves through a network of informal connections, driven by music—at least according to some accounts. The more sinister reading of these connections involves the state's motivations of surveillance. Die Firma, which is of course the pseudonym for the State Security Service, the *Staatssicherheitsdienst* or Stasi, kept its secret by telling it, naming itself. (Two members of the band were suspected of working as—and eventually revealed themselves to be—*inoffizielle Mitarbeiter*, which either did or did not, depending on point of view or points on a moral compass, compromise the status of the GDR *Kultband*). For Pankonin, the music is more important—he even describes it as "Deutsche Volksmusik in Reinstkultur" (German folk music in its purest cultural form) (75). How, then, do we read the critical voices, so full of irony, ambiguity, and ambivalence? It seems that surveillance was as much a part of the scene as performance, and still Pankonin's narrator stands by the band and its music, which has its "eigenes Gesicht" (75).[16]

The CD was released in 1993 on the dead horse label and mixed in the WYDOCKS studio on Schönhauser Allee 5, an address at the center of the scene.[17] The CD cover reads like a Hallmark card from the edge: Greetings are sent to familiar names: paths crossed with Freygang, Feeling B, Herbst in Peking, Tacheles (1987–1990), Inchtabokatables,[18] IchFunktion, and so on (back cover). The CD liner notes record some lyrics, photos of the band members in various leisure activities, and a philosophical paragraph about the relationship between states, subjects, and systems, some of which echoes passages from *Keynkampf*.[19] This was the first and last CD produced by Die Firma.

Apart from and in addition to the references made by the bands themselves to finality, endings, and last days, scholars and commentators have mimed this diction of finitude. In Olaf Leitner's "Rock Music in the GDR: An Epitaph," the GDR rock historian looks back and sings the "swan song"[20] of East German rock, while he attempts to specify the sounds and events that separate GDR music from a mimetic dependence on outside influence. Not surprisingly, Leitner zooms in on highly politicized, resistant musical moments, including the media feud between Erich Honecker and Udo Lindenberg, and rock musicians' participation in the "effective revolution" (39). Peter Wicke, founder and current director of the *Forschungszentrum populäre Musik* at Humboldt University in (East) Berlin, has written extensively on the aethetics and politics of rock music in the GDR.[21] Michael Rauhut's *Beat in der Grauzone: DDR-Rock 1964 bis 1972—Politik und Alltag* and *Schalmei und Lederjacke*, with its focus on the 1980s,[22] exemplify a balance of interpretation and archival research. What emerges from both books is an overview and a close-up of the government's constant negotiation with the forces of music and its potential impact on security issues, identity formation, and youth-cultural politics. In this regard, the interplay between public and private cultural life in the GDR assumes the significance of a social movement. While there are clear differences between the cultures of the First and Second Worlds,[23] the one that bears the most weight is their divergent relations to media and technology as constitutive elements of the public sphere. The debate about confederation or unification, the lambasting of Christa Wolf, the crisis of German intellectuals, the accusational mode that inspires confession, and the displacement of politics with moral law enforcement—these reactions obscure a crucial point: that the culture of everyday life did not depend on "intellectuals," narrowly defined as literary or scientific figures. If, as Peter Rossman and others have argued,[24] there were two classes of intellectuals in the GDR, the official and the unofficial, then contemporary definitions could benefit from adjusting the politics of inclusion and exclusion.[25] Music counts. It becomes clear, in the perfect vision of hindsight and the retroactive act of prophecy, that music articulates the public sphere. This articulation is specific to the bands' role in GDR history.

Any attempt to theorize the nature of *Öffentlichkeit* (public sphere, publicity) in the former GDR must consider a Habermasian model of the bourgeois public sphere, map it on to "really existing socialism," and ultimately reject it as a bad fit.[26] Certain universals simply seem not to be transferable across ideological, cultural, and economic boundaries. Yet, if we consider the historical events that culminated in the popular uprising of 1989, we must come to terms with the conceptual nature of the revolutionary project drafted by the "oppositional" groups of the former East. The eruption of the "private" into the "public" sphere defines the "revolution" that led to reunification. At that point, the collective unconscious of an entire people surfaced with the realization that they were "das Volk" (the people) so vaunted in the empty rhetoric of the SED. The demands of groups such as Neues Forum, Demokratie Jetzt, Initiative Frieden und Menschenrechte, and die Grünen included above all freedom of speech and association, freedom of assembly, autonomy of institutions, free elections, direct democracy[27]—in short, a civil society in the classical sense. The discourse echoed a Habermasian vocabulary: the exclusion of violence on both sides, the imperative of rational participation, the inclusion of the disenfranchised but universalist interests. Eventually, however, the remarginalization of these oppositional groups after the first general German-German election led to the inevitable conclusion that the *Volk* preferred a "DM-nationalism" (Habermas) to an experimental idea of civil society.[28]

Historically, the public sphere was occupied and orchestrated by the SED and its apparatus, though, as David Bathrick has argued, there was an emergent literary public sphere.[29] The monolithic media, the paranoid control over means of communication—from telephones to copiers to electric typewriters to cassettes—and the deployment of the Stasi in both official and unofficial capacities correspond to a Foucauldian definition of the relationship between knowledge and power. Any criticism from below was criminalized, unless, of course, that criticism was so peculiarly encoded as to bypass the hermeneutic circle of state socialist interpretation.[30]

This leads to the question of a split between public and private language. There was consensus (if silent, or so abstract as to be incomprehensible) that the public language spoken by the state had been evacuated of meaning. The argot of "Trashfoodpunk" (Pankonin) challenged the idiom of officialdom. Thus, the struggle for power—the power of and over semantics—must be considered as a predominantly linguistic struggle. In the GDR, the *Alltag* (everyday) did in fact become a site of resistance, however closely observed it may have been. For a moment, the collective desire of the people had an impact on the party and its fate. That instant signals the fleeting existence of an East German public sphere. In the context of Pankonin's music and cohort, however, that sphere was necessarily fragmented. The response to politics must be differentiated within the scene itself. One site, for example, is the squat Im Eimer, described in Pankonin's text; it constitutes an alternative reality: "Kein Chaos, sondern eine andere Ordnung" (not chaos, but another order) (43). The conditions of that subculture enabled the amateur bands to challenge with disorder the monopoly on music.[31]

The establishment (and failure) of independent labels after the fall of the Wall represented an effort by musicians to take control of the means of production and distribution of their "own" music. As Pankonin points out, bands tried to help each other make records, but eventually this effort proved futile (49). Some survive; others have already jousted with the free market and fallen off the horse. Owing in part to the (in some cases misleading) political construction of the music scene in the East, with few exceptions, there is almost no resonance or reception in the West. Other bands maintain their own labels and sublabels: they play the role of manager, promoter, and producer, defying the capitalist-commercial structures in place in the West. Still others, such as Pankonin, have taken up the pen.[32]

Extreme Unction

The ubiquitous compulsion to document and publicize the remains of the GDR before it disappears completely—to collect, collate, and codify this closed chapter of German history—is not least discernible in the music industry. Deutsche Schallplatten, once the only record studio in the GDR (the best-known label was AMIGA), has produced a series of re-releases, a twenty-volume "Rock aus Deutschland Ost" and "final," or post-*Wende*, concluding numbers on other series, such as "Kleeblatt" (which produced "die anderen bands") and "Hallo." The GDR fanzine "NM!MMES-SITSCH" released number 13 in the "Hallo" series with an ironic commentary:

> Hart aber Hallo, denn diese Platte heißt *HALLO 13*, weil sie sich direkt an euch wendet: *Hallo Leute! Hallo 13!* Pünktlich zum 20jährigen Jubiläum der einst mit großem Hallo begrüßten gleichnamigen, zwölfteiligen *Amiga*-Serie wollen wir unseren Eltern zeigen, daß doch noch etwas aus uns geworden ist. Und—*Na aber Hallo-Ballo*—da schlägt's glatt 13![33]

> Hard but Hallo, for this record is called Hallo 13, because it is a direct appeal to you: hallo people, hello 13. Punctually on the 20th anniversary of the 12-part Amiga series of the same name, once greeted with a big hello, we wanted to show our parents that we made something of ourselves. And—now hallo-ballo—and that makes an even 13!

Such musical moments, produced by relatively independent labels, proliferated in the period between the fall of the Wall and reunification. They reference a certain GDR-specific history while ironically noting their place in it as the last in the sequence.

Still, the time between the fall of the Wall and reunification was marked by a feeling of anarchy, optimism, and hope. Traces of that time can still be heard in the music, but we cannot overlook the Pirandello-esque predicament of bands in search of an audience in a variation on the theme of last rites.

Such an ultimate moment is marked by the production of the album in honor of the currency union, which took place on 1 July 1990. Meanwhile, in the ruins of the Eimer, the bands played on. The album cover features a tryptich of the bands in action, the individual shots framed by crumbling columns. The back cover lists the songs on side one by IchFunktion and Die Firma; a picture of Im Eimer divides this pair of bands from Freygang's side. There are no obvious common points, though IchFunktion's songs thematize power reversals, inverted heroes, and unlikely upheaval. One example of these themes is IchFunktion's "Beitrag zur Währungsunion" (Contribution to the currency union, the album's dedication):

"Hobin Rood" (2:10)

Der Schachkönig	The chess king
und die Herzdame	and the queen of hearts
die allcrimes are paid	the "allcrimes are paid"
aus dem Andererseits	from the other side
die gegen Wahrheit	against truth
und die Rechtecktypen	and the rectangular types
konnten ihm nichts anhaben	they had nothing on him
Hobin Rood ist bereit	Hobin Rood is ready
Er ließ sich lumpen	He mooched when he could
er befreite die Reichen	he freed the rich
er ist wieder da	he's back
Don't eat the rich	"Don't eat the rich"
er beklaut jetzt die Bauern	now he's robbing the farmers
er nimmts von den Armen	he steals from the poor
er besteigt mit seinen Ratten	and he boards the sinking ship
das sinkende Schiff	with his rats
Nehmt's den Armen,	Steal from the poor
gebt's den Reichen	give to the rich
Geld muß zu Geld	money stays with money
H. Rood schlampt für die Feigheit	H. Rood does a bad job for cowardice
denn er ist kein Held . . .[34]	for he is no hero . . .

Pankonin's lyrics transform Robin Hood into a contemporary political figure who robs the poor to feed the rich. The logic: no future, no hero. The frequent occurrence of the verb *schlampen*, to be slovenly, jackhammers the meaning of the inversion home while it parodies *kämpfen*, to struggle. The other texts, "Loser" and "Attila," similarly upset the status quo, though the haphazard lyrics defy consistent reading. Whether this piece fits into a punk anticorporate profile is debatable. The ironic and shifting position of Pankonin boggles the hermeneutic mind. This material is highly undecidable.

In homage to Johnny Rotten, perhaps, Pankonin sings the song of "no future," of the life of a loser, of the great, dark, meaningless future of negation: no future, no president, no heroes, no fun. If nothing else, the song decides that under the circumstances, having overslept for two-thirds of the future is preferable to staying awake. This stance, however, lacks the aggressive pugnacity of the "Null Bock" rhetoric from the generation of the same name. A chapter in Pankonin's book is titled "Die Summe aller Aktivitäten ist Null" (52). Negative logic reigns. Pankonin offers a negative philosophy of replacement politics.

In the chapter "Die Summe aller Farben ist weiß" (The sum of all colors is white) Pankonin reports on the concert. Under a subheading, "Die letzten Tage von Pompeji," he writes:

> Das Gefüge des östlichen Staatenverbandes war am Kippen. . . . Am Tag danach wurde das Radio interessanter. . . . Das Radio sagte zu mir: Wenn Du den Westen sehen willst, dann kannst Du das jetzt tun. Du brauchst dazu nur in die Tschechei zu fahren und kannst noch in dieser Nacht das sehen, wovon Du jahrelang heimlich und unklar geträumt hast. (34–36)

> The structure of the eastern alliance of states was about to tip over. . . . On the next day the radio got more interesting. . . . The radio told me: If you want to see the West, you can do so now. You just have to go to Czechoslovakia and tonight you can see what you've dreamed of secretly and vaguely for all these years.

With brisk historical references, Pankonin describes the moment of convergence between the public narrative and personal opportunity. His political consciousness filters the events (the destabilizing effects of glasnost and perestroika, the final GDR national holiday celebrated with fireworks, the opening of borders to the West) through the voice of the radio, which speaks directly to him. Pankonin, the GDR consumer of air waves, becomes the target audience for world news: he is directly affected. Suddenly, his secret dreams are put on display. Although this signals a personal shift in signification, the political drive toward stabilization (of meaning, among other things) is acknowledged. He reads the political change as no change, just a dis- and replacement: "Ich dachte: Der neue Staat macht den alten Staat zur Sau" (I thought, the new state is breaking up the old state, literally, "making it into a sow") (36). This opinion is followed by the lyrics to the song "Was soll ich bloß thunfisch?" (Just what should I tunafish?) (37), which critiques (seriously?) unhealthy anarchy and the curiosity of "Munter-Monika" (a play on the "Mundharmonika") and ends with the dentist's recommendation: " 'Go West' " (37). Music carries the burden of political action.

Pankonin's political parodies surface. While, for example, "Der Schänder" (one who desecrates or defiles) demonstrates, Pankonin goes to bed. He meets the alter egos of his two songs:

> Ich schämte mich gründlich wegen meiner Feigheit, ging in die Umkehrwelt, traf dort Atilla und Hobin Rood, und beging die Flucht nach Entenhausen (39).

> I was thoroughly ashamed of myself because of my cowardice, went to the world of reversals, ran into Atilla and Hobin Rood, and took flight to Entenhausen [German home of the Disney Duck family].

The music functions as political sublimation: instead of heading for the barricades, Pankonin's persona writes and performs songs about antiheroes, "losers," "Verlierer," and other "Nullen" (zeroes), as he calls them in the dedication of the song before the performance of "Loser" in the Last Days of Pompeii concert. The intertextuality between the album and Keynkampf provides an index for reading the politics of the music and its "scene." After the demonstrations, the house "im Eimer" was squatted, as is pointed out on the liner to the album, on 17 January 1990; the first concert took place on 18 March 1990, election Sunday. The album's self-presentation aligns the Eimer and the music it houses with political and historical moments in German-German relations. Back in Keynkampf, the final days of Pompeii are celebrated as negatively as possible with the old East sound: "Es spielte der heilige Verband Firma, Freygang, IchFunktion zum Untergang des alten Staates. Es klang, als fände das gesamte Konzert in einer riesigen Blechdose statt, das war der Sound des alten Ostens" (The holy alliance of Firma, Freygang, IchFunktion played for the demise of the old state. It sounded as though the entire concert took place in a huge tin can, that was the sound of the old East) (40). In this description, the tin-can sound of the old East provides a radical counterpoint to the symphonic strains of "euphoria" emanating from the concert of German-German unity. Pankonin melds the antiaesthetic form with an antipolitical content—German politics in the tin can.

The next segment belongs to Die Firma, which performs three songs, all of which appear on the CD Maschinenrepublik as well. Perhaps the most sinister of these is "Alte Helden," though "Faschist" comes close. Backed up by ominous minor chords and punctuated by a sound like that of a revving motor, the lead sings the lyrics in a tone between a low growl and a scream:

"Alte Helden" (3:56)

Ach, es sind die alten Helden schon längst zerredet.
und der Fortschritt klopft mit neuen Tönen an
uns're Tür, man schaltet ab die alten Revoluzzer
sind am Sattsein längst verblödet . . .
Ach die Liebe ist vor'm Mai
schon längst verbittert, die alte Gänsehaut,
ist geschliffen an der Zeit
Nur die Zweisamkeit noch nach dem
Orgasmus gleichsam zittert . . .[35]

Oh, the old heroes, long since talked to death.
And progress knocks in new tones at our door.
We turn off the old revolutionaries, stupefied on satiation . . .
Oh, love is gone, long since embittered.
The old goose-flesh is refined with time.
Only being alone together as it were trembles after the orgasm . . .

Whereas the first stanza marks a refusal to take the old heroes seriously, the second stanza makes the connection between political domination and sexual submission. There is nothing new about the relationship between sex and politics, personal and public power, but here Die Firma, "the company," the alias for the Stasi, turns on the party "revolutionaries" and critiques the opportunists who already come to power. Here, the prospect of political change signals that things will stay the same. The old heroes equal the new whores. All this commemorates and celebrates DIE LETZTEN TAGE VON POMPEJI.

Finally, on the second side, Freygang[36] performs five songs. Freygang, the only band in the triad that still plays, has a long and illustrious history in the GDR. The lead singer, André Greiner-Pol, began writing his own material in the early 1980s. During a two-year *Spielverbot* (prohibition from playing) for Freygang, Greiner-Pol functioned behind the scenes in founding the group Die Firma. The band began to play again in 1985 (with new members—two had gone to the West) and met with an enthusiastic reception. Greiner-Pol was arrested on stage in summer 1986 "wegen obszöner Äußerungen und Belästigung des Publikums, wegen Widerstand gegen polizeiliche Maßnahmen und Störung des sozialistischen Zusammenlebens" ("because of obscene remarks and pestering the audience, because of resisting police measures and disturbing socialist co-existence"). Gregor Gysi defended him, preventing a lengthy jail stay, but the singer was prohibited from performing. Still, he worked for the band Die Firma, founded the band Tacheles, and performed under the name "OK" in the

Soviet Union.[37] The band biography describes the album under consideration in the following way:

> "FREYGANG," "die FIRMA," "ICH-FUNKTION" und Unterstützung von "HERBST IN PEKING" drei Nächte Live IM EIMER; Wir schneiden mit und das definitiv letzte "Ost-Vinyl" in der Geschichte der DDR, noch mit Ost-Mark produziert, entsteht.

> Freygang, die Firma, IchFunktion [literally, ego function], with the support of Herbst in Peking, three nights live Im Eimer. We are recorded live and the definitively final "East-album" in the history of the GDR is made, still financed with the East Mark.

Thus the groups gather together to celebrate the only way they know how, according to the lead singer's address to the audience: they fête "die letzten paar Tage" in song and beer, "rumzusingen" and "ein bißchen was zu trinken" (to sing around the last few days, drink a little [introduction]). After the first number, "Das rollende Faß" (Rolling barrel), which is full of political (and, here I concede to Greiner-Pol, erotic) allusions—"wenn ich in den Himmel sehe, wenn ich an die Grenze gehe, wenn ich vor der Mauer stehe, wenn ich auf den Friedhof gehe" ("when I look at the sky, when I go to the edge, when I stand before the wall, when I go to the cemetery")—there is a shouted/sung list of dates: '31, '45, '29, '56, '61, then, '89, '89, '93, '39. The rolling barrel serves as an evocative image of history seen through Freygang's lens.

Then the band sings a song "aus der bleiernen Zeit—80er Jahre" ("from the leaden time, the '80s") called "Zwei Bier, Zwei Korn" (Two beers, two shots of rye schnapps). In this number, the signal of resignation, besides "retiring" and the bar order "zwei Bier, zwei Korn," is "Du hast deine Gitarre, schon längst verkauft" ("you sold your guitar a long time ago").[38] Freygang performs several other numbers: "Mörder" (Murderer), "Der König" (The king), and "Schrotthaufen" (Scrap-heap). In *Keynkampf*, Pankonin expresses respect for "Der König" (his name for Freygang's lead singer, André Greiner-Pol):

> Aber als der König auf die Bühne stieg und "Ich bin ein Mörder" sang, zog ein ordentlicher Schauer über meinen Rücken, und ich wußte, daß der Sound nichts zu sagen hatte. Hier war für einige Momente der Rock'n'Roll, nur das war wichtig. (40)[39]

> But when the king climbed on stage and sang "I am a murderer," I felt a real shudder go up my spine and I knew that the quality of the sound did not matter. Here, for a few moments, was rock 'n roll, and only that was important.

To generalize from this example, the live performance provided not only an opportunity for politics, but for real rock.

"IchFunktion ist der Einfluß der Sterne auf das persönliche Schicksal"
In the "Vorfunktion" (pre-function) of *Keynkampf* Pankonin narrates the extraterrestrial beginnings of his personal destiny: he is sentenced to life on earth in the twentieth century for negligently bringing a Soviet light bulb back from the future. His mission on the potato (earth):to find the "FF," the female figure for love, the game he must play on earth. In this introductory section, Pankonin's narrator comes of age with speed and precocity. He listens to his parents' albums by Mireille Mathieu and Frank Schöbel, the popular *Schlager* (hit song) singers; his parents give him a guitar, "Die kleine Liese," and he and his older brother watch the pop shows on Western television. After hearing the song "The Sixteens" by Sweet, he decides to become a "Rock 'n' Roller" when he grows up. Tschaka's words ("Ego function is the influence of the stars on personal fate," the heading above) persuade Pankonin to join the band IchFunktion, a high point of personal fate.

The logic of negation collapses into a radical politics of the oppressed. The narrative continues with the "first kiss of the negative energy source" (7). Again, he faces West to pray: "Im grau leuchtenden Fenster zur westlichen Welt kam ein Ausschnitt aus einem Kisskonzert. Was ich sah, war angenehm negativ" ("In a gray-lit window to the Western world came an excerpt from a Kiss concert. What I saw was pleasantly negative") (7). His political birth coincides with his viewing on television the film "Blutige Erdbeeren" (Bloody strawberries), which he describes as a documentary film about the battles between American students and the police: "Ich wollte kein Junge mehr sein, sondern ein Held" ("I didn't want to be a kid anymore, I wanted to be a hero") (8). The film feeds his political-magical fantasy:

> In den Märchenbüchern, die ich zu dieser Zeit gelesen habe, gab es immer einen Prinzen, der seine Prinzessin bekommt, wenn er einen Drachen erschlagen hat. Bei "Blutige Erdbeeren" war dieser Drache die Polizei. Wo war meine? (8).

> In the fairy-tale books that I read at the time, there was always a prince who got his princess if he could slay the dragon. In "Bloody Strawberries" the dragon was the police. Where was mine?

In tenth grade, he and a friend play with "Sprengkörper aus der Nazizeit. . . . Es knallte fürchterlich, und wir stellten uns dabei vor, Terroristen für eine gerechte Sache zu sein" ("Explosives from the Nazi period. . . .

There was a horrible crash, and we imagined that we were terrorists for a just cause") (8). His imagination is structured by negative musical energy and aggression, political justice, and radical fairy tales. The language of human types (FF, "der Schänder," the F.d.L.u.d.V., or "Fanatiker der Lügen und des Verrats," fanatics of lies and betrayal, 9), card games, court power constellations, royalty, monarchy, majesty, and chess contrasts and com-plements the idiom of boredom, the social welfare office, the army, the night shift. The words from the West German band Fehlfarben's influen-tial album *Monarchie und Alltag* (Monarchy and the everyday) provide a reference point for his life. Then there was punk; then there was a band:

> Von da ab begann ich in zwei Welten zu leben. Die eine ist ein Königreich, und dieses Königreich ist groß, schön und gerecht. Die zweite Welt ist die Welt der Zahlen, in dieser Welt gibt es Brot zum Leben und Spiele für alle. Es sind benachbarte Welten. Wenn sie sich zu streiten beginnen und trennen wollen, geht es mir schlecht (17).

> From then on, I began to live in two worlds. One is a monarchy, and this monarchy is big, beautiful, and just. The second world is the world of num-bers, in this world, there is bread to live and games for all. They are neigh-boring worlds. And when they start to fight with each other and want to separate, I don't do so well.

Pankonin alternates between reality and reverie against the backdrop of history. He develops a philosophy of resistance:

> Man könnte tagelang darüber diskutieren, wie man am besten in totalitären Systemen Widerstand leistet, ohne selbst zum Opfer oder Täter zu werden. Meine Devise war meist: SICH WEHREN, OHNE ZU STÖREN. Ich habe die Leute bewundert, die ihren Kopf hingehalten haben und für eine Veränderung im Knast gelandet sind. (72).

> You could talk for days about how you can best resist in totalitarian systems without becoming a victim or a perpetrator yourself. My motto was mostly: Defend yourself without disturbing. I admired people who stuck their necks out and for a change ended up in jail.

Although he himself is no hero, Pankonin retains respect for those who took risks. He has a place to occupy in the "Maschinenrepublik," even if it is home in bed.

In his introductory text to Die Firma's CD liner notes, "Wir sind die Kinder der Maschinenrepublik," Pankonin writes in the voice perhaps of a generation:

> Du hast den Weg aus dem System gesucht. Da wo Du herkommst, hat nie-mand geschrien. Der Schrei kam mit den Gesetzen des Systems, in dem Du

geboren wurdest. Du gehörst dazu und es gibt scheinbar keinen Ausweg. Du bist ein Kind im Getriebe und versuchst, mit Sand zu werfen. Es knirscht in der Maschine und plötzlich zerbricht sie. Arbeiter mit Halbglatzen und neuen Frisuren hasten durch den falschen Alltag und streichen die Trümmer der Maschine grau. Sie bauen die unbeschädigten Teile in die neue Maschine. Sie ist so groß, daß Du nicht glauben kannst, daß es noch Sand genug gibt, sie zu zerstören. Aber wenn niemand es versucht, bleibst Du ein Kind aus der Maschinenrepublik.

You sought the way out of the system. There, where you came from, no one screamed. The scream came with the rules of the system you were born in. You belong to it and there is apparently no way out. You are a child in the gears and you try to throw sand. It grinds in the machine and suddenly it breaks down. Workers with half-bald heads and new hair cuts rush through the false everyday and paint the ruins of the machine gray. They insert the undamaged parts into the new machine. It is so big that you can't believe there is enough sand to destroy it. But if no one tries, you remain a child of the machine republic.

For Pankonin, the songs and the music are the sand, friction that delays or defeats the system—whatever its political persuasion. And what of the new machine? Will there be enough sand?

Notes

A portion of this paper was presented to the DAAD seminar "Theorizing the Public Sphere," Ithaca, July 1994. I would like to thank the participants and the organizer, Peter Hohendahl, for their provocative questions and comments on that version. I owe a similar debt to the organizers, Michael Kennedy and Mayer Zald, and participants of the Sawyer Seminar "Social Movements and Social Change in a Globalized World" at the Advanced Studies Center, University of Michigan, Ann Arbor (fall 1995). I owe a debt of gratitude to Rex Joswig, André Greiner-Pol and Freygang, Delia Müller, and Michael Rauhut of Humboldt University for their generous assistance. All translations are my own, with thanks to Hubert Rast and Frauke Lenckos.

1. I base the information about the audience at the Eimer on an interview conducted in (East) Berlin with André Greiner-Pol and Tatjana Besson, 31 May 1995.

2. See Martin Watson, " 'Flüstern & Schreien': Punks, Rock Music and the Revolution in the GDR," in *German Life and Letters* 46, no. 2 (April 1993): 162–75.

3. Joswig, interview with author, 7 July 1995. I base the second half of this assertion on the liner notes in the booklet to the CD *Egotrip*, IchFunktion, 1993.

4. Though I access a Habermasian vocabulary, I acknowledge that its application to the events in the former GDR is an imperfect fit. In part, I hope to historicize the terms of "civil society" and "public sphere" in the former GDR with attention to the music scene, for the relationship between a universalizing theory and a specific history is in this and all cases problematic. I depart consciously from Jürgen Habermas's notion of a bourgeois public sphere with its principles of universal access

and interests. What there was of a potential GDR public sphere in 1989 has been displaced largely by the Western media and federal forms. Music, particularly rock music and its transmission, constituted an emerging forum for Eastern listeners, as in the extraordinary case of DT 64. The bands themselves established what Delia Müller, Freygang's current manager, referred to (citing Key Pankonin) as a "state within a state." She also pointed to the blues bands that preceded the bands I discuss here; they created, according to Müller, the *Freiraum* (space to be oneself) necessary for the subsequent scene. It is difficult to characterize these *Freiräume* from within the discourse of political science. Within those spaces, however, music functioned as a "Ventil, um uns über politische Mißstände lustig zu machen" ("an outlet for making fun of the deplorable state of political affairs," Müller, letter to the author, January 1997).

5. Notorious in this regard is André Greiner-Pol of Freygang. In his song "In stiller Trauer" (In quiet mourning) he writes a pastiche biography of an allegedly historical figure with a wife named Hannah and a daughter named Marlies. I assumed that there was a singular historical referent, and asked who it was, and Greiner-Pol responded that this was a "typical American question. It could be Krenz, Honecker, Gorbachev, Kohl." The interchangeability of the historical identities epitomizes Greiner-Pol's wordplay. When, for example, I asked about the political significance of certain lines, such as "wenn ich an die Grenze gehe" ("when I go to the edge"), he suggested instead an erotic interpretation.

6. See Simon Frith, "Popular Music and the Local State," in *Rock and Popular Music*, ed. Tony Bennett, Simon Frith, Lawrence Grossberg, John Shepherd, and Graeme Turner (London, 1993), 14–24, for a look at the politics of "local" music culture in Britain, specifically, at "making it" in a different context.

7. Herbst in Peking, for example, is engaged in individual and ongoing projects. The band members cannot, according to Joswig, sustain themselves as an institutional band, though they are raising money to play again. The key hindrance is financial, not creative (Joswig, interview with author, 31 May 1995). Since the mid-1990s, HIP has released *Das Jahr Schnee* (Plattenmei: EFA Medien, 1996); *Feuer Wasser & Posaunen* (Moloko: EFA Medien, 1998); and *Les fleurs du mal* (Moloko Plu: EFA Medien, 1999).

8. Featured are IchFunktion (Key Pankonin, vocals, guitar; Frank Schacker, guitar, vocals; Jens-Uwe Haupt, drums; Ralph Schaum, bass); Die Firma (Tatjana Galler-Besson, vocals, bass; Trötsch Tröger, vocals, keyboards; Faren St. Matern, vocals, bass; Paul Landers, guitar; Thomas Schreiber, drums); Freygang (André Greiner-Pol, vocals, guitar; Kay Lutter, bass; Kurt Schimmelpfenning, guitar; Egon Kener, guitar). The album was recorded from 28 to 30 June 1990 in "honor" of the currency union.

9. Peking Records is now defunct, though Joswig continues to reconvene the band for concerts and projects. See n. 7.

10. For further information about this band, see my "Born in the Bakschischrepublik? Rock and Politics in the GDR," in *Elective Affinities: Interdisciplinary Cultural Studies of German Unification*, ed. Ruth Starkman and Peter Tokovsky (Rochester, forthcoming).

11. Pankonin is a key figure, known as the best lyricist in the East. When I asked Greiner-Pol about Pankonin's role in Freygang, André tapped an index finger against his temple. "He's with us in our minds." Many of the songs appear on the CD *Egotrip*, a 1994 release produced for Dizzy Hornet Records (Berlin) and Nasty Vinyl and Kikeriki Records (Hannover).

12. Key Pankonin, *Keynkampf* (Berlin, 1993), 27. As he explains, "R.G.M. ist eine Abkürzung für Rock gegen Mittelmäßigkeit. Das klingt fast wie eine Partei. Es ist nur einer von vielen Namen für das Kind, das ich Freiheit nennen möchte. Aber die Freiheit gehört keiner Partei und schon keinen drei Buchstaben. Sie ist ein Teil des Lebens, wie die Liebe, der Haß und die Zeit. Alles gehört zusammen" (R.G.M. is an abbreviation for rock against mediocrity. It almost sounds like a political party. It is just one of many names for the child I'd like to call freedom. It is a part of life, like love, hate, and time. Everything belongs together).

13. In one song, "Hobin Rood," Pankonin refers to the "zweite Buch," possibly a reference to Hitler's "second book" of the same name. I thank Adam Tooze for help with this reference.

14. Pankonin understands the dialectic of resistance and system. In a section titled "Und wenn der Widerstand" (And if resistance) he talks about *Arbeitswiderstand* (operational or working resistor—an electrical term referring to the resistance generated by an instrument when it is turned on), without which the *Gitarrenverzerrer* (guitar distorter) doesn't function. And, he writes in "Direkt in die Raghandi" (direct in the "raghandi," a play on Indira Ghandi, after whom a street in East Berlin is named), "Und wenn der Widerstand / ein Arbeitswiderstand ist / gehört der Widerstand zum System" ("And if the resistance is a working resistor / the resistance belongs to the system"). Pankonin, *Keynkampf*, 72.

15. Pankonin was retraining to become a plumber in the early 1990s.

16. The bands are connected in another text, that of an interview with Aram Radomski and Jürgen Winkler about the Stasi involvement of Trötsch and Tatjana. See "Es hat niemandem genützt: Die Firma nach den Stasi-Offenbarungen," *NM!Messitsch* 5 (1992), 14–15. See also "Verrat als Performance?" in the same issue, pp. 16 and 31, with Winkler and Trötsch, who did not want to participate in the discussion with Freygang, Die Firma, and IchFunktion, as "Diese Zeit ist für ihn abgeschlossen" (16). In the first interview, there seemed to be consensus that issues of, for example, right-wing radicalism were more pressing than past Stasi involvement of individuals. Members of Freygang had been attacked at a gas station and sustained injuries. Tatjana expressed a willingness to discuss her role as an IM. The overall tone was conciliatory. In the second interview, Trötsch appeared distanced and cynical about his twelve-year stint with the Stasi. Still, he is not ostracized from the musical community. He worked on the Freygang CD *Golem* and still cooperates on projects with Joswig; he also began working on radio plays. Some assert that the band's affiliation with the Stasi could be heard in the song lyrics; Trötsch dismisses this idea. Other sources from within the "scene" attribute the break-ups to the revelations about Stasi involvement.

17. The house was a squat and an alternative center. Aljosha presided over the activities while working on his own music and film projects. He plays with the reconfigured Feeling B. I thank Michael Rauhut for his help with updating this information.

18. To demonstrate the level of interaction among bands, I cite the 1993 CD *White Sheep*, The Inchtabokatables, with one song by Tatjana ("Rosenrot") and one by Key Pankonin ("In die Raghandi"). The bass player Hans Tomato ("Herbst in Peking") was on a two-year loan to the "Inch."

19. On the CD, the "high voices" are sung by two children who have since formed their own band, Rebel Power, at ages fourteen and sixteen. I saw them perform at a three-day open-air concert in Steinbrücken, during Pentecost weekend 1995. They sang Firma songs, with Tatjana, such as "Kinder der Maschinenrepublik," "Europa,"

and their version of her "Wounded Knee." The audience responded enthusiastically to their postpunk GDR sound.

20. Olaf Leitner, "Rock Music in the GDR: An Epitaph," in *Rocking the State: Rock Music and Politics in Eastern Europe and Russia*, ed. Sabrina Petra Ramet (Boulder, 1994), 17–40. Leitner provides a quick sketch of the relationship between rock music, capitalist internationalist influence, and the SED-administrated aesthetic in the GDR. See also Olaf Leitner, *Rockszene DDR: Aspekte einer Massenkultur im Sozialismus* (Reinbek, 1983).

21. See, e.g., Peter Wicke and John Shepherd, " 'The Cabaret Is Dead': Rock Culture as State Enterprise—The Political Organization of Rock in East Germany," in *Rock and Popular Music*, ed. Tony Bennett, Simon Frith, Lawrence Grossberg, John Shepherd, and Graeme Turner (London, 1993), 25–36. Here Wicke and Shepherd zero in on the relationship between rock and the state, ending with a call for a reconceptualization of the study of popular music and its relationship to the means of production, commercialism, and so on.

22. Michael Rauhut, *Beat in der Grauzone: DDR-Rock 1964 bis 1972—Politik und Alltag* (Berlin, 1993). He also completed a book about the relation between music and politics during the 1980s. See *Schalmei und Lederjacke: Udo Lindenberg, BAP, Underground: Rock und Politik in den achtziger Jahren* (Berlin, 1996), esp. chap. 4, 179 f., for Rauhut's treatment of the relation between the music scene, the state, and the Stasi. Unfortunately I cannot treat Rauhut's work adequately at this time. Another work crucial to understanding the relation between music and politics is *Rockmusik und Politik: Analysen, Interviews und Dokuments*, ed. Peter Wicke and Lothar Müller (Berlin, 1996). Rauhut's contribution, "Ohr an Masse—Rockmusik im Fadenkreuz der Stasi" (28 f.) provides an overview of musical trends and the Stasi's reaction to them, especially punk (42 f.). See also Ronald Galenza and Heinz Havemeister, eds., *Wir wollen immer artig sein . . . Punk, New Wave, Hip-Hop, Independent-Szene in der DDR, 1980–1990* (Berlin, 1999), for contributions from musicians, fans, disc jockeys, and others on their experiences with the music scene and its politics.

23. See Fredric Jameson, "Utopia, Modernism, and Death," in *The Seeds of Time* (New York, 1994), 73–128.

24. Peter Rossman, "Zum 'Intellktuellenstreit': 'Intellectuals' in the Former GDR." *Michigan GermanicStudies* 31, nos. 1–2 (1995): 32–36 (special issue, Gegenwartsbewältigung, ed. Patricia A. Simpson). Rossman insists that there were two distinct groups of intellectuals in the GDR: the first consists of "official" figures, such as Christa Wolf, the second group up of intellectuals who "chose to remain in the GDR and work for change" (34). Many felt that Christa Wolf, who enjoyed a privileged position within GDR society, was in a poor position to encourage the general populace to stay. See also John C. Torpey, *Intellectuals, Socialism, and Dissent: The East German Opposition and Its Legacy* (Minneapolis, 1995).

25. See Andreas Huyssen, "After the Wall: The Failure of German Intellectuals," in *Twilight Memories: Marking Time in a Culture of Amnesia* (New York, 1995), 37–66.

26. Jürgen Habermas, *The Structural Transformation of the Public Sphere: An Inquiry into a Category of Bourgeois Society*, trans. Thomas Burger with the assistance of Frederick Lawrence (Cambridge, Mass., 1989).

27. See Konrad H. Jarausch, *The Rush to German Unity* (Oxford, 1994), 44 f. for a historical account of events, organizations, and causes leading to unification. The difficulty of a "history of the present" (Foucault) of which Jarausch writes is signifi-

cant, but, I think, in need of a supplementary treatment of the cultural communities (however riddled with Stasi IMs) that formed, for example, around the music scene.

28. Ibid., 106.

29. David Bathrick, *The Powers of Speech* (Lincoln, 1995). Bathrick describes three public spheres in the GDR: the official one orchestrated by the SED; one shaped by the West German media, especially television; and one that "consisted of the various unofficial public enclaves or counterofficial voices that sought to break into or establish dialogue with the officially dominating voices" (34). Bathrick includes jazz, rock, and punk musicians (among others) in this category.

30. Ulrike Poppe, "Citizens Movements in the GDR: Their Past and Future," *Michigan Germanic Studies* 31, nos. 1–2 (1995): 37–43 (special issue, Gegenwartsbewältigung, ed. Patricia A. Simpson).

31. See Watson, " 'Flüstern & Schreien,' " 165 f., for a discussion of the role played by the amateur bands. Since the publication of that article, a sequel has been released. The director, Dieter Schumann, and Aljosha, formerly of Feeling B, were planning a third film, though not strictly about the GDR music scene.

32. Rex Joswig was planning a book about music in the 1980s. See also n. 37.

33. Tape cover, Vielklang Musikproduktion, 1992, presented by NM!MESSITSCH and Elf, 99.

34. The two other songs by IchFunktion on the album are "Loser" and "Attila," both of which also appear on the band's only solo DC, *egotrip*. The lyrics to the former song lament the lack of future, the loss of innocence, the constant berating by authority figures: "Als die atomaren Wixer dir den / Finger in die Unschuld bohrten / und der gelbe Würger Streß, / der schrie dir nachts ins Ohr, / 'Du wirst nicht Präsident' " ("When the atomic wankers / stuck a finger into your innocence / and the yellow murderer stress, / it screamed into your ear at night, / 'You'll never become president' "); the singer realizes that he is born to lose. The refrain, sung in English, proclaims: "[I'm] No fun I was clean(now) / I'm a loser / No fun I was clean / I was born to lose." In the absence of sympathizers,the "self" in the song confesses that he has slept through two-thirds of his future, but, given the reprimanding speeches of the "old comrades" he also acknowledges that he would rather sleep. In the ominous "Attila," the first line, "Das Baby nervt seine Mama in den Schlaf" ("The baby wears his mother down to sleep") is repeated again and again. Examples of reversed relationships in the song include the North Sea swimming in a tanker, the sea flowing into oil, and Jacques Cousteau circling a shark that he cannot tear apart.

35. The text is by Trötsch.

36. Freygang assumes a role in Pankonin's text. The leader singer, referred to as the "king," is a major player in the events described therein.

37. The full history of Greiner-Pol and the bands cannot be recounted here, but it is illustrious. I base the information on "Freygang, Golem, featuring Machtmaschine Trötsch," a pamphlet provided by the band. It is crucial that Freygang is still performing before audiences of old and new fans. Before *Golem*, they released a CD titled *Die Kinder spielen weiter*, recorded live at the Knaack-Club (dead horse, 1993). The band continues to expand its horizons and intensify its strengths: Tatjana Besson and "Borstel" Vorpahl write and perform songs now along with Greiner-Pol. He and Tatjana appeared in Brecht's *Der Brotladen*, directed by Thomas Heise, in the Berliner Ensemble in 1993. The band sings a hair-raising version of the Brecht/Weill "Kanonensong" from the *Dreigroschenoper*. These are but a handful of high points. If

the apocalypse is at hand, Greiner-Pol will arrive on a motorcycle. For a full acount of the man and the band, see André Greiner-Pol, *Peitsche Osten Liebe: Das Freygang-Buch*, ed. Michael Rauhut (Berlin, 2000). For Greiner-Pol, making music remains of paramount importance. He founded the band in 1977; it lost its permission to perform in 1983 but was reinstated in 1985 before being banned permanently in 1986. The volume includes Rauhut's brief summary of Greiner-Pol's reluctant activity as an IM (47 f.) and an interview on this topic with the author. Freygang's most recent release is *Land unter* (1998).

38. The song is track 15 on *Aufbruch, Umbruch, Abbruch: Die letzten Jahre*, vol. 20 of *Rock aus Deutschland*, Deutsche Schallplatten GmbH, PSB 3088–2, LC 6056, 1992.

39. On rock, ritual, and *Rausch* (ecstasy), see Konstanze Kriese, "Rock'n'Ritual," in *PopScriptum 2. Beiträge zur populären Musik*, ed. Forschungszentrum Populäre Musik der Humboldt-Universität zu Berlin (Berlin, 1994), pp. 94–120.

ANDREAS GRAF

Translated by Annette Timm

Media Publics in the GDR: Unification and the Transformation of the Media, 1989–1991

With a bit of generosity, German unification might be construed as an idyllic experience. Must it not appear unbelievably harmonious if on an ordinary January day in 1991 a certain Mühlfenzl can be glimpsed sitting at the conference table of the *Neues Deutschland*, of all things, as he charmingly relates how much he has learned in the past few months, here in the east of the unified fatherland? On his right is seated the editor-in-chief of that paper, whose front page until recently had carried a masthead admonishing, "Workers of the world, unite." He can now be seen quoting strenuously from the Treaty Concerning the Attainment of German Unification, in which said proletarians do not receive the slightest mention. Mühlfenzl grins with Bavarian joviality, while the editor-in-chief joins in with Prussian correctness. With the help of coffee and sweets, all is at last well in Germany.[1]

One should not look twice, because on closer observation one notices that during those gloomy January days of 1991 the Envoy for Radio and Television Networks, Rudolf Mühlfenzl, was fulfilling his own prophecy.[2] By the time his contract ended, he had suggested, no one would like him any longer. If one looks yet more carefully, one can observe Mühlfenzl fulfilling the terms of his contract by liquidating the last big chunk of a nation that had been broken up by its people—paradoxically arousing feelings of homesickness for the old GDR among the very same people in the process. The chunk in question, called *Einrichtung* in the language of the Unification Treaty, consisted of the Radio Corporation of the GDR *(Rundfunk der DDR)* and the German Television Network *(Deutscher Fernsehfunk)*, which Mühlfenzl, in accordance with article 36, section 6 of the Unification Treaty, was instructed to dissolve or transfer "into public law institutions of one or several states."[3]

This activity, carried out by Mühlfenzl, was both legitimate and desirable. The participants outdid themselves in support of the so-called dual system: the orderly coexistence of public and private broadcasters. Nevertheless, all of them became increasingly more agitated as the shape of things to come was defined. As December 31, 1991, that magic moment ordained by the Unification Treaty, grew closer, lengthy debates became a luxury. Working out the pros and cons of various scenarios became ever more expensive and less productive. An obsession with speed became the dominant modality. A kind of inverted, vulgar Marxism prevailed, in the sense that the productive forces that were finally free of the fetters of socialism now came into their own.[4] The country, which had been predicated on slowdowns, now opted for a course of break-neck acceleration in order to resolve the arduous questions of what broadcasting reforms ought to be about. Years ago, the French philosopher Paul Virilio had described the acceleration of events as a powerful assault on human rights and as an extreme violation that had never been properly recognized or evaluated.[5]

Haste was necessary in deregulating broadcasting, was it not? Or could it be that the manner in which the West Germans appropriated the airwaves was all too typical of the wealth and of (especially) the poverty of German unification? A glance back at the impetuous march of historical events since the autumn of 1989 provides some minor recuperation from this particular German misery.

The Dawning of the Freedom of the Press

"We are the People!" exclaimed the demonstrators in Leipzig in October 1989, thus entering the arena of History. This slogan hit its mark. The street became a public stage. People in the GDR, and from the other part of Germany, as well as the rest of the world, were dumbfounded. "I never thought I'd live to see the day," said one observer at Berlin's Alexanderplatz on November 4, 1989. Half a million people had gathered of their own volition to support the numerous speakers and their ideas for extensive reforms. "It is," explained the author Stefan Heym, "as if someone had kicked open the window after all those years of cultural, economic and political stagnation. Those years of gloom and stench, of empty phrases and bureaucratic pettiness and tyranny. What a transformation!" A liberating impulse swept the land. The Wittenberg Minister and prominent dissident Friedrich Schorlemmer stated: "It's true, we lived in oppressive gloom—bowed down and lorded over for so many years. Today we have come here, more openly and self-confident, walking taller. We rediscover our true selves. From objects we are turning into subjects of political action. . . . Yesterday we still inhaled the stifling air of political stagnation, and it left us bereft of air. Today we are experiencing changes that leave us breathless."[6]

This day was, above all, a time of liberating communication, of courageous dissent against the authorities—since, after all, freedom is precocious. The authentic voice of the demonstrators on November 4, 1990: "With your politics, we'd better leave" (Eure Politik ist zum Davonlaufen); "He who lies once, will never be trusted again unless he breaks with the lie"; "Down with the lie!"; "Freedom of opinion"; "Freedom of the press"; "Free access to information"; "One can not simulate freedom"; "The wall in our heads must go"; "Don't let yourselves be used"; "We won't leave them in the lurch; we'll shove the hypocrites from their perch!"[7]

These slogans, displayed on protest banners, manifest the demand for freedom of opinion, information, and the press as one of the dominant themes of "the people." These demands quickly led to a call for a law governing the media in order to guarantee the newly won freedoms of speech in the sphere of communication.

The GDR never had a media law. Although article 27 of the GDR constitution affirmed that every citizen had the right "to express opinions freely and publicly" (item 1) and that "the freedom of the press, radio and television is guaranteed" (item 2),[8] these constitutional guarantees were neither elaborated by specific laws governing the media nor were they actually practiced. The resulting instrumentalization of information proved to be politically and socially disastrous, since it degraded both the subjective desires of the citizens and their wish to have influence on the media. The fusion of state and party in a double helix was the foundation of the GDR "guardian state,"[9] which regulated not only the allocation of informational resources but also their distribution. Freedom of opinion, of information, and of the press, therefore, remained congenial illusions and became, at best, freedom of inconsequential action.

The degree to which freedom of information appeared possible was determined for the citizens of the GDR by a secretary of the Central Committee of the SED responsible for broadcasting. His orders were implemented by the upper echelons of functionaries in the broadcasting corporations and by the members of the editorial offices. News was disseminated by the journalists. Power in the hands of these "representatives" thus became independent of those whom they were supposed to represent. Publicity functioned as a perfect mechanism to suppress what citizens did know about their state. Informed forgetting prevailed. All possibility for feedback was short-circuited. Despotism followed.[10] The results were disastrous for the political fabric of society, even if the disaster was neither quickly nor easily recognized.

The courage displayed by the media in disseminating information and upholding freedom of speech is an indicator of the morality of any given society as well as of the state of its civil institutions—ranging from education to science, art, and culture, to justice. The media are pressure gauges and guardians, cause and effect, translators and instigators. In the GDR, the spirit of superficiality accompanied a journalism that was, on one hand, reduced to rudimentary German and, on the other, loaded with stereotypes and platitudes. This was not without effect on the audiences. What the guardian state had attempted to create was less a dictatorial method of censorship—though it was this as well—than an apparatus to promote indifference among its citizens.

Media in the GDR: A Brief Overview
The centralized structure of the GDR media system, which was under the direct control of the state or, more specifically, the SED, was established in May 1945 under prerogatives of the Soviet Military Administration in Germany (SMAD).[11] On the evening of May 13, 1945, the first broadcast, "This Is Berlin Speaking" (*Hier redet Berlin*), was transmitted from the old radio station on Masurenallee in the English sector. At the time, it was the first and only German radio program in the four occupied zones. With this broadcast, the foundations were laid for the ultimate utilization of radio as a means of molding society into a Soviet-style socialism. Hans Mahle, later to become the general director of the Radio Broadcasting System in the Soviet sector, explained this goal succinctly: "The Central Committee's understanding was that radio must play a direct, operative and organizational role in the transformation of life in Germany."[12] The reconstruction of the broadcast system occurred over a very short span of time, but the system was subsequently reorganized several times. By 1989, the GDR Radio Broadcasting System broadcast from its center on the Nalepastraße in Berlin-Oberschöneweide on five cross-regional frequencies (Radio DDR I, DDR II, Berliner Rundfunk, Stimme der DDR, and Jugendradio DT 64). It also maintained twelve regional studios. In addition, there was a program for the Sorb minority and for the foreign service (Radio Berlin International). The regional stations were bound to the two programs of Radio DDR I and shared their frequency with Radio DDR II. Radio stations and studios were located in Rostock, Schwerin, Potsdam, Leipzig, Dresden, Cottbus, Weimar, Neubrandenburg, Frankfurt/Oder, Halle, Magdeburg, and Karl-Marx-Stadt (Chemnitz). In principle, each district had jurisdiction over its own broadcasting station. The exceptions were the three southwestern districts of Erfurt, Gera, and Suhl. Studios in Weimar, Gera, and Suhl broadcast over a single frequency

that served the entire region. By 1986, the broadcast volume had reached 79,140 program hours.

Television broadcasting in the GDR was an outgrowth of the radio broadcasting system. The first program, the news show *Aktuelle Kamera*, was aired on December 21, 1952. Subsequently the medium was slow to evolve. The first official television channel of the German Television Network (*Deutscher Fernsehfunk*, or *DFF*) was founded in 1956. On October 3, 1969, a second channel was chartered that evolved into an alternative program although it served the same fundamental functions (information, entertainment, education) as the existing service. Programming for both channels was, for the most part, produced at the studios in Berlin-Adlershof. No programs were produced regionally; studios outside Berlin (Rostock and Halle, among others) functioned simply as subcontracting services. By 1986, television broadcasts included a total of 8,320 program hours.

Unlike the Western occupation forces, the SMAD almost never granted press licenses to private persons but only to parties and mass organizations. The KPD (which, in 1946, became the SED) received priority. By 1986, there were thirty-nine daily papers, usually published five to six times a week with an average of six to eight pages each. The SED owned fifteen newspapers with 218 local publications; the Christian Democratic Union had six, the Liberal Democratic Party of Germany had five, the National Democratic Party of Germany had six, and the Democratic Farmer's Party had one newspaper. Even the Trade Union League, the Free German Youth, and the German Gymnastics and Sport League each had a daily newspaper at their disposal. The organization of the Sorb minority, Domovina, also had its own newspaper. The combined publications of the daily papers were officially recorded in 1987 as comprising 9.4 million issues. The majority of these were SED newspapers, numbering more than 6 million issues. By 1987 there were, in addition, 662 industry-related newspapers, published as organs of the respective local party administration with a combined total of 2 million issues. The publishing houses and their most important production facilities (typesetting and publishing) had been seized by the Soviet occupation forces and were later converted into cooperatives or enterprises owned by mass organizations (*Vereinigung Organisationseigener Betriebe* [VOB]) or state-owned enterprises (*Volkseigene Betriebe* [VEB]). The Central Publishing, Purchasing, and Revision Corporation (*Zentrale Druckerei-, Einkaufs- und Revisionsgesellschaft*, or *Zentrag*) was under the authority of the Central Committee of the SED. It controlled more than ninety publishing houses and newspaper and industry publishing enterprises that together comprised more than 90 percent of the publishing capacity of the GDR. The monopoly on advertising was controlled by the German Advertising and Classified Ad Society *(Deutsche Werbe- und Anzeigengesellschaft*, or *DEWAG)*, which was also a party-owned venture. The entire distribution of periodicals was handled by the monopolistic German postal service.

The General German News Service *(Allgemeiner Deutscher Nachrichtendienst* or *ADN)*, the central news agency of the GDR, played an essential role governing the mass media. By 1987 ADN possessed fourteen district editorial offices in the GDR and forty-seven foreign bureaus. The correspondents of ADN were accredited in eighty-seven countries.

Finally, one should mention the Deutsche Film AG, or DEFA, which was the first German production venture to receive a Soviet license after 1946. Until 1950, DEFA was operated as a Soviet joint-stock company with controlling interests held by the Ministry of the Film Industry of the USSR. After 1950, control of the industry once again fell into German hands, where it eventually came under the auspices of the Central Film Administration in the Ministry of Culture and was integrated into the media system.

Inevitably, the transformations of the autumn of 1989 called for the reconstruction of the GDR media apparatus. Consequently, in December 1989, the Cabinet appointed the Minister of Justice to the task of creating a new media law. On December 21, 1989, the Media Legislative Commission *(Mediengesetzgebungskommission)* was formed with fifty representatives from government ministries, the parties and groups represented at the Round Table, the churches, the professional organizations, and the media, as well as a collection of independent experts. At the outset, the commission agreed on a series of fundamental principles. Among these were the principles that new monopolies in the nascent media landscape would be forestalled; that the media's independence from the government and the state would be reinforced; that fundamental rights of speech and freedom of information—as guaranteed by the universal human rights protocols—would be fully protected; and that the media's responsibility to meet the informational, cultural, and educational needs of the population would be safeguarded. Freedom of the press was accordingly defined as a service-oriented freedom; that is, the media were set free in order to serve society. Further, there was consensus that GDR media relations should be constructed in a form compatible with those of (Western) Europe. These general guidelines notwithstanding, it became clear to the members of the commission that the formulation of a media law would require a more protracted effort. In consideration of these premises and fully aware of urgent pragmatic needs, the commission agreed that its first task would be to outline the fundamental principles of the freedoms of opinion, press, and information, which they would present to the East German parliament (the *Volkskammer*). On February 5, 1990, the parliament passed a statute listing a basic framework of principles that consisted of a preamble and seventeen articles, until such time as encompassing media legislation could be enacted.[13]

This resolution found acceptance among all political groups in the GDR. Konrad Weiß of Democracy Now described its statutes as a "carefully weighed and constructive compromise" that would pave the way for "a democratic transformation of the media landscape."[14] In this sense, it might justifiably be understood as the origin of the freedom of the press in the GDR. The statutes interpreted the citizens' demands for the right to free and comprehensive information primarily in cultural and not in economic terms; in the conflict between culture and commerce, it gave the former unequivocal priority.

However, the media statutes contained several gaps. Aware that insufficiency and ambiguity would be inevitable in an unstable situation and certain that published norms would provide no guarantees against abuses, the lawmakers created an institution unique in the history of the German media: the Media Control Council (*Medienkontrollrat*, or *MKR*). This organization was entrusted with oversight concerning the implementation of the parliamentary statutes. On February 13, 1990, the MKR was formed as an autonomous organ, independent of the state but sensitive to the influence of socially relevant groups and tendencies. The lawmakers were explicitly set against creating an agency with executive power (such as the old propaganda division *[Agitationsabteilung]* of the Central Committee of the SED), because they did not want to arouse anew anxieties of old about censorship of unsanctioned opinion. It was one of the functions of the MKR to recommend a course of action in the event that freedom of opinion, information, or the press was endangered. It served, among other things, as a watchdog organization. The council's recommendations were prescriptive for the government, a situation that proved to be not without complications. The Council was—as *die tageszeitung* labeled it in early April 1990—"a dog without teeth."[15] Media Councilor Wolfgang Kleinwächter gratefully accepted this characterization and answered all doubts about the competence of the council with these words: "A dog without teeth. This is in fact true. But this should not be regrettable, it should be desirable. The Media Control Council should do the barking, then the executive—be it the Cabinet, or the minister or other agencies responsible for the implementation of the law—can bite."[16] In fact, the MKR was a bit more than a mere watchdog organization. In a sense it

was to act as a guardian, a body with moral authority that had a mandate to protect the diversity of opinion and freedom of choice for the
sovereign media-consuming citizen and to guide the media in their development toward independence and away from government control. The
council was thus a transitional body but also the product of a compromise between the need to effectively secure the freedom of the press as
quickly as possible, on one hand, and the impossibility of solving all the
urgent political and legal problems on an ad hoc basis, on the other. The
mandate of the MKR was revised in four stages after March 18, 1990:
through a coalition draft, a governmental deposition from the first freely
elected minister president of the GDR, a letter from the parliamentary
chairmanship, and a letter from the Minister for Media Politics himself.
This should be emphasized in view of later objections that the allegedly
"weak legitimacy" of the MKR made it an "inertia-germinating relic of
the transitional period" that should be abolished quickly and vanish without consequence.

The council was assigned a series of specific tasks. It was to confirm the
minister president's appointments of general directors of radio and television. The directors, as well as the general director of ADN, were obligated
to report to the council. Thus, strategies for product advertising on radio
and television and the statutes governing it were repeatedly discussed. The
MKR also reacted promptly to questions concerning the distribution of
print media and was unequivocal in its suggestions.[17] The council's March
7, 1990, vote to create a distribution system in the GDR that was "open,
competitive, and independent of the publishing houses" was a clear statement aimed at establishing compatibility with the system in the Federal
Republic, where independence of delivery systems from publishing houses
and open competition are the norm. On March 28, the council once again
sent an open declaration to the Cabinet, demanding a legal guarantee that
the wholesale market for published works would remain "independent from
publishing houses" and seeking "an immediate formulation and implementation of the legal regulation of cartels following the model of the Federal
Republic."[18] The Ordinance on the Distribution of Media Materials in
the GDR, which was finally released on May 2, 1990, by the Minister of
Media Politics, Gottfried Müller,[19] signaled a conflict between the Media
Control Council and the intentions of the government.[20] This conflict
became more virulent when on June 13, 1990, the council refused to confirm Minister President Lothar de Maizière's choice for General Director
for Radio and Television, Gero Hammer, thereby thwarting the party's
interference in the media. The manner in which the Law Concerning the
Transformation of Radio Broadcasting came into existence is an indication

that, by this time, the conflict of interest between the state and the MKR had reached an all-time high.[21]

The MKR was an honest project, a mixture of resolution and ambition on one hand, inexperience and lack of professionalism on the other. This project very quickly broke down in the new era that followed the elections of March 18, 1990, when the grass-roots democratic elements of the revolutionary days immediately subsequent to the *Wende* were pushed back, once again, in favor of administrative methods. As long as the MKR existed, this setback was not quite as evident. The chair of the MKR was the former consistory president of the Protestant church of the province of Saxony, Martin Kramer, whose expertise Minister President de Maizière had already hoped to use within his advisory circle. Kramer chaired the interminably long public meetings; he gathered, encouraged, summarized, arranged, and advised. The MKR became a genuine political authority, a fact that was remarkably, yet revealingly, noticed only in the West—but there, this development was considered a threat.[22]

The process of democratization in the GDR had created a number of extralegal arenas of activity, which were exploited intensively. After the fall of 1989, managers and directors of Western publishing houses traveled with their judicial councilors to the GDR, where they signed preliminary contracts, promised technical assistance, exchanged technical know-how, and looked for likely objects for cooperation. These Westerners acted as if they had landed in the "Wild East," but their can-do mentality meant success.

The first case of such a *conquista* appeared early in 1990 in an improbable but significant area of business. The act itself suggested the impatience of the four most prominent West German publishing houses (together Bauer, Burda, Gruner & Jahr, and Springer controlled 70 percent of the market in the Federal Republic) to stake their claims in the East. By means of a covert alliance, the Big Four publishers and a monopolistic postal service succeeded in establishing a distribution and advertising joint venture that, if successful, would have put them in control of all deliveries of newspapers and magazines to East German newsstands.[23] Under the leadership of this faction's main West German competition, the Hamburg-based Jahreszeiten publishing house, approximately twenty other publishing companies, along with GDR politicians, the MKR, and the Round Table, led a storm of protest against the Big Four. As a result, the no-longer-secret negotiations were broken off. In early March, the four publishing giants, after having carved up the East among themselves, began independently marketing and distributing their own newspapers and magazines in the GDR. The fight for an open and comprehensive distribution system for the press, with free competition and independence from publishing houses, had begun. Apparently, the various machinations of the Big Four had a far-reaching goal. They were intended to use novel GDR regulations to overthrow the established balance of power in the Federal Republic.

Since October 1989, the GDR print media have also been driven into a new plane of existence.[24] The Western publishers followed three different strategies, all of which were directed toward the same goal: conquering the East German market with the intent of shaping the order of things in the West. Some offered unaltered West German editions of their publications to the East German market (others began publishing East German editions). A very few founded new newspapers. More commonly, however, the publishing giants took over elements of businesses or entire enterprises from Eastern publishers, especially those of the high-volume district newspapers of the SED and the minor bloc parties. In April 1991, it was noted that the "control of ownership interests in the very attractive market of regional newspapers in the new German provinces has been sown up."[25] Eleven former SED papers, with a total publication of three million issues, went to publishers from the West. It was not only the mammoth enterprises that gathered booty; even mid-sized Western publishing companies claimed their share. Two of the largest Eastern newspapers were not even offered in a public tender by the *Treuhand:* the *Freie Presse* of Chemnitz, with a print run of 600,000, was curiously taken "out of the competition" and handed over to the *Rheinpfalz* newspaper, based in chancellor Helmut Kohl's home town of Ludwigshafen, and the *Mitteldeutsche Zeitung* (print run 530,000), which appears in FDP foreign minister Hans-Dietrich Genscher's birthplace, Halle, was, by coincidence, absorbed by the publisher of the *Kölner Stadtanzeiger,* a publication known to be sympathetic to the FDP. Only a rogue would cry foul. At the denouement, which cannot be fully described here, we are left watching the expansionist drive of the big (West) German media enterprises shifting the balance of power among themselves and the various branches of the media, even if their eastward expansion failed to fulfill all their dreams.

In 1992, two and a half years after the structural upheavals began, the press in the East was more strongly concentrated than it had ever been in the former GDR. Instead of rationally ordering competition and creating a diversified market for newspapers, the new leaders had simply reorganized the monopolies. The *Treuhand* had been piloted only by concerns with its sale of former SED district newspapers, and as a result had been completely and fatally oblivious to the political situation of the media. Given this experience with the concentration of the press and regional monopolies, the atrophied diversity of information and the monopolization by publishers, should one not have given some thought to alternative models such as collegial solutions, cooperative enterprises, publicly legislated forms of organization, and communal responsibility? But these mundane concepts never stood a chance even in the old Federal Republic. As a result, the biggest media deal in postwar German history occurred practically without notice.[26] It was carried out not as a public but as a private venture. With this in mind, one can begin to understand the growing sense of alien control of the press in the new German states, a matter that prompted the fitting observation in the *Spiegel:* "The media-landscape in the ex-GDR remains as monochrome as it was before the *Wende*, only this time it is black instead of red."[27]

Yet the noisiest campaign on the media-political battlefield was conducted with regard to the electronic media, particularly radio and television broadcasting. Edginess and anxiety characterized not only the debates about the future of the German broadcasting landscape but also the unfolding events. All media politicians saw it as their mission to transform the centralized bureaucracy of party-sponsored broadcasting into a publicly legislated, decentralized federal system. They favored, moreover, the notion of a dual broadcasting system—the parallel coexistence of public and private broadcasting stations. Accordingly, Minister of the Media Müller (who, incidentally, worked in the same building that had housed not only Goebbels's Ministry of Reich Propaganda but also the Press and Information Department of the GDR government) felt that it was his duty to stipulate the conditions of the decision-making process as soon as possible. On May 6, 1990, Antenne Brandenburg had expeditiously aired the first (provisional) provincial broadcasts in East Germany. Sachsenradio, Radio Sachsen-Anhalt, Thüringen 1, and Radio Mecklenburg-Vorpommern followed on July 1. To accommodate a GDR-wide frequency for decentralized Länder (state) stations, Radio DDR II and Deutschlandsender, previously Stimme der DDR, merged on the June 16 to form DS Kultur. A provisional federal radio structure was thus created. All the politically responsible participants insisted that legislation was required posthaste. Yet this legislation fundamentally scrambled the steps of the reorganization of the media sector that had initially been envisioned. Minister Müller justified this state of affairs, stating: "Actually, it would have been very convenient, if one could have drafted a comprehensive media law. . . . But such an arrangement will not take place now because there are much more urgent demands for decisive action in certain areas. Thus, under the pressure of sometimes endless controversies, we decided to privilege radio and television—and create a law to govern it, so that the cornerstone of our efforts, the transition from a centralized broadcasting network to a federal, to be exact, to a regional radio and television network, could be secured."[28] Yet the new changeling, devised as a draft (*Referenten-Entwurf*) by civil servants who had been "borrowed" from the West under the direction of Minister Müller's media-political secretary, Manfred Becker, retained so many aspects of state-controlled radio that the public found it unacceptable.[29] The invective "apprentice's draft" (*Referendar- Entwurf*) circulated. Once again, all game plans began to falter, because this draft got nowhere. It vanished in the parliamentary committee on press and media until the end of the parliamentary summer holiday. When the Radio Network Reform Act (*Rundfunküberleitungsgesetz*) was finally handed down in September, it was repealed by article 36 of the Unification Treaty only two weeks later.

The Era of "the Institutional Entity"

The Ministry of the Media, marooned in the contradiction between ideal and means, had effectively achieved its initial goal of getting nowhere fast. The minister—more a man of promises than a pragmatic spirit—gave interviews here and there; he even held press conferences in Goebbels's Steinsaal. But by and large his administration remained amorphous and he increasingly hid behind noncommittal remarks designed to avoid injuring anyone, while his state secretary was noted mainly for his absence during periods of crucial decision making. And so began, with the Day of the Unification, on October 3, 1990, the era of the institutional entity, the *Einrichtung,* and with it the era of Mühlfenzl.

This leads right away to the question why the last parliament of the GDR did not elect an East German broadcasting commissioner for the radio network. This fact is especially puzzling since candidates such as DFF director Michael Albrecht and Konrad Weiß were considered. The truth of the matter is simple enough. The parliament wanted to act, but was not allowed to. At the appointed hour, Minister President de Maizière heeded the word of his master in Bonn and stepped on the brakes of his own party; the sparsely attended plenary session provided a welcome pretext. The authors of the Unification Treaty had very wisely prepared for this eventuality in the many rules and regulations that made up the treaty: "The Broadcasting Commissioner will be elected by the parliament under recommendation of the Minister President of the German Democratic Republic. If a vote is not taken by the parliament, the Broadcasting Commissioner will be determined by a majority among the representatives from the states . . . and the mayor of Berlin."[30] The state executors (*Landessprecher*) leading the newly created states—who would hold office in the new German states until the election of minister presidents and were currently preparing their constituencies for the coming events—fulfilled, at least temporarily, very important political functions. Among these functions was the election of the broadcasting commissioner, which took place on October 15. Then again, the electors, with the exception of Tino Schwierzina from Berlin, were not really duly elected representatives but simply members of various state administrations. No one questioned their legitimacy; but this was unnecessary. For the chairman, Federal Minister Günter Krause—soon after dubbed the "scandal minister" of 1993—it was enough if someone just said, as one delegate did: "I am Mr. Jones from Saxony. And I will participate in the vote" (*Ich bin der Sachse Schmitt. Ich mache die Wahl mit*). Mühlfenzl won the election with four ayes; Brandenburg dissented, and Berlin abstained.[31]

The restructuring of radio and television broadcasting was, on the whole, compromised by deadlock—a situation inseparable from the outcome of this election. It was well established that radio and television fell within the domain of the states. But during the first months of existence of the newly established states, problems with administration, personnel, and structural organization prevailed. In addition, the political system was under pressure from the mounting social and economic dislocations that came with unification. Media politics, having been a central concern of 1989, was now relegated to the bottom of the priority list. Furthermore, both the Eastern activists and the old professionals in the broadcasting business were suddenly shut out. After Mühlfenzl took office, neither the new directors of the provincial broadcasting networks nor the East Berlin business directors from Nalepastraße and Adlershof were allowed to act on their own initiative. Mühlfenzel's first mandate on taking office was a muzzling order.

With the exception of his press spokesperson, Mühlfenzl selected personnel from the West. Only Wernfried Maltusch functioned as a quasi– East German "advisor," though it was never officially admitted—and Maltusch happened to be a Stasi agent, *IM Maser*.[32] But most significantly, the envoy cultivated a kind of bunker mentality among his people. He himself almost never left his main office, so as not to run the risk of meeting his subordinates in-house or of gaining knowledge about urgent needs on location. His staff invaded the life of this "institutional entity" as storm troopers enter enemy territory—charging and retreating in search of data or documents. Issuing orders seemed to completely satisfy the envoy. The deputy director of the radio network at the time, Jörg Hildebrandt (whom Mühlfenzl fired due to an improperly fitting muzzle), described his experience as follows: "Arguments that opposed his convictions did not disturb him, because those who thought differently, especially those from East German bolshevik radio and television, didn't have any say to begin with. . . . Rudolf Mühlfenzl did not have an easy job. Probably any other envoy faced with the difficulties of overseeing these chaotic circumstances would have been equally unsuccessful. . . . The actual points of conflict resided at the political level and extended far beyond personal misunderstandings. . . . Mühlfenzl misunderstood his assignment from the Unification Treaty, be-cause he believed, as did the crew he had flown into the annexed terri-tory, that he had carte blanche to operate above and beyond the means of his constituency (listeners, audience, provincial politicians, program directors) and act merely at his own discretion."[33]

In the melee involving the media industries, public officials, and the peaceful revolutionaries—who had, in the meantime, assumed responsi-bility and demonstrated their expertise in the restructuring of the media—the latter were left out in the cold. Although Mühlfenzl declared that he was ready to "cooperate with the existing apparatus,"[34] he nevertheless depended entirely on his West German advisory staff, all of whom had earned their stripes as supporters of private radio and television. This would not necessarily have resulted in disaster, as long as there was a minimum of knowledge about the old GDR broadcasting system and an appreciation of the new East German situation, or at least a willingness to get to know them. After a few weeks it was apparent that the balance had already shifted toward Mühlfenzl's staff, as Albrecht's assertion that he was no longer being called upon demonstrates.[35] To be sure, the old GDR media really had no "substance," but what was created from scratch in the opening after 1989 never really got a chance. A sobering disillusionment. Scenes of a German-German marriage? Or simply a marriage of political patronage and nepotism? Whatever the label, it seems to me that Lothar Späth's nasty remark about the unconditional surrender of the GDR that preceded German unification also applies to the sphere of the media.

The Publicly Legislated Sisyphus and Its Consequences
For better or worse, I have been obliged to dish up all manner of nit-picking unpleasantness so far. The balance sheet is thus all the more surprising:

When the lights went out at Adlershof and Nalepastraße exactly at midnight on December 31, 1991, and the "institutional entity" ended its broadcasting activities, the State Treaty Concerning the Broadcasting System in Unified Germany (*Staatsvertrag über den Rundfunk im vereinten Deutschland*), which had been signed in Bonn on August 31, 1991, went into effect.[36] In Saxony, Saxony-Anhalt, and Thuringia the Mitteldeutsche Rundfunk (MDR) embarked on its broadcasting enterprise. In Branden-burg, the Ostdeutsche Rundfunk Brandenburg (ORB) was launched. Mecklenburg-Vorpommern was now served by the Norddeutsche Rund-funk (NDR). Only the private radio and television stations had to wait for their opportunity. The federal broadcasting system gained its footing as a sort of "limping dualism."[37]

Given the short period of time, this was an extraordinary organizational achievement. Many had been questioning the possibility of dismantling a centralized radio system that had served approximately sixteen million people and of building a new federal broadcasting organization from the ground up in only a few short months. But while in the East everything was undergoing radical transformation, in Western Germany nothing was affected by the new organization of the network.[38] All remained quiet on the Western front.

At the beginning of the unification process, the outlook was quite different. Back then many observers were still recommending that people take advantage of the fortuitous turn of events in the East and reconsider the West German radio system as well. In this context, they pointed to the perseverance of political parties in attempting to gain influence over the broadcasting system with the help of control commissioners, the continued expansion of the administrative apparatuses, the confusion resulting from the admission of private stations, the (missing) quality control in programming, and the lack of a thoroughly developed European vision for the media. This critical undertone, usually expressed in an idealistic spirit, was evident, for example, in the formulation of the sixth decision on the broadcasting network by the Federal Constitutional Court.[39] In this document, the chief justices emphatically recalled that the radio freedom secured by article 5 of the Basic Law of the Federal Republic is an "service-oriented freedom" (dienende Freiheit), meaning that it maintains a "position of responsibility with respect to the general public."[40] The principle of freedom from the state was emphasized in several passages,[41] and the distance from political parties was placed at a premium. The "socially representative control committees" are ordained as "administrators of the interests of the general public" and are "therefore not called upon to align programming according to specific interpretations or goals thereby promoting the concerns of specific interest groups."[42] The judges also expected a high degree of quality in programming;[43] even the private stations were not exempted from the responsibility of providing information, education, and cultural diversity for the public.[44]

At the end of 1991, there was precious little remaining of these self-critical reflections and of the judicial warnings—there were, at best, a few articles in professional journals whose significance only history can judge. All this, despite fundamental revision of the German Broadcasting System, despite the state governments' agreement for the establishment of public radio and television stations, despite four new laws concerning private radio and television, and despite six state treaties concerning the broadcasting system in unified Germany.[45]

First, the influence of the parties on radio and television did not diminish, but rather grew stronger. The triadic arrangement finally settled on for East Germany—the three-state MDR for CDU-ruled Saxony, Saxony-Anhalt, and Thuringia, the one-state ORB for SPD-FDP-Bündnis 90–ruled Brandenburg, and the marriage between CDU/FDP-ruled Mecklenburg-Vorpommern and the SPD-dominated NDR—would never have occurred without the political constellations created by the voters in the state elections of October 1990. The result was an uncontested partisan assault on the networks in the new states. The forty-three-member MDR broadcasting commission alone contains twelve party politicians, and of the ORB broadcasting commission's twenty-five members, five are delegates of political parties. The appeal to members to leave their party affiliations behind while participating in the control commissions was superseded by the world of everyday politics.

Second, the unification of the radio and television network led to a mushrooming of bureaucracies; two new directors were added to the existing administration of the West German *Arbeitsgemeinschaft der Rundfunkanstalten Deutschlands* (ARD), along with an additional series of new directors, deputy directors, division leaders, and so on. The fact that the ARD was hurdling headlong into an economic abyss leads one to question this centralized administration's organizational expertise. It is very probable that the ARD with its administrative maneuvering had lost out in the very real competition with the private stations. The solvent that will finally erode the conflict between publicly legislated and private providers is acid. Owing to a dearth of creative personnel and the exigency of prior debts, no new programming ideas were developed in public broadcasting. Those who sought to alleviate the economic stagnation, domestic predicaments, and inherent structural weaknesses by enlarging administrations will soon be faced with the quagmire of a bankrupt system. Private commercial competition is marching all over Germany's public broadcasting.

Third, the provincialism that was evident in the manner in which private radio and television providers were authorized has now been extended to the East. Private radio was and is supervised by state media institutions *(Landesmedienanstalten)*. Four more state media institutions, those in Saxony, Saxony-Anhalt, Thuringia, and Mecklenburg-Vorpommern, were appended to the eleven West German ones. Private radio and television failed in its efforts to break into the field of multistate frequencies and, hence, to expand its competencies to a national level. Only Brandenburg managed to escape—inasmuch as it merged with Berlin. These new media institutions are by no means "impoverished" agencies, at least financially, as they receive 2 percent of the fees generated by public radio; yet, there are few frequencies to go around. Stubbornly imitating the practice in the old (Western) states—giving a guarantee of land-based broadcasting capabilities in exchange for the general support of private stations for the respective state government—quickly led to a dead end in the new states. Private broadcasters circumvented all this using the Astra satellite, which fulfilled 70 percent of their needs without the complicated agreements required for land-based transmission. But satellite broadcasting notwithstanding, they did not escape the constraints of the state-based media institutions.

Fourth, debates about the quality of radio and television programming were a never-ending saga in the West, yet the subject of quality was scarcely broached in the endless discussions on the restructuring of broadcasting in the East. The now passé media forums debated matters of finances and subscriptions, people and parties, but ignored the subject of audiences and programs. Evasion of quality-related issues occurred despite their apparent timeliness.

Fifth, the frequently avowed European spirit remained obscured behind the wave of national anticipation that overwhelmed the Germans. They remained in a state of nearly total self-absorption. It would seem that most people are still far from adept at conceptualizing a unified Europe. But reality is ahead of the people in this particular case. Psychology still lags behind technology in an age of information, where the spread of diverse forms of telecommunication is no longer impeded by limitations of time and space.

"One could have thought this matter out, but one didn't want to," writes the director of Saarland radio, Manfred Buchwald. "Neither in the West, where the status quo is worshipped like an idol by its many supporters— nor in the East, where there was and is a lack of time and peace of mind."[46] The new beginning of East German broadcasting might have been such an opportunity, but the media politicians were not ready for this task. The fall of the Berlin Wall was beyond their ability to comprehend as a chance for a new beginning. They had not developed an agenda to handle a German-German media unification. Instead, they chose the path of least resistance. Hence, the entrenched West German media organization became the order of the day. Those on one side now feel and act like victors; those on the other side lack self-confidence and allow themselves to be treated accordingly. It would have been particularly important for East Germany to maintain its own voice, so that West and East German differences could have been reconciled. Some such solution might have required that East German journalists not only had a say but also had some responsibility for programming beyond the mere veto power that came with obstinacy. The result was a process of colonization, although it is well understood that any such process requires a considerable degree of self-colonization.

These are crazy times. The mass media as we have come to know them may well turn out to be a passing fad, but we treat them as permanent fixtures of the social landscape. In contemporary Germany, discussion is still focused on the multiplication of radio and television channels, video on demand, or computer games—in short, on simple forms of entertainment. But the future may well entail much more invasive electronic technologies that will permeate every aspect of life. Notions of an information society or of wired cities have come to embody this expectation.

Nobody can be sure which way the electronic media are heading. But *mediatization,* that is, the advancement of the electronic media markets, continues with uncanny velocity.[47] For those who are not timid Germany offers a unique market. With its 32 million television-viewing households and, except for the United States, the world's best infrastructure, including a cable network, satellite reception, and substantial buying power, the Federal Republic is Europe's television market of the future. If one counts the German-speaking neighbors, an investor could reach 100 million people in one of the most potent areas for business on earth. The Australian-British media baron Rupert Murdoch chose one of the best minds in the business when he began a partnership with Leo Kirch, whose programming assets include 18,000 feature films and video material for another 50,000 television hours. Together they are forerunners of the future of digital television in Europe. Digital information could become the most important and lucrative market of the twenty-first century, comprising a billion-dollar industry. The television of the not-so-far-off future will no longer be under the jurisdiction of broadcasting agencies but rather of telecommunications services, companies that will function as data banks. They are completely outside of the media architecture that has been created in the process of unification—and are a sign of things to come. These enterprises will warehouse digital, time-compressed films and reports that can be retrieved by the customer for a fee. The restrictive German media laws operative up to now would be useless. The fight was over radio and television, but the future is with the electronic media.

"So We Were Allowed to Believe That We Were Fighting"

Where were the intellectuals? What role did they play in these momentous transformations?[48]

In a grandiose act of nostalgia—as political missionaries and impractical idealists—the prominent GDR authors appeared before the masses on

November 4, 1989, and announced the happy news of democratic social-ism.[49] Spirit and power seemed to have once again magically converged. Authors such as Christa Wolf, Stefan Heym, and Christoph Hein were suddenly reveling in the communitarian utopias of Hölderlin, Schelling, and Hegel, as they had been sketched out in the "oldest systems program of German idealism," that of 1795. True, this was the time when the call of thousands ("We are staying here!") rang in everyone's ears. The experi-ence of the demonstrations in the early fall of 1989—when a democratic-socialist future seemed realistic—was still fresh in everyone's mind. But this was also a peculiarly one-sided view of the GDR that was flawed by the effort to prove a point while overlooking the realities of life. The intellectuals had long disregarded the social predicament of the masses; in fact, "the people" had long begun to feel abandoned. In the end, the people depended on themselves—and, now, were taken seriously. They had worked hard with old machines and in decrepit buildings. A hierarchy of parasites had reigned over them. When more and more people joined the Monday demonstrations, the newcomers were mostly disenchanted work-ers. They suppressed their own feelings of shame and disgrace and called, "Helmut, Help!" As Helmut Kohl announced the election on February 12, 1990, a huge sign floated over the masses: "Helmut, take us by the hand, lead us into economic wonderland." This sounds pathetic, but it was meant seriously. The *Volk* surrendered itself to the West Germans, while those who had long abandoned the *Volk* now suddenly wanted to behave like self-conscious and deliberating citizens of the GDR. Because of their earlier ignorance, these good citizens were condemned to obscurity. It seems to be practically a law of culture that the less political influence Germany's intellectuals have, the more elevated and wrong-headed their opinions become.

The Broadcasting Advisory Board (*Rundfunkbeirat*), which was attached to the "institutional entity," proved itself to be surprisingly inert. It was a collection of "18 recognized personalities of public life representative of socially relevant groups"[50]—not to be confused with the agile Media Control Council. This board should have envisioned itself as a corrective to Mühlfenzl, a supervisory agency, or a type of controlling organization, that possessed "a right to advise on all programming questions and a right to collaborate on all essential personnel, economic and budgetary ques-tions."[51] Many expectations and hopes rested on this board, but it failed to have any significant impact on developments. Nor was it meant to be that way. Its chairman, the poet and CDU Member of Parliament Uwe Grüning, contributed substantially to this outcome. As he said himself, he was not well-versed in these matters.[52] Thus, the media expert Mühlfenzl sat opposite a self-proclaimed amateur who posed no great challenge. Media experts were in fact very rare in East Germany. So why didn't they rely on someone who had taken a crash course in the algebra of the post-1989 media? In June 1991, Günter Gaus, the media expert who had been a delegate of the Brandenburg State, threw in the towel. He wanted nothing more to do with this "impotent organization," he explained.[53] In forging the new broadcasting system in the GDR, the Broadcasting Advisory Board did more harm than good. But its complacent resignation to the inefficacy, incompetence, and lack of creative direction in the remaking of East German broadcasting had serious consequences.

And the broadcasters themselves? A banner at the demonstration in the GDR in October 1989 proclaimed: "Half of the truth is the best means of diverting attention from the whole." In a GDR-Television program on January 22, 1990, titled "Plain Speaking on Our Own Affairs," Horst Mempel gave his interpretation: "Perhaps it was the politics of disinformation that was the worst of the many crimes against the people. This disinformation was a two-edged sword; the rape of the truth not only concealed all the other failures of the former leadership, it also obscured the blunders of the current power-elite."[54] One might also cite a bitter—yet muted—observation voiced by one of the producers of *Aktuelle Kamera*, the central news program of GDR-Television: "Politicians . . . made presentations on television. We were transfixed by them. We were obliged to cheer, obliged to do everything they wanted. . . . Whether this was effective, whether it moved anybody, whether it was good, these were not the deciding factors."[55]

Paraphrasing the Lord's prayer, the poet Wolfgang Hinkeldey caricatured the GDR media's proselytizing of false optimism:

ERFOLG UNSER, der	OUR SUCCESS, that
Du stehst in der Zeitung	You stand in this newspaper
Geheiligt werde dein Wortlaut	Hallowed be Your wording
Deine Ziffer melde	Your figures are received
Dein Optimismus blühe	Your optimism blooms
Wie im Rundfunk	On radio
Also auch im Fernsehen . . .	As on television . . .
Und führe uns nicht in Versuchung	And lead us not into temptation
sondern erlöse uns	But release us
Von allen Zweifeln	From all doubt
Denn Dein ist Genehmigung	For Thine is the permission
Und die Karriere	And the career
Also auch der Beifall	And therefore the applause
in Ewigkeit	Forever and ever
Hurra.	Hooray.[56]

The limited viewing audience of *Aktuelle Kamera*, estimated at a constant 5 percent of the viewing public, ensured that the lack of realism in news programming disturbed very few souls. Besides, the country had effectively been unified by the spillover of West German media into the GDR long before the *Wende*. One could have lived easily with these differentials in publicity in the East and the West, if only information had been the issue. But the critical potential of the East was forfeited. The structural inability of the GDR media system to discuss the need for social reform blotted out any potential for a critique of the system. It generated a series of monads that were incapable of creating a strategy for the overhaul of the whole system. Therefore, a transformation from within never took place, or if it did it was decidedly too late.

The media did not call for demonstrations in Berlin on November 4, 1989, but rather Berlin artists demanding freedom of speech and of assembly. Even at this late hour, the Oversight Committee for Radio of the GDR (*Staatliches Kommittee für Rundfunk beim Ministerrat der DDR*) —according to its name the top coordinating agency, but more aptly the top censorship organ of the GDR—was debating whether to broadcast the demonstrations nationwide. "It would be a compromise solution," wrote the chairman, Achim Becker, to Heinz Geggel, the director of the department *Agitation* in the Central Committee of the SED on November 1, 1989, "to carry the announcement on the FM-channel of Berlin Radio. This would serve the listeners in the Berlin area. On the remaining channels of the Berlin network—also in Berlin—we could broadcast the normal program of the Berlin area with such mass-appeal programs as the sports show. . . . I'm asking for your opinions and must remind you once again most emphatically that the entire collective of Berlin Radio supports this demand."[57]

I know many prominent people who happily placed themselves at the service of the state. I know of no cases of open, that is to say public, rebellion. I know only a few, only a very few, who abstained. Naturally there were some dissidents in the media who worked together on useful, respectable tasks—but a resistance with the necessary resolve or planning did not exist. The protesting of the managers in the media sector—much of it invented in hindsight in order to look good in the pubic eye—remained so general that they were unable to join forces in any useful way. And this was, in fact, the problem. A stratum of semi-protesters evolved, convinced of their critical self-consciousness, so much so that they were prepared to take part in all kinds of socialistic rites of self-improvement and even in some clandestine cabal. That is an unofficial model of how it worked. Everyone knew what no one was told and everything stayed as it always was. It is not analysis but despair that sows the seeds of resistance. For the majority of people in the GDR, there was no reason to despair. Daily life set the norms in tolerable amounts. The preparations for minor emergencies precluded a major one. The practice of confession necessarily became more attenuated in a country that clapped a hand over the mouths of the talkative. On one hand, the short-sighted machinators did not care what it was they worked on, and on the other, there was that questionable yet irrefutable maxim: If I don't do it, then someone else will.

With such compromising much was despoiled—too much, as became clear with hindsight. Compromises of this kind left too much unsaid. This lack of publicity affected the audiences. They remained in a perpetual state of unhappiness and dissatisfaction, unable to name or precluded from naming their predicament. They were themselves cogs in the machine that had engendered them. Drawing the line between the inherent impotence of the system and genuine personal guilt will remain a running theme in discussions about the GDR media for a long time to come. Where restrictions on speech prevail, words are intrinsically endowed with greater weight. Now it remains to be seen where they fall.

"And No Saviors, No Knights in Shining Armor, No Redeemer in Sight"

Intellectuals of the unified Germany are once again standing on the sidelines, indifferent and unable to devote themselves to the secular trends of the "mediatization" of social life. Walter Jens reached this verdict: "The so-called 'broadcasts' of the private stations (and, unfortunately, of others as well) are becoming ever more like commercials. It all comes out of the same pot; it is, I can only repeat, the same flagrant cynicism again and again."[58] Yet, is this not just a populist rendition of a state of affairs in order to voluntarily renounce the role of spirited opposition? "Television is the imperial agent of culture, that devours everything in its path; . . . it is not an isolated phenomenon. It is the flagship of a whole armada of de-realizations, the instigator of the great motto 'pretend as if.'"[59] The machinators actually should have grown suspicious when Bernd Guggenberger presented this and other theses in September 1993, but they swept these doubts under the rug. The anticipated *"general arrival* of data and pictures" will, according to Paul Virilio, mean "as fundamental a change for mankind" as "the generation of the *Homo erectus*. Only it no longer has anything to do with a 'positive evolution' towards a new kind of mobility, but rather a 'negative behavior-related convolution,' which culminates in the genus of a pathological immobility: the generation of a *Homo inertus* or, even worse, of a *Homo catatonicus.*"[60]

Who watches the warden? Who holds television's reins? The intellectuals' defenses are put to the test. It is their challenge to act up against the "disintegration of the social body into the few ubiquitous activists and an amorphous mass of the 'acted upon.' "[61] The shape of this development is becoming ever clearer, and intellectuals must take a stand.

Notes

1. "Bloße Übernahme oder Neugründung: Medienexperten über die Zukunft von Funk und Fernsehen," *Neues Deutschland* 10, 12–13 January 1991.

2. In 1991 Mühlfenzl was a seventy-one-year-old former editor-in-chief of the Bavarian Broadcasting Corporation. He had been a member of the Christlich Soziale Union since 1965 and a close friend of the late Franz Josef Strauß. He was repeatedly attacked for political cronyism. After his retirement he became a leading spokesperson for the privatization of the media.

3. Contract Between the Federal Republic of Germany and the German Democratic Republic Concerning the Attainment of German Unity (the Unification Treaty), in *Bulletin des Presse- und Informationsamtes der Bundesregierung* 104, 6 September 1990, 886.

4. The chief GDR negotiator for the unity accord, Günther Krause, offered a prime example of this kind of thinking when he said: "We engineers and communications specialists [*Informatiker*] . . . , we know the circuitry [*Regelmechanismen*] of systems, we can analyze their manageability [*Beherrschbarkeit*]." "DDR Unterhändler Günther Krause über Probleme der Einigung," *Der Spiegel*, 13 August 1990, 25–28, here 27.

5. Paul Virilio, *Geschwindigkeit und Politik: Ein Essay zur Dromologie* (Berlin, 1980).

6. *40 Jahre DDR-TschüSSED: 4.11.89, Katalog zur Ausstellung der "Initiativgruppe 4.11.89" im Museum für deutsche Geschichte, Berlin-Ost, und im Haus der Geschichte der Bundesrepublik Deutschland Bonn* (Bonn, 1990), 36.

7. Ibid.

8. Constitution of the German Democratic Republic, 6 April 1968, in the version of the law to amend and add to the Constitution of the German Democratic Republic of 7 October 1974 (Berlin, 1974), 29.

9. Rolf Henrich, *Der vormundschaftliche Staat* (Reinbek, 1989).

10. See, e.g., Ulrich Bürger, *Das sagen wir so natürlich nicht! Donnerstag-Argus bei Herrn Geggel* (Berlin, 1990); Stephan Pannen, *Die Weiterleiter: Funktion und Selbstverständniss ostdeutscher Journalisten* (Köln, 1992); Günter Simon, *Tisch-Zeiten: Aus den Notizen eines Chefredakteurs 1981 bis 1989* (Berlin, 1990).

11. See Jürgen Wilke, "Medien DDR," in *Fischer Lexikon Publizistik-Massenkommunikation*, ed. Elisabeth Noelle-Neumann, Winfried Schulz, and Jürgen Wilke (Frankfurt am Main, 1989), 156–69; Rolf Geserick, *40 Jahre Presse, Rundfunk und Kommunikationspolitik in der DDR* (Munich, 1989); Heike Riedel, *Hörfunk und Fernsehen in der DDR: Funktion, Struktur und Programm des Rundfunks in der DDR* (Cologne, 1977). For information regarding the "Samisdat" papers see Luise von Flotow, " 'Samizdat' in East Berlin," *Cross-Currents: A Yearbook of Central European History* 9 (1990): 197–218; Wolfgang Rüddenklau, "Behörden und Unternehmerunfreundlich:

Zum 5-jährigen Bestehen des 'telegraph': Ein Blick in die Vorgeschichte unserer Zeitschrift. Teil 1: Die 'Umweltblätter,'" *telegraph* 9 (1994): 10–18; Tom Sello, "Von den Umweltblättern zum Telegraph: Medien im Untergrund," in *Stattbuch Ost: Adieu ddr oder die Liebe zur Autonomie. Ein Wegweiser durch die Projektelandschaft* (Berlin, 1991), 85–88.

12. Quoted in Ernst Richter, "Entwicklungsetappen des Deutschen Demokratischen Rundfunks," *Schriftenreihe des Deutschen Demokratischen Rundfunks* 4, no. 2 (1970): 13.

13. Decision of the *Volkskammer* on guaranteeing freedoms of opinion, information, and the press on 5 Febuary 1990 in *Gesetzblatt der DDR*, pt. 1, no. 7 (12 February 1990). On the laws concerning the media see also Wolfgang Hoffmann-Riem, "Die Entwicklung der Medien und des Medienrechts im Gebiet der ehemaligen DDR," *Archiv für Presserecht* 22, no. 2 (1991): 472–81; Wolfgang Kleinwächter, "Die Vorbereitung für ein Mediengesetz der DDR," *Media Perspektiven* 3 (1990): 133–39; Heinz Odermann, "Der Umbruch und die Mediengesetzgebung in der DDR," *Rundfunk und Fernsehen* 38, no. 3 (1990): 377–84; Walter Schütz, "Der (gescheiterte) Regierungsentwurf für ein Rundfunküberleitungsgesetz der DDR: Chronik und Dokumente," *Rundfunk im Wandel: Festschrift für Winfried B. Lerg*, ed. Arnulf Kutsch, Christina Holtz-Blacha, and Franz R. Stuke (Berlin, 1993), 263–303; Karola Wille, "Medienrecht in der DDR—Vergangenheit und Gegenwart," *Zeitschrift für Urheber- und Medienrecht* 35 (1991): 15–20.

14. Quoted in Kleinwächter, "Vorbereitung," 136.

15. Ute Thon, "Medienkontrollrat—ein Wolf ohne Zähne," *die tageszeitung*, 3 April 1990.

16. Tape-recorded protocol of the meeting of the Media Control Commission on 18 April 1 1990 (copy in the possession of the author).

17. "Fundamental Principles on the Free Market System for the Press" [*Pressevertriebssystem*] of 7 March 1990 (copy in possession of the author).

18. Statement of the Media Control Commission to the Government, 28 March 1990 (copy in possession of the author).

19. See "Ruling on the retail trade of media materials [*Presseerzeugnisse*] in the GDR," in *Gesetzblatt der DDR*, pt. 1, no. 26, 15 May 1990.

20. The original intentions of the Media Control Council to establish a wholesale distribution system independent of publishing houses after the West German model was contradicted by Article 2 of the ordinance. Here one reads: "The Ministry for Media Politics can . . . upon request grant participation [of publishing houses] in the wholesale market of newspapers and magazines, if available distribution channels for media do not meet the demand in a particular area." Ibid. Only wholesalers operating independently of publishing houses could meet demand, since all others could not rely on large publishers for distribution. And this fact was well known to the minister, who was heavily influenced by large publishing houses.

21. An account that accepts the legend of "borrowed" West German media administrators can be found in Schütz, "Der (gescheiterte) Regierungsenwurf," 267.

22. See the obituaries: Katharina Bluhm, "Instrumente der Öffentlichkeit als vierte Gewalt," *Frankfurter Rundschau*, 18 September 1990; Jens Brüning, "Ein 'basisdemokratisches Relikt der Wende' löst sich auf," *Süddeutsche Zeitung*, 19 September 1990; Reinhart Bünger, "Beim Abschiedstrunk kam ein wenig Wehmut auf," *Frank-*

furter Rundschau, 21 September 1990; Ute Thon, "Medienkontrollrat tritt ab," *die tagezeitung,* 21 September 1990.

23. "Dokumentation zur Kontroverse um den Pressevertrieb in der DDR (Documentation concerning the controversy about distribution systems)," updated as of February 16, [19]90. *Media Perspektiven. Basisdaten. Daten zur Mediensituation in Deutschland* (1991): 42–58. Deposited with the Fond Medienkontrollrat des Instituut voor Sociale Geschiedenis, Amsterdam.

24. See, e.g., Maryellen Boyle, "The Revolt of the Communist Journalist: East Germany," *Media, Culture, and Society* 14 (1992): 133–39; Jürgen Grubitzsch, "Presselandschaft der DDR im Umbruch: Ausgangspunkte, erste Ergebnisse und Perspektiven," *Media Perspektiven* 3 (1990): 140–55; Klaus Michael, "Neue Verlage und Zeitschriften in Ostdeutschland," *Aus Politik und Zeitgeschichte,* 4 October 1991, 33–45.

25. "Zeitungsverkauf steht bevor: Treuhand will Entscheidung über Ost-Regionalblätter fällen," *Saarbrücker Zeitung,* 9 April 1991.

26. For overviews see Horst Röper, "Die Entwicklung des Tageszeitungsmarktes in Deutschland nach der Wende in der ehemaligen DDR," *Media Perspektiven* 7 (1991): 421–30; Horst Röper, "Daten zur Konzentration der Tagespresse in der Bundesrepublik Deutschland im I. Quartal 1991," ibid., 431–44; *Media Perspektiven.*

27. "Ruß aus der Hose," in *Der Spiegel* 17, 8 April 1991.

28. Quoted in Andreas and Heike Graf, "Der Medienkontrollrat—Insel der Stabilität im medienpolitischen Schlachtenlärm," in *Medien-Wende /Wende-Medien? Dokumentation des Wandels im DDR-Journalismus Oktober '89 –Oktober '90,* ed. Werner Claus (Berlin, 1991), 7–15, here 13.

29. See Uwe Kammann, "Dialektischer Pragmatismus der treuen Hand: Das DDR-Rundfunküberleitungsgesetz—ein Wechselbalg," *epd* [Evangelischer Pressedienst]; *Kirche und Rundfunk* 53 (7 July 1990): 3–4; Peter Leudts, "Nicht zu Ende gedacht: Zum Rundfunküberleitungsgesetz in der DDR," *Funk-Korrespondenz,* 13 July 1990, 1–2.

30. See note 3.

31. Reinhart Bünger, "'Guten Abend, ich bin der Sachse Schmitt, ich mache die Wahl mit': Wie Rudolf Mühlfenzl zum Rundfunkbeauftragten bestellt worden ist. Protokoll der Wahlmänner-Sitzung im Wortlaut," *Frankfurter Rundschau,* 22 October 1990.

32. Wernfried Maltusch agitated from the *Wende* until his discharge in the summer of 1990 as the deputy director of the Radio Network. Before this he was a colleague of Hubert Sydow, a member of the State Committee for Radio of the GDR Cabinet. See Erich Schmidt-Eenboom, *Schnüffler ohne Nase: Der BND : Die unheimliche Macht im Staate* (Düsseldorf, 1993).

33. Jörg Hildebrand, "Eine Lektion in Demokratie: Vom Ab- und Aufbau der ostdeutschen Rundfunkanstalten," in *Die Abwicklung der DDR,* ed. Heinz Ludwig Arnold and Frauke Meyer-Gosau (Göttingen, 1992), 64—70, here 68.

34. "'Ich, Mühlfenzl, die Einrichtung': Gespräch mit dem Beauftragten für den Rundfunk in der ehemaligen DDR," *Süddeutsche Zeitung,* 30 October 1990.

35. See "Neues Programm wackelt: Will Mühlfenzl den verbleibenden DFF-Kanal teilweise den Privaten zuschanzen," *Junge Welt,* 30 November 1990.

36. See "Staatsvertrag über den Rundfunk im vereinten Deutschland," *Media Perspektiven: Dokumentation* no. 3a (1991): 105–72.

37. Wolfgang Kleinwächter, "Deutsche Rundfunkneuordnung: Rückblick auf eine verpaßte Chance," *Funk-Korrespondenz*, 2 January 1992, 11–14, here 11.

38. To be more exact: one more deutschmark in fees for the construction of the networks in the new provinces and 7 percent of the programming in the ARD schedule reserved for ORB and MDR—there was an impact, after all.

39. See "Urteil des Bundesverfassungsgerichts vom 5. Februar 1991," *Media Perspektiven: Dokumentation*, no. 1 (1991): 1–48.

40. Ibid., 31.

41. Ibid., 29, 44.

42. Ibid., 45.

43. Ibid., 6–7.

44. Ibid., 29–30, 37–39.

45. One example would be Kleinwächter, "Deutsche Rundfunkneuordnung," 12–14.

46. Manfred Buchwald, "Bestandsaufnahme eines Neubeginns," in *So durften wir glauben zu kämpfen . . . Erfahrung mit DDR-Medien*, ed. Edith Spielhagen (Berlin 1993), 165–75, here 172.

47. For more on this see Winfried Schulz, "Die Transformation des Mediensystems in den Achtzigern: Epochale Trends und modifizierende Bedingungen," in *Rundfunk im Wandel: Festschrift für Winfried B. Lerg*, ed. Arnulf Kutsch, Christina Holtz-Blacha, and Franz R. Stuke (Berlin, 1993), 155–71.

48. The subheading refers to a sentence by Gislinde Schwarz that also provided the title of book about the ticklish history of the East German media. See her "Im Dienste der Frauen? Kühnheit und Anschmiegsamkeit der Frauenzeitschrift FÜR DICH," in *So durften wir glauben zu kämpfen . . . Erfahrung mit DDR-Medien*, ed. Edith Spielhagen (Berlin 1993), 191–200, here 195.

49. See *40 Jahre DDR*, supra n. 6, 36, 38–39, 55–57.

50. See note 3.

51. Ibid.

52. Feature, *DS-Kultur*, 9 January 1991, 6:05 P.M.

53. "Gaus verläßt Rundfunkbeirat," *Berliner Zeitung* 11 June 1991; see also Günter Gaus, "Abrechnung," *Freitag*, 21 June 1991.

54. Quoted in Peter Ludes, " 'Von mir hätten Sie immer nur die halbe Wahrheit bekommen': Interviews mit Journalisten des Deutschen Fernsehfunks der DDR," *Aus Politik und Zeitgeschichte: Beilage zur Wochenzeitung "Das Parlament,"* 19 April 1991, 21–31, here 29. See also Stefan Heym, "Je voller der Mund, desto leerer die Sprüche: Leben mit der Aktuellen Kamera," *Sinn und Form* 42, no. 2 (1990): 417–25; Peter Ludes and Georg Schütte, "Ost-westliche Begegnungen: Wie TV-Journalisten der alten DDR sich auf neue Arbeitsbedingungen einstellen," *Funk-Korrespondenz*, 15 October 1992, 1–3.

55. Quoted in Ludes, "Interviews," 29–30. Bernd Okun presents a general perspective and sketches some of the relationships between media and "Wende." See his "Medien und "Wende" in der DDR," *Comparativ* 1, no. 3 (1991): 11–25.

56. Quoted in Hans-Peter Klausenitzer, "Konkrete Prosa aus einem real existierenden Land," *Deutschland Archiv* 11, no. 2 (1979): 185.

57. "Staatliches Komitee für Rundfunk beim Ministerrat der DDR," in *Deutsches Rundfunkarchiv/Ost*, Berlin (in posession of the author), n.p.

58. Walter Jens, "Und bleibe, was ich bin: Ein Scheiß-Liberaler," *Die Zeit*, 5 March 1993.

59. Bernd Guggenberger, "Vom Bürger zum Zerstreuungspatienten: Zehn Thesen zur sozialen Macht des Fernsehens," in *Kongreßdokumentation: Reden und Beiträge*, ed. Medien-Forum Berlin-Brandenburg (Munich, 1993), 348–50, here 348–49.

60. Paul Virilio, *Rasender Stillstand: Essay* (Munich, 1992), 124–25.

61. Guggenberger, "Vom Bürger zum Zerstreuungspatienten," 349.

The Double Disappointment: Revolution, Unification, and German Intellectuals

The process of unification has profoundly disappointed the German intellectuals. The educated had spearheaded the demonstrations and dialogue that propelled the democratic awakening in the German Democratic Republic during the exciting fall of 1989. Even many academic supporters of the SED had been caught up in the drive toward renewal and reform. But the popular turn toward the German mark and the vote for unity with the West during the winter of 1990 disenchanted proponents of a Third Way. Swinging from hope into depression, many intellectuals lost their bearings and began to doubt their sagacity as well as their legitimacy. The unexpected disappearance of the GDR prompted acute self-questioning and a narcissistic nostalgia for the bad old days.[1]

As a result, intellectuals suffered a drastic loss of authority in the public's eyes. At the beginning, the leadership of educated dissenters in the civic revolution had lived up to the heroic image, and newspaper editorials had been full of praise for the civic courage of the dissidents. But their subsequent effort to reform socialism and their rejection of unification spurred widespread condemnation in the media. Revelations of Stasi complicity unleashed a wave of anti-intellectualism among the general population that disparaged all forms of leftist engagement. Forgetting their initial contribution, pragmatic critics fastened on the "failure of the explanatory class."[2]

The vagaries of intellectuals defy easy analysis. The ample literature about the educated is marked by conceptual fog and emotional hyperbole because commentators are in effect writing about their own group. Exaggerated expectations of superior insight and morality make intellectual betrayals seem particularly poignant. More often cited than read is Julian Benda's classic indictment La trahison des clercs. His charge of selling out for practical advantage has inspired a raft of warnings against conformism that intone, "Beware [of] intellectuals." Fewer impassioned voices have rushed to their defense in order to argue that "the presence of intellectuals in the modern state is crucial for democracy."[3]

How can one escape the vicious cycle of eulogizing or bashing intellectuals? Perhaps transatlantic distance can help break down the partisan identification with internal German concerns. A meta-perspective of reflecting about discourse instead of thinking within it is also essential. As an antidote to oversimplifications, distinctions are equally imperative: Speaking in a babble of contending voices, the educated fracture along ideological, geographic, gender, and generational lines. Judgments also have to be contextualized. The same critics can be brilliantly correct and obtusely wrong, depending on circumstances. Explaining the post-unity depression requires looking at the intellectuals' general structure and analyzing their specific German development.[4]

Meanings of "Intellectual"

The sociocultural formations of the educated have varied in name and content throughout history. In the German context, their evolution has followed a particular sequence: During the eighteenth century, the notion of a *Gelehrter*, which referred to a private scholar, steeped in knowledge and preoccupied with other-worldly concerns, predominated. In the nineteenth century, the concept of a *Gebildeter* gained prominence. Trained in neohumanist classics, this person pursued cultivation as a life goal and often sought to attain it through systematic scholarship. Collectively this stratum became known as the *Bildungsbürgertum*, a product of secondary education in the *Gymnasium*. After 1900, the term *Akademiker* came into vogue in order to denote graduates from universities and technical institutes. Reflecting greater numbers and confidence, this designation separated the educated from the propertied bourgeoisie and lower white-collar groups.[5]

In the twentieth century, the evolution of the educated took a surprising turn. The survival crisis of the Weimar Republic produced the slogan *Geistesarbeiter*. This was a Marxist neologism, later picked up by the Nazis as well, that likened "workers of the mind" to "workers of the fist." After the disasters of World War II, the self-consciously neutral word *Experte* became popular. It referred to technical or scientific expertise, compensating for the lack of a special designation for "professional" in the German language. These succeeding conceptions suggest that self-images and structures of the educated strata have changed dramatically over time. But the superseded formations have left behind remnants that created cleavages and debates.[6]

As the label of the cultured, the term *intellectual* suggests a radical stance. In its narrower sense, the notion originated in the Dreyfus Affair in France. The literati who joined in protest against the scandalous anti-Semitism of the military establishment considered themselves "intellectuals." When universalized, the concept designated the critical, progressive outlook of a self-selected group of educated *engagés*. In imperial Russia, the intelligentsia similarly became known as the revolutionary vanguard beyond liberal *zemstvo* (local self-government) professionals. In the West, this historical origin has given the term *intellectual* an attitudinal rather than a structural base. Its committed posture *(Haltung)* has acquired a certain cachet.[7]

For some sociologists, the notion of intellectuals has come to designate the entire group of educated persons. Karl Mannheim coined the concept of *freischwebende Intelligenz* (free-floating intelligence) as the designation for the entire knowledge-based stratum. Marxist-Leninist theoreticians similarly included anyone working with his mind in the intelligentsia. In the East, *die Intelligenz* was not confined to a certain political point of view but referred to a structurally defined stratum, comprised of the educated, that had clear statistical boundaries. But echoes of the radical origin of the term lingered in the implication that intellectuals ought to provide the leadership of the proletariat.[8]

In literary circles, the concept of intellectual refers to yet another group, the critical writers. This connotation tends to conflate engagement with structure by focusing on the producers of ideology. In their works of fiction or their essays, these literati are somehow supposed to speak for a larger audience. Unfortunately, this common usage elaborates neither membership criteria nor clear boundaries.[9] These shifting definitions result in conceptual chaos. If the meanings were identical, all leftists would have to be educated or write, and all literati would need to be on the Left. Polemicists abet the confusion since they like to tar all and sundry with the same brush.

All these conflicting usages proceed from the premise that the social stratum of intellectuals is based on cultural capital. It lives by words, deals in symbols and signs, and produces meaning, explanation, and guidance. Therefore, intellectuals are the guardians of tradition and of collective identity. As core of the noneconomic middle class, they are ensconced in education, the media, or the church. These particular livelihoods produce a curious combination of spiritual freedom and institutional dependence. In contrast to Mannheim's theory, intellectuals are not really free-floating but possess distinctive group interests. In claiming to represent collective social goods, they tend to advance their own sectoral concerns.[10]

In political terms, intellectuals often play a paradoxical role. Idealist engagement spurs them to become regime critics and to speak on behalf of disenfranchised groups. Their moral authority is primarily based on representation of fundamental values such as health, justice, or enlightenment. Yet the practical self-interest of university graduates counsels accommodation to the existing government in order to be rewarded with a share of power and certain privileges. Since their collective well-being derives from acceptance of their superior authority, they cannot stray too far from public sentiment. This ambivalent position produces possibilities for disinterested dissent as well as the temptations of self-serving complicity, no matter what the regime.[11]

In Germany, intellectuals were late to emerge as critics of the dominant *Bildungsbürgertum*. Although there were single precursors before and during the 1848 revolution, a group of educated radicals only arose around the turn of the twentieth century. Artistic bohemians formed a small but protean counterculture by seceding from the academy, writing shocking plays, or attacking the bourgeoisie in cartoons. In Peter Gay's felicitous phrase, many of these outsiders became insiders during the Weimar Republic. With the support of Socialists and Communists, leftist intellectuals captured the cultural establishment and founded new institutions such as the Bauhaus, the Hochschule für Politik, and the Theater am Schiffbauerdamm. But such experimentation provoked an intense rightist backlash that denounced decadence. In Ernst Jünger, Ernst von Salomon, and the *Tat* circle, the right created a new breed of anti-intellectual intellectuals.[12]

Only in the postwar period did the majority of the educated begin to identity themselves as intellectuals. Opposing the restoration of the *Bildungsbürgertum* in West Germany, the literati formulated a powerful critique of the Nazi past and the FRG present. Triggered by the student revolt, the cultural revolution of the late 1960s spawned the new social movements of feminism, environmentalism, and pacifism that changed academic styles and overturned the classical canon. During the 1970s, the reforms of the social-liberal coalition remade educated youths in a postnationalist and postmaterialist image. Even the neoconservative turn during the 1980s could not reinstate the remaining traditionalists to cultural hegemony. In the West, intellectuals on public salary were negatively integrated via their critique of the capitalist system.[13]

The GDR consciously broke with bourgeois traditions and created a new type of working-class intellectual in order to fashion a loyal *sozialistische Intelligenz*. With émigrés and Marxist partisans, the SED worked hard to make its brand of antifascism mandatory for the entire group of the educated. Because of mass emigration, the initial resistance of the

Bildungsbürger eventually waned. The *Aufbaugeneration* (rebuilding generation), which built the East German state, constructed a new social formation that even forced religious opponents to come to terms with the GDR. Only during the 1980s did "conspiratorial avantgardism" reduce the certainty of party intellectuals, while a new cohort of dissidents emerged to challenge the regime from within. In the East, a subservient intelligentsia received a great deal of government support as a reward for its prescribed radicalism.[14]

Civic Revolution Leadership

Different strands of intellectuals contributed to the democratic awakening in the East. Least involved were the Western leftists who accepted the existence of two states as a precondition for peace. Since many radicals saw the GDR as a better alternative, only a few Greens such as Petra Kelly or Social Democrats such as Erhard Eppler helped the emerging opposition. In spite of practical frustrations, most of the Eastern intelligentsia also believed Socialism to be a morally superior social system. But the politically involved envied Soviet perestroika and wanted to reform their system in order to make it function better. Although the educated generally agreed on the need for change, when it actually came they were surprised by its rapidity and extent.[15]

Critical writers sought to improve "real existing Socialism." In contrast to official celebrations of heroic workers, realistic portrayals of everyday conflicts intended to humanize the GDR. Authors such as Christa Wolf in *Kassandra*, Günter De Bruyn in *Märkische Forschungen*, and Christoph Hein in *Ritter der Tafelrunde* pointed out the difference between progressive rhetoric and repressive practice.[16] In a system with a controlled public sphere, their tolerated critique worked as a safety valve. By holding print runs much smaller than those of the popular media, the SED tried to keep subversive ideas from reaching the masses. But the party hoped to gain intellectuals' loyalty by permitting a limited debate in carefully selected circles. The authentic language of literature was therefore enormously important, since it created the only mirror that reflected some of the less pleasant sides of East German realities.[17]

These literati helped prepare the ground for the October rising. Following authors' readings, public discussions allowed the articulation of some complaints. Such gatherings sometimes had the unwanted result of encouraging real opposition to the regime. During the democratic awakening prominent writers served as opinion leaders in demanding free speech and civil rights. Well-known novelists, theater actors, and rock musicians signed countless petitions and organized demonstrations such as the memorable mass gathering at the Alexanderplatz on November 4. Later Western attacks during the *Literaturstreit* were largely beside the point. Of course, privileged literati were in some sense the court jesters of the regime. But they did also press for open dialogue, since wanting more freedom for themselves also required greater liberty for society.[18]

Party intellectuals wanted to remodel rather than abolish socialism. In contrast to the image promoted in its propaganda, the SED was not monolithic but rife with internal tensions between apparatchiks and educated reformers. Gorbachev's daring example increased internal debates, especially on the grass-roots level among artists and academics. One important milestone was the SPD-SED *Streitpapier*, which concerned itself with ideologies, since it was published in the GDR and provided alternative visions of democratic socialism. Another impetus was the prohibition of the magazine *Sputnik* and of Soviet films. Keeping perestroika out meant *Abgrenzung* not against the West but against the East, and it contradicted the slogans that urged learning from the Soviets. Such repression triggered protest resolutions and resignations from the party. In spite of growing ferment, the prohibition of factions kept the lid on and prevented the internal discussions from reaching the outside.[19]

During the civic revolution, SED reformers helped destabilize the regime from within. Already in the spring of 1989, theory groups at Humboldt University had begun to discuss alternative models of socialism. The product of these debates was a series of interesting papers on rebuilding society that tried to persuade the party leadership to reform its state. Restless intellectuals within the SED wanted to get rid of Honecker's post-Stalinist leadership and democratize the party in order to regain its credibility. During the critical confrontations in early October, functionaries who sympathized with their critique decided on a peaceful course in Dresden and Leipzig. In the late fall, separate "platforms" emerged, calling for radical renewal but clinging to SED leadership. They contributed to the transition toward the PDS but failed to achieve their goal of developing a radical but democratized socialist party.[20]

Opposition dissidents instead intended to construct a new, freer version of democratic socialism. Beginning in the early 1980s, circles of pacifists, environmentalists, and feminists had formed in the shelter of the Protestant Church. Many of these critics had been mobilized by GDR participation in Czech repression and by the expulsion of the popular satirist and performer Wolf Biermann. They were not necessarily religious, but they sought church protection since it provided the only quasi-public space. An ambivalent church hierarchy both controlled and shielded dissent. The opponents were products of the GDR in their thirties or forties who lived at the margins of official cultural institutions and often espoused an alternative lifestyle. Though the Stasi penetrated the dissident groups, they continued to forge ahead. When protest became too loud, its leaders were shipped to the West, decimating dissent. But persecution failed to stop the growth of a small opposition milieu.[21]

In the fall of 1989, once-marginal dissidents took the public lead. A few months earlier, there had only been a loose network of one hundred and fifty groups. The Stasi estimated that there were a few hundred committed opponents, supported by a couple of thousand sympathizers. But these activists had started an underground press and developed a set of peaceful tactics that relied on international media support to counter harassment. By risking their lives, these dissenters provided leadership for demonstrations and gradually attracted mass support. Though unable to unite, they penned the founding manifestoes of new groups such as the *Neue Forum*, *Demokratie Jetzt*, *SDP*, and the *Demokratischer Aufbruch*. Their central aim of creating a civil society sought to restore bourgeois civil liberties. But the opposition programs also incorporated many socialist aspirations and moved forward toward postnational and postmaterial aims.[22]

The intellectual reform effort culminated in the discussions of the *Runde Tisch* (Round Table) during the winter of 1989–90. Borrowed from Poland and Hungary, this institution promoted an apolitical means of building consensus for change. Technically, it represented a reluctant concession by the disintegrating Modrow government that it would share power with the new social forces. Since the Round Table carefully balanced dissident groups with SED affiliates and bloc parties, the debates were dominated by party reformers and opposition intellectuals. However, the government and the SED apparatus often dragged their feet in implementing decisions. Broadcast on television, the debates turned into something like a national town meeting. They focused not so much on practical politics as on fundamental decisions for a restructuring the public realm. Rather than seizing power, the Round Table supervised reform.[23]

The goal of these rebuilding efforts was a *Dritter Weg*—a third way between state socialism and rampant capitalism. In contrast to their counterparts in other Eastern countries, GDR intellectuals had not given up on socialism but sought to reinvigorate it. The Third Way appealed as a double negation of communism and capitalism that would combine their best elements in a Hegelian synthesis. Theoretically intriguing, this vague blend of socialism and democracy unfortunately lacked practicality. Even if Sweden was an attractive model, there was little understanding of the economic and political underpinnings of Scandinavian success. Though the Round Table conquered the Stasi hydra, it had no remedies for GDR deficits or for the collapse of the planned economy. Intellectuals failed to provide a convincing alternative to the combined introduction of parliamentarianism and market competition. In the end, deep-seated distrust between party reformers and opposition dissidents blocked an effective renewal of the GDR.[24]

The civic revolution of 1989 was high drama for the intellectuals. Writers, reformers, and dissidents openly rebelled against the dictatorship of the hated nomenclatura. Previously marginal critics gained power through citizen's committees and suddenly found themselves city councilmen, deputies, or even ministers. But formulating plans for a new society and simultaneously cleaning up SED debris severely overtaxed even the best-intentioned. As intellectuals, they preferred to rely on rhetoric and moral authority rather than grasping control and seizing government. They excelled in restoring authentic language, drafting resolutions, and leading public debates. In many ways, intellectuals had their finest hour in undermining the old regime and debating the course of renewal.[25]

Split into contending groups, the educated were therefore ineffective in managing the ensuing transition to democracy. Marxist reformers and opposition dissidents could not agree with previously silent technical experts and nationally minded *Bildungsbürger* on which direction and what measures to take. The broader group of the intelligentsia hoped to gain Western civic rights while maintaining their Eastern privileges. They joined the popular mobilization but abhorred chaos and had little patience for gambling on futuristic visions. At the same time, Western intellectuals were strangely perplexed by these unforeseen events. Instead of being gratified by the civic ferment, many had difficulty cutting their established SED ties. Unwilling to intervene, these radicals largely contented themselves with cheering from afar.[26]

Rejection of Unification

As a result of their sympathies for reforming socialism, most intellectuals opposed unification. In the West, only remnants of the *Bildungsbürgertum* or previous refugees clamored for tearing down the GDR as a separate state, but leftists dismissed these advocates of unity as unreconstructed nationalists and cold warriors. In the East, the refusal of writers, party reformers, and dissidents to confront division left the masses without a voice. Because of this reluctance, national aspirations of the East could only be articulated by the just barely transformed bloc parties of the old regime or by politicians from the West. The conservative victory in the March 1990 election therefore triggered a double disappointment: While intellectuals resented the repudiation of their previous leadership, the people were incensed about the lack of sensitivity of the educated.[27]

Deep-seated opposition to the search for a German national identity complicated intellectual responses to unity. Perhaps the educated had learned the lessons of repudiating the hypernationalism that had prevailed during World Wars I and II too well. In order to escape a troubling German identity, they had fled after 1945 into other causes such as European integration or communist internationalism. Some intellectuals had even developed an inverted nationalism of self-hatred in the hope of immunizing German culture against the possible recurrence of nationalism. In the West, Adenauer's support for European integration and economic success had created a substitute pride. The economic miracle and democratic cosmopolitanism avoided troubling questions about the Nazi past. In the East, the SED's internationalism sought to leave the old nationality behind in Communist solidarity. To cope with the identity deficit, the GDR propagated a socialist patriotism that annexed all progressive German traditions.[28]

Ingrained elitism also made the educated insensitive to popular aspirations. Though socialists claimed to speak for the people, most academics found them repugnant in actual life. They had an instinctive antipathy toward beer-drinking soccer fans, narrow-minded hobby gardeners, and cake-devouring matrons of the lower class. Western intellectuals would much rather have settled in a restored villa in Tuscany or participated at an interesting conference in Prague than travel to the drab GDR. With a more sophisticated lifestyle and postmaterialist values, many of the educated elites were ignorant of or, indeed, condescending toward the feelings of the deprived East German people. The democratic awakening in the fall reinforced the intellectuals' sense that they deserved to lead. Dissidents could not imagine that the same masses that had cheered them in October would desert them in March.[29]

Such political naiveté contributed to a fundamental failure of foresight. The same earnest idealism that motivated dissidents to oppose the post-Stalinist regime made it hard for them to compromise in solving the practical transition problems. While the Round Table debated the principles of a model constitution, professional politicians were busy campaigning in order to win the election. Intellectuals' expectations that a rapprochement between the German states would take years to achieve turned out to be utterly wrong owing to Chancellor Kohl's success in speeding up the timetable. Unification critics were convinced that German neighbors, most notably the Soviet Union, would never agree to an actual union.

When the Kohl-Gorbachev breakthrough resolved the "two-plus-four" disputes among the four World War II allies and the two German states, the diplomatic support for a slow transition coupled with neutralization disappeared. Even if they made mistakes, those who dared to act continually outmaneuvered those who only criticized.[30]

These intellectual blinders blocked sympathy for the shift in popular sentiment toward unity. When Easterners crossed the former Wall, they were dazzled by the material prosperity and the political freedom of the West. Whereas GDR intellectuals warned against unemployment and drugs, the populace saw a model state that they wanted to join. Privileged writers such as Stefan Heym disparaged public hopes for FRG-style consumerism as base materialism. In frantic appeals "for our country," Eastern intellectuals tried to plead for the maintenance of a separate state. When some of them finally embraced unity, they still wanted to slow down the merger through confederation schemes. Because during the winter they began to lag behind popular aspirations, writers, reformers, and dissidents gradually lost their mass following.[31]

Frantic warnings by Western intellectuals were of no more avail, either. The socialist novelist Günter Grass invoked the Auschwitz trauma to argue against any resurgence of German strength. The social moralist Jürgen Habermas denounced the popular deutschmark nationalism that was leading to a currency union. The postmodern novelist Patrick Süsskind found the French vastly more appealing than ugly East Germans in their baggy suits and stinking little Trabi cars. Only some neoconservatives such as Karl Heinz Bohrer, novelists such as Martin Walser, and émigrés such as Monika Maron dared to support unity in public statements. Reading any reference to a unified nation as a turn toward neo-Nazi sentiment, the bulk of the Western educated class lacked empathy for the Eastern choice of union with the FRG. Because they instinctively opposed unification, critical intellectuals squandered the opportunity to shape its course.[32]

The defeat of the Social Democrats and the dissidents (Bündnis 90) in the March election was the intellectuals' Waterloo. Mirroring the wishful thinking of many commentators, polls had predicted an SPD victory all through the campaign. It seemed plausible that the East German people would prefer a moderate shift from a repressive to a democratic form of socialism to a complete reversal of course. When the conservative victory proved the pundits wrong, some dissidents could only fall back on conspiracy theories. Either they blamed PDS foot-dragging or exaggerated CDU promises. The educated also found it easy to lampoon popular hopes for a better life. When asked for the reasons for the defeat in a television interview, the former Western Green Otto Schily simply pulled a banana out of his pocket. This disparaging of consumerism betrayed the impotent arrogance of the educated who could afford to reject its blandishments because their own needs were satisfied. Out of tune with national sentiment, many intellectuals marginalized themselves and began to grieve for their lost hopes.[33]

The shrillness of their criticism robbed such intellectual critiques of their credibility. The March election meant quick accession to the Federal Republic, giving article 23 of the Basic Law priority over article 146, which foresaw a constitutional assembly as a prerequisite for unification. Though technically correct, economists' warnings against a precipitous currency union failed to take popular pressure for a rapid merger into account. The demand that both systems meet halfway was also impractical, since it was not clear how a democracy could compromise with dictatorship. With the GDR crumbling further every day, the negotiating partners in the unification treaty were hardly equal. Although a drawn-out constitutional convention might have been more democratic, the collapse of the East required quick action to establish an orderly process of transition with the rules spelled out in a detailed document. The dream of disarmament and neutrality disappeared because Eastern neighbors preferred to control Germany through NATO membership. Though many of their objections eventually turned out to have merit, the intellectuals' rejection of unity rendered their strictures irrelevant.[34]

By opposing unification, the intellectuals suffered a disastrous loss of authority and public esteem. As a result, critical voices that had brought hundreds of thousands out into the streets in October 1989 were virtually ignored a year later. The reasons for this repudiation lie in the intellectuals' shifting relations to popular demands and in the changing context of debate. As long as the GDR lacked a public sphere, it was up to writers to articulate broader social aspirations. In the revolutionary phase the demands of reformers and dissidents therefore coincided for a glorious moment with the wishes of the majority. But their success in reestablishing civil rights, in a sense, rendered the intellectuals superfluous. By restoring free speech, they lost their control over public opinion, which turned out to have different priorities, once it could articulate them. The revived and transformed media and the politicians who had pressed for unity began to dominate the public debate.[35]

During the unification process, intellectuals more and more lost touch with the feelings of their popular supporters. Idealistic Eastern planning for a distant Third Way could not satisfy the hopes of GDR citizens for immediate prosperity. Moreover, Western preferences for postnational values could not appeal to people who saw unity as the most effective strategy for improving their lives. During the heady winter 1989–90 the public no longer wanted to hear predictions of doom but craved messages of hope. Western parties and their Eastern allies therefore took over the role of articulating popular desires, pushing critics unceremoniously aside. Instead of following reformers or dissidents, the East German people elected older *Bildungsbürger* or newer experts to lead the transition to the West.[36]

For the intellectuals German unification therefore turned into a triple disaster. The shutdown of Eastern institutions threatened their previously assured livelihood, since it cost many their jobs. The disappearance of the separate state removed the need for duplicating Western institutional efforts in culture or research. The dissolution of the Academy of Sciences, the purge of the universities, and the collapse of industrial research drastically reduced employment of academic personnel. Politically inspired liquidation *(Abwicklung)* dissolved entire institutions, such as departments of Marxism-Leninism, tarnished by the previous regime. Lack of finances stripped the disproportionately large stratum of the educated of its prior privileges and economic security. In desperate attacks, critics railed against the "intellectual decapitation" of the East.[37]

Moreover, unity threatened the identity of GDR intellectuals, whether they were conformist writers, socialist reformers, or civic dissidents. The rapid imposition of a different Western system devalued much of their cultural capital, since expertise in citing the Marxist-Leninist classics had now become useless. The unexpected collapse of the SED state destroyed the focus of their creativity, because the regime, which intellectuals loved to hate, was gone. Suddenly there was nothing more to defend or to criticize that was particularly theirs. Falling back on reflex condemnations of a Western capitalism that they did not understand was only a poor consolation. Because it seemed that many a life work had become pointless, cultural disorientation was profound. Responses among those concerned ranged from hyperadaptation to stubborn resistance. Expressed in the term *Besserwessi*, resentment against intellectual colonization was strong.[38]

Finally and perhaps most painfully, intellectuals lost their utopian dreams. The Eastern collapse destroyed many hopes for a better society, a different future, an alternative life. With the collapse of Communism, idealists saw their theoretical and political moorings cut, and Western radicals mourned the evident refutation of their alternative project of Socialism. They could only fume impotently at the triumphalism of capitalist apologists. When public appeals and vitriolic tracts failed to stop the merger, intellectuals shifted to proving that they had been right all along. In rehabilitating their critique, they took perverse pleasure in the veracity of the dire prophecies they had made during the transition crisis. In the

East, the bureaucratic and capitalistic nature of the merger renewed a sense of victimization that fed a GDR nostalgia. In the West, a disappointed Left redoubled its efforts to defend its previous agenda of cosmopolitan enlightenment.[39]

Implications of Unity

To many intellectuals, the irresistible trajectory from revolution to unification seemed like a trick of history. The Hungarian theoretician György Konrad had predicted during the 1970s that the intelligentsia was on the way to achieving class power. In an influential book he argued that technocrats were supposed to reform the post-Stalinist system gradually from within and that bureaucratic compromise would open space for intellectual critique. With its speed and extent, the East European upheaval validated and superseded these brilliant forecasts. Intellectuals did play a major role in bringing down post-Stalinism, but the rapid change had an unexpected result. The restoration of parliamentary politics and market economics returned their intellectual promoters to a subsidiary role. After an important interlude, in which the educated occupied center stage, a new group of pragmatic politicians and capitalists took over once again.[40]

Western expectations for the future were equally mistaken. Both neo-Marxist theories of the new classes and liberal prophecies concerning post-industrial society had envisaged increasing intellectual power. Inspired by the experience of 1968, the former talked about a common front between proletarianized intellectuals and the working class. Although this forecast might describe the alliance that overthrew Communism, it did not anticipate the return of capitalist democracy. Based on impressions of advancing technology, the latter predicted the triumph of a revived professionalism. But those who expected the ascendancy of the experts failed to foresee the renewed commitment to a civil society. Therefore capitalists crowing about the fall of Communism does not understand the actual reasons for the Western victory. The rebuilding of the East is taking neither neo-Marxist hopes nor postindustrial rhetoric into account. The theoretical implications of this rupture have yet to be worked out.[41]

The unification shock has in effect marginalized German intellectuals. The unexpected swing from revolutionary elation to unification depression has turned the educated inward upon themselves. All they have left is the memory of the elation of the democratic awakening and a deep-seated fear of the problems of a united Germany. For the moment, the collapse of the socialist utopia and the rejection of unification have discredited their public critiques. The profound failure of perception and of empathy has made both policy makers and the general public less responsive to intellectual warnings. Among the educated themselves, the surprising result of the civic revolution has resurrected old self-doubts. At present, the intellectuals are therefore embattled as much from within as from without.[42]

Wallowing in self-pity, various kinds of intellectuals are struggling to discover a new role. Eastern writers have been slow to recover their voice, largely in opposition to the West. Hemmed in by neo-Stalinist hard-liners, reform Marxists are agonizing about whether to make the PDS a radical opposition within or against the capitalist system. Former dissidents resent their reduced impact on parliamentary politics within a hybrid Green Party dominated by the old states. Western intellectuals are still figuring out how to deal with their surprise at finding themselves in a national state that they had long thought past. Instead of being able to fight for European integration or Third World concerns, they are now confronted with their backward, nationalistic cousins. A minority of neoconservative thinkers tries to use unification to restore their intellectual ascendancy.[43] In heated controversies such as the Goldhagen debate or the "Black Book on communism," the educated are mounting a confused effort to reorder the universe, to come to grips with the enormous changes.[44]

Coping with the unexpected present is complicated by the recurrence of an ugly past. After unification, Germans have had to come to terms with a double history of Nazi and Stalinist oppression. Discoveries of Soviet reuse of concentration camps and tales of persecution by regime victims have reopened the old question of totalitarianism. On the face of it, similarities abound: Both the Third Reich and the GDR were police states that suppressed opposition and destroyed civil society. But there are nonetheless considerable differences as well: Marxism preserved elements of a progressive humanitarian legacy. Since the rulers of the GDR had four decades to shape mentalities, they eventually shifted to less violent means. East Germany never unleashed a world war or a holocaust. Yet the voluntary support of intellectuals for the GDR poses the question of intellectual complicity with greater urgency.[45]

Shocking revelations of Stasi collaboration are only an extreme case of this problem of complicity. Historians of the Third Reich have shown how nationalist academics, especially doctors and engineers, voluntarily worked with the SS. Hence the surprise of the literary community at Stasi betrayals is somewhat difficult to understand. It was predictable that an organization in which hundreds of thousands of members who ceaselessly collected information would also target intellectuals. In some ways the attention of the secret service to dissidents and writers was a backhanded compliment from the regime. Unlike the oblivious West, the SED was preoccupied with the intellectual potential for opposition. The Third Reich analogy suggests that motives of collaboration were a mixture of idealism and self-interest. The Stasi hysteria has fractured intellectuals once more into two groups: moralists who insist on punishment and pragmatists who would rather forget.[46]

How can intellectuals regain their critical authority? As a result of their adjustment difficulties, many Eastern observers recall the vanished GDR with a rosy sense of nostalgia and are beginning to develop a defensive identity (*Trotzidentität*). But some postunification developments are offering a fresh opportunity for more constructive criticism, since they are disproving conservative claims of success. For instance, the creative destruction of the Eastern economy is beginning to rehabilitate a traditional Marxist attack on capitalism. Widespread unemployment and the fiscally driven dismantling of parts of the welfare state are gradually restoring a mass base for leftist appeals. Similarly, xenophobic attacks on foreigners are reviving an abhorrence of the potential dangers of a revival of nationalism. The anti-asylum hysteria has in turn been fostering a renewed dedication to multiculturalism and immigration reform. By proving the correctness of some original criticisms, the postunification problems are gradually starting to restore to intellectuals some public credibility.[47]

Instead of pouting, intellectuals need to recover their nerve by reflecting more dispassionately on their role in the German upheaval. The intoxicating democratic awakening of October 1989 does show the enormous power of critics when they represent broader aspirations for civil rights. The ferment of ideas during the winter of 1989–90 did produce the outlines of a postindustrial civil society that would transcend the present FRG order. In order to help give it direction, the intellectuals now need to jump over their own shadow and accept unification, however little they may have wanted it. They should also probe the reasons for their own misperceptions, which put them at such odds with the aspirations of the majority of the people. Only when they have understood the causes for their own failure in leadership will intellectuals regain their public authority and recapture the initiative in social debates. With such a troubled past, problematic present, and uncertain future, the united Germany desperately requires their critical voice.[48]

Notes

1. Since this essay only begins to explore the role of the intellectuals, the notes will be kept to a minimum. For the context see Konrad H. Jarausch, *Die unverhoffte Einheit 1989–1990* (Frankfurt, 1995), and *After Unity: Reconfiguring German Identities*

(Providence, 1997). See also Jan-Werner Müller, *Another Country: German Intellectuals, Unification, and National Identity* (New Haven, 2000).

2. Stefan Heym and Werner Heiduczek, eds., *Die sanfte Revolution* (Leipzig, 1990) versus Wolf Lepenies, *Folgen einer unerhörten Begebenheit* (Berlin, 1992). See also Andreas Huyssen, "After the Wall: The Future of German Intellectuals," *New German Critique* 52 (1991): 108–43.

3. Julien Benda, *La trahison des clercs* (Paris, 1927, rev. ed., 1947), and Paul Johnson, *The Intellectuals* (London, 1988) versus Bernard-Henri Lévy, *Eloge des intellectuels* (Paris, 1987).

4. For the methodological orientation see Michael Geyer and Konrad H. Jarausch, "The Future of the German Past: Transatlantic Reflections for the 1990s," *Central European History* 22 (1989): 229–59.

5. Rudolf Vierhaus, "Umrisse einer Sozialgeschichte der Gebildeten in Deutschland," *Quellen und Forschungen aus italienischen Archiven und Bibliotheken* 60 (1980): 395 ff.; Werner Conze and Jürgen Kocka, eds., *Bildungsbürgertum in 19. Jahrhundert* (Stuttgart, 1985).

6. Konrad H. Jarausch, *The Unfree Professions: German Lawyers, Teachers, and Engineers, 1900–1950* (New York, 1990), 4–8; Charles E. McClelland, *The German Experience of Professionalization* (Cambridge, 1991), 15–20.

7. Christophe Charle, *Naissance des "Intellectuels," 1880–1900* (Paris, 1990); Vladimir Nahirny, *The Russian Intelligentsia: From Torment to Silence* (New Brunswick, 1983).

8. Karl Mannheim, *Ideology and Utopia: An Introduction to the Sociology of Knowledge* (New York, 1955); Theodor Geiger, *Aufgaben und Stellung der Intelligenz in der Gesellschaft* (New York, 1975, repr.); and Jürgen Kuczynski, *Die Intelligenz: Studien zur Soziologie und Geschichte ihrer Großen* (Berlin, 1987), 11–30.

9. Nahirny, *Russian Intelligentsia*, 35–36. See also the essay by Frank Trommler in this collection.

10. Pierre Bourdieu, *Die feinen Unterschiede: Kritik der gesellschaftlichen Urteilskraft* (Frankfurt am Main, 1987); Pierre Bourdieu, *Les Héritiers: Les étudiants et la culture* (Paris, 1964); Fritz K. Ringer, *Education and Society in Modern Europe* (Bloomington, 1979).

11. Konrad H. Jarausch, "Die Krise des deutschen Bildungsbürgertums im ersten Drittel des 20. Jahrhunderts," in *Bildungsbürger und bürgerliche Gesellschaft im 19. Jahrhundert. Deutschland im europäischen Vergleich*, ed. Jürgen Kocka (Munich, 1988), 3:124–146.

12. Fritz K. Ringer, *The Decline of the German Mandarins: The German Academic Community, 1890–1933* (Cambridge, Mass.,1969); Michael Stark, ed., *Deutsche Intellektuelle 1910–1933* (Heidelberg, 1984).

13. Hauke Brunkhorst, *Der Intellektuelle im Land der Mandarine* (Frankfurt, 1987), 94–111; the research project by Hannes Siegrist on postwar professions in West Germany; and Jarausch, *Unfree Professions*, 202–16.

14. Rainer Land and Ralf Possekel,"Intellektuelle aus der DDR: Kulturelle Identität und Umbruch," *Berliner Debatte INITIAL* 1 (1992); Rainer Land and Ralf Possekel, *'Namenlose Stimmen waren uns voraus': Politische Diskurse von Intellektuellen aus der DDR* (Bochum, 1994); see also Ralph Jessen, *Akademische Elite und Kommunistische Diktatur: Die ostdeutsche Hochschullehrerschaft in der Ulbricht-Ära* (Göttingen, 1999).

15. Jürgen Kuczynski, *Schwierige Jahre—mit einem besseren Ende? Tagebuchblätter 1987 bis 1989* (Berlin, 1990); Markus Wolf, *In eigenem Auftrag: Bekenntnisse und Einsichten* (Munich, 1991); Fritz Klein, *Drinnen und draussen: Ein Historiker in der DDR* (Frankfurt, 2000).

16. Christa Wolf, *Kassandra* (Berlin Ost, 1983); Günter de Bruyn, *Märkische Forschungen* (Halle, 1978); Christoph Hein, *Die Ritter der Tafelrunde* (Frankfurt, 1989); Stefan Wolle, *Die heile Welt der Diktatur: Alltag und Herrschaft in der DDR 1971–1989.* (Berlin, 1998).

17. Christiane Lemke, *Die Ursachen des Umbruchs 1989: Politische Sozialisation in der ehemaligen DDR* (Opladen, 1991); Antonia Grunenberg, *Aufbruch der inneren Mauer* (Bremen, 1990); Simone Barck, Martina Langermann, and Siegfried Lokatis, *Jedes Buch ein Abenteuer: Zensur-System und literarische Öffentlichkeit in der DDR bis End der sechziger Jahre* (Berlin, 1997).

18. Annegret Hahn et al., eds., *4. November '89* (Frankfurt, 1990); Karl Deiritz and Hannes Krauss, eds., *Der deutsch-deutsche Literaturstreit oder "Freunde, es spricht sich schlecht mit gebundener Zunge"* (Hamburg, 1991).

19. Heinrich Bortfeldt, *Von der SED zur PDS: Wandlung zur Demokratie?* (Bonn, 1992), 13–43.

20. Rainer Land, ed., *Das Umbaupapier (DDR): Argumente gegen die Wiedervereinigung* (Berlin, 1990); Gregor Gysi and Thomas Falkner, *Sturm aufs grosse Haus* (Berlin, 1990).

21. Gerhard Besier and Stephan Wolf, eds., *"Pfarrer, Christen und Katholiken": Das Ministerium für Staatssicherheit der ehemaligen DDR und die Kirchen,* 2d ed. (Neunkirchen, 1992); Wolfgang Rüddenklau, *Störenfried: DDR-Opposition 1986–1989* (Berlin, 1992); Erhart Neubert, *Geschichte der Opposition der DDR 1949–1989* (Berlin, 1997).

22. Armin Mitter and Stefan Wolle, eds., *"Ich liebe Euch doch alle": Befehle und Lageberichte des MfS Januar–November 1989* (Berlin, 1990); Helmut Müller-Enbergs et al., eds., *Von der Illegalität ins Parlament. Werdegang und Konzepte der neuen Bürgerbewegungen,* (Berlin, 1991).

23. Helmut Herles and Ewald Rose, eds., *Vom Runden Tisch zum Parlament* (Bonn, 1990); Uwe Thaysen, *Der Runde Tisch. Oder: Wo blieb das Volk?* (Opladen, 1990).

24. Gregor Gysi, ed., *Wir brauchen einen dritten Weg: Selbstverständnis und Programm der PDS* (Hamburg, 1990); Ralf Dahrendorf, *Reflections on the Revolution in Europe* (New York, 1990), 58–60.

25. Jarausch, *Rush to German Unity,* 33–114; Charles S. Maier, *Dissolution: The Crisis of Communism and the End of East Germany* (Princeton, 1997).

26. Jens Reich, *Abschied von den Lebenslügen: Die Intelligenz und die Macht* (Berlin, 1992); John Torpey, *Intellectuals, Socialism, and Dissent: The East German Opposition and Its Legacy* (Minneapolis, 1995).

27. Interviews in Dirk Phillipsen, ed., *"We Were the People": Voices from East Germany's Revolutionary Autumn of 1989* (Durham, 1982). Compare Konrad H. Jarausch, "Die postnationale Nation: Zum Identitätswandel der Deutschen, 1945–1995," *Historicum* (spring 1995): 30–35.

28. Charles S. Maier, *The Unmasterable Past: History, Holocaust, and German National Identity* (Cambridge, Mass., 1988); Helmut Meier and Walter Schmidt, eds., *Erbe und Tradition in der DDR: Die Diskussion der Historiker* (Berlin, 1988). See also

Bernd Giesen, *Intellectuals and the German Nation: Identity in a German Axial Age* (Cambridge, 1998).

29. Reich, *Abschied von den Lebenslügen*, 50–67.

30. Klaus Hartung, *Neunzehnhundertneunundachtzig: Ortbesichtigungen nach einer Epochenwende* (Frankfurt, 1990); Ulrich Albrecht, *Die Abwicklung der DDR* (Opladen, 1992); Philip Zelikow and Condoleeza Rice, *Germany Unified and Europe Transformed: A Study in Statecraft* (Cambridge, Mass., 1995).

31. John Borneman, *After the Wall: East Meets West in the New Berlin* (Berlin, 1991). For some of the texts see Konrad Jarausch and Volker Gransow, eds., *Uniting Germany: Documents and Debates* (Providence, 1994).

32. As examples see Günter Grass, *Deutscher Lastenausgleich: Wider das dumpfe Einheitsgebot* (Berlin, 1990). and Jürgen Habermas, *Die nachholende Revolution* (Frankfurt, 1990) versus Martin Walser, *Über Deutschland reden* (Frankfurt, 1989). and Peter Schneider, *Extreme Mittellage: Eine Reise durch das deutsche Nationalgefühl* (Hamburg, 1990). See also Müller, *Another Country*, 64 ff.

33. Russel J. Dalton , ed., *The New Germany Votes: Unification and the Creation of the New German Party System* (Providence, 1993); Jarausch, *Rush to German Unity*, 115–34.

34. Wolfgang Schäuble, *Der Vertrag: Wie ich über die deutsche Einheit verhandelte* (Stuttgart, 1991); Horst Teltschik, *329 Tage* (Berlin, 1991).

35. Compare Helga Königsdorf, *1989, Oder ein Moment der Schönheit* (Berlin, 1990) with Helga Königsdorf, *Adieu DDR: Protokolle eines Abschieds* (Hamburg, 1990). See also Rainer Bohn et al., eds., *Mauer Show: Das Ende der DDR, die deutsche Einheit und die Medien* (Berlin, 1992).

36. Gert-Joachim Glaeßner, *Der schwierige Weg zur Demokratie: Vom Ende der DDR zur Deutschen Einheit*, 2d ed. (Opladen, 1991).

37. Jürgen Kocka, "Folgen der deutschen Einigung für die Geschichts- und Sozialwissenschaften," *Deutschland Archiv* 25 (1992): 793–802; Kristie Macrakis, "Wissenschaft and Political Unification in the New Germany," in *From Two to One*, ed. Humboldt Stiftung (Bonn, 1992), 72 ff.; Konrad H. Jarausch, "La destruction créatrice: Transformer le système universitaire est-allemand," *Civilisations* (winter 2000–2001).

38. Hans-Joachim Maaz, *Der Gefühlsstau: Ein Psychogramm der DDR* (Berlin, 1990); Hans-Joachim Maaz, *Das gestürzte Volk oder die unglückliche Einheit* (Berlin, 1991); Johannes M. Becker, *Ein Land geht in den Westen* (Bonn, 1991).

39. Heinz Kallabis, *Ade, DDR! Tagebuchblätter, 7. Oktober 1989–8. Mai 1990* (Berlin, 1990); Wolfgang Fritz Haug, *Versuch beim täglichen Verlieren des Bodens unter den Füssen neuen Grund zu gewinnen: Das Perestrojka Journal* (Hamburg, 1990). See also Erhard Crome, "DDR Perzeptionen: Kontext und Zugangsmuster," *Berliner Debatte. Initial* 9 (1998): 45–58.

40. György Konrad and Ivan Szelenyi, *The Intellectuals on the Road to Class Power* (New York, 1979); György Konrad and Ivan Szelenyi, "Intellectuals and Domination in Post-Communist Societies," in *Social Theory for a Changing Society*, ed. Pierre Bourdieu and James S. Coleman (New York, 1991).

41. Alvin W. Gouldner, *The Future of Intellectuals and the Rise of the New Class* (New York, 1981); Daniel Bell, *The Coming of Post-Industrial Society* (New York, 1976); Arnd Bauernkämper and Petra Styckow, "Entwurf für die Konzeption eines

sozialwissenschaftlichen SFB: Umbruchsgesellschaft. Bestimmungsfaktoren von Kontinuität und Kontingenz des Systemwandels in Ostmittel und Osteuropa" (Berlin, 1998).

42. Wolf Lepenies, "Deutsche Zustände zwei Jahre nach der Revolution: Grenzen der Gemeinschaft," *Mitteilungen des Deutschen Germanistenverbandes* (December 1991), 4–16; Ulrich Wickert, ed., *Angst vor Deutschland* (Hamburg, 1990).

43. Peter Glotz, *Der Irrweg des Nationalstaats* (Stuttgart, 1990), or Thomas Schmid, *Staatsbegräbnis: Von ziviler Gesellschaft* (Berlin, 1990) versus Arnulf Baring, *Deutschland, was nun?* (Berlin, 1991); Michael Stürmer, *Die Grenzen der Macht. Begegnung der Deutschen mit der Geschichte* (Berlin, 1992). Compare Konrad H. Jarausch, "Normalisierung oder Re-Nationalisierung. Zur Umdeutung der deutschen Vergangenheit," *Geschichte und Gesellschaft* 21 (1995): 559–72.

44. Malte Lehming, "Das Goldhagen Phänomen," *Der Tagesspiegel*, 26 June 1998; Reinhard Mohr, "Die Wirklichkeit ausgepfiffen," *Der Spiegel* 27, 29 June 1996; Stephen Brockmann, "The Good Person of Germany as a Post-Unification Discursive Phenomenon," *German Politics and Society* 15 (1998): 1–25.

45. Eberhard Jäckel, "Die doppelte Vergangenheit," *Der Spiegel* 52, 23 December 1991: 39–43; Ernst Nolte, "Die fortwirkende Verblendung," *FAZ* 45, 22 February 1992; Jürgen Habermas, "Bemerkungen zu einer verworrenen Diskussion," *Die Zeit* 15, 3 April 1992; Konrad H. Jarausch, ed., *Dictatorship as Experience: Toward a Socio-Cultural History of the GDR* (Providence, 1998).

46. "Politische Kultur im vereinigten Deutschland," *Utopie kreativ* (January 1992); Katja Schmidt and Martin Ottmers, "Zu Tisch mit dem Teufel": Auseinandersetzungen um die Integrität von Literatur und Kirche in der DDR (Hagen, 1992); issues of *Zwiegespräch: Beiträge zur Aufarbeitung der Staatssicherheits-Vergangenheit* (Berlin, 1991–); Albrecht Schönherr, ed., *Ein Volk am Pranger? Die Deutschen auf der Suche nach einer politischen Kultur* (Berlin, 1992).

47. As examples of recent responses, see Daniela Dahn, *Vorwärts und nicht vergessen: Vom Unbehagen in die Einheit* (Berlin, 1996); Hans Misselwitz, *Nicht länger mit dem Gesicht nach Westen. Das neue Selbstbewußtsein der Ostdeutschen* (Bonn, 1996); Richard Schroeder, *Vom Gebrauch der Freiheit: Gedanken über Deutschland nach der Vereinigung* (Stuttgart, 1996). Compare Konrad H. Jarausch, "Toward a Postsocialist Politics?" in *The Crisis of Socialism in Europe*, ed. Christiane Lemke and Gary Marks (Durham, 1992), 228–39.

48. Reich, *Abschied von den Lebenslügen*, 154–76; Gunter Hofmann and Werner A. Perger, *Richard von Weiszäcker im Gespräch* (Frankfurt, 1992), 54–57. See also Müller, *Another Country*, 266–85.

MITCHELL G. ASH

Becoming Normal, Modern, and German (Again?)

There is much talk of normalization in Germany today. That is ironic, since that is exactly what is not happening. Admittedly, some signs point that way. The Western allies have left Berlin, the Russians have left eastern Germany, and ordinary people do not seem to be very sad, or even care very much, about it. Tempelhof Airport has been converted from American military use to civilian commuter flights with little fuss. The "Palace of Tears," formerly a busy border checkpoint at Friedrichstraße station in East Berlin, where many couples and families were once forced to separate at midnight, has become a pop concert venue. In fact, the situation is anything but "normal." The xenophobic violence in Rostock, Hoyerswerda, Mölln, and elsewhere in the 1990s was the worst that postwar Germany, East or West, had seen; numerous gruesome attacks on foreigners since then have shown that such violence was not a temporary flare-up but an endemic feature of postunification German society. The willingness of East Germans to endure a de facto unemployment rate of more than 30 percent without protest would not ordinarily be considered "normal," either. Whatever the word could possibly mean in the circumstances is part of what needs to be discussed.

"Normalcy" talk implies a peculiar combination of perspectives. Used in domestic affairs, it suggests that the political, social, and cultural institutions of the former Federal Republic, and even the mentalities of its people, constitute norms to which the East Germans should strive to adapt. At the same time, talk of becoming a normal nation in foreign policy, most obvious in the debate on Germany's present and future military role, means that in this context the West German past is not regarded as a norm worth continuing but rather as a state of clientage to be left behind as soon as possible. Is this ordinary intellectual confusion—or a double game? A new discourse is emerging in which multiple meanings of words such as *normal, modern,* and even *German* are combining in peculiar ways.

By now it has become clear even to casual observers that the unification treaty was only the beginning of a complex process that will take considerably longer, cost far more, and have further-reaching results than most politicians originally thought. In fact, a fundamental change is taking place in the character of German politics, with obvious implications for social and cultural life. Although the living standards even of unemployed eastern Germans have been raised with the help of transfer payments and extensive government subsidies from the West, in the "old" Federal Republic a rich, self-satisfied people is starting to realize that the future may hold a struggle over the distribution of relative scarcity, rather than of surpluses. Wolf Lepenies accurately depicted West Germans' initial response to their new circumstances in his now widely cited formulation, "the non-results of an extraordinary event" (*die Folgenlosigkeit einer unerhörten Begebenheit*).[1] This phrase describes many West Germans' tendency, and wish, to go on as before, as though the accession (*Beitritt*) of the new German states will and should lead only to an expansion of the old Federal Republic and not to a new, fundamentally changed national entity. According to Lepenies, behind talk of normalcy and normalization lies a new restoration mentality— not only ordinary West German ignorance of East Germany but willful ignorance, feelings of self-righteousness and superiority, and rigid negation of any alternatives to the fastest possible Westgermanification of everything in the new states. This analysis has lost none of its force since it first appeared.

In the new states of eastern Germany, the initial experience of unification after deutschmark euphoria for a great many people has been one of destruction and loss, not only of social institutions and jobs but of a way of living. As a result, differences between East and West Germans have come to light that were there before for anyone willing to look, but had been studiously overlooked by wishful thinkers claiming that this was, after all, still one people with a common culture. Ironically, precisely that mutual ignorance, or mutual self-delusion, is what made the slogan *Wir sind ein Volk* and the resulting rapid unification in the form of *Beitritt* possible. In the East this worked because so many of *das Volk* really believed that they could have the deutschmark's purchasing power and freedom to travel while retaining the advantages and apparent security of the GDR's social welfare network. In the West some politicians, at least, really believed they could finance it all on the cheap, thus preserving and even extending Germany's wealth while achieving equal living standards in five years.

The size and complexity of the economic, social, cultural, and psychological changes involved should have made talk of rapid normalization seem wildly utopian even in 1990. That so many people shared such hopes anyway bespeaks the motivating power of wishful thinking. Of course politicians were warned by economic experts of the potential danger to the East German economy of suddenly introducing the deutschmark; of course they ignored those warnings for reasons of short-term political advantage. But the reason they thought they could get away with it was that they deluded themselves as well, in particular about the costs and the time needed to recover from deutschmark shock. Such illusions may even have been necessary in order to get so much done in so little time.

Nevertheless, Germany is a new political force, now the most populous, and for the time being still one of the more prosperous, nations in western and central Europe, with full sovereignty for the first time since 1945. It would be strange if its leaders did not seek ways of expressing their new potency, the problems of unification notwithstanding. Despite talk in the United States of burden sharing, the initiative for Germans to participate in United Nations peacekeeping or peacemaking forces, or to take a seat on the Security Council came primarily from the German government. The forces driving Germans to push for what they call a "normal"—in fact, more prominent—role in world affairs are primarily domestic. German actionism, and hesitancy to act, abroad cannot be understood without considering the multiple difficulties and deficits of unification at home. As both the asylum debate of the early 1990s and the immigration debate since then show, in the new world economy it is no longer possible—if it ever was—to separate domestic and foreign policy. Germans' behavior at home directly affects their country's image abroad. Moreover, the practical credibility of German initiatives for a normal role abroad depends in part on the perception that the new Germany's political elite will not become overly self-absorbed in unification's problems. But that is just what is happening; and those problems are not going away.

I want to discuss three issues that impinge in one way or another on the current reshaping—or the struggle to resist a reshaping—of German political culture:

1. the new or renewed discourse of modernization that was initially offered as part of the intellectual justification for institutional normalization after unification;

2. the transformation in higher education, which illustrates the problematic character of normalization understood as the uncritical importation or imposition of *status quo ante* West German structures; and

3. the impact of modernization and normalization discourse on the reconstruction of German identities, as exemplified in competing images of the German past.

Normalization and the Discourse of Modernization

Modernization talk was prominent in social scientists' early analyses of unification. Initially, such talk appeared in conjunction with discussions of unification as a sort of human "experiment."[2] Tempting as it is for academics to write this way, there is more than a little irony involved. After all, the March 1990 elections went the way they did because so many East German voters vehemently rejected the idea of becoming "experimental animals" (*Versuchskaninchen*) for peaceful revolutionaries' utopian hopes of a better GDR. What they have received is an experiment, too, only no one has put it to them in such terms—an experiment in more or less guided social transformation and integration on a scale far larger in scope than that attempted in the Federal Republic with the incoming Germans from Pomerania and Silesia in the 1950s.

Modernization talk is a variety of such technocratic discourse. It is something of a shock for an American child of the 1960s to find this term being used with such impunity. Thirty years ago, such talk had a political function in American social science—legitimating the imposition of American power and technological models on the developing world. Use of the term with regard to German unification implied, intentionally or not, that the Eastern Germans are not "modern"—that, like "primitive" inhabitants of the Third World, they are in need not only of skills training or retraining but of a behavioral and mental overhaul.

One of many examples is an essay published in July 1992 by University of Siegen sociologist Rainer Geißler, in which he lists, in textbook fashion, ten characteristics of GDR social structure, eight of which he labels "modernization deficits" and two—the status of women and the level of occupational qualification—"modernization head starts" (*Vorsprünge*).[3] In the case of women, he acknowledges that one of these head starts has already turned into a deficit and that in this respect "the West German social structure also has need of modernization." But he insists that, on balance, modernization means "adapting the East German social structure to the West German model" and that this will work if East Germans change their "social mentality" by showing "a greater willingness to independent initiative and criticism." Important here, as in older versions of modernization talk, is the emphasis on proper attitudes. If these are not forthcoming, a cover story is already in place, blaming the benighted natives—in this case, Eastern Germans too accustomed to the seeming security of a planned economy and society—for the experiment's failure.[4]

This marks a rather sudden transformation in talk about an area that had been agreed to be the most advanced in the socialist world only a few years earlier. In another paper that appeared in 1992, Stefan Hradil, a recent president of the German Sociological Association, makes a more sophisticated distinction between "objective" and "subjective" modernization, at least grudgingly conceding that the GDR was some kind of modern society after all and that the current transformation needs to be considered in rather less Manichean terms.[5] Hradil acknowledges, for example, that in both East and West German societies technological innovation was believed to be the motor of higher production and social progress. But he notes, correctly, that the two societies were quite different by the time of unification. The GDR followed, with some variations, a Soviet model of classical industrial society, including a fixation on gender-specific family roles despite the high participation of women in production. By the 1970s and 1980s, the FRG had developed the more decentralized production patterns, lifestyle pluralism, and subjective "free spaces" (*Freiräume*) allegedly characteristic of "post-industrial" society.

Hradil makes no mention of the niches that many East Germans claim to have created for themselves under socialism, or of the flexibility, negotiating ability, and improvisation skills they may have acquired in the process.[6] Instead of asking whether all East Germans can or wish to become West German–style consumers, or questioning the extent of the "subjective control" some West German imagine they have over their lifestyles, he presents advancement to the lifestyle "paradigm" as a goal for eastern Germans to achieve. The persistence of linear thinking and of the idea of progress in what was supposed to be the age of postmodern plurality is remarkable.

A brief look at the transformation in higher education in the new German states indicates how inappropriate, indeed dysfunctional, modernization discourse can be when it is translated into policy.

Normalization in Higher Education and Science Policy

The fundamental issue in intra-German relations since unification is the apparent contradiction between the supposed priorities of rapid technocratic administrative reorganization and the democratic, or rather plebiscitary, legitimation of the results. Higher education and science policy are important examples of the problems involved in reconciling these priorities, since both the training of future technocrats and—at least in the east, supposedly—the formation of a new generation of democrats is at stake. Initial discussions of this and related issues focused on what Jürgen Habermas called an "exchange" or replacement of elites *(Elitenwechsel)*.[7] As will be shown below, the term is at best only partially accurate in this case; moreover, vast personnel changes have occurred together with the elimination and reshaping of institutional structures, which may have more powerful long-term effects.

The development of higher education and science policy in the new German states since unification can be divided into three overlapping stages.[8] The first might be called the "heroic" stage, lasting from unification to early 1991. Predominant in this period were attempts to restructure the entire higher education and research landscape of the former GDR with a few spectacular measures, including the dissolution of the Academy of Sciences and the abolition and selective refounding *(Abwicklung und Neugründung)* of specific university departments, all undertaken either in ignorance or in dismissive disregard of efforts at reform from below. In the universities, the ostensible legal basis for these measures was an at best questionable application of provisions in the Unification Treaty that mandated either the closing or the takeover of East German state institutions by December 31, 1990.[9] The selection of particular departments for *Abwicklung* was based in part on two populistic, wishful, and misinformed assumptions about science in general and about the social system of science in the GDR: (1) that whereas disciplines such as philosophy, law, history, pedagogy, and the social sciences were thoroughly "tainted" ideologically, others were not; (2) that moral or political probity and scientific competence go together.

The result was confusion and inconsistency. Few objected to the elimination of Marxism-Leninism institutes, which occurred before unification. But the lists of other departments and institutes designated for *Abwicklung* differed in the various states for no obvious reason. Apart from certain exceptions, the "cultural sciences" *(Kulturwissenschaften)*, such as anthropology, German and foreign languages and literatures, and art history, were generally spared from *Abwicklung* lists, even though Marxist-Leninist dictates were as firmly established there as in history or philosophy. In addition, the naive assumption that the natural and medical sciences are necessarily value-neutral gave an initial reprieve to many internationally known SED party loyalists in those disciplines.

In the second, more "prosaic" or "legalistic" stage, which began in the spring of 1991, attempts were made to put policy on a more detailed and coherent legal basis than that provided by the Unification Treaty alone. In this period, the new states passed provisional, and later permanent, higher education laws, while Berlin amended its existing law, mandating conformity with West Germany's framework higher education statute (*Hochschulrahmengesetz*, or HRG).[10] This created, temporarily, a two-class professoriate consisting of "professors according to new law" (*Professoren neuen Rechts*) and "professors according to previous law" (*Professoren bisherigen Rechts*). Ironically, by mandating majorities of full professors on university committees, the new laws also overrode many earlier efforts by East German faculty and students to democratize university governance. Although the mandate to conform with the HRG was accepted, however, the guidelines for doing so differed among the new states. At the level of structural change, state governments responded to local pressures by retaining more of the older institutions than the Federal Science Council (*Wissenschaftsrat*) had recommended. Brandenburg's law even founded three new universities, combining and upgrading existing institutions in Potsdam and Cottbus while creating a new European university in Frankfurt/Oder. This was clearly a political act in a poor state.

Stage three is often presented as a straightforward institutional and personnel "renewal" based primarily on West German patterns, as mandated by the laws just described. In reality, institutional and personnel restructuring and the passage of the higher education laws designed to legitimate the results proceeded in parallel, while financial constraints simultaneously forced deep cuts in *Länder* budgets in this as in other areas. Two results are that, contrary to still-current emphasis on political firings for collaboration either with the Stasi or the SED, dismissals of otherwise positively evaluated staff for budgetary reasons greatly outnumber dismissals for political or moral reasons, and that in many cases the remaining East German academics are forced to compete with West Germans for a greatly reduced number of positions. Nonetheless, contrary to talk of wholesale elite replacement, the percentages of eastern Germans now in the professorial rank varies widely by type of discipline. Predictably, the highest ratio of West Germans exists in disciplines already singled out for *Abwicklung* in the first months after unification, such as philosophy, history, and law, whereas the lowest is in the natural and medical sciences. A relatively high percentage of Eastern Germans, however, has also been retained in the humanistic disciplines not previously singled out for *Abwicklung*, the "cultural sciences" mentioned above.[11] In this respect, the results are thus as much an artifact of stage one policy decisions as of essential truths about the moral or political corruptibility of science as such under socialism.

The potential of transitions for producing innovations is well known, and this one is no exception. All of the new states have moved to found specialized training academies (*Fachhochschulen*), in part to ease some of the enrollment pressure on the universities. Many universities, most notably

Halle and Potsdam, have established cooperative relationships with nearby Max Planck institutes and other extrauniversity research centers. Saxony's minister for science and art, Hans-Joachim Meyer, has announced ambitious plans to establish a multiversity resembling the American model by adding medicine and humanities to the technical faculties at the Technical University in Dresden. The new European University "Viadrina" in Frankfurt/Oder, already mentioned, though small and by no means financially secure, has reached out in innovative ways to Germany's eastern neighbor by enrolling hundreds of Polish students and has promoted particularly promising interdisciplinary efforts in its new Faculty of Cultural Studies.[12] Finally, at the new University of Erfurt in Thuringia, rector Peter Glotz, a former Social Democratic parliamentarian and higher education expert, appointed well-known scholars to constitute a "Max Weber Kolleg" for advanced study and research in history and the social sciences before he suddenly departed in 1999 to take a professorship in Switzerland.

Nonetheless, the complications and contradictions of present policy are evident; some of these could easily be generalized to other policy areas. The strongest driving force behind the imposition of West German structures and norms, as well as the real or perceived pressure to accept the recommendations of the *Wissenschaftsrat*, is the continuing financial dependence of the new *Länder* on the federal government. The threat to the constitutional principle of state autonomy in cultural affairs (*Kulturhoheit der Länder*) is obvious. But the self-assertion of *Länder* autonomy—and the primacy of local politics—in the face of extreme financial constraints is equally evident. Examples include the effort to retain full universities, including faculties of medicine and dentistry, in both Rostock and Greifswald in Mecklenburg/Lower Pomerania, despite contrary recommendations from the *Wissenschaftsrat*, or in the founding of three new universities in Brandenburg, already mentioned.

Equally fundamental is the tension between science or higher education policy (*Wissenschafts-* or *Hochschulpolitik*) and social or labor policy priorities (*Sozial- und Beschäftigungspolitik*). The most obvious examples of this are the efforts to "salvage" at least some of the former GDR Academy of Sciences staff members who were positively evaluated by the *Wissenschaftsrat*. The results have been mixed at best. Some scientists have been integrated into existing West German research institutions, and many others have been placed in new Max Planck institutes and research groups or in other jointly funded federal-state research operations. But the so-called WIP program, designed to integrate former academy researchers into the universities, has been a nearly complete failure.[13] The point is that it is unclear whether salvaging research jobs or cushioning the socioeconomic blow for the less fortunate with short-term projects and work-creation schemes will produce high-quality science or scholarship. By the same token, though it is often asserted that the universities in the new states were overstaffed, no one dares to predict what effect the personnel reductions now under way there will have on the quality of instruction, particularly since enrollments are increasing at the same time.

A tension with broader implications for political culture is that between the urge to achieve what appear to be politically desirable and morally "clean" solutions and the norms of the legal state. This was the stone over which the initial *Abwicklung* stumbled in Berlin. In response to a suit from Humboldt University, an administrative court ruled that the Unification Treaty did not allow such a step, if nothing more was intended than the refounding of university departments under their old names but with new personnel. The *Abwicklung* as such was not challenged in court outside Berlin, but lawsuits against dismissals of individuals in other universities continued to occupy university and state administrations for years, blocking innovation. The mixed results of legally mandated personnel "renewal" reported above suggest that neither legislative nor juridical instruments are designed to yield the kind of political and moral clarity that was evidently desired.

The most significant short-term impact of all this on the emerging political culture of the new Germany is a negative one—the often-remarked loss of the opportunity to reexamine and reform the scientific and scholarly landscape in the West as well as in the East.[14] Of course, the opportunity for critical reexamination was not actually lost but was stoutly resisted by science and university leaders in West Germany, who are fearful of competition in some cases and also worried, quite rightly, that some policy mechanisms now being tried out in the East, for example systematic evaluation of university and research institutes, will eventually be turned back on them.

This, along with financial pressure from Bonn, is surely the primary reason for the rigid emphasis on what Saxony's Minister Meyer once sardonically, but appropriately, called a "transvaluation of values" (*Umwertung aller Werte*).[15] He meant by this the sudden transformation in the evaluation of the West German system, widely acknowledged as late as 1988 to be in deep difficulty and then presented to the East quite literally as a gift from on high. This began to change by 1992, as major media began to revive talk of a crisis in higher education. It is more than slightly ironic to read complaints about overfilled seminars and lecture halls in the West while teaching personnel are being dismissed "for lack of need" in the East. But the term "transvaluation of values" also refers to the experience of East

German scholars, as standards, goals, and even methods suddenly change in many disciplines.

This leads to questions about the impact of these transformations on the political culture of academic life. Will the emerging mixture of East and West German personnel, largely unintended in this form, yield a functioning community of scholars, much less provide a living example of "democratic" political culture? Reviews of results thus far have been mixed, to say the least. The most extreme case of near-total conflict is that of the historians at Humboldt University, where newly appointed West Germans confronted their court-reinstated East German predecessors head-on.[16] Natural scientists, on the other hand—those with jobs, at least—appear to be more optimistic about the future. Some hope to participate in coming innovations, perhaps even leapfrogging over Western competition by acquiring the latest technologies with financial help from Bonn.

With the imposition of West German models of higher education on the new states, it is fair to say that West German problems, as well as West German debates over such issues as university governance, are also being introduced, for better or for worse. Paradoxical as it may sound, normalization in this case has meant the importation of crisis; Jens Reich calls it "the cloning of a dinosaur."[17] Potential for significant innovations is evident, and it would be unwise to underestimate the integrative power of the German social state. But an impression of improvisation, and widespread frustration, remain. Perhaps it is inappropriate to expect a high level of careful planning in transition periods, when improvisation is the norm. What induces cynicism is the contrast between the impression of arbitrary guesswork or rough and ready improvisation and the technocratic rhetoric of rational control. When those adversely affected hear these changes being called "modernization" or "renewal," that cynicism can only grow.

Reconstructing Historical Identities

Those who are aware of the varied pace and results of industrialization in European and world history should realize that it is impossible in principle for people with a social and cultural history of their own simply to repeat all the stages through which another society has already passed. Nonetheless, modernization talk appears to be on the way to becoming important in postwar German social and political history as well. In this case, the status of nonmodern "otherness" is accorded to both the GDR and the Nazi regime. Hans Mommsen, for example, claims that Nazism exemplifies only an "illusory (*vorgetäuschte*) modernization," despite its prominent use of rational planning and technological organization.[18] He and others refuse to call the Nazi regime "modern" because it lacked both liberal-democratic institutions and moral restraints.

Mommsen and other West German historians, like the social scientists already mentioned, apparently want to identify modernization as Westgermanization and give it an unambiguously positive connotation. This would make it easy to move from thinking of Nazism as "illusory" modernization to comparing the Nazi and East German systems and classifying the latter, too, as in some sense not quite modern. One example comes from an essay on the social history of the GDR that uses the term "de-differentiation" (*Entdifferenzierung*) to contrast the politically dominated economy and society of the GDR with Western pluralistic societies, while avoiding the politically loaded word "totalitarian."[19]

An alternative to such awkward formulations would be to consider the FRG and the GDR, perhaps even the Nazi regime, as different though not entirely incompatible structurings of modernity that existed not as yes or no opposites, but in definable historical relations with one another. It would then be necessary to examine continuities from Nazism in both Germanies, and also the ways in which East and West German societies interacted with one another. And it would also be necessary to break with cold war imagery and teleological models of history, to reconsider not only German historians' but also ordinary Germans' historical self-consciousness, if anything like a common identity is to emerge.

Here is where politically formed discourses currently clash most forcefully. Many writers and politicians agree on the importance of history in the political culture of the new Germany. Usable pasts are being created for public consumption at a remarkable rate in the memoir literature coming both from leading Western actors and the former East German leadership.[20] Amusing as it might be to dissect the apologist mythologies instantiated in many of these texts, I want instead to consider an issue that will surely be of greater importance in the long run. That is the transformation in the discourse and meaning of "mastering" or "dealing with the past" (*Vergangenheitsbewältigung*), marked by a subtle change in both its subject and its object. Whereas West Germans constantly were and still are being dunned never to forget the Nazi past, East Germans are now being pressured to confront both the Nazi and the Stasi pasts.[21]

It is now common to speak contemptuously of the "compulsory antifascism" (*verordnete Antifaschismus*) of the GDR regime. This acknowledges, rightly, that the East German state's historical claim to legitimacy as the political incarnation of antifascism on German soil had lost much of its force by 1989, degenerating into empty rituals and street names evoking heroes few remembered any longer. But at the same time, users of this phrase generally give no clear idea of what should have happened instead; should antifascism not have been ordered, or should there have been no antifascism? Nor do they suggest what should replace those rituals now, or show any awareness of the more subtle coercion and memory-shaping involved in the constant focus on the White Rose and the Twentieth of July conspiracies and the consistent downplaying of working-class resistance in the West.[22] The issue here, nota bene, is not the actual importance or effectiveness of the various resistance movements as debated by historians, but the contemporary use of historical imagery for political education.

Embedded in references to "compulsory antifascism" is a largely unexamined claim: that official standpoints and propaganda had little impact on the historical views or memories of ordinary people. Alexander von Plato suggests that this is true of both Germanies. Instead, he argues, "positive" experiences, for example, in the Hitler Youth or the League of German Girls, were "banned to the *Stammtische*" or *Kaffeekränzchen*.[23] I would add that this is also true of many West and East Germans' most powerful negative experiences, those of Allied bombings, forced repatriation, and rape. The first two of these lived on in stories parents or grandparents told one another, and maybe their children; the rapes were banned to still deeper recesses of wounded women's memories. Von Plato argues that an analogous process is occurring now, as positively remembered experiences, for example, in the Young Pioneers or even the Free German Youth, are dismissed as "GDR nostalgia." If unification continues to take the form of a West German conquest, he warns, a new community of self-styled victims could result, and in historical memories a corresponding tendency would emerge to accentuate the positive aspects of life in the GDR.

My own claim, one that is also relevant for Germany's image abroad, is that the sorrowful poses of regret that have served to maintain the Federal Republic's credibility as a civilized nation for two generations will not work for ordinary East Germans. Indeed, here "normalization" will mean reworking the historical imagery of all Germans, not imposing West German images on East Germans. Such a reworking will need to acknowledge that the penitent sinner stance was foreign to most West Germans, too. They were indeed incapable of mourning, not only because they wanted to deny responsibility for the murder of the Jews, as Alexander and Margarete Mitscherlich claimed decades ago, but because the *subjective legitimacy* of their own experiences of massive death and loss at the end of the war was largely denied to them in official rituals and discourse. Many West German historians have attached themselves to the noble pedagogical project of "working up the past," because they assume that the results affirm the value of democracy over dictatorship. By making this commitment historians and others have too often lost sight of a fundamental pedagogical principle: the need to meet prospective pupils on their own ground, starting with their knowledge and experiences. Instead, teachers, when they have dealt with the Nazi period at all, have often substituted for these experiences those of Nazism's victims. This is *morally* legitimate, but *pedagogically* questionable.

Imposing this West German modus on East Germans and adding a requirement to mourn the "Stalinist" past as well will fail, if what is wanted is a genuine attitudinal and behavioral change and not only proper responses on survey questionnaires. Of course, the latter may be all that is wanted, but even if that is the case the prospects for such a strategy are not good. Perhaps the capacity of Germans to see themselves as (pseudo) victims is infinitely extendible. It may be possible to impose the rituals of sobersided regret for the Nazi past on the East Germans, and they may go along either sincerely or for show, as many West Germans have done. But the ritual is becoming empty and boring, if not deeply problematic, for young West Germans already; for East Germans, it will seem all too similar, if not in outward appearance and political content then in its emotional thrust, to the "compulsory antifascism" they already encountered under the previous regime. Perhaps this is one reason for the near-complete absence of East Germans from the recent debates over Daniel Goldhagen's *Hitler's Willing Executioners* and the construction of a central Holocaust memorial in Berlin.

The leading current candidate to replace compulsory antifascism in East German hearts and minds is talk of *Vergangenheitsbewältigung* in a new connotation—facing the Stasi past. The Stasi issue has served a multitude of functions, some of them out of synch with the others and none of them without problems. Thanks in part to sensational media reports, accusations of collaboration with the Stasi appeared at first to be a convenient lever for getting rid of political and other competitors in the new states. But the ambiguous outcome of the affair surrounding Brandenburg's prime minister, Manfred Stolpe, the exposure of some West German academics as "informal cooperators," and the recent controversy over whether to publish Stasi records of telephone conversations involving former chancellor Helmut Kohl regarding possibly illegal contributions to the CDU indicate the probable limits of that particular function.

The Stasi issue is also the last refuge of the otherwise defeated peaceful revolutionaries of 1989. The Stasi archives are the only place in which a former dissident, Joachim Gauck, and his co-workers have been able to acquire both political influence and moral authority in the new Germany. Yet here, despite the best efforts of Bündnis 90 leftists to avoid talking like cold warriors, an uncomfortable convergence looms between former dissidents from the East clinging to this vestige of power and legitimacy and equally self-righteous arch-conservatives from the West anxious to clear the decks for their own reasons. Last but not least, the opening of Stasi files on individuals to those who were observed and persecuted and the resulting exposure of "informal cooperators" is a venture in political education unprecedented not only in German but in all of modern history. This event has had positive, and for some at least, unexpectedly nonviolent results so far. Yet even here, there is a danger that once-active dissidents and their former friends will be fobbed off with an exercise in navel-gazing and their political or cultural impact further defused.

A critical East German historian, Rainer Eckert, rightly argues that focusing on the Stasi alone is insufficient and that an adequate working through of the GDR past must include a functional analysis of the Socialist Unity party, state, and Stasi apparatuses and all their interconnections.[24] Nonetheless, he insists that even such an analysis must begin with individuals' personal involvements with the regime. Quoting the West German publicist Ralph Giordano, he warns that East Germans will incur "a second guilt" alongside that of suppressing the Nazi past if they fail to confront the errors and sins of the past. But he notes, sadly, that this is not what is happening among his former teachers. Instead, the court-reinstated historians at Humboldt University, like many others who had influential positions in the past, indulge in an all-too-imaginable—and utterly normal—variety of immunization and exculpation strategies, including stonewalling, silence, and denial.

Work in progress by Werner Weidenfeld and Felix Philipp Lutz suggests that common general accounts of East Germans' experiences are actually more valid for single generations.[25] Thus, they write, it is primarily the "founder generation," and not all East Germans, as von Plato suggests, that maintains that the GDR alone paid for Germany's defeat in World War II. Eckert claims that life in the GDR induced a "permanent schizophrenia" (*Dauerschizophrenie*), combining positive experiences in party youth organizations with later suppression of individual identity and criticism. Weidenfeld and Lutz attribute this mentality to Eckert's own generation, the one born after the founding of the GDR.

Such generational differences complicate attempts to forecast Germans' future historical identities. An obvious prediction is that Eckert's experience will become typical as the older generation's antifascist commitment becomes a shibboleth interfering with a deeper personal confrontation with the past. In response to the need to justify their lives, the second and third GDR generations, too, could join the search for positive sides to their GDR experience and pass on these reconstructed memories to their children. One report about the children of former activists enrolled at historic Schulpforta Gymnasium suggests that this is already happening.[26] In the younger generations, lack of credible role models or perspectives for the future could lead to rejection of all authority.

Needed here, as elsewhere, will be new terminologies with different moral loadings. These are not likely to come from the current West German political class. If Eckert's experience is typical, we cannot expect them to come from those among the younger generation who were persecuted by the former regime, either. The reconstitution of Germany's historical self-image is a long-term project. One hopes that it will become a joint venture by older and younger East and West Germans, together with sympathetic foreigners. In the current climate, one can only wish, but cannot guarantee, that East and West Germans will eventually go beyond cold war dualisms of good and evil, free and unfree, and begin to acknowledge the human complexity of one anothers' pasts.

Conclusion: Normalcy, Germany, and Europe

Can craziness be normal? Talk of sick or healthy politics or societies has its problems, but for those inclined to detect ironies in human affairs the current situation has the look and feel of a classic double bind in both domestic and foreign affairs. Inside the new Germany, East Germans are constantly being told to stop being so passive, to show more initiative, and to learn the rules of West German political *Streitkultur*. At the same time they hear, sometimes from the very same administrators who ordered them around earlier, what this or that law or regulation does not permit (for example, repairing your own apartment because there are conflicting property claims on the building). Family therapists would call this a double bind.

A parallel double bind can be observed in Germany's efforts to emerge from its former client status and create a new role for itself in world affairs. Textbook symptoms were criticism of the German government's alleged passivity and many Germans' pacifism in the Gulf conflict of 1991, followed by equally touchy reactions to German actionism in Europe, such as Hans-Dietrich Genscher's push for recognition of Slovenia and Croatia, now widely depicted as one of the proximate causes of the war in the former Yugoslav federation. Surely there is nothing wrong with criticizing a NATO ally or a European Community partner, but critics who send such seemingly mixed messages ought not to be surprised if the reaction appears confused or unreasonable. What is wanted, apparently, is German "responsibility," meaning plenty of action as well as money, but under the careful observation and, if possible, also the control of non-Germans—a continuation of limited sovereignty by other means. Whether that is what will result from the inclusion of German troops in U.N. peacekeeping forces remains to be seen. The current strategy in Bonn is evidently to expand Germany's role gradually beyond checkbook diplomacy, but within the framework of extraterritorial organizations and on the condition that Germany has more to say in the policy decisions of just those organizations.

The historian Christian Meier has called the new Germany "a nation that refuses to be one" (eine Nation, die keine sein will).[27] Will or should Germany become a "normal" nation state with an ordinary European past and a bright European future? Caution and skepticism are clearly justified. David Blackbourn and Geoff Eley argued effectively years ago that Germany could not have become a normal nation state after the unification of 1871, because there is no such thing as a normal nation state; differences in national circumstances offset any attempt to present a single country, for example, Britain, as such a norm.[28] Some might ask whether the nation state is obsolete anyway and whether a new, united Europe will not overcome such antiquated notions. That is what Robert Schuman dreamed, but human beings live primarily in villages, neighborhoods, or regions, only secondarily in nations, and at best tertiarily in continents. Thus far only a tiny minority of intellectuals, politicians, and businesspeople think of themselves as Europeans. If such an overarching European identity emerges at all, whether in the form of a Europe of nations or of regions, it will take longer still than German unification.

In current debates, invoking "Europe is an immunization strategy to avoid focusing too sharply on local issues and difficulties. Talk of regionalism, on the other hand, helps Länder politicians place themselves in opposition to Bonn, hence to sharpen their own political profiles, and, paradoxically, also to put the new states in line for regional aid from the European Community. Talk of Europe is not likely to make much of an impression on rowdies in Rostock, Hoyerswerda, Magdeburg, Guben, or Mölln. Even the most optimistic scenario for European integration foresees long-term unemployment for millions of East Germans and the export of lower-paying jobs to the cheaper parts of the European Union and beyond. Whatever happens to the Maastricht Treaty, the current dilemmas in Germany—and thus the current pressures or temptations to channel domestic tensions into foreign policy or its domestic counterparts, such as the so-called asylum issues and immigration and the inability to develop a common political culture capable of consensus rather than conflict—are likely to continue for some time.

Talk of normalization puts the desired state of normalcy some time in the future. But confusion, contradiction, and improvisation are precisely what is normal in times of transition. Even the built landscape one sees while traveling through the new German states creates a mixed impression. Many façades are newly renovated, with well-kept gardens indicating their owners' striving for at least the image of West German petty bourgeois existence; some are still in a pre-1989, if not pre-1945, state of decay. Behind many unrenovated façades, however, are new businesses and service firms of every stripe, with high-tech software and Deutsche Telekom's best switching equipment. The situation in the hearts and minds of many East and West Germans is equally mixed. "Normality" in these circumstances remains a mixed marriage of past and future; such relationships only look abnormal to more conventional eyes.

It would be better to cast aside such coercive frames of reference and convert the vocabulary of normalization into a more neutral terminology of reconstruction and renewal. It would definitely be better to stop making the transformation now under way look more orderly and rational than it is with terms such as "modernization" and to acknowledge with some humility that not only politicians but also the self-styled experts, academics included, are in over their heads. It is by no means certain whether the result in Eastern Germany will be a permanent *Mezzogiorno* (that is, a mixture of high modernity, deep poverty, and out-migration of the most productive younger workers) or something slightly better. In any case the political culture of the new Germany will not be nearly as much like that of the old Federal Republic as terms such as "normalization" suggest.

Notes

1. Wolf Lepenies, *Folgen einer unerhörten Begebenheit: Die Deutschen nach der Vereinigung* (Berlin, 1992), esp. 25–28.

2. Wolfgang Zapf, "Der Untergang der DDR und die soziologische Theorie der Modernisierung," in *Experiment Vereinigung—Ein sozialer Großversuch*, ed. B. Giesen and Claus Leggewie (Berlin, 1991), 38–51.

3. Rainer Geißler, "Die ostdeutsche Sozialstruktur unter Modernisierungsdruck," *Aus Politik und Zeitgeschichte: Beilage zur Wochenzeitung 'Das Parlament'*, B 29–39/92 (10 July 1992), 15–28.

4. For the most prominent version of that story, presented, ironically, by an East German psychotherapist, see Hans-Joachim Maaz, *Der Gefühlsstau: Ein Psychogramm der DDR* (Berlin, 1990); Hans-Joachim Maaz, *Das gestürzte Volk, oder: Die unglückliche Einheit* (Berlin, 1991).

5. Stefan Hradil, "Die 'objektive' und die 'subjektive' Modernisierung: Der Wandel der westdeutschen Sozialstruktur und die Widervereinigung," *Aus Politik und Zeitgeschichte: Beilage zur Wochenzeitung 'Das Parlament'*, B 29–39/92 (10 July 1992), 3–14.

6. For the claim that East Germans have brought just such supposedly "postmodern" lifestyle capabilities into the new Germany, see Wolfgang Engler, *Die ungewollte Moderne—Ost-West Passagen* (Frankfurt am Main, 1995).

7. See, e.g., Jürgen Habermas, "Die normativen Defizite der Vereinigung," in *Vergangenheit als Zukunft*, ed. Michael Haller (Zürich, 1990).

8. Mitchell G. Ash, "Higher Education in the New German States: Renewal or the Importation of Crisis?" in *German Universities Past and Future: Crisis or Renewal?* ed. Mitchell G. Ash (Providence, 1997), 84–109. See also Renate Mayntz, ed., *Aufbruch und Reform von oben: Ostdeutsche Universitäten im Transformationsprozeß* (Frankfurt am Main, 1994); Gertraude Buck-Bechler and Heidrun Jahn, eds., *Hochschulerneuerung in den neuen Bundesländern: Bilanz nach vier Jahren* (Weinheim, 1994); Gunnar Berg et al., eds., *Zur Situation der Universitäten und außeruniversitären Forschungseinrichtungen in den neuen Ländern*, special issue of *Nova Acta Leopoldina*, n.s. 71, no. 220 (1994): Wolfgang Schluchter, *Neubeginn durch Anpassung? Studien zum ostdeutschen Übergang.* (Frankfurt am Main, 1996); Gertraude Buck-Bechler et al., eds., *Die Hochschulen in den neuen Ländern der Bundesrepublik Deutschland: Ein Handbuch der Hochschulerneuerung* (Weinheim, 1997); Alfons Söllner and Ralf Walkenhaus, eds., *Ostprofile: Universitätsentwicklungen in den neuen Bundesländern* (Opladen, 1998).

9. Peter Quint, *The Imperfect Union: Constitutional Structures of German Unification* (Princeton, 1997), chap. 13.

10. Karl-Heinrich Hall, "Die Hochschulgesetzgebung der neuen Länder als Rahmenbedingung der Neustrukturierung," in Mayntz, *Aufbruch und Reform von oben*, 165–90; Quint, *Imperfect Union*.

11. For data supporting these statements, see Ash, "Higher Education in the New German States."

12. On Frankfurt/Oder, see Hans N. Weiler, "Wissenschaft an der Grenze: Zum besonderen Profil der Europa-Universität Viadrina in Frankfurt/Oder," in *Ostprofile: Universitätsentwicklungen in den neuen Bundesländern*, ed. Alfons Söllner and Ralf Walkenhaus (Opladen, 1998), 80–100; on Erfurt, see Klaus D. Wolf, " 'Universität beginnt im Kopf': Zur Genesis der Universitäten Bayreuth und Erfurt," in ibid., 124–39; Peter Glotz, "Die Erfurter Idee: Hochschulpolitik in den neuen Ländern," in ibid., 140–43.

13. "WIP-Memorandum: Verwirklichung des Wissenschaftler-Integrationsprogramms (WIP) im Hochschulerneuerungsprogramm (HEP)," *Das Hochschulwesen* 2 (1995): 95–100.

14. Dieter Simon, "Die Quintessenz—der Wissenschaftsrat in den neuen Bundesländern: Eine vorwärtsgewandte Rückschau," *Aus Politik und Zeitgeschichte. Beilage zur Wochenzeitung 'Das Parlament'*, B 51/92 (11 December 1992); Dieter Simon, "Verscheudert und verschludert," *Die Zeit*, no. 15 (7 April 1995), 49.

15. Hans Joachim Meyer, "Higher Education Reform in the New German States," paper presented to the German Studies Association, Los Angeles, California, 24 September 1991.

16. Kurt Pätzold, "What New Start? The End of Historical Study in the GDR," *German History* 10 (1992): 392–404; Gerhard A. Ritter, "The Reconstruction of History at the Humboldt University: A Reply," *German History* 11 (1993): 339–45; Mitchell G. Ash, "Geschichtswissenschaft, Geschichtskultur und der ostdeutsche Historikerstreit," *Geschichte und Gesellschaft* 24 (1998): 283–304.

17. Jens Reich, "Die Einheit: Gelungen und gescheitert," *Die Zeit* 38, 15 September 1995, 58.

18. Hans Mommsen, "Nationalsozialismus als vorgetäuschte Modernisierung," in *Der Nationalsozialismus und die deutsche Gesellschaft: Ausgewählte Aufsätze* (Reinbek, 1991), 405–27.

19. Ralph Jessen, "Die Gesellschaft im Staatssozialismus: Probleme einer Sozialgeschichte der DDR," *Geschichte und Gesellschaft* 21 (1995): 96–110, esp. 101; for the term *Entdifferenzierung* Jessen cites Ilya Surbar, "War der reale Sozialismus modern?" *Kölner Zeitschrift für Soziologie und Sozialpsychologie* 43 (1991): 415–32. See also Detlef Pollack, "Die konstitutive Widersprüchlichkeit der DDR," *Geschichte und Gesellschaft* 24 (1997): 110–31; Konrad Jarausch, "Realer Sozialismus als Fürsorgediktatur: Zur begrifflichen Einordnung der DDR" *Aus Politik und Zeitgeschichte* B20–98 (8 May 1998): 33–46.

20. See, among many others, Wolfgang Schaeuble, *Der Vertrag: Wie ich über die deutsche Einheit verhandelte* (Stuttgart, 1991); Hans-Dietrich Genscher, *Erinnerungen* (Berlin, 1995); Günther Mittag, *Um jeden Preis: Im Spannungsfeld zweier Systeme* (Berlin, 1991).

21. Jürgen Habermas, "Was bedeutet 'Aufarbeitung der Vergangenheit' heute?" in *Die Normalität einer Berliner Republik* (Frankfurt am Main, 1995), 21–46; Klaus Sühl, ed, *Vergangenheitsbewältigung 1945/1989: Ein umöglicher Vergleich?* (Berlin, 1994).

22. For examples, see the special issue commemorating 20 July 1944 in *Zeitschrift für Geschichtswissenschaft* 44 (1994).

23. Alexander von Plato, "Eine zweite 'Entnazifizierung'? Zur Verarbeitung politischer Umwälzungen in Deutschland 1945 und 1989," in *Wendezeiten—Zeitenwende: Zur 'Entnazifizierung' und 'Entstalinisierung,'* ed. Rainer Eckert, Alexander von Plato, and Jörn Schütrumpf (Hamburg, 1991), 7–32.

24. "Entnazifizierung offiziell und inoffiziell: Die SBZ 1945 und die DDR 1989," in Eckert, von Plato, and Schütrumpf, *Wendezeiten—Zeitenwende*, 33–52; Rainer Eckert, "Vergangenheitsbewältigung oder überwältigt uns die Vergangenheit? Oder: Auf einem Sumpf ist schlecht bauen," *Internationale wissenschaftliche Korrespondez (IWK) zur Geschichte der deutschen Arbeiterbewegung* 2 (1992): 228–32.

25. Werner Weidenfeld and Felix Philipp Lutz, "Die gespaltene Nation: Das Geschichtsbewußtsein der Deutschen nach der Einheit," *Aus Politik und Zeitgeschichte: Beilage zur Wochenzeitung 'Das Parlament'*, B 31–32/92 (24 July 1992): 3–22. This initial study is based on results from narrative interviews with more than two hundred West and East Germans and survey data from more than two thousand West Germans. For a more complete report, see Felix Philipp Lutz, *Das Geschichtsbewußtsein der Deutschen: Grundlagen der politischen Kultur in Ost und West* (Cologne, 2000).

26. Peter Meier-Bergfeld, "Als Wessi-Lehrer abgelehnt," *Der Tagesspiegel*, 3 September 1992.

27. Christian Meier, *Die Nation, die keine sein will* (Munich, 1991).

28. David Blackbourn and Geoff Eley, *The Peculiarities of German History* (Oxford, 1984).

Nation, Race, and Immigration: German Identities After Unification

Nationalism today is at once obsolete and current.
—Theodor W. Adorno

The Antinationalist Consensus

More than three decades ago the existentialist philosopher Karl Jaspers, author of an important though little-known book about German guilt *(Die Schuldfrage)*,[1] claimed that the history of German nationalism was finished and done with. National unity, he argued, was forever lost as a result of the guilt of the German state, and to him the demand for reunification was nothing but a denial of what had happened during the Third Reich.[2] Jaspers's critique was directed against a then-strident conservative discourse of reunification that was coupled with the bellicose nonrecognition of the GDR and the demand, especially by the organizations of Eastern refugees *(Vertriebenenverbände)*, to keep the question of the Eastern borders open. He was the first to articulate an argument against a unified German nation-state that has since been widely adopted in Germany, even though at the time Jaspers himself was rejected by the Right and mostly ignored by the Left.

Although the division of Germany in 1949 into two states was the political result of the emerging cold war superpower confrontation and had nothing much to do with retribution for the crimes of the Third Reich, a rhetoric of punishment regarding the question of national unity became the basis for a broad left-liberal consensus in the Federal Republic beginning in the 1960s, from Jaspers to Grass and Habermas and the vast majority of the cultural and academic establishment. Any proper coming to terms with the past *(Vergangenheitsbewältigung)*, it seemed, was predicated on the end of the German nation-state. In the 1950s, of course, the Social Democrats had an emphatically affirmative position on national unity, and the building of the Berlin wall stirred up a strong wave of national sentiment. Eventually, however, a strong antinationalism took hold, affecting the political and literary culture in fundamental ways. Nation, nation-state, and nationalism were short-circuited, and their history in Germany was judged exclusively from the telos they had reached in the Third Reich and in Auschwitz. German nationhood and unification became nonissues for many. The existence of more than one German state was increasingly accepted across the political spectrum, and some never stopped to point out with glee that in the long wave of German history the unified nation-state had only been a brief episode after all. When the question of German nationhood surfaced at all, usually it was more in a cultural than a political sense: thus the debate over whether there was only one or whether there were two German literatures or, later, the debate between Grass and Heym about a German *Kulturnation* that might transcend the political division. It bears remembering that this antinationalist consensus, with its thoroughgoing critique of all the German traditions (and by no means only conservative ones) that opposed German culture to Western civilization and argued for German exceptionalism *(Sonderweg)*, was an essential component in the successful Westernization of the Federal Republic, its embrace of liberal lifestyles, democratic institutions, and a political identity based on the constitution. At the same time, there always was a fundamental contradiction. The antinationalist consensus clashed head-on with the reunification clause of the Basic Law of 1949, which remained the normative basis of West German politics, even if its realization was pragmatically postponed in the day-to-day life of Ostpolitik from Brandt via Schmidt to Helmut Kohl. In 1989, before the fall of the Wall, reunification was not something anybody held out much hope for or even thought possible in the short term. The consensus among all parties in the 1980s still was Brandt's "policy of small steps," designed to ease life for the East Germans and to build a network of intra-German relations that would outlast any further superpower freezes. When the Greens proposed to do away with the claim to reunification altogether, it was like calling the others' bluff. Of course, the proposal was not successful, but in practice the constitutional demand for reunification had been reduced to achieving a modest measure of freedom for the East Germans (for example, the easing of travel restrictions) through a calibrated politics of rapprochement and interdependency. Unification itself was left to the incalculable whims of history, and history indeed took care of it.

The Return of Nationhood

Thus in 1990 the question of German nationhood returned with a vengeance and took everybody by surprise.[3] After the collapse of the SED
regime the East Germans voted for unification with the Federal Republic,
and the Basic Law provided the political and legal basis for this process,
which was achieved with lightning speed. Forty-five years after the end of
Hitler's war Germany was again a sovereign nation-state. East and West
Germans are united on a territory with stable borders in the east and
in the west. The western part of the country, confiding in the strength
of its economy, has shouldered the enormous burden of currency union
(against the advice of most economic experts), institutional unification,
and reconstruction.

Since unification, however, the process seems to have gone into reverse.
The abyss between East and West Germans seems larger than ever. The
rebuilding of East Germany, accompanied by much Western arrogance,
selfishness, and insensitivity, has stalled, with unemployment in some parts
of East Germany running as high as 40 percent. Structural economic difficulties have emerged to an extent unanticipated even by the doomsayers of
1990, and the social and psychological integration of the two Germanies
seems further away than ever. At a time when the progress of European
unification has slowed significantly as well, to a large measure owing to
economic difficulties stemming from German unification, there is a rise
of various nationalist discourses on the right, accompanied by rampant
violence against foreigners in both parts of Germany: Hoyerswerda, Rostock, Mölln, and Solingen.[4] Often the police seem curiously ineffective,
the courts indecisive in prosecuting offenders, and the politicians and some
of the media less concerned with the victims than with understanding the
perpetrators. Those who promote the slogan "Germany to the Germans"
count adherents not only on the far right. Indeed, the discourse of nation
in Germany has fallen back into a register all too well-known from German history.

Nevertheless it would be too simplistic to assume that an inherently
xenophobic and racist national character is reasserting itself. The numerous candlelight marches against xenophobia demonstrate, in their own
problematic ways, that there is at least a strong moral opposition to nationalist xenophobia.[5] But the problem is not a moral one. It is structural
and political, and thoroughly of current making. Xenophobia in Germany
will continue to run out of control as long as the state refuses, for reasons
of short-term electoral gain, to use its monopoly of juridical and police
power against criminal offenders, as it did to great effect against the left-
wing terrorists of the 1970s. The nurturing ground of xenophobia can

only be dried out through a political process that clearly articulates issues of immigration and citizenship as separate from political asylum and in relation to national interest. Asylum, immigration, and citizenship are the primary discursive terrains on which German national identity is currently being rewritten. The almost exclusive focus on asylum, however, and the general oblivion to issues of citizenship and immigration, are reason to worry about the democratic future of Germany. Thus the manipulative and outright demagogic attacks on Germany's extremely liberal and constitutionally grounded political asylum law have resulted in a reprehensible and impractical "compromise" that hollows out the individual right to asylum and may still prove to be unconstitutional. The insidiously exclusive focus on the asylum question nurtures the delusion that "Germany is not an immigration country," and it highlights the absence of an immigration law that would begin to regulate the influx of foreigners who currently must claim political persecution in order to gain legal entry.

The current debate on German nationhood, with few exceptions, is hardly more promising. It has barely begun to free itself from ingrained argumentative patterns that are inadequate to the current situation of Germany in Europe and in the world. In different ways, both the new nationalists and the antinationalists are heavily mortgaged to the politics of the past. The nationalists, to the extent that they have an articulated position at all, reproduce delusions of national grandeur—Germany as a central European power in Bismarckian terms or worse—and the adamant postnationalists and critics of unification remain tied nostalgically to what I would call the post-fascist exceptionalism of the old Federal Republic, thus representing what George Orwell in 1945 called "negative nationalism." Since 1990, these have been the two sides of the same coin.

It may be significant that so far it has mainly been liberal observers from abroad who see unification as Germany's second chance in this century (Fritz Stern), as an institutional, constitutional opportunity (Ralf Dahrendorf).[6] Despite worries about the rise of the new nationalism in Germany, linked as it is to the new nationalisms in France and in Eastern Europe, and despite its damaging effect on European integration, I tend to share Stern's and Dahrendorf's point of view. My argument is at a time when Germany is again a nation-state and in desperate need of national reconciliation between East Germans and West Germans, and between Germans and their long-time immigrants, the question of German nationhood must be understood as a key political challenge across the ideological spectrum, a challenge to the democratic parties and institutions as well as to the antinationalist cultural and academic Left. Nationhood *and* democracy, not its contradiction, nationhood *and* modernity, not its inherent opposite—

that is the field of political contestation that will determine whether Germany continues on the path of Westernization or falls back into the anti-Western, antidemocratic mode that is so prominent in the right-wing discourse. As some in Germany have begun to argue,[7] the question of nationhood must not be abandoned to a still-marginal right wing that seeks to undermine the democratic consensus and that has been successful so far in exploiting inevitable insecurities and instabilities in the wake of unification. Those who harbor fantasies of a new Bismarckian Reich as the major power in central Europe called upon to colonize the East and to dominate the EC threaten a vital political consensus that is built on the two pillars of integration into the West and reconciliation with the East.

Westernization and reconciliation in the broadest sense, though never complete, have functioned as powerful forces of "normalization" in Germany, and it is this kind of normalization, one that recognizes rather than forgets the crimes of the past and that remains committed to a constitutional, democratic form of government, that could provide the basis for a more stable and secure sense of German national identity.

National Identity and European Integration

But how does one approach this notoriously shifting concept of national identity?[8] Any discussion of nationhood and national identity must recognize that it moves on extremely slippery terrain. The concept of nationhood never functions alone, but in relation to other signifiers in a semantic chain including patriotism and chauvinism, civic spirit and ethnocentrism, democracy and authoritarianism, constitutional rights and xenophobic exclusions. Indeed, as Etienne Balibar has argued, the discourses of race and nation are never very far apart, and racism is not merely a perversion of nationalism but "always a necessary tendency in [its] constitution."[9] In addition, we have come to understand how racism and sexism are linked and how nationalism itself has had a strong impact on codifications of gender and sexuality.[10] The notion of nationhood is indeed fundamentally ambiguous, a "modern Janus," as Tom Nairn has called it,[11] and its negative constituents may be enough of an incentive for anybody to stick with their antinationalist or postnationalist convictions.

Most critical observers these days agree that nationhood, like race, is primarily a political construct, not a natural given or essence. Constructs are subject to change over time, can be contested and shaped through political processes. This insight must be constructively exploited by the democratic Left today if it does not want to end up either sidelined or sucked into nationalist sentiment as it was in 1914 and as it was again, on a lesser scale, in the asylum compromise. Clearly the move toward

European unification and internationalism in the decades since World War II has greatly benefited from the cold war. Thus it has been argued that the superpower confrontation put any number of nationalisms into a kind of historical deep-freeze by imposing bloc affiliations, creating international structures, and limiting the field of action of national players. Since the collapse of the Soviet Union we have been witnessing an explosive mix of old nationalisms revived, both in eastern and western Europe, and we are entering into new power politics nationalisms that threaten to undo the advances toward supranational structures. The violent breakup of Yugoslavia is the case in point. It not only illustrates the paralysis of Europeans when a common foreign policy toward a murderous conflict in Europe would be in order. It has also resurrected old allegiances between the Germans and the Croats, the British and the Serbs, thus adding fuel to German-British animosities that pull this war on the geographic margins of Europe right into the center of European politics. The victims are the Bosnian Muslims on whose behalf there yet has to be a single major demonstration in Germany or, for that matter, elsewhere in western Europe. The drawn-out tragedy of Bosnia represents a breakdown of European integration far more serious than the sudden death of the Maastricht agreement. Europe has accepted ethnic cleansing in an area that provided a living example of multicultural integration. The difference between Serbian nationalism, bent on outward conquest and genocide, and a western European populism that calls for internal ethnic cleansing on the basis of a new differentialist racism is only one of degree and direction. Europe in general, not only its eastern "liberated" parts, is faced with a resurgence of nationalisms not thought possible only a few years ago. In this situation it would be a serious political abdication for the democratic Left not to occupy the question of nationhood, not to try to make use of the potentially constructive side that builds community, guarantees civil rights, and integrates populations. Europeanism and regionalism, two alternatives to nationalism that are privileged by the postnationalists, are and have always been not really alternatives at all but necessary supplements to nationalism and always implied in it. The emerging internationalism of the European right wing should remind us that fascism was not just the telos of German nationalism but itself projected a version of European unification. The decision to opt for a European identity in order to avoid the Germanness in question, so typical of postwar intellectuals, was always a delusion, necessary perhaps in the postwar decades but politically self-destructive today. Europe was always the privileged space in which modern nationhood took shape.[12] Rather than representing an alternative to nationalism, Europe was always its very condition of possibility, just as it enabled empire and colonialism. The mechanisms separating the non-European as barbarian, primitive, and uncivilized were ultimately not that different from the ways in which European nations perceived each other. The traditional national border conflicts that led to intra-European wars have now, it seems, simply been displaced to the outside: Europe, for all its divergent national identities, cultures, and languages, as one meta-nation vis-à-vis the migrations from other continents.[13] Fortress Europe as the contemporary reinscription of nineteenth-century fictions of national autonomy: this is the danger of a Europe dominated by the right wing. Bosnia, at any rate, is already "outside."

Thus, to prevent further "regression" to a nationalism of megalomania, resentment, and aggression in Germany, all those who favor an open society and identify with the democratic, constitutional, and Westernized culture of the Federal Republic might do well to engage in a debate about a potentially alternative and positive notion of nationhood. A democratic concept of nationhood would emphasize negotiated heterogeneity rather than an always fictional ethnic or cultural homogeneity. It would acknowledge the abyss between West and East Germans and devise ways to bridge it, including for instance the simple acknowledgment that major mistakes were made in the process of unification itself. It would accept the reality of immigration and devise reasonable ways to control it. Even with Berlin as capital, it would draw on the strong tradition of federalism rather than on centralism, build on the structures and institutions of the old Federal Republic, and continue on the now more difficult path toward a multinational, united Europe.

Blocked Discourses
There is a perverse paradox here. When Germany was divided, the question of German nationhood had become increasingly theoretical, and, at least in the West, the notion that the nation unified in one state had merely been a short-lived episode in the long wave of German history had been thoroughly internalized, especially by the postwar generations. East and West Germans had come to live with rather separate identities. They were even somewhat exotic to each other and acknowledged each other in their differences. One such difference was that the SED regime tried unsuccessfully to instill a class-based sense of a socialist German nation in the East Germans, whereas the West Germans, in the 1980s, indulged in a debate about national identity that had nothing at all to do with the East Germans. The identity at stake in the FRG after the electoral *Wende* of 1982 was, rather, the left-liberal identity of the Federal Republic, which seemed to many to be threatened by the conservative government. Bitburg,

the historians' debate, Kohl's plan for two German history museums, the Jenninger affair, and the many official memorials marking anniversaries of key events in the history of the Third Reich (1933/83, 1945/85, 1938/88, 1939/89) all became issues of national public debate, but the nation was the old Federal Republic.[14] October 3, 1990, the day of unification, which was not celebrated with much nationalist exuberance, let alone jingoism, primarily marks not the happy conclusion of an unhappy national division but rather the sharpening of the national question, the opening up of new fissures and faultlines in the problematic of nation. Before 1990 there were two German states but presumably one nation. There now is again one German nation-state, but two national identities, FRG and GDR, within what is supposed to be one nation. If in the 1980s debate on national identity the emphasis was on the word *identity* and *national* remained restricted by political circumstances and featured more of a cultural slant, now the emphasis inevitably falls on the word *national* in the political sense. But the totally unanticipated, even unimagined unification of Germany as a fully sovereign nation-state now has Germans befuddled as to what *nation* actually might mean under current circumstances. Forty years of understatement, abstention, or outright taboo are claiming their dues, and the absence of political vision among the political elites is fanning the fires of the kind of retrograde nationalism that the Federal Republic thought it had successfully exorcised.

The process of rethinking German nationhood has barely begun, although it is subterraneously energizing all of the current political debates in Germany, from asylum to military participation in U.N. missions, from social and economic policy to Bosnia and European unification. Any attempt to move beyond the stifling and dangerous stalemate in the discourse of nationhood must begin by identifying the blockages to a new approach. Here I distinguish three major forms of inability and unwillingness to deal with the question of German nationhood that look to the future rather than to the past. The first blockage can be squarely located in the official government discourse. Despite the widespread and highly significant hesitations regarding the question whether Bonn or Berlin should be the capital of Germany, official discourse in Bonn simply takes nationhood and national unity for granted as if Germany had just been returned to a natural state of things. That this view is not limited to the conservatives is demonstrated by Willy Brandt's understandably euphoric statement in the wake of the falling of the Wall: "What belongs together is now growing together." Proponents of this "naturalist" view forget or repress the fact that ever since the building of the Wall in 1961 the existence of two German states had become second nature and unification was nothing but a nostalgic phantasm, ritualistically conjured up on a West German national holiday such as June 17 (the anniversary of the 1953 uprising in the GDR) but not thought to be in the realm of the possible or even, as far as the younger generations were concerned, the desirable. It is symptomatic that with all the research done on the GDR over the years, there never was a single think tank developing scenarios of reunification. The term *reunification* itself, which suggests a return to some prior, more natural state, is actually symptomatic of this forgetting of the enormousness of this social experiment and of the lack of reflection on what separated the two Germanies for more than forty years.

Significantly, the identity of the new nation was first sought in nothing but economic strength and high living standards, exactly the element that primarily defined West Germany before unification and that presumably was all the East Germans wanted. The first things Kohl promised in the euphoria of unification in 1990 were identical salary levels and identical living standards in East and West within a few years with no sacrifices necessary on anybody's part. Since unification this discourse of economic national unity has collapsed under the weight of adverse economic conditions: a national debt proportionately larger than that of the United States, increased taxes with further tax hikes on the horizon, dramatically rising unemployment, increasing awareness of an aging infrastructure in the West, and a weakening of the national fetish: the deutschmark. Many but not all of these problems are a consequence of ill-advised priorities carved in stone at the time of unification: the 1:1 exchange rate at currency union, the policy of returning property to former owners rather than compensating them (*Eigentum vor Entschädigung*), the often hasty and counterproductive Treuhand privatizations. In the context of a global recession, which in Germany was only postponed by the unification boomlet, Helmut Kohl's house of cards is gone and his failure to make a hard-nosed call for sacrifice and national solidarity—which might have been heeded by a majority in the West in 1989–90—now comes to haunt the political class, whose credibility and competence ratings are lower than ever.

The West German chauvinism of prosperity, boosted as it was by the greed of the 1980s, can now be hidden behind the argument that the taxpayers should not be held accountable for the mistakes of the politicians. Anxieties about the economic future are on the rise in the still incredibly wealthy West, and they are heightened by the political instabilities in central and eastern Europe. As the image of instant European integration has faded, some reasonable definition of German nationhood is all the more urgently needed to prevent further division between East and West Germans, Germans and foreigners living in Germany, East and

West German *Länder*, and communities and the federal government. However strongly bound the EC nations still are into the web of supranational organizations such as NATO, the European parliament, and the Helsinki accords, the nation-state remains a major political force in Europe and will continue to set the political agenda in the foreseeable future. European unification itself will have to be thoroughly rethought. Bonn's 1990 slogan about a European Germany does not do justice to the current political constellations.

The second obstacle to the new discourse is the refusal to address the problematic of nationhood altogether (except in order to fight the Right), along with the conviction that the Germans are beyond nationhood. This mostly liberal and left-wing discourse remains tied by way of simple reversal and similar lack of reflection to the ritualistic national discourse of the conservatives. It simply rejects what they celebrate and thus perpetuates an intellectual stance that made a lot of political sense in the 1950s and 1960s but has outlived its usefulness. In its strategies of denial and evasion, it could be called the Hallstein doctrine of the Left. The Hallstein doctrine of the 1950s and 1960s was a policy of nonrecognition of the GDR that caused politicians to address the other German state as the "so-called GDR" or the "zone" or even "central Germany," suggesting that the Oder-Neiße line would not remain the border with Poland. The current nonrecognition of nationhood as a political challenge again ignores the East Germans and remains tied nostalgically to the old FRG, except that by now the rhetoric of punishment for the crimes of the Third Reich has been transmuted into a rhetoric of German superiority. Thus one could argue, meanly, that the Hallstein doctrine of the Left is just another version of the claim to German exceptionalism and comparable to the old conservative Sonderweg thesis in that it, too, claims German superiority, in this case over those who still adhere to a self-understanding as nation: the French, the British, the Americans, and many others.

This most recent kind of German exceptionalism is located primarily among a middle-aged generation of intellectuals, journalists, and professionals whose political identity was defined during the 1950s and 1960s and whose work has contributed significantly to the strength of West German democracy over the years. The lived refutation of traditional conservative notions of Germanness was certainly a prerequisite to the successful Westernization of the FRG. This generation's fierce antinationalist stance has been more than successful in that it has denationalized a majority of Germans to the extent that many of them prefer to feel European rather than German, a preference that in its own paradoxical way is of course peculiar to the Germans.[15]

Jürgen Habermas, one of the major proponents of such a postnational identity, thus will accept a constitutional patriotism only, and he rejects the earlier predominant notions of a *Volksnation*, with its focus on homogeneous ethnicity, and *Kulturnation*, with its emphasis on the exceptionality of German culture in relation to Western civilization.[16] Understandably wary of amorphous cultural identity politics and historically aware of the dangers of nationalist discourse altogether, Habermas holds out the idea of Europe and the universalist European ideal of constitutional rights as a panacea for the vicissitudes of German national identity. To me, the question here is not whether Habermas is right or wrong. Constitutional rights are indeed nonnegotiable as the basis of identity in a democratic society, but it is not negligible that the only legal authority that can guarantee constitutional rights is still the democratic nation-state and its institutions. In the absence of functioning supranational political units, the nation-state is still a fact of life, and it will produce forms of belonging and identity needs that cannot in all instances be satisfied by the abstract-universalist principles of the constitution. In some ways, the very notion of constitutional patriotism, first coined by Dolf Sternberger in 1982, remains tied to the culture of the old Federal Republic with its studied rejection of the national. Today, at any rate, as the struggle to unify the two parts of the country economically, legally, culturally, and psychologically confronts all Germans with extremely difficult tasks, a broader vision of Germany's role in the world is clearly called for. All of the current debates on the reconstruction of the East, on the uses and abuses of the German military, on asylum, on policy toward Bosnia, on European integration and, and on the deutschmark do indeed define a sense of German nationhood, whether one wants to admit it or not. Forms of national identity will emerge from those debates and from the actions taken or omitted. National identity will be a field of contesting discourses, and as long as the political sphere, parties, and parliamentary representation are organized primarily on a national basis, it is dangerously short-sighted to keep proclaiming that "we are beyond that," a position that has understandably been seen as "postnational arrogance." Replacing a lost socialist or progressively liberal internationalism with a constitutional universalism combined with a commitment to Europe does not do away with the problem of nation at all. To acknowledge this, however, is not to dismiss the idea of a constitutional patriotism. It merely tries to place it in a broader field of reference. Patriotic commitment to the German constitution, though a founding element in the redefinition of German identities, by itself is not enough to address the hard questions of cultural identity, historical memory, immigration, and race.

The third obstacle to a new approach to German nationhood is the rabidly nationalist discourse of the new right-wing organizations, the skin-heads and other disenfranchised segments of the population, both in the eastern and the western *Länder*.[17] With its anti-Semitism and racism, its street violence and cowardly nighttime fire-bombings, and its phantasm of ethnic autonomy and purity, this is of course the revivalist nationalist discourse that reminds the world of the Nazis and triggers warnings of a Fourth Reich. It does not advance new approaches to nationhood, but it is grist for the mill of the postnationalists whose convictions it reinforces. The range of potential electoral support of the new "respectable" right-wing parties, who try hard, though not persuasively, to keep their distance from street violence, is far from clear. Their new differentialist racism—acknowledging cultural difference in order to expel it from the national body—clearly has wide appeal, and it has parallels in France, Italy, and England. Although the Right has enjoyed some electoral successes in state parliaments, polls taken after the murders of Turks in Mölln and Solingen indicate that much of that support is soft. The attacks on foreigners, however, have continued unabated in the first half of this year, and the general dissatisfaction with the traditional parties is undiminished.

Much will depend on how the political, intellectual, and media elites in Germany will shape the discourse about the problems facing the unified country. So far the radical right, aided by conservative Bonn politicians such as Rühe and Schäuble, has scored a major political success in dis-placing the debate about German nationhood to the discursive terrain of asylum legislation. It is indeed in this debate that German nationhood is being redefined. After all, the rationale for Germany's extremely liberal asylum law was the recognition that political asylum had been the only life-line for thousands of refugees from Nazi terror. The founders of the Federal Republic wanted to pay back Germany's debt, as it were, with article 16 of the Basic Law, which guarantees unlimited political asylum. Dismantling this law in response to public pressure and prejudice fanned by short-term party interests is thus indirectly a denial of Germany's past that plays into the hands of the right-wing revisionists. The new asylum "compromise," which does away with the unlimited right to political asylum, clearly is a success for those who claim Germany for the Germans.

Citizenship, Immigration, and Asylum

Perhaps changing the practice of asylum in Germany was unavoidable in light of the expected south-north and east-west migrations and in light of the fact that the extent of the current influx is already larger than that of all other European countries combined. But the practice of asylum could have been changed in a different way. The political pressure could have been taken off the asylum legislation by separating asylum from immigration and moving toward immigration quotas. Although that would not have solved all the practical problems, it would have given a clear indication that the Germans are willing to abandon the delusion that "Germany is not a country of immigration," like the old Hallstein doctrine a denial of reality. It would also have required that the country accept a different definition of German citizenship, one that puts the emphasis on length of residency rather than blood lineage and ethnic descent, *ius soli* rather than *ius sanguinis*.[18] It took two years and several thousand attacks on foreigners and dozens of dead and injured for Bonn and the media to recognize that the 1913 law that still defines German citizenship via blood lineage should be repealed or modified to permit at least second- and third- generation foreigners to claim German citizenship if they so desire. It remains to be seen if the current rethinking of citizenship will result in a much-needed further Westernization of Germany or if it will produce as foul a compromise as the asylum debate has.

Citizenship, asylum, and immigration are key to current redefinitions of German nationhood and will provide us with a strong means of judging German politics in years to come. Achieving nationhood will have to be understood as a process of negotiating identity and heterogeneity outside of the parameters of the ethnic myth and including all the foreigners who live and work in Germany and have made Germany their second *Heimat*. The 1913 law that defines German citizenship on the basis of *ius sanguinis* rather than *ius soli* should be abolished and replaced by a "normalized" law closer to the practice of Western nations such as France. This, of course, is the task of a democratic Left that is under pressure on this very issue in France itself, where the conservatives want to make the rules governing citizenship closer to the German model. Thus politically progressive action on citizenship and immigration in Germany today may well have significant implications for Europe. At any rate, the absence of a Western-type practice of naturalization in Germany is a major political deficit, and it burdens the search for national identity with a heavy mortgage from the past. By defining citizenship via blood lineage and descent, this law not only gives credence to the phantasm of uncontaminated Germanness. Worse, it constructs this phantasm in the first place. As long as settled second- and third-generation immigrants, who went to school in Germany, work in Germany, watch German television, and have become part of German culture in a multitude of hybrid ways, can be considered less German than foreign-born ethnic Germans from the Volga or Romania who no longer speak the language and whose ideas of Germanness are in a pre-modern time warp, the fires of xenophobia will continue to be fanned. Of course, there is no guarantee that changing the rules governing citizenship will have an immediate effect on the radical right wing. In the short run it might make things worse. One can only hope that the political class will articulate this necessary change in policy in such a way that the majority of Germans perceive the current situation for what it is: a massive deficit in Westernization.[19]

My political point here is simple. If the radical Right has been able to determine the agenda of the debate on Germanness vis-à-vis the asylum issue, it is because liturgical incantation and an equally ritualistic taboo are still the two major forms the discourse of nationhood takes in Germany today. But this is exactly where both the antinationalist intellectuals and the fumbling politicians in Bonn are in danger of repeating that German history they both ostensibly want to avoid. For as Rainer M. Lepsius has shown, the problem with German definitions of nation was always the lack of clearly defined content (contrary to France, England or the United States), and this lack threatens again to lead to grave consequences if the discourse of nation is abandoned to the antidemocratic Right, where it is energized by racist hatred, resentment, and violence.[20] Paradoxically, it is again (as after 1918) the lack of a stable sense of national identity and statehood in Germany that energizes the violence against those who do not "belong." The history of German nationalism that has to be overcome is one that always bought national hegemony at the expense of an internal enemy: in the Second Reich it was the working class, later the Jews, today the "foreigners." That is why the "German question" today is the question of asylum and immigration and why there can be no meaningful political discussion of these matters apart from a discussion of the fissures in German identity and in the German nation.

The Xenophobic Triangle
If the asylum debate, energized as it was by xenophobia, fire bombings, beatings, and German fears of being "foreignized" (*Überfremdung*), in one very obvious sense is about German national identity, it also has an insidious hidden dimension: the growing intensity of resentment between East and West Germans.[21] My hypothesis is that the astonishing levels of physical and verbal violence against foreigners, including widespread fellow-traveling in xenophobia, result to a large extent from a complex displacement of an inner-German problematic that right-wing ideologues are successful in exploiting. At issue is not just the scapegoating of foreigners by the East Germans who now experience themselves as second-class citizens, as colonized by the victorious West, or for that matter by the

West Germans who fear for their living standard and, like everybody else in Europe, face an uncertain political future. These are important factors, but what is at issue on a deeper level is, rather, the displacement onto the non-Germans of forty years of an inner-German hostility in which another kind of foreign body was identified as the source of most problems: the other Germany. The whole *Ossi-Wessi* split, symptomatically expressed in this infantilized language, is not so much a function of objectively sep-arate developments since the late 1940s, nor is it only the result of the current problems with unification. Those issues, one would think, could be rationally discussed and dealt with. Rather, rhe unwillingness even to engage in such rational discussions can be attributed to the fact that, on the psychosocial level, the other Germany was always inscribed as the other in one's own sense of being either a West or an East German. The inability of a postwar German to belong could always be blamed on that other German, the thief of one's own potential identity.[22] And that bad, other German could be found either on the other side of the Wall or, through a complex web of political identifications, on one's own side. Thus the West German Left was always and without differentiation accused by the conservatives of identifying with the GDR. And dissidents in the GDR could always be accused of being enemies of socialism or agents of Western revanchism: the internal enemy as an agent of an "outside" power that also happened to be German. National identity was always fractured in this way, and it remains to be explored to what extent the success of denationalization in both Germanies was fueled by such sub-terranean conflicts, which destroyed older forms of national identity as much as they added another chapter to the history of German self-hatreds. Unification, of course, dismantled the external form of this mechanism, but it displaced its substance onto another terrain. The new thieves of German identity—thieves of "our" tax money, "our" jobs, "our" homes and so on—are the foreigners. Only this triangulation of foreigners, East Germans, and West Germans fully explains the intensity of the escalation in xenophobia since unification.

Such inner-German hostilities show how the historical identity of the GDR is inescapably intertwined with that of the FRG. But Germans have barely begun to understand that, indulging instead in replays of the blaming game. Thus the West Germans use the Stasi revelations to make the East Germans "other" yet one more time, with the added dimension of using the Stasi to compare the GDR to the Third Reich and thus writing yet another chapter of a displaced coping with the past. The East Germans in turn insist on their GDR identity more than ever and transfer their antagonism from the SED state, which they and not the Bonn government dismantled in the peaceful revolution, to the Bonn republic, democratic institutions, and Americanization. Indeed, one state, but two nations, a potential powder keg of conflicts and political instability. It is this common heritage and recent resurrection of cold war attitudes and patterns of thought on both sides, together with the stubbornly postnational discourse in the West and the lack of vision of the political class, that blocks what is needed most: national reconciliation, integration, and solidarity, all public qualities that the political culture of the 1980s did little to encourage.

If the question of citizenship and immigration is one major discursive terrain on which a new democratic understanding of German national identity may be shaped today, the question of German history and memory is the other. However, the ideological trench warfare over history and memory is about as stifling as that about nation. The right-wing demand for a positive identification with German traditions that precede the Third Reich seeks to relativize that period of German history, to isolate it, and to redeem a German nationalism untainted by the "perversions" of the Hitler years. This attempt must be opposed with arguments that emphasize linkages between the specific kind of German nineteenth-century ethnic nationalism and the Aryan ideology of the Nazis without collapsing the two. But the call for an identification with tradition and historical memory is not per se a right-wing enterprise. The predominant left-wing response to this question of German traditions is too caught up in he rituals of antifascism that have been recharged by the new Right, the latest object of negative desire. The positions of the democratic Left on German history are actually much better founded than the apocalyptic tone of the current political debate would lead one to believe. New understandings of German history evolved in the GDR as well as in the FRG, and there is no doubt that Marxist cultural and literary history, with its orthodoxies and even more with its heterodoxies, has contributed substantially to the emergence of progressive views of the German traditions in West Germany since the 1960s. All of the new social movements in Germany, up to and including the opposition movement in the GDR, have reappropriated traditions, constructed alternative memories, and searched the national past for materials that would support their political and cultural claims. German unification will be no exception to the rule that all historical upheavals will result in a rewriting of history and tradition. The question is not if but how and to what extent identificatory memories will be reshaped. It will be interesting to see how eventually an all-German dialogue not mired in mutual recriminations will give rise to a new texture of national memory.

Postnationalism and Normalization

As in the nationhood debate, here too the position of the postnationalists and constitutional patriots hampers the emergence of such a dialogue. When Jürgen Habermas argues that citizenship is not conceptually tied to nationhood and that "the nation of citizens does not derive its identity from ethnic or cultural properties, but from the praxis of citizens who actively exercise their civil rights," he underestimates the legitimate need of East and West Germans to secure a common history that has a lot to do with cultural properties and national history.[23] Clearly, Habermas (for good reason) has no use for the old notion of a German *Kulturnation* with its anti-Western implications, its class-based notion of high culture, and its populist ethnic, if not racist, connotations. But to see the exercise of civil rights as separate from cultural properties or from the praxis of culture altogether is not very persuasive. Exercising one's civil rights will always involve cultural properties, traditions, memories, and language. Memory is indeed central to constitutional patriotism itself. The very notion of constitutional patriotism carries political and moral force because it has drawn political conclusions from the memory of the uniqueness of the Shoah, and Habermas himself over the years has proved to be one of the most eloquent critics of those who want to "normalize" German history by excising the memory of Auschwitz either through relativization or denial.

The emphatic postnationalism on the Left is of course fired up by one keyword: *normalization*. It is still haunted by the historians' debate of 1986.[24] But the revisionist history advanced by Ernst Nolte and Andreas Hillgruber clearly did not win the day.[25] Its absurdities were too blatant, and they were effectively exposed in a wide-ranging public debate. There is no need to be apocalyptic about normalization. Thus if one increasingly hears these days that Germans should identify with other, better traditions, that they cannot be expected to walk in sackcloth and ashes forever (as if they ever had), and that restitution (*Wiedergutmachung*) has been concluded, this does not mean that the revisionists finally achieved the victory denied them in 1986. After all, this type of discourse, often coupled with an anti-Semitism of resentment ("The Germans will never forgive the Jews for Auschwitz"), is not exactly new.[26] That it is being voiced with increased hostility since unification is not surprising to anybody who is aware of the contorted history of anti- and philo-Semitism in the Federal Republic. In order to oppose this kind of discourse, however, one must admit to notions of national responsibility and national guilt, as Karl Jaspers argued as early as 1946. The discourse of nationhood is indispensable here too: the crimes of the Third Reich were not committed "in the name of Germany," as Bonn-speak all too frequently has it, but by ordinary Germans. The Shoah is ineradicably part of German history and German memory. Curiously, nobody has made the argument that the denial of German national identity and the emphatic commitment to Europe could itself be seen as a flight from this history. The reason, of course, is that the postnationalists are also the ones who insist most adamantly on preserving the memory of German responsibility. And yet, there is an inconsistency here that points to the unbearable nature of a burden too heavy even for those who acknowledge it.

At the same time, we must not forget that it was in the struggles of the 1960s for a more democratic Germany that Auschwitz became part of German national consciousness, although the fierce antinationalism of that critical generation would not have permitted such phrasing at the time. But why resist such a thought now? As international as the movements of the 1960s were in France, the United States, and Germany, each one did have its own national elements, and in the FRG the demand to work through the fascist past and the Holocaust were central to the demands for a more democratic Germany in the years of the Great Coalition, the APO (extraparliamentary opposition), and the student movement. However problematic some of the German discussions and treatments of the Shoah may have been at the time, the memory of Auschwitz was indelibly inscribed into German national identity in those years, and even the current advocates of forgetting—as long as they are publicly opposed, and they are, vociferously—actually reinforce rather than weaken the legibility of that inscription.[27] Memory, of course, is a very tenuous and fragile thing, and it needs to be buttressed with the help of institutions of documentation, preservation, and participatory debate. But given the extraordinary intensity of public memory and debate in the 1980s (from the explosive reception of the television series *Holocaust* via Bitburg, the historians' debate, and the Third Reich anniversaries all the way to the Wannsee Conference anniversary of 1992 and the media debate about the new Holocaust museum in Washington), I am not worried that right-wing strategies of denial have had much of an impact. This is not to say that they should not be fought every step of the way. One strategically productive way of fighting them would be for the democratic Left to reoccupy the discursive terrain of nationhood and recognize that the democratization of Germany, indissolubly coupled with the recognition of a murderous history, has already given the new Germany a national identity that is worth preserving and building on.

Notes

This essay first appeared in Andreas Huyssen, Twilight Memories: Marking Time in a Culture of Amnesia (New York, 1995), 67–84. Copyright 1995 by Andreas Huyssen. Reproduced by permission of Routledge, Inc., part of The Taylor & Francis Group.

1. Karl Jaspers, Die Schuldfrage (1946; reprint, Munich, 1987).

2. Karl Jaspers, Freiheit und Wiedervereinigung (Munich, 1960), 110–11. On Jaspers and reunification see most recently Wolfgang Schneider, Tanz der Derwische: Vom Umgang mit der Vergangenheit im wiedervereinigten Deutschland (Lüneburg, 1992), 93–100.

3. For a thorough account of unification see Peter H. Merkl, German Unification in European Context (University Park, Pa., 1993). The politically most astute assessment of 1989–90, written during the events, still is Klaus Hartung, Neunzehnhundertneunundachtzig (Frankfurt am Main, 1991).

4. For a thorough analysis of the recent pogroms see Hajo Funke, Brandstifter (Göttingen, 1993).

5. For a polemically negative view of the candlelight marches see Eike Geisel, "Triumph des guten Willens," die tageszeitung, 12 December 1992.

6. Fritz Stern, "Deutschland um 1900—und eine zweite Chance," in Deutschlands Weg in die Moderne: Politik, Gesellschaft und Kultur im 19. Jahrhundert, ed. Wofang Hardtwig and Harm-Hinrich Brandt (Munich, 1993), 32–44; Ralf Dahrendorf, "Die Sache mit der Nation," Merkur 44 (October–November 1990): 823–34.

7. See, e.g., Dieter Henrich, Nach dem Ende der Teilung: Über Identitäten und Intellektualität in Deutschland (Frankfurt am Main, 1993); Christian Meier, Die Nation, die keine sein will (Munich, 1991); Christian Meier, "Halbwegs anständig über die Runden kommen, ohne daß zu viele zurückbleiben," in Politik ohne Projekt? Nachdenken über Deutschland, ed. Siegfried Unseld (Frankfurt am Main, 1993); Petra Braitling and Walter Reese-Schäfer, eds., Universalismus, Nationalismus und die neue Einheit der Deutschen (Frankfurt am Main, 1991). See also my earlier essay "The Inevitability of Nation: German Intellectuals After Unification," written in September 1991 after the pogrom of Hoyerswerda and published in October 61 (spring 1992): 65–82.

8. Recent works that have proved helpful to me in approaching this question include Benedict Anderson, Imagined Communities (London, 1983); Ernest Gellner, Nations and Nationalism (Oxford, 1983); Anthony D. Smith, Theories of Nationalism (New York, 1983); Tom Nairn, The Break-Up of Britain: Crisis and Neo-Nationalism (London, 1977); Peter Alter, Nationalismus (Frankfurt am Main, 1985); Homi K. Bhabha, ed., Nation and Narration (New York, 1990); Slavoj Zizek, "Republics of Gilead," New Left Review 183 (September–October 1990): 50–62; Julia Kristeva, Nations Without Nationalism (New York, 1993). Not useful at all is Leah Greenfeld's Nationalism: Five Roads to Modernity (Cambridge, Mass., 1992). For a semantic history see the article by Reinhart Koselleck et al., "Volk, Nation, Nationalismus, Masse," in Geschichtliche Grundbegriffe: Historisches Lexikon zur politisch-sozialen Sprache in Deutschland (Stuttgart, 1992), 7:141–431.

9. Etienne Balibar, "Racism and Nationalism," in Race, Nation, Class: Ambiguous Identities, ed. E. Balibar and I. Wallerstein (London, 1991), 37, 48.

10. Balibar, "Racism and Nationalism," 49; George Mosse, Nationalism and Sexuality: Middle-Class Morality and Sexual Norms in Modern Europe (Madison, Wis., 1985);

Andrew Parker, Mary Russo, Doris Sommer, and Patricia Yaeger, eds., *Nationalisms and Sexualities* (New York, 1992).

11.Nairn, *Break-Up of Britain*.

12. See Michael Geyer, "Historical Fictions of Autonomy and the Europeanization of National History," *Central European History* 22 (1989): 316–42.

13. For a perceptive essay on the problem of migration see Hans Magnus Enzensberger, *Die große Wanderung* (Frankfurt am Main, 1992).

14. On the changing role of the concept of nation in the FRG see Wolfgang J. Mommsen, *Nation und Geschichte: Über die Deutschen und die deutsche Frage* (Munich, 1990).

15. For a historical analysis of intellectuals and their codifications of German national identity see Bernhard Giesen, *Die Intellektuellen und die Nation* (Frankfurt am Main, 1993). Paul Noack offers a sharp critique of German intellectuals today in *Deutschland, deine Intellektuellen: Die Kunst, sich ins Abseits zu stellen* (Frankfurt am Main, 1993). On the breakdown of West Germany's prevalent left-liberal consensus during and after unification see Andreas Huyssen, "After the Wall: The Failure of German Intellectuals," *New German Critique* 52 (winter 1991): 109–43, reprinted in *Twilight Memories: Marking Time in a Culture of Amnesia*. (New York, 1995).

16. See especially Jürgen Habermas, "Yet Again: German Identity," *New German Critique* 52 (winter 1991): 84–101; Jürgen Habermas, "Citizenship and National Identity: Some Reflections on the Future of Europe," *Praxis International* 12, no. 1 (April 1992): 1–19.

17. Among the many publications on this topic see Hajo Funke, *Brandstifter*; Matthias von Hellfeld, *Die Nation erwacht: Zur Trendwende der deutschen politischen Kultur* (Cologne, 1993).

18. See the superb study by Rogers Brubaker, *Citizenship and Nationhood in France and Germany* (Cambridge, 1992); for a thorough legal comparison of the United States with Germany see Gerald L. Neumann, "'We Are the People': Alien Suffrage in German and American Perspective," *Michigan Journal of International Law* 13, no. 2 (winter 1992): 259–335.

19. For one of the few enlightened discussions of citizenship and immigration in Germany today see Daniel Cohn-Bendit and Thomas Schmid, *Heimat Babylon: Das Wagnis der multikulturellen Demokratie* (Hamburg, 1992). See also Bahman Nirumand, ed., *Angst vor den Deutschen* (Reinbek, 1992); Daniel Cohn-Bendit, et al., *Einwanderbares Deutschland* (Frankfurt am Main, 1991).

20. For a good summary see M. Rainer Lepsius, "Nation und Nationalismus in Deutschland," in *Grenzfälle: Über neuen und alten Nationalismus*, ed. Michael Jeismann and Henning Ritter (Leipzig, 1993), 193–214.

21. For a recent sociological profile of East and West Germans since reunification see Ulrich Becker, Horst Becker, and Walter Ruhland, *Zwischen Angst und Aufbruch* (Düsseldorf, 1992).

22. On this idea of blaming the thief of one's identity see Slavoj Zizek, "Republics of Gilead," *New Left Review* 183 (September–October 1990): 50–62.

23. Habermas, "Citizenship and National Identity," 3.

24. For a good example how the historians' debate can overdetermine reactions to current events, in this case the asylum debate, see Jürgen Habermas, "Die zweite Lebenslüge der Bundesrepublik: Wir sind wieder 'normal' geworden," first published in *Die Zeit* (11 December 1992) and translated in *New Left Review* 197 (January–

February 1993): 58–66 as "The Second Life Fiction of the Federal Republic: We Have Become 'Normal' Again."

25. For documentation and discussion of key texts of the debate see *New German Critique* 44 (spring–summer 1988). For a thorough analysis see Charles S. Maier, *The Unmasterable Past: History, Holocaust, and German National Identity* (Cambridge, Mass., 1988).

26. On the history of German anti-Semitism and philo-Semitism in the late 1940s and 1950s see Frank Stern, *Im Anfang war Auschwitz: Antisemitismus und Philosemitismus im deutschen Nachkrieg* (Gerlingen, 1991). See also Frank Stern's reflection on unification and its aftermath in his essay "The 'Jewish Question' in the 'German Question,'" *New German Critique* 52 (winter 1991): 155–72.

27. For a critique of left-wing discussions of the Holocaust see the special issue on Germans and Jews, *New German Critique* 19 (winter 1990) and Anson Rabinbach and Jack Zipes, eds., *Germans and Jews Since the Holocaust* (New York, 1986).

Education After the Cold War: Remembrance, Repetition, and Right-Wing Violence

Measuring Successful Education

In 1966, Theodor Adorno wrote for German radio a manuscript titled *Erziehung nach Auschwitz* (Education After Auschwitz). In this essay Adorno maintains that all considerations are secondary to the question about what to do to avoid a repetition of Auschwitz. "The barbarism [which he identifies with "the principle of Auschwitz"] continues," he writes, "as long as the conditions which might produce a relapse continue in their essence to persist." His goal is to isolate the mechanisms that made Auschwitz possible, and in this vein, he concludes, "the climate that is most supportive for a revival . . . is a reawakened nationalism." The role of intellectuals, he maintains, is, on one hand, to educate children, and on the other, to engage in a "general enlightenment" that would "create a spiritual, cultural, and social atmosphere that would prevent a repetition. . . . The single, truthful force against the principle of Auschwitz," he continues, "would be autonomy, if I may employ the Kantian expression: the strength for reflection, for self-determination, for not-going-along." In fact, this last element, the willingness to work against the collective interest, is the one that Adorno singles out as most important for the prevention of a repetition of the principle of Auschwitz.[1]

I cite Adorno here because since the end of the cold war, we have been confronted with a problem similar to the one he faced following World War II and the Holocaust: How might one remember without repeating? How might one act so that the mechanisms responsible for particularly barbaric or grotesque episodes in our history do not repeat themselves? "Never again Auschwitz" indeed may ring a bit hollow in light of the kinds of massacres we saw in Cambodia during the cold war and the "ethnic cleansing" that we witnessed in Rwanda and Bosnia. My comparison of the Holocaust with other, more contemporary genocides is not meant to deny its singularity—that, in the words of Saul Friedlander, it marks "some kind of outer limit of state criminality."[2] But in order to prevent the operation of its "principle," that barbarism Adorno sought to identify, we should not wait until barbarism reaches "some kind of outer limit." And in the spirit of Adorno's conceptualization, the racial violence and genocide in Bosnia is, I think it fair to say without in any way relativizing or trivializing the horror of Nazi annihilation policies, the operation of the principle of Auschwitz.

In Germany, the birthplace of the principle, however, something has changed since Auschwitz.[3] The argument often made that education in the two Germanies since 1945 has utterly failed is, I think, clearly wrong. I say this not to minimize the significance of the more than two thousand acts of violence perpetrated against foreigners in both 1991 and 1992, including the bombing and burning of homes for asylum seekers and the seventeen murders by right-wing groups, of whom eight of the victims were foreigners. Indeed, the Office of Constitutional Protection estimated at that time that political parties of the radical right in eastern and western Germany had about forty thousand members, of whom six thousand were ready to use violence.[4] Equally if not more disturbing than these specific acts of murder has been the acceptance, often extending to support, of this violence by a large number of German bystanders.

Does this wave of violence illustrate a repetition compulsion? Ignatz Bubis, chairperson of the Central Council of Jews in Germany, recently put this violence into a different framework, concluding that it is an example of "[not] of too many right-wing extremists, but [of] too few democrats."[5] Here Bubis is observing from a decidedly West German perspective, which maintains that the proper response to fascism is more democracy. The official position in the German Democratic Republic (GDR) maintained that the proper response to fascism entailed the elimination of capitalism and antifascist education, especially in the schools.[6] Neither perspective, we might note, emphasized Adorno's prescription that autonomy and resistance to "going along" were needed to prevent a repetition. From Adorno's perspective, these violent events and the reactions to them in the unified Germany would be a good test of successful postwar education. In the fall of 1992, several million East and West Germans demonstrated publicly their unwillingness to go along, organizing peaceful marches and demanding that politicians and police take resolute action to stop the violence. Following these demonstrations, politicians and significant numbers of relatively apolitical citizens have been spurred into action against this new wave of right-wing violence. This action alone did not stop the violence, though it did demonstrate an unwillingness to go along. One may criticize the kinds and effectiveness of the various responses, but let us for a moment remain with the mass rallies. If these demonstrations, with participants from the East and West, are indicative of a more autonomous citizenry, then from what do they result? In what way did either more democracy or the elimination of capitalism and antifascism contribute to this result?

Today a "repetition compulsion," a further turn to violence in Germany—at its most extreme, like the scenes in the early nineties in Bosnia-Herzegovina—is extremely unlikely. This most recent violence in Germany was not a repetition of old antagonisms suddenly allowed to resurface but a new phenomenon, a product not of fascism and World War II but of the cold war. Before going on, I want to emphasize that, despite the post-unification growth of neonationalist movements in Germany, the accompanying violence is not a product of "nationalism." Adorno had identified nationalism as the single factor most likely to bring about another Auschwitz. For Serbia and Croatia today, as well as for parts of the former Soviet Union, Adorno's analysis seems to hold true: the resurrection of nationalism prepares the way for the principle of Auschwitz.[7] In Germany, by contrast, unification has provoked a spirited debate on nationalism's nature and history, its dangers and accomplishments. Nationalism has not become a mass rallying cry that unifies a majority against some externally hypostatized other, partly, I think, because of successful education over the course of the past forty-five years.[8] The question remains, though, where exactly, when, and for what reasons has education been successful? And exactly what is the cause of the renewed violence in Germany?

Education Oriented to the Past

If we agree that violence is not an individual psychological pathology but a cultural predisposition dependent on social mechanisms and a particular social milieu for expression, then our analysis of violence must be directed to these social mechanisms and this milieu. And that milieu today is not simply post-Auschwitz but also post-cold war. Hence "education after Auschwitz" must be regarded as an ongoing historical task to which we must now add "education after the cold war." My task, then, is considerably more modest than was Adorno's; it presupposes an extension of Adorno's analysis and not its completion.

In order to extend Adorno's analysis, we must first recognize that the origins and functioning of the cold war cannot be attributed to nationalism but, rather, to three factors: a particular kind of supranational ideological, segmentary bloc-building; a particular kind of symbiotic relationship between small, dependent client states and superpower, welfare-state superpowers; and exploitation of the perhaps universal human tendency to create mirror images by projecting one's own lack or inadequacy onto others. The division of Germany and the dual organization resulting from it were not a planned or necessary consequence of losing World War II and certainly not a penalty for Auschwitz, which the Allies were only too eager to forget within a few years after the end of the war.[9] Rather, this division was a planned and necessary consequence of the cold war.[10] Resistance to the cold war would have entailed, following Adorno's critique, reflecting on these factors and asserting autonomy with regard to the use and abuse of the mechanisms that made them possible.[11] For the remainder of this essay, I would like to focus on Adorno's critique of behavior—failure to reflect and willingness to go along—among East German intellectuals during the cold war, and thereby shed light on the conditions that made possible a cold war and on how one might educate so as to prevent its repetition. Finally, I will bring this analysis to bear on the cold war origins of right-wing violence in the newly unified Germany.

I shall begin with the observation that the two arguably most influential postwar writer-intellectuals in Germany, the West German Günter Grass and the East German Christa Wolf, have had difficulty reorienting themselves since November 1989. Both Grass and Wolf, we might note, became great writers in their personal confrontation with the mechanisms that made the Holocaust possible. *Die Blechtrommel* (The tin drum) by Grass and *Kindheitsmuster* (Patterns of childhood) by Wolf were undoubtedly essential reorienting texts for several generations of Germans in East and West. They provided a new, critical reading of the German past and thus an opening to an alternative future. My point is, however, that neither author was able to follow his or her insights into the Nazi past with the same kind of analysis of either the Federal Republic (FRG) or the GDR during the cold war. Both saw German division following World War II as a result and necessary consequence of German fascism and Auschwitz. Neither was able to see this division as a product of the cold war, with its own mechanisms, strategies, and social logic. Hence, both authors viewed unification through a lens focused on the horrors of the Nazi past and the dangers of its repetition; this view simultaneously filtered out analysis of the opportunities for the present and future that might open up if the cold war division ended.

Grass and Wolf belong to a generation that oriented itself in and derived its moral authority from its ability to respond to its collective past, primarily World War II and the Holocaust, as if they were on the side of good and as if this past were the embodiment of evil. Their acute ability to reflect on the past, on 1933–1945, was not matched by an equal acumen in reflecting on the present, on 1945–1989, precisely because their generation did not have, and could not create, the distance necessary for the same kind of analysis of their present. From today's perspective, the datedness of much of their work is attributable to an unsuccessful distancing from their own present. About the present they wrote ideologically. By *ideological* I do not mean loyal to the regime, *staatsnah*, an accusation often made unfairly against Wolf, who admitted to writing reports for the state security in 1959 and 1960.[12] In fact Wolf devoted much of her writing to a critique of actually existing socialism in the GDR. And Grass was a consistent critic of the Federal Republic. Rather, I mean ideology as thought "organized by a principle of occultation," as Claude Lefort writes, "thereby suppressing all the signs that could destroy the sense of certainty."[13] Grass and Wolf wrote about the FRG and the GDR as if they possessed a knowledge of the present—objectifiable and representable—that arose from its own order of things, not dependent on a distance between themselves and their ongoing histories. In writing about the Nazi period their work was much more relational, circumspect, and distanced. This distance constantly reinforced a view that their own ideas could supposedly objectify and make intelligible the Nazi past as an isolable period of history. For the majority of Germans, who are at least twenty years younger than either Grass or Wolf, the period 1933–1945 no longer remains the point of orientation. For them, the cold war experience is that point. And for even younger Germans, who seek orientation for life after 1989, both authors belong to another era.

Cold War Education in the German Democratic Republic

To understand why this is so, one would have to analyze the interaction of West and East German intellectuals as they constructed themselves as separate *Szene* (milieux).[14] Here I will narrow my focus to East German intellectuals and analyze separately three generations who were active in the cold war. I follow a typology made by Rainer Land and Ralf Possekel in a recent monograph.[15] The first generation of intellectuals in the former GDR is presently of Erich Honecker's age; in other words, most members are no longer living. This generation—and here I am limiting myself to those in or near positions of power, for example, Johannes R. Becher, Anna Seghers, and Stefan Hermlin—was composed mostly of committed Communists. Its members experienced class conflict at the end of the Weimar period, often worked in the antifascist resistance, and suffered under or at least encountered and had to make an arrangement with Stalinist repression either in the USSR or later in East Germany. They returned to the Soviet Zone and contributed to the early building of the state. This generation produced very few dissidents (the most well-known being Robert Havemann, Wolfgang Leonard, and Stefan Heym), because most had been trained in the habit of obeying party discipline, which was assumed to transcend individual or national interests. Those who worked close to Walter Ulbricht, and later Honecker, leaders who themselves were by no means intellectuals, were afflicted by what we might call the Kissinger effect, maximizing the principle of proximity to power as an end in itself, irrespective of the content of this power. Those unwilling to serve the repressive apparatuses of the state tended to remain silent rather than disobey the party. Land and Possekel have referred to this arrangement as one of " 'communicative' silence."[16] It was precisely this atmosphere of taboos, marked by agreed-upon silences, that increasingly characterized the behavior of this generation of intellectuals as the GDR and the cold war took concrete form.

This generation was the last to work in the nineteenth-century tradition of intellectuals. The West German sociologist Wolf Lepenies has characterized intellectuals generally—I would restrict his schema to those educated before World War II—as torn between melancholy and utopia. He writes that intellectuals tend to be critical and dissatisfied, constant complainers about present conditions. They tend to "suffer, correctly, on the condition of the world," and thus have a basically melancholic temperament.[17] Alternately, writes Lepenies, in order to escape melancholy, they think up utopias. For this pre-war generation of intellectuals, the melancholy was replaced with hope as they worked to realize a socialist utopia in the GDR. But this utopia had already clearly gone adrift by the early 1950s. What held it on course—in the minds of these intellectuals— was, on one hand, party discipline, and on the other, a conviction that they were committed antifascists and thus involved in negating the principle of Auschwitz. Party discipline supposedly steered people in a progressive, future-oriented direction. And the halo accompanying the antifascist self, an identification with the Soviets as victims of fascism, sealed one off from having to think about the past.[18] Both mechanisms, party discipline and identification with the antifascist Soviet Union, worked to foreclose consideration of and reflection about the specific nature of German fascism and about its further reproduction in the GDR. These mechanisms fostered the illusion that the GDR and its people had been inoculated against potential strains of fascism. The avoidance of this ultimate evil, in the eyes of this generation, was sufficient to ground and justify both self and community. As we know with the benefit of hindsight, party membership and antifascism tended to reduce raison d'être to raison d'état.

Moreover, for this generation of East German intellectuals, the Federal Republic served as the alter-ego of the antifascist. Since the FRG never thematized capitalism or antifascism, but instead represented itself as "democratic," the GDR responded by calling it "a merely formal democracy" compared to its own true democracy in the "better Germany." Sigrid Meuschel argues that this view made for a basic anti-Western attitude, resulting in a "symbiosis between antifascism and Stalinism."[19] Critical intellectuals and the party never coalesced into a protest movement for democratization in the GDR, as they did in Poland and Hungary in 1956 and in the 1980s, because, as Meuschel argues, the possibilities for social improvement of the disadvantaged classes were coupled to a subaltern position vis-à-vis party nomenclatura. Hence, the "strength for reflection, for self-determination, for not-going-along," which Adorno had emphasized as the "single, truthful force against the principle of Auschwitz," was displaced onto resistance against an isolable past, making it unnecessary for this generation to reflect critically on their own postwar behavior or on the present.

The second group, whose members came of age in the 1950s, is commonly called the *Aufbau* (reconstruction) generation. They had experienced neither class conflict nor the Communist idealism of their predecessors. Instead, the new state, the GDR, claimed to be founded in the interests of its youth, to create a "better Germany" through a reeducation of its youth. Some of the members of this generation had graduated from the *Arbeiter- und Bauern-Fakultäten* (worker and farmer faculties) set up to educate children from working-class and peasant families for positions of leadership. Indeed most GDR intellectuals were a new historical class; most came not from bourgeois but from working-class or lower-class white-collar families. Ultimately, however, they exercised minimal power in the GDR, for the old Communists of the first generation continued to rule up to one month before the Wall came down.

Among politburo members, for example, only Egon Krenz represented the Aufbau generation. A friend of mine who studied existential philosophy in the early 1980s knew the Krenz family well and told me the following story. He had had many conversations with Krenz, on many different topics. Once in a discussion of Marxism they reached a point where they were confronted with a direct contradiction between theory and practice in the GDR. Krenz replied to my friend, "When I am confronted with these situations, it is best to sit firmly in the saddle and hold the reins tight." Krenz, who can hardly be called an intellectual, nonetheless shared with intellectuals of this generation inherited taboos on public expression of opinion along with a sense of obligation to praise the party in a kind of Orwellian partyspeak in public discourse. The public domain in the GDR shrank over the years, so that by the 1970s the realm of the social had become smaller and had been privatized. Günter Gaus coined the term *Nischengesellschaft* to refer to this retreat to and elaboration of the private sphere.[20]

This second generation of intellectuals also shared with their elders a moral commitment to the state and to the East German society as a morally superior model and an alternative to the Federal Republic. In their service to the state, they frequently employed the naive notion that knowledge equals power. Inspired by the idea of "scientific Marxism," one could supposedly discover the laws of nature and direct them to the benefit of humanity. Yet the knowledge that they put at the disposal of the state—primarily in economics, demography, education, psychology, administration, and political science—did not so much serve for general enlightenment, as many had hoped, but was often put to use by the state and its security apparatus, the Stasi, to make the exercise of authority more effective. Even for the state, however, this knowledge did not always lead to more effective administration. For example, economists consistently misled Walter Ulbricht in the 1950s by propounding a theory that socialism would be able to *überholen ohne einzuholen*, overtake capitalism without having to catch up to it. Likewise, political scientists misled leaders of the state by propagating a theory that linked unproblematically capitalism to imperialism, and a theory of state legitimacy that assumed a reconciliation of democracy with the idea of dictatorship by an avant-garde party. In short, knowledge often did not equal power. Instead it more frequently served to legitimate faulty theories of order, planning, administration, psychology, education, and the like. And where knowledge was "correct," or *gesichertes Wissen* (secure knowledge), in East German terminology, as in the psychology or medicine employed by the Stasi to create fear or destabilize the personalities of suspected dissidents, it often worked against the long-term interests of East German society and merely in the interests of short-term state stability and a ruling elite from an older generation.

The state's reaction to what the most critical intellectuals of this generation said and wrote was either to isolate them within or exile them to West Germany. In exile, intellectuals such as Rudolf Bahro and Wolf Biermann did not function as diasporic intellectuals waiting to return, widely read or heard in dissident circles in their country of origin (as was the case with many exiled Polish, Czech, Hungarian, and Russian intellectuals). Instead they were integrated into certain *Szene* in West Germany and remained largely cut off from their potential audience in the GDR until the opening of the Wall.

In the late summer of 1989, as the consequences of Gorbachev's reforms became increasingly clear to the world, this Aufbau generation, along with a few critical intellectuals of a prior generation, began preparing to take over power from the old leadership. What prompted them to move quickly was the flight across the borders of Hungary and into the embassies in Eastern Europe, mostly by members of the third generation of East Germans, intellectuals and nonintellectuals alike, who shared a disrespect for and total lack of loyalty to the "East German project." The reaction of the different generations of intellectuals to this flight is rather telling.

Most of the generation of old Communists were unable to respond to this crisis. Their disorientation, in my opinion, was the basic reason why they lost their will to rule and continually capitulated to opposition demands in the summer and fall of 1989 without resorting to a "China solution."[21] The writer Stefan Heym, one of the few dissidents among his cohort with an audience in the West and the East, became a self-proclaimed spokesman for the East German "masses" in the Western media, in particular for *Der Spiegel*. He reacted to events of fall 1989 by calling for a proper education of the masses concerning the socialist project and later criticizing East Germans for their "cannibalistic lust" after consumer goods. For this message he found only a tiny audience in the East. And in the West, he was criticized pointedly by the ex-GDR author Monika Maron, who had resettled in Hamburg, for intellectual arrogance and "disrespect of the people."[22]

Members of the reconstruction generation who had organized the mass demonstration of between 600,000 and one million on November 4, 1989, in Berlin also called for a reinvigoration of socialism. Like Heym, they also, following this demonstration, had problems finding an audience. Lepenies calls these people "heroes for five days," from November 4 to the opening of the Wall on November 9.[23] The real heroes, he concludes, are the thousands who fled into the embassies and across the Hungarian border. They were the ones who totally destabilized the regime and quickened its final collapse, and few among them were intellectuals.

Here we arrive at a controversial question with respect to the role of this third generation in the collapse of the GDR. Were the people who risked their lives and fled the GDR in September and October 1989, and who through 1992 continued to flee the ex-GDR at the rate of approximately two thousand per week, heroes or victims of a false seduction? In other words, were they heroes for fleeing the GDR and precipitating the end of the cold war, or was this more a cowardly flight to capitalism, a succumbing to the seduction of the sirens of Western abundance?[24] The vast majority of the people who engaged in this flight were, as I mentioned, members of a third generation of GDR citizens. And the intellectuals among them were predominantly children of the new social classes that were constituted by the Aufbau generation. They were without personal memory of the two world wars or the Third Reich. Instead, one might argue, they are complete products not only of the cold war but also of education after Auschwitz in the GDR.

Education After Auschwitz
Land and Possekel divide the intellectuals among this third generation into a group of non-Marxists and a group that they claim is characterized by a mentality of "conspirative avant-gardism."[25] The non-Marxists, who formed the basis of what were in the 1980s called *Basisgruppen*, attempted to work outside and often in opposition to the state; above all, they tried to "not go along." They criticized the masses for being totally coopted by the state, the ruling Socialist Unity Party for being incapable of reforming itself, the state-recognized artists and intellectuals for being corrupted (in other words, trading acquiescence in return for travel privileges to the West), and the society in which they lived for being based on lies. Because the GDR's public domain had been so dramatically shrunken in size, the voice of this group of intellectuals and their critique had a small hearing among the people; these critics remained totally marginalized. Most members of the church and other, one might say, "normal" members (in GDR slang, *Stino:* stink normal) of the society actually disliked social critics. During my initial fieldwork, the GDR stumbled through a series of highly publicized confrontations with "dissidents" from 1987 to 1989. At that time I rarely heard expressions of support for the more radical system critics, such as Bärbel Bohley or Freya Klier. And the few who did express support for and solidarity with the more radical opposition often stressed to me that they felt relatively isolated and were not part of a "silent majority" who thought differently. Hence the younger critics in the GDR often relied on contacts with West German or "Western" intellectuals, myself included, for emotional and moral support, as well as to take their "voice" outside the confines of private gatherings in apartments, artistic happenings, or church-supported events. This group of East Germans, I might add, is the one in which Timothy Garton Ash, who along with Milan Kundera was perhaps the "official voice" on Eastern Europe for the free West, cultivated an interest, and to whom he gave voice in his reporting on East Germany and Eastern Europe for *Granta* and for the *New York Review of Books*.[26] The problem with Ash's work is that he so closely identified with these dissidents that during the heady days of the collapse of East European regimes he was not able to put their voices in the larger context of a widespread social disapproval of critical positions and thus understand the ultimate weakness of dissidents' authority claims.[27]

The intellectuals characterized by conspirative avant-gardism agreed with much of the critique of the non-Marxists, but instead of moving outside the state and the party, they developed a conspirative mentality to work in and around it. (Sascha Anderson, the dissident and Stasi informant, is perhaps the extreme example of such a mentality.) For example, many worked with the Stasi as IM, unofficial co-workers, because the Stasi was the only official institution willing to address the taboo topics and problems of the society. It seemed as if the Stasi was genuinely interested in reform, whereas the party and the state apparatus were controlled by an aging elite who categorically refused to acknowledge any problems whatsoever. The Protestant Church and many of its members were also involved in this conspirative activity. In the 1960s the leadership of the church made a new, cooperative arrangement with the state, yielding its staunch oppositional role in order to redefine itself as "the church in socialism." From 1990 to 1993, governmental and media investigations of Manfred Stolpe, the minister-president of Brandenburg and former representative elected by the church to deal with the state, came to revolve around the question whether his, and the church's, conspirative attitude actually made him, to use Lepenies' phrase, a hero or a betrayer of the people.[28]

To be sure, the flight across the Hungarian border was a heroic act insofar as it quickened the collapse of a nondemocratic regime and the end of the cold war. The fact that most people were motivated for this flight by hopes for a better material life should not, as I've written elsewhere, lead us to condemn them.[29] They sought what they imagined could be had but what they themselves lacked. How are people supposed to know the value of political freedoms before they have experienced them? And even when the nonintellectual masses have experienced political freedom, this is no guarantee that they will grant freedom the value of an absolute. I would be more willing to condemn individuals who had already enjoyed bourgeois freedoms but then were willing to give them up (a good number of examples in the United States come to mind) than I would be willing to criticize East Germans for not prioritizing freedoms that they had never experienced.

Some German intellectuals of what I have called the first and second generations have criticized this third generation precisely for fleeing the republic and thus in part being responsible for the negative consequences of unification. Certainly unity was rushed and many of the humiliations and actual harms suffered by East Germans could have been avoided. The brain drain from East to West and the takeover or closing of most publishing houses and newspapers, for example, have indeed made "self-realization" more difficult for most East Germans. East German intellectuals have felt singled out by the wholesale delegitimation of entire biographies, often on spurious grounds, such as having been a committed Communist. Furthermore, they have been victimized by what many call *Siegerjustiz* (justice of the victors), which has accompanied *die Abwicklung,* the evaluation, closing, and dissolution of academies and research divisions in the universities.[30] At the same time this official *Abwicklung,* this bringing to completion, has strengthened the *Schadenfreude* or *Besserwisserei* of the West Germans. Current East German intellectual humiliation and loss, however, are not intended results of the desire by the masses for bananas and automobiles and the right to travel in the West. It is not as if only workers and youths had an appetite for bananas and Mercedes; this taste is one they shared with adult intellectuals.

A more interesting question is: In what way did education in the GDR contribute to this flight? Specifically, what might we conclude from the end of the GDR about antifascist education? One must grant that, given the amount of right-wing violence in unified Germany, the success of education after Auschwitz—to be autonomous, to not go along—has been a limited one. Studies seem to show an equal percentage of youths in West and East with a positive attitude toward the Nazi period, though the reasons for these attitudes are different. The West German political leadership had rejected the notion of "collective guilt" and affinity with American culture and the Wirtschaftswunder to distance oneself from the Nazi period. In the East, antifascist education became a pillar of identity. In 1988, for example, "resistance fighters" held 36,000 discussions with more than 1.6 million in attendance. In the 1980s approximately 200,000 eighth graders in schools visited yearly one of three concentration camps: Buchenwald, Ravensbrück, or Sachsenhausen.[31]

Many observers have argued, as does Wilfried Schubarth, that the GDR discredited antifascism because it "administered, instrumentalized, monopolized, and ritualized" it.[32] But do not these characteristics hold for all formal education? Schooling is always for a purpose and thus administered and instrumentalized. To be sure, there is a need for a more effective pedagogy to educate about fascism, but there really is no evidence that this clumsy form of administered antifascism has caused right-wing violence. The cause of this violence is more likely to be found in the events surrounding the terms of unity itself, such as loss of authority due to the end of cold war ideological props, or dislocations and uncertainties in life courses expectancies. And to the extent that millions of people oppose this violence (similar not-going-along was rare in the Nazi period), this also has to be attributed not to lessons of the Nazi period but to achievements of postwar education. I am most inclined to think that the GDR's education system, to the extent one can attribute cause specifically to it, produced not fascist behavior but cynicism and distance from all authority, therefore precipitating the kind of flight that occurred in the fall of 1989.

Education After the Cold War

I would add yet another defense for those who fled and are still fleeing the areas of what was called the "East bloc" for what was and is still known as "the West." They reacted, and are reacting, to the finality of personal destinies mapped out by the conservative regimes in the East and to restrictions on freedom of movement of ideas and peoples—both central structures of the cold war. The penetration of international borders, by ideas or people or capital, was always—especially when achieved by those in the East—an ultimate heretical act during the cold war phase of the nation-state system. For many people in the West, tourists and businessmen being exemplary cases, this penetration was, of course, a privilege and "right" of living in the "free world." This old world order was an extension of and particular take on the Westphalian system of independent and sovereign, though insecure, nation-states. It was concerned with securing borders and boundaries, with formulating the rule and enforcing the law. In order to represent itself as a paradigm of security and order, the most active of the cold war regimes actually fostered instability and insecurity elsewhere, among other peoples, as a mirror and justification for their own orderliness. In Europe, the social welfare state and the West-East divide (NATO versus Warsaw Pact) were the pillars of this order of closed societies, of group identities reassembled in a segmentary lineage structure where each side's self-definition presupposed the dangerous and anxious other. These identities were organized as national families in which all nationals enjoyed certain formal rights and predictable futures as legal subjects within a particular territory, joined to other nationals in higher-order coalitions. Although social welfare states characterized both East and West, the nature of the legal subject and his or her rights privileged those in the West over those in the East. And the West's system of rights was able to maintain itself only with a basic asymmetry: all nonnationals or "aliens" who did not have access to these rules, and whose very inability to express themselves in terms of the rules reassured Western legal subjects of their own reality and intelligibility, were legitimately excluded from these rights, these territories, and these futures.

The geographical movement of Germans from East to West, constant during the cold war but accelerated since the summer of 1989, was not largely a response of the poor to their economic plight, nor of the persecuted to their lack of freedom—as a large number of American scholars in various disciplines would like to imagine (and as they are now being told by people of the Eastern bloc in radically revised accounts of what life was "really like" before the opening). This movement is a fairly direct and immediate response to the collapsing cold war order, more specifically to the inherent instability at the core of the West's system of rights and privileges. The new homelessness and dislocation throughout the former Eastern bloc is also indicative of a more generalized condition of the new world order being constructed. This emerging order signifies, I would argue, the end not of the nation-state but of its specific welfare state form and of the East-West divide as structuring principles of the cold war. The collapse of these two principles has unsettled both domestic order and international relations, as has the dissolution of the Warsaw Pact and the disintegration of the set of alter egos in the East. The decentering of rules and penetration of borders are no longer isolated or exceptional acts, as they were during the cold war, for they are becoming new generative principles, acted out not merely by the resettlers from eastern to western Germany, nor merely by waves of refugees and asylum seekers, but also by national and supranational businesses and legal regimes. I am by no means original in emphasizing that the condition of homelessness, a new nomadism, has been long regarded as an adaptive reaction to modernity.[33] As both people and capital increasingly resort to this adaptive strategy, homelessness is perhaps now entering a new stage. It is in this light that I see the East German "heroes": not as asserting autonomy in the Kantian sense, nor concerned with reflection or "not going along" in the manner that Adorno stressed. They asserted "exit," to employ a term from Albert Hirschman's much-abused framework of "voice, loyalty, exit."[34] This exit caused a welcome collapse of a particular system of domination. But it also was part of a panic, a massive flight from a reflective self. It was not a "voicing" in Hirschman's sense, for voice formation, he writes, "depends on the potential for collective action."[35] Unlike most of the participants in the demonstrations in Leipzig and East Berlin who were intent on reformulating the nature of the collective to which they belonged, those who fled were primarily motivated by a desire to assume an already constituted voice elsewhere, that of the West German.

My intellectual defense of this flight necessarily ends here, for this flight was not only a rejection of fixity and cold war order but also a seduction by consumer culture and escape from a confrontation with one's historical self. Nonetheless I cannot identify with the critique lodged against these resettlers by some East German intellectuals. Rather, this younger generation of East Germans points intellectuals in a direction we must go in education after the cold war. First, we must take seriously their critique of what they fled—the conditions of confinement, closure, and exclusion on which the welfare state depends, the immobility imposed on them that was a precondition for the survival of the national insecurity state during the cold war. And second, we must critique what they fled to—the phantasmic "civic culture" of the liberal West, with its elections, private life, and consumer culture. The creation of civic cultures is hardly a panacea for the world's problems. It solves neither intolerance nor poverty. Francis Fukuyama's prediction of an ideological consensus in favor of secular liberal democracy has proved to be a liberal conceit.[36] The idea that democracy in its liberal capitalist form has become an ultimate form of governance serves to obscure the different understandings and uses being made of "democracy," "the people," "markets," and "privatization" for illiberal purposes. Many of the liberal regimes that replaced those "actually existing socialist" regimes in 1989 and 1990 have already become footnotes to a continuous history of displacements. Other than the staging of formal elections, some of these regimes no longer even pretend to democratic legitimation. Even in eastern Germany, the future of liberal capitalism and its relation to democracy remains an open question. Indeed, the sanctification of Chancellor Helmut Kohl (until his party finance scandal), his reincarnation as the Bismarckian national father, suggests a conflation of historical authority structures rather than a simple displacement of authoritarianism into stable democratic form.

Let us return to my original question about right-wing violence and education after the cold war. My major argument has been that this violence, in both East and West, must be understood not as a repetition of repressed aggression and traditions rooted in Auschwitz but as generated by the disintegration of mechanisms of the cold war order. Racist and nationalist thinking in the GDR, which Schubarth identifies with "an accentuated ethnocentric superiority claim coupled with a massive fear and hate of foreigners,"[37] are not "survivals" of the past but regenerated forms of group belonging. They are being regenerated because of post-unity problems: lost orientation, fear of the future, economic and status insecurities growing out of present concerns. Under these conditions, intellectuals have a responsibility to take seriously insecurities—regardless of their real status or origin—instead of demonizing or humiliating Ossis, or trivializing their concerns. Since most East German intellectuals have lost much of their authority, if not their jobs, this educational responsibility to provide orientation during a time of increased insecurity falls primarily to the West Germans.

As the mechanisms that structured authority during the cold war crumble, remembering alone will not—in locating either the cause of violence or its solution—lead to new authority structures. The new authority structures that seek to manage conflictual and multiple identifications, are, in my opinion, being created within a new "regime of the market," with its emphases on mobility and exchangeability, where local and global actors often work in tandem instead of in opposition. That this domain is one from which classical German intellectuals (Marx is, of course, an exception) have traditionally distanced themselves accounts in part for why they have had little to contribute. This leads the sociologist Bernard Giesen to argue that the compensatory role of *Kultur*, as formulated by the intellectuals that have made up German *Bildungsbürgertum* (educated bourgeoisie) for the past two hundred years, is no longer necessary in a united Germany. He concludes that in the future "the field of this national identity will be determined by the bureaucracies of the ministries, where plans for the institutional reconstruction are drawn up and the costs of unity calculated, calculated anew and more or less artificially financed."[38] The problem with Giesen's formulation is that he assumes that national identity is solely a product of intranational forces, whereas national identity has always been an international affair, always constituted partly by (em)migration, international exchange, and wars.[39] By this, I do not mean to exaggerate the interconnectedness of the world, nor to minimize the significance of the role of German-identified actors in German affairs.

In my personal encounters with West Berlin intellectuals, as well as in my reading of essays and viewing of television talk shows and documentary and feature films, I have found the most frequent reaction to right-wing violence is one of alarm coupled with *Schadenfreude*. The joy over the other's harm is, of course, not joy over violence against foreigners, which everyone abhors, but a smugness about where the danger lies—elsewhere, particularly in the East, especially among disaffected nonbourgeois youth. For example, in a book of essays by West Berlin and West German authors titled *Der rasende Mob. Die Ossis zwischen Selbstmitleid und Barbarei* (The raging mob: Ossis between self-pity and barbarism), satire is employed to critique rampant hatred of foreigners and self-pity in the East.[40] Yet one must ask why the authors (intellectuals?) stubbornly refuse to engage in any self-critique, why they cannot define a position for themselves as bourgeois (West) German intellectuals of 1992—except as the empty contrasting (and cool) sign to the abominable (and overheated) Ossi. "The most embarrassing thing about the GDR," writes Michael O.R. Kröher in the opening essay, "is the people who live there."[41] He means to be funny, but the question is: Who is laughing at whose expense? Although it is perhaps too much to still expect a noncoercive exchange between East and West intellectuals, a minimal condition of future exchange would be a more reflexive stance than has been evident to date with regard to the mutual constitution of subjects during and since the

cold war. Intellectuals can and should regain a voice in this reconstruction by articulating and by self-reflectively positioning themselves with
and against what are often misleadingly called the "common interests of
the market."

Notes

*An earlier version of this essay appeared in John Borneman, Subversions of International
Order: Studies in the Political Anthropology of Culture (Albany: State University of
New York Press, 1998), 221–45. Reprinted by permission of the State University of New
York Press; © 1998 State University of New York; all rights reserved. A shorter version of
the essay was initially delivered at a Social Science Research Council conference organized
by Susan Gal entitled "Intellectuals in Political Life," held February 12–14, 1993, at
Rutgers University. All translations from the German are mine unless otherwise noted.*

1. Theodor W. Adorno, "Erziehung nach Auschwitz," (repr.) *Die Zeit*, 1 January
1993, 53.

2. Saul Friedlander, "A Conflict of Memories? The New German Debates About
the 'Final Solution,'" in *Memory, History, and the Extermination of the Jews in Europe*,
ed. Friedlander (Bloomington, 1993), 22–41.

3. John Borneman, "Towards a Theory of Ethnic Cleansing: Territorial Sovereignty, Heterosexuality, and Europe," in *Subversions of International Order: Studies in the
Political Anthropology of Culture*, ed. John Bornemann (Albany, 1998): 273–318.

4. *The Week in Germany*, 12 November 1992, 1.

5. *The Week in Germany*, 1 May 1995, 2.

6. This position can no longer be articulated because the terms of unification—
e.g., threatened or actual unemployment, loss of audience, attacks on intellectual integrity, projected homogenization of East German elites—have involved a great deal
of silencing of East German intellectuals who expected to have a career in the unified
Germany; see John Borneman, "Time-Space Compression and the Continental Divide in German Subjectivity," *New Formations* 3, no. 1 (winter 1993): 102–18 For a
documentation and analysis of an East German exhibit on the "myth of anti-fascism,"
Kulturamt Prenzlauer Berg, ed., see *Mythos Antifaschismus: Ein Traditionskabinett wird
kommentiert* (Berlin, 1992).

7. I do not mean to imply that the genocidal war against the Muslims in Bosnia
was the result of "survivals," a revival of tribal hatreds. Instead, the antagonisms that
generated and triggered this conflict must be sought in the post–cold war order, where
Serbs and Croats asserted and exercised the only going principle of international
order: territorial sovereignty through national self-determination. See Borneman,
"Towards a Theory of Ethnic Cleansing."

8. Michael Geyer has made a similar argument in an essay on "the stigma of
violence" in twentieth-century Germany. Geyer writes that because difference in
Germany "remained traumatically linked to the violent process of segregation, exclusion and annihilation in the Third Reich, [postwar society was marked by] the
inability to distinguish between violent exclusion and the play of difference." The
1980s mark a "moment of rupture" with "the national project as the pursuit of unity

and coherence of the nation," by which he means the possibilities for "an opening for [either] a nationalizing expansion of the unitary ideal with its resulting exclusion of the unwanted and unfit [or] a chance for the discovery of the play of difference in German histories." See Michael Geyer, "The Stigma of Violence, Nationalism, and War in Twentieth-Century Germany," *German Studies Review* special issue (winter 1992): 75–110.

9. Clemens Vollnhals, ed., *Entnazifizierung: Politische Säuberung und Rehabilitierung in den vier Besatzungszonen 1945–1949* (Munich, 1991); Klaus-Dietmar Henke and Hans Woller, *Politische Säuberung in Europa: Die Abrechnung mit Faschismus und Kollaboration nach dem Zweiten Weltkrieg* (Munich, 1991).

10. John Borneman, *Belonging in the Two Berlins: Kin, State, Nation* (Cambridge, 1992); Dietrich Staritz, *Geschichte der DDR 1949–1985* (Frankfurt am Main, 1985).

11. John Borneman, "Trouble in the Kitchen: Totalitarianism, Love, and Resistance to Authority," in *Moralizing States and the Ethnography of the Present*, ed. Sally Falk Moore (Washington, D.C., 1993), 93–118.

12. For a documentation see Christa Wolf, *Akteneinsicht Christa Wolf: Zerspiegel und Dialog einer Dokumentation* (Hamburg, 1993).

13. Claude Lefort, *The Political Forms of Modern Society: Bureaucracy, Democracy, Totalitarianism* (Cambridge, Mass., 1986), 202–3.

14. My omission of West German intellectuals from this analysis is in no way meant to infer that East German intellectuals were primarily or more responsible for the cold war than West German ones. As Wolfgang Haug has pointed out, criticism since unity has been "an illumination of a dead order of rule by a living one" rather than in how both sides were caught in the net of the cold war (Wolfgang F. Haug, "Die Wiederkehr des Unerwarteten," in *Erinnern, Wiederholen, Durcharbeiten: Zur Psycho-Analyse deutscher Wenden*, ed. Brigitte Rauschenbach [Berlin, 1992], 276–85, here 284). I have written elsewhere that East and West Germans during the cold war were part of a "dual organization" formed through the interaction and asymmetrical exchanges between the two halves (Borneman, *Belonging in the Two Berlins* and John Borneman, *After the Wall: East Meets West in the New Berlin* [New York, 1991]). An analysis of the specific role of West German intellectuals reaches beyond the scope of this essay. It would differ fundamentally from my account of East German intellectuals. Because both generational conflict and forms of political authority were structured differently in East and West, opportunities for autonomy and mechanisms for change were also dissimilar.

15. Rainer Land and Ralf Possekel, *Intellektuelle aus der DDR: Diskurs und Identität* (Berlin, 1992).

16. Ibid., 18.

17. Wolf Lepenies, *Aufstieg und Fall der Intellektuellen in Europa* (Berlin, 1992), 14.

18. I should note here that the West German identification with "America," "the West," and "American democracy" served a similar function: that of granting West Germans the illusion of immunity from fascism through distance from their specifically German national context.

19. Sigrid Meuschel, "Antifaschistischer Stalinismus," in *Erinnern, Wiederholen, Durcharbeiten: Zur Psycho-Analyse deutscher Wenden*, ed. Brigitte Rauschenbach (Berlin, 1992), 163–71.

20. Günter Gaus, *Wo Deutschland liegt: Eine Ortsbestimmung* (Hamburg, 1983), 156–233.

21. See, e.g., the analysis by Stefan Wolle of Eric Mielke, former head of the State Security (Stasi), in the period when the regime's authority wasdisintegrating. Wolle concludes that in August and September 1989, the documents "show [Mielke to be] a confused and helpless old man who no longer understands the world. He hangs on stubbornly to his old thought and speech pattern and yet senses that his time has run out." Stefan Wolle, "Operativer Vorgang 'Herbstrevolution': War die Wende des Jahres 1989 eine Verschwörung der Stasi?" in *Die Ohnmacht der Allmächtigen. Geheimdienste und politische Polizei in der modernen Gesellschaft*, ed. Bernd Florath, Armin Mitter, and Stefan Wolle (Berlin, 1992), 234–40, here 238.

22. Monika Maron, "Das neue Elend der Intellektuellen," in *Nach Maßgabe meiner Begreifungskraft* (Frankfurt am Main, 1993), 80–90.

23. Lepenies, *Aufstieg und Fall der Intellektuellen in Europa*, 56–61.

24. Borneman, *After the Wall*.

25. Land and Possekel, *Intellektuelle aus der DDR*, 22–26.

26. Timothy Garton Ash, *The Uses of Adversity: Essays on the Fate of Central Europe* (New York, 1989), and *The Magic Lantern: The Revolution of '89 Witnessed in Warsaw, Budapest, Berlin, and Prague* (New York, 1990).

27. Ash admits, "[E]ven here my account is largely from inside the opposition movements and from among so-called 'ordinary people' on the streets" (*Magic Lantern*, 21). Though he may have had a great deal of contact with "ordinary people" before the fall of 1989, his reportage after the fall of 1989 concentrates almost exclusively on public figures, in particular members of the various oppositions. In all of the former East-Central European countries except East Germany, many of these very intellectuals whom he knew moved into positions of power in 1990. Yet, between 1991 and 1993, most had lost these positions. For my own perspective on the relationship of dissidents to totalitarianism and authority during the cold war, see Borneman, "Trouble in the Kitchen."

28. The state security actually listed Stolpe as an IM and even awarded him a bronze medal for service. Stolpe, however, insists—and is supported on this claim by his colleagues in the church and by his former contacts in the Stasi—that he never worked for the Stasi and that if he had been an IM, he would have received for his service a gold instead of a silver medal.

29. Borneman, *After the Wall*, 248–54.

30. On justice, see John Borneman, "Uniting the German Nation: Law, Narrative, and Historicity," *American Ethnologist* 20 (1993): 288–311 and *Settling Accounts: Violence, Justice, and Accountability in Postsocialist Europe* (Princeton, 1997); Lothar Bisky, Uwe-Jens Heuer, and Michael Schumann, eds., *Rücksichten: Politische und juristische Aspekte der DDR-Geschichte* (Hamburg, 1993); on intellectuals, see Wolf Lepenies, "Alles rechtens—nichts mit rechten Dingen," *Die Zeit*, 11 December 1992, 87–88; on the Treuhand, see Peter Christ and Ralf Neubauer, *Kolonie im eigenen Land: Die Treuhand, Bonn und die Wirtschaftskatastrophe* (Berlin, 1991); for a documentation of discrimination, see Wolfgang Richter, *Weissbuch: Unfrieden in Deutschland* (n.p., 1992). A very vivid example of this confrontation with freedom is the case of Horst Klinkmann, reported by Rainer Frenkel, "Der Riss im Leben des Horst Klinkmann," *Die Zeit*, 2 April 1993, 44. Born in 1935 and raised as an orphan, Klinkmann was an internationally acclaimed researcher in the transplantation of artificial organs. He had been director of the clinic for internal medicine at the University of Rostock in the GDR, as well as guest professor in many foreign countries. In 1990, he was the

first democratically elected president of the Academy of Sciences of the GDR, and thus the official discussion partner in the unification of the sciences in the two Germanies. In May 1992, he was dismissed from his post because of unproved suspicions that he had worked for the Stasi, as well as for activities as an SED party member, which supposedly compromised his scientific work, resulting in "Fehlverhalten" (lit.: erroneous behavior).

31. Winfried Schubarth, "Antifaschismus in der DDR—Mythos oder Realität?" *Erinnern, Wiederholen, Durcharbeiten*, 172–79.

32. Ibid., 173.

33. Gilles Deleuze and Félix Guattari, *Anti-Oedipus and Schizophrenia*, trans. Robert Hurley, Mark Seem, and Helen Lane (New York, 1977).

34. Albert O. Hirschman, *Exit, Voice and Loyalty: Responses to Declines in Firms, Organizations, and States* (Cambridge, Mass., 1970).

35. Albert O. Hirschman, *Rival View of Market Society* (Cambridge, Mass., 1986).

36. Francis Fukuyama, *The End of History and the Last Man* (New York, 1992).

37. Schubarth, "Antifascismus in der DDR," 177.

38. Bernhard Giesen, *Die Intellektuellen und die Nation: Eine deutsche Achsenzeit* Frankfurt am Main, 1993), 253–54.

39. Charles Tilly, *Coercion, Capital, and European States, AD 990–1992* (Cambridge, Mass., 1990).

40. Klaus Bitterman, ed., *Der rasende Mob: Die Ossis zwischen Selbstmitleid und Barbarei* (Berlin, 1993).

41. Michael O. R. Kröher, "Nichts gegen die da drüben," in ibid., 12–30, here 12.

The Long Good-bye:
German Culture Wars in the Nineties

The turmoil of German opinions and sentiments during the past decade is stunning and bewildering. Contrary to initial expectations, the fact of unification has neither settled acrimony nor led to a state of "normalization." Instead, unification has added an edge of unpredictability. In part, bringing easterners and westerners into one nation challenged identities that seemed all but self-evident, although they had remained strangely unarticulated while they existed. Many easterners and westerners only discovered after the fact that they had possessed rather distinct collective identities.[1] In part, establishing normalcy in the emergent Berlin Republic created novel responsibilities for Germany that challenge old self-perceptions. In particular, the open exercise of power proved difficult to reconcile with the image Germans had made of their country as a peaceable kingdom.[2] Both resulted in the breakup of political and cultural allegiances that had taken on a solidity that also became appreciated only after the fact. The disarray of German opinions and sentiments is the expression of the acrimonious remaking of German society and identity in the process of unification. Its most telling metaphor is the traffic accident.[3]

If it was all but evident before 1989 which sentiments and opinions move which kinds of Germans in East and West and where the contending parties would fit in the overall political and cultural spectrum, after 1989 individual orientations, much as the general direction of the nation, became more difficult to pin down. The signposts that have guided public opinion through the long postwar period have begun to disappear. There is no longer a self-evident German "mainstream," but a "profound intellectual, moral, and social disarray of Germans."[4]

The main cause of this disorientation is the unforeseen and, for the most part, unwanted discontinuity between the present and the recent past. One might think that the effects of abrupt change are more readily evident for the East, where the collapse of the communist regime and the accession to the Federal Republic have led to a deep rupture of institutional as well as social, economic, and cultural continuities. But there, actually one can find a rather stubborn and tenacious defense, if not of the old regime, then of the old ways and the old days. This is a highly creative and remarkably adaptive insistence on a discrete identity that is made up from scraps of experience that are fused into a new collective identity.[5] The sentiment is commonly captured in the blanket condemnation of nostalgia for the East *(Ostalgie)*. But it proves to be an effective mechanism of sheltering identities against the abrupt transformation of outlook and perception.

In contrast, continuity was proclaimed as official policy in the West. After all, it was the Federal Republic that incorporated the GDR in the shape of the so-called "five new states." It even gave continuity constitutional sanction when the parliament decided to retain the West German Basic Law, with minor changes worked out in committee, over and against efforts to elect a new constitutional assembly with the intent to constitute anew the political nation after unification. However, the public has increasingly realized that nothing has stayed quite the same with unification. "BRD ade!" was undoubtedly meant as a catchy book title in 1992, but it proved to be an apt prognostication.[6] The longer the process of unification was dragging on, proving that the integration of East and West was a treacherous proposition, the more the Federal Republic was becoming something of the past as well. The more Berlin acquired a tangible reality as a new capital, the easier it proved to shed the Federal Republic's past.

Change still does not come easily. For a while, the political process seemed to be grinding to a halt. The intellectual elites tended to be among the advocates of the status quo—best exemplified in the defense of the GDR by leading East German literati and by the cautious and, indeed, reluctant acceptance (as opposed to the active construction) of the image and reality of the emergent Berlin Republic by someone like Jürgen Habermas.[7] The call for change—and radical change at that—initially came from the Right, which insisted that a nation had yet to be created where there had been none before.[8] It looked for a while as if the only available alternatives would be either paralysis or a refounding of the nation on nationalist principles. But by the mid-nineties this perturbing scenario had begun to change. References to 1989 were increasingly used as license to debate and to visualize a remaking of German society beyond what nationalists of all stripes had to offer in terms of national identity. At the end of the decade, it seemed the country was changing faster than its imagination. Rather than continuity and stability, punctuated by calls for a nationalist revival, we find a tumultuous process of remaking German society that is accompanied, slowly and gingerly, by the production of ever more elaborate ideas and images to fit this emergent reality.[9]

This transformation was and is accompanied by a stunning array of public debates and controversies. They range from the responsibility of intellectuals, xenophobia and multiculturalism, the culture of memory and German national identity, the out-of-area use of the Bundeswehr, globalization and industrial competitiveness, unemployment and the welfare state, to issues of citizenship, to mention just the more politically important ones. Concurrently, one finds lengthy and controversial disquisitions about the nature of modernity, the meaning of tradition, the powers of capitalism, the illusions of ideology, and a veritable tour d'horizon through twentieth-century German culture—all this not as academic exercise but as (curiously unacknowledged) media and commercial culture. Although each one can be read separately, their sum is bigger than each individual part. Hence, rather than concentrate on one or the other public controversy, it seems a useful exercise to trace the contours of what is an altogether baffling, indeed, stupefying progression of public debates. Their rapid-fire intensity and recurrence in all areas of public life is striking. It is surely appropriate, as has been argued repeatedly, to think of this process as the formation of a national identity.[10] But it may well be the case that what we see in its infancy is not the reemergence or restoration of older identities but the formation of a new national code in a communicative situation that differs significantly from the preceding ones.[11]

From *Wendezeit* to *Zeitenwende* and Beyond

Any observer will readily confirm how quickly and how naturally it came to be assumed in 1990 that the Federal Republic would expand to incorporate, within a reasonably brief period of time, what had been a separate state, the German Democratic Republic, and would now become the "*fünf neue Länder,*" the five new states.[12] This supposition was all the more striking since very few had conceived of such a thing prior to October 1989. But by the spring of 1990 the expectation of unity (Willy Brandt: *Jetzt muß zusammenwachsen, was zusammengehört*)[13] was not just a popular fable to which the West added a touch of caution (it shouldn't cost too much) and the East a sense of urgency (it couldn't go fast enough). Neither was it simply a matter of political boasting during the first all-German election campaign in 1990, when a hapless loser (Oskar Lafontaine of the Social Democratic Party) was easily outwitted by a seasoned federal chancellor (Helmut Kohl, Christian Democratic Union) who promised wealth and happiness to everybody and a "flowering industrial landscape" (*blühende*

Industrielandschaft) within four years (the next election), thereby fulfilling, at long last, the utopia of the GDR, whose national anthem—with the key line "resurrected from ruins" *(Auferstanden aus Ruinen)*—now seemed to come true under changed circumstances.

And why not? Few doubted German industry. The deutschmark had become a national symbol of stability. And few questioned the German discipline that was to make the rebuilding possible. The rejection of the communist regime and its peaceful overthrow seemed to indicate the long-awaited maturation of democracy in Germany. The country had had its own homemade democratic revolution, which allayed any fears that West German constitutionalism was merely a matter of the general economic well-being of its population—a "fair-weather democracy" *(Schönwetter-Demokratie).*[14] As if to outdo politics and popular opinion, social scientists rushed forward to proclaim that, with a bit of belt-tightening here and there, the transformation of the East was not only possible but also feasible and quickly attainable.[15] The East became a laboratory for overcoming delayed modernization. It was to repeat for East Germany what the federal Republic had done for the German past—make all of Germany a truly modern country. Also, the expanse of the East seemed to be growing almost daily. The initial perspectives went far beyond Germany. In contrast to what appeared as a meek and reticent American policy, attributed, at the time, to the softness of the dollar and a decline of American power in accordance with the "imperial overstretch" theory of Paul Kennedy,[16] it appeared well within reach for the Germans to salvage eastern Europe and even Russia. In the heat of the moment, some even spoke of a return to a traditional German mission of eastern colonization.[17] There was a lot of this kind of talk in the heady days of 1989–90. If there is a deeper meaning to any of this, it is that in 1989–90 the German past had been redeemed through a democratic revolution and the sky was the limit.

These high spirits engendered a word game. Protest in the GDR had accomplished a *Wende,* a "reversal" resulting in the collapse of the communist regime. The model Germans from the West would now achieve a *Wende in der Wende,* a turn within the reversal. This was to suggest that, if the people of the GDR had taken the first step by bringing down their regime, the West would take the next step and help provide the democracy—and in this context, shed the left-liberal tendencies that had dominated postwar German culture. This was a piece of crafty politicking that entailed suppressing the eastern dissidents and dreamers who had hoped for a third way, a reformed and humane GDR that, though no longer communist, would also not be quite the "throw-away" society of the West, with its crass materialism and all-pervasive consumerism.[18] This strategy also meant to challenge all those in the West who hesitated in the face of unification because they feared it would bring back a past that had been overcome.[19] But above all it entailed pushing ahead with the jubilant endorsement of the majority of Germans. Whatever the hard edge of such ideas, a sense of boundless optimism and a "can-do" attitude ruled the day.

The oppositional spirit on the Right was not satisfied with a rollback of the GDR. The slogan of the *Wende in der Wende* quickly took on a more programmatic and partisan character. It was no longer simply an issue of bringing the two Germanies together in one nation-state (although the latter proved to be treacherous enough). The slogan became a call for re-making both Germanies, so that a unified Germany would, at long last, "be-come a wholly normal country."[20] This train of thought about "normalcy" suggested that a unified Germany would deliberately leave behind the *juste milieu* of the Federal Republic, as it was now called derogatively, and start anew both as an emphatically sovereign nation and as a distinct national culture.[21] This cluster of ideas and arguments reversed the modernization agenda that both the CDU government and the social scientific estab-lishment had pursued. First, it involved reasserting what was perceived as the "natural" and traditional position of Germany in the middle of Europe and, to that end, overcoming the postwar German "forgetfulness of power-politics."[22] Second, it assumed a more active and self-interested stance in Europe as well as preparing the domestic political ground for a new mission for of the German army—both at home and abroad—beyond the confines of NATO.[23] Third, it included a reassessment of Germany's external com-mitments and dependencies, in particular, in relation to the United States. Fourth, a lengthy debate ensued on the limitations of the constitutional guarantee of asylum and on immigration.[24] And finally, this unhappiness with the prevailing defense of the status quo was also the context for the attacks on postwar West German culture as an overly moral culture of contrition. The *Literaturstreit* (mostly directed against GDR intellectu-als[25] and the parallel debate on national identity (against West German "constitutionalists" like Habermas)[26] were the two foremost examples. One might add to this the charges against the relaxed morals and the political sentimentalism of the youth rebellion of the sixties, which challenged the remnants of the new social movements.[27] The latter would emerge as the first grand debate of the new millennium. The most far-reaching revisions, though, came with the effort to undo the memory culture of the Federal Republic, which had become the cornerstone if not of the popular, then surely of the public and intellectual identity of Germany and its people.

The very profusion of these debates suggests that there was considerable doubt about the initial optimism concerning the speed and the scope of unification. This doubt mingled, quite manifestly, with the effort to use unification as a lever for changing the pre-1989 status quo. This effort originated, for the most part, from a right-of-center establishment that used the newly gained stature of the unified Germany to clamor for a more nationally self-conscious and power-driven German policy. It satisfied populist desires for an altogether more exclusive Germany for the Germans and coincided with a mainstream wish for self-assertion, both individually and collectively. This welter of initiatives used unification in order to re-locate the dominant postwar consensus toward the Right. The success of these efforts was rather mixed. It did serious though not lasting damage to the reputation of GDR literature and to some of the icons of West German culture such as Günter Grass.[28] However, it was unable to move the center of gravity of the national consensus. The limits of success have to do with a great reluctance to abandon the status quo on one hand and the persistent tendency of these establishment initiatives to be hijacked by a radical Right on the other. It was one thing for a Hans Magnus Enzensberger to worry about immigration, but a very different thing to have these worries explode in violent riots.[29] Martin Walser's doubts about the postwar culture of contrition engendered sharp disputes but were also open to appropriation for much more radical ends.[30] The difficulty of controlling debates and demarcating boundaries time and again limited the potency of these challenges to the status quo.

This fluidity of boundaries on the Right is particularly evident in the debate on literature, which had the political and social activism of postwar literature as its subject. This debate was launched in the pages of the *Frankfurter Allgemeine Zeitung* and *Die Zeit*, picking up and broadening debates that started in the late seventies and eighties with Karl Heinz Bohrer, the editor of the public culture journal *Der Merkur*, as one of its main protagonists.[31] It ran into an altogether half-hearted defense, but it also had to tussle with much more distinctly Rightist points of view. Most famously, Hans-Jürgen Syberberg unleashed his diatribe against all postwar works of art as expressions of materialism, consumerism, and capitalism and of the captivity of the German spirit, cowed by defeat and Holocaust guilt.[32] Syberberg's all-out debunking of postwar culture gained a sudden lease on life, because his utopia of a "genuine" and more "existential" art now came to be associated with the East—as the site of a more traditional, more community-centered, and ultimately more spiritual way of life.[33] It took Botho Strauß's famous essay on tragedy to insinuate the goal—the pursuit of a more mysterious, sacrificial, and aesthetic existence.[34] This yearning for a more vital and, ultimately, a purer life articulated a spirit and took up a language of "resistance" that captured a young, "new" Right that looked at the older generation with disdain. But the pervasive debate concerning Strauß's quite hermetic piece also suggests that his call for pathos tapped a sensibility that extended far beyond the Right—which in turn has led Karl Heinz Bohrer to praise irony and cosmopolitan wit as antidotes to German seriousness.[35] The opposition of an "ironic West" and a "tragic East" has become canonic.[36]

Bohrer has been quite consistent in his argument.[37] He hated the post-war therapeutic culture with a vengeance—and from all appearances he still does. In order to be consistent, however, he had to shift weight, as it were, from his right to his left foot, from German pathos to French irony. But his defense of a more aesthetic culture now confronts a new essentialism that seeks out culture as the German preserve of authenticity. Botho Strauß has located himself at this seam between aestheticism and essentialism. Whether the Right is concerned with aesthetics or with a rather more palpable—and trivial—revival of Germandom remains to be seen. As it stands, this fluid field of actors has staked a new claim to the tradition of the *Kulturnation*.

As long as the official optimism and the popular enthusiasm for unification prevailed, these debates could be put aside as controversies among various kinds of eggheads. But unification proved to be far more difficult than initially assumed. The troubles of unification were hardly a result of the West Germans' decision to deliver their democracy and their economy wholesale, which was the source of enduring complaints about the arrogance of the *Besserwessies* (Western nitwits) and the alleged colonization of the East.[38] Neither was the difficulty mere griping from all those in the East who had expected more and better things faster. Rather, unification did not go as planned. The German East did not industrialize and modernize as expected. Quite apart from the realization that the damage done by socialist economics was more seriously than expected and that the East German rust belts would do no better than their western counterparts, recovery and renewal meant abandoning economic institutions and disbanding social relations. It entailed changing the ways of going about one's affairs in everyday life.[39] With unemployment rising, homes threatened, daycare for children abolished, and pensions and health payments not catching up with the cost of living, loyalty toward the new nation was difficult to achieve. Solidarity and neighborliness (the community spirit that both the Right and the neo-marxist Left saw embodied in the GDR) were in short supply under the impact of a new competitiveness that soured social relations.[40] The list of hazards of unification is long, and the reaction to them was drastic. It is not just that the initial excitement gave way to a great deal of surliness and petulance, if not worse. Rather, it seemed that the social fabric of German society was run down rather than refurbished.

Although the east-west differential remained a significant factor, East Germany was not exceptional. Rather, East Germans became the exemplary victims of a pattern of restructuring social and economic life that had been in evidence throughout the western industrial world since the seventies. As far as Germany was concerned, this cycle of structural change seemed temporarily suspended in the unification boom (which amounted to a huge pump-priming process), but the overall trend was not broken. The "flourishing industrial landscape" of which Helmut Kohl spoke was a twentieth-century memory that was passing fast. The harsher and more existential life the literati were dreaming about proved to be the hard-luck existence of all those who lost out in the process of unification or those who had fled or immigrated to Germany because it was still, notwithstanding a marginal existence and the threat of xenophobic violence, the better and safer place to be. The margins of society widened considerably. With this widening came the fear that this new inequality would be the source of violence—and predictably it was presumed that these margins were violent and criminal, though in fact the major acts of violence occurred when the "good society" let lose its hooligans to patrol the boundaries.[41]

It is in this much rougher climate of the nineties that the left-of-center intellectuals faced the denouement of their convictions. In part, the economists and sociologists had to realize that, even in the rare cases when they were right, their insights did not matter in the face of political and social exigencies. Also, progressive academics soon had to discover that there was a distinct shortage of ideas about reforming academia in the East and that they were just barely a match for their more conservative colleagues in the battle over who would control the universities. Most important, though, they approached with great discomfort a condition they had coveted for a long time. They now were masters of their own memory and of their own destiny. There was no more cold war framework to hem them in—no more protectors to pay tribute to. The Americans, for one thing, had all but abandoned—the Gulf War was the watershed—the niceties that they had reserved for minor client states in better days and started to play hardball, whether in economic and military relations or, for that matter, in memory politics. The moment of truth came when American lawyers (backed up by "self-serving" politicians, as it was regularly noted) rudely punctured the artifice of German memory culture and asked the German government and industry to put money where their spirit had been. Quite apart from the troubles with a more self-assertive Right, these intrusions of realism into an intellectual culture that had seemed all but triumphant in the late eighties (when it could claim to have won the *Historikerstreit*) deflated it thoroughly. With the public controversies about German participation in the intervention against Serbia this round of debate had gone full circle.[42] The preservation of peace and order, it was now acknowledged, might entail war. German memory culture was no guarantee against violence.

This is the background for a second cluster of debates and controversies that swirled around the themes of *Orientierungslosigkeit* and *Unübersichtlichkeit*, a lack of direction and purpose in politics and culture. Again, the gyrations of this field of debate are illustrative for the kind of change unification engendered, for initially, the themes were brought up in a turn against both postmodern arbitrariness and the challenges of a rationally organized and rationally debating society.[43] But in the course of unification, they were taken over by a diverse array of opinion-makers. There were those who now argued that the West could not possibly remain the West if the East no longer was the East; that is, since both German postwar histories were so conditioned by the cold war division, neither could survive the end of the other. The most extravagant argument of this kind insisted that the terminal crisis of socialism would only initiate the global crisis of capitalism— a Fukuyama "end of history" in reverse, and so much more flamboyantly Nietzschean and entertaining.[44] In short, there had always been enough people to argue that things were too good to remain what they were— and hence had to be changed. But now more and more commentators began to argue that the Germans will have to change their ways if they want to persist. The assumption now was that "after the end of the East-West conflict we live in a period of upheaval" (*Umbruch*) that "requires that we put together (*zusammenbauen*), similarly to 1945, an entirely new state"—and an entirely new economy, a thoroughly reformed society, and a revitalized culture.[45]

German debate has come to call this phenomenon, often with apocalyptic overtones, *Zeitenwende*, which is to say, in the first instance, that the bottom had fallen out from under the unification process. Then again, the notion of *Zeitenwende* alludes to much more than that. It suggests that Germany has moved from a unification crisis to a veritable *Kulturkrise*. Surprisingly, this crisis-talk has been "occupied" not by the Right, but by the liberal center.[46] Industry is bound to change in order to stay competitive— and, with it, the national sense of work and of self-worth defined by work. Politics will have to change in order to cope with the disenchantment of voters—and with it a political system with its people's parties, which had guaranteed stability for the past forty years. Social welfare will have to be altered in order to guarantee a minimum of social security—and with it the welfare state that had provided for the security of the nation. But crisis-talk is contagious. If one believes the media, the Bundesbahn, the Bundesbank, national television, even the local zoos are caught in a crisis of transformation.[47] In the new century, the Germans would learn that they could not even trust their sausages and their meat.

Throughout the eighties, the theme of a profound rupture of social relations and cultural values had languished on the margins as a predictable Christian-conservative theme, but in the wake of unification, it was articulated most clearly in the pages of *Die Zeit*, with some eminent and quite unlikely commentators, such as Helmut Schmidt, thinking aloud that two thousand years of Christian values are disappearing in the black hole of a united Germany.[48] Even if we take this rhetoric of millennial upheaval with a grain of salt it is persistent enough and its recurrence at a crucial juncture in German history is predictable enough to be taken seriously.[49] Thus, the editor of *Die Zeit*, Marion Dönhoff, and her co-editor, former German chancellor Helmut Schmidt, aimed at capturing this sentiment when they endorsed a manifesto that observed that "we Germans remain an endangered people."[50] They feared that the Germans may, yet again, get out of control, because they no longer quite knew where they stand as individuals and as a nation. They were profoundly convinced that this lack of orientation *(Orientierungslosigkeit)*[51] derived from a weak and unformed identity.[52] And they deduced that this weakness may cause havoc, because it always has been that way: "We [the Germans] have a tendency to excessive sentiments, to excitedness and to hubris." Complaining bitterly about the dangers of a new irrationalism, Dönhoff and Schmidt's manifesto continues to elaborate on the problems facing contemporary Germany:

> The citizens are frustrated. Government and opposition are without energy and vision. Most everything is left to happenstance. It is as if history gushes [*rasen*] by us like an unchanneled white-water river, while we, standing on the riverbank, raise the alarmed question as to where all this should lead. Everyone has the wish that it be thought about [*daß darüber nachgedacht wird*], how the world will look or, in any case, how the world should look, and what we have to do in order to get there.[53]

One might read this as a particularly cunning piece of politics designed to steal the thunder from the Right. But it is more likely that Dönhoff's "Manifesto: Because the Country Must Change" exemplifies a widespread sense of politics in which the "state" is called upon to solve basic social and cultural issues in order not to expose the nation to undue danger. As is so often the case, the politics of averting social panic becomes the very source of it. The "unacceptably large unemployment, the huge immigration of foreigners which result in xenophobia and moral decay [*Zersetzung*] at home and a decline of standing and influence in the world" are counted among the pressing political issues to be solved.[54]

In case of doubt, the state is called upon to provide the solution. If Dönhoff and Schmidt packaged this idea in an old-fashioned language of decay and deviance that reminded the reader uncomfortably of the first half of the twentieth century, a younger generation has formulated the same programmatic stance into a more palatable language at least as far as Europe is concerned: "In the future, we seek protection not against the state, but wish that the state may protect us—against private criminality, against privatized misuse of data, against the excesses of individualization and the creeping dissolution of social togetherness that come with it, as well as against the insatiable imperatives of flexibilization that result from global capitalism."[55]

This quest for neoregulationism is a characteristic if diffuse feature of a variety of German debates on social, economic, and cultural issues. It is the social-liberal response to the structural remaking of Germany of which unification has become a part. This cluster of debates has the reformation of the welfare state and the integration of minorities as its subjects. New topics such as protection against globalization, gene technology, and the information society, because they amount to an "unwanted game which is to be played in order to avoid worse," are replacing older ones.[56] Security, redefined as shelter against an anarchic world of markets, has become a key theme. There are all sorts of new "invasions"—of the nation, of the economy, of the individual and his or her body—to deal with. The common feature of all these debates is a profound distrust of the self-regulatory capabilities of society and the presumption that "naturally" it will take the state to maintain a well-ordered society. Due to the tendency (articulated explicitly in the Manifesto) to think of a society left to its own devices as unstable, if not prone to deviance, the slippage between the quest for social justice and law and order is inadvertent and recurs as a matter of course. In the nineties, the Staatsnation has returned from the left-liberal center as agent of regulation and as protector against an anarchic world.

With the Kulturnation coming from the Right and the Staatsnation coming from the Left we have an example for the confusion that leads some German observers to the conclusion that the sky is caving in. For though it is a recovery of a more distant German past, it also entails a reversal of roles. These roles, however, are still inchoate and highly unstable. More realistically we might say that old alliances are falling apart and unexpected and previously unimaginable coalescences of ideas are taking shape. All this points to a "structural transformation of the public sphere" as it has emerged in postwar Germany. This, of course, presumes that there has been such a sphere in the first place, which is a proposition that, ironically, the author of *The Structural Transformation of the Public Sphere* would have considered highly unlikely, if not outright impossible when he wrote his path-breaking *Habilitation* in 1962.[57] Then again, in 1962 nobody would have thought that an academic exercise could possibly become a public event, promoted by a rapidly expanding culture industry.

The Power of Intellectuals?

If we believe an influential strand of opinion in postunification Germany, there is no intellectual culture of the GDR worth remembering.[58] And if we listen to another strand of criticism, there may well not be much of an intellectual culture in contemporary Germany to contend with.[59] Learned opinion has weighed in heavily to the same effect. The "literary-cultural" intelligence has lost its "function" and, hence, is bound to fall.[60] The tenor of commentary in Germany is perhaps somewhat more muted than in France, but the notion of a "dusk" setting in upon intellectuals was, and is, widespread.[61] Hence, it would seem a more accurate rendition of German thought on the state of intellectuals in contemporary Germany to speak of their crisis rather than their power.

The prevailing crisis talk provides us with an opportunity to clarify the kind of intellectuals we are talking about and, more generally, what tools are required in order to talk about them. For the debate on intellectuals slips uncomfortably between two levels of analysis and their respective discursive apparatuses. On one level, it is argued that the very notion of the "modern" intellectual—whether we locate "his" origins in the late eighteenth or the late nineteenth century—is exhausted and has come to an end.[62] If this were the case, it would make sense to put the thunder and lightning of a *Götterdämmerung* aside, stop complaining about television, and go on to assess the new "intelligence" of an information age.[63] If, on the other hand, one wants to understand German intellectuals in the nineties, it is more useful to think about the configuration of the eastern and western intellectual scene as it developed over the past fifty years.

The latter entails not talking about intellectuals as such, because they are about as interesting as a sack of potatoes (which is to say that in case of doubt it is good to have them). What matters are cultural configurations in which intellectuals are capable of exerting palpable influence and of shaping what people—not all, but enough of them to make a difference—think about themselves and the world, including what they identify as "the nation." Such configurations do not exist naturally or, for that matter, by virtue of tradition.[64] Rather, it takes, for one thing, a certain makeup of cultural institutions, a certain social composition, and a consensual mission that makes intellectuals part of a web of interaction. For another, it needs a certain transparency of the public domain that allows intellectuals to exert influence. Neither of these conditions was self-evidently present in Germany after 1945. However, there is enough evidence to suggest that powerful intellectual configurations did fall into place in both East and West Germany whose respective features have become much clearer, now that they are in the process of change and, indeed, disappearance.

Not to make too fine a point, the East German intellectuals got their pedestal knocked out from under them—and this proved true for the "official" intellectuals (whether critical of the regime or not), the dissidents, and expellees inasmuch as they have remained tied to the GDR. The pervasive nature of the calamity suggests that the entire configuration of an intelligentsia was breaking apart rather than that a specific position or element (that is, conformists and regime supporters) was being removed. The dissolution, build-down, and transformation—all summed up in the term *Abwicklung*—of cultural and academic institutions as well as the remaking of the media sector figured prominently in the unmaking of East German intellectuals.[65] For one thing, it hit the bread-and-butter intellectuals more than the stars and thus highlights the depth of the field of intellectuals. For another, the build-down made abundantly clear how dependent the entire sphere, including the dissenters, was on access to state-supplied resources and institutions. The autonomy of intellectuals was highly contingent. The build-down further cut into the composition of the intellectual class, affecting the humanities and social sciences in the academy and the literary culture far more than scientific knowledge and technical expertise. The disqualification of a great deal of professional or "expert" knowledge (in law and business, but also technology) should, however, warn against too clean a distinction between literary-cultural intellectuals and experts. In any case, the main point is that with the (GDR) state-sponsored infrastructure curtailed, the entire intellectual configuration unraveled. The dependence of the intellectuals on the state is striking. It sheds a peculiar light on the claim for autonomy, which was championed most forcefully by the literary establishment. It was an autonomy claimed against the state by intellectuals who depended on the state—and, as it turns out, have a difficult time of thinking themselves beyond the state.

In the end, the decisive factor in the unmaking of East German intellectuals proved to be the loss of their raison d'être. For however diverse the East German intelligentsia was, the entire cultural configuration pivoted on the ability of a literary elite to represent Germany—which is what they came to do remarkably successfully.[66] The centrality of literary intelligence, which formed a distinct sphere in conflict with academy-based metadisciplines such as philosophy on one hand and history on the other, was a source of considerable friction. The GDR mass public just barely tolerated it. But literary-cultural intelligence became the capstone of GDR intellectual culture—and when it crumbled, the entire cultural setup collapsed. In hindsight the diversity of the aesthetic visions of a Christa Wolf, Günter de Bruyn, Wolf Biermann, or Heiner Müller are emerging very clearly. But so is the overarching commonality of their mission or project. East German intellectuals gained their cultural capital from representing the "other" Germany. They were invested with the traditions of Weimar cultural heroes and, more generally, with the spirit of German Enlightenment culture, which was taken as the road to recovery and salvation, as an articulation of the "other" and better Germany.[67] They had come to represent, moreover, the ideal of the autonomous intellectual, unconstrained by West German media capitalism, in opposition to the state, and critical of the cold war. The cultural capital thus accrued was used effectively to capture public sentiment. Not everyone read these writers, and they were always on the verge of an interdict by the regime, but socialist humanism gained wide currency. It became a key element for the self-identification of eastern and western intellectual publics who readily recognized each other's value in this artifice of words and images they had in common. It was a magnificent artifice in which East and West reinforced each other, shaping a public culture in the wake of the war.[68] Aesthetic and cultural reason intertwined to form what Germans readily identified as virtuous art and, hence, at once precious and useful.[69] It took this compelling artifice (and the requisite delivery) to make literary-cultural intellectuals powerful—more powerful, in any case, than any number of experts and professionals.

The plain fact of the matter is that this bubble burst. Hopes for a third Germany between capitalism and state socialism were squashed. The entanglements with the Stasi cast doubt on the autonomous and critical role of intellectuals. Last but not least, the collapse of the GDR left the literary intellectuals no other choice than to go to the market—which is where the more successful ones had been all along, but now they had lost their aura. What collapsed in 1989–90 was the aura of representativeness of East German intellectuals that had held the entire configuration in place.

The dominant West German intellectuals articulated many of the same concerns as their East German equivalents. This western group found its identity in recovering an enlightened humanism from the physical, cultural, and spiritual destruction of the war. Although it toyed with proletarian righteousness off and on, it ultimately pursued a rather bürgerlich ideal, which has led some critics to suspect them as representatives of the complacent affluence of the nineteenth-century French juste milieu. This assessment, however, underestimates the zeal and the mission of West German intellectuals who emerged slowly and remained embattled throughout the long postwar years.[70] They gained their reason and their reasoning from the effort of undoing the Nazi past.[71] Perhaps the most outstanding feature of the entire configuration was its interventionist and oppositional zeal, which contrasted with the altogether more "elevated," representational quality of East German intellectuals and put them at odds with a liberal governmental group, defenders of constitutionality, among whose members Karl Dietrich Bracher or, for that matter, the American Fritz Stern figured most prominently—quite apart from running into the full-blown opposition not simply of conservative academics but all those who, like Helmut Schelsky, dreaded the fusion of the political, the social, and the cultural as "fascist." The sheer aggressiveness of this intellectual culture can hardly be overemphasized. The interventionist intellectuals—the most evident candidates are the writers Heinrich Böll and Günter Grass, the philosopher and social theorist Jürgen Habermas, the psychologists Alexander and Margarete Mitscherlich, the historians Fritz Fischer and Hans-Ulrich Wehler, and, perhaps most of all, public intellectuals such as Hans Magnus Enzensberger—set out to transform society and stylized themselves in opposition to prevailing politics, which they, in turn, characterized as preserving fascist mentalities. The very best of them were superb polemicists. If their activism caught on in the context of the debate on a set of laws concerning the a state of emergency (*Notstandsgesetze*), it found its most telling expression in the rebellion against the generation of the fathers (and mothers), and it had lasting impact as a culture of memory, egged on by an investigative history.[72]

This intellectual activism started out as literary and historical provocation before it settled into being a more learned enlightenment.[73] When Günter Grass launched his aesthetic attack on what Germans considered speakable and unspeakable, be it sex, the past, or the "East," and when he said things in ways that were unheard of, he rattled not just the literary and political establishment but the nation.[74] Fritz Fischer was no less shocking for his argument concerning German war guilt, even if he had no particular wish to scandalize.[75] Of course, it took an audience ready and eager to accept and reject (and the latter was the majority to spread the fame) what these and other West German cultural heroes said to make it the cultural revolution that it was.[76] West German intellectuals depended on this popular support (and on controversy) much as the East Germans depended on the state.[77]

The "new" intellectuals clearly saw themselves as guardians of the nation when they declared society (*Gesellschaft*) their domain. They were, in any case, not what Rainer M. Lepsius, one of the most influential West German sociologists, had laid down as definition and norm for what intellectuals ought to be.[78] They aimed not at establishing a consensus of values but at challenging society and transforming politics; they did not care to open up alternate ways of interpreting the world, but thought of themselves as establishing the truth in a world full of deception that could serve as norm and referent for the remaking of society. Fortunately, they did not know for sure nor could they ever agree on what was good for society, and this kept a vigorous debate going despite a great deal of finger-wagging. Still, this configuration of intellectuals established itself by launching into the world and setting it right. They constituted a public providing models and images (and a smattering of arguments) for all those who stood at factory doors to distribute leaflets or on soapboxes to explain the disaster of nuclear energy or nuclear weapons. They gave meaning and purpose to teachers and educators and shaped an expansive cohort of public intellectuals in a minor key—the many journalists and freelance writers and researchers who became a force in their own right in the seventies and eighties. It thus seems quite appropriate to characterize key members of this intellectual scene—such as Habermas, Grass, or Wehler—as princes in an enlightened aristocracy who defined themselves by their service or duty to society, which they understood as furthering the public education of the people.

The phenomenal success of this scene was driven by the dramatic expansion of the educational sector, with the goal of a classless higher education, and the opening up of cultural institutions with the effect of an uneasy coalescence of high and low culture. Two aspects of this development are of particular import. First, the expansion of the educational and cultural institutions brought into alignment what had been traditionally oppositional camps: literary elites on one hand and academics on the other.[79] The fissures between the two remained, but their leading representatives made common cause in the education of the nation. Second, the expansion of educational opportunities and the desegregation of high culture created a constituency of the well-educated that formed less a class or stratum than a sphere of discussion and debate that identified its members as part of a broad-based meritocracy—and since education was expanding so dramatically, one could at times think of this sphere as a mass culture. If it was not quite that, it still produced something tactile and tangible. Older class and gender divisions (and a much-underrated urban-rural, Protestant-Catholic divide) were folded into a new social identity that took its cues from their enlightenment princes but otherwise developed a thick everyday culture that is most commonly associated with, but not limited to, the new social movements. An educated society emerged that had the clout—an elite, institutions, a mass base, and a raison d'être—to define itself as the public culture that formed a distinctly West German nation.

The intellectual and, one might even be inclined to say, spiritual force that moved this diverse group and its audience (and thus made a public sphere happen) was the effort of undoing and overcoming the legacies and effects of the Third Reich and Nazism. Initially this amounted to a frontal attack on Nazis and their recrudescence in the fifties.[80] A distinctly enlightening public sphere formed with the intent of not simply blocking Nazis but overcoming the corrosion of cultural values and moral norms as well as the misuse of knowledge that both produced Nazism and was its main legacy. The enlightening activism was endowed with a Whiggish sense of progress—configured as either marxist or Weberian—in which Nazism and all its attending ideological and political formations were seen as part of an older world in decay. It was so distinctly—some would say anachronistically—an enlightening culture because moral reform and the reconstitution of civility were its very essence. This moral impulse extended into what one might see as a "romantic" and "irrational" countermovement (like the environmental and pacifist movements). The latter remained tied to the overall agenda of melioration and moral improvement, even as it toyed with and occasionally crossed over into a language of anti-enlightenment. In any case, inasmuch as this enlightening public sphere had an influence, it gained and exerted it in the form of a moral imperative for German society to become aware of and overcome the societal and cultural legacies of Nazism, war, and genocide.

The peculiar power of the enlightening public sphere consisted in its ability to convince a sufficiently large number of people that conversion was a good and necessary thing in order to overcome the past. The new enlightenment of the seventies and eighties had all the trappings of a secular religion. It does not at all surprise that the self-perception of this public was different. In claiming that the new enlightenment necessarily followed from the devastation of war and genocide, its main proponents naturalized what effectively was a competitive situation. They understood themselves as, by necessity, the spirit that could move Germany beyond the legacies of the Third Reich and that, because of the effective destruction of civility and culture, was destined to proselytize a new culture. The missionary fervor of this public, much as its appeal, cannot be underestimated.

The tensions within this configuration have caught public attention more than has the overall thrust to convert German society into a better, postfascist nation. Subcultures of all kinds splintered off from the dominant configuration. The older guard of rationalists fought a younger cohort of "romantics" tooth and nail over issues of gender, multiculturalism, and everyday history. Neither can the boundaries and exclusions of this public culture be overlooked. Despite its expansiveness and its ability to cross traditional divisions in German society, it always remained a meritocratic culture with a tendency to castigate the masses—if not for mass consumption, then for their craving for security or their lack of convictions.[81] It remained stunningly male. It also elicited virulent counterattacks from a more conservative camp whose mainstay was initially in the universities but increasingly also in the "reputable" media—for their intrusion into the political realm, for their heavy-handed enlightenment moralism, for their celebration of public as opposed to more purely aesthetic and scholarly values, and not least for their "antinational" politics of contrition.[82] In short, this cultural configuration was enwrapped in a thick tangle of confrontations and engagements.

It would seem appropriate, then, to recover the competitiveness of attempts to capture the public. The ability of this new public sphere to marginalize alternatives and oppositions and to elide the very issue of marginalization is one of the best indicator of its power. But there were limits. As mentioned, it ran up against a more conservative and Christian camp and vociferous academic detractors of the new clerisy. It is altogether more important, though, that the new enlightenment never really caught on to a much more Catholic, shame- rather than guilt-driven culture of memory and stayed aloof from the transformation of popular culture.[83] It never came to grips with a more entertainment-oriented culture.

None of this diminished the power of its intellectual elites. But they fell on harder times in the nineties. Unification and the difficulties of orientation in a united Germany were part of the issue, all the more since quite a few of the princes had come out against a united Germany.[84] Perhaps more important, they made no bones about their distaste for the new populism of Chancellor Kohl's unification policies.[85] Their visceral opposition seemed vindicated during the rash of xenophobic violence that ran like a brush fire through the newly unified country. But the damage was done. The easy presumption that the intellectuals could speak for the people whom they took to task collapsed. The breach was widened by an all-out offensive by conservative states, public institutions, and media, with competing claims on "the nation" as the banner issue.[86] Unification opened up a new field of competition. The incorporation of East Germany became the sectarian battle ground in the fight over change in the West German balance of culture and power. It was a battle over meaning and identity as much as it was over jobs and media control. Whoever expanded faster and whoever captured (or was capable of defining) eastern German sentiment better would emerge on top. An editorial of the *Frankfurter Allgemeine Zeitung*, the national liberal opinion maker, made no bones about the main thrust of the post-1989 debates over the future of the intellectuals. German intellectuals were engaged in a *Kulturkampf*.[87] The editorial portrayed this cultural struggle as an opportunity for a rollback of the left-liberal progressivism of the old Federal Republic, a reversal of fortunes of what the editors considered West and East German postwar orthodoxy—*Gesinnungsliteratur* (moralizing literature) and *Betroffenheitskult* (sentimentalism, search for authenticity).[88]

In the end, neither side won these culture wars. The East German intellectuals got mauled badly. The old guard of West German intellectuals and counterintellectuals are still doing battle and are still capable of raising a storm.[89] But the configuration within which these battles made sense is rapidly falling apart. The institutions that have formed the backbone of postwar intellectual culture have been turned upside down with the privatization of radio, television, and last but not least telecommunications, the globalization of the publishing industry, and the mass-marketization of culture as commodity and of knowledge as intelligence. Higher education is bound to change, if only because the unsolved problems of a mass university, vastly aggravated by unification, have rendered the educational system dysfunctional. The mostly municipal and state-centered public cultures of the stage, of libraries, and of public education are in serious crisis due to massive cutbacks. In short, the entire infrastructure of postwar culture has come under serious strain. In their own way, West German intellectuals had to discover that they could not rely on society in maintaining the fiction of a public culture the intellectuals thought was their own.[90]

The meritocratic ideal and spiritual center of this culture has gone up in smoke even faster. Knowledge still gives one the passkey to upward mobility, but the presumption that a "critical," humanist knowledge would make the difference has evaporated. Although it never actually was a sociological reality, it now seems that even the belief has vanished.[91] The most important indicator of change, though, is the inability to sustain the effort of remaking Germany into a better society, which German intellectuals tend to discuss as crisis of utopian designs.[92] The zeal is still there. But the goal has become uncertain, as the debate on asylum and immigration or, for that matter, the out-of-area use of the German military suggests. Not least, a vociferous and, indeed, venomous populist opposition has been forming which has challenged the intellectuals as so many talking heads one can do without. This challenge, in conjunction with the other woes, indicates that the notion of the intellectual as the guardian of society is no longer accepted.

Is this the end of "the intellectual"? The problem of the old antagonists of the Federal Republic and of the virtuous counterpublic of the former GDR is that they needed each other and fed off each other but now are faced with a much younger generation that shows none of the compunctions of the old. At the same time, all of them depended in equal measure on the real and imagined constraints imposed by the climate of the cold war on Germany's politics and culture. With (the presumption of) these constraints removed, the stakes have increased dramatically. The emergent controversies of the nineties concerned themselves with the norms and standards of public conduct in Germany—who should articulate and who should police them.[93] Last but not least, they are struggles over the powers of the state—how and by whom they should be used. It has become quite common to think of these controversies as identity wars or cultural wars. But it is more to the point to think of them as conflicts over self-determination. After all, it is now for the Germans to figure out what they want to do with themselves after having become sovereign. They now have themselves, in the present, to contend with. It turns out that this is a daunting task for politicians and intellectuals alike, a task for which both the eastern and the western past had left them remarkably unprepared. But they never stopped talking and writing. Not only have all efforts to expunge the memory of the disastrous collapse of civility in twentieth-century Germany been rebuffed, but the memory of this rupture of civility is the source of some of the most energetic new thinking and writing that is emerging from Germany. It is too early to write about the German "enigma of arrival."[94] But it is safe to say that it pays to watch out for it.

Notes

1. Lothar Probst, ed., *Differenz in der Einheit: Über die kulturellen Unterschiede der Deutschen in Ost und West* (Berlin, 1999).

2. Andrei S. Markovits and Simon Reich, *The German Predicament: Memory and Power in the New Europe* (Ithaca, 1997).

3. Durs Grünbein, *Den teuren Toten: 33 Epitaphe* (Frankfurt am Main, 1994).

4. Klaus Scherpe,"The German Intelligentsia in a Time of Change," *European Studies Journal* 10 (1993): 297–311; Claudia Mayer-Iswandy, "Ästhetik und Macht: Zur dikursiven Unordnung im vereinten Deutschland," *German Studies Review* 19, no. 3 (1996): 501–23.

5. Wolfgang Engler, *Die Ostdeutschen: Kunde von einem verlorenen Land* (Berlin, 1999).

6. Otthein Ramstedt and Gert Schmidt, eds., *BRD ade! Vierzig Jahre in Rück-Ansichten* (Frankfurt am Main, 1992).

7. Jürgen Habermas, *A Berlin Republic: Writings on Germany*, trans. Steven Randall (Lincoln, 1997). The German original was published in 1995. On Habermas, see Jan-Werner Müller, *Another Country: German Intellectuals, Unification, and National Identity* (New Haven, 2000).

8. Heimo Schwilk and Ulrich Schacht, eds., *Die selbstbewusste Nation: "Anschwellender Bocksgesang" und weitere Beiträge zu einer deutschen Debatte* (Berlin, 1994).

9. Gabriele Goettle, *Deutsche Sitten: Erkundungen in Ost und West* (Frankfurt am Main, 1991), Goettle, *Freibank: Kultur minderer Güte, amtlich geprüft* (Frankfurt am Main, 1995), and Goettle, *Deutsche Spuren: Erkenntnisse aus Ost und West* (Frankfurt am Main, 1998) trace a distinct progression.

10. See the special issue "One Nation—Which Past? Historiography and German Identities in the 1990s," ed. Christhard Hoffmann, *German Politics and Society* 15, no. 2 (1997); Müller, *Another Country*.

11. Bernhard Giesen, *Intellectuals and the German Nation: Collective Identity in an Axial Age*, trans. Nicholas Levis and Amos Weisz (New York, 1998); Peter Glotz, *Die beschleunigte Gesellschaft: Kulturkämpfe im digitalen Kapitalismus* (Munich, 1999).

12. Konrad H. Jarausch, *The Rush to German Unity* (New York, 1994).

13. Willy Brandt, ". . . was zusammengehört." *Reden zu Deutschland* (Bonn, 1990).

14. Jürgen Kocka, *Die Vereinigungskrise: Zur Geschichte der Gegenwart* (Göttingen, 1995).

15. In the first critical assessment: Claus Offe, *Der Tunnel am Ende des Lichts: Erkundungen der politischen Transformation im Neuen Deutschland* (Frankfurt, 1994).

16. Paul Kennedy, *The Rise and Fall of the Great Powers: Economic Change and Military Conflict from 1500 to 2000* (New York, 1987).

17. Arnulf Baring, *Unser neuer Größenwahn: Deutschland zwischen Ost und West* (Stuttgart, 1989).

18. Jens Reich, *Rückkehr nach Europa: Bericht zur neuen Lage der deutschen Nation* (Munich, 1991); Lothar Probst, *Ostdeutsche Bürgerbewegungen und Perspektiven der Demokratie: Entstehung, Bedeutung, Zukunft* (Cologne, 1993).

19. Christian Meier, *Die Nation, die keine sein will* (Munich, 1991).

20. Hans-Peter Schwarz, "Das Ende der Identitätsneurose," *Rheinischer Merkur*, 7 September 1990, and, in contrast, Jürgen Habermas, "Wir sind wieder 'normal' geworden," *Die Zeit*, 18 December 1992; Stefan Berger, "Der Dogmatismus des Normalen," *Frankfurter Rundschau*, 26 April 1996.

21. Karl Heinz Bohrer, "Provinzialismus (I–VI)," *Merkur* 44 (1990): 1096–1102; 45 (1991), 255–61, 348–56, 537–45, 710–27, 1059–67.

22. Hans-Peter Schwarz, *Die Zentralmacht Europas: Deutschlands Rückkehr auf die Weltbühne* (Berlin, 1994), and Schwarz, *Die gezähmten Deutschen: Von der Machtbesessenheit zur Machtvergessenheit* (Stuttgart, 1995).

23. John S. Duffield, *Political Culture, International Institutions, and German Security Policy After Unification* (Stanford, 1998); Andrei S. Markovits and Simon Reich, *The German Predicament: Memory and Power in the New Europa* (Ithaca, 1997).

24. Klaus J. Bade, ed., *Das Manifest der 60: Deutschland und die Einwanderung* (Munich, 1994).

25. Karl Deiritz and Hannes Krauss, eds., *Der deutsch-deutsche Literaturstreit oder "Freunde, es spricht sich schlecht mit gebundener Zunge": Analysen und Materialien* (Frankfurt am Main, 1991).

26. Konrad H. Jarausch, "Normalisierung oder Re-Nationalisierung? Zur Umdeutung der deutschen Vergangenheit," *Geschichte und Gesellschaft* 21 (1995): 559–72.

27. Cora Stephan, *Der Betroffenheitskult: Eine politische Sittengeschichte* (Berlin, 1993).

28. Fritz J. Raddatz, "Günter Grass, deutscher Dichter," *Die Zeit*, 10 October 1997, 1, 6.

29. Hans Magnus Enzensberger, *Aussichten auf den Bürgerkrieg* (Frankfurt am Main, 1993).

30. Frank Schirrmacher, ed., *Die Walser-Bubis-Debatte: Eine Dokumentation* (Frankfurt am Main, 1999). For a candid reflection on this tension see Martin Walser, "Über das Selbstgespräch: Ein flagranter Versuch." *Die Zeit*, 13 January 2000, 42–43.

31. A good summary is Karl Heinz Bohrer, "Provinzialismus," *Merkur* 44 (1990): 1096–1102; see also Müller, *Another Country*, 177–98.

32. Hans-Jürgen Syberberg, *Vom Unglück und Glück der Kunst in Deutschland nach dem letzten Kriege* (Munich, 1990).

33. Ibid., 90–91.

34. Botho Strauß, "Anschwellender Bocksgesang, " *Der Spiegel*, 8 February 1993, 202–7. See also Stephen Brockmann, "The Good Person of Germany as a Post-Unification Discursive Phenomenon," *German Politics and Society* 15 (1998): 1–25.

35. Karl Heinz Bohrer, ed., *Sprachen der Ironie—Sprachen des Ernstes* (Frankfurt am Main, 2000).

36. Michael Weck, "Der ironische Westen und der tragische Osten," *Kursbuch* 109 (1992): 133–46.

37. Karl Heinz Bohrer, *Die gefährdete Phantasie* (Munich, 1970), and Bohrer, *Plötzlichkeit Zum Augenblick des ästhetischen Scheins* (Frankfurt am Main, 1981) (Suddenness: On the moment of aesthetic appearance, trans. Ruth Crowley [New York, 1994]).

38. Wolfgang Dümcke and Fritz Vilmar, eds., *Die Kolonialisierung der DDR: Kritische Analysen und Alternativen des Einigungsprozesses* (Münster, 1995).

39. Kurt Biedenkopf, "Kurt Biedenkopf und der Abschied von der 'Aufholjagd': Wie sich der sächsische Ministerpräsident die unterschiedliche ökonomische und soziale Entwicklung in Ost und West vorstellt," *Frankfurter Rundschau*, 27 March 1992.

40. Barbara Einhorn, *Cinderella Goes to Market: Citizenship, Gender, and Women's Movements in Eastern Europe* (New York, 1993); Ellen E. Berry, ed., *Postcommunism and the Body Politic* (New York, 1995).

41. Joyce Marie Mushaben, *From Post-War to Post-Wall Generations: Changing Attitudes Toward the National Question and NATO in the Federal Republic of Germany* (Boulder, 1998), esp. 315–59.

42. Jan Ross, "Die Geister, die der Krieg rief," *Die Zeit* 17 June 1999, 11–4.

43. Hauke Brunkhorst, *Der entzauberte Intellektuelle: Über die neue Beliebigkeit des Denkens* (Hamburg, 1990).

44. Francis Fukuyama, *The End of History and the Last Man* (New York, 1992); Robert Kurz, *Der Kollaps der Modernisierung* (Frankfurt, 1991); Robert Kurz, *Der Letzte macht das Licht aus: Zur Krise von Demokratie und Marktwirtschaft* (Berlin, 1993).

45. [Arnulf Baring,] "Sind die Liberalen noch zu retten?" *Die Woche* [Beilage], 17 March 1994.

46. Thomas E. Schmidt, "Die Geburt konservativer Bürgerethik aus dem Geist

der Kulturkritik," *Freibeuter* 61 (1994): 80–89, speaks of *Liberalkonservatismus* but overlooks the left-wing strands of the debate on values.

47. For literature proper: Robert Weninger and Brigitte Rossbacher, eds., *Wendezeiten, Zeitenwende: Positionsbestimmungen zur deutschsprachigen Literatur 1945–1995* (Tübingen, 1997).

48. "Alte Tugenden, neue Werte," [Roundtable], *Die Zeit*, 24 December 1994.

49. Karl Dietrich Bracher, "Zeitgeschichtliche Anmerkungen zum 'Zeitenbruch' von 1989/90," *Neue Züricher Zeitung*, 20 January 1991.

50. Marion Dönhoff et al., *Ein Manifest: Weil das Land sich ändern muss* (Reinbek, 1992), 113. The manifesto was signed by an unusual combination of personalities: Marion Dönhoff (editor, *Die Zeit*), Meinhard Miegel (executive director, Institut für Wirtschaft und Gesellschaft), Wilhelm Nölling (president, State Central Bank of Hamburg), Edzard Reuter (CEO, Daimler Benz), Helmut Schmidt (former chancellor and editor, *Die Zeit*), Richard Schröder (former dissident, professor of theology, Humboldt University Berlin), Wolfgang Thierse (former dissident, SPD member of parliament), and Ernst Ulrich von Weizsäcker (director, Institut für Klima, Umwelt, und Energie).

51. Jörg Calließ, ed., *Historische Orientierung nach der Epochenwende* (Loccum, 1993).

52. Werner Weidenfeld, "Identität," in *Handwörterbuch zur deutschen Einheit*, ed. Werner Weidenfeld (Frankfurt, 1992), 376–83.

53. Dönhoff, *Manifesto*, 9.

54. Ibid.

55. Susanne Gaschke, "Vater Staat und seine Kinder," *Die Zeit*, 7 October 1999, 45.

56. The vox populi puts it this way: "Of course, it is strange. We Europeans have reached a point where we all want to be. We join the social market economy with cultural diversity and have an eye for the environment. This is not the case in the United States which has the consequence that globalization threatens our values. And since only the victor can change the rules, we must, under current conditions, become as efficient as the United States, if we want a world order that reflects European values." "Ein ungewolltes Spiel mitspielen, um Schlimmeres zu verhüten: Europa und die Veränderungen des Weltmarktes—Votrag von Professor Franz Josef Rademacher beim Jahrestag des TÜV," *Darmstädter Echo*, 3 April 2000, 7.

57. Jürgen Habermas, *Strukturwandel der Öffentlichkeit: Untersuchungen zu einer Kategorie der bürgerlichen Gesellschaft* (Neuwied, 1962), rev. German ed. 1990. (The structural transformation of the public sphere: An inquiry into a category of bourgeois society, trans. Thomas Burger [Cambridge, Mass., 1989]).

58. Sabine Brandt, "Wer spricht vom Versagen der Briefträger: 'Etwas echt Deutsches': Die Frage nach den Fehlleistungen der Intellektuellen," *Frankfurter Allgemeine Zeitung* 11 December 1992, 35; Thomas Anz, ed., *"Es geht nicht um Christa Wolf": Der Literaturstreit im Vereinigten Deutschland* (Munich, 1991).

59. Frank Schirrmacher, "Das Prinzip Handwerk: Zurück zur Kunst nach Jahrzehnten des Dilletantismus," *Frankfurter Allgemeine Zeitung*, 5 March 1995; Eckhard Henscheid, "Weltwachgeister; Planstellen deutscher Literatur (I)," *Frankfurter Allgemeine Zeitung*, 4 January 1994, and his " 'Der Softie als Rambo'; Planstellen deutscher Literatur (II)," ibid., 6 January 1994.

60. Wolf Lepenies, *Aufstieg und Fall der Intellektuellen in Europa* (Frankfurt, 1992), 63.

61. Martin Meyer, ed., *Intellektuellendämmerung: Beiträge zur neuesten Zeit des Geistes* (Munich, 1992).

62. Jean-François Lyotard, *Tombeau de l'intellectuel, et autres papiers* (Paris, 1984).

63. I am deliberately speaking of "intelligence," because one of the key signatures of the new intellect is the dissolution of the "modern" linking of subjectivity and knowledge. "Cogito ergo sum" is no longer the issue. In a world of interactive, artificial, and human intelligences, the subject is being thought.

64. I take the "rediscovery" of German intellectuals in the Wilhelmine Empire as a successful example of this kind of analysis. See Gangolf Hübinger and Wolfgang J. Mommsen, eds., *Intellektuelle im Kaiserreich* (Frankfurt am Main, 1993); Wolfgang J. Mommsen, *Bürgerliche Kultur und künstlerische Avantgarde* (Frankfurt am Main, 1994).

65. The *Abwicklung* is still a highly contested subject about which there is little agreement. Its consequences, however, were clearly foreseen by Heinz Ludwig Arnold and Frauke Meyer-Gosau, eds., *Die Abwicklung der DDR* (Göttingen, 1992).

66. Stephen Brockmann, "Literature and Convergence," in *Beyond 1989: Re-Reading German Literary History Since 1945*, ed. Keith Bullivant (Providence, 1997), 49–67.

67. Keith Bullivant, "The End of the Dream of the 'Other Germany': The 'German Question' in West German Letters," in *1870/71–1989/90: German Unifications and the Change of Literary Discourse*, ed. Walter Pape (Berlin, 1993), 303–19.

68. Cora Stephan, ed., *Wir Kollaborateure: Der Westen und die deutschen Vergangenheiten* (Reinbek, 1992).

69. Bernd Hüppauf, "Moral oder Sprache: DDR-Literatur vor der Moderne," in *Literatur in der DDR: Rückblicke*, ed. Heinz-Ludwig Arnold (Munich, 1991); Wolfgang Emmerich, "Affirmation-Utopie-Melancholie: Versuch einer Bilanz von vierzig Jahren DDR Literatur," *German Studies Review* 14 (1991): 325–44.

70. The critical position is marked by Frank Schirrmacher, "Abschied von der Literatur der Bundesrepublik," *Frankfurter Allgemeine Zeitung*, 2 October 1990, and in the countercritique as in Wolfram Schütte, "Auf dem Schrotthaufen der Geschichte: Zu einer denkwürdig-voreiligen Verabschiedung der bundesdeutschen Literatur," *Frankfurter Rundschau*, 20 October 1989; Ulrich Greiner, "Die deutsche Gesinnungsästhetik," *Die Zeit*, 2 November 1990; Eberhard Rathgeb and Thomas Steinfeld, "Egalitäre Bundesrepublik: Die politische Ästhetik kultureller Ereignisse," *Merkur* 49 (1995): 865–74.

71. Jürgen Habermas, "Einleitung," in *Geistige Situation der Zeit*, ed. Jürgen Habermas, vol. 1: *Nation und Republik* (Frankfurt, 1979), 7–35; Siegfried Mews, "Moralist versus Pragmatist? Heinrich Böll and Güter Grass as Political Writers," in *Coping with the Past: Germany and Austria After 1945*, ed. Kathy Harms et al. (Madison, 1990), 140–54.

72. Edgar Wolfrum, *Geschichtspolitik in der Bundesrepublik Deutschland: Der Weg zur bundesrepublikanischen Erinnerung 1948–1990* (Darmstadt, 1999).

73. Klaus Wagenbach, ed., *Vaterland, Muttersprache: Deutsche Schriftsteller und ihr Staat seit 1945* (Berlin, 1994); Helmut L. Müller, *Die literarische Republik: Westdeutsche Schriftsteller und die Politik* (Weinheim, 1982).

74. Günter Grass, *Die Blechtrommel* (Darmstadt, 1960) (The tin drum, trans. Ralph Manheim [New York, 1963]).

75. Fritz Fischer, *Griff nach der Weltmacht: Die Kriegszielpolitik des kaiserlichen*

Deutschland 1914–18 (Düsseldorf, 1962) (Germany's aims in the first world war [New York, 1967]).

76. Clemens Albrecht et al., *Die intellektuelle Gründung der Bundesrepublik: Eine Wirkungsgeschichte der Frankfurter Schule* (Frankfurt am Main, 1999).

77. Again, this becomes most evident in the critique of this populism that is the subject of one of the most influential essays of the nineties, Botho Strauß, "Anschwellender Bocksgesang," *Der Spiegel,* 8 February 1993, 202–7. A brief discussion of the context is Jay J. Rosellini, "A Revival of Conservative Literature? The "Spiegel-Symposium 1993" and Beyond," in *Beyond 1989: Re-Reading German Literary History since 1945,* ed. Keith Bullivant (Providence, 1997), 109–28.

78. Rainer M. Lepsius, "Kritik als Beruf: Zur Soziologie der Intellektuellen," *Kölner Zeitschrift für Soziologie und Sozialpsychologie* 16 (1964): 75–91.

79. Hauke Brunkhorst, *Der Intellektuelle im Land der Mandarine* (Frankfurt am Main, 1987); Wolf Lepenies, *Between Literature and Science: The Rise of Sociology* (Cambridge, 1988).

80. Norbert Frei, *Vergangenheitspolitik: Die Anfänge der Bundesrepublik und die NS-Vergangenheit* (Munich, 1996); Jürgen Danyel, ed., *Die geteilte Vergangenheit: Zum Umgang mit Nationalsozialismus und Widerstand in beiden deutschen Staaten* (Berlin, 1995); Jochen Vogt, *"Die Erinnerung ist unsere Aufgabe": Über Literatur, Moral and Politik 1945–1990* (Opladen, 1991).

81. John Carey, *The Intellectuals and the Masses: Pride and Prejudice Among the Literary Intelligentsia 1880–1939* (London, 1992) is the classic example. The issue is picked up, somewhat surprisingly, by Peter Slotterdijk, *Die Verachtung der Massen: Versuch über Kulturkämpfe in der modernen Gesellschaft* (Frankfurt am Main, 2000).

82. Helmut Schelsky, *Die Arbeit tun die anderen: Klassenkampf u. Priesterherrschaft die Intellektuellen* (Opladen, 1975); Kurt Sontheimer, *Das Elend unserer Intellektuellen: Linke Theorie in der Bundesrepublik Deutschland* (Hamburg, 1976).

83. Michael Geyer, "The Politics of Memory in Contemporary Germany," in *Radical Evil,* ed. Joan Copjec (London, 1996), 169–200.

84. Most famously Günter Grass, *Deutscher Lastenausgleich: Wider das dumpfe Einheitsgebot: Reden und Gespräche* (Frankfurt am Main, 1990).

85. Wolfgang Herles, *Nationalrausch: Szenen aus dem gesamtdeutschen Machtkampf* (Munich, 1990).

86. Jan-Werner Müller, "Preparing for the Political: German Intellectuals Confront the 'Berlin Republic,'" *New German Critique* 72 (1997): 151–76, makes the important point that the talk about the nation is, in fact, talk about the state. One of the most interesting and telling texts of this kind is Dieter Henrich, *Eine Republik Deutschland: Reflexionen auf dem Weg aus der deutschen Teilung* (Frankfurt am Main, 1990).

87. Eckhard Fuhr, "Ein Kulturkampf," *Frankfurter Allgemeine Zeitung,* 26 September 1993. See also John Ely,"The *Frankfurter Allgemeine Zeitung* and Contemporary National-Conservatism," *German Politics and Society* 13, no. 2 (1995): 81–121.

88. Frank Schirrmacher, "Abschied von der Literatur der Bundesrepublik: Neue Pässe, Neue Identitäten, neue Lebensläufe: Über die Kündigung einiger Mythen des westdeutschen Bewußtseins," *Frankfurter Allgemeine Zeitung,* 2 October 1990; Ulrich Greiner, "Was bleibt? Bleibt was?," *Die Zeit,* 1 June 1990; Ulrich Greiner, "Die deutsche Gesinnungsästhetik," *Die Zeit,* 2 November 1990; Karl Heinz Bohrer, "Kulturschutzgebiet DDR?" *Merkur* 10–11 (1990): 1015–17.

89. Peter Sloterdijk, *Regeln für den Menschenpark: Ein Antwortschreiben zu Heideggers Brief über den Humanismus* (Frankfurt am Main, 1999), with a fulsome attack against "critical theory"—and the debate in *Die Zeit* 36–40, 2 September–7 October 1999

90. It is one of the fascinating sideshows that the West German cultural sector has always been a predominantly commercial sector and that the enlightenment public culture depended, to a large degree, on a commercial publishing and media industry. Andreas Johannes Wiesand, "The state of the Kulturstaat: Ideas, Theses, and Facts from a German and European Perspective," in *The Cultural Legitimacy of the Federal Republic: Assessing the Kulturstaat,* ed. Frank Trommler (Washington, D.C., 1999).

91. I take Peter Sloterdik, ed., *Vor der Jahrtausendwende: Berichte zur Lage der Zukunft,* 2 vols. (Frankfurt am Main, 1990), as a symptomatic text that contrasts and compares with Jürgen Habermas, ed., *Stichworte zur geistigen Situation der Zeit,* 2 vols. (Frankfurt am Main, 1979).

92. Werner von Bergen and Walter H. Pehle, eds., *Denken im Zwiespalt: Über den Verrat von Intellektuellen im 20. Jahrhundert* (Frankfurt am Main 1996).

93. Heinz Bude, *Die ironische Nation: Soziologie als Zeitdiagnose* (Hamburg, 1999).

94. V. S. Naipaul, *The Enigma of Arrival* (New York, 1987).

ALEXANDER KLUGE

Translated by Devin Pendas

The Moment of Tragic Recognition
with a Happy Ending

**Why the Public Sphere Is a Common Good Which Cannot Be
Sold at Any Price in the World (Common Good = Personal Property
Belonging to Each One of Us)**

In the eighteenth century the public sphere had yet to emancipate itself
from the state and other powers. In his essay "What Does It Mean to
Orient One's Self in Thought?" Immanuel Kant put it this way: "[T]he
external power which deprives people of their freedom to *communicate*
their thoughts publicly also deprives them of the freedom to *think* because
the only guarantee for the 'validity' of our thinking actually lies in the
fact that we think, as it were, in community with others with whom we
mutually share our thoughts."[1]

Thinking is not thinking if it is limited to monologue; the reply, the
acknowledgment of my thought in the response of others, above all, is
thinking. Since I cannot live without thinking (and, as Heinrich von
Kleist said, this also means "the discriminating faculty of emotions"), the
elementary ability to have an exchange with others, to create a public
sphere, is necessary for living. It is not pathos but praxis that makes a rich
and diverse public sphere a prerequisite for my ability to trust myself, and
trusting myself I can then trust others. The production of this trust is both
the function and the lifeblood of the public sphere.

Gotthold Ephraim Lessing wanted to expand these ideas even further.
He argued that for a thinker it is not sufficient to sit, free and alone, in
his study, think something, and then have it published. Rather, he needs
the foil of those actually present, a public sphere that derives from the
stage. As we know, he wanted to found a national theater in Hamburg.
This plan created misunderstandings with the city. All that remains of the
project is the monument we see in the Gänsemarkt: a verdigrised statue
of Lessing sitting in a relaxed pose, like an enterprising person, lightly

resting one hand on his knee, and a finger holding his place in a book. And so every day he looks out at the hustle and bustle of the Gänsemarkt and its strange new buildings. A public that is absent on Sunday, returns again early Monday, and disappears again in the evenings—that is what characterizes Hamburg's inner-city public sphere.

At this point I would like to pose a rhetorical question: What about the public sphere makes it a kind of personal property that should not be sold at any price? that makes it a property as personal as the air we breathe and as unsalable as one's life history? For I cannot sell a person, and neither can we sell our hopes.

In reality, however, the following happens: In the face of immediate danger, discussion groups who lay claim to public status develop in niches provided by the church. After a while, it becomes clear that, if they practice nonviolence, if they do not give the state the legitimation necessary to deploy armed force, then the members of this public sphere have the power to bring down the state.

The flip side of this image is that, a few weeks later, in precisely the same place, this public sphere belongs to other people; that these people fly other flags and propose other slogans; and that this public sphere, too, dissolves quite fast. As happened after November 9, 1918, the upheaval lasts until shortly after Christmas or New Year's Eve. There follows the January crisis, the turn within the turn (die Wende in der Wende). Back in 1919, the image of the National Assembly replaced that of the Councils (Räte) or the Round Tables (Runde Tische), both of which sought, in full knowledge of the catastrophe of World War I, to mediate between the immediate experience of individuals and the entity of the state.

Very similar concerns emerged after November 9, 1989, and, again, after the March 1990 elections. In the end, the media could endlessly multiply and disseminate the events, as they originally had taken place, to the constituents of an indirect public sphere of the Federal Republic who were not engaged in and directly affected by the events. The original situation was gone with the wind and could no longer be ascertained.

An important figure in this short-lived public sphere was Jens Reich. Formerly a scientist, he participated in the revolt and, for six weeks, his voice was heard by millions of people. We are both the sons of doctors, raised in the same city; he is the son of Dr. Reich and I of Dr. Kluge. Yes, our fathers held themselves to the standard of good physicians, beloved by the people, making nighttime house calls and such. And we sons inherited their pride. A good deal of our persistence comes from the persistence of our fathers, who visited patients in emergencies even on Christmas Eve. This ethos gives rise to a certain attitude that we seek to emulate.

The public sphere that remains of what I hesitate to call the former German Democratic Republic has today become a marketplace. All kinds of opportunities are created to hand over broad segments of the public sphere to anyone who has the means to invest, so that an immediate and autonomous public sphere is no longer even viable as a project. Heiner Müller, the president of the Academy of the Arts (formerly the Prussian Academy), resides there alone and hopes that he can rescue this institution—as a piece of public life. But the academy is interested in anything but promoting public life or enriching it with new business. Instead, it seems to be burdened with mistrust and a lack of self-trust.

So what is the use value of the public? Of a public sphere whose beginnings are short-lived and that seems to be subject to spontaneous processes of disintegration? Two observations can be made about the weakness of the public sphere.

In the *Hamburg Dramaturgy*, Lessing defends Shakespeare's themes against French tragedy's doctrine of virtue.[2] A father is deserted by all his daughters, save one, and it is she who dies. A man sets out from Wittenberg sensing that his father has been murdered; his step-father has dishonored his mother. Othello's uncontrollable jealousy is spawned by a wager between two men; the deadly conspiracy begins as a game. Shakespeare's plots correspond to experiences that derive their power from the sphere of intimacy. These intimate spheres are the great sources of substance in every society. The public sphere cannot accept these expressions of emotion directly. It prefers diluted expressions and evasive strategies when it comes to the powers of the intimate. This is one cause of its weakness.

On the other side, we observe the current explosion of free enterprise in the former GDR. The second great sphere of lived experience obviously consists of commercial enterprise and the production process. Our activities in the commercial sphere fill the lion's share of our lifetime. This second sphere of experience is also constituted privately. By itself this energy does not strive toward public exchange, understanding with others, or community. The principle of privatization defines the two most important sources of what people do during their lifetimes. This means that the public must constitute itself from energies that are weaker than the forces that derive from the two major private spheres and for whom the will of the majority counts only to a limited extent.

At this point, an antagonism arises that *further* weakens the public sphere: the authority of the republic (*Gemeinwesen*) derives from its claim to represent the whole. The public, in turn, which subtends the community, therefore cannot admit that it is composed of mere fragments.

I can demonstrate to you the price every public broadcasting and tele-vision station pays to maintain its high level of legitimation. It is supposed to report on everything and to provide an additional window in the room where everything essential in the world is shown, but this is precisely what it cannot do as an institution of public law. This mandate leads to the phenomenon that Bert Brecht describes in his fable of the laurel tree, which was trimmed into an ever more perfect shape until it completely disappeared.[3] That is to say that the public sphere has an intrinsic tendency to void itself and to weaken. It is in this respect that Hannah Arendt's point in her Lessing lecture is so important: Lessing valorizes human feelings that are considered *weaker* and yet are also more continuous and have their specific quality in a certain stubbornness, as, for example, friendship, hospitality, the need to gossip, the need to exchange all sorts of intelligence without any particular purpose.[4] The forms of sociability among human beings—as social beings—that do not prevail in catastrophic situations and are withdrawn like the feelers of a snail in case of danger are precisely the ones we need in order to found human community and a public sphere. This relates to the problem that the public sphere cannot by itself invent the tools, means, and idioms it needs in order to manage and renew the exchange of public communication. That is, for the production of these tools of publicness—films, books, discourses, public situations and their transformation—it is always necessary to loop back to subjectivity and intimacy, for this is where the instruments are built that make the public in the public sphere rich in substance. This is Lessing's opinion about the work of poetry: the poetic enables the mediation between the immediate, the subjective, and the individual on one hand and the general on the other.

The Principle of "Tragic Recognition"

A tragedy, says Lessing, is a "dramatic poem." Since Brecht did not really deal with tragedy and Heiner Müller does not write theory, Lessing is the last author to be concerned with drama (that is, with the representation of elementary emotional conflicts in the form of publicly performed action) in a theoretically grounded fashion, in the *Hamburg Dramaturgy* among other places.

I find particularly striking a passage of nearly thirty pages that is devoted to the fourteenth chapter of Aristotle's *Poetics*.[5] According to Aristotle, there is a hierarchy of "events that elicit fear and pity," which is to say, make successful tragedy.[6] Every one of these events, says Lessing, citing Aristotle, turn on conflicts between enemies, between friends, or between people who are indifferent toward each other. In order to yield a "dramatic profit" adequate to the stage, tragic action must occur between friends.

A brother must kill, mistreat, or intend to mistreat his brother, a son his father, a mother her son, or a son his mother.

In this sense, according to Lessing, four classes of tragedy come into existence. In the first class—one thinks of *Emilia Galotti*—events are reported in which the act is committed wittingly and in full knowledge of the person affected, but not carried to completion. In fact, Emilia Galotti's father would have had to overthrow or kill the prince, but this did not happen. Instead he killed his own flesh and blood, his daughter. This is, so to speak, tragedy of the first kind, not the highest according to Aristotle.[7] Tragedies of the second kind arise when the act is consciously undertaken and actually carried out. This is the case with every murder plot. The third kind is produced "when the act is undertaken and carried out unconsciously, without full knowledge of the circumstances and the actor recognizes the person whom he kills too late." And the fourth class of tragedy, the highest according to Aristotle—and the reason why I am telling you this and which surprised me greatly—is when an unconsciously undertaken action does not succeed, because "the people entangled therein recognize one another in the nick of time." This is the case in the story of *Merope*, a play by Sophocles that did not survive the burning of the library at Alexandria. Lessing reconstructed its plot from indirect sources.

A king is attacked by a bandit neighbor. The usurper kills him and all of his children save one, who is hidden in a remote location. The queen is forced to marry the usurper. He, however, cannot feel safe as long as the last royal child of the old regime has not also been killed. A youth appears at court whom Merope takes to be the hired murderer of her last child. She wants to kill this assassin and, as we read, to "rip his heart out with her teeth." As she is about to plunge her dagger into his heart, she recognizes the supposed assassin as her son. According to tradition, the people of Athens were more upset and moved by the tragedy of Merope, which ends happily, than by the terrifying ending of any other play. A tragic conflict resolves itself in amicability and good will. There is a happy ending, a reunification. And this occupies Lessing for thirty pages.[8]

I call attention to this passage because it demonstrates the objective of Lessing's demand for a well-grounded, theoretical examination of drama— an exploration of the ability of art to express a defense of practical experience against something that is merely asserted onstage. This concept is at the core of Lessing's concept of critique.

In the nineteenth century, the dramatic tradition founded by Lessing was continued in quite a different manner, resulting in a rigid abstraction of value. In a kind of spiritual Bonapartism, enormous masses and colossal accumulations of both horror and pity were built up, each isolated from the other. Thus, every drama became the competitor of every other in the attempt to arrange its fifth act so as to maximize effects of pity. This is also the world of opera. This is how Verdi and Puccini deployed the genre.

This accumulation of horror and pity is not, however, of the sort with which Lessing's *Hamburg Dramaturgy* is concerned, because there balance is at issue. Lessing's concern goes back to antiquity, to the question, "What must I fear, what must I love?" It is concerned with the *Socratic* question, in turn introducing the theme of pity, which is not yet considered a separate ideal. As Hannah Arendt elaborated in her Lessing lecture, in antiquity pity was no more considered a virtue than was envy. And terror in itself was not seen as anything valuable at all. What mattered was the balance, the ability to let oneself be seized by pity in the midst of terror and in the midst of pity not to relinquish the memory of terror's bitterness.

Pity derives from that which I love and must not lose, fear from the terror that I might lose my way, that I am no longer in agreement with myself and therefore go to pieces. In this situation, the hierarchy of dramatic forms dissolves into a rich world of reflections, of balances, of calibrations and countercalibrations. This is, in Lessing's words, the "education of senti-ments," the core of a pleasurable, public contemplation that connects the intimate with the public.

This draws attention to the fact that no other generation has been able to view its own century as an open landscape of experience like ours. And yet, our metaphors, our dramatic representations, but also our news reports lack the expressive capacity to disseminate this experience. I want to suggest this discrepancy with two examples. They also illuminate the explosion of material power and substance that the classical canon of forms is not capable of dealing with and that will sooner or later break down this canon so that new forms will emerge.

I begin with two observations that are associated with Lessing's dramatic poem *Nathan the Wise*.[9] Lessing wrote this piece in a period when he was directly threatened with censorship. Therefore, he transposed the location of the drama to the Near East, into a timeless, fairy-tale realm so as to remove it from actuality. One look at the television news suggests that, in the meantime, the subject of the Near and Middle East has become less suitable for such magic transposition.

There is something else, though. The classical drama, with which Less-ing was concerned, identified social conflicts with persons. In the ancien régime, this identification corresponds to the public perception of the sovereign as a living embodiment of the people. This is why Lessing re-peatedly gives the impression that humanity could be educated if it were possible to better educate the rulers. It is, in short, considerably less mistaken to interpret world events on the basis of individual confrontations in the twelfth century, which is the setting for Nathan the Wise, or even in the eighteenth century, in which Lessing wrote, than would be the case today.

If one transfers the metaphor of "personal entanglement," intrinsic to drama, from the stage to the Middle East in the 1990s and attempts, as with Lessing's drama, to name the three contending forces among which it is unclear which of the three rings of Nathan the Wise is the right one, then the Muslims do not correspond to Saladin II but rather to Saddam Hussein, that is, to Iraq as a regime. A heavily armed Israel takes the place of Nathan. For the Templars, the white knights, we may choose George Bush or the UN coalition. It is abundantly clear, however, that this is not a personal but a systemic conflict, that the human actors (including Saddam Hussein) stand, as it were, beside the events, while acting on the world's stage as if they were directing them.

Until this day, the quest for truth, the question of who has the legitimating power to judge, awaits the better judges and will do so for the next thousand years. There seems to be astonishingly little that is new in the old conflict. But the form in which it is narrated will not be that of a dramatic poem. News systems such as CNN, Der Spiegel, the Washington Post report on it, but—and this is why we are gathered here on the occasion of the Lessing Prize—something is missing in these news narratives which, in the classical public sphere, was appended by the composers and the poets. What is missing is the element of recognition, the happy turn for the good, that defines Aristotle's fourth kind of tragedy. Stated simply, the news reports lack a sense of human interconnectedness, and hence also a potential for a defense of too much of a good thing.

I was very happy that, in their decision, the jury quoted a metaphor from one of my stories, and that is the concept of a "strategy from below."[10] I want to briefly recall this image. During an air raid in 1945, a woman, Gerda Baethe, sits in the basement with her children and, in that moment, can think of no way to protect them. The bomber squadron that for some—from her perspective completely abstract—reason is bombing the city is a systemic power of extraordinary effectiveness. Even experienced bomb disposal experts cannot deal with the results of decades of technological development that rain down from the skies. The bombs have to first arrive before the bomb defuser can defuse them. Even he, as an expert, cannot respond any differently than a layman while he is sitting in an air raid shelter being bombed. His professional knowledge is useless. There is no human relationship between those sitting in an air raid shelter and a bomber squadron. I cannot capitulate, I cannot defend myself, I cannot repent, I cannot respond, I cannot protect that which I love. And it does not even make sense that I am afraid.

This is what the teacher, Frau Baethe, said to herself in her basement. For a moment she wondered whether praying would help. But what should she pray for? That the bombs not fall on her and her children but instead on her neighbors? That would be a very unholy request, depriving the prayer of its power. In such micro-dramas there is no plan for action that one might pursue in a linear, logical way. The same situation arises during the occupation of a country, like the one we are currently practicing in our own, or during the frenzy following a world soccer championship. These events constitute a systemic totality (*Zusammenhang*) that dispenses violence out of its systemic context; and next to it, below or inside the abstraction, is the human being who cannot respond to it whatever he or she might do. This is what I consider *tragic*. This tragedy cannot be played out as a drama, though; it takes the form of monadic units that smash into each other in such a way, however, that one unit strikes and the other cannot strike back.

Dramas of this sort demand an account. Gerda Baethe draws such a balance when she considers: When was the last point in time that I could, in cooperation with others, have developed a defense against the powers that now threaten to kill me and my children? She comes to the realization that perhaps in 1928 (in the story it is 1945, and now it is 1990) it might have been possible, together with many others, by taking different measures than she actually took, to protect her children in this moment of danger in 1945.

The unity of location, time and action, which is another subject of the *Hamburg Dramaturgy*, is ruptured as a temporal and logical bond, in the conflict between life worlds and system worlds. At the same time, there is a whole network of new logical and temporal bonds that interrelate in an indirect and therefore relativistic order, as they refer to completely different moments in time and are situated in different locations. What was once a single location is now dissolved.

I would like to translate Lessing's metaphor of the three rings into yet another form, because it is very important to me that you understand the static quality of stage drama correctly—because this stasis does not imply that, under real conditions, anything ever stands still. To this end, I will briefly tell you the story of three men.

In 1941, there was a rumor that Japanese submarines were nearing the Pacific coast of the United States. Therefore, preparations were made to repel the enemy and people were drafted. Los Angeles and the surrounding areas were under strict blackout orders.

At the time there were three men in the metropolitan region of the city whom I will describe more closely. First, Walther Bade. Walther Bade is an astronomer, and he sat in his extremely cold room—observatories are kept cold so that the lenses do not fog—on Mount Wilson, all bundled up as if he were in Siberia, and observed the stars. Because of the blackout, he could do this in great detail. Thanks to this help, he studied the starry heaven above us and discovered that the galaxies are actually twice as far away as anyone had thought up to that time. He took the correct measure of that structure in which we live, surrounded by an extremely cold world outside. In one night in 1941, he took us further from a Ptolemaic worldview than Copernicus had. He is an enlightener (*Aufklärer*), an enlightener concerned with distance, an enlightener by scientific means.

At this same time, there was another man named David Miles, a private detective. He was drafted and was ordered to guard corporate buildings. They drafted the fox to guard the chicken coop. Because he was an excessively curious man, he used the telephones he was supposed to be guarding to make long-distance telephone calls. He called the day-side of our planet and closely followed the progress of the Japanese offensive. He made calls to telephone exchanges in northern Singapore, to Ceylon, to the vicinity of Manila, pushed very far into the provinces, into the local. Much of what he learned might have been based on misunderstanding, because he could not speak all of these languages; rather, he listened for the tone of voice or whether he could make out gunfire in the distance above the incomprehensible Spanish.

Thus he oriented himself, and the pathos that lies in his effort is that he did so in an unmediated form. He did not rely on reports by news agencies or on reports prepared for him by the newspapers. But, as a witness to these times, he worked his way by telephone into the crisis spots, and if people had wanted to know where they could flee to, if anyone had asked him, he would have known.

There is a third man in this curious "unity of place and time." He was later awarded the Lessing Prize—Max Horkheimer. At that time, he worked at night; he could not fall asleep. He doubted whether he would wake up again. He extended every day as long as he could and wrote, as we know, the notes that later went into the *Dialectic of Enlightenment*.[11] He had discovered a sentence by Karl Marx that reads: "The result of all of our discoveries and all our progress seems to be that material forces have been equipped with spiritual life and human existence has been stultified into a material force."[12] When human beings are nothing but consumers anymore, when they are cannon fodder in a war, then they have certainly become a material force, just as dead labor can be accumulated to fill the 186th generation of an IBM computer with spiritual life, for the labor of countless preceding generations lies hidden therein. This accumulated material power has a spiritual life; it is a spiritual life that marches separately but is capable of striking united.

The latter sentence does not appear in any of Marx's collected works, but it is a sentence that the Stasi might just as well have found. The Stasi people recently discovered a manuscript in London but it was not passed on to the Politburo because no one thought that newly discovered sentences by Marx could affect them. Horkheimer was of the opinion that one should not be sadistic in the name of truth (*wahrheitssadistisch*).[13] He put this phrase in his notebook every night during the blackout. By "sadistically truthful" he meant that there are realities which, if they were reported realistically, would cause such deep injuries that we have to decelerate information about them, so that experience can catch up with them. With this notion he described what a metaphor does, what poetry produces. In the face of unbearable experience, poetry shapes the vessels, labyrinths, threads, in which terror decelerates enough so that our sense experience can deal with it without being injured; so that the feelers of the snail, our sense perceptions, remain extended, although human beings as a species are not equipped for experiencing terror. The feelers are bent on experiencing happiness; they want this with every fiber of their being. In this regard, all feelings are antirealist and directed against experiencing terror. At the same time, we must invent forms that can decelerate terror so that human beings can deal with it.

I have listed here three highly subjective intellects, which represent three fragments of the Enlightenment. They never spoke with one another. According to the standard of verisimilitude, upon which Lessing insisted for dramatic scenes, there is also no conceivable constellation in which they could have met. All they have in common is time and place as the total context of blindness (*Verblendungszusammenhang*). In other years this systemic blinding would be triggered by the mass media, but in this year, in 1941, it was due to a blackout.

What matters here is the category of linkage, or relationality (*Zusammenhang*), at work both in poetic production and in the shaping of actual everyday situations. Seen from the perspective of emancipation, subjective qualities appear disconnected. Yet, if they are mobilized by advertising, a television series, or a propaganda campaign, that is, from the perspective of nonemancipation, the same qualities are linked and interrelated. Now, the chance for a spontaneous turn toward a happy ending, for autonomy, for tragic recognition and Lessing's sobriety (*Sachlichkeit*), is only possible from the perspective of emancipation. The project of the Enlightenment and the project of poetics are, in this perspective, necessary allies, and the less these projects can be realized in practice the more strongly we can sense this alliance.

In her Lessing lecture, "On Humanity in Dark Times," Hannah Arendt offered the following definition: "Tragedy shows the reversal of action into suffering."[14] In this respect, and this is the core of what I want to say, tragedy has left the stage of the theater and has ended up in real life, worldwide. But it cannot attain any form there—neither location, nor time, nor action. A new, open situation arises, for even suffering loses its ostensibly necessary form, just as it has lost its form of rationalization. In this situation, which provides new possibilities for action, for curiosity, and for poetic capacities, the recognition of the authentic, of the subjective, and of good will has a particular form—at first glance, it looks like naiveté.

I take a sentence from Kant's essay *On Perpetual Peace, Appendix I*: "The rights of man must be held sacred, however great a sacrifice the ruling power may have to make."[15] This attitude took hold in a lot of people's heads for six weeks last autumn. It unleashed a revolution. These people destroyed the image of a closed system that I had taken for a reality. More than one hundred years ago, though, when Kant's sentence was written, it seemed not quite realistic—in a word, naïve. This is because it was published but none of its promise was fulfilled. Suddenly, however, what the sentence describes became a reality and a power to be reckoned with.

In the context of the events of 1989, there was a demonstration in Leipzig in which people carried signs saying, "We are the people," just as the individual who, in the seventeenth century, played sovereign said of himself, *"L'état, c'est moi."* For precisely these absolutist reasons, Bert Brecht never spoke of the people but always of the population. The word "population," however, would be a lot less attractive as a slogan. "We are a population" sounds like a syllogism. It is also evident that something is missing. The sentence would actually have to read: "We are a population, and we possess a public sphere in which autonomy is possible—one in which we use our capacity to reason without the guidance of others."

Before something new oppresses me, after the demolition of the old, which had pushed me away from myself, there must be a glimpse of that tragic recognition that we humans—all humans—have for the authentic, for the subjective, for the otherness in other persons and for good will. Something like that may trigger catharsis as in *Merope*. It reunites terror and sensibility. A population without this vessel of sense-perception, without the real stage of the public, cannot develop self-confidence.

This is what Lessing's optimistic attitude refers to. It is the prerequisite for all rigorous poetics in the twentieth century. And this faith is tied to skepticism in the face of closed system worlds that function as if they were real. They are countered, Lessing says, by the antirealism of feeling.

It is for the sake of this skepticism, for this system of tolerances, that we need an independent public sphere. The public allows us to manufacture the tools that enable communication and make mutual understanding possible. And that is why the public sphere is a "common good which cannot be sold for any price in the world." Therefore, anyone who accumulates possessions for him- or herself in the public sphere, be it in the form of a public-law institution or as a private entrepreneur, is a trustee. We are the people and the public as long as we keep open the direct path and the unmediated communication between subjectivity and community. In this lies the moment of tragic, happy recognition.

Editor's Notes

1. Immanuel Kant, "Was heisst: sich im Denken orientieren?" in Immanuel Kant, *Werke in zehn Bänden*, ed. Wilhelm Weischedel (Darmstadt, 1981), 5:280, emphasis added. Originally published in the *Berlinische Monatsschrift*, Berlin, October 1786. Kant states: "Der Freiheit zu denken ist erstlich der bürgerliche Zwang engegengesetzt. Zwar sagte man: die Freiheit zu sprechen, oder zu schreiben, könne uns zwar durch obere Gewalt, aber die Freiheit zu denken durch sie gar nicht genommen werden. Allein wie viel und mit welcher Richtigkeit würden wir wohl denken, wenn wir nicht gleichsam in Gemeinschaft mit Andern, denen wir unsere und die uns ihre Gedanken mitteilen, dächten! Also kann man wohl sagen, dass diejenige äussere Gewalt, welche die Freiheit, seine Gedanken öffentlich mitzuteilen, den Menschen entreisst, ihnen auch die Freiheit zu denken nehme."

2. Gotthold Ephraim Lessing, *Hamburgische Dramaturgie*, in *Werke uns Briefe in zwölf Bänden*, ed. Wilfried Barner, vol. 6: *Werke 1767–1769*, ed. Klaus Bohnen (Frankfurt am Main, 1985) (Hamburg dramaturgy [New York, 1962]).

3. Bertolt Brecht, "Geschichten vom Herrn Keuner," in Bertholt Brecht, *Gesammelte Werke* (Frankfurt am Main, 1967), 12:373–415, here 385. The title of Brecht's story is "Form und Stoff."

4. Hannah Arendt, *Von der Menschlichkeit in finsteren Zeiten: Gedanken zu Lessing* (Munich, 1960) ("On humanity in dark times: Thoughts about Lessing," in Men in dark times [New York, 1968]), 3–31, here 20.

5. Lessing, *Hamburg Dramaturgy*. On the fourteenth chapter of Aristotle's *Poetics*, see especially essays 37–39. On the subject of pity, see especially essays 74–78.

6. Aristotle, *The Poetics of Aristotle: Translation and Commentary*, trans. Stephen Halliwell (Chapel Hill, N.C., 1987), chaps. 14, 45–47.

7. Ibid., chap. 14.

8. Lessing, *Hamburg Dramaturgy*; see esp. essays 74–78.

9. Gotthold Ephraim Lessing, *Nathan der Weise*, in *Werke und Briefe*, vol. 9: *Werke 1778–1780*, ed. Klaus Bohnen and Arno Schilson (Frankfurt am Main, 1993), 483–667 (Nathan the wise: A dramatic poem, ed. Ellen Frothingham [2d rev. ed., New York, 1989]).

10. Alexander Kluge, *Neue Geschichten. Hefte 1–18: Unheimlichkeit der Zeit* (Frankfurt am Main, 1977), 55–59. The story is part 2 of fasc. 2: *Der Luftangriff auf Halberstadt am 8. April 1945.* Its title is "Strategy from Below." See also Alexander Kluge and Oskar Negt, *Geschichte und Eigensinn* (Frankfurt am Main, 1981), 787–91.

11. Max Horkheimer and Theodor W. Adorno, *Dialektik der Aufklärung,* in Max Horkheimer, *Gesammelte Schriften,* ed. Gunzelin Schmid Noerr (Frankfurt am Main, 1987), 5:13–292 (Dialectic of enlightenment [New York, 1972]).

12. Karl Marx, "Speech at the Anniversary of the People's Paper, April 14, 1856," in *The Marx-Engels Reader,* 2d ed. (New York, 1978), 577–78. The English original of the speech states: "In our days, everthing seems pregnant with its contrary. Machinery gifted with the wonderful power of shortening and fructifying human labor, we behold starving and overworking it. The new fangled sources of wealth, by some weird spell, are turned into sources of want. The victories of art seem bought by the loss of character. At the same pace that mankind masters nature, man seems to become enslaved to other men or to his own infamy. Even the pure light of science seems unable to shine but on the dark background of ignorance. All our invention and progress seem to result in endowing material forces with intellectual life, and in stultfying human life into a material force."

13. Max Horkheimer, "Aufzeichnungen und Entwürfe zur *Dialektik der Aufklärung* —1939–1942," in Horkheimer, *Gesammelte Schriften,* ed. Gunzelin Schmid Noerr (Frankfurt am Main, 1987), 12:250–325.

14. Arendt, "On Humanity in Dark Times," 20.

15. Immanuel Kant, "Perpetual Peace: A Philosophical Sketch," in *Kant's Political Writings,* ed. Hans Reiss (Cambridge, 1970), 125.

Mitchell G. Ash is professor of history at the University of Vienna. He has previously taught in the history department of the University of Iowa, the history of science department of the University of Göttingen, and the science studies department of the University of Vienna. Among his recent publications are *Gestalt Psychology in German Culture, 1890–1967: Holism and the Quest for Objectivity* (1995), as well as two edited volumes: *Forced Migration and Scientific Change: German-Speaking Emigré Scientists and Scholars After 1933* (1996) and *German Universities Past and Future: Crisis or Renewal?* (1997; German ed. 1999).

Simone Barck, born in 1944, studied Germanic and Slavic literatures and languages in Rostock and Greifswald and was, between 1970 and 1991, a researcher at the Zentralinstitut für Literaturgeschichte der Akademie der Wissenschaften der DDR. She completed her Dr. sc.phil. in 1986. She has written extensively on the literature of the Weimar Republic, exile literature, theory of literature, GDR literature, and women's literature. Most recently she coauthored *Jedes Buch ein Abenteuer: Zensur-System und literarische Öffentlichkeit in der DDR bis Ende der sechziger Jahre* (1997) with Martina Langermann and Siegfried Lokatis.. She is a member of the Zentrum für Zeithistorische Forschung in Potsdam.

David Bathrick did his graduate work at the University of Chicago and is currently professor of German studies and chair of the Department of Theater, Film, and Dance at Cornell University. His field of research is twentieth-century German literature, theater, and film with special focus on the Weimar Republic, the Third Reich, and the GDR. He serves as editor of the journal *New German Critique*. His most recent book is *The Power of Speech: The Politics of Culture in the GDR* (1995). He is currently finishing a book on visual culture in the Third Reich.

John Borneman is professor of anthropology at Princeton University. He completed his graduate studies in anthropology at Harvard University. His early ethnographic research in Berlin both before and since 1989 resulted in publication of *Belonging in the Two Berlins: Kin, State, Nation* (1992). His most recent publications include *Settling Accounts: Violence, Justice, and Accountability in Postsocialist States* (1997) and *Subversions of International Order: Studies in the Political Anthropology of Culture* (1998). His scholarly interests encompass culture and international order, sexuality, and national and European identifications, as well as the anthropology of memory work. He is currently doing research in Lebanon.

Dorothea Dornhof, born in Leipzig in 1951, began her career as a bookseller, subsequently studied cultural sciences and aesthetics at Humboldt University, worked as a journalist for the Berliner Rundfunk, and completed her doctorate at Humboldt University with a dissertation titled "Baukasten für kritische Eingriffe: Zur Funktion

des Dokumentarischen im literarischen und theoretischen Werk Hans Magnus En-
zensbergers," which was published as *Hans Magnus Enzensberger: Erinnerungen an die
Zukunft* (1988). She was a member of the Zentralinstitut für Literaturgeschichte at the
Akademie der Wissenschaften in Berlin and subsequently was a research fellow at the
Förderungsgesellschaft wissenschaftliche Neuvorhaben. Her main interests and publi-
cations focus on the politics, history, and theory of contemporary West German and
East German literature as well as on women's literature and femininity as a paradigm
for aesthetics since the Enlightenment. She is working on a book, *Demons of Modern
Knowledge*. She has held teaching positions at the FU Berlin (German literature),
Humboldt University (theater), University of Chicago (German Studies), and Monash
University (German Studies, Melbourne) and is currently assistant professor at the
Institut für Kulturwissenschaften at Humboldt University in Berlin.

Michael Geyer, born in 1947, studied history and German literatures at the University
of Freiburg. He is currently professor of contemporary European history at the Univer-
sity of Chicago. His earlier publications focus on military history and include *Deutsche
Rüstungspolitik, 1860–1980* (1984). More recently, he has edited (together with Konrad
Jarausch) a special issue of *Central European History* (1989) titled "German Histories:
Challenges in Theory, Practice, and Technique" as well as (together with John Boyer)
Resistance Against the Third Reich, 1933–1990 (1994), with an essay titled "Resistance
as On-Going Project: Visions of Order, Obligations to Strangers, Struggles for Civil
Society." He is currently working with Konrad Jarausch on a book-length essay about
twentieth-century German history.

Andreas Graf was born in 1952 in Ebersbach/Oberlausitz. He studied history at the
University of Rostock and completed his dissertation, "Anarchismus in der Weimarer
Republik: Tendenzen—Organisationen—Personen," at Humboldt University in Berlin,
where he was a member of the Arbeitskreis Friedens- und Konfliktforschung in the
Social Science Division. He served as the managing executive of the Media Control
Council in 1990–91. He also was a cofounder of the Unabhängige Historiker-Verband
and a member of the Commission of Experts on the Memorials of the State Brandenburg. He is on the editorial committee of the journal *Internationale Wissenschaftliche Korrespondenz zur Geschichte der Arbeiterbewegung*. His publications deal with the history
of anarchism, the political police, Soviet internment camps in the Soviet Zone and the
GDR, as well as media politics. Currently he is research fellow at the Forschungsstelle
Widerstandsgeschichte at the Freie Universität and the Gedenkstätte deutscher Widerstand, both in Berlin.

Dietrich Hohmann, born in Apolda (Thuringia) in 1939, has lived in Werder/Havel
since 1961. He studied chemical engineering and, between 1961 and 1979, was employed in various positions in the chemical industry. In 1978–79 he spent a year at
the Institut für Literatur in Leipzig and since 1979 has been a writer. Among his
publications are short stories, poems, scripts for television, and documentary films, as
well as translations, including *Londoner Skizzen* (travelogue, 1973), *Blaue Sonnenblumen*
(short stories, 1982), *Große Jungen weinen nicht* (novel, 1984), and *Ich, Robert Burns*
(biographical novel, 1991). Since 1991 he has been the administrative director of
the Sozialdemokratische Gemeinschaft für Kommunalpolitik im Land Brandenburg.
He has completed a novel about the 1970s in the GDR ("Einer oder das Schwe-

dengeschäft") and is currently working on a novel focusing on the theme of perpe-trators/victims and victors/vanquished.

Andreas Huyssen studied in Munich, Paris, and Zurich and is Villard Professor of Ger-man and Comparative Literature and director of the Center for Comparative Literature and Society at Columbia University in New York. He is an editor of *New German Critique* and the author of books, in German, on romantic poetics and the drama of the *Sturm und Drang*. He coedited *The Technological Imagination* (1980) with Teresa de Lauretis and Kathleen Woodward, *Postmoderne: Zeichen eines kulturellen Wandels* (1986) with Klaus Scherpe, and *Modernity and the Text: Revisions of German Modernism* (1989) with David Bathrick. He is the author of *After the Great Divide: Modernism, Mass Culture, Postmodernism* (1986) and of *Twilight Memories: Marking Time in a Culture of Amnesia* (1995). His most recent collection of essays, on global memory culture, urban space, and the new Berlin, were published in Brazil as *Seduzidos pela memoria* (2000).

Konrad Jarausch, born in 1941, is a graduate of the University of Wisconsin and has been Lurcy Professor of European Civilization at the University of North Carolina, Chapel Hill, since 1983 and director of the Zentrum für Zeithistorische Forschung in Potsdam since 1998. He has published widely on all aspects of German history. Among his best-known books are *The Enigmatic Chancellor: Bethmann Hollweg and the Hubris of Imperial Germany, 1856–1921* (1973), *Students, Society, and Politics in Imperial Germany: The Rise of Academic Illiberalism* (1982), *The Unfree Professions: German Lawyers, Teach-ers, and Engineers, 1900–1950* (1990), and *Quantitative Methods for Historians* (1991), *The Rush to German Unity* (1993), *Uniting Germany: Documents and Debates* (1994), and *After Unity: Reconfiguring German Identities* (1997). His latest books are *Dictatorship as Experience: Towards a Socio-Cultural History of the GDR* (1999), *Weg im dem Untergang: Der innere Zerfall der DDR* (1999), and *Versäumte Fragen: Deutsche Historiker im Schatten des Nationalsozialismus* (2000). He is currently working on twentieth-century German history.

Alexander Kluge, born in 1932 in Halberstadt, graduated from the University of Frank-furt in 1955 with a doctorate in law and a minor in sacred music. He is best known as a writer of prose fiction, a filmmaker, a spokesman for the Oberhausen group, which founded "Young German Cinema," a media theorist and, since 1983, an independent television producer. His first feature film, *Abschied von Gestern* (Yesterday girl, 1986) is based on the short story "Anita G." from his volume of short stories *Lebensläufe* (196?); *Life Stories*, 198x). Since then he has signed his name to at least seven more feature films (including *Germany in Autumn, Strongman Ferdinand, The Patriot, Power of Feeling*), eight collections of stories, essays, and scripts, and, in collaboration with Oskar Negt, two theoretical works, *Öffentlichkeit und Erfahrung* (1972 [Public sphere and Experi-ence, 1993]) and *Geschichte und Eigensinn* (History and Obstinancy/Self-Will, 1981), and hundreds of television programs such as *Ten to Eleven* on the commercial station SAT 1. Most recently he published two conversations with Heiner Müller: *Ich schulde der Welt einen Toten* (1995) and *Ich bin ein Landvermesser* (1996). He is the recipient of prestigious literary awards, including the Lessing Prize of the City of Hamburg, on which occasion he gave the speech translated here.

Loren Kruger was educated at the University of Cape Town (South Africa), the Insti-tut d'études théâtrales (Paris), the Institut für Theaterwissenschaft (F.U. Berlin), and

Cornell University, where she received a Ph.D. in comparative literature. She teaches drama and critical theory at the University of Chicago and is former editor of *Theatre Journal* (1995–99). Her publications include *The National Stage* (1992), the translation of *The Institutions of Art: Essays by Peter and Christa Bürger* (1992), the edition of *The Autobiography of Leontine Sagan* (the director of *Mädchen in Uniform*) (1996), and *The Drama of South Africa* (1999), as well as articles in journals such as *Diaspora, Frakcija, Poetics Today, Rethinking Marxism,* and *Theater der Zeit.* Her current research projects include an investigation of the theatrical culture of the cold war, of which the essay published in this volume forms a part.

Martina Langermann, born in 1961, studied Germanistik in Greifswald, where she received her doctorate in German literatures and languages. From 1987 to 1991 she held a research position at the Zentralinstitut für Literaturgeschichte at the Akademie der Wissenschaften der DDR. Since 1993 she has been associated with the Forschungs-schwerpunkt Zeithistorische Studien in Potsdam and with Humboldt University. She has published on GDR literature, mainly on Anna Seghers and on the anti-war novel, and most recently, with Simone Barck and Siegfried Lokatis, *Jedes Buch ein Abenteuer: Zensur-System und literarische Öffentlichkeit in der DDR bis Ende der sechziger Jahre* (1997).

Siegfried Lokatis, born in Essen in 1956, studied history, philosophy, archaeology, and oriental studies at the Ruhr-Universität Bochum, where he completed his doctorate. Among his publications are *Hanseatische Verlagsanstalt: Politisches Buchmarketing im "Dritten Reich"* (1992) and, most recently, with Simone Barck and Martina Langermann, *Jedes Buch ein Abenteuer: Zensur-System und literarische Öffentlichkeit in der DDR bis Ende der sechziger Jahre* (1997). Since 1993 he has been a member of the Zentrum für Zeithistorische Forschung in Potsdam.

Patricia Anne Simpson received her Ph.D. in 1988 from the Department of Germanic Languages and Literatures at Yale University. She is currently visiting assistant professor of German at Kenyon College. Her publications include essays on German classicism and romanticism, as well as contemporary literature, theory, and popular culture. She is working on a project about the politics of punk in the GDR and has edited a volume on responses to the fall of the Berlin Wall. She is also preparing a study of philosophy and literature under the title *The Poetics of Power, The Ethics of Violence: Theories of* Gewalt *in German Romanticism.*

Frank Trommler, born in Zwickau (Saxony), received his Ph.D. from the University of Munich. Between 1967 and 1969 he taught at Harvard University and, since 1970, has taught at the University of Pennsylvania as a professor of German and comparative literature. In 1980–1986 and again in 1995–1997 he chaired the German department. Since 1995 he has also directed the Humanities Program at the American Institute for Contemporary German Studies in Washington, D.C. He has published widely in the areas of nineteenth- and twentieth-century German literature, theater, and culture; socialist literature; German-American cultural relations; modernism in literature; technology; and the arts. Among his publications are *Sozialistische Literatur in Deutschland: Ein historischer Überblick* (1976); *Kultur der Weimarer Republik,* with Jost Hermand (1978); *America and the Germans,* coedited with J. McVeigh (1985); *"Mit uns zieht die neue Zeit": Der Mythos Jugend,* coedited with T. Koebner and R. Janz (1985); *Germanistik in den USA* (1989); *Thematics reconsidered* (1995); and *Revisiting Zero Hour 1945: The Emergence of Postwar German Culture,* coedited with S. Brockmann (1996). He is currently reassessing and comparing American and German concepts of modernity in literature, technology, arts, and design.

Katie Trumpener is a comparatist who attended graduate school at Harvard and Stanford Universities. She is professor of Germanic studies, English, comparative literature, and cinema and media studies at the University of Chicago. Her first book, *Bardic Nationalism: The Romantic Novel and the British Empire* (1997), received the British Academy's Rosemary Crawshay Prize and the Modern Language Association's prize for a first book. Her second book, *The Divided Screen: The Cinemas of Postwar Germany* (forthcoming), attempts a synthetic, comparative account of the East and West German cinemas. Her new book project centers on European modernists and their nannies; she plans a future book on the attempts of GDR writers and filmmakers to re-situate German culture in relation to Eastern Europe.

Films

9 Days in One Year, dir. Mikhail Romm (USSR, 1961), b/w, 111 mins.

Abschied von Gestern (Yesterday's Girl), dir. Alexander Kluge (Federal Republic of Germany, 1966), b/w, 90 mins.

The Accused/The Defendant (Obzalovany), dir. Elmar Klos and Ján Kadár (Czechoslovakia, 1960), b/w, 93 mins.

The Apartment, dir. Billy Wilder (USA, 1960), color, 125 mins.

Ashes and Diamonds, dir. Andrej Wadja (Poland, 1958), b/w, 105 mins.

L'Avventura, dir. Michelangelo Antonioni (Italy, France, 1960), b/w, 145 mins.

Ballad of a Soldier (Ballada o Soldate), dir. Grigori Chukrai (USSR, 1959), b/w, 89 mins.

Band à Part, dir. Jean-Luc Godard (France, 1964), b/w, 95 mins.

Berlin um die Ecke, dir. Gerhard Klein (German Democratic Republic, 1965), b/w, 88 mins.

Blackboard Jungle, dir. Richard Brooks (USA, 1955), b/w, 102 mins.

Brot der frühen Jahre, dir. Herbert Vesely (Federal Republic of Germany, 1962), color, 89 mins.

Die Brücke, dir. Bernhard Wicki (Federal Republic of Germany, 1959), b/w, 105 mins.

Die Buntkarierten, dir. Kurt Maetzig (German Democratic Republic, 1949), b/w, 105 mins.

The Cassandra Cat (Az prijde kocour), dir. Vojtech Jasny (Czechoslovakia, 1963), color, 91 mins.

The Ceremony, dir. Nagisa Oshima (Japan, 1970), color, 122 mins.

The Confrontation (Fényes Szelek), dir. Miklos Janscó (Hungary, 1968), b/w, 86 mins.

The Cranes Are Flying, dir. Mikhail Kalantazov (USSR, 1957), b/w, 94 mins.

Cruel Story of Youth, dir. Nagisa Oshima (Japan, 1960), color, 96 mins.

Denk bloß nicht ich heule, dir. Frank Vogel (German Democratic Republic, 1965), b/w, 91 mins.

La dolce vita (The Sweet Life), dir. Frederico Fellini (Italy, 1960), b/w, 167 mins.

Dr. Strangelove: Or, How I Learned to Stop Worrying and Love the Bomb, dir. Stanley Kubrick (Great Britain, 1964), b/w, 93 mins.

Ehe im Schatten (Marriage in the Shadows), dir. Kurt Maetzig (German Democratic Republic, 1947), b/w, 105 mins.

Einheit SPD-KPD, dir. Kurt Maetzig (German Democratic Republic, 1946), b/w, 19 mins.

Ernst Thälmann, Sohn seiner Klasse, dir. Kurt Maetzig (German Democratic Republic, 1954), color, 124 mins.

Familie Benthin, dir. Kurt Maetzig and Dudow Slatan (German Democratic Republic, 1950), b/w, 98 mins.

The Four Hundred Blows (Les quatre cents coups), dir. François Truffaut (France, 1959), b/w, 99 mins.

Fünf Patronenhülsen (Five Empty Cartridges), dir. Frank Beyer (German Democratic Republic, 1960), b/w, 87 mins.

Himmel ohne Sterne, dir. Helmut Käutner (Federal Republic of Germany, 1955), b/w, 109 mins.

Hiroshima Mon Amour, dir. Alain Resnais (France, Japan, 1959), b/w, 89 mins.

Interrogation (Przesluchanie), dir. Ryszard Bugajski (Poland, 1982), color, 118 mins.

Ivan's Childhood/My Name Is Ivan, dir. Andrej Tarkovsky (USSR, 1962), b/w, 95 mins.

Jahrgang '45, dir. Jürgen Böttcher (German Democratic Republic, 1965), b/w, 94 mins.

Judgment at Nürnberg, dir. Stanley Kramer (USA, 1961), b/w, 187 mins.

Kanal (Canal), dir. Andrzej Wajda (Poland, 1957), b/w, 95 mins.

Das Kaninchen bin ich, dir. Kurt Maetzig (German Democratic Republic, 1965), b/w, 105 mins.

Karbid und Sauerampfer, dir. Frank Beyer (German Democratic Republic, 1963), b/w, 85 mins.

Karla, dir. Hermann Zschoche (German Democratic Republic, 1965), b/w, 128 mins.

Die Legende von Paul und Paula, dir. Heiner Carow (German Democratic Republic, 1979), b/w, 106 mins.

Mutter Krausens Fahrt ins Glück, dir. Piel Jutzi (Germany, 1929), b/w, 121 mins.

Night and Fog in Japan, dir. Nagisa Oshima (Japan, 1960), color, 107 mins.

Orpheus, dir. Jean Cocteau (France, 1949), b/w, 96 mins.

Port of Call (Hamnstad), dir. Ingmar Bergman (Sweden, 1948), b/w, 100 mins.

Rebel Without a Cause, dir. Nicholas Ray (USA, 1955), color, 111 mins.

The Red and the White (Csillagosok, Katoník), dir. Miklos Janscó (Hungary, 1968), b/w, 92 mins.

Rocco and His Brothers, dir. Luchino Visconti (Italy, France, 1960), b/w, 170 mins.

Rosen für den Staatsanwalt, dir. Wolfgang Staudte (Federal Republic of Germany, 1959), color, 94 mins.

Salaire de la Peur (Wages of Fear), dir. Henri-Georges Clouzot (Italy, 1953), b/w, 131 mins.

Saturday Night and Sunday Morning, dir. Karel Reisz (Great Britain, 1960), b/w, 89 mins.

Die Schauspielerin, dir. Siegfried Kühn (German Democratic Republic, 1988), color, 87 mins.

Schlösser und Katen (Part I: Der krumme Anton; Part II: Annegrets Heimkehr), dir. Kurt Maetzig (German Democratic Republic, 1956), b/w, 204 mins.

Smiles of a Summer Night (Sommarnattens Leende), dir. Ingmar Bergman (Sweden, 1955), b/w, 108 mins.

Sonntagsfahrer, dir. Gerhard Klein (German Democratic Republic, 1963), b/w, 87 mins.

Spur der Steine, dir. Frank Beyer (German Democratic Republic, 1966), b/w, 129 mins.

Summer with Monika (Monika), dir. Ingmar Bergman (Sweden, 1952), b/w, 82 mins.

Tom Jones, dir. Tony Richardson (Great Britain, 1963), color, 121 mins.

The Travelling Players (O Thiassos), dir. Theo Angelopoulous (Greece, 1975), color, 230 mins.

Die Verlobte, dir. Günter Ruckert and Günter Reisch (German Democratic Republic, 1980), color, 105 mins.

Viridiana, dir. Luis Bunuel (Spain, 1961), b/w, 90 mins.

Wenn du groß bist, lieber Adam, dir. Egon Günther (German Democratic Republic, 1965), b/w, 78 mins.

West Side Story, dir. Robert Wise and Jerome Robbins (USA, 1961), color, 150 mins.

The Young Stranger, dir. John Frankenheimer (USA, 1957), b/w, 84 mins.

Audio Recordings

Adorno, Theodor W. "Engagement oder Autonomie von Kunst," Radio Bremen (Bremen, March 1962), radio broadcast.

Braun, Volker. "Kahlschlag: Auswertung eines Plenums, oder Paul Verner liest 'Die Kipper' von Volker Braun. Aus dem Tonbandprotokoll des 11. Plenums des ZK der SED vom 15. bis 18. Dezember 1965," Studio für elektro-akustische Musik at the Berlin Akademie der Künste (Berlin, 1990), cassette tape.

Die Firma. *Kinder der Maschinenrepublik*, prod. WYDOCKS Studio, GEMA LC5899, deadhorse (Berlin, 1993).

Die Firma, Freygang, and Ichfunktion. *Die letzen Tage von Pompeji*, Peking Records LC7896 (Recorded live "Im Eimer," Berlin, 1990).

Freygang, *Aufbruch, Umbruch, Abbruch: Die letzten Jahre*. Vol. 20 of *Rock aus Deutschland*, Deutsche Schallplatten GmbH, PSB 3088–2, LC 6056, [Berlin] 1992.

Freygang. *Die Kinder spielen weiter*, prod. Multiple-Noise Studio Seeba und Detlef, Flint Records, GEMA 5899, deadhorse (Recorded live in Knaak-Club, Berlin, 1993).

Freygang. *Golem*, prod. Ja Skutnik and Freygang, Skutnik Musikverlag (Berlin, 1995).

Herbst in Peking. *Das Jahr Schnee*. ASIN: B00000B0K9 (Plattenmei: EFA Medien, 1996).

Herbst in Peking. *Feuer, Wasser & Posaunen*. ASIN: B0000260BC (Moloko: EFA Medien, 1998).

Herbst in Peking. *Les fleurs du mal*. ASIN: B000028E67 (Moloko Plu, EFA Medien, 1999).

Ichfunktion. *egotrip*, prod. Tschaka and Rexin, Dizzy Hornet Records, Nasty Vinyl, Kikeriki Records, LC5704, SPV 77–83732 ([Berlin], 1994).

The Inchtabokatables. *White Sheep*, prod. Len Davies and Haje Roesink, Costbar/Autogram Records, LC5944, CLCD-6304, EFA CD 11890–26 ([Berlin], 1993), compact disc.

Müller, Heiner. "Bertolt Brecht's *Fatzer*," Berliner Rundfunk (Berlin, February 1988), radio broadcast.

Müller, Heiner. Texte gelesen von 42 Berliner Schauspielern: Live-Mitschnitt der öffentlichen Lesungen vom 3.–9.1.1996 im Berliner Ensemble, Berliner Ensemble @-Henschel Schauspiel Theaterverlag and Radio Brandenburg, eds., 3CD, ISBN:3–89581-010-X [1996].

Magazine and Newspaper Articles

Adorno, Theodor W. "Erziehung nach Auschwitz (reprint)," *Die Zeit*, 48/1, 1 January 1993.

"Alte Tugenden, neue Werte," [Roundtable], *Die Zeit*, 24 December 1994.

Anderson, Sascha. "'Das ist nicht so einfach': Gespräch von Iris Radisch mit Sascha Anderson," *Die Zeit*, 46/45, 1 November 1991.

Assheuer, Thomas. "Was ist deutsch?" *Die Zeit* 54/40, 30 September 1999.

"'Auf der Stasi-Schiene gegen die kritischen Kultur,' Gespräch mit den PEN-Präsidenten Gerd Heidenreich," *Süddeutsche Zeitung*, 2 March 1992.

Baier, Lothar. "Selbstverstümmelnder Literatenschmäh: Über den neuen deutschen Intellektuellenhaß," *Freitag*, 29 January 1993.

[Baring, Arnulf]. "Sind die Liberalen noch zu retten?" *Die Woche*, 17 March 1994.

Becher, Johannes R. "Vom sinnvollen Einsatz der Macht," *Neues Deutschland*, 26 October 1957.

Berger, Stefan. "Der Dogmatismus des Normalen," *Frankfurter Rundschau*, 26 April 1996.

Biedenkopf, Kurt. "Kurt Biedenkopf und der Abschied von der 'Aufholjagd': Wie sich der sächsische Ministerpräsident die unterschiedliche ökonomische und soziale Entwicklung in Ost und West vorstellt," *Frankfurter Rundschau*, 27 March 1992.

Bierman, Wolf. "à la lanterne, à la lanterne!" *Der Spiegel*, 46/39, 21 September 1992.

———. "Der Lichtblick im gräßlichen Fatalismus der Geschichte: Rede zur Verleihung des Büchner Preises," *Die Zeit*, 46/44, 25 October 1991.

———. "Laß o Welt, o laß mich sein: Rede zum Erich Mörike Preis," *Die Zeit*, 46/47, 15 November 1991.

———. "Nur wer sich ändert, bleibt sich treu: Der Streit um Christa Wolf, das Ende der DDR, das Elend der Intellektuellen. Das alles ist auch komisch," *Die Zeit*, 46/35, 24 August 1990.

"Bloße Übernahme oder Neugründung. Medienexperten über die Zukunft von Funk und Fernsehen," *Neues Deutschland*, 12–13 January 1991.

Bluhm, Katharina. "Instrumente der Öffentlichkeit als vierte Gewalt," *Frankfurter Rundschau*, 18 September 1990.

Bohley, Bärbel. "Vergewaltigung des Themas. Das Beispiel Biermann und das Beispiel Anderson," *die andere*, 6 November 1991.

Böhme, Andrea and Stefan Willeke. "Nichts als die Wahrheit?" *Die Zeit*, 55/27, 10 February 2000.

Bracher, Karl Dietrich. "Zeitgeschichtliche Anmerkungen zum 'Zeitenbruch' von 1989/90." *Neue Züricher Zeitung*, 20 January 1991.

Brandt, Sabine. "Wer spricht vom Versagen der Briefträger; 'Etwas echt Deutsches': Die Frage nach den Fehlleistungen der Intellektuellen," *Frankfurter Allgemeine Zeitung*, 11 December 1992.

Brecht, Bertolt. "Kulturpolitik und Akademie der Künste," *Neues Deutschland*, 12 August 1953.

Brüning, Jens. "Ein 'basisdemokratisches Relikt der Wende' löst sich auf," *Süddeutsche Zeitung*, 19 September 1990.

Bünger, Reinhart. "Beim Abschiedstrunk kam ein wenig Wehmut auf," *Frankfurter Rundschau*, 21 September 1990.

———. "'Guten Abend, ich bin der Sachse Schmitt, ich mache die Wahl mit.' Wie Rudolf Mühlfenzl zum Rundfunkbeauftragten bestellt worden ist. Protokoll der Wahlmänner-Sitzung im Wortlaut," *Frankfurter Rundschau*, 22 October 1990.

Corino, Karl. "Vom Leichengift der Stasi. Die DDR-Literatur hat an Glaubwürdigkeit verloren. Eine Entgegnung," *Süddeutsche Zeitung*, 12 June 1991.

de Bruyn, Günter. "Dieses Mißtrauen gegen mich selbst: Schwierigkeiten beim Schreiben der Wahrheit. Ein Beitrag zum Umgang mit den Stasi-Akten," *Frankfurter Allgemeine Zeitung*, 18 February 1993.

Detje, Robin. "Heiner Müller und die Stasi: Der große Dichter schrumpft, XV 3470/78," *Die Zeit*, 48/3, 15 January 1993.

Dieckmann, Friedrich. "Trauersache Geheimes Deutschland. Wanderer über viele

Bühnen im zerrissenen Zentrum: Totenfeier in Berlin," *Frankfurter Allgemeine Zeitung*, 18 January 1996.

————. "Von der Volksbühnenbewegung zum Subventionstheater," *Theater der Zeit*, August 1991.

"Ein ungewolltes Spiel mitspielen, um Schlimmeres zu verhüten. Europa und die Veränderungen des Weltmarktes—Votrag von Professor Franz Josef Rademacher beim Jahrestag des TÜV," *Darmstädter Echo*, 3 April 2000.

Enderlein, H. P. "Zusammenarbeit schließt Meinungsstreit ein," *Theater der Zeit*, August 1989.

"Es hat niemandem genützt. Die Firma nach den Stasi-Offenbarungen," *NM!Messitsch* 5 (1992): 14–15.

Frenkel, Rainer. "Der Riss im Leben des Horst Klinkmann," *Die Zeit*, 48/14, 2 April 1993.

Fuchs, Jürgen. "Maßnahme Totenhaus," *Der Spiegel*, 45/ 52, 23 December 1991.

Fuchs, Jürgen, and Klaus Hensel. "Heraus aus der Lüge und Ehrlichkeit herstellen: Der Schriftsteller und die Stasi-Spitzel," *Frankfurter Rundschau*, 21 December 1991.

Funk, Werner, and Hanswerner Kilz, eds. "Der lange Arm der Staatssicherheit," *Der Spiegel*, 44/13, 26 March 1990.

————. "Ruß aus der Hose," *Der Spiegel*, 45/15, 8 April 1991.

Fuhr, Eckhard. "Ein Kulturkampf," *Frankfurter Allgemeine Zeitung*, 26 September 1993.

Gaschke, Susanne. "Vater Staat und seine Kinder," *Die Zeit*, 54/41, 7 October 1999.

"Gaus verläßt Rundfunkbeirat," *Berliner Zeitung*, 11 June 1991.

Gaus, Günter. "Abrechnung," *Freitag*, 21 June 1991.

Geisel, Eike. "Triumph des guten Willens," *die tageszeitung*, 12 December 1992.

Gorek, Bert Papenfuß. " 'One always loves the cat in the bag': Gespräch mit Bascha Mika und Ute Scheub," *die tageszeitung*, 29 January 1992.

Grass, Günter. "Kurze Rede eines vaterlandslosen Gesellen," *Die Zeit*, 45/7, 9 February 1990.

————. "Nötige Kritik oder Hinrichtungen: Gespräch mit Hellmuth Karasek und Rolf Becker," *Der Spiegel*, 44/29, 16 July 1990.

Gratzik, Paul. "Müller und Maiglöckchen," *Wochenpost*, 2 April 1992.

Greiner, Ulrich. "Die deutsche Gesinnungsästhetik: Noch einmal. Christa Wolf und der deutsche Literaturstreit/Eine Zwischenbilanz," *Die Zeit*, 45/46, 2 November 1990.

————. "Mangel an Feingefühl: Einen ZEIT-Kontroverse über Christa Wolf und ihre neue Erzählung 'Was bleibt,' " *Die Zeit*, 45/23, 1 June 1990.

————. "Plädoyer für Schluß der Stasi-Debatte," *Die Zeit*, 48/ 7, 5 February 1993.

Greiner, Ulrich, and Volker Hage. " 'Es gibt längst die neue Mauer': Ein Zeit-Gespräch mit Günter Grass und Christoph Hein," *Die Zeit*, 47/7, 7 February 1992.

Grünbein, Durs. "Im Namen der Füchse: Gibt es eine neue literarische Zensur?" *Frankfurter Allgemeine Zeitung*, 26 November 1991.

Habermas, Jürgen. "Die andere Zerstörung der Vernunft: Über die Defizite der deutschen Vereinigung und über die Rolle der intellektuellen Kritik," *Die Zeit*, 46/20, 17 May 1991.

————. "Bemerkungen zu einer verworrenen Diskussion," *Die Zeit*, 47/15, 3 April 1992.

————. "Wir sind wieder 'normal' geworden (Die zweite Lebenslüge der Bundesrepublik)," *Die Zeit*, 47/51, 11 December 1992.

Hage, Volker. "Kunstvolle Prosa: Eine ZEIT-Kontroverse über Christa Wolf und ihre neue Erzählung," *Die Zeit*, 45/23, 1 June 1990.

Hauser, Oskar. "Demagogie oder nur Unkenntnis," *Neues Deutschland*, 7 November 1989.

Hein, Christoph. "Achten auf den Nachtfrost," *Süddeutsche Zeitung*, 7/8 March 1992.

———. "Die DDR auf Knien und mit weißer Flagge in die Einheit: Der DDR-Schriftsteller Christoph Hein über sein Land, die Intellektuellen und das Volk," *die tageszeitung*, 17 March 1990.

———. "Warum ich in der DDR geblieben bin," *Theater Heute*, April 1992.

———. "Waschzwang ist da, also muß gewaschen werden," *Freitag*, 29 January 1993.

Henscheid, Eckard. "'Der Softie als Rambo': Planstellen deutscher Literatur (II)," *Frankfurter Allgemeine Zeitung*, 6 January 1994.

———. "Weltwachgeister: Planstellen deutscher Literatur (I)," *Frankfurter Allgemeine Zeitung*, 4 January 1994.

Hermlin, Stephan. "'Der Erbe von Lenin und Franz von Assissi': Interview mit Stephan Hermlin," *Der Tagesspiegel*, 6 February 1993.

Herzinger, Rudolf. "Staubwolken im Nichts," *Die Zeit* 51/28, 5 July 1996.

Heym, Stefan. "Aschermittwoch in der DDR," *Der Spiegel*, 43/49, 4 December 1989.

———. "Hurrah für den Pöbel," *Der Spiegel*, 43/45, 6 November 1989.

———. "Die Wahrheit und nichts als die Wahrheit. Ein Plädoyer für die Gerechtigkeit im Umgang mit den Stasi-Akten," *Berliner Zeitung*, 9/10 November 1991.

Hildebrandt, Dieter. "Wer spricht da von Exil?" *Die Zeit*, 39/8, 24 February 1984.

Hoffmann, Hans-Joachim. "Commemorative Address on Brecht's 90th Birthday, 10 February 1988," *Theater der Zeit*, April 1988.

Hoffmeyer, Miriam. "Krieg der Metaphern: Götz Friedrich in Klauser, Käthe Reichel wettert gegen die Demokratie: Kulturniks sind wegen Entwurf zum Nachtragshaushalt schockiert," *die tageszeitung* (electronic ed.), 15 March 1996.

"'Ich, Mühlfenzl, die Einrichtung': Gespräch mit dem Beauftragten für den Rundfunk in der ehemaligen DDR," *Süddeutsche Zeitung*, 30 October 1990.

Jäckel, Eberhard. "Die doppelte Vergangenheit," *Der Spiegel*, 45/52, 23 December 1991.

Jens, Walter. "Plädoyer gegen die Preisgabe der DDR Kultur: Fünf Forderungen an die Intellektuellen des geeinten Deutschland. Rede in Potsdam am 11.5.1990," *Süddeutsche Zeitung*, 16/17 May 1990.

———. "Und bleibe, was ich bin: Ein Scheiß-Liberaler," *Die Zeit*, 48/10, 5 March 1993.

Jochen-Kopke, Fritz. "Wem gehört Brechts Theater?" *Wochenpost* (electronic ed.), 20 April 1995.

John, Hans Rainer. "Die Legende von Paul und Paula (Review)," *Theater der Zeit*, January 1984.

Kammann, Uwe. "Dialektischer Pragmatismus der treuen Hand: Das DDR-Rundfunküberleitungsgesetz—ein Wechselbalg," *epd [Evangelisher Pressedienst]. Kirche und Rundfunk*, 53, 7 July 1990.

Kampe, Dieter, and Rainer Pörtner. "DDR Unterhändler Günter Krause über Probleme der Einigung," *Der Spiegel*, 44/33, 13 August 1990.

Kant, Hermann. "Bonus und Malus, von Grass und Persil: Zu einem Spiegel-Gespräch," *Neues Deutschland*, 21/22, July 1990.

Kinzer, Stephen. "Dueling Playwrights at Bertolt Brecht's Berliner Ensemble," *New York Times*, 25 June 1995.

Kleinwächter, Wolfgang. "Deutsche Rundfunkneuordnung: Rückblick auf eine verpaßte Chance," *Funk-Korrespondez*, 2 January 1992.

Klier, Freya. "Heiner Müller und der deutsche Wolf im braven Hund," *die tageszeitung*, 18 January 1993.

Kohse, Petra. "Ein sächsicher Römer. Gestern wurde der Dichter und Theaterleiter Heiner Müller auf dem Dorotheenstädtischen Friedhof in Berlin beerdigt: Ein angemessen ratloser Abschied," *die tageszeitung*, 17 January 1996.

Kramer, Jane. "Letter from Europe," *New Yorker*, 25 May 1992.

Krug, Hartmut. "Auch Theater sind sterblich," *Theater Heute*, January 1992.

Kunert, Günter. "Weltfremd und blind: Zum Streit um die Literatur der DDR," *Frankfurter Allgemeine Zeitung*, 30 June 1990.

Lattmann, Gunhild. "Jetzt ist die Kraftprobe unerhört," *Theater der Zeit*, October 1989.

Lehming, Malte. "Das Goldhagen Phänomen." *Der Tagesspiegel*, 26 June 1998.

Lepenies, Wolf. "Alles rechtens—nichts mit rechten Dingen," *Die Zeit*, 47/51, 11 December 1992.

Leudts, Peter. "Nicht zu Ende gedacht," *Funk-Korrespondenz*, 13 July 1990.

Lüttke, Hans. "Sonnabend-Demo Positives und Negatives entnommen," *Neues Deutschland*, 7 November 1989.

Maron, Monika. "Die Schriftsteller und das Volk," *Der Spiegel*, 44/7, 12 February 1990.

Meier-Bergfeld, Peter. "Als Wessi-Lehrer abgelehnt," *Der Tagesspiegel*, 3 September 1992.

Menge, Marlies. "Sägen am eigenen Ast: 'Distel'-Chefin Gisela Oechelhaeuser—oder: Kabarett als Überlebenstrategie," *Die Zeit*, 48/19, 7 May 1993.

Merschmeier, Michael. "Heiner und 'Heiner': Im Dickicht der Stasi. Ein deutsches Leben?" *Theater Heute*, February 1993.

Mohr, Rienhard. "Die Wirklichkeit ausgepfiffen," *Der Spiegel*, 53/27, 29 June 1998.

Morgner, Martin, and Liane Düsterhöft. "Theater unter dem Dach [Interview with Liane Düsterhöft]," *Theater der Zeit*, March 1991.

"Die Müller Überschwemmung," *Der Spiegel*, 51/3, 15 January 1996.

Müller, Heiner. "Gegen die Hysterie der Macht, Erkärungen Heiner Müllers und seines Anwalts zum Stasi Vorwurf," *Der Tagesspiegel*, 15 January 1993.

———. "Nun scheint es, daß die Freiheit erstmal ins nächste Kaufhaus führt," *Der Spiegel*, 43/49, 4 December 1989.

———. "Ohne Hoffnung, ohne Verzweiflung," *Der Spiegel*, 49/43, 4 December 1989.

———. "Plädoyer für den Widerspruch," *Neues Deutschland*, 14 December 1989.

"Nach vier Wochen hatten die mich klein," *Berliner Zeitung*, 18/19 January 1992.

"Neues Programm wackelt: Will Mühlfenzl den verbleibenden DFF-Kanal teilweise den Privaten zuschanzen," *Junge Welt*, 30 November 1990.

Nolte, Ernst. "Die fortwirkende Verblendung," *Frankfurter Allgemeine Zeitung*, 22 February 1992.

Novak, Helga. "Offener Brief an Sara Kirsch, Wolf Biermann und Jürgen Fuchs," *Der Spiegel*, 45/44, 28 October 1991.

"Die Opfer der Diktatur sitzen nicht in Talk Shows: Gespräch von Jürgen Serke mit Jürgen Fuchs," *Welt*, 4 November 1991.

"Politische Kultur im Vereinigten Deutschland," *Utopie kreativ*, January 1992.

Raddatz, Fritz J. "Äußerung Christa Wolfs in der Fernsehsendung 'Kulturreport' vom 24. Januar," *Die Zeit*, 48/5, 29 January 1993.

————. "Es geht. Geht es? Eindrücke vom zweiten Berliner Ost-West-Treffen der Schriftsteller," *Die Zeit*, 38/19, 13 May 1983.

————. "Günter Grass, deutscher Dichter." *Die Zeit* 52/42, 10 October 1997.

————. "Von der Beschädigung der Literatur durch ihre Urheber," *Die Zeit*, 48/5, 29 January 1993.

Radisch, Iris. "Krieg der Köpfe, Heiner Müller und die Stasi: Die Westdeutschen zählen Quittungen, die Ostdeutschen verteidigen ihre Geschichte. Der Dichter liest Kafka und die Akten schweigen," *Die Zeit*, 48/5, 29 January 1993.

Rathenow, Lutz. "Operativer Vorgang Assistent: Stasi," *Stern*, 9 January 1992.

Reich, Jens. "Die Einheit: Gelungen und gescheitert," *Die Zeit*, 50/38, 15 September 1995.

Rockwell, John. "Berliner Ensemble in the 90's: Brecht's Old House Is Divided," *New York Times*, 9 February 1993.

Ross, Jan. "Abschied von den Lebenslügen: Jens Reich und Heiner Müller diskutieren in Berlin über die Rolle der Intellektuellen," *Frankfurter Allgemeine Zeitung*, 2 April 1992.

————. "Die Geister, die der Krieg rief," *Die Zeit*, 17 June 1999.

Rühle, Günter. "Die Zeit des Übergangs," *Theater der Zeit*, June 1991.

Schaller, Henning. "Neu anfangen, unsere Chance," *Theater der Zeit*, February 1990.

Schedlinski, Rainer. " 'Dem Druck, immer mehr sagen zu müssen, hielt ich nicht stand': Literatur, Staatssicherheit und der Prenzlauer Berg," *Frankfurter Allgemeine Zeitung*, 14 January 1992.

Schiewe, Siehard. "Zurück zum Dogma," *Spandauer Volksblatt Berlin*, 20 July 1966.

Schirrmacher, Frank. "Abschied von der Literatur der Bundesrepublik," *Frankfurter Allgemeine Zeitung*, 2 October 1990.

————. "Dem Druck des härteren strengeren Lebens standhalten: Christa Wolf Aufsätze, Reden, und ihre jüngste Erzählung 'Was Bleibt,' " *Frankfurter Allgemeine Zeitung*, 2 July 1990.

————. "Ein grausames Spiel: Der Fall Anderson und die Stasi-Akten," *Frankfurter Allgemeine Zeitung*, 20 October 1991.

————. "Fälle Wolf und Müller," *Frankfurter Allgemeine Zeitung*, 21 January 1993.

————. "Literatur und Staatssicherheit," *Frankfurter Allgemeine Zeitung*, 28 January 1993.

————. "Das Prinzip Handwerk: Zurück zur Kunst nach Jahrzehnten des Dilletantismus," *Frankfurter Allgemeine Zeitung*, 5 March 1995.

————. "Verdacht und Verrat. Die Stasi-Vergangenheit verändert die literarische Szene," *Frankfurter Allgemeine Zeitung*, 5 November 1991.

Schlesinger, Klaus. "Ich gestehe! Ich verlange! Ein Lehrstück über die Macht des Gerüchts, oder: Etwas bleibt immer hängen," *Die Zeit*, 47/8, 14 February 1992.

————. "Ich war ein Roman: Blick auf eine Kolportage," *Die Zeit*, 47/10, 17 March 1992.

Schmid, Thomas. "Pinscherseligkeit: Über die deutschen Intellektuellen und ihre Unfähigkeit mit der jüngsten Geschichte zurechtzukommen," *Die Zeit*, 47/16, 3 April 1992.

Schmitter, Elke. "Heiner Müller Stasi-Gespräche: Ein Anarchist paktiert. Ein Mann für gewisse Stunden," *die tageszeitung*, 12 January 1993.

Schneider, Karl. "Das Ensemble," *Theater der Zeit*, February 1989.

Schneider, Peter. "Gefangen in der Geschichte," *Der Spiegel*, 47/3, 18 January 1993.

Schöder, Richard. "Es ist doch nicht alles schlecht. Einspruch gegen Jürgen Habermas: Auch im Faktischen steckt manchmal ein bißchen Vernunft," *Die Zeit*, 46/23, 7 June 1991.

————. "Die Gesellschaft läßt sich nicht therapieren: Was heißt Vergangenheitsbewältigung im Osten?" *Franfurter Allgemeine Zeitung*, 2 February 1993.

Schütte, Wolfram. "Auf dem Schrotthaufen der Geschichte: Zu einer denkwürdigvoreiligen Verabschiedung der bundesdeutschen Literatur,'" *Frankfurter Rundschau*, 20 October 1989.

————. "Reißwolf: Zu einem Eilverfahren beim Umgang mit der DDR-Literatur," *Frankfurter Rundschau*, 8 June 1990.

————. "Zum Eingeständnis Andersons," *Frankfurter Rundschau*, 2 November 1991.

Schwarz, Hans-Peter. "Das Ende der Identitätsneurose," *Rheinischer Merkur*, 7 September 1990.

Seyfarth, Ingrid. "Die Saison 1989–1990," *Theater der Zeit*, September 1990.

Siemons, Mark. "Mit Derrida über den Fluß," *Frankfurter Allgemeine Zeitung*, 4 January 1996.

Simon, Annette. "Fremd im eigenen Land," *Die Zeit* 54/25, 17 June 1999.

Simon, Dieter. "Verschleudert und verschludert," *Die Zeit*, 50/15, 7 April 1995.

Speicher, Stephan. "Die gekränkte Würde der Ostdeutschen: Monika Marons Angriff auf ihre Landsleute. Eine Diskussion in Potsdam," *Frankfurter Allgemeine Zeitung*, 15 September 1992.

"Standpunkte," *Theater der Zeit*, March 1990.

Strauß, Botho. "Anschwellender Bocksgesang," *Der Spiegel*, 47/7, 8 February 1993.

Thron, Ute. "Medienkontrollrat—ein Wolf ohne Zähne," *die tageszeitung*, 3 April 1990.

————. "Medienkontrollrat tritt ab," *die tageszeitung*, 21 September 1990.

Tragelehn, B. K., and Lothar Trolle. "Rechtfertigungsreden sind überflüssig. B. K. Tragelehn und Lothar Trolle über die Stasi-Vorwurfe gegenüber Heiner Müller," *Berliner Zeitung*, 20 January 1993.

"Verrat als Performance?" *NM!Messitsch* 5 (1992): 16, 31.

Walser, Martin. "Über das Selbstgespräch: Ein flagranter Versuch," *Die Zeit* 55/3, 13 January 2000.

Waschinsky, Peter. "Die Off-Theaterszene vor und nach der Wende," *Theater der Zeit*, August 1990.

————. "Die real existierende (?) freie Theaterszene," *Theater der Zeit*, August 1990.

Weinraub, Bernhard. "Heinrich Böll Wins Nobel for Literature," *New York Times*, 20 October 1972.

Wekwerth, Manfred. "Die Welt braucht Veränderung," *Theater der Zeit*, December 1989.

Wille, Franz, and Ulrich Roloff-Momin. "Weniger Staat, mehr Verantwortung [Interview with Ulrich Roloff-Momin]," *Theater Heute*, May 1993.

Wolf, Christa. "Eine Auskunft," *Berliner Zeitung*, 21 January 1993.

"Zeitungsverkauf steht bevor: Treuhand will Entscheidung über Ost-Regionalblätter fällen," *Saarbrücker Zeitung*, 9 April 1991.

Books and Journal Articles

Adorno, Theodor W. *Noten zur Literatur*. Frankfurt am Main, 1980.

Agde, Günter, ed. *Kahlschlag: Das 11. Plenum des ZK der SED 1965. Studien und Dokumente*. Berlin, 1991.

Albrecht, Clemens et al. *Die intellektuelle Gründung der Bundesrepublik: Eine Wirkungs-geschichte der Frankfurter Schule.* Frankfurt am Main, 1999.

Albrecht, Richard. *Das Bedürfnis nach echten Geschichten: Zur zeitgenössischen Unterhal-tungsliteratur in der DDR.* Frankfurt am Main, 1987.

Albrecht, Ulrich. *Die Abwicklung der DDR.* Opladen, 1992.

Alter, Peter. *Nationalismus.* Frankfurt am Main, 1985.

Anderson, Benedict. *Imagined Communities.* London, 1983.

Anderson, Sascha. "Quelle IMB David Metzer." In *MachtSpiele: Literatur und Staatsicher-heit im Fokus Prenzlauer Berg,* edited by Peter Böthig and Klaus Michael. Leipzig, 1993: 250–75.

Anderson, Sascha, and Elke Erb, eds. *Berührung is nur eine Randerscheinung: Neue Lite-ratur aus der DDR.* Cologne, 1985.

Anz, Thomas, ed. *"Es geht nicht um Christa Wolf": Der Literaturstreit im vereinigten Deutschland.* Munich, 1991.

Arendt, Hannah. *The Human Condition.* Chicago, 1958.

———. *Men in Dark Times.* New York, 1968.

———. *Von der Menschlichkeit in finsteren Zeiten: Gedanken zu Lessing.* Munich, 1960 ("On Humanity in Dark Times: Thoughts About Lessing," in *Men in Dark Times* [New York, 1968], 3–31).

Aristotle. *The Poetics of Aristotle: Translation and Commentary.* Trans. Stephen Halli-well. Chapel Hill, N.C., 1987.

Arnold, Heinz Ludwig, ed. *Literatur in der DDR: Rückblicke.* Munich, 1991.

Arnold, Heinz Ludwig, and Frauke Meyer-Gosau, eds. *Die Abwicklung der DDR.* Göttingen, 1992.

Aron, Raymond. *The Opium of the Intellectuals.* Garden City, N.Y., 1957.

Ash, Mitchell G. "Geschichtswissenschaft, Geschichtskultur und der ostdeutsche Hi-storikerstreit." *Geschichte und Gesellschaft* 24 (1998): 283–304.

———. "Higher Education in the New German States: Renewal or the Importation of Crisis?" In *German Universities Past and Future: Crisis or Renewal?* edited by Mitchell G. Ash. Providence, 1997, 84–109.

Ash, Timothy Garton. *The Magic Lantern: The Revolution of '89 Witnessed in Warsaw, Budapest, Berlin, and Prague.* New York, 1990.

———. *The Uses of Adversity: Essays on the Fate of Central Europe.* New York, 1989.

Assmann, Aleida. *Arbeit am nationalen Gedächtnis: Eine kurze Geschichte der deutschen Bildungsidee.* Frankfurt am Main, 1993.

Bade, Klaus J., ed. *Das Manifest der 60: Deutschland und die Einwanderung.* Munich, 1994.

Bahner, Werner. *Beitrag zum Sprachbewußtsein in der spanischen Literatur des 16. und 17. Jahrhunderts.* Berlin, 1956.

Bahro, Rudolf. *Alternative: Zur Kritik des real existierenden Sozialismus.* Frankfurt am Main, 1977.

Baier, Lothar. "Fighter und Sozialarbeiter oder die neue Kunst des rechten Einteilens." *Freibeuter* 53 (1992): 44–52.

Balibar, Etienne. "Racism and Nationalism." In *Race, Nation, Class: Ambiguous Identi-ties,* edited by E. Balibar and I. Wallerstein. London, 1991.

Barck, Simone, Martina Langermann, and Siegfried Lokatis. *Jedes Buch ein Abenteuer: Zensur-System und literarische Öffentlichkeit in der DDR bis Ende der sechziger Jahre.* Berlin, 1997.

Baring, Arnulf. *Deutschland, was nun?* Berlin, 1991.

————. *Unser neuer Größenwahn: Deutschland zwischen Ost und West.* Stuttgart, 1989.

Bathrick, David. *The Powers of Speech: The Politics of Culture in the GDR.* Lincoln, 1995.

Bauman, Zygmunt. *Legislators and Interpreters: On Modernity, Post-Modernity, and Intellectuals.* Ithaca, 1987.

Baumert, Heinz. "Das verbotene Heft: Filmwissenschaftliche Mitteilungen, 2/1965." In *Kahlschlag: Das 11. Plenum des ZK der SED 1965: Studien und Dokumente,* edited by Günter Agde. Berlin, 1991: 189–200.

Baumert, Heinz, and Hermann Herlinghaus. *20 Jahre DEFA-Spielfilm.* Berlin, 1968.

Bayer, Isabel, and Wolfgang Engel. "Diesseits der Hoffnung, jenseits der Furcht" (Interview with Wolfgang Engel). In *Theater 1990: Jahrbuch der Zeitschrift Theater Heute.* Seelze, 1990, 47–51.

Becher, Johannes R. *Erziehung zur Freiheit: Gedanken und Betrachtungen.* Berlin, 1946.

————. "Macht der Literatur." In *Von der Größe unserer Literatur,* edited by Johannes R. Becher. Leipzig, 1971: 224–33.

————. "Von der Größe unserer Literatur." In *4. Deutscher Schriftstellerkongreß,* edited by Deutscher Schriftstellerverband. Protokolle 1 & 2, 1956: 11–39.

————. "Von der Größe unserer Literatur der Arbeiterklasse." In *Gesammelte Werke,* edited by Johannes R. Becher Archiv der Akademie der Künste, vol. 18. Berlin, 1981: 499–534.

Becker, Johannes M. *Ein Land geht in den Westen.* Bonn, 1991.

Becker, Peter von. "Nach Sachsen, nach Sachsen: Eindrücke in Dresden und Leipzig, über Aufführungen der beiden größten Schauspielhäuser außerhalb der Hauptstadt." In *Theater 1988: Jahrbuch der Zeitschrift Theater Heute.* Seelze, 1988: 36–41.

————. "Theaterspielen im neuen Deutschland." In *Theater 1990: Jahrbuch der Zeitschrift Theater Heute.* Seelze, 1990: 128.

Becker, Ulrich, Horst Becker, and Walter Ruhland. *Zwischen Angst und Aufbruch.* Düsseldorf, 1992.

Beckermann, Thomas. "'Die Diktatur repräsentiert das Abwesende nicht': Essay on Monika Maron, Wolfgang Hilbig and Gert Neumann." In *German Literature at a Time of Change: 1989–1990: German Unity and German Identity in a Literary Perspective,* edited by Arthur Williams, Stuart Parkes, and Roland Smith. Bern, 1991: 97–116.

"Befehl Nr. 333 der SMAD über die Gründung von Gesellschaftswissenschaftlichen Fakultäten von 2. Dezember 1946." In *Dokumente der Sowjetischen Militäradministration im Deutschland zum Hoch- und Fachschulwesen 1945–1949,* edited by Gotfried Handel and Roland Köhler. Studien zur Hochschulentwicklung, vol. 57. Berlin, 1975: 56–61.

Bell, Daniel. *The Coming of Post-Industrial Society* (New York, 1976).

Benda, Julien. *La trahison des clercs,* rev. ed. [1927] Paris, 1947 (The treason of the intellectuals. Trans. Herbert Read. [New York, 1969]).

Berendse, Gerri-Jan. "Outcast in Berlin: Opposition durch Entziehung bei der jüngeren Generation." *Zeitschrift für Germanistik,* n.s. 1 (1991): 21–27.

Berg, Gunnar, et al. "Zur Situation der Universitäten und außeruniversitären Forschungseinrichtungen in den neuen Ländern." *Nova Acta Leopoldina,* n.s. 71 (220) (1994).

Bergen, Werner von, and Walter H. Pehle, eds. *Denken im Zwiespalt: Über den Verrat von Intellektuellen im 20. Jahrhundert*. Frankfurt am Main, 1996.

Berry, Ellen E. *Postcommunism and the Body Politic*. New York, 1995.

Besier, Gerhard, and Stephan Wolf, eds. *"Pfarrer, Christen und Katholiken": Das Ministerium für Staatssicherheit der ehemaligen DDR und die Kirchen*. 2d ed. Neunkirchen, 1992.

Bhabha, Homi K., ed. *Nation and Narration*. New York, 1990.

Bialas, Wolfgang. "Ostdeutsche Diskurse und die Weimarer Republik: Variationen zum Verhältnis von Geist und Macht." In *Die Weimarer Republik zwischen Metropole und Provinz: Intellektuellendiskurse zur politischen Kultur*, edited by Wolfgang Bialas and Burkhard Stenzel. Weimar, 1996.

―――. *Vom unfreien Schweben zum freien Fall: Ostdeutsche Intellektuelle im gesellschaftlichen Umbruch*. Frankfurt am Main, 1996.

Bialas, Wolfgang, and Eckhardt Fuchs, eds. *Macht und Geist: Intellektuelle in der Zwischenkriegszeit*. Leipzig, 1995.

Bierman, Wolf. *Der Sturz des Daedalus oder Eizes für die Eingeborenen der Fidschi-Insel über den IM Judas Ischariot und den Kuddelmuddel in Deutschland seit dem Golfkrieg*. Cologne, 1992.

Bilanz einer Ausstellung: Dokumentation der Kontroverse um die Ausstellung "Vernichtungskrieg. Verbrechen der Wehrmacht 1941 bis 1944." Edited by Kulturreferat, Landeshauptstadt München. Munich, 1998.

Bisky, Lothar, Uwe-Jens Heuer, and Michael Schumann, eds. *Rücksichten: Politische und juristische Aspekte der DDR-Geschichte*. Hamburg, 1993.

Bitov, Andrei. *A Captive of the Caucasus*. Trans. Susan Brownsberger. New York, 1992.

―――. *The Monkey Link: A Pilgrimage Story*. Trans. Susan Brownsberger. New York, 1995.

―――. *Pushkin House*. Trans. Susan Brownsberger. Ann Arbor, 1990.

―――. *Ten Short Stories*. Trans. Susan Brownsberger. Moscow, 1991.

Bitterman, Klaus, ed. *Der rasende Mob: Die Ossis zwischen Selbstmitleid und Barbarei*. Berlin, 1993.

Blackbourn, David, and Geoff Eley. *The Peculiarities of German History*. Oxford, 1984.

Bloch, Ernst. *Das Princip Hoffnung*, 3 vols. [1954–1959]; Frankfurt am Main, 1977 (The principle of hope. Trans. Neville Plaice, Steven Plaice, and Paul Knight [Cambridge, Mass., 1986]).

Blunk, Harry, Dirk Jungnickel, and Berend von Nottbeck, eds. *Filmland der DDR: Ein Reader zur Geschichte, Funktion, und Wirkung der DEFA*. Cologne, 1990.

Bodek, Janusz. "Ein 'Geflecht aus Schuld und Rache'? Die Kontroversen um Fassbinders Der Müll, die Stadt und der Tod." In *Deutsche Nachkriegsliteratur und der Holocaust*, edited by Stephan Braese et al. Frankfurt am Main, 1998: 351–84.

Boden, Petra. "Strukturen der Lenkung von Literatur: Das Gesetz zum Schutz der Berufsbeschreibung Schriftsteller." In *MachtSpiele: Literatur und Staatsicherheit*, edited by Peter Böthig and Klaus Michael. Leipzig, 1993: 217–27.

―――. "Universitätsgermanistik in der SBZ/DDR: Personalpolitik und struktureller Wandel 1945–1965." In *Geschichte der Deutschen Literaturwissenschaft 1945–1965*, edited by Rainer Rosenberg and Petra Boden. Berlin, 1996: 119–56.

Bogdal, Klaus Michael. "Wer darf sprechen." In *Der deutsch-deutsche Literaturstreit oder "Freunde, es spricht sich schlecht mit gebundener Zunge,"* edited by Karl Deiritz and Hannes Krauss. Hamburg, 1991: 40–49.

Böhme, Hans-Ludwig. "Dresden im Herbst—eine Fotodokumentation." In *Theater 1990: Jahrbuch der Zeitschrift Theater Heute*. Seelze, 1990: 132–37.

Böhme, Petra. "Öffentliche Bibliotheken in den neuen Bundesländern." *Mitteilungen aus der kulturwissenschaftlichen Forschung* 32 (1993): 452–59.

Bohn, Rainer, et al., eds. *Mauer Show: Das Ende der DDR, die deutsche Einheit und die Medien*. Berlin, 1992.

Bohrer, Karl-Heinz. "Die Ästhetik im Ausgang ihrer Unmündigkeit." *Merkur* 44 (1990): 851–65.

———. *Die gefährdete Phantasie*. Munich, 1970.

———. "Kulturschutzgebiet DDR." *Merkur* 500 (1990): 1015–18.

———. *Plötzlichkeit: Zum Augenblick des ästhetischen Scheins*. Frankfurt am Main, 1981 (Suddenness: On the moment of aesthetic appearance. Trans. Ruth Crowley [New York, 1994]).

———. "Provinzialismus" (I–VI)." *Merkur* 44 (1990): 1096–1102; 45 (1991): 255–61, 348–56, 537–45, 710–27, 1059–67.

Bohrer, Karl Heinz, ed. *Sprachen der Ironie—Sprachen des Ernstes*. Frankfurt am Main, 2000.

Böll, Heinrich. *Ansichten eines Clowns*. Cologne, 1963 (The clown. Trans. Leila Vennewitz [New York, 1965]).

———. *Billiard um Halbzehn*. Cologne, 1959 (Billiards at half past nine. Trans. Patrick Bowers [London, 1961]).

———. *Haus ohne Hüter*. Cologne, 1954 (The unguarded house. Trans. Marvyn Saville [London, 1957]).

———. *Und sagte kein einziges Wort*. Cologne, 1953 (And never said a word. Trans. Leila Vennewitz [New York, 1978]).

———. *Wo warst Du Adam?* Opladen, 1951 (And where were you, Adam? Trans. Marvyn Saville [Evanston, IL, 1994]).

Borneman, John. *After the Wall: East Meets West in the New Berlin*. New York, 1991.

———. *Belonging in the Two Berlins: Kin, State, Nation*. Cambridge, Mass., 1992.

———. *Settling Accounts: Violence, Justice, and Accountability in Postsocialist Europe*. Princeton, 1997.

———. "Time-Space Compression and the Continental Divide in German Subjectivity." *New Formations* 3, no. 1 (winter 1993): 102–18.

———. "Towards a Theory of Ethnic Cleansing: Territorial Sovereignty, Heterosexuality, and Europe." In *Subversions of International Order: Studies in the Political Anthropology of Culture*, edited by John Bornemann. Albany, N.Y.,1998: 273–318.

———. "Trouble in the Kitchen: Totalitarianism, Love, and Resistance to Authority." In *Moralizing States and the Ethnography of the Present*, edited by Sally Falk Moore. Washington, D. C., 1993: 93–118.

———. "Uniting the German Nation: Law, Narrative, and Historicity." *American Ethnologist* 20 (1993): 288–311.

Bortfeldt, Heinrich. *Von der SED zur PDS: Wandlung zur Demokratie?* Bonn, 1992.

Bos, Ellen. *Leserbriefe in Tageszeitungen der DDR*. Opladen, 1992.

Böthig, Peter, and Klaus Michael, eds. *MachtSpiele: Literatur und Staatsicherheit im Fokus Prenzlauer Berg*. Leipzig, 1993.

Bourdieu, Pierre. *Acts of Resistance: Against the Tyranny of the Market*. New York, 1998.

―――. *Die feinen Unterschiede: Kritik der gesellschaftlichen Urteilskraft.* Frankfurt am Main, 1987.

―――. "Die historische Genese einer reinen Ästhetik." *Merkur* 46, no. 11 (1992): 967–79.

―――. *Die Intellektuellen und die Macht.* Hamburg, 1991.

―――. "L'emprise du journalisme." *Actes de la recherche en sciences sociales* 101–2 (1994): 3–9.

―――. *Les Héritiers: Les étudians et la culture.* Paris, 1964.

―――. *On Television.* New York, 1998.

―――. *Sozialer Raum und Klassen.* Frankfurt am Main, 1985.

Bovery, Margret. *Der Verrat im XX. Jahrhundert,* 4 vols. Reinbek, 1956 (*Treason in the Twentieth Century* [New York, 1963]).

Boyle, Maryellen. "The Revolt of the Communist Journalist: East Germany." *Media, Culture, and Society* 14 (1992): 133–39.

Brady, Philip, and Ian Wallace, eds. *Prenzlauer Berg: Bohemia in East Berlin?* Amsterdam, 1995.

Braitling, Petra, and Walter Reese-Schäfer, eds. *Universalismus, Nationalismus und die neue Einheit der Deutschen.* Frankfurt am Main, 1991.

Brandt, Willy. " . . . was zusammengehört." In *Reden zu Deutschland.* Bonn, 1990.

Brasch, Thomas. "Und über uns schließt sich ein Himmel aus Stahl." In *Vor den Vätern sterben die Söhne,* edited by Thomas Brasch. Berlin, 1977: 27–60.

Bräuer, Siegfried, and Clemens Vollnhals, eds. *"In der DDR gibt es keine Zensur": Die Evangelische Verlagsanstalt und die Praxis der Druckgenehmigung 1954–1989.* Leipzig, 1995.

Braun, Volker. "Die Kunst als Streit der Interne." In *Theater 1988: Jahrbuch der Zeitschrift Theater Heute.* Seelze, 1988: 130–31.

Brecht, Bertolt. *Arbeitsjournal.* Frankfurt am Main, 1981.

―――. *Gedichte,* vol. 3. Berlin, 1978.

―――. *Gesammelte Werke.* Frankfurt am Main, 1967.

Brickner, Richard M. *Is Germany Incurable?* Philadelphia, 1943.

Brie, André, Michael Brie, Wilfried Ettl, and Dieter Segert. "Elf Thesen zur Krise der DDR und der SED." In *Das Umbaupapier (DDR): Argumente gegen die Wiedervereinigung,* edited by Rainer Land. Berlin, 1990: 155.

Brockmann, Stephen. "The Good Person of Germany as a Post-Unification Discursive Phenomenon." *German Politics and Society* 15 (1998): 1–25.

―――. "Literature and Convergence." In *Beyond 1989: Re-Reading German Literary History Since 1945,* edited by Keith Bullivant. Providence, 1997: 49–67.

―――. *Literature and German Unification.* Cambridge, U.K.,1999.

Brubaker, Rogers. *Citizenship and Nationhood in France and Germany.* Cambridge, U.K., 1992.

Brunkhorst, Horst. *Der entzauberte Intellektuelle. Über die neue Beliebigkeit des Denkens.* Hamburg, 1990.

―――. "The Intellectual in Mandarin Country: The West German Case." In *Intellectuals in Liberal Democracies: Political Influence and Social Involvement,* edited by Alain G. Gagnon. New York, 1987: 121–42.

―――. *Der Intellektuelle im Land der Mandarine.* Frankfurt am Main, 1987.

―――. "Das Verschwinden der Sozialwissenschaften aus dem 'geistigen Leben.'" *Literaturmagazin* 15 (1985): 69–81.

Bude, Heinz. *Die ironische Nation: Soziologie als Zeitdiagnose.* Hamburg, 1999.

Büchner, Georg. *Werke und Briefe.* Munich, 1980.

Buchwald, Manfred. "Bestandsaufnahme eines Neubeginns." In *So durften wir glauben zu kämpfen . . . Erfahrung mit DDR-Medien,* edited by Edith Spielhagen. Berlin, 1993: 165–75.

Buck-Bechler, Gertraude, ed. *Die Hochschulen in den neuen Ländern der Bundesrepublik Deutschland: Ein Handbuch der Hochschulerneuerung.* Weinheim, 1997.

Buck-Bechler, Gertraude, and Heidrun Jahn, eds. *Hochschulerneuerung in den neuen Bundesländern: Bilanz nach vier Jahren.* Weinheim, 1994.

Bürger, Ulrich. *Das sagen wir so natürlich nicht! Donnerstag-Argus bein Herrn Geggel.* Berlin, 1990.

Büscher, Wolfgang, and Peter Wensierski. *Null Bock auf DDR: Aussteigerjugend im anderen Deutschland.* Hamburg, 1984.

Bullivant, Keith. "The End of the Dream of the 'Other Germany': The 'German Question' in West German Letters." In *1870/71 – 1989/90: German Unifications and the Change of Literary Discourse,* edited by Walter Pape. Berlin, 1993: 303–19.

Calließ, Jörg , ed. *Historische Orientierung nach der Epochenwende.* Loccum, 1993.

Carey, John. *The Intellectuals and the Masses: Pride and Prejudice Among the Literary Intelligentsia, 1880–1939.* London, 1992.

Caysa, Volker, et al., eds. *"Hoffnung kann enttäuscht werden": Ernst Bloch in Leipzig.* Frankfurt am Main, 1992.

Charle, Christophe. *Les intellectuels en Europe au XIXe siècle: Essai d'histoire comparée.* Paris, 1996.

Charle, Christophe. *Naissance des "Intellectuels," 1880–1900.* Paris, 1990.

Christ, Peter, and Ralf Neubauer. *Kolonie im eigenen Land: Die Treuhand, Bonn und die Wirtschaftskatastrophe.* Berlin, 1991.

Cohn-Bendit, Daniel, et al., eds. *Einwanderbares Deutschland.* Frankfurt am Main, 1991.

Cohn-Bendit, Daniel, and Thomas Schmid. *Heimat Babylon: Das Wagnis der multikulturellen Demokratie.* Hamburg, 1992.

Conze, Werner, and Jürgen Kocka, eds. *Bildungsbürgertum in 19. Jahrhundert.* Stuttgart, 1985.

Corino, Karl, ed. *"Die Akte Kant," "Martin," der Stasi, und die Literatur in Ost und West.* Hamburg, 1995.

Crome, Erhard. "DDR Perzeptionen: Kontext und Zugangsmuster." *Berliner Debatte: Initial 9* (1998): 45–58.

Dahlke, Birgit. "Avant-gardist, Mediator, and . . . Mentor?" *Women in GermanYearbook* 13 (1997): 123–32.

Dahn, Daniela. *Westwärts und nicht vergessen: Vom Unbehagen in der Einheit.* Berlin, 1996.

Dahn, Daniela, and Barbara Erdmann. *Wir bleiben hier, oder, Wem gehört der Osten: Vom Kampf um Häuser und Wohnungen in den neuen Bundesländern.* Reinbek, 1994.

Dahrendorf, Ralf. "Einführung in die Soziologie." *Soziale Welt* 40 (1989): 1–10.

———. *Reflections on the Revolution in Europe.* New York, 1990.

———. "Die Sache mit der Nation." *Merkur* 44 (1990): 823–34.

Dalos, György. *Ungarn: Vom Roten Stern zur Stephanuskrone.* Frankfurt am Main, 1991.

Dalton, Russel J. *Two German Electorates?* Berkeley, 1992.

———, ed. *The New Germany Votes: Unification and the Creation of the New German Party System.* Providence, 1993.

Danyel, Jürgen, ed. *Die geteilte Vergangenheit: Zum Umgang mit Nationalsozialismus und Widerstand in beiden deutschen Staaten.* Berlin, 1995.

Darnton, Robert. *Berlin Journal, 1989–1990.* New York, 1991.

———. "Censorship, a Comparative View: France, 1789—East Germany, 1989." *Representations* 49 (winter 1995): 40–49.

"Daten zur Mediensituation in Deutschland." *Media Perspektiven* (1991): 42–58.

de Bruyn, Günter. "Als der Krieg Ausbrach." *Liber: Europäische Kulturzeitschrift* 1 (October 1989): 4.

DEFA. *Auf Neuen Wegen: 5 Jahre Forschrittlicher Deutscher Film.* Berlin, 1951.

Deiritz, Karl, and Hannes Krauss, eds. *Der deutsch-deutsche Literaturstreit oder "Freunde, es spricht sich schlecht mit gebundener Zunge."* Hamburg, 1991.

Deleuze, Gilles, and Félix Guattari. *Anti-Oedipus and Schizophrenia.* Trans. Robert Hurley, Mark Seem, and Helen Lane. New York, 1977.

Domdey, Horst. "DDR-Literatur as Literatur der Epochenillusion." In *Die DDR im vierzigsten Jahr* (=22. Tagung zum Stand der DDR-Forschung in der Bundesrepublik). Cologne, 1989: 137–48.

Dönhoff, Marion, et al. *Ein Manifest: Weil das Land sich ändern muss.* Reinbek, 1992.

Döring, Stefan, and Egmont Hesse. "Introview: Egmont Hesse-Stefan Döring." In *Sprache & Antwort: Stimmen und Texte einer andere Literatur aus der DDR,* edited by Egmont Hesse. Frankfurt am Main, 1988.

Dornhof, Dorothea. "Von der 'Gelehrtenrepublik' zur marxistischen Forschungsgemeinschaft an der Akademie der Wissenschaften: Das Institut für deutsche Sprache und Literatur." In *Deutsche Literaturwissenschaft 1945–1965: Fallstudien zu Institutionen, Diskursen, Personen,* edited by Petra Boden and Rainer Rosenberg. Berlin, 1997: 173–203.

Drescher, Angela, ed. *Dokumentationen zu Christa Wolf, "Nachdenken über Christa T."* Hamburg, 1991.

Duffield, John S. *Political Culture, International Institutions, and German Security Policy after Unification.* Stanford, 1998.

Dümcke, Wolfgang, and Fritz Vilmar, eds. *Die Kolonialisierung der DDR: Kritische Analysen und Alternativen des Einigungsprozesses.* Münster, 1995.

Eckert, Detlef. "Die Volkswirtschaft der DDR im Spannungsfeld der Reformen." In *Kahlschlag: Das 11. Plenum des ZK der SED 1965. Studien und Dokumente,* edited by Günter Agde. Berlin, 1991: 20–32.

Eckert, Rainer. "Entnazifizierung offiziell und inoffiziell: Die SBZ 1945 und die DDR 1989." In *Wendezeiten-Zeitenwende. Zur 'Entnazifizierung' und 'Entstalinisierung',* edited by Rainer Eckert, Alexander von Plato, and Jörn Schütrumpf. Hamburg, 1991: 33–52.

———. "Vergangenheitsbewältigung oder überwältigt uns die Vergangeheit? Oder: Auf einem Sumpf ist schlecht bauen." *Internationale wissenschaftliche Korrespondenz (IWK) zur Geschichte der deutschen Arbeiterbewegung* 2 (1992): 228–32.

Eigler, Friederike. "At the Margins of East Berlin's 'Counter-Culture': Elke Erb's Winkelzüge and Gabriele Kachold's zügel los." *Women in German Yearbook* 9 (1993): 146–61.

Einhorn, Barbara. *Cinderella goes to Market: Citizenship, Gender, and Women's Movements in Eastern Europe.* New York, 1993.

Elsaesser, Thomas. *New Geman Cinema: A History.* New Brunswick, 1989.

Elster, Jan, Claus Offe, and Ulrich K. Preuss. *Institutional Design in Post-communist Societies: Rebuilding the Ship at Sea.* New York, 1998.

Ely, John. "The *Frankfurter Allgemeine Zeitung* and Contemporary National-Conservatism." *German Politics and Society* 13, no. 2 (1995): 81–121.

Emmerich, Wolfgang. "Affirmation-Utopie-Melancholie: Versuch einer Bilanz von vierzig Jahren DDR Literatur." *German Studies Review* 14 (1991): 325–44.

———. *Kleine Literaturgeschichte der DDR: Erweiterte Neuausgabe.* Leipzig, 1996.

———. "Die Literatur der DDR." In *Deutsche Literaturgeschichte von den Anfängen bis zur Gegenwart,* edited by Wolfgang Benlin et al. Stuttgart, 1992: 462.

Engler, Wolfgang. *Die Ostdeutschen: Kunde von einem verlorenen Land.* Berlin, 1999.

———. *Die ungewollte Moderne—Ost-West Passagen.* Frankfurt am Main, 1995.

Enquete Kommission, ed. *Aufarbeitung von Geschichte und Folgen der SED-Diktatur in Deutschland.* 9 vols. Frankfurt am Main, 1995.

Enzensberger, Hans Magnus. *Aussichten auf den Bürgerkrieg.* Frankfurt am Main, 1993.

———. "Gemeinplätze, die neueste Literatur betreffend." *Kursbuch* 15 (1968): 187–97.

———. *Die große Wanderung.* Frankfurt am Main, 1992.

Erb, Elke. "DDR und aus: Bemerken zu den Angriffen auf Christa Wolf." *Litfass* 49 (1990): 24–33.

———. *Kastanienallee.* Salzburg, 1988.

———. *Menschsein, nicht.* Basel, 1998.

———. *Sachverstand.* Basel, 2000.

———. *Unschuld, du Licht meiner Augen.* Göttingen, 1994.

———. "Vorwort." In *Berührung ist nur eine Randerscheinung: Neue Literatur aus der DDR,* edited by Sascha Anderson and Elke Erb. Cologne, 1985: 14–15.

———. *Der wilde Forst, der tiefe Wald.* Göttingen, 1995.

———. *Winkelzüge oder nicht vermutete, aufschlussreiche Verhältnisse.* Berlin, 1991.

———. *Winkelzüge oder nicht vermutete aufschlussreiche Verhältnisse,* with drawings by Angela Hampel. Berlin, 1992.

Erbe, Günter. *Der verfemte Moderne: Die Auseinandersetzung mit dem "Modernismus" in Kulturpolitik, Literaturwissenschaft und Literatur der DDR.* Opladen, 1993.

Erpenbeck, Fritz. "Formalismus und Dekadenz (1949)." In *Dokumente zur Kunst-, Literatur-, und Kulturpolitik der SED,* edited by Elmar Schubbe. Stuttgart, 1972: 109–13.

Esslin, Martin. *Bertolt Brecht: A Choice of Evils.* London, 1962.

Faktor, Jan. "Der große Ost-West-Sturm, oder Wo leben die letzten Gerechten." *CONstruktiv* 2 (1991): 30–31.

Feige, Hans Uwe. "Hans Mayers Vertreibung von der Karl-Marx-Universität Leipzig." *Deutschlandarchiv* 24, no. 7 (1991): 730–32.

Felsmann, Barbara, and Annett Gröschner, eds. *Durchgangszimmer Prenzlauer Berg: Eine Berliner Künstlersozialgeschichte in Selbstauskünften.* Berlin, 1999.

Film-Autoren-Kongreß, Deutsche. *Der Deutsche Film: Fragen-Forderungen-Aussichten. Bericht vom ersten Deutschen Film-Autoren-Kongreß 6–9 Juni 1947.* Berlin, 1947.

Filmreihe, Südwest 3. *Verbotene Filme der DDR.* Baden-Baden, 1991.

Fischer, Fritz. *Griff nach der Weltmacht: Die Kriegszielpolitik des kaiserlichen Deutschland 1914–18.* Düsseldorf, 1962 (*Germany's Aims in the First World War* [New York, 1967]).

Flotow, Luise von. "'Samizdat' in East Berlin." *Cross-Currents: A Yearbook of Central European History* 9 (1990): 197–218.

40 Jahre DDR - TschüSSED: 4.11.89. Katalog zur Ausstellung der "Initiativgruppe 4.11.89" im Museum für deutsche Geschichte, Berlin-Ost, und im Haus der Geschichte der Bundesrepublik Deutschland Bonn. Bonn, 1990.

Foucault, Michel. *Sexualität und Wahrheit*. Vol. 1. Frankfurt am Main, 1986 (The history of sexuality. Trans. Robert Hurley, vol. 1 [New York, 1978]).

Frank, Lawrence K. "The Historian as Therapist." In *Society as the Patient: Essays on Culture and Personality*. New Brunswick, 1948: 298–307.

Franke, Konrad. "'Deine Darstellung ist uns wesensfremd': Romane der 6oer Jahre in den Mühlen der DDR-Zensur." In *"Literaturentwicklungsprozesse": Die Zensur der Literatur in der DDR*, edited by Ernest Wichner and Herbert Wisener. Frankfurt am Main, 1993: 101–27.

Frei, Norbert. *Vergangenheitspolitik: Die Anfänge der Bundesrepublik und die NS-Vergangenheit*. Munich, 1996.

Freund, Rudolf, and Michael Hanisch, eds. *Mutter Kraussens Fahrt ins Glück: Filmprotokoll und Materialien*. Berlin, 1976.

Friedlander, Saul. "A Conflict of Memories? The New German Debates About the 'Final Solution.'" In *Memory, History, and the Extermination of the Jews in Europe*. Bloomington, 1993: 22–41.

Fries, Fritz Rudolf, and Kurt Batt. *Bemerkungen anhand eines Fundes oder das Mächen aus der Flasche: Texte zur Literatur*. Berlin, 1985.

Frith, Simon. "Popular Music and the Local State." In *Rock and Popular Music*, edited by Simon Frith, Tony Bennett, Lawrence Grossberg, John Shepherd, and Graeme Turner. London, 1993: 14–24.

Fuegi, John. *Bertolt Brecht: Chaos According to Plan*. Cambridge, U.K.,1989.

Fukuyama, Francis. *The End of History and the Last Man*. New York, 1992.

Fulbrook, Mary. *German National Identity After the Holocaust*. Cambridge, U.K., 1999.

Funke, Hajo. *Brandstifter*. Göttingen, 1993.

Für den Aufschwung der forschrittlichen deutschen Filmkunst. Berlin, 1952.

Furet, François. *Le passé d'une illusion: Essai sur l'idée communiste au XXe siècle*. Paris, 1995 (*The Passing of an Illusion: The Idea of Communism in the Twentieth Century* [Chicago, 1999]).

Furet, François, and Ernst Nolte. *"Feindliche Nähe": Kommunismus und Faschismus im 20. Jahrhundert*. Munich, 1998.

Furet, François, and Pierre Rosanvallon, eds. *La République du centre: La fin de l'exception française*. Paris, 1988.

Galenza, Ronald, and Heinz Havemeister, eds. *Wir wollen immer artig sein . . . Punk, New Wave, HipHop, Independent-Szene in der DDR, 1980–1990*. Berlin, 1999.

Gaus, Günter. *Kein einig Vaterland: Texte von 1991 bis 1998*. Berlin, 1998.

———. *Wo Deutschland liegt: Eine Ortsbestimmung*. Hamburg, 1983.

Geiger, Theodor. *Aufgaben und Stellung der Intelligenz in der Gesellschaft*. New York, 1975.

Geißler, Rainer. "Die ostdeutsche Sozialstruktur unter Modernisierungsdruck." *Aus Politik und Zeitgeschichte. Beilage zur Wochenzeitung "Das Parlament"* B29–39/92 (10 July 1992): 15–28.

Gellner, Ernest. *Nations and Nationalism*. Oxford, 1983.

Genscher, Hans-Dietrich. *Erinnerungen*. Berlin, 1995.

Germany, Federal Republic of, Ministry for Intra-German Relations, ed. *DDR-Handbuch*. Cologne, 1985.

Germany, German Democratic Republic of. *Constitution of the German Democratic Republic*, April 6, 1968, in the version of the law to amend and add to the Constitution of the German Democratic Republic of October 7, 1974. Berlin, 1974.

Gersch, Wolfgang. "Film in der DDR: Die verlorene Alternative." In *Geschichte des deutschen Films*, edited by Wolfgang Jacobsen, Anton Kaes, and Hans Helmut Prizler. Stuttgart, 1993: 323–64.

———. *Film und Fernsehkunst der DDR: Traditionen-Beispiele-Tendenzen*. Berlin/DDR, 1979.

Geserick, Rolf. *40 Jahre Presse, Rundfunk und Kommunikationspolitik in der DDR*. Munich, 1989.

Geyer, Michael. "Geschichte als Wissenschaft für ein Zeitalter der Unübersichtlichkeit." In *Nach dem Erdbeben: (Re)Konstruktionen ost-deutscher Geschichte und Geschichtswissenschaft*, edited by Konrad Jarausch and Matthias Middell. Leipzig, 1994: 38–65.

———. "Historical Fictions of Autonomy and the Europeanization of National History." *Central European History* 22 (1989): 316–42.

———. "The Politics of Memory in Contemporary Germany." In *Radical Evil*, edited by Joan Copjec. London, 1996: 169–200.

———. "The Stigma of Violence, Nationalism, and War in Twentieth-Century Germany." *German Studies Review* (winter 1992): 75–110.

Geyer, Michael, and Konrad H. Jarausch. "The Future of the German Past: Transatlantic Reflections for the 1990s." *Central European History* 22 (1989): 229–59.

Giesen, Bernhard. *Die Intellektuellen und die Nation: Eine deutsche Achsenzeit*. Frankfurt am Main, 1993 (Intellectuals and the German nation: Collective identity in an axial age. Trans. Nicholas Levis and Amos Weisz [New York, 1998]).

Gill, David, and Ulrich Schröter, eds. *Das Ministerium für Staatssicherheit: Anatomie des Mielke Imperiums*. Berlin, 1991.

Glaeßner, Gert-Joachim. *Der schwierige Weg zur Demokratie: Vom Ende der DDR zur deutschen Einheit*, 2d ed. Opladen, 1991.

Glotz, Peter. *Die beschleunigte Gesellschaft: Kulturkämpfe im digitalen Kapitalismus*. Munich, 1999.

———. "Die Erfurter Idee: Hochschulpolitik in den neuen Ländern." In *Ostprofile: Universitätsentwicklung in den neuen Bundesländern*, ed. Alfons Söllner and Ralf Walkenhaus. Opladen, 1998: 140–43.

———. *Der Irrweg des Nationalstaats*. Stuttgart, 1990.

———. *Die Jahre der Verdrossenheit. Politisches Tagebuch 1993/94*. Stuttgart, 1996.

Goettle, Gabriele. *Deutsche Sitten: Erkundungen in Ost und West*. Frankfurt am Main, 1991.

———. *Deutsche Spuren: Erkenntnisse aus Ost und West*. Frankfurt am Main, 1998.

———. *Freibank: Kultur minderer Güte, amtlich geprüft*. Frankfurt am Main, 1995.

Göhler, Helmut. *Stand und Tendenzen des Lesens in der DDR*. Berlin, 1983.

———, ed. *Buch—Lektüre—Leser: Erkundungen zum Lesen*. Berlin, 1989.

Gould, Daniel J., ed. *Post New Wave Cinema in the Soviet Union*. Bloomington, 1989.

Gouldner, Alvin W. *The Future of Intellectuals and the Rise of the New Class*. New York, 1981.

Graf, Andreas, and Heike Graf. "Der Medienkontrollrat—Insel der Stabilität im medienpolitischen Schlachtenlärm." In *Medien-Wende—Wende-Medien? Dokumentation des Wandels im DDR-Journalismus Oktober '89 – Oktober '90*, edited by Werner Claus. Berlin, 1991: 7–15.

Grass, Günter. *Die Blechtrommel*. Darmstadt, 1960 (The tin drum. Trans. Ralph Manheim [New York, 1963]).

———. *Deutscher Lastenausgleich: Wider das dumpfe Einheitsgebot*. Berlin, 1990.

Greenfeld, Leah. *Nationalism: Five Roads to Modernity*. Cambridge, Mass., 1992.

Greiner, Bernhard. " 'Sentimentaler Stoff und fantastische Form': Zur Erneuerung frühromantischer Tradition im Roman der DDR." In *DDR-Roman und Literaturgesellschaft*, edited by Jos Hoogeveen and Gerd Labriosse. Amsterdam, 1981: 249–328.

Greiner-Pol, André. *Peitsche Osten Liebe: Das Freygang-Buch*, ed. Michael Rauhut. Berlin, 2000.

Gries, Rainer. "Nostalgie-Legende-Zukunft? Geschichtskultur und Produktkultur in Ostdeutschland." *Universitas* 51 (1996): 102–15.

Grubitzsch, Jürgen. "Presseland der DDR im Umbruch: Ausgangspunkte, erste Ergebnisse und Perspektiven." *Media Perspektiven* 3 (1909): 140–55.

Grünbein, Durs. *Den teuren Toten: 33 Epitaphe*. Frankfurt am Main, 1994.

Grunenberg, Antonia. *Aufbruch der inneren Mauer*. Bremen, 1990.

———. "In den Räumen der Sprache: Gedankenbilder zur Literatur Gert Neumanns." In *Die Andere Sprache: Neue DDR-Literatur der 80er Jahre*, edited by Heinz Ludwig Arnold and Gerhard Wolf. Sonderband Text und Kritik. Munich, 1990.

Guggenberger, Bernd. "Vom Bürger zum Zerstreuungspatienten. Zehn Thesen zur sozialen Macht des Fernsehens." In *Kongreßdokumentation: Reden und Beiträge, Medien-Forum Berlin-Brandenburg '93*. Munich, 1993: 348–50.

Gysi, Gregor, ed. *Wir brauchen einen dritten Weg: Selbstverständnis und Programm der PDS*. Hamburg, 1990.

Gysi, Gregor, and Thomas Falkner. *Sturm aufs grosse Haus*. Berlin, 1990.

Habermas, Jürgen. *A Berlin Republic: Writings on Germany*. Trans. Steven Randall. Lincoln, 1997.

———. "Citizenship and National Identity: Some Reflections on the Future of Europe." *Praxis International* 12, no. 1 (April 1992): 1–19.

———. "Einleitung." In *Geistige Situation der Zeit*, edited by Jürgen Habermas. Frankfurt, 1979: 1:7–35.

———. *Die nachholende Revolution*. Frankfurt am Main, 1990.

———. *Die neue Unübersichtlichkeit*. Frankfurt am Main, 1985.

———. "Die normative Defizite der Vereinigung." In *Vergangenheit als Zukunft*, edited by Michael Haller. Zurich, 1990.

———. "The Second Life of the Federal Republic: We Have Become 'Normal' Again." *New Left Review* 197 (January–February 1993): 58–66.

———. *Strukturwandel der Öffentlichkeit: Untersuchungen zu einer Kategorie der bürgerlichen Gesellschaft*. Rev. ed. Neuwied, 1990 (The structural transformation of the public sphere: An inquiry into a category of bourgeois society. Trans. Thomas Burger [Cambridge, Mass., 1989]).

———. *Vergangenheit als Zukunft*. Ed. Michael Haller. Zurich, 1990 (The past as future. Trans. Max Pensky [Lincoln, 1994]).

———. "Was bedeutet 'Aufarbeitung der Vergangenheit' heute?" In *Die Normalität einer Berliner Republik*. Frankfurt am Main, 1995: 21–46.

———. "Yet Again: German Identity—A Unified Nation of Angry DM-Burghers." *New German Critique* 52 (1991): 84–101.

———, ed. *Stichworte zur geistigen Situation der Zeit*. 2 vols. Frankfurt am Main, 1979.

Hager, Kurt. "Weimar Nostalgia (July 1957)." In *Dokumente zur Kunst-, Literatur- und Kulturpolitik der SED*, edited by Elmar Schubbe. Stuttgart, 1972: 540.

Hahn, Annegret, et al., eds. *November '89*. Frankfurt am Main, 1990.

Hall, Karl-Heinrich. "Die Hochschulgesetzgebung der neuen Länder als Rahmenbedingungen der Neustrukturierung." In *Aufbruch und Reform von oben: Ostdeutsche Universitäten im Transformationsprozeß*, edited by Renate Mayntz. Frankfurt am Main, 1994: 165–90.

Hallberg, Robert von, ed. *Literary Intellectuals and the Dissolution of the State: Professionalism and Conformity in the GDR*. Trans. Kenneth J. Northcott. Chicago, 1996.

Hamburger Institut für Sozialforschung, ed., *Besucher einer Ausstellung: Die Ausstellung "Vernichtungskrieg. Verbrechen der Wehrmacht 1941 bis 1944" in Interview und Gespräch*. Hamburg, 1998.

Hames, Peter. *The Czechoslovak New Wave*. Berkeley, 1985.

Handke, Peter. *Eine winterliche Reise zu den Flüssen Donau, Save, Morawa und Drina, oder, Gerechtigkeit für Serbien*. Frankfurt am Main, 1996.

———. *Mein Jahr in der Niemandsbucht: Ein Märchen aus den neuen Zeiten*. Frankfurt am Main, 1994.

———. *Sommerlicher Nachtrag zu einer winterlichen Reise*. Frankfurt am Main, 1996.

———. *Zurüstungen für die Unsterblichkeit: Ein Königsdrama*. Frankfurt am Main, 1997.

Hansen, Miriam. "Space of History, Language of Time: Kluge's *Yesterday Girl* (1966)." In *German Film and Literature: Adaptions Transformations*, edited by Eric Rentschler. New York, 1985: 193–216.

Hardtwig, Wolfgang, and Heinrich August Winkler, eds. *Deutsche Entfremdung: Zum Befinden in Ost und West*. Munich, 1994.

Harich, Wolfgang. "Es geht um den Realismus." In *Dokumente zur Kunst-, Literatur- und Kulturpolitik der SED*, edited by Elmar Schubbe. Stuttgart, 1972: 292–96.

———. *Keine Schwierigkeiten mit der Wahrheit: Zur nationalkommunistischen Opposition 1956 in der DDR*. Berlin, 1993.

Harig, Gerhard. "Die Erkenntnistheorie des Marxismus (1945)." In *Ausgewählte philosophische Schriften 1934–1959*. Leipzig, 1973: 61–75.

Hartmann, Anneli. "Schreiben in der Tradition der Avantgarde: Neue Lyrik in der DDR." *Amsterdamer Beiträge zur neueren Germanistik* 26 (1988): 1–37.

Hartung, Klaus. "Im Spiegelkabinett der Vereinigung: Die neue deutsche Täter-Opfer-Ordnung und die alten Fluchten aus der Realität." In *Wir Kollaborateure: Der Westen und die deutschen Vergangenheiten*, edited by Cora Stephan. Reinbek, 1992.

———. *Neunzehnhundertneunundachtzig*. Frankfurt am Main, 1991.

Haufe, Gerda, and Karl Bruckmeier, eds. *Die Bürgerbewegungen in der DDR und in den ostdeutschen Bundesländern*. Opladen, 1993.

Haug, Wolfgang Fritz. *Der Hilflose Antifaschismus: Zur Kritik der Vorlesungsreihen über Wissenschaft und NS an deutschen Universitäten*. Frankfurt am Main, 1967.

———. *Versuch beim täglichen Verlieren des Bodens unter den Füssen neuen Grund zu gewinnen: Das Perestrojka*. Hamburg, 1990.

———. "Die Wiederkehr des Unerwarteten." In *Erinnern, Wiederholen, Durcharbeiten:*

Zur Psycho-Analyse deutscher Wenden, edited by Brigitte Rauschenbach. Berlin, 1992: 276–85.

Haußmann, Leander. "Man wechselt nicht so leicht die Feinde." In *Theater 1990: Jahrbuch der Zeitschrift Theater Heute*. Seelze, 1990: 31–32.

Hecht, Werner, ed. *Materialien zum Leben des Galilei*. Frankfurt am Main, 1977.

Heimann, Thomas. *DEFA, Künstler und SED-Kulturpolitik: Zum Verhältniß von Kulturpolitik und Filmproduktion in der SBZ/DDR 1945 bis 1959*. Berlin, 1994.

Hein, Christoph. *Die Ritter der Tafelrunde*. Frankfurt am Main, 1989.

Hell, Julia. *Post-fascist Fantasies: Psychoanalysis, History, and the Literature of East Germany*. Durham, N.C., 1997.

Hellfeld, Mattias von. *Die Nation erwacht: Zur Trendwende der deutschen politischen Kultur*. Cologne, 1993.

Henke, Klaus-Dietmar, and Hans Woller, eds. *Politische Säuberung in Europa: Die Abrechnung mit Faschismus und Kollaboration nach dem Zweiten Weltkrieg*. Munich, 1991.

Henrich, Dieter. *Eine Republik Deutschland: Reflexionen auf dem Weg aus der deutschen Teilung*. Frankfurt am Main, 1990.

———. *Nach dem Ende der Teilung: Über Identitäten und Intellektualität in Deutschland*. Frankfurt am Main, 1993.

Henrich, Rolf. *Der vormundschaftliche Staat*. Reinbek, 1989.

Herf, Jeffrey. "German Communism, the Discourse of 'Antifascist Resistance,' and the Jewish Catastrophe." In *Resistance Against the Third Reich, 1933–1990*, edited by Michael Geyer and John Boyer. Chicago, 1994: 257–94.

Herles, Helmut, and Ewald Rose, eds. *Vom Runden Tisch zum Parlament*. Bonn, 1990.

Herles, Wolfgang. *Nationalrausch: Szenen aus dem gesamtdeutschen Machtkampf*. Munich, 1990.

Hermand, Jost. *Kultur im Wiederaufbau: Die Bundesrepublik Deutschland. 1945 bis 1965*. Frankfurt am Main, 1989.

Hewison, Robert. *Heritage Culture*. London, 1987.

Heym, Stefan. "Ash Wednesday in the GDR." *New German Critique* 52 (winter 1991): 31–36.

———. "Je voller der Mund, desto leerer die Sprüche: Leben mit der Aktuellen Kamera." *Sinn und Form* 42, no.2 (1990): 417–25.

———. "Das Volk will echten Realismus!" In *Dokumente zur Kunst-, Literatur-, und Kulturpolitik der SED*, edited by Elmar Schubbe. Stuttgart, 1972: 298–99.

Heym, Stefan, et al. "Für das Land." In *Literatur der DDR: Ein Rückblick*, edited by Heinz Ludwig Arnold and Frauke Meyer-Gosau. Munich, 1991: 301.

Heym, Stefan, and Werner Heiduczek, eds. *Die sanfte Revolution*. Leipzig, 1990.

Hilbig, Wolfgang. *Das Provisorium*. Frankfurt am Main, 2000.

Hildebrand, Jörg. "Eine Lektion in Demokratie: Vom Ab- und Aufbau der ostdeutschen Rundfunkanstalten." In *Die Abwicklung der DDR*, edited by Heinz Ludwig Arnold and Frauke Meyer-Gosau. Göttingen, 1992: 64–70.

Hinrichs, Reimar. "Patient DDR." *Kursbuch* 101 (1990): 57–65.

Hirschman, Albert O. "Abwanderung, Widerspruch, und das Schicksal der Deutschen Demokratischen Republik: Ein Essay zur konzeptuellen Geschichte." *Leviathan* 20 (1992): 330–58.

———. *Exit, Voice, and Loyalty: Responses to Declines in Firms, Organizations, and States*. Cambridge, Mass., 1970.

———. *Rival View of Market Society*. Cambridge, Mass., 1986.

Hoffmann, Christhard, ed. "One Nation—Which Past? Historiography and German Identities in the 1990s." *German Politics and Society* 15, no. 2 (1997): 17–31.

Hoffmann, Hans-Joachim. "Culture in the GDR: Unity and Diversity." *World Marxist Review* 30 (1987): 94–100.

———. "Das Sicherste ist die Veränderung." In *Theater 1988: Jahrbuch der Zeitschrift Theater Heute*. Seelze, 1988: 10–20.

Hoffmann, Hilmar. "Am Ende und am Anfang: Theater im Deutschland: Bilanz der Teilung." In *Vom Aufbruch zur Wende: Theater in der DDR*, edited by Knut Lennarz. Velber, 1992: 94–101.

Hoffmann-Riem, Wolfgang. "Die Entwicklung der Medien und des Medienrechts im Gebiet der ehemaligen DDR." *Archiv für Presserecht* 22, no. 2 (1991): 472–81.

Hofmann, Gunter, and Werner A. Perger. *Richard von Weiszäcker im Gespräch*. Frankfurt am Main, 1992.

Hohmann, Dietrich. *Ich, Robert Burns*. Berlin, 1991.

Holzweißig, Günter. *Massenmedien in der DDR*. Berlin, 1984.

Honecker, Erich. *Bericht des ZK der SED an den X Parteitag der SED*. Berlin, 1981.

Höpke, Klaus. *Probe für das Leben*. Halle, 1971.

Horkheimer, Max. "Aufzeichnungen und Entwürfe zur Dialektik der Aufklärung—1939–1942." In *Gesammelte Schriften*, edited by Gunzelin Schmid Noerr. Frankfurt am Main, 1987: 12:250–325.

Horkheimer, Max, and Theodor W. Adorno. *Dialektik der Aufklärung*. Ed. Gunzelin Schmid Noerr, 5:13–292, in Max Horkheimer, *Gesammelte Schriften*. Frankfurt am Main, 1987 (*Dialectic of Enlightenment* [New York, 1972]).

Hornbostel, Stefan. "Kein Land in Sicht—Von den neuen Schwierigkeiten, ein Intellektueller zu sein." *Leviathan* 24 (1996): 493–520.

Hörnigk, Therese. "Die erste Bitterfelder Konferenz: Programm und Praxis der sozialistischen Kulturrevolution am Ende der Übergangsperiode." In *Literarisches Leben in der DDR 1945 bis 1960*, edited by Inge Münz-Koenen. Berlin, 1980: 196–243.

Hradil, Stefan. "Die 'objektive' und die 'subjektive' Modernisierung: Der Wandel der westdeutschen Sozialstruktur und die Wiedervereinigung," *Aus Politik und Zeitgeschichte: Beilage zur Wochenzeitung "Das Parlament,"* B29–39/92 (10 July 1992): 3–14.

Hübinger, Gangolf, and Wolfgang J. Mommsen, eds. *Intellektuelle im Kaiserreich*. Frankfurt am Main, 1993.

Humann, Klaus, ed. *Schweigen is Schuld: Ein Lesebuch der Verlagsinitiative gegen Gewalt und Fremdenhaß*. Frankfurt am Main, 1993.

Hüppauf, Bernd. "Moral oder Sprache: DDR-Literatur vor der Moderne." In *Literatur in der DDR: Rückblicke*, edited by Heinz-Ludwig Arnold. Munich, 1991.

Huyssen, Andreas. "After the Wall: The Failure of German Intellectuals," *New German Critique* 52 (winter 1991): 109–43, reprinted in *Twilight Memories. Marking Time in a Culture of Amnesia*. New York, 1995: 37–66.

———. "The Inevitability of Nation: German Intellectuals After Unification." *October* 61 (spring 1992): 65–82.

———. "Das Versagen der deutschen Intellektuellen." In *Der deutsch-deutscher Literaturstreit oder "Freunde, es spricht sich schlecht mit gebundener Zunge,"* edited by Karl Deiritz and Hannes Krauss. Hamburg, 1991.

Irrlitz, Gerd. "Ankunft der Utopie." *Sinn und Form* 42, no. 5 (1990): 930–35.

————. "Ein Beginn vor dem Anfang: Philosophie in Ostdeutschland 1945–1950." In *Wissenschaft im geteilten Deutschland: Restauration oder Neubeginn nach 1945*, edited by Walter H. Pehle and Peter Sillem. Frankfurt am Main, 1992: 113–24.

Jaeggi, Urs. *Versuch über den Verrat*. Neuwied, 1984.

Jäger, Manfred. "Auskünfte: Heiner Müller und Christa Wolf zu Stasi-Kontakten." *Deutschlandarchiv* 26, no. 2 (February 1993): 142–46.

Jäger, Wolfgang, and Ingeborg Villinger, eds. *Die Intellektuellen und die deutsche Einheit*. Freiburg, 1997.

Jameson, Fredric. "Utopia, Modernism, and Death." In *The Seeds of Time*. New York, 1994: 73–128.

Janka, Walter. " . . . bis zur Verhaftung": Erinnerungen eines deutschen Verlegers. Berlin, 1993.

————. *Schwierigkeiten mit der Wahrheit*. Reinbek, 1990.

Jansen, Peter W., and Wolfram Schütte, eds. *Film in der DDR*. Munich, 1977.

Jarausch, Konrad H. "Die Krise des deutschen Bildungsbürgertums im ersten Drittel des 20. Jahrhunderts." In *Bildungsbürger und bürgerliche Gesellschaft im 19. Jahrhundert: Deutschland im europäischen Vergleich*, edited by Jürgen Kocka. Munich, 1988: 3:124–46.

————. "Normalisierung oder Re-Nationalisierung: Zur Umdeutung der deutschen Vergangenheit." *Geschichte und Gesellschaft* 21 (1995): 559–72.

————. "Die postnationale Nation: Zum Identitätswandel der Deutschen, 1945–1995." *Historicum* (spring 1995): 30–35.

————. "Realer Sozialismus als Fürsorgediktatur: Zur begrifflichen Einordnung der DDR." *Aus Politik und Zeitgeschichte* B20–98 (8 May 1998): 33–46.

————. *The Rush to German Unity*. New York, 1994.

————. "Toward a Postsocialist Politics?" In *The Crisis of Socialism in Europe*, edited by Christiane Lemke and Gary Marks. Durham, N.C., 1992: 228–39.

————. *The Unfree Professions: German Lawyers, Teachers, and Engineers, 1900–1950*. New York, 1990.

————. *Die unverhoffte Einheit 1989–1990*. Frankfurt am Main, 1995.

————, ed. *After Unity: Reconfiguring German Identities*. Providence, 1997.

————. *Dictatorship as Experience: Toward a Socio-Cultural History of the GDR*. Providence, 1998.

————. *Zwischen Parteilichkeit und Professionalität: Bilanz der Geschichtswissenschaft der DDR*. Berlin, 1991.

Jarausch, Konrad H., and Volker Gransow, eds. *Uniting Germany: Documents and Debates*. Providence, 1994.

Jaspers, Karl. *Freiheit und Wiedervereinigung*. Munich, 1960.

————. *Die geistige Situation der Zeit [1931]*. Berlin and New York, 1979 (*Man in the Modern Age* [New York, 1978]).

————. *Die Schuldfrage*. Heidelberg, 1946 (*The Question of German Guilt* [New York, 1961]).

Jessen, Ralph. "Die Gesellschaft im Staatssozialismus: Probleme einer Sozialgeschichte der DDR." *Geschichte und Gesellschaft* 21 (1995): 96–110.

Johnson, Paul. *The Intellectuals*. London, 1988.

Joppke, Christian. *East German Dissidents and the Revolution of 1989: Social Movement in a Leninist Regime*. New York, 1995.

Judt, Tony. *Past Imperfect: French Intellectuals, 1944–1956*. Berkeley, 1992.

Kachold, Gabriele. "Das Gesetz der Szene." *Kontext* 5 (1989).

Kallabis, Heinz. *Ade, DDR! Tagebuchblätter, 7. Oktober 1989–8. Mai 1990*. Berlin, 1990.

Kant, Immanuel. "Grundlegung zur Metaphysik der Sitten." In *Werke*, edited by Wilhelm Weischedel. Darmstadt, 1961: 6:11–102.

———. "Perpetual Peace: A Philosophical Sketch." In *Kant's Political Writings*, edited by Hans Reiss. Cambridge, U.K., 1970.

———. "Was heisst: Sich im Denken orientieren?" In *Werke im zehn Bänden*, edited by Wilhelm Weischedel. vol. 5 Darmstadt, 1981: 265–33.

Kapferer, Norbert. *Das Feindbild der marxistisch-leninistischen Philosophie in der DDR 1945–1988*. Darmstadt, 1990.

Kaufmann, Hans. *DEFA-Frühling findet vorläufig nicht statt*. Cologne, 1966.

———. *Politisches Gedicht und klassische Dichtung: Heinrich Heine, Deutschland, ein Wintermärchen*. Berlin, 1958.

Kennedy, Paul. *The Rise and Fall of the Great Powers: Economic Change and Military Conflict from 1500 to 2000*. New York, 1987.

Kershaw, Baz. *The Politics of Performance: Radical Theatre as Cultural Intervention*. London, 1992.

Kersten, Heinz. "Entwicklungslinien." In *Film in der DDR*, edited by Peter W. Jansen and Wolfram Schütte. Munich, 1977: 7–56.

———. *Das Filmwesen in der sowjetischen Besatzungszone*. Bonn, 1954.

———. "Schatten über Babelsberg." *Filmkritik* 10, no. 3 (March 1966): 164–66; 10, no. 4 (April 1966): 232–34; 10, no. 5 (May 1966): 250–53.

———. *Die Spielfilm-Produktion in der SBZ*. Bonn, 1964.

Klatt, Gudrun. " 'Modebuch' und Diskussionen 'über das leben selbst': Ulrich Plenzdorfs *Die neuen Leiden des Jungen W.*" In *Werke und Wirkungen: DDR-Literatur in der Diskussion*, edited by Inge Münz-Koenen. Leipzig, 1987: 361–98.

———. "Schriftsteller-Literatur-Leser: Zur Literaturdiskussion am Beginn der sechziger Jahre in der Zeitschrift 'Junge Kunst.' " *Weimarer Beiträge* 23, 10 (1977): 23–44.

Klausenitzer, Hans-Peter. "Konkrete Prosa aus einem real existierenden Land." *Deutschland Archiv* 11, no. 2 (1979): 185.

Klein, Fritz. *Drinnen und draussen: Ein Historiker in der DDR*. Frankfurt am Main, 2000.

Kleinwächter, Wolfgang. "Die Vorbereitung für ein Mediengesetz der DDR." *Media Perspektiven* 3 (1990): 133–39.

Kleist, Heinrich von. "Über die allmähliche Verfertigung der Gedanken beim Reden." In *Sämtliche Werke und Briefe*. Munich, 1983: 2:315–18.

Klemperer, Victor. *LTI: Notizbuch eines Philologen*. Leipzig, 1946.

Klier, Freya. *Abreiß-Kalender: Ein deutsch-deutsches Tagebuch*. Munich, 1988.

Kluge, Alexander. "It Is an Error That the Dead Are Dead." *New German Critique* 73 (1998): 5–11.

———. *Neue Geschichten: Hefte 1–18. Unheimlichkeit der Zeit*. Frankfurt am Main, 1977.

———, ed. *Bestandsaufnahme: Utopie Film*. Frankfurt am Main, 1983.

Kluge, Alexander, and Heiner Müller. *"Ich schulde der Welt einen Toten": Gespräche*. Hamburg, 1995.

———. *Ich bin ein Landvermesser: Gespräche mit Heiner Mueller*. Hamburg, 1996.

Kluge, Alexander, and Oskar Negt. *Geschichte und Eigensinn*. Frankfurt am Main, 1981.

Knoth, Nikola. "Das 11. Plenum-Wirtschafts-oder Kulturplenum?" In *Kahlschlag: Das*

11. *Plenum des ZK der SED 1965. Studien und Dokumente*, edited by Günter Agde. Berlin, 1991: 64–68.

Koch, Hans. *Unsere Literaturgesellschaft*. Berlin, 1965.

Kocka, Jürgen. "Folgen der deutschen Einigung für die Geschichts-und Sozialwissenschaften." *Deutschland Archiv* 25 (1992): 793–802.

———. *Die Vereinigungskrise: Zur Geschichte der Gegenwart*. Göttingen, 1995.

Koestler, N. "Intelligenz und höhere Bildung im geteilten Polen." In *Bildungsbürgertum im 19. Jahrhundert*, edited by Werner Conze and Jürgen Kocka. Stuttgart, 1985: 1:186–206.

Kolbe, Uwe. "Die Heimat der Dissidenten: Nachbemerkungen zum Phantom der DDR-Opposition." In *Der deutsch-deutsche Literaturstreit*, edited by Karl Deiritz and Hannes Krauss. Frankfurt am Main, 1991: 33–39.

König, Helmut, Michael Kohlstruck, and Andreas Wöll, eds. *Vergangenheitsbewältigung am Ende des zwanzigsten Jahrhunderts* (=Leviathan Sonderheft 18/1998). Opladen, 1998.

Königsdorf, Helga. *Adieu DDR: Protokolle eines Abschieds*. Hamburg, 1990.

———. *1989, Oder ein Moment der Schönheit*. Berlin, 1990.

Konrad, György, and Ivan Szelenyi. "Intellectuals and Domination in Post-Communist Societies." In *Social Theory for a Changing Society*, edited by Pierre Bourdieu and James S. Coleman. New York, 1991.

———. *The Intellectuals on the Road to Class Power*. New York, 1979.

Koselleck, Reinhart, et al. "Volk, Nation, Nationalismus, Masse." In *Geschichtliche Grundbegriffe: Historisches Lexikon zur politisch-sozialen Sprache in Deutschland*. Stuttgart, 1992: 7:141–431.

Koziol, Andreas, and Rainer Schedlinski, eds. *Abriss der Ariadnefabrik*. Berlin, 1990.

Krauss, Werner. "Literaturgeschichte als geschichtlicher Auftrag." In *Werner Kraus: Das wissenschaftliche Werk*, edited by Manfred Naumann, vol. 1, *Literaturtheorie, Philosophie, Politik*. Berlin, 1984: 7–61.

———. "Der Stand der romantischen Literaturgeschichte an der Leipziger Universität." In *Werner Kraus: Das wissenschaftliche Werk*, edited by Manfred Naumann, vol. 1, *Literaturtheorie, Philosophie, Politik*. Berlin, 1984: 62–66.

———, ed. *Grundposition der französischen Aufklärung*. Neue Beiträge zur Literaturwissenschaft, vol. 1. Berlin, 1955.

Krawczyk, Stephan. "We'll Keep Playing." *Across Frontiers* 4, nos. 2–3 (1988): 39–40.

Krenzlin, Leonore. "Vom Jugendkommuniqué zur Dichterschelte." In *Kahlschlag: Das 11. Plenum des ZK der SED 1965. Studien und Dokumente*, edited by Günter Agde. Berlin, 1991: 148–58.

Kriese, Konstanze. "Rock'n'Ritual." In *PopScriptum 2*, edited by Forschungszentrum Populäre Musik der Humboldt-Universität zu Berlin. Beiträge zur populären Musik. Berlin, 1994: 94–120.

Kristeva, Julia. *Nations Without Nationalism*. New York, 1993.

Kröher, Michael O. R. "Nichts gegen die da drüben." In *Der rasende Mob: Die Ossis zwischen Selbstmitleid und Barbarei*, edited by Klaus Bitterman. Berlin, 1993: 12–30.

Krug, Hartmut. "Aufbruch-Stimmung, Morgenluft? Aspekte jüngerer DDR-Dramatik." In *Theater 1988: Jahrbuch der Zeitschrift Theater Heute*. Seelze, 1988: 59.

Krug, Manfred. *Abgehauen: Ein Mitschnitt und ein Tagebuch*. Düsseldorf, 1996.

Krüger, Hans Peter. "Ohne Versöhnung handeln, nur nicht leben: Zur Diskussion um DDR-Intellektuelle." *Sinn und Form* 44, 1 (1992): 40–50.

————. "Rückblick auf die DDR-Philosophie der 70er und 80er Jahre." In *Demission der Helden: Kritiker von innen, 1983–1992*, edited by Hans Peter Krüger. Berlin, 1992: 79–103.

Kruger, Loren. "Heterophony as Critique: Brecht, Müller, and Radio Fatzer." *Brecht Yearbook* 17 (1992): 235–51.

————. "Placing the Occasion: Raymond Williams and Performing Culture." In *Views Beyond the Border Country: Essays on Raymond Williams*, edited by Dennis Dworkin and Leslie Roman. New York, 1993: 51–73.

Kuberski, Angela, ed. *Wir treten aus unseren Rollen heraus: Dokumente zum Aufbruch 1989*. Berlin, 1990.

Kuczynski, Jürgen. *Die Intelligenz: Studien zur Soziologie und Geschichte ihrer Großen.* Berlin, 1987.

————. *Schwierige Jahre—mit einem besseren Ende? Tagebuchblätter 1987 bis 1989.* Berlin, 1990.

Kühn, Gertraude, Karl Tümmler, and Walter Wimmer, eds. *Film und revolutionäre Arbeiterbewegung in Deutschland 1918–1932*. 2 vols. Berlin/DDR, 1975.

Kulick, Holger. "Grautöne: Der Amoklauf Sascha Andersons. Aus drei Gesprächen." In *MachtSpiele: Literatur und Staatssicherheit im Fokus Prenzlauer Berg*, edited by Peter Böthig and Klaus Michael. Leipzig, 1993.

Kulturamt, Prenzlauer Berg, ed. *Mythos Antifaschismus: Ein Traditionskabinett wird kommentiert.* Berlin, 1992.

Kurella, Alfred. "Ästhetische Restauration?" *Sonntag* 6 (1947): 12.

————. "Einflüsse der Dekadenz." In *Dokumente zur Kunst-, Literatur-, und Kulturpolitik der SED*, edited by Elmar Schubbe. Stuttgart, 1972.

Kurz, Robert. *Der Kollaps der Modernisierung.* Frankfurt, 1991.

————. *Der Letzte macht das Licht aus: Zur Krise von Demokratie und Marktwirtschaft.* Berlin, 1993.

Ladd, H. Brian. *The Ghosts of Berlin: Confronting German History in the Urban Landscape.* Chicago, 1997.

Lämmert, Eberhard. "Germanistik: Eine deutsche Wissenschaft." In *Nationalismus in Germanistik und Dichtung: Dokumentation des Germanistentags im München vom 17. – 20. 10 1966*, edited by Benno von Wiese and R. Henß. Berlin, 1967: 15–36.

Land, Rainer, ed. *Das Umbaupapier (DDR): Argumente gegen die Wiedervereinigung.* Berlin, 1990.

Land, Rainer and Ralf Possekel. "Intellektuelle aus der DDR: Kulturelle Identität und Umbruch." *Berliner Debatte INITIAL* 1 (1992).

————. *"Namenlose Stimmen waren uns voraus": Politische Diskurse von Intellektuellen aus der DDR.* Bochum, 1994.

Latchinen, Sewan. "Germoney: Die BRDigung der DDR." In *Theater 1990: Jahrbuch der Zeitschrift Theater Heute*. Seelze, 1990: 30–31.

Le Carré, John. *The Spy Who Came in from the Cold.* New York, 1963.

Lefort, Claude. *The Political Forms of Modern Society: Bureaucracy, Democracy, Totalitarianism.* Cambridge, Mass., 1986.

Lehnert, Herbert. "Fiktionalität und autobiographische Motive: Zu Christa Wolfs Erzählung *Was bleibt.*" *Weimarer Beiträge* 3 (March 1991): 423–44.

Leitner, Olaf. "Rock Music in the GDR: An Epitaph." In *Rocking the State: Rock Music and Politics in Eastern Europe and Russia*, edited by Sabrina Petra Ramet. Boulder, 1994: 17–40.

———. *Rockszene DDR: Aspekte einer Massenkultur im Sozialismus*. Reinbeck, 1983.

Leming, Warren. "Tui-Memorandum: Brecht and the *New York Times*." *Communications from the International Brecht Society* 22, no. 1 (1993): 5–6.

Lemke, Christiane. *Die Ursachen des Umbruchs 1989: Politische Sozialisation in der ehemaligen DDR*. Opladen, 1991.

Lenin, V. I., "State and Revolution." In *The Lenin Anthology*, edited by Robert C. Tucker. New York, 1985.

Lennarz, Knut, ed. *Vom Aufbruch zur Wende: Theater in der DDR*. Velber, 1992.

Lenz, Siegfried. *Deutschstunde*. Hamburg, 1968 (*The German Lesson* [New York, 1971]).

Leonhard, Sigrun D. "Testing the Borders: East German Film Between Individualism and Social Commitment." In *Post New Wave Cinema in the Soviet Union*, edited by Daniel J. Gould. Bloomington, 1989: 55–101.

Leonhard, Wolfgang. *Die Revolution entläßt ihre Kinder*. Cologne, 1955.

Lepenies, Wolf. *Aufstieg und Fall der Intellektuellen in Europa*. Berlin, 1992.

———. *Between Literature and Science: The Rise of Sociology*. Cambridge, U.K., 1988.

———. "Deutsche Zustände zwei Jahre nach der Revolution: Grenzen der Gemeinschaft." *Mitteilungen des Deutschen Germanistenverbandes* (December 1991): 4–16.

———. "Das Ende der Utopie und die Rückkehr der Melancholie: Blick auf die Intellektuellen eines alten Kontinents." In *Intellektuellendämmerung*, edited by Martin Meyer. Munich, 1992: 15–26.

———. "Epilog: Soziologie und Anti-Soziologie im Nationalsozialismus und danach." In *Die drei Kulturen: Soziologie zwischen Literatur und Wissenschaft*. Reinbek, 1988: 403–22.

———. *Folgen einer unerhörten Begebenheit: Die Deutschen nach der Vereinigung*. Berlin, 1992.

———. "Motive Max Webers im Werk von Thomas Mann." In *Die drei Kulturen: Soziologie zwischen Literatur und Wissenschaft*. Reinbek, 1988: 357–75.

Lepsius, Rainer M. "Kritik als Beruf: Zur Soziologie der Intellektuellen." *Kölner Zeitschrift für Soziologie und Sozialpsychologie* 16 (1964): 75–91.

———. "Nation und Nationalismus in Deutschland." In *Grenzfälle: Über neuen und alten Nationalismus*, edited by Michael Jeismann and Henning Ritter. Leipzig, 1993: 193–214.

"Lese-Land." *Neue Deutsche Literatur* 39, no. 1 (1991): 172.

Leserförderung im Sozialismus: Ergebnisse einer internationalen wissenschaftlichen Konferenz anläßlich der iba [Internationale Buchkunst-Ausstellung], May 19–20, 1982 in Leipzig, edited by Internationale Buchkunst-Ausstellung. Leipzig, 1983.

Leseverhalten in Deutschland 1992/93: Repräsentativstudie zum Lese- und Meinungsverhalten der erwachsenen Bevölkerung im vereinigten Deutschland, [conducted by the] Stiftung Lesen. Mainz, 1993.

Lessing, Gotthold Ephraim. *Hamburgische Dramaturgie*, ed. Wilfried Barner. In *Werke und Briefe*, vol. 6:*Werke 1767–1769*. Edited by Klaus Bohnen. Frankfurt am Main, 1962 (*Hamburg Dramaturgy* [New York, 1962]).

———. *Nathan der Weise*, ed. Klaus Bohnen and Arno Schilson. In *Werke und Briefe*, vol. 9: *Werke 1778–1780*. Frankfurt am Main, 1993. (Nathan the Wise: A dramatic poem. Trans. and ed. Ellen Frothingham, 2nd rev. ed. [New York, 1989]).

Lévy, Bernard-Henri. *Eloge des intellectuels*. Paris, 1987.

Lewis, Alison. "Unity Begins Together: Analyzing the Trauma of German Unification." *New German Critique* 64 (1995): 135–59.

Liehm, Mira, and Antonin Liehm. *The Most Important Act*. Berkeley, 1977.

Lifshitz, Michail. *Karl Marx und die Ästhetik*. Dresden, 1960.

———. *Marx und Engels über Kunst und Literatur: Eine Sammlung aus ihren Schriften*. Berlin, 1948.

Linklater, Beth. "Erotic Provocations: Gabriele Stötzer-Kachold's Reclaiming of the Female Body." *Women in German Yearbook* 13 (1997): 151–70

Loest, Erich. *Der vierte Zensor*. Cologne, 1984.

———. *Der Zorn des Schafes*. Künzelsau, 1990.

Löffler, Dietrich. "Perspektive des Lesers im Zeitalter der Medien." In *Leser und Lesen in Gegenwart und Zukunft: Beiträge einer internationalen wissenschaftlichen Konferenz des Institutes für Verlagswesen und Buchhandel der Karl-Marx-Universität anläßlich der iba [Internationale Buchkunst-Ausstellung] 1989*, edited by Jutta Duclaud. Leipzig, 1990.

Lokatis, Siegfried. "Dietz: Probleme der Ideologiewirtschaft im zentralen Parteiverlag der SED." In *Von der Aufgabe der Freiheit: Festschrift für Hans Mommsen*, edited by Christian Jansen, Lutz Niethammer, and Bernd Weisbrod. Berlin, 1995: 533–48.

———. "Verlagspolitik zwischen Plan und Zensur: Das 'Amt für Literatur und Verlagswesen' oder die schwere Geburt des Literaturapparates in der DDR." In *Historische DDR Forschung*, edited by Jürgen Kocka. Berlin, 1994: 303–25.

———. "Zur Rolle der Massenorganisationen in der Diktatur: Praktische Probleme der Kunstverbreitung in der DDR." In *Auf der Suche nach dem verlorenen Staat: Die Kunst der Parteien und Massenorganisationen*, edited by Monika Flacke. Berlin, 1994: 78–89.

Ludes, Peter. " 'Von mir hätten Sie immer nur die halbe Wahrheit bekommen': Interviews mit Journalisten der Deutschen Fernsehfunks der DDR." In *Aus Politik und Zeitgeschichte* B17 (19 April 1991): 21–31.

Ludwig, Andreas. "Objektkultur und DDR-Gesellschaft: Aspekte einer Wahrnehmung des Alltags." *Aus Politik und Zeitgeschichte* B28 (1999): 3–11.

Lukács, Georg. *Geschichte und Klassenbewußtsein*. Berlin, 1923 (History and class consciousness. Trans. Rodney Livingstone [Cambridge, Mass., 1971]).

———. *Die Zerstörung der Vernunft*. Berlin, 1953 (The destruction of reason. Trans. Peter Palmer [Atlantic Highlands, N.J., 1981]).

Lüthy, Herbert. "Vom armen BB." *Der Monat* 4, no. 44 (May 1952): 115–44.

Lutz, Felix Philipp. *Das Geschichtsbewustsein der Deutschen: Grundlagen der politischen Kultur in Ost und West*. Cologne, 2000.

Lutze, Peter C. *Alexander Kluge: The Last Modernist*. Detroit, 1998.

Lyotard, Jean François. *Tombeau de l'intellectuel et autres papiers*. Paris, 1984.

Maaz, Hans-Joachim. *Der Gefühlsstau: Ein Psychogramm der DDR*. Berlin, 1990.

———. *Das gestürzte Volk, oder Die unglückliche Einheit*. Berlin, 1991.

Mabee, Barbara. "Footprints Revisited, or 'Life in the Changed Space That I Don't Know': Elke Erb's Poetry Since 1989." *Studies in 20th Century Literature* [special issue] 21, no. 1 (winter 1997): 161–85.

Macrakis, Kristie. "*Wissenschaft* and Political Unification in the New Germany." In *From Two to One*, edited by Humboldt Stiftung. Bonn, 1992.

Maetzig, Kurt. *Filmarbeit, Gespräche, Reden, Schriften*. Ed. Günter Agde. Berlin, 1987.

Magenau, Jörg. "Strukturelle Befangenheiten: Die Intellektuellen-Debatte." In *Verrat an der Kunst? Rückblicke auf die DDR-Literatur*, edited by Karl Deiritz and Hannes Krauss. Berlin, 1993: 48–53.

Maier, Charles S. *Dissolution: The Crisis of Communism and the End of East Germany*. Princeton, 1997.

———. *The Unmasterable Past: History, Holocaust, and German National Identity*. Cambridge, Mass., 1988.

Mannheim, Karl. *Ideology and Utopia: An Introduction to the Sociology of Knowledge*. New York, 1955.

Markovits, Andrei S., and Simon Reich. *The German Predicament: Memory and Power in the New Europe*. Ithaca, 1997.

Markovits, Andrei S., Seyla Benhabib, and Moishe Postone. "Symposium on Rainer Werner Fassbinder's "Garbage, the City, and Death." *New German Critique* 38 (1986): 3–27.

Maron, Monika. "Das neue Elend der Intellektuellen." In *Nach Maßgabe meiner Begreifungskraft*. Frankfurt am Main, 1993: 80–90.

Marx, Karl. "Speech at the Anniversary of the People's Paper, April 14, 1856." In *The Marx-Engels Reader*, edited by Robert C. Tucker. New York, 1978: 577–78.

Marx, Karl, and Friedrich Engels. *Werke, Ergänzungsband Erster Teil*. Berlin, 1968.

Mayer, Hans. *Ansichten zur Literatur der Zeit*. Reinbeck, 1963.

———. *Ein Deutscher auf Widerruf. Erinnerungen*, vol. 2 Frankfurt am Main, 1984.

———. *Der Turmbau von Babel: Erinnerungen an die Deutsche Demokratische Republik*. Frankfurt am Main, 1993.

———. "Zur Gegenwartslage unserer Literatur (1956)." In *Zur deutschen Literatur der Zeit. Zusammenhänge. Schriftsteller. Bücher*. Hamburg, 1967: 365–73.

———, ed. *Studien zur deutschen Literatur*. Berlin, 1955.

Mayer-Iswandy, Claudia. "Ästhetik und Macht: Zur dikursiven Unordnung im vereinten Deutschland." *German Studies Review* 19, no. 3 (1996): 501–23.

Mayntz, Renate, ed. *Aufbruch und Reform von oben: Ostdeutsche Universitäten im Transformationsprozeß*. Frankfurt am Main, 1994.

McClelland, Charles E. *The German Experience of Professionalization*. Cambridge, U.K., 1991.

Meier, Christian. "Halbwegs anständig über die Runden kommen, ohne daß zu viele zurückbleiben." In *Politik ohne Projekt? Nachdenken über Deutschland*, edited by Siegfried Unseld. Frankfurt am Main, 1993.

———. *Die Nation, die keine sein will*. Munich, 1991.

Meier, Helmut, and Walter Schmidt, eds. *Erbe und Tradtion in der DDR: Die Diskussion der Historiker*. Berlin, 1988.

Mendelssohn, Peter de. *Der Geist in der Despotie: Versuche über die moralischen Möglichkeiten der Intellektuellen in der totalitären Gesellschaft*. Frankfurt am Main, 1987.

Merkl, Peter H. *German Unification in European Context*. University Park, Pa., 1993.

Merleau-Ponty, Maurice. *Humanism and Terror: An Essay on the Communist Problem*. Boston, 1969.

Meuschel, Sigrid. "Antifaschistischer Stalinismus." In *Erinnern, Wiederholen, Durchar-*

beiten: Zur Psycho-Analyse deutscher Wenden, edited by Brigitte Rauschenbach. Berlin, 1992: 163–71.

Meuschel, Sigrid. *Legitimation und Parteiherrschaft in der DDR: Zum Paradox von Stabilität und Revolution in der DDR, 1945–1989.* Frankfurt am Main, 1992.

Meuschel, Sigrid. "Überlegungen zu einer Herrschafts- und Gesellschaftsgeschichte der DDR." *Geschichte und Gesellschaft* 19 (1993): 5–14.

Mews, Siegfried. "Moralist versus Pragmatist? Heinrich Böll and Güter Grass as Political Writers." In *Coping with the Past: Germany and Austria after 1945*, edited by Kathy Harms et al. Madison, 1990: 140–54.

Meyer, Martin, ed. *Intellektuellendämmerung: Beiträge zur neuesten Zeit des Geistes.* Munich, 1992.

Michael, Klaus. "Eine verschollene Anthologie: Zentralkomitee, Staatssicherheit und die Geschichte eines Buches." In *MachtSpiele: Literatur und Staatsicherheit*, edited by Peter Böthig and Klaus Michael. Leipzig, 1993: 202–16.

———. "Feindbild Literatur: Die Biermann-Affäre, Staatssicherheit und die Herausbildung einer literarischen Alternativkultur in der DDR." *Aus Politik und Zeitgeschichte: Beilage zur Wochenzeitung "Das Parlament"* B 22–23/93 (28 May 1993): 23–31.

———. "Neue Verlage und Zeitschriften in Ostdeutschland." *Aus Politik und Zeitgeschichte: Beilage zur Wochenzeitung "Das Parlament"* 41–42 (4 October 1991): 33–45.

Michael, Klaus, and Thomas Wohlfahrt, eds. *Vogel oder Käfig sein: Kunst und Literatur aus unabhängigen Zeitschriften in der DDR, 1979–1989.* Berlin, 1991.

Michalek, Boleslaw, and Frank Turaj. *The Modern Cinema of Poland.* Bloomington, 1988.

Misselwitz, Hans. *Nicht länger mit dem Gesicht nach Westen: Das neue Selbstbewußtsein der Ostdeutschen.* Bonn, 1996.

Mitscherlich, Alexander, and Margarete Mitscherlich. *Die Unfähigkeit zu trauern.* Munich, 1967.

Mittag, Günther. *Um jeden Preis: Im Spannungsfeld zweier Systeme.* Berlin, 1991.

Mittenzwei, Werner. "Brecht und die Probleme der deutschen Klassik." *Sinn und Form* 25, no. 1 (1973): 135–68.

———. "Zur Kafka-Konferenz 1963." In *Kahlschlag: Das 11. Plenum des ZK der SED 1965. Studien und Dokumente*, edited by Günter Agde. Berlin, 1991: 84–92.

Mitter, Armin, and Stefan Wolle, eds. *"Ich liebe Euch doch alle": Befehle und Lageberichte des MfS Januar–November 1989.* Berlin, 1991.

Mommsen, Hans. "Nationalsozialismus als vorgetäuschte Modernisierung." In *Der Nationalsozialismus und die deutsche Gesellschaft: Ausgewählte Aufsätze.* Reinbek, 1991: 405–27.

Mommsen, Theodor. *Römische Geschichte*, vol. 5. Berlin, 1885.

Mommsen, Wolfgang J. *Bürgerliche Kultur und künstlerische Avantgarde.* Frankfurt am Main, 1994.

———. *Nation und Geschichte: Über die Deutschen und die deutsche Frage.* Munich, 1990.

Morawitz, Silvia. "Die Freiheit des Gesprächs . . ." In *Abriss der Ariadnefabrik*, edited by Andreas Koziol and Rainer Schedlinski. Berlin, 1990: 255–58.

Mortier, Jean. "Ein Buchmarkt mit neuen Strukturen: Zur Verlagspolitik und Buchplannung in der SBZ, 1945–1949." In *Frühe DDR-Literatur*, edited by Klaus Scherpe and Lutz Winckler. Hamburg, 1988: 62–80.

Mosse, George. *Nationalism and Sexuality: Middle-Class Morality and Sexual Norms in Modern Europe*. Madison, 1985.

Mückenberger, Christiane, ed. *Prädikat: Besonders schädlich. Das Kaninchen bin ich. Denk bloß nicht, ich heule. Filmtexte*. Berlin, 1990.

————. *Zur Geschichte des DEFA-Spielfilms 1946–9: Eine Dokumentation*. 2 vols. Potsdam, 1976, 1981.

Mückenberger, Christiane, and Günter Jordan. *"Sie sehen selbst, Sie hören selbst . . .": Die DEFA von ihren Anfängen bis 1949*. Marburg, 1994.

Müller, André. *Kreuzzug gegen Brecht: Die Kampagne in der Bundesrepublik 1961/62*. Darmstadt, 1963.

Müller, Harald. "Deutschland, ein Fernsehmärchen." In *Theater 1990: Jahrbuch der Zeitschrift Theater Heute*. Seelze, 1990: 23–24.

————, ed. *DDR-Theater des Umbruchs*. Berlin, 1990.

Müller, Heiner. *Germania 3: Gespenster am Toten Mann*. Ed. Stephan Suschke. Cologne, 1996.

————. *Hamletmachine and Other Texts for the Stage*. Ed. and trans. Carl Weber. New York, 1989.

————. *Krieg ohne Schlacht: Leben in zwei Diktaturen*. Cologne, 1992.

————. "Das Leben stört natürlich ständig: Ein Gespräch mit Heiner Müller." *Freibeuter* 47 (1990): 91–98.

————. "Das Liebesleben der Hyänen." In *Was von den Träumen blieb: Eine Bilanz der sozialistischen Utopie*, edited by Thomas Grimm. Berlin, 1993: 7–8.

————. "Mommsens Block." In *Drucksachen des Berliner Ensembles*. Berlin, 1993.

Müller, Helmut L. *Die literarische Republik: Westdeutsche Schriftsteller und die Politik*. Weinheim, 1982.

Müller, Jan. "Preparing for the Political: German Intellectuals Confront the 'Berlin Republic.'" *New German Critique* 72 (1997): 151–76

Müller, Jan-Werner. *Another Country: German Intellectuals and National Identity*. New Haven, 2000.

Müller-Enbergs, Helmut, et al., eds. *Von der Illegalität ins Parlament: Werdegang und Konzepte der neuen Bürgerbewegungen*. Berlin, 1991.

Münkler, Herfried, Hans Grünberger, and Kathrin Mayer, ed. *Nationenbildung: Die Nationalisierung Europas im Diskurs humanistischer Intellektueller: Italien und Deutschland*. Berlin, 1998.

Münz-Koenen, Inge, ed. *Werke und Wirkungen: DDR-Literatur in der Diskussion*. Leipzig, 1987.

Murry, Bruce. *Film and the German Left in the Weimar Republic*. Austin, 1990.

Muschg, Adolf. *Literatur als Therapie? Ein Exkurs über das Heilsame und das Unheilbare: Frankfurter Vorlesungen*. Frankfurt am Main, 1981.

Mushaben, Joyce Marie. *From Post-War to Post-Wall Generations: Changing Attitudes Toward the National Question and NATO in the Federal Republic of Germany*. Boulder, 1998.

Myritz, Reinhard. "Zwischen Umbruch und Konsolidierung: Zur Entwicklung der Hochschullandschaft in den neuen Bundesländern." *Deutschlandarchiv* 26 (1993): 657–73.

Mytze, Andreas W., ed. *Europäische Ideen: Stasi Sachen 3*. Berlin, 1993.

Nahirny, Vladimir. *The Russian Intelligentsia: From Torment to Silence*. New Brunswick, 1983.

Naipaul, V. S. *The Enigma of Arrival*. New York, 1987.

Nairn, Tom. *The Break-Up of Britain: Crisis and Neo-Nationalism*. London, 1977.

Naumann, Klaus. *Der Krieg als Text: Das Jahr 1945 im kulturellen Gedächtnis der Presse*. Hamburg, 1998.

Naumann, Manfred, ed. *Gesellschaft-Literatur-Lesen: Literaturrezeption in theoretischer Sicht*. Berlin, 1973.

Nettl, J. P. "Ideas, Intellectuals, and Structures of Dissent." In *On Intellectuals: Theoretical Case Studies*, edited by Philip Rieff. Garden City, N.Y., 1969: 53–122.

Neubert, Ehrhart. *Geschichte der Opposition der DDR 1949–1989*. Berlin, 1997.

Neumann, Gerald L. " 'We Are the People': Alien Suffrage in German and American Perspective." *Michigan Journal of International Law* 13, no. 2 (winter 1992): 259–335.

Neumann, Gert. "Anfangstext einer Lesung (Dresden, Heilige Geist Kirche, September 1984)." In *Abriss der Ariadnefabrik*, edited by Andreas Koziol and Rainer Schedlinski. Berlin, 1990: 146–48.

———. *Anschlag*. Cologne, 1999.

———. *Elf Uhr*. Frankfurt am Main, 1981.

———. "Gespräch und Widerstand: Das nabeloonische Chaos." In *"Literaturentwicklungsprozesse": Die Zensur der Literatur in der DDR*, edited by Ernst Wichner and Herbert Wisener. Frankfurt am Main, 1993: 144–65.

———. *Die Klandestinität des Kesselreiniger: Ein Versuch des Sprechens*. Frankfurt am Main, 1989.

———. *Die Schuld der Worte*. Rostock, 1989.

———. *Übungen jenseits der Möglichkeit*. Frankfurt am Main, 1991.

Niemann, Heinz. *Meinungsforschung in der DDR: Die geheime Berichte des Instituts für Meinungsforschung und das Politbüro der SED*. Cologne, 1993.

Nirumand, Bahman, ed. *Angst vor den Deutschen*. Reinbek, 1992.

Noack, Paul. *Deutschland, deine Intellektuellen: Die Kunst, sich ins Abseits zu stellen*. Frankfurt am Main, 1993.

Noelle-Neumann, Elisabeth, Winfried Schulz, and Jürgen Wilke, eds. *Publizistik-Massenkommunikation*. Frankfurt am Main, 1989.

Odermann, Heinz. "Der Umbruch und die Mediengesetzgebung in der DDR." *Rundfunk und Fernsehen* 38, no. 3 (1990): 377–84.

Offe, Claus. *Der Tunnel am Ende des Lichts: Erkundungen der politischen Transformation im Neuen Deutschland*. Frankfurt, 1994.

Okun, Bernd. "Medien und 'Wende' in der DDR." *Comparativ* 1, no. 3 (1991): 11–25.

Orwell, George. *Nineteen Eighty Four*. New York, 1949.

Oswald, Horst. *Literatur, Kritik und Leser*. Berlin, 1969.

Pankonin, Key. *Keynkampf*. Berlin, 1993.

Pannen, Stephan. *Die Weiterleiter: Funktion und Selbstverständniss ostdeutscher Journalisten*. Cologne, 1992.

Parker, Andrew, et al., eds. *Nationalisms and Sexualities*. New York, 1992.

Pätzold, Kurt. "What New Start? The End of Historical Study in the GDR." *German History* 10 (1992): 392–404.

Paul, David, ed. *Politics, Art, and Commitment in the Eastern European Cinema*. New York, 1983.

Pehle, Walter H., and Peter Sillem, eds. *Wissenschaft im geteilten Deutschland: Restauration oder Neubeginn nach 1945*. Frankfurt am Main, 1992.

Phillipsen, Dirk, ed. *"We Were the People": Voices from East Germany's Revolutionary Autumn of 1989*. Durham, 1982.

Plato, Alexander von. "Eine zweite 'Entnazifizierung'? Zur Verarbeitung politischer Umwälzungen in Deutschland 1945 und 1989." In *Wendezeiten-Zeitenwende: Zur 'Entnazifizierung' und 'Entstalinisierung'*, edited by Rainer Eckert, Alexander von Plato, and Jörn Schütrumpf. Hamburg, 1991: 7–32.

Plenzdorf, Ulrich. *Filme*. Frankfurt am Main, 1990.

———. *Die Legende von Paul und Paula: Filmerzählung*. Frankfurt am Main, 1974.

Plenzdorf, Ulrich, Klaus Schlesinger, and Martin Stade, eds. *Berliner Geschichte. "Operativer Schwerpunkt Selbstverlag." Eine Autoren-Anthologie: Wie sie entstand und von der Stasi verhindert wurde*. Frankfurt am Main, 1995.

Pollack, Detlef. "Die konstitutive Widersprüchlichkeit der DDR." *Geschichte und Gesellschaft* 24 (1997): 110–31.

Poppe, Ulrike. "Citizens Movements in the GDR: Their Past and Future." *Michigan Germanic Studies* 31, nos. 1–2 (1995): 37–43.

Probst, Lothar. *Ostdeutsche Bürgerbewegungen und Perspektiven der Demokratie: Entstehung, Bedeutung, Zukunft*. Cologne, 1993.

———, ed. *Differenz in der Einheit: Über die kulturellen Unterschiede der Deutschen in Ost und West*. Berlin, 1999.

Rabinbach, Anson, and Jack Zipes, eds. *Germans and Jews Since the Holocaust*. New York, 1986.

Ramstedt, Otthein, and Gert Schmidt, eds. *BRD ade! Vierzig Jahre in Rück-Ansichten*. Frankfurt am Main, 1992.

Rathgeb, Eberhard, and Thomas Steinfeld. "Egalitäre Bundesrepublik: Die politische Ästhetik kultureller Ereignisse." *Merkur* 49 (1995): 865–74.

Rauhut, Michael. *Beat in der Grauzone: DDR-Rock 1964 bis 1972—Politik und Alltag*. Berlin, 1993.

———. "DDR-Beatmusik zwischen Engagement und Repression." In *Kahlschlag: Das 11. Plenum des ZK der SED 1965. Studien und Dokumente*, edited by Günter Agde. Berlin, 1991: 52–63.

———. *Schalmei und Lederjacke: Udo Lindenberg, BAP, Underground: Rock und Politik in den achtziger Jahren*. Berlin, 1996.

Reich, Jens. *Abschied von den Lebenslügen: Die Intelligenz und die Macht*. Berlin, 1992.

———. *Rückkehr nach Europa. Bericht zur neuen Lage der deutschen Nation*. Munich, 1991.

Rentschler, Eric. *West German Cinema in the Course of Time*. Bedford Hills, 1984.

———, ed. *West German Filmmakers on Film: Visions and Voices*. New York, 1988.

Reso, Martin. *Der geteilte Himmel und seine Kritiker*. Halle, 1965.

Richter, Erika. "Zwischen Mauerbau und Kahlschlag, 1961 bis 1969." In *Das zweite Leben der Filmstadt Babelsberg: DEFA Spielfilme 1946–1992*, edited by Rolf Schenk. Berlin, 1994.

Richter, Ernst. "Enwicklungsetappen des Deutschen Demokratischen Rundfunks." *Schriftenreihe des Deutschen Demokratischen Rundfunks* 4, no. 2 (1970): 13.

Richter, Wolfgang. *Unfrieden in Deutschland*. N.p.: Gesellschaft zum Schutz von Bürgerrecht und Menschenwürde, 1992.

Riedel, Heike. *Hörfunk und Fernsehen in der DDR: Funktion, Struktur und Programm des Rundfunks in der DDR*. Cologne, 1977.

Riedel, Manfred. "Die Sage vom guten Anfang: Über ein Kapitel deutscher Literaturgeschichte." *Sinn und Form* 44, no. 4 (1992): 520–34.

Rieff, Philip *The Triumph of the Therapeutic: Uses of Faith After Freud*. Chicago, 1966.

Riesman, David. *The Lonely Crowd: A Study of the Changing American Character*. New Haven, 1950.

Ringer, Fritz K. *The Decline of the German Mandarins: The German Academic Community, 1890–1933*. Cambridge, Mass., 1969.

———. *Education and Society in Modern Europe*. Bloomington, 1979.

Ritter, Gerhard A. "The Reconstruction of History at the Humboldt University: A Reply." *German History* 11 (1993): 339–45.

Robbins, Bruce. "Espionage as Vocation: Raymond William's Loyalties." In *Intellectuals: Aesthetics, Politics, Academics*. Minneapolis, 1990.

Roesler, Jörg. "Gab es sozialistische Formen der Mitbestimmung und Selbstverwirklichung in Betrieben der DDR? Zur Rolle der Brigaden in der betrieblichen Hierarchie und im Leben der Arbeiter." *Utopie Kreativ* 31–32 (1993): 122–39.

Rohrwasser, Michael. *Der Stalinismus und die Renegaten: Die Literatur der Exkommunisten*. Stuttgart, 1991.

Röper, Horst. "Daten zur Konzentration der Tagespresse in der Bundesrepublik Deutschland im I. Quartal 1991." *Media Perspektiven* 7 (1991): 431–44.

———. "Die Entwicklung des Tageszeitungsmarktes in Deutschland nach der Wende in der ehemaligen DDR." *Media Perspektiven* 7 (1991): 421–30.

Rosenberg, Rainer. "Der ritualisierte Diskurs: Das Modell der offiziellen sowjetischen Literaturtheorie der 50er Jahre." *Zeitschrift für Germanistik*, n.s. 3, no. 1 (1993): 99–109.

Rosellini, Jay J. "A Revival of Conservative Literature? The 'Spiegel-Symposium 1993' and Beyond." In *Beyond 1989: Re-Reading German Literary History Since 1945*, edited by Keith Bullivant. Providence, 1997: 109–28.

Rossman, Peter. "Zum 'Intellektuellenstreit': Intellectuals in the Former GDR." *Michigan Germanic Studies* 31, no. 1–2 (1995): 32–36.

Rüddenklau, Wolfgang. "Behörden und Unternehmerunfreundlich. Zum 5-jährigen Bestehen des 'telegraph': ein Blick in die Vorgeschichte unserer Zeitschrift. Teil 1: Die 'Umweltblätter.'" *telegraph* 9 (1994): 10–18.

———. *Störenfried: DDR-Opposition 1986–1989*. Berlin, 1992.

Sa'adah, Anne. *Germany's Second Chance: Trust, Justice, and Democratization*. Cambridge, Mass., 1998.

Säße, Günter. "Der Kampf gegen die Versteinerung der Materie Wirklichkeit durch die Sprache: Zur Systematik sprachthematisierender Literatur aus Anlaß von Gert Neumanns *Elf Uhr*." In *Die Schuld der Worte*, edited by Paul Gerhard Klussmann and Heinrich Mohr. Bonn, 1987: 196–219.

Scharfschwert, Jürgen. *Literatur und Literaturwissenschaft in der DDR*. Stuttgart, 1982.

Schäuble, Wolfgang. *Der Vertrag: Wie ich über die deutsche Einheit verhandelte*. Stuttgart, 1991.

Schedlinski, Rainer. *die arroganz der ohnmacht: aufsätze und zeitungsbeiträge 1989 und 1990*. Berlin, 1991.

———. *letzte bilder*. Reinbek, 1990.

———. *die männer/der frauen*. Berlin, 1991.

————. *die rationen des ja und des nein: gedichte*. Frankfurt am Main, 1990.

————. "Die Unzugänglichkeit der Macht." *Neue deutsche Literatur* 40, no. 474 (June 1992): 75–105.

————. "zwischen nostalgie und utopie." *ariadnefabrik* 5 (1989): 29.

Schelsky, Helmut. *Die Arbeit tun die Anderen: Klassenkampf und Priesterherrschaft der Intellektuellen*. Munich, 1977.

Schenk, Ralf, ed. *Das zweite Leben der Filmstadt Babelsberg: DEFA-Spielfilme 1946–1992*. Berlin, 1994.

Scherpe, Klaus. "The German Intelligentsia in a Time of Change." *European Studies Journal* 10 (1993): 297–311.

Scherstjanoi, Elke. " 'Von der Sowjetunion lernen . . .' " In *Kahlschlag: Das 11. Plenum des ZK der SED 1965. Studien und Dokumente*, edited by Günter Agde. Berlin, 1991: 39–51.

Schildt, Axel. *Ankunft im Westen: Ein Essay zur Erfolgsgeschichte der Bundesrepublik*. Frankfurt am Main, 1999.

Schiller, Dieter. "Zu Begriff und Problem der Literaturgesellschaft." In *Studien zur Literaturgeschichte und Literaturtheorie*, edited by Hans Günter Thalheim and U. Wertheim. Berlin, 1970: 291–332.

Schirrmacher, Frank, ed. *Die Walser-Bubis-Debatte: Eine Dokumentation*. Frankfurt am Main, 1999.

Schlenstedt, Dieter. *Wirkungsästhetische Analysen*. Berlin, 1979.

Schluchter, Wolfgang. *Neubeginn durch Anpassung? Studien zum ostdeutschen Übergang*. Frankfurt am Main, 1996.

Schmaus, Cornelia. "Wie spiele ich weiter." In *Theater 1990: Jahrbuch der Zeitschrift Theater Heute*. Seelze, 1990: 32–33.

Schmid, Thomas. *Staatsbegräbnis: Von ziviler Gesellschaft*. Berlin, 1990.

Schmidt, Thomas E. "Die Geburt konservativer Bürgerethik aus dem Geist der Kulturkritik." *Freibeuter* 61 (1994): 80–89.

Schmidt-Eenboom, Erich. *Schnüffler ohne Nase: Der BND: Die unheimliche Macht im Staate*. Düsseldorf, 1993.

Schmitz, Walter. "Über Gert Neumann." In *Verhaftet: Dresdner Poetikvorlesungen*, ed. Gert Neumann. Dresden, 1999: 97–131.

Schneider, Rolf. "Selbstmitleid und Selbstbetrug." In *Theater 1990: Jahrbuch der Zeitschrift Theater Heute*. Seelze, 1990: 138–40.

Schneider, Wolfgang. *Tanz der Derwische: Vom Umgang mit der Vergangenheit im wiedervereinigten Deutschland*. Lüneburg, 1992.

Schölling, Traute. " 'On with the Show'? The Transition to Post-Socialist Theatre in Eastern Germany." *Theatre Journal* 45, no. 1 (1993): 30–31.

Schönherr, Albrecht, ed. *Ein Volk am Pranger? Die Deutschen auf der Suche nach einer politischen Kultur*. Berlin, 1992.

Schroeder, Richard. *Vom Gebrauch der Freiheit: Gedanken über Deutschland nach der Vereinigung*. Stuttgart, 1996.

Schubart, Wolfgang. "Zur Entwicklung der marxistisch-leninistischen Philosophie." *Deutsche Zeitschrift für Philosophie* 5, no. 6 (1959): 701–20.

Schubarth, Winfried. "Antifaschismus in der DDR—Mythos oder Realität?" In *Erinnern, Wiederholen, Durcharbeiten: Zur Psycho-Analyse deutscher Wenden*, edited by Brigitte Rauschenbach. Berlin, 1992: 172–79.

Schultz, Winfried. "Die Transformation des Mediensystems in den Achtzigern:

Epochale Trends und modifizierende Bedingungen." In *Rundfunk im Wandel: Festschrift für Winfried B. Lerg*, edited by Arnulf Kutsch, Christina Holtz-Blacha, and Franz R. Stuke. Berlin, 1993: 155–71.

Schulz, Günter, ed. *Film-Archiv 4: DEFA-Spielfilme I: 1946–1964. Filmographie*, Berlin, 1989.

Schumacher, Ernst. *Die dramatischen Versuche Bertolt Brechts 1918–1933*. Ed. Werner Kraus and Hans Meyer. Berlin, 1956.

Schütz, Walter. "Der (gescheiterte) Regierungsentwurf für ein Rundfunküberleitungs-gesetz der DDR: Chronik und Dokumente." In *Rundfunk im Wandel: Festschrift für Winfried B. Lerg*, edited by Arnulf Kutsch, Christina Holtz-Blacha, and Franz R. Stuke. Berlin, 1993: 263–303.

Schwarz, Gislinde. "Im Dienste der Frauen? Kühnheit und Anschmiegsamkeit der Frauenzeitschrift FÜR DICH." In *So durften wir glauben zu kämpfen . . . Erfahrung mit DDR-Medien*, edited by Edith Spielhagen. Berlin, 1993: 191–200.

Schwarz, Hans-Peter. *Die gezähmten Deutschen: Von der Machtbesessenheit zur Machtvergessenheit*. Stuttgart, 1995.

————. *Die Zentralmacht Europas: Deutschlands Rückkehr auf die Weltbühne*. Berlin, 1994.

Schwilk, Heimo, and Ulrich Schacht, eds. *Die selbstbewusste Nation: "Anschwellender Bocksgesang" und weitere Beiträge zu einer deutschen Debatte*. Berlin, 1994.

SED, Parteihochschule Karl Marx beim ZK der, ed. *Der Marxismus-Leninismus über die Rolle, das Wesen und die Bedeutung für Literatur und Kunst*. Kleinmachnow, 1953.

Sello, Tom. "Von den Umweltblättern zum Telegraph: Medien im Untergrund." In *Stattbuch Ost: Adieu DDR oder die Liebe zur Autonomie*. Berlin, 1991: 85–88.

Semprun, Jorge. *The Long Voyage*. Trans. Richard Seaver. New York, 1990 (*Le Grande Voyage* [1963]).

Silberman, Marc. "A Postmodernized Brecht?" *Theatre Journal* 45, no. 1 (1993): 1–19.

Simon, Dieter. "Die Quintessenz - der Wissenschaftsrat in den neuen Bundesländern: Eine vorwärtsgewandte Rückschau." *Aus Politik und Zeitgeschichte* B 51/92 (11 December 1992): 1–14.

Simon, Günter. *Tisch-Zeiten: Aus den Notizen eines Chefredakteurs 1981 bis 1989*. Berlin, 1990.

Simpson, Patricia A. "Born in the Bakschischrepublik? Rock and Politics in the GDR." In *Elective Affinities: Interdisciplinary Cultural Studies of German Unification*, edited by Ruth Starkman and Peter Tokovsky. Ann Arbor, 1999.

————. "Entropie, Ästhetik und Ethik im Prenzlauer Berg." In *MachtSpiele: Literatur und Staatsicherheit im Fokus Prenzlauer Berg*, edited by Peter Böthig and Klaus Michael. Leipzig, 1993: 50–59.

————. "Die Sprache der Geduld: Produzierendes Denken bei Elke Erb." In *Zwischen Gestern und Morgen: Schriftstellerinnen der DDR aus amerikanischer Sicht*, edited by Ute Brandes. Berlin, 1992: 263–276.

————. "State of the Art: Alternative Theatre in the GDR." *Modern Drama* 33, 1 (1990): 131.

Sloterdijk, Peter, *Regeln für den Menschenpark: Ein Antwortschreiben zu Heideggers Brief über den Humanismus*. Frankfurt am Main, 1999.

————. *Die Verachtung der Massen: Versuch über Kulturkämpfe in der modernen Gesellschaft*. Frankfurt am Main, 2000.

————. *Vor der Jahrtausendwende: Berichte zur Lage der Zukunft*. 2 vols. Frankfurt am Main, 1990.

Smith, Anthony D., *Theories of Nationalism*. New York, 1983.

Söllner, Alfons, and Ralf Walkenhaus, eds. *Ostprofile: Universitätsentwicklung in den neuen Bundesländern*. Opladen, 1998.

"Soll man Brecht spielen: Antworten an Friedrich Tolberg." *Der Monat* 14, no. 161 (1962): 57–64.

Sommer, Dietrich. *Leseerfahrung—Lebenserfahrung: Literatursoziologische Untersuchungen*. Berlin, 1983.

————, ed. *Funktion und Wirkung: Soziologische Untersuchungen zur Literatur und Kunst*. Berlin, 1978.

Sontheimer, Kurt. *Das Elend unserer Intellektuellen: Linke Theorie in der Bundesrepublik Deutschland*. Hamburg, 1976.

Spritzer, Leo. "Das Eigene und das Fremde: Über Philologie und Nationalismus." *Die Wandlung* 1 (1946): 576–94.

"Staatsvertrag über den Rundfunk im vereinten Deutschland." In *Dokumentation: Daten zur Mediensituation in Deutschland*, special issue of *Media Perspektiven* 3a (1991): 105–72.

Städtke, Klaus. "Beispiele der Deformation wissenschaftlichen Denkens in den Geisteswissenschaften der frühen DDR." *Zeitschrift für Sozialwissenschaft* 19, no. 1 (1991): 32–43.

Staritz, Dietrich. *Geschichte der DDR 1949–1985*. Frankfurt am Main, 1985.

Stark, Michael, ed. *Deutsche Intellektuelle, 1910–1933: Aufrufe, Pamphlete, Betrachtungen*. Heidelberg, 1984.

Steimle, Uwe. *Uns fragt ja keener: Ostalgie; Texte für Ilse Bähnert und Günter Zieschong*. Berlin, 1997.

Steiner, George. *Von realer Gegenwart: Hat unser Sprechen Inhalt*. Munich, 1990.

Stephan, Cora. *Der Betroffenheitskult: Eine politische Sittengeschichte*. Berlin, 1993.

————. *Wir Kollaborateure: Der Westen und die deutschen Vergangenheiten*. Reinbek, 1992.

Stern, Frank. *Im Anfang war Auschwitz: Antisemitismus und Philosemitismus im deutschen Nachkrieg*. Gerlingen, 1991.

————. "The 'Jewish Question' in the 'German Question.'" *New German Critique* 52 (winter 1991): 155–72.

Stern, Fritz. "Deutschland um 1900—und eine zweite Chance." In *Deutschlands Weg in die Moderne: Politik, Gesellschaft und Kultur im 19. Jahrhundert*, edited by Wolfgang Hardtwig and Harm-Hinrich Brandt. Munich, 1993: 32–44.

Sternberger, Dolf, Gerhard Storz, and Wilhelm Emanuel. *Aus dem Wörterbuch des Unmenschen*, rev. ed. Munich, 1970.

Stötzer-Kachold, Gabriele. *Erfurter Roulette*. Munich, 1995.

————. *grenzen los fremd gehen*. Berlin, 1992.

————. *zügel los: prosa*. Frankfurt am Main, 1990.

Strasser, Johano. "Intellektuellendämmerung? Anmerkungen zu einem Machtkampf im deutschen Feuilleton." *Neue Deutsche Literatur* 40, no. 10 (1992): 110–27.

Strittmatter, Erwin. *Die Lage in den Lüften: Aus Tagebüchern*. Berlin, 1990.

Stürmer, Michael. *Die Grenzen der Macht: Begegnung der Deutschen mit der Geschichte*. Berlin, 1992.

Sühl, Klaus, ed. *Vergangenheitsbewältigung 1945/1989: Ein unmöglicher Vergleich?* Berlin, 1994.

Suny, Ronald G., and Michael D. Kennedy, eds. *Intellectuals and the Articulation of the Nation.* Ann Arbor, 1999.

Surbar, Ilya. "War der reale Sozialismus modern?" *Kölner Zeitschrift für Soziologie und Sozialpsychologie* 43 (1991): 415–32.

Syberberg, Hans Jürgen. *Vom Unglück und Glück der Kunst in Deutschland nach dem letzten Kriege.* Munich, 1990.

Sylvester, Regine, ed. *The Forbidden Films.* Goethe Institute, 1992.

Szyrocki, Marian. *Martin Opitz.* Ed. Werner Kraus and Hans Meyer. Berlin, 1956.

Teltschik, Horst. *329 Tage.* Berlin, 1991.

Thalheim, Hans-Günter et al., eds. *Geschichte der deutschen Literatur: Von den Anfängen bis zur Gegenwart.* Berlin, 1965–83.

Thaysen, Uwe. *Der Runde Tisch. Oder: Wo blieb das Volk?* Opladen, 1990.

Thierse, Wolfgang, and Dieter Kliche. "DDR-Literaturwissenschaft in den 70er Jahren: Bemerkungen zur Entwicklung ihrer Positionen und Methoden." *Weimarer Beiträge* 31, no. 2 (1985): 267–308.

Thöns, Magdalena, and Kerstin Thöns. "Präsidialratssitzung am 3. Juni 1953." In *SED und Intellektuelle in der DDR der 50er Jahre: Kulturbund-Protokolle*, edited by Magdalena and Kerstin Thöns. Cologne, 1990.

Thulin, Michael [Klaus Michael]. "Sprache und Sprachkritik: Die Literatur des Prenzlauer Bergs in Berlin/DDR." In *Die Andere Sprache: Neue DDR-Literatur der 80er Jahre*, edited by Heinz Ludwig Arnold and Gerhard Wolf, special issue of *Text + Kritik* (1990).

Tilly, Charles. *Coercion, Capital, and European States, AD 990–1992.* Cambridge, Mass., 1990.

Torberg, Friedrich. "Soll man Brecht im Westen spielen?" *Der Monat* 14, no. 159 (1962): 56–62.

Torpey, John C. *Intellectuals, Socialism, and Dissent: The East German Opposition and Its Legacy.* Minneapolis, 1995.

Trommler, Frank. "Between Normality and Resistance: Catastrophic Gradualism in Nazi Germany." In *Resistance Against the Third Reich, 1933–1990*, edited by Michael Geyer and John W. Boyer. Chicago, 1994: 119–38.

———. "Die nachgeholte Résistance: Politik und Gruppenethos im historischen Zusammenhang." In *Die Gruppe 47 in der Geschichte der Bundesrepublik*, edited by Justus Fetscher. Würzburg, 1991: 9–22.

———. "What Should Remain? Exploring the Literary Contributions to Postwar German History." In *Beyond 1989: Re-reading German Literary History Since 1945*, edited by Keith Bullivant. Providence, 1997: 153–76.

Trumpener, Katie. *The Divided Screen: The Cinemas of Postwar Germany.* Forthcoming.

———. "Moving DEFA into Eastern Europe." In *Moving Images of East Germany: Past and Future*, edited by Barton Byg. Forthcoming.

———. "Old Movies: Cinema as Palimpsest in GDR Fiction," *New German Critique* (forthcoming).

———. "Reconstructing the New German Cinema: Social Subjects and Critical Documentaries." *German Politics and Society* 18 (fall 1989): 37–53.

Ulbricht, Walter. "Einige Probleme der Kulturrevolution." In *Dokumente zur Kunst-,*

Literatur-, und Kulturpolitik der SED, edited by Elmar Schubbe. Stuttgart, 1972: 534.

———. "Der Kampf gegen den Formalismus in der Kunst und Literatur: Für eine fortschrittliche deutsche Kultur." In *Dokumente zur Kunst-, Literatur-, und Kulturpolitik der SED*, edited by Elmar Schubbe. Stuttgart, 1972: 178–86.

———. "Der Weg zur Sicherung des Friedens (1959)." In *Dokumente zur Kunst-, Literatur-, und Kulturpolitik der SED*, edited by Elmar Schubbe. Stuttgart, 1972: 543.

"Urteil des Bundesverfassungsgerichts vom 5. Februar 1991." *Media Perspektiven: Dokumentation* 1 (1991): 1–48.

Vierhaus, Rudolf. "Umrisse einer Sozialgeschichte der Gebildeten in Deutschland." *Quellen und Forschungen aus italienischen Archiven und Bibliotheken* 60 (1980): 385 ff.

Vinke, Hermann, ed. *Akteneinsicht Christa Wolf: Zerrspiegel und Dialog. Eine Dokumentation*. Hamburg, 1993.

Virilio, Paul. *Geschwindigkeit und Politik: Ein Essay zur Dromologie*. Berlin, 1980.

———. *Rasender Stillstand. Essay*. Munich, 1992.

Vogt, Jochen. *'Die Erinnerung ist unsere Aufgabe': Über Literatur, Moral and Politik 1945–1990*. Opladen, 1991.

Vollnhals, Clemens, ed. *Entnazifizierung: Politische Säuberung und Rehabilitierung in den vier Besatzungszonen 1945–1949*. Munich, 1991.

Wagenbach, Klaus, ed. *Vaterland, Muttersprache: Deutsche Schriftsteller und ihr Staat seit 1945*. Berlin, 1994.

Walser, Martin. *Extreme Mittellage: Eine Reise durch das deutsche Nationalgefühl*. Hamburg, 1990.

Walther, Joachim. *Sicherungsbereich Literatur: Schriftsteller und Staatssicherheit in der Deutschen Demokratischen Republik*. Berlin, 1996.

———, ed. *Protokoll eines Tribunals: Die Ausschlüsse aus dem DDR-Schiftstellerverband 1979*. Reinbek, 1991.

Walther, Joachim, and Sabine von Prittwitz. "Mielke und die Musen: Die Organization der Überwachung." *Text und Kritik* 120 (1993): 74–88.

Walzer, Michael. *The Company of Critics: Social Criticism and Political Commitment in the Twentieth Century*. New York, 1988.

Watson, Martin. "'Flüstern & Schreien': Punks, Rock Music and the Revolution in the GDR." *German Life and Letters* 46, no. 2 (April 1993): 162–75.

Weber, Carl, ed. *Hamletmaschine and Other Texts for the Stage by Heiner Müller*. Trans. Carl Weber. New York, 1984.

Weck, Michael. "Der ironische Westen und der tragische Osten." *Kursbuch* 109 (1992): 133–46.

Weidenfeld, Werner, and Felix Philipp Lutz. "Die gespaltene Nation: Das Geschichtsbewußtsein der Deutschen nach der Einheit." *Aus Politik und Zeitgeschichte* B 31–32 (24 July 1992): 3–22.

Weiler, Hans N. "Wisenschaft an der Grenze: Zum besonderen Profil der Europa-Universität Viadrina in Frankfurt/Oder." In *Ostprofile: Universitätsentwicklung in den neuen Bundesländern*, edited by Alfons Söllner and Ralf Walkenhaus. Opladen, 1998: 80–100.

Weninger, Robert, and Brigitte Rossbacher, eds. *Wendezeiten, Zeitenwende: Positionsbestimmungen zur deutschsprachigen Literatur 1945–1995*. Tübingen, 1997.

Wertheim, Ursula. *Friedrich Schiller—Dichter der Nation, 1759–1805: Sein Leben, sein Werk, seine Zeit in Bildern und Dokumente*. Berlin, 1959.

———. *Schillers "Fiesko" und "Don Carlos": Zu Problemen des historischen Stoffes* (Weimar, 1958).

Wertheim, Ursula, and Edith Braemer. *Studien zur deutschen Klassik*. Berlin, 1960.

Whitfield, Stephen J. *The Culture of the Cold War*. Baltimore, 1991.

Wichner, Ernst. "'Und unverständlich wird mein ganzer Text': Anmerkungen zu einer zensurgestreuten 'Nationalliteratur.'" In *"Literaturentwicklungsprozesse": Die Zensur der Literatur in der DDR*, edited by Ernest Wichner and Herbert Wiesner. Frankfurt am Main, 1993: 199–216.

Wichner, Ernest, and Herbert Wisener, eds. *"Literaturentwicklungsprozesse": Die Zensur der Literatur in der DDR*. Frankfurt am Main, 1993.

Wicke, Peter, and Lothar Müller, eds. *Rockmusik und Politik: Analysen, Interviews und Dokumente*. Berlin, 1996.

Wicke, Peter, and John Shepherd. "'The Cabaret Is Dead': Rock Culture as State Enterprise—The Political Organization of Rock in East Germany." In *Rock and Popular Music*, edited by Simon Frith, Tony Bennett, Lawrence Grossberg, John Shepherd, and Graeme Turner. London, 1993: 25–36.

Wickert, Ulrich, ed. *Angst vor Deutschland*. Hamburg, 1990.

Wiesand, Andreas Johannes. "The State of the Kulturstaat: Ideas, Theses, and Facts from a German and European Perspective." In *The Cultural Legitimacy of the Federal Republic: Assessing the Kulturstaat*, edited by Frank Trommler. Washington, D.C., 1999.

Wilke, Jürgen. "Medien DDR." In *Fischer Lexikon Publizistik-Massenkommunikation*, edited by Elisabeth Noelle-Neumann, Winfried Schulz, and Jürgen Wilke. Frankfurt am Main, 1989: 156–69.

Wilkering, Albert. *DEFA: Betriebsgeschichte des VEB DEFA Studio für Spielfilme*, 3 vols. Potsdam, 1981.

Wille, Karola. "Medienrecht in der DDR-Vergangenheit und Gegenwart." *Zeitschrift für Urheber- und Medienrecht* 35 (1991): 15–20.

Willett, John. "Two Political Excursions." In *Brecht in Context*. London, 1985: 210–21.

Williams, Raymond. "Brecht and Beyond." In *Politics and Letters*. London, 1981: 219–24.

Winkler, Lutz. "Der Geist an der Macht? Kulturnation und intellektueller Hegemonieanspruch." In *Les intellectuels et l'état sous la république de Weimar*, edited by Manfred Gangl and Hélène Roussel. Rennes, 1993: 219–31.

"WIP-Memorandum: Verwirklichung des Wissenschaftler-Integrationsprogramms (WIP) im Hochschulerneuerungsprogramm (HEP)." *Das Hochschulwesen* 2 (1995): 95–100.

Wittstock, Uwe. *Über die Fähigkeit zu trauern: Das Bild der Wandlung im Prosawerk von Christa Wolf und Franz Fühmann*. Frankfurt am Main, 1987.

Wolf, Christa. *Auf dem Weg nach Tabou: Texte 1990–1994*. Cologne, 1994 (*Parting from Phantoms: Selected Writings, 1990–1994* [Chicago, 1997]).

———. *Der geteilte Himmel*. Halle, 1963 (*Divided Heaven* [New York, 1976]).

———. "Interview." *Weimarer Beiträge* 6 (1974): 90–112.

———. "Interview with Myself." In *The Author's Dimension: Selected Essays*, edited by Alexander Stephan. New York, 1993: 16–19.

———. *Kassandra*. East Berlin, 1983.

————. *Nachdenken über Christa T.* Halle, 1968 (*The Quest for Christa T.* [New York, 1970]).

————. *Was bleibt.* Frankfurt am Main, 1990 (*What Remains & Other Stories* [Chicago, 1993]).

Wolf, Gerhard. "gegen sprache mit sprache—mit-sprache gegen-sprache. Thesen mit Zitaten und Notizen zu einem literarischen Prozess." In *Die Andere Sprache:. Neue DDR-Literatur der 80er Jahre,* edited by Heinz Ludwig Arnold and Gerhard Wolf, special issue of *Text + Kritik* (1990).

Wolf, Klaus D. " 'Universität beginnt im Kopf': Zur Genesis der Universitäten Bayreuth und Erfurt." In *Ostprofile: Universitätsentwicklung in den neuen Bundesländern,* edited by Alfons Söllner and Ralf Walkenhaus. Opladen, 1998: 124–39.

Wolf, Markus. *In eigenem Auftrag: Bekenntnisse und Einsichten.* Munich, 1991.

Wolfrum, Edgar. *Geschichtspolitik in der Bundesrepublik Deutschland: Der Weg zur bundesrepublikanischen Erinnerung 1948–1990.* Darmstadt, 1999.

Wolle, Stefan. *Die heile Welt der Diktatur: Alltag und Herrschaft in der DDR 1971–1989.* Berlin, 1998.

————. "Operativer Vorgang 'Herbstrevolution': War die Wende des Jahres 1989 eine Verschwörung der Stasi?" In *Die Ohnmacht der Allmächtigen: Geheimdienste und politische Polizei in der modernen Gesellschaft,* edited by Bernd Florath, Armin Mitter, and Stefan Wolle. Berlin, 1992: 234–40.

Wurm, Carsten. *Jeden Tag ein Buch: 50 Jahre Aufbau-Verlag.* Berlin, 1995.

Zapf, Wolfgang. "Der Untergang der DDR und die soziologische Theorie der Modernisierung." In *Experiment Vereinigung—Ein sozialer Großversuch,* edited by Bernd Giesen and Claus Leggewie. Berlin, 1991: 38–51.

Zelikow, Philip, and Condoleeza Rice. *Germany Unified and Europe Transformed: A Study in Statecraft.* Cambridge, Mass., 1995.

Zentralinstitut für Bibliothekswesen, ed. *Internationale Beratung der Spezialisten sozialistischer Länder für die Forschung auf dem Gebiet des Lesens und der Bibliotheksbenutzung, November 17–22, 1980 in Berlin.* Berlin, 1982.

Zipser, Richard, ed. *Fragebogen: Zensur.* Leipzig, 1995.

Žižek, Slavoj. "Republics of Gilead." *New Left Review* 183 (September–October 1990): 50–62.

Zwerenz, Gerhard. *Der Widerspruch: Autobiographischer Bericht.* Frankfurt am Main, 1974.

Zwiegespräch: Beiträge zur Aufarbeitung der Staatssicherheit-Vergangenheit. Berlin, 1991.

Unpublished Sources

"Abteilung Schöne Literatur, Kunst und Musik, 21.1.1958." Bundesarchiv Potsdam, DR 1/1223.

Ackermann, Anton. "Rede vor Angehörigen der Intelligenz." 15 October 1946, SAPMO-BA, ZPA NL/109/14:40.

Bauernkämper, Arnd, and Petra Srzckow. "Entwurf für die Konzeption eines sozialwissenschaftlichen SFB: Umbruchsgesellschaft. Bestimmungsfaktoren von Kontinuität und Kontingenz des Systemwandels in Ostmittel und Osteuropa." 1998.

Böthig, Peter. "Differenz und Revolte: Literatur aus der DDR in den 80er Jahren. Untersuchungen an den Rändern eines Diskurses." Ph.D. diss., Humboldt Universität zu Berlin, 1993.

Feinstein, Joshua. "The Triumph of the Ordinary: Depictions of Daily Life in the East German Cinema, 1956–1966." PhD. diss., Stanford University, 1995.

Jessen, Ralph. "Akademische Elite und Kommunistische Diktatur: Studien zur Geschichte der Hochschullehrerschaft in der Ulbricht-Ära." Habilitationsschrift, Freie Universität Berlin, 1998.

"Hauptreferat Buchhandel, 22.5.1954: Werbung für Bücher durch den Zugfunk." Bundesarchiv, DR 1/1896.

"Hausmitteilung des Amtes für Literatur und Verlagswesen vom 20.10.1955." Bundesarchiv, DR 1/1906.

Meyer, Hans Joachim. "Higher Education Reform in the New German States." Paper presented at the German Studies Association conference, Los Angeles, 24 September 1991.

"Nachtrag zur Statistik über die Entwicklung der belletristischen Buchproduktion, 13.10.1960." Bundesarchiv, DR 1/1275.

"Protokolle der Literaturarbeitsgemeinschaft der belletristischen Verlage von 1958." Bundesarchiv, DR 1/1224.

Mühlberg, Dietrich. "Über kulturelle Differenzen zwischen Deutschen in Ost und West." 1998.

Rossman, Peter. "Zum 'Intellektuellenstreit,'" paper presented at the conference on "Gegenwartsbewältigung," [University of Michigan], Ann Arbor, 25–27 October 1990.

Schmidt, Katja, and Martin Ottmers. "Zu Tisch mit dem Teufel." In *Auseinandersetzungen um die Integrität von Literatur und Kirche in der DDR*. Fern-Universität Hagen, 1992.

"Stenographisches Protokoll der 30. Tagung des ZK der SED." Bundesarchiv, ZPA IV/2/1/252:109.

Ulbricht, Walter. "Beratung mit Genossen Gesellschaftwissenschaftlern (18 April 1954)," SAPMO-BA, ZPA, Abteilung Wissenschaft beim ZK der SED, IV/2/904/33.

"Verordnung über die Förderung und Intensivierung der an den Universitäten und Hochschulen der DDR betriebenen Forschungen." SAPMO-BA, ZPA Bestand Abteilung Wissenschaft IV2/904/373:36–37.

"Walter Victor's address to the Ministry of Culture, 10.7.1959." Bundesarchiv, DR 1/1278.

ZK der DDR. *Das 15. Plenum des Zentralkomitees der SED vom 24. Juli bis 26. Juli 1953: Nun für den persönlichen Gebrauch bestimmt.* Ed. ZK der SED Berlin. Berlin, 1953.

Abwicklung, 287, 300, 301, 303, 346, 367, 378n. 65
Academic life, impact of unification on, 304
Academic mandarins, 39, 40, 41
Academy of Sciences, 287, 300
Academy of the Arts, 383
Ackermann, Anton, 68
Acting Institute, Berlin, 193
Adenauer, Konrad, 284
Adorno, Theodor W., 45, 336; critique of Brecht, 205n. 19; *Erziehung nach Auschwitz* (Education After Auschwitz), 335; on nationalism, 314, 337; on self-determination, 335, 338, 341
Advanced worker-reader, 93
Advertising, 254, 256
Aesthetics of moral conviction (*Gesinnungsästhetik*), 186
Akademie-Verlag, 98
Akademiker, 277
Aktuelle Kamera, 253, 268, 269
Albrecht, Michael, 260, 262
Albrecht, Richard, 104
Alltag, as a site of resistance, 234
"Alte Helden," 238–39
Alternative theater, in unified Germany, 201–2
AMIGA, 235
Andersch, Alfred, 44
Anderson, Sascha, 154; as an IM, 6, 37, 138, 140–41, 161, 345; Prenzlauer Berg and, 138, 140
Antifascism, in the GDR, 63–70, 305–6, 336, 346–47
Antifeminism, 67
Anti-intellectualism, 67–68
Antimodernism, 73
Antinationalism, 19, 315, 323, 327, 331
Anti-Semitism, 325, 330
APO (extraparliamentary opposition), 331
Arbeiter und Bauern Fakultät, 341

Arbeitsgemeinschaft der Rundfunkanstalten Deutschlands (ARD), 264
Arbeitsgruppen, 123
Arbeitsstelle für Geschichte der deutschen und französischen Aufklärung, 87n. 49
Arendt, Erich, 144
Arendt, Hannah, 4, 139, 186, 384, 386; "On Humanity in Dark Times," 391
Ariadnefabrik, 156, 160, 169
Aristotle: *Poetics*, 384, 385
Arrabal, Fernando: *Picnic*, 193
Ash, Mitchell, 19
Ash, Timothy Garton, 344
Association of German Authors, 223
Association of Theater Practitioners, 193
Astra satellite, 265
Asylum debate, 297, 310, 317, 318, 327, 359
Asylum law, 325
Aufbaugeneration (reconstruction generation), 280, 341–43
Aufbau Verlag, 68, 99, 133n. 6
Auschwitz, 10, 19, 213, 331
Automatic utterance, 165
Avant-garde: East German intellectuals, 160, 344, 345; SED opposition to, 79

Bahner, Werner, 86n. 40
Bahro, Rudolf, 69, 82, 342; *Die Alternative*, 145
Baier, Lother, 50
"Bakschischrepublik," 229
Balibar, Etienne, 318
Barck, Simone, 13
Basic Law, 263, 315, 316, 325, 356
"Basisgruppen," 344
Bathrick, David, 13, 14, 234
Batt, Kurt, 110n. 38
Bauhaus, 279
Becher, Johannes R., 36, 52, 64–65, 69, 72, 399; concept of new reader, 92; concept of reading nation, 89–90, 94; *Education for Freedom*, 65

Becker, Achim, 269
Becker, Jurek, 36, 137n. 22
Becker, Manfred, 260
Beckett, Samuel: Waiting for Godot, 190
"Beitrag zur Währungsunion," 236
Benda, Julien: La trahison des clercs (The Treason of the intellectuals), 12, 35, 36, 37, 47, 276–77
Benjamin, Walter, 63, 144
Benn, Gottfried, 44
Berlin, new, 5
Berliner Ensemble, 183, 190, 196, 198, 199, 206n. 31
Berliner Rundfunk, 195
Berlin Film Festival, 117
Berlin Puppet Theater, 196, 197
Berlin Wall, 44, 50, 53, 121, 187
Bernhardt, Thomas, 200
Berufsverbot, 7, 193
Besserwessis, 230, 287
Besson, Benno, 189
Besson, Tatjana, 245n. 16, 245n. 18, 247n. 37
Beyer, Frank, 116, 136n. 18, 136n. 19; Fünf Patronenhülsen (Five empty cartridges), 124, 130; Spur der Steine (Traces of stones), 126
Biermann, Wolf, 368; attack on Anderson, 6; commitment to remake society, 13; in exile, 342; expulsion, 36, 69, 82, 145, 151, 191, 207n. 37, 281
Bildung, 2
Bildungsbürger, 277, 279, 280, 283, 350
Bildungsroman, 54
Bismarck, Otto von, 7
Bitov, Andrei, 213
Bitterfeld Conference, 103
Bitterfelder Weg, 55, 92, 93, 99, 103, 121
"Black Book on communism," 289
Blackbourn, David, 310
Blacklisting, 116
Bloch, Ernst, 36, 69, 75, 77, 79, 81, 120, 144
Bobo in White Wooden Houses, 229
Bobrowski, Johannes, 129
Bohley, Bärbel, 344
Bohrer, Karl Heinz, 285, 360, 361
Böll, Heinrich, 12, 38, 369; Ansichten eines Clowns (The clown), 42; Haus ohner Hüter (The unguarded house), 42; therapeutic discourse, 39, 40, 44, 51; Und sagte kein einziges Wort (And never said a word), 42; Wo warst du, Adam? (Where were you, Adam?), 42

Book production and distribution, state planning of, 95–103
Book shortage, 94–95, 98, 101–3
Borneman, John, 19
Bosnia, 319, 320, 335, 336, 337, 351n. 7
Böttcher, Jürgen, 116, 136n. 18; Jahrgang 45 (Born in '45), 124–25
Bourdieu, Pierre, 20, 68
Bracher, Karl Dietrich, 369
Brandenburg, Antenne, 259
Brandenburg literature prize, 225
Brandenburg's law, 301
Brandt, Willy, 315, 321, 357
Brasch, Thomas, 36
Braun, Volker, 99, 129; Lenins Tod, 190
Brecht, Bertolt, 16, 36, 53, 148, 149, 184, 391; appropriation by state as cold war weapon, 187; attacks on, 187, 205n. 16; Berliner Ensemble, 206n. 31; challenge to SED cultural policy, 188; contribution to the discourse of Kulturpolitik, 188–89; dedication to socialism, 64; fable of the laurel tree, 384; Fatzer material, 195; Die Massnahme (Measures Taken), 200
Brecht-Schall, Barbara, 199, 206n. 31
Brigade movement, 92–93
Broadcasting, 252–253: advertising, 256; deregulation, 18, 250, 259–62; federal system, 262–66; private radio and television, 264–65
Broadcasting Advisory Board (Rundfunkbeirat), 267–68
Brunkhorst, Hauke, 20
Brussig, Thomas: Helden wie wir (Heroes like us), 200–201
Bubis, Ignatz, 7, 336
Buch, Lektüre, Lesen, 105
Buchenwald, 27, 346
Büchner, Georg, 184
Buchwald, Manfred, 265
Bugajski, Ryszard: Interrogation, 137n. 21
Bundesbürger, 31
Bundeswehr, 9
Bündnis 90, 307
Bunge, Hans, 149

Cabaret, 194
Cambodia, 335
Carow, Heiner, 115–16
Castorf, Frank, 201
Censorship, 95–97, 110n. 31
Centers for National Research and Commemoration of Classical German

Literature (Nationale Forschungs- und Gedenkstätten der klassischen deutschen Literatur), 72
Central Council of Jews in Germany, 336
Central Film Administration, Ministry of Culture, 254
Christoph Links Press, 200
Cinema, East German: documentary and short-film units, 128; exposure to foreign and experimental films, 124, 135n. 14; government intervention, 115–17, 121; innovation after New wave, 128; neue Tendenzen (new tendencies), 122–23; New wave, 14, 122–31; return to visual and narrative realism, 129
Cinema, West German, 116–17, 123, 125
Citizenship: defined via blood lineage, 326–27; and German national identity, 317, 357
Civic cultures, 349
Civil rights, 330
Clandestine language, 154, 171–76
Classicism, cult of in GDR, 70, 72, 78–83
Closed system, 391, 392
Clouzot, Henri-Georges: Salaire de la Peur (Wages of fear), 124
Coca-Colonization, 53
Cold war: collapsing order of, 348, 349; and concept of treason, 35; education after, 347–51; education during, 339–43; effect on nationalism, 19, 319; origins and functioning of, 337–38; securities of, 10
Collage, 129
Collective guilt, 346
Commercial sphere, 383
"Communicative silence," 340
Congress on Cultural Freedom, 186
Conspirative avant-gardism, 160, 344, 345
Constitutional patriotism, 324, 330
Contributions on the German Classics, 72
Croatia, 309, 337
Croats, 351n. 7
Cult bands, 227
Cultural capital, generation of in Federal Republic, 198, 199–200, 201
Cultural Commission, 102
Cultural sciences (Kulturwissenschaften), 300, 301
Cultural socialism, 94
Culture, education, and science, offices of, 71, 72
Culture clubs, 194
Culture of memory, in Federal Republic, 8–9, 357, 359, 372

Culture wars, post-unification, 373, 374
Currency union, 227, 228, 229, 236, 285, 286, 296–97
Curtius, Ernst Robert, 78
Czech New Wave, 124

Dahrendorf, Ralf, 45–46, 317
Daimler, 4
De Bruyn, Günter, 51, 54, 99, 192, 368; Märkische Forschungen, 280
DEFA (Deutsche Filmaktiengesellschaft), 113, 254; Central Committee attack on, 115, 116, 120–21; connection to new developments in world cinema, 134n. 14; documentary studios, 128; influence of international films on, 123; influence of the twenties on the sixties, 129; loss of political daring, 137n. 21; reorganization of institutional structures, 123
Dehler, Peter, 201
De Maizière, Lothar, 256, 257, 260
Democracy, secular liberal, 349
Democracy Now (Demokratie Jetzt), 234, 255, 282
Demokratischer Aufbruch, 282
Depth psychology, 41
Descartes, René, 59, 82
De-Stalinization: in Eastern Europe, 118–19; in GDR, 119–20
Deutsche Filmaktiengesellschaft. See DEFA (Deutsche Filmaktiengesellschaft)
Deutsche Schallplatten, 235
Deutsches Theater, 183, 190, 198
Deutschlandsender, 75
Deutschmark: nationalism, 285; as national symbol of stability, 358; unification, 296–97; weakening of, 322
Dietze, Walter, 86n. 40, 87n. 49, 101
Dietz Verlag, 100, 102–3
Digital information, 266
Discourse: of modernization, 298–99; of nationhood, 65, 321–25; therapeutic, 12, 38–49, 51
Djacenko, Boris: Herz und Asche, Bd. 2, 109n. 27
Documentary theater, 199
La Dolce Vita, 124
Domovina, 253
Dönhoff, Marion, 364, 365
Döring, Stefan, 155
Dornhof, Dorothea, 12
Double bind, position of East Germans in new state, 309

Drama, 384
Dresden State Theater, 190, 191, 197, 198
Dreyfus Affair, 278
Dritter Weg (Third Way), 282
DS Kultur, 259

Eastern Europe: collapsing order of cold war, 348; cultural "thaw" of 1956–1962, 118
East German Intellectuals. See Intellectuals, East German
East Germany. See German Democratic Republic (GDR)
East Mark, conversion of. See Currency union
Eckert, Rainer, 308
Education: after Auschwitz, 344–47; after the cold war, 347–51; oriented to the past, 337–39. See also Higher education
Education for Freedom (Becher), 65
Egotrip, 247n. 34
Eisler, Hanns, 36, 134n. 11
Eleventh Plenum, 94
Eley, Geoff, 310
Elites, "exchange" or replacement of, 300, 301
Elitism, 284
Emilia Galotti, 385
Emmerich, Klaus, 200
Engel, Wolfgang, 190–91; Faust, 200
Enlightenment, 390
Enquete Commission, 2
Enzensberger, Hans Magnus, 44, 45, 360, 369
Eppler, Erhard, 280
Erb, Elke, 156, 160; Berührung ist nur eine Randerscheinung (Touching is only a marginal thing), 153; "Das Unternehmen Schreiben" (The writing enterprise), 161–63
Ernst-Busch-Schauspielschule, 199
Essentialism, 361
Esslin, Martin, 186; Bertolt Brecht: A Choice of Evils, 187
Ethnic cleansing, 319, 335
European parliament, 323
European unification, 310, 316; and national identity, 318–20
European University, 302
Exceptionalism, 323, 324
Existentialism, 123
Experte, 277
Expressionism, 44–45, 123

Fachhochschulen, 301
FDGB (Trade Union), 100
FDJ (Free German Youth), 75, 100, 194, 195

Federal Constitutional Court, decision on the broadcasting network, 263
Federal Republic of Germany (FRG), 7; anti-authoritarian movement, 122; chauvinism of prosperity, 322; cultural capital generation, 198, 199–200, 201; debate about national identity in the 1980s, 320–21; and East German publishing market, 257–58; educational expansion, 370–71; film subsidy system, 123; indictment of East German intellectual complicity, 184–87; intellectuals (See Intellectuals, West German); memory culture, 8–9, 357, 359, 372; mode of dealing with Nazi past, 306–7; new cinema, 116–17, 123, 125; nostalgia, 7; unification and, 3–4, 5, 296; Westernization of, 315. See also Germany, unified
Federal Science Council (Wissenschaftsrat), 301
Feeling B, 232
Fehlfarben, 242
Fellini, Federico, 124
Festschrift, 87n. 49
Die Firma, 228–30, 232, 236, 238–39
Fischer, Fritz, 369
Fluxus, 129
"Forbidden Films," 118
Forschungszentrum populäre Musik, 233
Foucault, Michel Paul, 155; notion of power, 63; panoptic eye, 151
Fourth German Writer's Congress, 72, 89
Frankfurt, as global marketplace, 5
Frankfurter Allgemeine Zeitung (FAZ), 6, 360, 373
Frankfurt exchange, merger with London, 4
Frankfurt-Oder, 201
Frankfurt School, 129, 144
Franz Mehring Institute, University of Leipzig, 73–74
Free German Youth (FDJ), 75, 100, 194, 195
Free spaces (Freiräume), 299
Freie Presse, 258
Freie Szene, 201–2
Freie theater, 194–95
Freiräume, 244n. 4
Freischwebende Intelligenz (free-floating intelligence), 278
French filmmaking, 124
Freyer, Hans, 40
Freygang, 228, 229, 232, 236, 239–41, 247n. 37
Friedlander, Saul, 336

Frings, Theodor, 74
Fromm, Erich, 63
Fuchs, Jürgen, 145
Fühmann, Franz, 51, 148
Fukuyama, Francis, 349
Functionalization, 121
"Fünf neue Länder" (five new states), 357
Funktion und Wirkung, 104
Furet, François, 8, 10, 12
Für unser Land (For Our Country), 47

Gänsemarkt, 381
Gauck, Joachim, 307
Gaus, Günter, 268, 341
Gay, Peter, 279
Gebildeter, 277
Gegenwartsbewältigung, 10
Geggel, Heinz, 269
Geißler, Rainer, 298
Geistesarbeiter, 277
Gelehrter, 277
General German News Service (*Allgemeiner
    Deutscher Nachrichtendienst* or ADN), 254
Genscher, Hans-Dietrich, 258, 309
German Academy of Science (*Deutsche
    Akademie der Wissenschaften der DDR*), 71
German Advertising and Classified Ad Society
    (*Deutsche Werbe- und Anzeigengesellschaft*,
    or *DEWAG*), 254
German classicism, 66, 350
German Democratic Republic (GDR):
    antifascism, 63–70, 305–6, 336, 346–47;
    cinema, 14, 115–17, 121, 122–23, 124,
    128, 129, 134n. 14, 135n. 14; constitution,
    206n. 29; culture, education, and science,
    offices of, 71, 72; culture in the sixties and
    seventies, 12; de-Stalinization, 119–20;
    education, 337–47; esteem of reading, 53;
    founding myth of, 63; history of literary
    opposition, 143–47; ideological control of
    universities, 73; institutional reorientation
    of humanities, 70–71; intellectuals (*See*
    Intellectuals, East German); letters to the
    editor, encouragement of in 1960s, 92, 93;
    link of language to power, 144; literary
    circles, 92; as literary-political experiment,
    95–97; media, 7, 18, 252–71; "new reader,"
    105–6; nostalgia for, 5, 200, 288, 290, 306;
    notion of reading nation, 13, 53, 88–91,
    107–8; November 1989 demonstration,
    18, 48, 195, 233, 250–51, 281, 283, 343,
    382; Petition law of 1961, 93; public
    funding for intellectual work, 44; public

sphere, 233–34, 243n. 4, 247n. 29, 286;
    publishing, 29–30, 97–103, 253–54; "real
    readers," 103–8; regional literature, 11;
    regulation of information, 251–52; socialist
    national literature, 79–83, 102, 103–5,
    129; state socialism, 67; Theater Jury,
    193; Theater Workshop, 193; unification
    impacts, 3–4, 296, 383; workers' uprising,
    120. *See also* Socialist Unity Party (SED);
    State Security Service (Stasi)
German Enlightenment, 368
German language, absence of adequate,
    174–75
German Language Association, 71
German superiority, 323
German Television Network (*Deutscher
    Fernsehfunk*, or *DFF*), 249, 253
German thought, juxtaposition of rationalism
    and irrationalism in, 66–67
Germany, division of in 1949, 314
Germany, unified: absence of immigration law,
    317; blockages to nationhood discourse,
    321–25; consequences of unification,
    4–6, 221–26; culture wars, 373; debate
    on national identity, 316–18, 321–25,
    350, 357, 359; disappointments of
    unification, 276–77, 361–62; discontinuity
    between present and recent past, 355–56;
    discourse of economic national unity,
    65, 322; discovery of East German
    cultural scene, 8; early optimism, 357–59;
    efforts to change status quo, 360; as an
    "experiment," 298; higher education,
    299–304, 373; intellectuals in, 366–74;
    logic of rationalization, 198, 199; media,
    249–50; quest for neoregulationism, 365;
    reconstruction of historical identities,
    304–9, 329; resentment between East
    and West Germans, 327–29; resistance
    to change, 3, 5–6; right-wing violence,
    295, 325, 336–37, 346, 349; structural
    transformation, 365–66; theater, 197–203.
    See also National identity; Normalization
Germoney, 197
Gesellschaft-Literatur-Lesen, 91
Gesellschaftswissenschaften, 62
Gesichertes Wissen (secure knowledge), 342
Gesinnungsästhetik (aesthetics of moral
    conviction), 186
Giesen, Bernard, 350
Giordano, Ralph, 308
Glasnost, destabilizing effects of, 237
Globalization, 357

Glotz, Peter, 302
Godard, Jean-Luc, 216
Goethe, Johann, 79, 190
Goethe Institute, 117
Goldhagen, Daniel: *Hitler's Willing Executioners*, 307
Goldhagen debate, 289
Gorbachev, Mikhail, 281, 285, 342
Götz, Rainald, 15
Graf, Andreas, 18
Gräf, Roland, 135n. 14
Gramsci, Antonio, 144
Granta, 344
Grass, Günter, 46–47, 86n. 40, 360; *Die Blechtrommel* (The tin drum), 338; criticism of FRG, 339; focus on the Nazi past, 338–39; interventionism, 369, 370; opposition to unification, 285; therapeutic literature, 44
Great Coalition, 331
Green Party, 289
Greiner, Ulrich, 186, 204n. 14
Greiner-Pol, André, 239–40, 244n. 5, 247n. 37
Groß, Jürgen: *Parteifreund*, 191
Group 47, 41, 43
Die Grünen, 234
Grüning, Uwe, 267
Guattari, Felix, 17, 212
Guggenberger, Bernd, 270
Gulf war, 9, 309, 362
Günther, Egon, 136n. 18; *Wenn du groß bist, lieber Adam* (When you're grown up, dear Adam), 124
Gymnasium, 277
Gysi, Gregor, 239

Habermas, Jürgen, 6, 356; *Der andere Zerstörung der Vernunft* (The other destruction of reason), 50; on "exchange" of elites, 300; image of Stasi, 138, 139, 140; on nationhood debate, 285, 324, 330; *neue Unübersichtlichkeit*, 5
Hacks, Peter, 149; *Die Sorgen und die Macht*, 86n. 40
Hager, Kurt, 72, 78, 113
"Hallo," 235
Hallstein doctrine, 323, 326
Hammer, Gero, 256
Handke, Peter, 2
Harich, Wolfgang, 69, 79, 120, 188
Härtling, Peter, 46
Haug, Wolfgang, 352n. 14

Hauptmann, Gerhart: *Die Weber*, 201
Haußmann, Leander, 210n. 62
Havel, Vaclav, 145
Havemann, Robert, 69, 82, 113, 120, 145, 339
Hebbel, Friedrich: *Nibelungen*, 190
Hegen, Iduna, 195
Heiduczek, Werner: *Tod am Meer*, 109n. 27
Hein, Christoph, 14, 47, 267; *Ritter der Tafelrunde* (Knights of the Round Table), 190, 280
Helsinki accords, 323
Herbst in Peking, 232, 244n. 7
Hermlin, Stefan, 148, 339
Heym, Stefan, 47, 184, 188, 189, 229, 250, 267, 285, 343
High culture, desegregation of, 370
Higher education, in unified Germany: "heroic" stage, 300; "legalistic" stage, 300–301; normalization and, 297, 299–304; personnel "renewal," 301, 303; problems of, aggravated by unification, 373; tension with social or labor policy priorities, 302–3; "transvaluation of values," 303–4
Hildebrandt, Jörg, 261
Hillgruber, Andreas, 330
Hinkeldey, Wolfgang, 268
Hinrichs, Reimar: "Patient DDR," 48
Hinstorff Verlag, 99
Hirschman, Albert, 348
Historicism, 78
History of German Literature: From the Beginnings to the Present, 82
Hitler, Adolf: *Mein Kampf*, 231
Hochhuth, Rolf: *Die Hebamme*, 210n. 59; *Der Stellvertreter*, 210n. 59; *Weissis in Weimar*, 210n. 59; *Wessis in Wewimar*, 199
Hochschule der Künste, 199
Hochschule für Politik, 279
Hochschulrahmengesetz (HRG), 301
Hoffmann, Hans Joachim, 190–92
Hohmann, Dietrich, 11–12, 17; "An Attempt at an Exemplary Report on H," 27–34; "The Consequences of Unification According to H," 221–26
Holocaust, 42, 335–36
Holocaust, 331
Holocaust memorial, Berlin, 307
Holocaust museum, Washington, 331
Home Army (Poland), 119
Homelessness, as adaptive reaction to modernity, 348
Honecker, Erich, 47, 55, 91, 113, 196, 233, 281, 339, 340

Höpcke, Klaus, 91
Horkheimer, Max, 63; *Dialectic of Enlightenment*, 389–90
"Hour Zero," 43
Hradil, Stefan, 299
Huchel, Peter, 144
Humanities, institutional reorientation in the GDR, 70–71
Humboldt University, 303, 304, 308
Hungarian uprising, 69, 102, 120, 187
Huyssen, Andreas, 19

IchFunktion, 228, 229, 230, 232, 236, 241, 247n. 34
IM (unofficial informant), 138, 141–42, 223, 226n. 1, 245n. 16, 345, 353n. 28
Im Eimer, 229, 234, 236, 238
Immigration, 310, 317, 320, 326, 359, 364
"Imperial overstretch" theory, 358
Inchtabokatables, 232, 245n. 18
Individual psychology, shift to social-psychological analysis, 42–43
Initiative 4 November, 183
Initiative Frieden und Menschenrechte, 234
Institute for Social Sciences (*Institut für Gesellschaftswissenschaften*), 72
Institute for the History of National Literatures (*Institut für die Geschichte der Nationalliteraturen*), 74
Institute of Marxism-Leninism, 72
Institute of Modern German Literature (*Institut für neuere Deutsche Literatur*), 74
Intellectuals: meanings of throughout German history, 277–80; in unified Germany, 6–7, 366–74
Intellectuals, East German: accommodation to the SED, 1–2, 8, 61–63, 68–69, 340; aesthetics of interiority and therapy, 12; antifascism, 63–70; anti-Westernism, 341; attempt to balance power with culture, 63–65; *Aufbau* (reconstruction) generation, 280, 341–43; centrality of literary-cultural intelligence, 2, 367–68; civic revolution leadership, 280–83; conspirative avant-gardism, 160, 344, 345; disparate tendencies of opposition and conformity, 15, 73, 144–45, 146–47; facing the Stasi past, 307–8; first generation of, 13, 339–41; hope for utopian socialism, 13, 145–47, 340; identification with Soviet Union, 340; implications of unification for, 4–5, 288–90, 345–46, 351n. 6, 367–68; indictment by West German critics,

184–87; language and resistance, 160–76; media assessment of role of in GDR, 59–60; newest generation of, 153–58; non-Marxists, 344; rejection of unification, 267–77, 283–88; role in generating a language of legitimation, 148–49; role in transforming media, 266–71; Stasi collaboration, 35–39, 289–90; third generation, 145–46, 343–48. See also Theater intellectuals; Writers
Intellectuals, West German, 279, 352n. 14; activism, 368–70; continuity of elites, 64; enlightening public sphere, 369–72; opposition to unification, 285, 372; postwar attitude of resistance, 43–44; reaction to right-wing violence, 350
Interiority/inwardness (*Innerlichkeit*), 12, 41, 53
Intimacy, spheres of, 383

Jahreszeiten, 257
Janka, Walter, 68, 69, 99, 133n. 6
Jarausch, Konrad, 18, 19
Jasny, Vojtech: *The Cassandra Cat*, 124
Jaspers, Karl, 330; *Die Schuldfrage* (The question of German guilt), 40, 314; *Zur geistigen Situation der Zeit* (Man in the modern age), 40
Jens, Walter, 46, 270
Jentzsch, Cornelia, 172
John, Erhard, 86n. 40
John, Hans Rainer, 193
Johnson, Uwe, 44
Joswig, Rex, 227, 228
Jünger, Ernst, 44, 149, 279
Jünger, Harri, 86n. 40
Just, Gustav, 68, 75
Jutzi, Piel: *Mutter Krausens Fahrt ins Glück* (Mother Krausen's journey to happiness), 130

Kafka, Franz, 14, 149
Kafka conference, 129
Kaiser, Georg, 149
Das Kaninchen bin ich (I am the rabbit), 125–26, 127
Die Kaninchenfilme ("the rabbit films"), 116, 117, 118, 122, 124–31
Kant, Hermann, 46
Kant, Immanuel, 216; *On Perpetual Peace, Appendix I*, 391; "What Does It Mean to Orient One's Self in Thought?" 381
Kantorowicz, Alfred, 69, 79

Karge, Manfred, 189
Karla, 126, 130
Karl Marx University, 74, 86n. 40
Kelly, Petra, 280
Kennedy, Paul, 358
Kershaw, Baz, 210n. 62
Khrushchev, Nikita, 118, 120, 122
Kinder der Maschinenrepublik (Children of the
    machinery republic) (Die Firma), 232–33
Kirch, Leo, 266
Kirsch, Sarah, 36
Kissinger effect, 340
"Kleeblatt," 235
Klein, Gerhard, 136n. 18; Berlin um die Ecke
    (Berlin around the corner), 126; Der Fall
    Gleiwitz (The Gleiwitz affair), 123–24;
    neorealism, 121, 123; Sonntags fahrer
    (Sunday drivers), 136n. 19; youth oriented
    films, 116, 123
Kleinwächter, Wolfgang, 255
Klier, Freya, 185, 192–95, 344
Klinkmann, Horst, 353n. 30
Kluge, Alexander, 16, 17, 20; Abschied von
    Gestern (Yesterday girl), 125–26
Koch, Hans, 91
Koeppen, Wolfgang, 44
Kofler, Leo, 79
Kohl, Helmut, 4, 47, 258, 267, 307, 357, 362;
    sanctification of, 349; unification and, 3,
    284, 285, 322
Kohlhaase, Wolfgang, 134n. 11
Kolbe, Uwe: The Homeland of Dissidents:
    Afterthoughts Concerning the Phantom of
    GDR Opposition, 145–46
Kollektivwesen Literatur, 90
Kölner Stadtanzeiger, 258
Konrad, György, 288
Koonen, Alissa, 207n. 41
Korff, Hermann August, 74, 79
KPD. See Socialist Unity Party (SED)
Krake, image of Stasi as, 139
Kramer, Martin, 257
Krass, Werner, 86n. 40
Krause, Günter, 261, 271n. 4
Krauss, Werner, 73, 76–78, 79, 82, 87n. 49
Krawczyk, Stephan, 185, 192–95
Kremer, Fritz, 134n. 11
Krenz, Egon, 341
Kroetz, Franz Xaver, 200
Kröher, Michael O. R., 350
Krug, Manfred, 207n. 37
Kruger, Loren, 15
Kultur, 350

Kulturbrauerei, 202
Kulturbund zur demokratischen Erneuerung
    Deutschlands (Cultural Alliance for the
    Democratic Renewal of Germany), 68, 89
Kulturkampf, 7, 373
Kulturkrise, 363
Kulturnation, 63–64, 68, 71, 315, 324, 330,
    361, 365
Kulturpolitik, 28, 223
Kundera, Milan, 344
Kunert, Günter, 36, 144, 148
Kunze, Reiner, 36
Kurella, Alfred, 36, 51, 52, 75, 79, 86n. 39
Kursbuch, 45, 48

Labor movement, 79
Lafontaine, Oskar, 4, 357
Lamberz, Werner, 191, 207n. 37
Lämmert, Eberhard, 71
Land, Rainer, 339, 340
Lang, Alexander, 190
Langermann, Martina, 13
Langhoff, Matthias, 189, 199
Language: clandestine, 154, 171–76; German,
    absence of adequate, 174–75; and power,
    143, 144–47, 148–49, 155–58, 160–61,
    173; as prerequisite for social critique, 154;
    of silence, 166, 170–76, 340; socialism and,
    169–76; split between public and private,
    234; of treason, 48; truth and, 171, 172,
    175; and unconscious, 161–63, 168
Law Concerning the Transformation of Radio
    Broadcasting, 256–57
Le Carré, John, 38
Lefort, Claude, 339
Lehnert, Herbert, 151
Lehrstück, 200
Leipzig, 15
Leipzig School, 79
Leitner, Olaf: "Rock Music in the GDR: An
    Epitaph," 233
Lem, Stanislaw, 106
Lenin, Vladimir, 67
Lennarz, Knut, 191
Lenz, Siegfried, 46
Leonard, Wolfgang, 339
Lepenies, Wolf, 61, 296, 340, 343, 345
Lepsius, Rainer M., 327, 370
Leseland GDR, 53, 89
Lessing, Gotthold Ephraim: Hamburg
    Dramaturgy, 383, 384–86, 388; Nathan the
    Wise, 386–87; on need for public sphere,
    381–82

Lettrism, 129
Die Letzten Tage von Pompeji (The last days of
    Pompeii), 227–28, 229–30
Lewis, Jerry, 124
Life world (Lebenswelt), 46
Lifshitz, Michail: "Encouragement of the
    Positive and the Disparagement of
    Decadence," 79; Marx und Engels über
    Kunst und Literatur, 73
Lindenberg, Udo, 233
"Literary History as Historical Mission"
    (Literaturgeschichte als geschichtlicher
    Auftrag) (Krauss), 77, 87n. 49
Literary scholarship, East Germany: avant-
    garde, 161–76; dominance by state, 62–63;
    socialist national, 79–83, 129; as a social
    science, 39, 70–78
Literary scholarship, West Germany: rise of
    therapeutic discourse, 39–47
Literary societies, 92, 94
Literaturgesellschaft, 88
LKG, 101, 102
Löffler, Dietrich, 105
Lokatis, Siegfried, 13
London, Jack, 106
Lukács, Georg, 36, 66, 79, 81, 144; Geschichte
    und Klassenbewußtsein (History and class
    consciousness), 52
Luther, Martin, 59
Lutz, Felix Philipp, 308
Luxemburg, Rosa, 192, 193–94

Maastricht Treaty, 310
Maaz, Hans-Joachim: Der Gefühlsstau, 48
Maetzig, Kurt, 115, 116, 123, 125, 136n. 18;
    Ehe im Schatten (Marriage in the shadows),
    136n. 19, 137n. 21; Das Kaninchen bin ich
    (I am the rabbit), 116
Mahle, Hans, 252
Main Administration for Publishing and
    Booksellers (Hauptverwaltung Verlage und
    Buchhandel), 95–99
Maltusch, Wernfried, 261, 273n. 32
Mandarins, academic, 39, 40, 41
Mann, Heinrich, 37
Mann, Thomas, 36, 39
Mannesmann, 4
Mannheim, Karl, 278
Marcuse, Herbert, 45, 63, 155
Markov, Walter, 77, 79
Maron, Monika, 49, 204n. 6, 285, 343
Marquardt, Fritz, 199
Marx, Karl, 144, 389

Marxism-Leninism: as an education for
    freedom, 64–65; dominance of in
    scholarship, 72, 74; as integral part of
    university curricula, 73; literary theory,
    70–83; "scientific," 342; social science, 75,
    78–79
Marxism-Leninism on the Role, the Essence, and
    the Meaning of Literature and Art, 73
Maschinenrepublik, 238
Max Planck institutes, 302
Mayer, Hans, 73–76, 77, 78; Ansichten zur
    Literatur der Zeit, 86n. 40; defense of
    Western modernism, 85n. 38; expulsion,
    69; Leipzig School, 79; Neue Beiträge zur
    Literaturwissenschaft, 87n. 49; reprisals
    against, 75–76, 86n. 40; revisionism,
    81–82
Mecklenburg State Theater, 193
Media, East German: after unification,
    262–66; assessment of intellectuals, 59–60;
    destruction of monopoly by the state, 18;
    era of the institutional entity, 260–62;
    interest in scandal, 7; legislation, 254–55;
    role of intellectuals in, 266–71. See also
    Broadcasting; Press; Publishing, East
    German
Media Control Council (Medienkontrollrat, or
    MKR), 255–57, 267, 272n. 20
Media Legislative Comission (Mediengesetzge-
    bungskommission), 254–55
Mediatization, 266
Meier, Christian, 310
Memoir literature, 305
Memory: of Auschwitz, 331; constitutional
    patriotism and, 330; culture of, 8–9, 357,
    359, 362, 372
Mempel, Horst, 268
Der Merkur, 360
Merope, 391
Meuschel, Sigrid, 341
Meyer, Hans-Joachim, 302
Michael, Klaus, 163
Michnik, Adam, 170
Mielke, Eric, 353n. 21
Mikado, 156
Minetti, Hans-Peter, 193
Ministry for State Security, 223
Ministry of Culture, 29, 68, 95, 185
Ministry of the Media, 260
Mitscherlich, Alexander and Margarete, 41,
    42, 50, 306, 369; Der Unfähigkeit zu trauern
    (The inability to mourn), 42–43
Mitte, 198

Mitteldeutscher Rundfunk (MDR), 262, 264
Mitteldeutscher Verlag, 99, 103
Mitteldeutsche Zeitung, 258
Mittenzwei, Werner, 79
Modernity: exclusion from GDR literary
scholarship, 79, 82; postwar culture of, 44
Modernization, 298–99, 305, 358, 359
Modrow, Hans, 190, 191, 197
Mölln, 325
Mommsen, Hans, 304
Monarchie und Alltag (Monarchy and the
everyday), 242
Monday demonstrations, 267
Montage, 129
Morawitz, Silvia, 170
Mühe, Ulrich, 203n. 3
Mühlfenzl, Rudolf, 249–50, 260, 261–62, 267,
271n. 2
Müller, Delia, 244n. 4
Müller, Gottfried, 256, 259
Müller, Heiner, 16, 17, 54, 368, 384;
"autobiographical" works, 147–48,
153; *Bau*, 201; blocks and pushes to
productivity, 213–15; clash with the party
over *The Peasants*, 149; criticism of artists'
privileges, 184; *Crusade Against Brecht*,
187; ideological nonconformity, 144,
185; *Der Lohndrücker* (The wagebuster),
190; management of Berliner Ensemble,
199–200; "Mommsen's Block," 212,
213–14; obituary for, 212–17; president
of Academy of the Arts, 383; protest of
Biermann's disenfranchisement, 207n. 37;
radio version of Brecht's *Fatzer* material,
195; relationship to the GDR, 148, 149,
150; self-criticism, 150; self-defense,
208n. 49; Stasi connections, 36, 138–39,
140, 141–42; theory of an "aesthetics of
material," 149; *War Without Battle: Life
Under Two Dictatorships*, 148–51
Multiculturalism, 357
Murdoch, Rupert, 266
Muschg, Adolf: *Literatur als Therapie?*
(Literature as therapy?), 46
Music, East German, 227–43; after unification,
229; celebration of currency union,
227–28, 229–30; between the fall of the
Wall and unification, 235–41; independent
record labels after fall of wall, 235; rock,
233, 246n. 21, 246n. 22

Nachgeholter Widerstand, 43
Nairn, Tom, 318

National identity: alternative notion of, 320;
dangers of a revival of, 290; debate on in
unified Germany, 316–18, 321–25, 350,
357, 359; and European integration, 318–
20; impact on gender roles, 318; Jaspers
on, 314; negative, 284; obsolescence of,
310; as a political construct, 318; and
the principle of Auschwitz, 335, 337; of
self-hatred, 284
Nationalpreisträger, 128
National Socialism: failure of German writers
and intellectuals to resist, 43; as illusory
modernization, 304–5; literary scholarship
under, 71; overcoming the legacies of, 371
"National Socialism in Germanic Literary
Studies and Poetics," 71
NATO, 46, 323
Naturalization, absence of in Germany, 326
"Negative nationalism," 317
Neo-Nazi organizations, 43
Neorealism, 121, 123
Neubert, Wolfgang, 86n. 40
Neue Beiträge zur Literaturwissenschaft, 87n. 49
Neue Deutsche Literatur, 88, 89, 104
Neue Forum, 282
Die neuen Leiden des Jungen W, 94
Neues Deutschland, 69, 191, 249
Neues Forum, 234
Neue Unübersichtlichkeit, 5
Neugründung, 300
Neumann, Gert, 15, 160; clandestine
language, 154, 156–57, 161, 170–76; *Elf
Uhr*, 169; "Die Ethik der Sätze," 172;
Die Klandestinität der Kesselreiniger (The
clandestinity of the boiler cleaners), 169,
171–72; *Die Schuld der Worte* (The guilt of
words), 169
Neutsch, Erik, 99
New Economic System *(Neues Ökonomisches
System)*, 121–22, 124
New Forum, 183, 195
New German Cinema, 116–17, 123, 125
"New Reader," 92–94
Newspapers, 253
New wave cinema: in Eastern Europe, 118–19;
in GDR, 14, 122–31; western, 128–29
New York Review of Books, 344
Nietzsche, Friedrich, 66
Nischengesellschaft, 342
"NM!MMESSITSCH," 235
Nolte, Ernst, 10, 330
Norddeutsche Rundfunk (NDR), 262, 264
Normalization: and the discourse of

modernization, 298–99; of East German theater, 201–3; in higher education and science policy, 299–304; lack of, 295–96, 310–11, 355; and postnationalism, 330–31

Nostalgia: East German, 5, 200–201, 288, 290, 306, 356; West German, 7

November 1989 demonstration, 18, 48, 195, 233, 250–51, 281, 283, 343, 382

"Null Bock," 237

NVA (Armed Forces), 100

Oberhausen manifesto, 123

October rising, 280

Oder-Neiße line, 323

Öffentlichkeit, 233

Office of Constitutional Protection, 336

"Open Letter to German Artists" (Brecht), 188

Opera, 386

Order 333, 73

Ordinance on the Distribution of Media Materials in the GDR, 256

Organizational (organisationseigene) publishers, 100

Orientierungslosigkeit, 5, 363, 364

Orwell, George, 37, 49, 317

Ostalgie, 5, 200–201, 288, 290, 306, 356

Ostdeutsche Rundfunk Brandenburg (ORB), 262, 264

Oversight Committee for Radio of the GDR (Staatliches Kommittee für Rundfunk beim Ministerrat der DDR), 269

"Palace of Tears," 295

Palitzsch, Peter, 189, 199

Pankonin, Key, 236–38, 244n. 11, 245n. 14, 245n. 18; Keynkampf, 230–32, 235, 238, 241–43

Panopticon, 140

Panoptic society, 151, 157

Paper, allocation of as means of literary-political control, 99–100

Party University Karl Marx, 73

Pässe/Parolen (Passports, passwords) (Klier and Krawczyk), 192, 194

Peking Records, 229, 244n. 9

Perestroika, 237, 280, 281

Peterson, Sebastian, 201

Petition law of 1961, 93

Peymann, Claus, 200

Pfefferberg, 198

Photocopying, 29

Piscator, Ernst, 210n. 59

Plenzdorf, Ulrich, 137n. 22, 185; Freiheitsberaubung (Robbed of freedom), 192; Legend vom Glück ohne Ende, 193; Die Legend von Paul und Paula, 207n. 39

Poetry, work of, 384

Poland: crackdown on filmmaking, 119; crackdown on intellectuals, 47

"Polish School" of filmmaking, 118–19

Pop art, 129

Possekel, Ralf, 339, 340, 344

Postnationalism, 323–24, 330–31

Power, language and, 143, 144–47, 148–49, 155–58, 160–61, 173

Power relations, 63, 168

Prenzlauer Berg, 14, 17, 53; alternative cultural Szene, 160; Anderson and, 138, 140; disavowal of working within the system, 143; function of, 156; immunity of, 195; poetry of, 161–69; radical critique of the older dissidents, 145, 153

Press: after unification, 258–59; freedom of in GDR, 254–55. See also Media

Prime Time Spät Ausgabe, 20

"Progressive arts" (fortschrittliche Kunst), 188

Protestant Church, conspirative activity, 281, 345

Public broadcasting, 264

Public sphere: as a common good, 381–84; East German, 233–34, 243n. 4, 247n. 29, 286

Publishing, East German: book shortage, 94–95, 98, 101–3; hierarchy of, 100; profiling of, 98; state control of, 29–30, 97–103, 253–54; thematic plans, 98; use of censorship as excuse, 96–97

Publishing, in unified Germany, 32

Punks, 17, 18

Puppet theaters, 195–96

Racism, 325; nationalism and, 318; sexism and, 318

Radio Corporation of the GDR (Rundfunk der DDR), 249, 252–53

Radio Network Reform Act (Rundfunküberleitungsgesetz), 259

Ramba Zamba, 202

Rammstein, 229

Des rasende Mob. Die Ossis zwischen Selbstmitleid und Barbarei (The raging mob: Ossis between self-pity and barbarism), 350

Rathenow, Lutz, 141

Rationalization, logic of, 198, 199

Rauhut, Michael: *Beat in der Grauzone: DDR-Rock 1964 bis 1972—Politik und Alltag* and *Schalmei und Lederjacke*, 233

Ravensbrück, 346

Readers: as democratic censors, 92–93; "New," 92–94; "real," 103–8

Reading nation, 13, 53, 88–91, 107–8

Realsozialismus, 185

Rebel Power, 245n. 19

Reform socialism, 13, 145–47, 340

Regalfilme, 116

Reich, Jens, 18, 304, 382; *Abschied von den Lebenslügen*, 54–55, 62

Reich, Wilhelm, 129

Reichel, Käthe, 199

Reisch, Günther: *Die Verlobte* (The fiancée), 137n. 21

Resnais, Alain, 113–14, 117

Retro cult, 7

Revisionism, 81–82

Revolt of 1989, 48

Revolution of 1989, 18, 48, 195, 233, 250–51, 281, 283, 343, 382

Rheinpfalz, 258

Richter, Hans Werner, 43

Riesman, David, 42

Riesz, Karol: *Saturday Night and Sunday Morning*, 125

"Rock aus Deutschland Ost," 235

Rock music, relation to the state, 233, 246n. 21, 246n. 22. See also Music, East German

Roloff-Momin, Ulrich, 199, 208n. 55

Romanticism, 66

Rossman, Peter, 233

"Rowdytum," 116, 127

Der Ruf, 40

Rühe, 325

Runde Tische (Round Tables), 47, 257, 282–83, 284, 382

Rwanda, 335

Sachsenhausen, 346

Salomon, Ernst von, 279

Sartre, Jean-Paul, 43, 144

Satellite broadcasting, 265

SCHADEN, 156

Schädlich, Hans-Joachim, 36

Schall, Ekkehart, 206n. 31

Schall, Johanna, 203n. 3

Schedlinski, Rainer, 138, 154, 160, 161; "The Dilemma of the Enlightenment," 155; (*etmal*) ("*x-times*"), 164; *die rationen des ja und des nein* (the ratios/rations of the yes

and the no), 163–66; Stasi connections, 140, 141

Schelsky, Helmut, 43, 45, 48, 369; *Die Arbeit tun die anderen: Klassenkampf und Priesterherrschaft der Intellektuellen*, 40; indictment of Böll, 40–41; vendetta against the left-wing intelligentsia, 41–42

Schiller, Dieter, 91

Schiller, Friedrich, 79

Schiller Theater, 198, 199

Schily, Otto, 285

Schirrmacher, Frank, 6, 186, 208n. 49

Schleef, Einar, 199, 200

Schlesinger, Klaus, 137n. 22

Schmidt, Helmut, 47, 364, 365

Schmitt, Carl, 149

Schneider, Rolf, 204n. 12

Schnelle, Kurt, 86n. 40

Scholz, Gerhard, 79

Schorlemmer, Friedrich, 250

Schröder, Richard, 49

Schroth, Christoph, 190, 193

Schubarth, Wilfried, 346, 349

Schubert, Götz, 210n. 62

Schuhmann, Klaus, 86n. 40

Schulpforta Gymnasium, 309

Schultze, Dieter, 208n. 49

Schuman, Robert, 310

Schütz, Helga, 137n. 22

Schwierzina, Tino, 261

Science policy: "heroic" stage, 300; institutional and personnel "renewal," 301; "legalistic" stage, 300–301; normalization and, 299–304

Scientific Marxism, 342

SDP, 282

SED. See Socialist Unity Party (SED)

Seghers, Anna, 36, 53, 64, 339

Self-censorship, 30

Self-publication, 29

Self-realization, 52

Semprun, Jorge, 113; *Le Grande Voyage*, 131n. 1

Serbia, 319, 337, 351n. 7

Sex-Pol movement, 129

Shakespeare, William, 200, 383

Shoah, 330, 331

Sign and signified, 163

Silence, language of, 166, 170–76, 340

Silone, Ignazio, 37

Simpson, Patricia Anne, 15, 17

Skin-heads, 325

Sklavensprache, 197

Slovenia, 309
Social Democrats, 285, 315
Socialism: cultural, 94; language and, 169–76; reform, 145; state, 67
Socialist humanism, 368
Socialist literature, 79–83, 102, 103–5, 129
Socialist realism, 127, 187, 188
Socialist Unity Party (SED), 1, 8, 183; attempt at cultural revolution, 121, 185; attempt to repress unauthorized speech, 183; benevolent despotism, 188–92; campaign against formalism, 187–88; communist isolationism, 120; control of art and literature, 29; control of publishing, 280; crackdown on cinema, 127–28; cultural-political offensive of 1957, 102; dominance of Central Committee and Politburo, 206n. 29; Eleventh Plenum, 127; elimination of social-democratic elements, 66; initial campaign against intellectuals, 65–66; intellectuals within, 281; *Kampfkonferenz* (battle conference), 115–16, 120; newspapers, 253; orchestration of public sphere, 234; *Reformvermeidungspolitik*, 53; use of intellectuals to bolster legitimacy of state, 187; and writers, 54–55; youth policy of 1963 and 1964, 122
Social science: literary scholarship as a, 39, 70–78; Marxism-Leninism, 75, 78–79; withering of, 46
Social welfare policy, 39, 45
Sociologists, conflict with writers, 39–40
Solingen, 325
Sonderweg thesis, 323
Sonnenalle, 210n. 62
Sonntag, 68, 75, 86n. 39
Sonntags fahrer (Sunday drivers), 136n. 19
Sophocles: *Merope*, 385
Soviet Military Administration (SMAD), 66, 73, 252, 253
Späth, Lothar, 262
Der Spiegel, 139, 343
Spiegel TV, 142
Spielverbot, 239
Sprachmacht (language power), 170–71, 172
Sputnik, 281
Squat, 229
Staatliche Kunstkommission (State Art Commission), 68
Staatsnation, 365
Staatsoper, 198
Staatsverleumdung, 193
Stalin, Joseph, 120

Stasidichter, 143
State Security Service (Stasi), 390; as agent of social work, 39; dissolution of, 54; image of, 157; IMs (unofficial informants), 138, 141–42, 223, 226n. 1, 245n. 16, 345, 353n. 28; interest in reform, 345; post-Wall image of, 139–40; relations with East German intellectuals, 1–2; surveillance of Klier, 193; ubiquity of, 49
State Treaty Concerning the Broadcasting System in Unified Germany (*Staatsvertrag über den Rundfunk im vereinten Deutschland*), 262
"Statute for the Promotion and Intensification of Research at Universities and Colleges in the GDR," 80
Steiner, George: "The Cleric of Treason," 38
Stern, Fritz, 317, 369
Stern, Kurt, 134n. 11
Sternberger, Dolf, 324
Stiftung Lesen, 108
Stolpe, Manfred, 307, 345, 353n. 28
Stötzer-Kachold, Gabriele, 15, 160, 161; "Das Gesetz der Szene" ("The law of the scene"), 166–69
Stötzl, Christof, 199
Strauß, Botho, 360–61
A Streetcar Named Desire, 201
Streitpapier, 281
Streller, Siefried, 86n. 40
Strittmatter, Erwin, 111n. 46
Structural-functionalism, 127
Student movement, 41, 43, 45, 129, 331
Surveillance, 151, 165, 166, 193, 223, 232
Süsskind, Patrick, 285
Swedish Academy, 41
"Swords into Ploughshares," 194
Syberberg, Hans-Jürgen, 360
Sydow, Hubert, 273n. 32
Systems theory, 127

Tacheles, 198, 232, 239
Tairov, Alexander, 207n. 41
Tat circle, 279
Technical University, Dresden, 302
Telecommunications, 373
Television, 9, 94, 215, 247n. 29, 253
Tempelhof Airport, 295.
Theater: after unification, 197–203; documentary, 199; in the GDR, 15, 183–97. *See also* Theater intellectuals
Theater am Schiffbauerdamm, 279
Theater der Zeit, 193, 202

Theater Heute, 190, 192, 194, 200, 202
Theater im Palast der Republik, 192
Theater intellectuals: ambiguity of role in social change, 183–86; limited solidarity for those ostracized by the SED, 194; on the margins of legitimate publicity, 192–93; privileged dissent, 189–92, 195–97
Theaterpatie, 202
Theater unter dem Dach, 195, 198, 201, 202
Thematic Plan (*Themenplan*), 98–99
Therapeutic discourse, 12, 38–49, 51
Third Reich, 7, 146, 289, 315. *See also* National Socialism
Third Way, 282, 286
"This Is Berlin Speaking" (*Hier redet Berlin*), 252
Thulin, Michael (pseud. Michael, Klaus), 163–64, 197
Thürk, Harry, 106
Tomato, Hans, 245n. 18
Tragedy, four classes of, 385
Tragelehn, B. K., 189, 208n. 49
Tragic recognition, principle of, 384–92
Transfer payments, 296
"Trashfoodpunk," 231, 234
Treason: concept of, 12, 35, 36, 37, 52; language of, 48; paradigm of, 38
Treaty Concerning the Attainment of German Unification, 249
Treuhand, 258
Trolle, Lothar, 208n. 49
Trommler, Frank, 12, 13
Trötsch, 245n. 16
Trotzidentität, 290
Trumpener, Katie, 13, 14
Truth: controlled by power relations, 168; language and, 171, 172, 175
Tschaka, 230
Twentieth of July conspiracy, 306
Twentieth Party Congress, Soviet Communist Party, 68
"Two-plus-four" disputes, 285

Ulbricht, Walter, 55, 68, 94, 113, 120, 187, 188, 340, 342
Unconscious, language and, 161–63
UND, 156
Unemployment, 9, 295, 322, 357, 361, 364
Unification. *See* Germany, unified; National identity; Normalization
United Nations, 297
Universities: ideological control of in GDR, 73. *See also* Higher education

University of Erfurt, Thuringia, 302
Unpersonen (nonpersons), 86n. 40
Unübersichtlichkeit, 363

Vergangenheitsbewältigung, 8, 10, 49
Vergesellschaftung, 10
Verne, Jules, 106
"Viadrina," 302
Victim file, 142
Virilio, Paul, 250, 270
Vishnevsky, Vsevolod, 207n. 41; *Optimistic Tragedy*, 193
Vodafone, 4
Vogel, Frank: *Denk bloß nicht ich heule* (Just don't think I'll cry), 126, 127
Volk, 48, 234, 267, 296
Volksbühne, 183, 198, 201
Volksnation, 324
Von Kleist, Heinrich, 3, 381; *Penthesilea*, 190
Von Plato, Alexander, 306, 308

Währungsunion. See Currency union
Wajda, Andrzej: *Kanal*, 119
Walser, Martin, 6, 44, 46, 285, 360
Wannsee Conference anniversary, 331
Warsaw Ghetto, 27
Warsaw Pact, dissolution of, 348
Waschinsky, Peter, 194
Weber, Max, 39
Wehler, Hans-Ulrich, 369, 370
Weidenfeld, Werner, 308
Weigel, Helene, 206n. 31
Weimar Centers for National Research and Commemoration of Classical German Literature (*Nationale Forschungs- und Gedenkstätten der klassischen deutschen Literatur*), 78
Weimarer Beiträge, 72
Weimarer Gedenkstätte zur Erforschung der deutschen Literatur, 87n. 49
Weimar Republic, 130, 131, 279
Weimar school, 40, 79
Weiß, Konrad, 255, 260
Weiss, Peter, 44
Wekwerth, Manfred, 189–90, 199, 206n. 31; *Galileo Galilei*, 206n. 30
Weltoffenheit, 117
Wende, 63, 358
Wende in der Wende, 358, 359, 382
West German intellectuals. *See* Intellectuals, West German
West Germany. *See* Federal Republic of Germany (FRG)

White Rose conspiracy, 306
White Sheep, 245n. 18
Wicke, Peter, 233
Winkelzüge oder nicht vermutete, aufschlußreiche Verhältnisse (Shady moves or not anticipated, conclusive relationships), 162
WIP program, 302
Wir treten aus unseren Rollen heraus, 196
Wissenschaft, 43, 45
Wissenschaftsrat, 302
Wissenschaftssprache, 45
Wittenberg Church Conference, 194
Wladyslaw Gomulka, 118–19
Wolf, Christa, 6, 38, 99, 189, 267, 368; antifascist identification, 148, 184; attacks on by younger generation, 14; "autobiographical" works, 147–48, 153; critique of GDR, 142–43, 339; dream of reform socialism, 145; focus on the Nazi past, 338–39; *Der geteilte Himmel* (The divided heaven), 50–51, 52; *Kassandra*, 280; *Kindheitsmuster* (Patterns of childhood), 338; *Nachdenken über Christa T.* (The quest for Christa T.), 51, 52, 111n. 46; privileged position within GDR society, 246n. 24; protest of Biermann's disenfranchisement, 207n. 37; *Selbstinterview* (Interview with myself), 52–53, 54; socialist modernist literature, 129; speech at November 1989 demonstration, 47; Stasi connections, 138–39, 140, 141–42; therapeutic discourse, 12, 39, 51; *Was bleibt* (What remains), 47, 138, 154–55

Wolf, Friedrich, 53
Wolf, Gerhard, 156
Wolf, Konrad, 116, 123
Wolfram, Gerhardt, 191
Wolle, Stefan, 353n. 21
Work, writing as, 173–74
World War I, 213
Writers, 278; conflict with academic mandarins, 39–40; role of in demise of GDR, 53–54; SED and, 36, 54–55. *See also* Intellectuals, East German; Intellectuals, West German
Writer's Union (East German), 69, 88, 151

Xenophobia, 316–17, 327, 357, 364

Youth culture, 125, 126
Youth policy, 122
Youth theaters, 195–96
Yugoslav federation, 309
Yugoslavia, 319

Zadek, Peter, 199
Die Zeit, 154, 360, 364
Zeitenwende, 363
Zinnober, 195, 202
Die Zitty, 202
Zöger, Heinz, 68
Zola, Emile, 37
Zörger, Heinz, 75
Zschoche, Hermann, 136n. 18; *Karla*, 126, 130
Zweig, Arnold, 36, 53
Zwerenz, Gerhard, 36, 51–52

Learning Resources
Centre